The Apocalypse
in English Renaissance
thought and literature

The Three Woes of the Apocalypse. Reproduced from *The Kitto Bible* by permission of The Huntington Library, San Marino, California

C. A. PATRIDES
JOSEPH WITTREICH
   editors

The Apocalypse
in
English Renaissance
thought and literature

patterns, antecedents and repercussions

Manchester University Press

© Manchester University Press 1984

Published by Manchester University Press,
Oxford Road, Manchester M13 9PL
and 51 Washington Street, Dover, N.H. 03820, USA

British Library cataloguing in publication data

The Apocalypse in English Renaissance thought and
  literature.
  1. Eschatology   2. England – Intellectual life – 16th century
  3. England – Intellectual life – 17th century
  I. Patrides, C.A.   II. Wittreich, Joseph
  192   DA320

ISBN 0-7190-0958-8 (cased)   0-7190-1730-0 (paperback)

Filmset in Photina by August Filmsetting, Haydock

Printed in Great Britain
by Butler & Tanner Ltd, Frome

Contents

Preface	*vii*
The Contributors	*ix*

I THE BACKGROUND

1	Early Apocalypticism: the ongoing debate BERNARD MCGINN	2
2	The development of apocalyptic thought: medieval attitudes MARJORIE REEVES	40

II THE APOCALYPSE IN RENAISSANCE ENGLAND AND EUROPE

3	Some uses of Apocalypse in the magisterial Reformers JAROSLAV PELIKAN	74
4	The political dimension of apocalyptic thought BERNARD CAPP	93
5	Revelation and two seventeenth century commentators MICHAEL MURRIN	125

III THE APOCALYPSE IN RENAISSANCE ENGLISH LITERATURE

6	*The Faerie Queene*: An Elizabethan Apocalypse FLORENCE SANDLER	148
7	'Image of that horror': the Apocalypse in *King Lear* JOSEPH WITTREICH	175
8	'Something like Prophetick strain': apocalyptic configurations in Milton C. A. PATRIDES	207

IV THE AFTERMATH

9 Queuing and Waiting: the Apocalypse in England, 1660–1750 PAUL J. KORSHIN 240

10 Transatlantic extensions: apocalyptic in early New England STEPHEN J. STEIN 266

11 Ambiguous revelations: the Apocalypse and Victorian literature MARY WILSON CARPENTER *and* GEORGE P. LANDOW 299

12 The millenarian structure of *The Communist Manifesto* ERNEST L. TUVESON 323

13 Apocalypse: theme and variations M. H. ABRAMS 342

The Apocalypse: a bibliography JOSEPH WITTREICH 369
Index nominum 441

Preface

> The Book of Revelation is an Apocalypsis, not an Apocrypsis, but a mystery made manifest. . . . This book ought to be more diligently searched into.

As if in response to the plea ventured in 1617 by Richard Bernard,[1] the Book of Revelation had been so 'diligently searched into' that it had already affected the thought and the literature of Europe both East and West. Vast as the subject is, it may be doubted whether any single individual could attempt much more than a superficial survey of it. The task, we felt, had to be a cooperative one; for only the congregated talents of divers scholars could successfully study the impact of apocalyptic thought in general and of the Book of Revelation in particular.

The fourteen scholars responsible for the pages that follow were from the outset cognizant of the pivot of our joint enterprise, namely, the thought and the literature of Renaissance England in its European context, here reflected in the centrally placed Parts II and III. However, since apocalyptic thought during the Renaissance depends on the cumulative heritage of the past, another Part – here, the very first – was necessarily devoted to the variegated background. At the same time, since apocalyptic thought may scarcely be said to have expired with the Renaissance, still another Part – here, the very last – was devoted to the significant 'extensions' of the apocalyptic tradition through the nineteenth century in both Europe and America. Finally, the spacious bibliography at the end of the volume (pp. 369–440) indicates that even the present enterprise does not exhaust the considerable dimensions of the subject. As rightly it has been said by George Seferis, the modern Greek poet and Nobel laureate, 'The Apocalypse is the text not of one era and one generation, but of all eras and all generations.'[2]

Acknowledgment is made, with gratitude, for four awards that enabled us to complete the present volume: in Patrides's case, a stipend from the National

Endowment of the Humanities and a grant from the American Council of Learned Societies; and in Wittreich's case, a University of Maryland Provost's Fellowship and a Henry E. Huntington Library Fellowship. We are also grateful to Professor Mary Ann Radzinowicz of Cornell University for her counsel at a crucial stage of our work; to the editors of *English Language Notes* for permission to expand the version of Patrides' essay published in the Special Milton Issue of March 1982; and the Henry E. Huntington Library and Art Gallery, San Marino, California, and the Widener Library, Harvard University.

C.A.P.
J.W.

NOTES

1 *A Key of Knowledge for the Opening of the Secret Mysteries of St. Johns Mysticall Revelation* (London, 1617), sig. E^v, p. 1.
2 In the Prologue to his translation of the Book of Revelation into modern Greek: ʹΗ Ἀποκάλυψη τοῦ Ἰωάννη *(Athens, 1966).*

The contributors

M. H. ABRAMS Class of 1916 Professor of English Literature, Cornell University
BERNARD CAPP Senior Lecturer in History, University of Warwick
MARY WILSON CARPENTER Lecturer, Harvard University
PAUL J. KORSHIN Professor of English Literature, University of Pennsylvania
GEORGE P. LANDOW Professor of English Literature, Brown University
BERNARD MCGINN Professor of Historical Theology, The University of Chicago
MICHAEL MURRIN Associate Professor of English Literature, The University of Chicago
C. A. PATRIDES G. B. Harrison Professor of English Literature, The University of Michigan at Ann Arbor
JAROSLAV PELIKAN Sterling Professor of History, Yale University
MARJORIE REEVES, FBA Honorary Fellow of St. Anne's College, Oxford
FLORENCE SANDLER Professor of English Literature, The University of Puget Sound
STEPHEN J. STEIN Professor of Religious Studies and American Studies, Indiana University
ERNEST L. TUVESON Professor of English Literature, The University of California at Berkeley
JOSEPH WITTREICH Professor of English Literature, The University of Maryland

I
The background

BERNARD McGINN

1 Early Apocalypticism: the ongoing debate

In 1960 the German theologian Ernst Käsemann declared, 'Apocalyptic – since the preaching of Jesus cannot really be described as theology – was the mother of all Christian theology.'[1] Käsemann's remark was not totally novel: the importance of the eschatological (or, more properly, apocalyptic) element in the preaching of Jesus and the formation of the church had been recognized since the time of Samuel Reimarus at the end of the eighteenth century; but Käsemann's seminal article indicated that the evaluation of the role of apocalypticism in early Christianity was to enter a new phase about 1960. The same holds true for studies of the role of apocalypticism in Intertestamental Judaism. Stimulated by the discovery of the Dead Sea Scrolls in 1947, many issues concerning the origins and influence of early Jewish apocalypticism were obviously in need of a fresh look.

The volume of materials published on Jewish and early Christian apocalypticism over the past twenty years has been impressive, and it falls within the purview of many disciplines – Biblical studies, Judaica, Patristics, the History of Religions, to name just the major areas. It would be difficult to find anyone who is master of all of these fields; but, on the other hand, the history of apocalyptic traditions has frequently suffered from a compartmentalization in which scholars have been tempted to gain increasing mastery over ever-shrinking domains. A premise of this collection of essays is the necessity for a synthetic view as the proper background for detailed study of special epochs and topics, and hence there seems to be a place for an essay seeking to give a picture of recent trends in scholarship on the origins of apocalypticism and its influence on early Christianity. This essay is primarily an historiographical one, a summary of the state of the question,[2] though I shall not hesitate to take positions on some rather controversial issues. I take comfort in the admission of one recent Biblical scholar who said: 'Among students of both Testaments, Jewish apocalyptic remains an unsolved riddle.'[3]

I THE GENRE APOCALYPSE

The problem of what we mean by apocalypticism (or 'apocalyptic' – a theological transplant from the German *Apokalyptik*) is complicated by the fact that it can be formulated in two ways. One begins from the attempt to determine an essence or message ('What is apocalypticism?'), the other asks about a form of literature ('What is an apocalypse?') and seeks to describe the content as the second step. Traditionally, German scholars and an earlier generation of British and American exegetes followed the first option; more recently, considerable attention has been given to the second, especially in American biblical studies. In a forceful 'Postscript' to a 1976 article, M. E. Stone argued that '. . . a great deal of the current discussion of apocalypticism and of the apocalypses is being carried on in the midst of semantic confusion of the first order', specifically, the tendency to think that apocalypticism as generally understood was in some way coterminous with the content of the texts that can be called apocalypses. Stone went on to affirm that 'As long as we remember that by explaining "apocalyptic eschatology" we have not explained the apocalypses, there is hope for the future of the discussion.'[4] Other recent investigators have emphasized the same point.[5]

This observation seems to be a necessary methodological starting point, but we should note that distinction need not imply divorce. If we wish to understand apocalypticism as a form of eschatology (as shall be argued below), and if we are prepared to admit that it is separable from apocalyptic form, then we must still ponder the fact that most scholars are in agreement that this particular way of viewing history and its End came to birth within the literary form of apocalypse. Even if one were to adopt Stone's exaggerated position that the only true apocalyptic apocalypses are Daniel, the Apocalypse of John and IV Esdras,[6] it should still be observed that these are also the most influential apocalypses in later Western traditions. But the point remains: we must begin from a discussion of what contemporary Biblical scholars have to tell us about the genre apocalypse and then move on to investigate the complexities of how the genre relates to apocalypticism conceived as a particular form of eschatology.

One eminent Old Testament scholar, Gerhard von Rad, has denied that apocalypse as such can be said to constitute a distinctive literary genre.[7] This view can scarcely be maintained in the light of recent research. The most complete survey of the genre question is the fourteenth volume of *Semeia* entitled *Apocalypse: the Morphology of a Genre*, containing detailed studies of the Jewish and early Christian apocalypses, and briefer surveys of the Gnostic, Greek and Latin, Rabbinic and Persian apocalypses and related texts.[8] In the light of this survey, a tentative definition is advanced, as well as an analysis of basic types and sub-classes.

> "Apocalypse" is a genre of revelatory literature with a narrative framework, in which a revelation is mediated by an otherworldly being to a human recipient, disclosing a transcendent reality which is both temporal, insofar as it envisages eschatological salvation, and spatial, insofar as it involves another, supernatural world.[9]

The fundamental discrimination of types is made on the basis of the manner of revelation, that is, whether the seer goes on an otherworldly journey or not, whereas the distinction of sub-classes is based upon the eschatological content of the message received, that is (within each type), whether the revelation involves (a) a review of history, as well as its coming crisis and transformation, or (b) crisis and transformation without a general review of history, or (c) a purely personal eschatology.[10]

This is not the place to investigate the textual analyses upon which the definition and typology are based. Some might question the criteria upon which a distinction in the mode of revelation is chosen as the ground for distinguishing the two main types while a discrimination in content determines the sub-classes; nevertheless, the distinction between the 'historical' and the 'heavenly' types does highlight an important insight gradually emerging from current scholarship, namely, that apocalypse as a genre was the source not only of later apocalyptic traditions in Western thought, but also of significant elements in later Jewish and Christian mysticism.[11]

The determination of what an apocalypse is must be, to some degree, a scholarly construct, although one that cannot proceed independently from the investigation of the texts that call themselves apocalypses. Part of the problem is that the use of the term apocalypse, or revelation, as a self-description can be misleading. Many apocalypses (e.g., the Book of Watchers in I Enoch 1–36) do not. Still other texts (e.g., the Apocalypse of Moses) have little relation in form or content to what are considered apocalypses and apocalyptic eschatology. One way to approach the question of genre and the relation of genre to content is to address revelations of any kind with a series of questions that will serve to differentiate the particular kind of revelation that we can call apocalypse in the proper sense from other forms of the communication of hidden wisdom, e.g., oracles, testaments, Sibyllines, etc. I would suggest the following five questions as a useful introductory tool for this task: who reveals? to whom? how, or under what circumstances? what? and for what purpose? The first three questions primarily concern the form of revelation, while the fourth and fifth move on to questions of content which involve more complex issues and are thus much less tractable to generally agreed upon answers.

Among the Intertestamental Jewish apocalypses (the *Semeia* volume counts fifteen such texts) it is the universal rule that the revelation is conveyed to mankind through the agency of a heavenly mediator, usually an angel.[12] This rule is generally true of the later Christian examples as well, although some make the Risen Christ the mediator of the message. The revelation is made to a human sage who in the Jewish apocalypses is invariably pseudonymous, that is, he is identified with a long-dead holy man of renown, such as Enoch, Daniel and Moses. Pseudonymity has been much discussed in literature on apocalypticism.[13] There is agreement that its fundamental intent was to give the revelation added authority and frequently to heighten the authenticity of historical accounts disguised as prophecies (*vaticinia ex eventu*). Once again, a few Christian apocalypses, notably the Apocalypse of John, are exceptions; but pseudonymity is one of the most persistent characteristics of Western apocalypticism, being found in many subsequent apocalyptic prophecies that are not formally apocalypses. Of course, pseudonymity was not restricted to apocalypses, but was a widespread phenomenon in the Hellenistic period.

The manner of revelation, the circumstances under which the message is conveyed, is a more complicated area. The message can be seen in a vision (e.g., Daniel 7–12, and almost all the Jewish apocalypses), whether the vision is given in a dream, in waking life, or when rapt into heaven; it can also be conveyed in the form of a speech (e.g., I Enoch 72–82), or through a dialogue with the heavenly intermediate (e.g., II Baruch). The surviving Jewish apocalypses, with one exception,[14] mix both kinds of revelation. The visionary character of apocalypse as a genre guarantees that apocalypses make heavy use of symbols as a means of communicating their hidden message. Cosmic symbols of various sorts – animal symbols, number symbols, colour symbols, and symbolic human figures – are found throughout the Jewish apocalypses and their Christian counterparts.[15] Scholars with little sympathy for apocalypticism have attacked the artificial 'allegorical' aspect of apocalyptic symbolism,[16] and some texts do exhibit a cloying proliferation of images with one-dimensional meanings (e.g., the Animal Apocalypse of I Enoch 85–90); but much of the symbolism found in the ancient apocalypses is rich and complex and has testified to its power of evocation by continued use and reinterpretation in later religion, art and literature.

Another important characteristic of apocalypses is the 'bookish' nature of the revealed message. In several cases the revelation was originally contained in written tablets or books;[17] in others the seer's obligation to write the message down is noted.[18] Apocalypticism, in J. Z. Smith's apt phrase,[19] is a 'scribal phenomenon' insofar as the message revealed is to be communicated to its potential audience primarily through the written rather than the spoken word. Once again, it is important to note that this mode of presenting apocalyptic eschatology will long survive the demise of apocalypse as a literary genre.

II APOCALYPTIC ESCHATOLOGY

When we turn to the question of what is revealed in the Jewish apocalypses, we enter into the controversial area of the relation of the genre to what we have been calling apocalypticism, that is, to a distinctive form of teaching about history and its approaching End. There can be no doubt that a significant number of the Jewish apocalypses contain teaching that corresponds with what would be recognized as apocalypticism by most authors. M. E. Stone, as we have seen, would reduce the number of Jewish apocalyptic apocalypses to two (Daniel 7–12 and IV Esdras); W. Schmithals lists six,[20] while J. Collins, the author of the section on 'The Jewish Apocalypses' in the *Semeia* volume, also has six, those texts which represent his Type Ia, i.e., 'Historical Apocalypses with no Otherworldly Journey'.[21] It is precisely these texts, of course, along with the closely related Apocalypse of John from the New Testament,[22] that have formed the core sources for later Christian apocalypticism down to the present day.

Several options are possible at this point. One might argue that the 'historical' apocalypses are a distinct genre and thus make one type of apocalypse coincide with what has been traditionally seen as apocalyptic content.[23] Alternatively, given the wealth of non-historical material revealed in the apocalypses (e.g., heavenly secrets, lists of speculative materials, etc.), M. E. Stone suggests that apocalypse was originally created as a vehicle for communicating 'speculative' wisdom, and that a shift of interest to historical and eschatological concerns took place at the time of the crisis caused by the persecution of Antiochus IV.[24] What seems clear is that the content of apocalypses in Intertestamental Judaism was always multi-dimensional, and that any simple separation out of the historical apocalyptical content is to some extent arbitrary. The apocalyptic authors used their new tool to convey a wealth of revealed wisdom, not least the secrets about God's plan for history and the impending End.

An ideal text to illustrate the richness of the teaching conveyed in the apocalypses is the compilation known as I Enoch, or Ethiopic Enoch, since the text in its entirety survives only in that language. The discovery of portions of the Aramaic original at Qumran has stimulated much work on the book in recent years. It is now agreed that parts of I Enoch are the oldest surviving apocalypses and indeed the oldest extant extra-canonical Jewish books – a unique witness to Judaism in the third century BC.[25]

I Enoch is made up of at least five separate documents.[26] Chapters 1–36 form the Book of Watchers, or heavenly beings, and seem to have been composed on the basis of diverse sources and traditions in the third century.[27] In form it is certainly an apocalypse. Enoch, a righteous man, '. . . saw a holy vision in the heavens which the angels showed to me' (1.2). The vision is presented under the theme of the coming '. . . day of distress (which is appointed) for the removal of all the wicked and impious' (1.1), and the theme of judgment occurs frequently (e.g. 1.5–9, 10.14–21, 16.1, 18.6, 19.1, 22.4, 25.4, 27.3–4). But there is much else. Chapters 6–11 tell the story of the fall of the angelic Watchers, their corruption of mankind and their judgement, while Chapters 12–16 tell of Enoch's flight to heaven, the earliest Jewish ascent vision (especially chapter 14). The heavenly journeys of Enoch described in chapters 17–36 are highly speculative in content, containing learned material on angelology, meteorology, geography and astronomy, as well as eschatology.

Similar in character and also probably third century in date is the Book of Heavenly Luminaries, or Astronomical Book, contained in I Enoch 72–82 and which is found in a more extensive form in the Aramaic material from Qumran. The emphasis here is on esoteric astronomical and calendrical wisdom revealed by the angel Uriel and written down by Enoch,[28] but there are eschatological dimensions as well, such as reference to the coming judgment of sinners and the signs which precede it (80.2–8), and also to a new creation which is to last forever (72.1). Looking at the two earliest surviving apocalypses, it is difficult to deny M. E. Stone's contention that 'speculative interests . . . are one of the core elements of the Jewish apocalypses',[29] but significant elements of the historical, political and eschatological interests of later apocalypticism are not lacking, either.[30]

Two other apocalypses embedded in I Enoch and apparently of somewhat later date abandon the heavenly journey form and the speculative interests of these earliest texts and turn their attention primarily to revelations of the course of history and its coming judgment. Both apocalypses are usually seen as approximately Maccabean in date (i.e., c. 160 BC) and thus contemporary with the Book of Daniel. The Apocalypse of Weeks of I Enoch 93 and 91.12–17 may antedate the Maccabean revolt of 166. It is a sketch of world history divided into ten weeks, the earliest apocalyptic *ex eventu* historical review. The writer's own era of the middle of the seventh week is an age of apostasy (93.9), to be followed by a judgement of sinners and reward of the just in the eighth week (91.12–13), and a two-stage universal judgment (men and angels) in the ninth and tenth weeks (91.14–15). World Transformation and eternal reward for the just closes the picture (91.16–17). The Apocalypse of Weeks is contained in a longer section known as the Letter of Enoch, or Book of Exhortation (I Enoch 91–104), which R. H. Charles dated to the first century BC.[31] This section contains many of the formal elements of apocalypses and shows interest in apocalyptic eschatology, but is unusual in its stress on homiletic exhortation. Maccabean in date is the section known as the Dream Visions (I Enoch 83–90), consisting of a vision of cosmic destruction (chapters 83–4) which is formally closer to Old Testament prophecy than to an apocalypse, and the Animal Apocalypse (chapters 85–90), an allegorical review of history including an account of the coming judgment (90.24–7) and the restored messianic kingdom in which the just will reign (90.28 et seq.).

The final part of I Enoch, the Similitudes of Enoch (chapters 37–71), is later, probably dating from about the beginning of the Christian era. It involves a heavenly journey (39.3, 52.1) without a review of history, but shows a strong interest in cosmic eschatology, especially coming judgment (e.g., 38–9, 20.1–2, 60.7–25, 69.27), and also in contemporary political events (e.g., 56.5–8). There are speculative concerns in this apocalypse, too, as evidenced by the astronomical secrets in chapters 41–4.[32]

The apocalyptic eschatology that dominates the Animal Apocalypse and the Apocalypse of Weeks and that is present in various ways in the other parts of I Enoch is also evident in the second half of the canonical Book of Daniel, the apocalyptic visions of chapters 7–12. It is now agreed that Daniel is composed of two parts, the stories about the sage in chapters 1–6, which are probably earlier in date, and the three apocalyptic visions written down and combined with the traditional stories during the Maccabean revolt of 167–4 BC.[33] The Daniel stories are not formally apocalypses, but chapter two contains an important image that was to be influential in later apocalyptical speculation, Nebuchadnezzer's dream of the statue composed of four metals and the stone that destroyed it. This scheme of four world empires and the messianic kingdom that destroys them is a Jewish adaptation of Near Eastern political oracle composed in opposition to Hellenistic rule.[34]

The properly apocalyptic part of Daniel has three visions interpreted by angels. The first of these begins with four great beasts arising from the sea (7.1–8, a parallel to the four empires of chapter 2), followed by a heavenly epiphany of the Ancient of Days in council, the coming of the Son of Man and the final victory over the fourth beast (7.9–14). Although there is considerable dispute about the meaning of all the elements, recent study has made clear the connections of the vision with Canaanite myths of the victory of Baal over the forces of chaos.[35] The vision of chapter 8 is an allegory reminiscent of I Enoch's Animal Apocalypse, pitting a ram representing Persia against a hegoat and his horns figuring Alexander the Great and his successors. The final great vision of chapters 10–12 (chapter 9 is an intervening prayer) is a narrative communicated to Daniel by an angel who recounts in terms of *ex eventu* prophecy the history of the Hellenistic kingdoms concluding with a detailed account of the career of Antiochus IV Epiphanes, whose persecution of the Jews is painted as that of a final eschatological enemy, a proto-Antichrist (11.36–45). The prophecy of Antiochus's death (11.45) leads to a prediction of cosmic judgement and a subsequent resurrection of the dead '. . . some to everlasting life, some to shame and everlasting disgrace' (12.2), the earliest datable reference to the resurrection.[36]

Some of the characteristics of the message of these visions should be noted. Daniel is not interested in the speculative astronomical and geographical wisdom of the earlier Enoch texts, nor does he actually journey to heaven; but he does share with these earlier texts an interest in the heavenly world and especially in its angelic inhabitants. Second, Daniel is fascinated with contemporary politics and the course of history in the Hellenistic period. Although a review of world history is not found in each of the visions, their interlocking character presupposes a structured view of the historical process. Third, Daniel is obsessed with the desire to work out the time remaining until the judgement and resurrection. Indeed, the Danielic variations on the time remaining to the persecutor (the famed three-and-a-half times, or years, of 7.25, 9.27 and 12.7, interpreted as 1290 days in 12.11 and 1335 days in 12.12) were to provide rich fare for subsequent ingenuity and speculation.[37] Finally, Daniel's vision forms a classic presentation of an eschatological pattern of present crisis-coming judgement-final vindication that will become central to apocalypticism.[38]

One other Jewish apocalypse of a strongly historical character deserves note, if only because its translation into Latin assured it considerable influence in later Western apocalyptic traditions. IV Esdras (or Ezra) dates from the end of the great period of Jewish apocalypticism, being written in the late first century AD and reflecting the Fall of Jerusalem in the year 70. The work has seven sections.[39] The first three (3.1–5.19, 5.20–6.34 and 6.35–9.25) are dialogues between the seer and an angel centring on problems of theodicy, but with an interest in the coming End and the signs that will precede it (e.g., 5.1–13, 6.13–24, 9.1–6). The third dialogue contains a description of the events of the Endtime that involves a four-hundred-year earthly messianic kingdom (7.26–30) to be followed by a general resurrection and judgement (7.31–44). IV Esdras seems to react against the speculative tradition in its insistence that mere man cannot hope to know the secrets of the heavenly world (e.g., 4.1–8 and 6.33–4), and it shows a similar scepticism toward attempts to determine the precise time remaining until the End (e.g., 4.51–2).

Three striking allegorical visions follow the dialogue: the vision of the mourning woman (9.26–10.59), the eagle vision (10.60–12.51) and the vision of the man from the sea, a messiah figure (13.1–58). The book closes with a dialogue (chapter 14) where God commands the scribe to write down his message in ninety-four books, twenty-four to be made public (the books of the Old Testament) and seventy to be hidden. The use of *ex eventu* prophecy with strong political concerns (the famous eagle vision contains a detailed account of Roman history),[40] as well as the pervasiveness of the triple eschatological pattern of crisis–judgement–vindication,[41] mark these visions as typical of apocalyptic eschatology.

This brief survey of three key Jewish apocalyptic texts gives at least some indication of the complexity of the message contained.[42] Concerning the speculative content of the apocalypses, I. Gruenwald has noted '. . . we may once again surmise that a number of parallel, sometimes even conflicting, traditions with regard to the revelation of cosmological secrets were circulating among the apocalypticists'.[43] We might well broaden this observation. Apocalypses were a type of revelation that could be used to reveal many mysteries – they could even be used to reveal that there were some revelations too exalted for man to know (as in IV Esdras and in Mk. 13.32 and parallels). This variety is as much present in the revelations about the course of history and its End as it is in other aspects of the message of the apocalypses. When we look at what is revealed in the apocalypses, then, the hunt for any single apocalyptic mentality seems illusory.[44] Apocalypse is one form of revelation in an age avid for revelations, something that was true for Gentile as well as Jew. The genre was designed to achieve many ends, only some of which should be properly called apocalypticism in the sense of apocalyptic eschatology.

Since the fundamental concern of this essay is to see what Jewish and early Christian apocalyptic eschatology contributed to later Christian apocalyptic traditions down to the Renaissance and beyond, we must now take a closer look at the eschatology found in the more 'historical' apocalypses to determine both the main contours of their view of history and the variety found within this broad picture.

The first essential characteristic is the deterministic view of history implied or expressed by the apocalypticists. They believed that God had predetermined the course of history; the future was set no matter what man might do, '... because he [God] controls the times and what happens in them' (IV Esdras 13.58). In contrast to the prophetic view in which Nineveh's repentance might stay God's hand, the apocalyptic author saw all the real decisions as already made. The Lord might choose to reveal all or part of his plan regarding history's fate, but he does not change his mind. World-historical determinism, however, is not individual determinism.[45] An important theme of Jewish apocalypticism was the call for ethical choice between good and evil, or perhaps better, the call for the elect to persevere in their choice of the good, no matter what the cost in terms of disfavour, ostracism, persecution or death. This coexistence of cosmic determinism and individual free decision permeates the history of apocalypticism in the West.

A second indispensable characteristic of apocalyptic eschatology is the divinely predetermined pattern of crisis–judgement–vindication that marks the End. Apocalypses that show any interest in history at all have some variation on this pattern, that is, they see the present time as one of some form of crisis (most frequently, the growth of evil and the persecution of the just); they look forward to judgement in which the wicked are punished and the just approved;[46] and finally, they expect a triumphant vindication of the sufferings of the just, most commonly in terms of personal immortality,[47] but frequently also including the resurrection of the body, the establishment of the messianic kingdom and the transformation of the universe. The elements of this general pattern adopt a wide variety of forms; it would be impossible to pursue all the ramifications here. What I am claiming is that without a divinely-determined sense of history (whether actual historical reviews are present or not), and without triple-act drama of crisis–judgment–vindication for the coming End, there is no apocalyptic *eschatology*, though there may be other forms of apocalyptic teaching.

The conviction of the apocalypticists that the triple drama has already begun is another fundamental mark of apocalyptic eschatology, but one that can be present in so many ways that its importance is more difficult to assess than the first two characteristics. A conviction of the imminence of the End, a strong sense that the time is short, has traditionally been seen as the hallmark of apocalyptic thought. But the notion of imminence grows complex and ambiguous as we begin to investigate apocalyptic texts. Some historical apocalypses, such as Daniel, believe that it is possible to calculate the time remaining, while others, like IV Esdras, show a consciousness of living in the last times, but warn against any attempts at calculation. This tension continues through the history of apocalypticism. There are apocalypses that announce God's coming judgment and look forward to some form of personal and/or communal vindication without displaying any explicit sense of how near or far the denouement may be (the Book of Watchers seems to fit this category). However, the vast majority of the Jewish apocalypses that contain a good measure of apocalyptic eschatology in the sense of our first two characteristics also convey a sense that the final events have begun, whether the conclusion is near or still down the road. There is thus a form of 'psychological' imminence in apocalyptic eschatology from its origins. The apocalyptic author addresses his audience within a temporal framework that calls for and confirms decisions made in the light of the approaching End of history.

The predetermined nature of the apocalyptic view of history implies other characteristics frequently, but not universally, made explicit in the Jewish apocalypses. Among these is the sense of history as a unity, something that G. von Rad saw as the greatest contribution of apocalypticism, its special splendor.[48] But here, too, the variation is considerable. A number of historical apocalypses contain little or no investigation of the structure of world history through some sort of historical review or a determination of the succession of world ages. Nonetheless, it might be argued that all the apocalypses that show some interest in history imply a sense of its totality. If God has predetermined what will happen, especially at the End, can what has already taken place be any less bound to his will?

Similarly, much has been made of the dualism of the apocalyptic view of history, both the dualism of the two ages or Aeons – this age and the age to come –[49] and the dualism of the struggle between good and evil throughout history. Both forms of dualism are expressions of the predeterminism of apocalyptic history. Apocalypticists tend to see a definitive break in the irruption of divine judgment into history; the coming age is not a goal toward which history is building, but a new beginning sent by God. But the old age, just as much as the one to come, are both manifestations of the divine will – the one tending to destruction through judgment, the other, inchoatively present in the just, to be crowned with glory. The dramatic conflict between good and evil powers played out in both the angelic and human arenas throughout the course of history does seem at times to be portrayed almost in forms of a cosmic dualism, and this has led some investigators to search for Persian roots of Jewish apocalypticism, a position now generally suspect. In the Jewish and Christian apocalypses, the struggle between good and evil is always conducted under divine mandate. God controls the keys of the future: good will be rewarded, evil punished, no matter how things appear now. Apocalyptic eschatology bears a heavy weight of theodicy, whether this is implicit or made clear.

Finally, apocalypses differ considerably about what kind of history they are interested in and how they present it. The more mystical, heavenly-journey apocalypses at times contain accounts of the primordial history of creation and the origins of man, but they rarely have much concern for current events. The historical apocalypses, such as Daniel 7–12 and IV Esdras, are tied to political concerns by means of *ex eventu* prophecies in ways that frequently allow them to be dated with considerable accuracy. The literalism with which the author of Daniel painted his allegorical picture of the struggle between the Seleucid and Ptolemaic kings is a good example of a characteristic that was to remain of great importance in later apocalyptic eschatology. Apocalypticists believed that it was not only possible, but obligatory, to search the signs of the times for the marks of God's will displayed in history.

III THE ORIGINS OF APOCALYPTICISM

On the basis of the foregoing sketch, we are now in a position to ask when and under what circumstances such a view of history and eschatology arose. This area has been one of intense debate in recent years. Even if we could find a satisfactory answer to the question of origins, which at the present seems unlikely, the determination of where a thing comes from is not its total explanation, and may even be so partial as to be misleading. To say that Jesus was a carpenter's son from Galilee is not to say the last word about him.

The main questions about the origins of apocalypticism seem to be three. First, there is the question of what elements in the Old Testament are the major sources of apocalypticism. Second, there is the issue of how important extra-Jewish sources of the Hellenistic age may be. Finally, we can ask how far apocalypticism is a radically new departure from the past rather than an expected development from earlier traditions.

English scholars of the previous generation, such as H. H. Rowley, S. B. Frost, and D. S. Russell stressed the connection between Old Testament prophecy and apocalypticism;[50] but a long-standing tradition in German scholarship that emphasized a break between prophecy and what came after it is well illustrated by G. von Rad's argument that the apocalypticist's view of history was incompatible with that of the prophets and that its origins should be sought in Old Testament Wisdom traditions instead.[51] Despite von Rad's position as the premier Old Testament theologian of the day, many were not satisfied with his arguments. Recently, a strong counter-position has re-emphasized the connection between prophecy and apocalypticism, but with a distinctive new twist. Building upon the earlier approach of the *Religionsgeschichtlicheschule* of H. Gunkel and W. Bousset, as well as the influential work of S. Mowinckel, recent studies of F. M. Cross, P. D. Hanson and others have seen an influx of the themes of Canaanite myth into prophetic eschatology through the medium of the royal cult as the major source for Jewish apocalypticism.[52] Hanson would also argue from a number of late prophetic texts, such as Isaiah 56–66 and Zechariah 9–14, that apocalyptic eschatology was actually born in the sixth century BC rather than the third.[53]

The question of the relation of the full range of the teaching of the apocalypses to Wisdom traditions has received new investigation in recent years. Von Rad's thesis conceived Wisdom in a rather narrow sense; more recently, scholars who have emphasized the importance of the speculative, especially the cosmological and astronomical, element in the Jewish apocalypses have pointed to possible connections with Mesopotamian Wisdom circles.[54] In any case, it seems wise to remember with I. Gruenwald that '... apocalyptic cannot be adequately explained in the light of *either* Prophecy or Wisdom. Apocalyptic is much too complex a phenomenon to be explained by an either/or theory'.[55]

The second question concerns the extent to which non-Jewish sources may have influenced the origins of apocalyptic eschatology. Simplistic notions of a wholesale invasion of Persian religious ideas into post-exilic Judaism as the determining factor in the rise of apocalypticism are now generally discounted,[56] and even the more guarded approach of G. Widengren, who argues that the early apocalypticists were influenced by 'a lot of central Iranian teaching' which they then proceeded to read back into the Old Testament, seems out of favor.[57] If there are outside influences of importance, Canaanite mythology (at a considerable remove) and Near Eastern Wisdom traditions (in a manner not yet really analyzed) seem to be the prime candidates, as already mentioned, although some Persian connections cannot be ruled out.[58] It should be noted, though, that these outside influences, however strong they may be, should not be looked upon as alien incursions into 'pure' normative Old Testament religion – Canaanite mythology had long been domesticated in some strata of Israelite religion and a wide variety of Wisdom traditions were present in

Judaism and in the Hellenistic world in which the Jews lived.

An understanding of the Eastern Mediterranean world after Alexander the Great is crucial for a fruitful investigation of the origins of apocalyptic eschatology. In 1966, H.-D. Betz argued that 'We have to free ourselves from the idea of treating apocalypticism as an isolated and purely inner-Jewish phenomenon. Rather we must learn to understand apocalypticism as a peculiar manifestation within the entire course of Hellenistic–oriental syncretism.'[59] Whether one agrees with the term syncretism or not, there can be no denying that the past decade has seen a number of scholars try to analyse the significance of Jewish apocalypticism within the wider framework of the religious developments of the Hellenistic era.[60] Among these has been J. Z. Smith, who sees the development of 'apocalyptic situations' in various places in the Near East attendant upon the crisis of the cessation of native kingship under the Hellenistic rulers.[61] For Smith, apocalyptic is the outcome of a long 'trajectory' of scribal concern with the role of kingship that in Egypt can be traced back as far as the Neferti oracle of the nineteenth century BC. The variety of apocalypticisms in the Hellenistic Near East is to be understood as a continuum of individual reactions to a general trauma rather than as the product of syncretism. Smith's essay is an important contribution to the discussion, but seems to need further consideration from two aspects: first, the role of Old Testament prophecy in the special 'trajectory' toward Jewish apocalyptic (Smith tend to emphasize Wisdom); and second, further discrimination of the content and functions of the various national apocalypticisms. Crudely put, are we dealing with species of one genus, or related genera?

There is no easy answer to the question of whether apocalypticism was a new phenomenon that burst upon the scene in the Intertestamental period or a gradual evolution from ancient sources. Those scholars that are drawn to the analysis of the development of structures and traditions (the *longue durée* of religion) will tend to emphasize continuities; those that seek to penetrate to the inner essence of a particular phenomenon will look for decisive breaks where new situations produce new creations. Any answer worth taking seriously should contain elements of both kinds of explanation; but in light of the fact that apocalypse as a genre cannot be said to predate the third century BC,[62] and also considering the disagreement that still exists about how far earlier prophetic texts really do embrace the basic message of apocalyptic eschatology,[63] it seems better to call the prophetic and Wisdom antecedents 'proto-apocalyptic' and to hold that the rise of apocalypse as a genre and apocalypticism as a form of eschatology were products of Judaism in the third and second centuries BC.

Scripture scholars customarily search for the 'Sitz im Leben', or the circumstances in the life of a group or community which gave rise to and transmitted a particular text or genre. The search for the 'Sitz im Leben' of apocalypse as a literary type, as well as for the context and setting of the individual apocalypses, has been a highly conjectural and controversy-ridden endeavor. Some points of possible consensus have emerged, but they tend to be general.

As M. E. Stone has pointed out, the centuries between 400 and 200 BC 'remain somewhat obscure', despite the new material from Qumran. The relative abundance of evidence that we have after *c.* 200 BC indicates that radical changes had taken place in Jewish religious life during the preceding period.[64] Given this paucity of information concerning the third century, the search for particular groups, communities or political parties that were the bearers of proto-apocalyptic or apocalyptic traditions is largely a matter of learned conjecture. We are better informed about the Maccabean period where Daniel provides some specific, if debatable, information on the group to which the seer belonged and the intentions he had in writing down his visions. Several places in Daniel praise the *maskîlîm* (e.g., 11.33–5, 12.3), and J. Collins affirms 'There is no serious doubt among scholars that the author of Daniel 7–12 understood himself as one of these *maskîlîm*, or wise teachers.'[65] The question is whether it is possible to make a more precise identification of the 'wise teachers'. One traditional interpretation has been to equate the *maskîlîm* with the *hasidîm*, a group of scribes noted for their adherence to the Law and mentioned in the Books of Maccabees;[66] but Collins has rejected this on convincing grounds, arguing that the *maskîlîm* in Daniel are indeed learned men, but ones who advocated 'active but not militant resistance' to Antiochus,[67] while according to 2 Maccabees 14.6, the *hasidîm* joined with the Maccabees in armed resistance. R. H. Charles suggested long ago that elements of the Animal Apocalypse indicate a favorable view of the *hasidîm* and a pro-Maccabean stance (especially I Enoch 90.9),[68] and hence that text rather than Daniel seems to be a better candidate for hasidean origin. Thus, there appears to have been a number of learned scribal circles with varying attitudes of resistance to the Hellenizing program of Antiochus IV, and at least several of these produced apocalypses.[69] One thing is clear from the second-century texts and also from the highly speculative contents of the third-century apocalypses: apocalypses as a literary genre and the apocalyptic message, both in its speculative and historical dimensions, were not necessarily popular, lower class phenomena directed to the disenfranchised outcasts of society, but were produced by circles of learned savants for an apparently varied audience.[70]

How far it is possible to attribute political motivation to the third-century apocalypses is uncertain,[71] but there can be no question of the political interests of the second-century texts. The Apocalypse of Animals, Daniel 7–12 and the Testament of Moses (not an apocalypse in form, but a text containing apocalyptic eschatology)[72] are all Maccabean in date and are examples of political rhetoric in the sense that they are designed to move groups to adopt particular responses or courses of action in the face of the events of the moment.

The events and circumstances that triggered the responses of these early apocalypticists have been traditionally seen as severe national crises or traumas, and insofar as some kind of present crisis forms the first act in the triple drama of the End in apocalyptic eschatology, the emphasis on crisis is well taken. Yet the crisis orientation of apocalypticism has been used to support a number of rigid historical and sociological models which have not been helpful either to our understanding of early Jewish apocalypticism or to many subsequent chapters in the history of apocalyptic expectations.[73] Some important qualifications concerning the crisis orientation need to be made. First, crisis is more in the eye of the apocalypticist than in the mind of the historian, that is, there is no simple relation between the type of magnitude of a natural, political and/or social disaster and the apocalyptic response it may provoke. Great historical disasters have had little or no effect on apocalyptic beliefs and movements; seemingly minor dislocations have assumed major roles. There are no general rules for understanding why some crises have been accompanied by a rich outpouring of apocalyptic expectations and others have not. We must begin from the scribal leaders and authors to find out (if possible) why they were predisposed to look for crisis; their interpretation of events is never mere reaction to external stimuli. Second, crisis can be viewed as an ongoing condition or situation as much as a dramatic new event (e.g., the gradually building sinful state of mankind, as seems to be the case in I Enoch 1–36). Third, crisis does not provoke a single response among the apocalypticists, especially one that should always be conceived as violently opposed to the ruling powers – a revolutionary, or proto-revolutionary, ideology. Given the fact of Hellenistic and then Roman oppression of the Jews, it should not be surprising that the Jewish apocalypses generally express a negative attitude toward the ruling powers; but, as A. Collins has shown, these negative attitudes range across a wide gamut from active resistance to passive acceptance of suffering.[74] I have elsewhere tried to show that when apocalypticism was used by the dominant state religion (as Christianity became in the fourth century AD), it frequently encouraged support of the establishment in what were seen as times of great need.[75]

We have spoken thus far about apocalyptic circles and groups that can only be described in rather general fashion on the basis of a few surviving texts. It is also possible to identify a specific 'apocalyptic community' whose literature and archeological remains are known in considerable detail, namely, the Qumran sectarians.[76] The studies of Qumran and its literature are many, and there are also many points under dispute'. F. M. Cross has suggested that the community originated c. 150 BC, when a group of the *hasidîm* split with the Maccabeans over the question of the High Priestly office.[77] Whether or not this was the case, there can be no question of the interest of the sectarians in a wide range of apocalyptic literature. There are anomalies in Qumran's relation to apocalypticism, however, which serve to show how difficult it is to be definitive about the 'Sitz im Leben' (i.e., life setting) of Jewish apocalyptic eschatology. For one thing, the Qumran community itself cannot be directly tied to the production of any known apocalypse, though literature that is clearly theirs, such as the Community Rule, the Damascus Document, the War Scroll and the Thanksgiving Hymns, contain much apocalyptic eschatology. This, plus the evidence of texts like the Testament of Moses already noted, supports the conclusion that from a rather early date, apocalypse as a literary form and apocalypticism as a type of eschatology had considerable independence from each other. There are elements of the eschatology of Qumran, such as the stress on the predestination of individuals,[78] which seem to differ from the standard patterns of other Jewish apocalypticism, and the very complexity of the apocalyptic beliefs found in the community (divergent tendencies sometimes being present in the same document) can lead us to affirm, along with J. Collins, '. . . that the underlying structure was more important than any specific formulation'.[79] The same can be said for all Intertestamental Jewish apocalypticism.[80]

IV APOCALYPTICISM AND CHRISTIAN ORIGINS

It is difficult to deny that the creation of the genre apocalypse and the spread of apocalyptic eschatology were among the most significant features of Intertestamental Judaism. An even more important contribution of the Intertestamental era was the production of a new religious tradition, that of Christianity. The relation between apocalypticism and Christianity presents many problems. How influential was apocalypticism on the preaching of Jesus? Was Christianity originally an apocalyptic sect within Judaism? What role did the genre apocalypse play in early Christianity? Do the contents of early Christian apocalypses reflect similar patterns to those of the Jewish revelations, especially in the area of eschatology?

The major initial problem is Jesus. Was he an apocalypticist or not? Or better, to what extent was his message, insofar as we can recover it, an apocalyptic one? Paraphrasing the conclusion of John's Gospel, one can say that if all the views on this question were written down, the world itself would not suffice to hold the literature. Generations of biblical scholars have devoted themselves to the determination of the criteria to be used to discriminate the more or less authentic Jesus material in the Synoptic Gospels from the productions of the Christian community. Much recent research into the life of Jesus has taken its departure from the centrality of a criterion of dissimilarity, i.e., that the best yardstick for determining those aspects of the Gospels that originated in the preaching of Jesus is their departure from what might be expected from contemporary Judaism or from the nascent church.[81] The implementation of this approach, which is based in part upon the usually undefended premise that Jesus could not have made the impression he did if he said what others did, has tended to reduce the role of apocalyptic in Jesus's message.

All scholars, of course, admit that Jesus made use of the language and themes of his times, and that these included many apocalyptic elements; but the tendency today is to claim that he did not necessarily use them in an apocalyptic way. The crucial issue is the announcement of the coming of the kingdom of God, an image which has a rich background in Intertestamental apocalyptic. From 1892, the date of the publication of J. Weiss's *Die Predigt Jesu vom Reiche Gottes*, this admission has been the touchstone of those who saw Jesus primarily as an apocalyptic preacher, a 'consistent' eschatologist whose message was centered on imminent expectation of the coming of the messianic kingdom.[82] Exegetes of the past two decades have moved more in the direction of what is frequently called 'realized' eschatology, i.e., the stress upon the kingdom as being already present in some way in the very preaching of Jesus.[83] The sayings concerning the kingdom attributed to Jesus in the Synoptics contain elements of both future expectation and present realization, but the application of the criterion of dissimilarity has tended to cast doubt on how much of the future element can be ascribed to Jesus. As N. Perrin put it, '... almost all the elements in the tradition which give a definite *form* to the future expectation in the teaching of Jesus fail the test of authenticity'.[84]

This view represents a fairly wide consensus, at least in German and American biblical scholarship, as can be seen through a glance at a few other summary statements. E. Käsemann, in the 1961 article already noted, saw Jesus as beginning from the apocalyptic message of John, but argued that '... His own preaching was not constitutively stamped by apocalyptic but proclaimed the immediate nearness of God'.[85] For the German theologian, it was the apostolic community which put Christian belief into the framework of apocalypticism and thus made it 'the mother of all Christian theology'. R. W. Funk in a 1969 paper summarized this tendency by affirming that any merely chronological reading of Jesus's language about the now and future kingdom was a mistake.[86]

It should be pointed out that not all agree with removing Jesus from the consistent-eschatological perspective so easily. Both on the theological and the exegetical level, some have argued that future-oriented apocalyptic still played a large role in Jesus's preaching. Theologically, this view has been championed by W. Pannenberg and his group, though on doubtful premises;[87] and on the exegetical side, there has been the major study of L. Hartman, *Prophecy Interpreted*. Hartman analysed the most noted apocalyptic text of the Synoptic Gospels, the 'Little Apocalypse' of Mark 13, Matthew 24–5 and Luke 21, in which Jesus speaks about the coming End and the signs which will precede it. He argues that underlying this text, as well as the allied apocalyptic sections of

I and II Thessalonians, was a paraenetic interpretation of elements of Daniel built around two apocalyptic themes: first, an account of the signs of the End involving the Antichrist's activity, the coming of the Abomination of Desolation and warnings against false prophets; and second, the announcement of the glorious return of the Son of Man to gather the faithful into heaven.[88] Hartman saw the 'Sitz im Leben' of this underlying text as a Christian scribal circle prior to 50 AD,[89] and at the end of his book he raised the question if the speech could be thought to go back to the teaching of Jesus. His conclusion is that the judgment whether the *form* of the discourse comes from Jesus depends upon '. . . the image the scholar has of Jesus and his work', but he does not hesitate to affirm that '. . . it can hardly be doubted that a good deal of what came to be included in the discourse during the history of its tradition consists of *verba Christi* or derives from them'.[90]

The question of the extent to which Jesus preached an apocalyptic message is not fully settled, even though the dominant tendency in recent research has been adverse to seeing him as fundamentally apocalyptic in outlook. Even if Jesus did preach apocalyptic eschatology, there is no evidence that he wrote it down, something that would distinguish his activity from that of the scribal circles that were the typical purveyors of apocalypticism.

Whatever may be said about Jesus, there seems to be little disagreement about earliest Christianity. 'We may take for granted', says R. W. Funk, 'that the earliest church shared the imminent apocalyptic expectations of contemporary sectarian Judaism for which Paul is a later and secondary witness.'[91] I doubt if any New Testament scholar would disagree with this assessment, but as soon as we ask to what extent and over what time period earliest Christianity shared these expectations, differences of opinion begin to appear.

Judging on the basis of crucial New Testament texts stretching over the half-century between 50 and 100 AD, we can demonstrate that apocalyptic eschatology played a crucial role in developing Christianity, but by no means exhausted the total meaning of the Christian religion. Speculation that prior to the production of the New Testament there existed a stage of purely apocalyptic Christianity in which Christ's Resurrection was understood only according to one apocalyptic mode both goes beyond the evidence at our disposal and presupposes a rigid and simplistic notion of the nature of apocalypticism. We would do well to heed the words of H.-D. Betz: 'In reality, the problem as to what kinds of apocalypticism have influenced early Christianity, and what the results were, is presently much discussed and far from being settled.'[92]

The investigation of the apocalyptic elements in earliest Christianity has been pursued in a number of recent works.[93] To survey the range of opinions, let alone to try to evaluate them, is outside the scope of this essay. Since our concern has been the study of what early apocalyptic traditions contributed to later Western developments, we can limit ourselves to a consideration of the parts of the New Testament that have been most important for later apocalypticism.

The earliest of these texts are the apocalyptic segments of I and II Thessalonians (4.13–5.11 and 2.1–12 respectively). There is no doubt that I Thessalonians is authentically Pauline, and its date of *c.* 50 AD makes it the earliest surviving Christian document. Its message revolves around belief that God has raised his Son Jesus from the dead and that the Risen Lord will soon return to judge the world and bring 'full attainment of salvation' (5.9) to his followers. The text makes it clear that while Paul, like Jesus in the Synoptics, eschews any attempt to calculate the time of the coming of the Lord's Day (e.g., 5.2), he believes that it will take place in the lifetime of his audience (4.15). It is more difficult to evaluate the apocalyptic expectations of II Thessalonians. Many would hold that it is not authentically Pauline, because it seems to indicate a less imminent sense of the Parousia, or glorious return of Christ, than I Thessalonians.[94] This epistle also gives us the first full Christian account of the final eschatological enemy, later called the Antichrist,[95] whose advent and persecution are seen as the necessary precondition for the Lord's advent.

Paul did not invent the figure of the Antichrist. The detailed treatment of II Thessalonians presupposes an extensive evolution in Intertestamental literature and an earlier Christian development whose lines are not altogether clear to us. Many years ago, W. Bousset stressed the mythological background to the final enemy in Near Eastern cosmogonic stories concerning the primordial dragon opponent of the creator God.[96] There can be no denying the importance of the mythic elements in Antichrist traditions, but Bousset's treatment tended to rely too heavily on claims regarding oral traditions as against written texts, and he neglected the role that symbolic interpretations of historical figures (e.g., Antiochus IV as the 'little horn' of Daniel 7.8) had upon the gradually evolving beliefs in a final supreme foe. II Thessalonians 2.1–12 was only one of a host of Old and New Testament texts that later traditions used as sources for the coming and career of the Antichrist.[97]

The second crucial New Testament witness is the apocalyptic sayings and discourses ascribed to Jesus in the Synoptics, especially the 'Little Apocalypse'. Whether or not this text goes back to the preaching of Jesus, its importance for subsequent Western apocalypticism is undeniable. Apocalypse as a literary genre was the product of Intertestamental Judaism; the Gospel was the creation of early Christianity. But there is a real relation between the two forms, at least if we follow Norman Perrin, who has suggested that the first Gospel, that of Mark (*c.* 69 AD), is organized according to three stages of an apocalyptic drama. The difference is that Mark used narratives of the ministry of Jesus to convey his message rather than the traditional apocalyptic visions.[98] The subsequent Synoptic Gospels distance themselves further from the traditional form of apocalypse. Matthew, a product of the Hellenistic Jewish mission around 80 AD, makes use of Mark and an early collection of the sayings of Jesus (known as Q) from apocalyptic Palestinian Christianity. He structured his account so that the time of Jesus was seen as the sacred time of the formation of the church, in short '. . . at the hands of Matthew the apocalypse has become a foundation myth'.[99] Luke, writing in a more Hellenistic context about the same time, moves in the same direction, though with accounts and special sources of his own.

The theory that a brief Jewish apocalypse lay behind the 'Little Apocalypse' of Mark 13 and its parallels was advanced as long ago as 1864, and an extensive controversial literature has developed on the question.[100] According to the view of L. Hartman discussed above, the underlying Jewish–Christian apocalypse can best be seen in Mark 13.5b–8, 12–16, 19–22 and 24–27; but it was the longer version of the discourse found in Matthew that subsequent generations usually used when they wished to cite Jesus's message about the End. The first part of Matthew's version (24.4–26) sticks fairly close to Mark, but Matthew then adds apocalyptic material taken from Q (24.36–51), as well as a series of parables on the ten virgins, the talents and the judgment in chapter 25 that are distinctive to his rendition. Luke's version is even closer to Mark in general structure, but shows enough independence in detail to argue that it is not a copy, but a reworking of another witness to the original underlying text.[101]

The Apocalypse, or Revelation, of John, the final book of the New Testament, had been a source of scandal to many both ancient and modern,[102] but it remains the most influential of all apocalyptic texts. Without minimizing the value of earlier work done on this greatest of apocalypses, especially the classic commentaries of W. Bousset (1906) and R. H. Charles (1920), we must concentrate here only on some aspects of the recent discussion of the book.

There have been those who have doubted whether the Apocalypse is really an apocalypse, because it lacks some of the features of Jewish apocalypses.[103] Not only does the author abandon pseudonymity, but he also encloses his message within the framework of a letter sent to the seven churches in Asia Minor rather than figuratively hiding it until the hour of need. But there can be no real doubt that John's work is a true apocalypse, if one with some unusual features. Most of the special characteristics flow from the fact that John thought of himself as a prophet (e.g., 1.3 and 22.7); and, as P. Vielhauer has suggested, he is an important witness to the revival of prophecy in early Christianity.[104] John can speak in his own voice as a messenger of Jesus Christ (1.1), the ultimate source of revelation; there is no need for an appeal to ancient sages since Jesus has risen. The lessening of some themes found in the historical Jewish apocalypses, such as the restricted role given to *ex eventu* prophecy (present, however, in 17.9–12 and perhaps a few other places), flows from the fact that John and his audience had no need to be convinced that they were living in the last times.[105]

The features that we have pointed to as essential to apocalyptic eschatology are evident in the work. First, the stress upon the divinely determined course of history (e.g., 1.1), and second, the adherence to the triple drama of crisis–judgment–vindication.[106] The mediated character of John's visions and his concern for both the historical and the otherworldly dimensions of the apocalyptic message place the work squarely in line with Intertestamental apocalypses.[107]

Granted that the Apocalypse is apocalyptic in both form and content, we must still confront questions concerning its authorship, time of composition, and especially its unity and structure. Although later Christian tradition identified the John of the Apocalypse with John the beloved disciple, and this was an important element in its reception by the main Christian tradition,[108] this identification is clearly impossible. Modern scholars generally agree that the author was a Christian prophet living in Asia Minor and writing in the time of Domitian, i.e., c. 90–95 AD.[109] The problem of the unity and structure of the work is a difficult one. It is hard to think of anyone who on first reading the Apocalypse would not be confused by its structure. Former generations of scholars have sometimes thought of John more as a redactor of a variety of early sources than as a literary artist who at times chose to incorporate previous compositions and traditions into his work. There have been theories of the work that have seen it either a mere compilation of sources, or a revision of one primary work, or a redactional composite of oral and written traditions.[110] One modern theory postulates that the many doublets in the book are the result of a collation of two apocalypses written by the same author at different times.[111] There is, however, a consensus among the most recent interpreters that the Apocalypse is a unity, whatever use it may make of some earlier written sources, and there is some agreement that the notion of recapitulation, i.e., the repetition of the same series of events from different perspectives, enables us to solve most of the difficulties and problems of the structure.[112]

Given the subtlety of the repetitive and interlocking patterns which John used in the composition of his work, no outline of the Apocalypse will probably ever be totally adequate and convincing, but we can say that series of sevens provide the broad lines of the structure. Not only is the whole prefaced by the letters to the seven churches (2.1–3.22), but the main body can be divided into five series of sevens: the seven seals (6.1–8.5), the seven trumpets (8.2–11.19), seven unnumbered visions (12.1–15.4), the seven bowls (15.1–16.21) and a final seven unnumbered visions (19.11–21.8).[113] Almost all would agree that the seals, trumpets and bowls form a recapitulative progression in which the triple drama of persecution, judgment and the triumph of the Lamb and his followers is driven home over and over again. It can also be said that the visions break down into two broad parts: chapters 1–11, beginning with the vision of the Risen Christ and continuing with the vision of the closed scroll, and chapters 12–22, which seem to be related to the content of the open scroll in the angel's hand in 10.2–11.

The variety of ways in which the Apocalypse has been read during the course of Christian history are many. J. M. Court has recently detailed eight types of exegesis: chiliastic, allegorical, recapitulative, historical–prophetic, eschatological, historical–contemporary, literary and comparative.[114] These modes of exegesis are not discrete entities, but usually intermingle in many ways so that while most modern exegetes would agree that a good interpretation should be true to the traditional (i.e. mythological), the eschatological and the historical elements of the book,[115] few would come up with quite the same weighting of these components. Lately there have been important studies of the mythic dimension, and also the symbolic character of the presentation of the message; but others have emphasized a strongly political reading.[116] Clearly, the approaches are not mutually exclusive: in the Apocalypse and throughout apocalyptic literature, myth becomes a way of reading contemporary history and taking a stance toward it.

John wrote in a time of persecution to give courage to his fellow Christians, and he wrote from a deeply anti-Roman point of view similar to that of the Jewish Zealots but not shared by all in the early church. Like the Book of Daniel, the Apocalypse makes use of the imagery of holy war,[117] but not to encourage open rebellion, as did the Zealots, but rather to advocate passive resistance and '. . . a martyr's death, which hastens the end, because a fixed number of martyrs must die before the eschatological battle can be initiated'.[118] Differences of opinion will continue as to how much *ex eventu* reference to contemporary events may be found in the book, and as to how strongly the political aspects of the message should be stressed; but no one would want to deny that the Apocalypse was a call to decision in the midst of a time of trial. Of course, it is also an eschatological book, a book of the future.[119] While John adheres to the evangelical rejection of trying to set a definite time for the judgment of Rome and the return of Christ, the entire message is presented under the shadow of the imminent vindication of those who have washed their robes in the blood of the Lamb – 'The one who guarantees these revelations repeats his promise: I shall indeed be with you soon. Amen; come, Lord Jesus' (22.20).

V PATRISTIC APOCALYPTICISM

John's Apocalypse is not the only early Christian apocalypse. Surprisingly, if we follow the listings provided by the *Semeia* volume, there are even more early Christian apocalypses than Jewish ones,[120] and whereas apocalypse as a genre tends to die out in Judaism early in the second century AD, Christian apocalypses flourish through the second and third centuries and persist much longer, at least in Eastern Christianity.

The later Christian apocalypses have been little studied in comparison with their Jewish predecessors.[121] Taken as a group, they show a greater proportion of texts with purely personal eschatology; indeed, as the careful analysis of A. Collins has shown, one important type of historical apocalypse, that based on a visionary experience without an otherworldly journey but including an *ex eventu* review of world history, virtually vanishes from the scene.[122] But if we subtract the element of *ex eventu* reviews (which Christian apocalypticists of the early period may have felt unnecessary given their conviction that Jesus's rising from the grave marked the beginning of the End), a good proportion of the early Christian apocalypses display the characteristic triple apocalyptic pattern of crisis–judgment–vindication.[123] John's Apocalypse falls into this group (it even includes some *ex eventu* prophecy), and the type continues into the second century AD, as shown by the Shepherd of Hermas, a text which some circles in the church considered canonical. It is also found in the third century, as in the case of the apocalypse known as the Testament of the Lord.

Hermas is a complex document divided into a series of five visions mediated to the seer (apparently not pseudonymous) by three celestial beings, followed by collections of mandates and similitudes containing the revelation and ethical instruction given by the final mediator, an angel in the form of a shepherd. Both the form and the content of the work argue that it is an apocalypse.[124] There are no reviews of history,[125] but there is a sense of present persecution centering on martyrdom and the expectation of imminent eschatological judgment (e.g., Vision III.viii.9). The world will be destroyed by fire, sinners will be punished eternally, and the just will be received into everlasting glory with the angels. Hermas was most likely written in several stages between *c.* 90 and 140 AD. Its sense of historical crisis as a sign of the presence of the apocalyptic final drama appears in a more heightened fashion in another second-century apocalypse, the Apocalypse of Peter, especially if we accept the argument that its situation reflects Bar Kochba's persecution of Palestinian Christians.[126] The Testament of the Lord, a discourse of the Risen Christ to the disciples, also includes reference to persecutions, probably of third-century date, a detailed account of the apocalyptic signs (especially the career of the Antichrist) and descriptions of the coming fiery judgment of sinners and the resurrection and reward of the just.[127] It is evidence that at least some circles in third-century Christianity had apocalyptic beliefs that were similar to those of John and still expressed them in the same literary genre.

As Christianity passed into its second century of existence, though, it seems that the Christian apocalypses tended to lose interest in the public and historical dimensions of eschatology and to give more attention to the fate of the individual soul in the afterlife.[128] A. Collins lists five later Christian apocalypses without otherworldly journeys that display purely personal eschatology, and no less than eight examples of apocalypses involving transport to the heavens and description of the afterlife without any concern for the coming judgment of history.[129] Most of these texts are little known and difficult to date; indeed, 'It is possible that none of the eight date to the first three centuries of the common era.'[130] If, as I. Gruenwald has argued, the theosophical and speculative elements of the Intertestamental Jewish apocalypses fed into the great stream of Merkavah mysticism (i.e., mysticism based on the chariot vision of Ezechiel) that begins in Judaism in the second century of the Christian era,[131] a somewhat analogous movement seems to have taken place in third-century Christianity as the genre apocalypse became more and more the vehicle for visions of heaven and hell.[132]

The most important of the later Christian apocalypses is a good illustration of this transition, for although it contains two elements of apocalyptic eschatology, it is primarily a vision of the other world. The Vision of Paul was widely read in the Middle Ages,[133] and it is extant in a number of languages. The work recalls II Corinthians 12.1–5 by announcing itself as 'The revelation of the holy apostle Paul: the things which were revealed to him when he went up even to the third heaven and was caught up into Paradise and heard unspeakable words.'[134] After an introduction (chapters 1–2) telling of the miraculous discovery of the text in 388 AD, Paul conveys a message concerning creation's appeal to God against man's sinfulness (chapters 3–10). A lengthy account (chapters 11–51) of his journey to the other world in the company of an angel follows. This section is mostly devoted to a description of the geography of the extra-terrestrial regions and the punishments and rewards that await souls, but there are elements of the last two acts of the apocalyptic drama in the expectation of the coming day of judgment and destruction (chapters 16, 18), the general resurrection (chapters 14–15) and the millennial kingdom which will descend to replace the old earth (chapters 21–2). What is most striking about the Vision of Paul is its indifference to current history, something which makes it impossible to date from internal evidence. A reference to an Apocalypse of Paul in Origen suggests a third-century date, at least for the core of the work.[135]

Given this tendency in second- and third-century Christian apocalypses, it might be thought that with the conversion of the empire and the changes undergone by Christianity in the fourth century, the genre apocalypse might either vanish from the scene or become solely a type of vision of the other world, whether mediated or not. This seems to be the case in the Latin West, but not in Greek East. So little study has been done on the later Byzantine apocalypses (there are at least three Apocalypses of John, two of Mary, two of Esdras and seven of Daniel) that we cannot be sure of the dating of many of them, nor can we say how far they fit the genre apocalypse as we have been using it. A number of them do display real apocalyptic eschatology, including *ex eventu* periodizations of history.[136]

Our concern throughout has centered more on apocalypticism than on the literary form apocalypse, and hence the story does not end for Western apocalypticism when apocalyptic form dies out. Right from the start, apocalyptic eschatology also appeared in writings that were not apocalyptic in form. In the second century AD, apocalyptic eschatological content begins to appear in a wide range of patristic writings, especially in exegetical works, either in passages embedded in longer works or, from the third century, in full-fledged commentaries.[137] Throughout the subsequent history of Christian apocalypticism, new revelation about the End was frequently disguised as exegesis, not necessarily a totally new development, given how later Jewish apocalypses and early Christian ones had frequently included interpretations of earlier works. During the patristic period, we also get the beginning of dogmatic treatises devoted to eschatological questions.

Some parts of early patristic texts look very much like brief apocalypses which may have had an independent existence before becoming incorporated into formally different works. A good example is the final chapter of the Didache, or Teaching of the Twelve Apostles, a document that appears to date partly from the late first century and partly from the first half of the second. Chapters 1–6 are a moral catechism of Jewish or Jewish–Christian origin on the two ways (a theme also found in the Qumran texts); chapters 7–15 contain the earliest 'church order', or manual of ecclesiastical life and organization. Chapter 16 is a brief quasi-apocalypse (it is in the form of an address rather than a mediated vision) which makes use of Matthew and II Thessalonians. What is distinctive of this text, like the later Vision of Paul, is the lack of any reference to the historical situation of the author.[138] Apocalyptic has lost immediacy by incorporation into an ecclesiastical-moral treatise.

More significant than the apocalypses embedded in other works are the themes of apocalyptic eschatology found in a broad range of early patristic literature. Among these elements, given the lack of *ex eventu* schemes of world history in the Christian apocalypses, it is surprising to find an interest in the structure of history and the delimitation of the ages of the world.[139] One schema is dominant, that of the World or Cosmic Week, the division of history into six periods of a thousand years each, followed by a seventh thousand-year period representing the Sabbath. This pattern appears to have been a Jewish creation, though with possible influence from the astrological speculations of the Iranians and Babylonians. It occurs in II Enoch 32.2–33.2, an apocalypse which appears to come from Egyptian Judaism of the first century AD.[140] The scheme was absorbed into Christianity quite early, as the Epistle of Barnabas, chapter 15 (early second century AD, also probably from Egypt), shows. The pattern appears in a number of second-century authors,[141] and Hippolytus (c. 200) used it to show that Christ's first coming was in the middle and not at the end of the sixth millennium,[142] a position that shows a cool attitude toward any sense of an imminent return. The Cosmic Week recurs in third-century

Latin authors,[143] and in the early fourth century, Lactantius, the author of the most complete and interesting summary of early Christian apocalypticism (*Divine Institutes*, Book 7), also included it (7.14 and 25).[144]

The pattern was adopted by Augustine, but with two significant alterations: the Bishop of Hippo identified the sixth thousand-year period with the time of the church, and he insisted that this period was not to be taken in a literal sense. No calculations were possible about how long the final age would last.[145] Augustine's use assured that World-Week pattern would become the most popular medieval periodization of history. Many later uses of the schema were not apocalyptic in character, but the way was always open for attempts to read the signs of the times as indications of the imminent end of the sixth age and the coming of the Lord.[146]

The twentieth chapter of John's Apocalypse had predicted that an angel would descend to bind Satan in the abyss for a thousand years and that the martyrs would be raised from the dead to reign with Christ for the same period (20.1–6). This chiliastic hope was one of the most potent things John contributed to later apocalyptic speculation. The Apocalypse does not contain reference to the Cosmic Week, and this fact tends to support the contention of J. Daniélou that although Cosmic Week and chiliastic kingdom were soon combined in patristic thought, John's millennium was conceived as a return to the earthly Paradise of pleasures developed independently among the Christians of Asia Minor.[147]

The background to the Christian chiliasm (the doctrine of the return of Christ to reign on earth for a thousand years) must be sought in Jewish apocalyptic speculation about the messianic kingdom; its subsequent history was to be a long and controversial one.[148] The millennial kingdom is not absent from other early Christian apocalypses,[149] but it is in the commentaries, treatises and homilies of the Fathers that the struggle over the proper understanding of Apocalypse 20 was fought out. Irenaeus (*Against Heresies* 5.33.3) and Eusebius (*Church History* 3.39.11–12) mention the witness of Papias, an early Asian bishop, to the belief that Jesus himself had spoken of the millennial kingdom and its riches. This *logion* about the fruitfulness of the kingdom is based upon a theme that goes back to the origins of apocalypticism and appears in I Enoch 10.18–19. I Enoch also predicts that in the coming era '... the righteous will live until they beget thousands' (10.17), a notion that reappears in some later Christian speculations about the millennium. These traditions are usually associated with the first-century heretic Cerinthus and are condemned as a crude invitation to sexual license,[150] but they still appear in a number of Christian sources, such as Nepos of Arsinoe, Commodian and Lactantius.[151] It appears that early Christian belief in the return of the Lord to earth and his reign with the saints was universal, though it was understood in a wide variety of ways ranging from the materialistic to the highly spiritual.[152] Justin, Irenaeus, Tertullian, Methodius, Victorinus, Lactantius and many others were all chiliasts in one sense or another; Origen alone seems to have given a totally spiritual reading of Apoc. 20.1–6.[153]

The decisive challenge to early Christian chiliasm came toward the end of the fourth century and in the early fifth in the writings of Tyconius, Jerome and above all, Augustine. Tyconius, a north African Donatist who flourished about 380, was the first to compose a comprehensive spiritualizing commentary on the Apocalypse.[154] Although his commentary no longer survives, its popularity with later exegetes allows some reconstruction, and its influence on Augustine was great. Gennadius of Marseilles tells us that Tyconius not only '... explained John's Apocalypse anew, understanding the whole in a spiritual sense without anything carnal in it', but that he also '... removed the idea of a thousand-year future kingdom of the just on earth'.[155] Jerome, too, was highly suspicious of any form of chiliasm, and even re-edited the early Apocalypse commentary of Victorinus of Pettau (d. 304) to remove any trace of the dangerous doctrine.[156] Augustine, who had shared the mildest form of belief in the millennial kingdom in his early years,[157] turned against such a view in his later writings, especially in the Letter to Hesychius (Letter 199) and *The City of God*. The latter's 20.7–10 identifies the thousand-year reign with the time of the church on earth and provides a total spiritual interpretation of the details of John's vision. Augustine's views were decisive, because reappearances of belief in a literal millennium are rare in medieval and Renaissance Christian history; but Christian millenarianism in the broad sense, that is, various forms of hope for some coming ideal period of history, either before or after Christ's Parousia, by no means ended with Augustine.

A third theme of apocalyptic eschatology, the story of the Antichrist, also demonstrates the continuing development of apocalypticism in the patristic period and the fact that much of this development must be looked for outside the genre of apocalypse. We have already noted some early stages in Antichrist traditions; a few later chapters will be highlighted here. The first involves the relation between the persecuting emperor Nero (54–68 AD) and the Final Enemy. The mysterious circumstances surrounding Nero's death gave rise to rumors that he had not perished, but had fled to the East and would return leading an oriental army to defeat the Romans. As time went on, it was easy to see how these stories and the appearance of various Nero impostors gave rise to the legend that the vile emperor had indeed died, but that he would rise again to persecute the just and bring destruction to the world. The traditions identifying the *Nero redivivus* with the Antichrist are present in the Apocalypse, especially in the account of the seven-headed beast in 17.3–11 and the beast from the sea in 13.1–10,[158] and they are also found in a number of other Christian texts from the first and second centuries.[159]

The later history of this identification was a factor in the double Antichrist views that are found in the third century, but may well go back to earlier traditions. Complete descriptions of Antichrist's career are found in second-century authors like Irenaeus (*Against Heresies* 5.25–30), and later in the third century in Hippolytus, whose *Treatise on Christ and Antichrist* is the first independent survey. These accounts are remarkable for the wealth of detail they add to the scattered scriptural references: they witness to the importance of the Antichrist legend in early Christianity. In the third-century Latin poet Commodian we find a belief in two final Antichrists – a *Nero redivivus* who will come from the East and destroy the Roman empire, and a Jewish Antichrist born from the tribe of Dan who will reign as a false teacher from Jerusalem (a picture based on II Thessalonians).[160] In the fourth century, a similar doubling can be found in Lactantius and Sulpicius Severus.[161] Interest in the Antichrist is not lacking in the Christian apocalypses. Half these texts still adhere in some way to the threefold eschatological pattern of apocalypticism, and in a number of these works, the crisis stage of the pattern contains a description of the Antichrist and his activity, in several cases including physical portraits.[162]

The end of the fourth century also marked a parting of the ways in the history of Antichrist mythology, and once again Tyconius and Augustine are key figures. Tyconius believed in the advent of a final personal Antichrist, and he even thought that the persecution of the Donatists was a sign of his coming; but the brunt of the African's exegesis, based on the many Antichrists theme of the First Epistle of John I (e.g., 2.18–23, 4.3), was to stress a spiritual interpretation of the Antichrist as the aggregating body of evil within the church.[163] Augustine, too, believed in a final single Antichrist (*City of God*, 18.53, 20.19, 23 and 30), but true to the principles of his anti-apocalyptic theology of history, he refused to speculate on the time of his coming and was cool to most of the legendary accretions to his career.

This brief survey of some of the themes of early Christian apocalypticism is meant to be suggestive and not exhaustive. I have not tried to weigh the degree to which individual patristic authors did or did not adhere to an imminent expectation of the Parousia, because I believe that it is artificial to make this the sole touchstone of apocalypticism. Many authors of the post-100 AD period give us little indication of when they thought Christ would return; others expect a considerable time to intervene, and still others continued to trust in an imminent End to history. One could argue that there were apocalypticists in all three groups.

I have also deliberately refrained from trying to evaluate how far sectarian groups within Christianity, especially the Montanists in the late second century and the Donatists in the fourth (at least their extreme members), can be considered as being inspired by apocalypticism.[164] This is not because I doubt that there were indeed important apocalyptic dimensions to both groups, but because our evidence is controversial in both cases, and also because the concentration upon sectarians as the only apocalypticists in Christianity post-150 AD has tended to divert attention from the role of apocalyptic eschatology in the mainstream of the early church. This essay has been largely concerned with texts rather than with groups, if only because texts continue to be read when groups die out.

The evidence so briefly presented suggests some correction, or at least modification, to two commonly asserted positions concerning early Christian apocalypticism. The first is that which affirms that the earliest stage of Christianity should be seen solely as an apocalyptic sect within Judaism (a simplification of Käsemann's view, but one easy to make); the second is the claim that the delay of the Parousia led to an abandonment of the apocalyptic mentality in second-century Christianity and a basic shift in perspective. I believe that both these positions are misleading simplifications.

There can be no question that the return of the Risen Lord was central to the belief of the first Christians; but it goes beyond the evidence at our disposal to think that the Parousia was always understood in the same way, or according to the same timetable, even before our written records start *c.* 50 AD. If Jesus himself is not to be understood primarily as an apocalyptic preacher, is it not possible that some of his first followers also were not fundamentally apocalypticists, though, like Jesus, they, too, made use of apocalyptic themes in a number of ways? The evidence of the New Testament documents bears out the view that Christianity was highly complex, socially and intellectually, from the start. Apocalyptic elements occur both early (I Thessalonians) and late (the Apocalypse) in the New Testament; non-apocalyptic understandings are present in the developing theology of the synoptic Gospels at an early stage, and in the rather late Johannine literature. It seems too simple to claim that 'apocalyptic was the mother of all Christian theology', as such scholars as G. Ebeling and E. Fuchs responded to E. Käsemann early in the 1960s.[165]

If earliest Christianity was more than an apocalyptic sect, then the thesis of the 'de-eschatologization' of primitive Christianity advanced by M. Werner in his brilliant book, *The Formation of Christian Dogma* (German original, 1941), becomes highly dubious. According to Werner, the crisis in the delay of the Parousia led in the second century to the abandonment of the original consistent-eschatological foundation of Christian belief and its replacement by a new theoretical construction based on the doctrine of the institution of the sacraments through the death of Jesus. Werner's thesis, presented with a combination of broad dialectical simplicity and intricacy of detail, has been attractive to many historians of doctrine, and even seems to haunt the background of some social scientific portrayals of early Christianity's transition from a millenarian cult to a universal religion.[166] The fundamental failure of such views is a false application of Occam's razor – a desire to introduce simplicity at any cost, even in the face of contradictory evidence. Who would deny there is evidence for the loss of a sense of the imminence of the Parousia in second- and third-century Christianity? But what do we do with the fact that many Christians apparently continued to believe in such imminence, and that most of the major theologians and ecclesiastical leaders of the second and third centuries (think of Justin, Irenaeus, Tertullian, perhaps Hippolytus, Cyprian) considered apocalyptic eschatology to be an important part of Christian belief, whether or not they indulged in speculation about how much time remained until the End? One has to wait until the late fourth century in the West to find a systematic anti-apocalypticism. But even Augustine's authority, as the subsequent essays in this volume will show, was not enough to remove the apocalyptic element from Western religious history. The vibrant symbols of Daniel and John and a host of other texts and traditions remained to prompt new visions in the ages to come.[167]

NOTES

1 Ernst Käsemann, 'The Beginnings of Christian Theology', in *Apocalypticism: Journal for Theology and Church*, vol. 6, ed. R. W. Funk (1961), p. 40.
2 Two useful historiographical surveys are Klaus Koch, *The Rediscovery of Apocalyptic* (Naperville, 1972); and Paul D. Hanson, 'Prolegomena to the Study of Jewish Apocalyptic', in *Magnalia Dei: The Mighty Acts of God (G. E. Wright Memorial)*, eds F. M. Cross, W. Lemke and P. D. Miller (1976), pp. 389–413.
3 P. D. Hanson, 'Prolegomena', p. 389.
4 Michael E. Stone, 'Lists of Revealed Things in Apocalyptic Literature', in *Magnalia Dei* (as above, note 2), pp. 439, 443.
5 E.g., Paul D. Hanson, *The Dawn of Apocalyptic* (Philadelphia, 1975), pp. 29–30.
6 M. E. Stone, 'Lists', p. 439.
7 Gerhard von Rad, *Theologie des Alten Testaments* (Munich, 1965), vol. 2, p. 330.
8 *Semeia*, vol. 14, *Apocalypse: the Morphology of a Genre*, ed. John J. Collins (Missoula, 1979).
9 Ibid., p. 9. For some previous attempts to characterize the form, see K. Koch, *The Rediscovery of Apocalyptic*, pp. 23–8; and D. S. Russell, *The Method and Message of Jewish Apocalyptic* (Philadelphia, 1964), ch. IV.
10 John J. Collins, 'Introduction: Towards the Morphology of a Genre', in *Apocalypse: the Morphology of a Genre*, pp. 1–19.
11 On the Jewish side, see Ithamar Gruenwald, *Apocalyptic and Merkavah Mysticism* (Leiden/Cologne, 1980).
12 John J. Collins, 'The Jewish Apocalypses', in *Apocalypse. The Morphology of a Genre*, pp. 21–59.
13 E.g., H. H. Rowley, *The Relevance of Apocalyptic* (1964), pp. 40–2; D. S. Russell, *The Method and Message*, pp. 127–39; K. Koch, *The Rediscovery*, p. 26; John J. Collins, 'Pseudonymity, Historical Reviews and the Genre of the Apocalypse of John', *The Catholic Biblical Quarterly*, XXXIX (1977), pp. 329–43.
14 The Animal Apocalypse of I Enoch 85–90, to be discussed below.
15 For some aspects of apocalyptic symbolism, see e.g., John J. Collins, 'The Symbolism of Transcendence in Jewish Apocalyptic', *Biblical Research*, XXIX (1974), pp. 5–22; Bernard McGinn, 'Symbolism in the Thought of Joachim of Fiore', in *Prophecy and Millenarianism. Essays in Honour of Marjorie Reeves*, ed. A. Williams (1980), pp. 143–64; and with special reference to the Apocalypse of

John, Gilles Quispel, *The Secret Book of Revelation* (1979); and Ugo Vanni, 'Il simbolismo nell'Apocalisse', *Gregorianum*, LXI (1980), pp. 461–505.

16 E.g., Norman Perrin, 'Wisdom and Apocalyptic in the Message of Jesus', *Proceedings of the Society of Biblical Literature*, II (1972), pp. 543–72.
17 E.g., I Enoch 39.2, 93.1–2, 103.2–3; Daniel 12.4; Apocalypse 10.8–11.
18 E.g., I Enoch 74.2, 82.1; IV Esdras 12.37, 14.37–47; Apocalypse 22.
19 Jonathan Z. Smith, 'Wisdom and Apocalyptic', in *Religious Syncretisms in Antiquity*, ed. Birgir A. Pearson (Missoula, 1975), p. 154.
20 Walter Schmithals, *The Apocalyptic Movement* (Nashville, 1975), pp. 189–200.
21 *Apocalypse: Morphology of a Genre*, pp. 14, 22–3. These are Daniel 7–12, the Animal Apocalypse and the Apocalypse of Weeks from I Enoch, Jubilees 23, IV Esdras and II Baruch.
22 *Apocalypse: Morphology of a Genre*, pp. 70–2, lists this as a Type Ib.
23 J. Collins discusses this possibility, but rejects it in *Apocalypse: Morphology of a Genre*, pp. 16, 23–4, and 27.
24 Michael E. Stone, *Scriptures, Sects and Visions. A Profile of Judaism from Ezra to the Jewish Revolts* (Philadelphia, 1980), pp. 41–7.
25 J. T. Milik published the Aramaic fragments in *The Book of Enoch* (Oxford, 1976). M. A. Knibb put out a new edition and translation of the Ethiopic text in *The Ethiopic Book of Enoch* (Oxford, 1978), 2 vols. The Knibb translation will be used here.
26 For an introduction, see M. E. Stone, 'The Book of Enoch and Judaism in the Third Century B.C.E.', *The Catholic Biblical Quarterly*, XL (1978), pp. 479–92.
27 Considerable work has been done on the text of late. E.g., G. W. E. Nickelsburg, 'Apocalyptic and Myth in I Enoch 6–11', *Journal of Biblical Literature*, XCVI (1977), pp. 383–405; P. D. Hanson, 'Rebellion in Heaven, Azazel and Euhemeristic Heroes in Enoch 6–11', ibid., pp. 195–233; and D. Suter, 'Fallen Angel, Fallen Priest: the Problem of Family Purity in I Enoch 6–16', *Hebrew Union College Annual*, L (1979), pp. 115–35.
28 See M. E. Stone, 'Lists of Revealed Things' (as above, note 4), p. 426.
29 M. E. Stone, 'The Book of Enoch and Judaism in the Third Century', (as above, note 26), p. 487.
30 For suggestions regarding the historical and political references in the Book of Watchers, see G. Nickelsburg, 'Apocalyptic and Myth' (as in note 27), p. 391; and D. Suter, 'Fallen Angel, Fallen Priest' (as in note 27), pp. 119–24, 134.
31 R. H. Charles, *The Apocrypha and Pseudepigrapha of the Old Testament in English* (Oxford, 1913), p. 171. More recently, see G. W. E. Nickelsburg, 'The Apocalyptic Message of I Enoch 92–105', *The Catholic Biblical Quarterly*, XXXIX (1977), pp. 309–28.
32 The Appearance of a 'Son of Man' in the Similitudes of Enoch (e.g., chapters 46, 48, 62, 69 and 71) has provoked a rich literature that cannot be discussed here.
33 The literature on Daniel is very large. Among recent commentaries and studies, see John J. Collins, *The Apocalyptic Vision of the Book of Daniel* (Missoula, 1977); and Andre Lacocque, *The Book of Daniel* (Atlanta, 1979).
34 See Collins, *The Apocalyptic Vision*, pp. 36–46, for a summary, and also for access to the literature on this oracle.
35 Collins, ibid., pp. 96–106.
36 This is probably not to be conceived of as a universal resurrection. See G. W. E. Nickelsburg, *Resurrection, Immortality and Eternal Life in Intertestamental Judaism*

(Cambridge, MA, 1972), pp. 11–27.
37 Nor can we forget the 2300 evenings and mornings (i.e., 1150 days) of Daniel 8.14. On medieval attempts to deal with some of the discrepancies in Daniel, see Robert E. Lerner, 'Refreshment of the Saints: the Time after Antichrist as a Station for Earthly Progress in Medieval Thought', *Traditio*, XXXII (1976), pp. 97–144.
38 See especially J. Collins, *The Apocalyptic Vision*, ch. IV, 'History and Eschatology'.
39 The apocalypse proper is found in chapters 3–14; chapters 1–2 and 15–16 are not part of the original text. For a study and translation, see Jacob M. Myers, I and II Esdras (1974). See also E. Breech, 'These Fragments I have Shored against my Ruins: the Form and Function of 4 Ezra', *Journal of Biblical Literature*, XCII (1973), pp. 267–74.
40 The eagle is identified with the fourth kingdom of Daniel 7. For a review of some attempts to work out the details of the vision, see J. M. Myers, ibid., pp. 288–302.
41 There are also some explicit appeals to schemes of world history, e.g., 14.11–12.
42 For a more complete survey of Jewish apocalyptic texts, see J. Collins, 'The Jewish Apocalypses' (see above, note 12).
43 I. Gruenwald, *Apocalyptic and Merkavah Mysticism*, p. 14.
44 A recent representative of the search for a single apocalyptic mentality is W. Schmithals, *The Apocalyptic Movement*.
45 J. Collins, *The Apocalyptic Vision*, p. 88: 'In apocalyptic literature, the course of history is predetermined, but the fate of individuals is not.'
46 *Apocalypse: The Morphology of a Genre*, p. 25: 'The only temporal feature which is common to all apocalypses is the expectation of a future judgment in which the wicked are punished and the good rewarded.'
47 Ibid., p. 9: '. . . personal afterlife is the most consistent aspect of the eschatology of the apocalypses'.
48 G. von Rad, *Old Testament Theology* (1965), vol. 2, p. 304.
49 E.g., W. Schmithals, *The Apocalyptic Movement*, pp. 23–8.
50 H. H. Rowley, *The Relevance of Apocalyptic*, ch. 1; S. B. Frost, *Old Testament Apocalyptic* (1952) (Frost later abandoned this view); and D. S. Russell, *The Method and Message of Jewish Apocalyptic*, ch. VII.
51 G. von Rad, *Old Testament Theology* (1965), vol. 2, pp. 303–8.
52 See P. D. Hanson, 'Prolegomena' (as in note 2 above), pp. 397–401; F. M. Cross, 'New Directions in the Study of Apocalyptic' in *Apocalypticism* (as above in note 1), pp. 157–65; and P. D. Hanson, 'Jewish Apocalyptic against its Near Eastern Environment', *Revue Biblique*, LXXVIII (1971), pp. 31–58.
53 See *The Dawn of Apocalyptic* (note 5 above).
54 E.g., M. E. Stone, *Scriptures, Sects and Visions*, pp. 39–46; J. J. Collins, *The Apocalyptic Vision*, pp. 54–9; and 'Cosmos and Salvation: Jewish Wisdom and Apocalyptic in the Hellenistic Age', *History of Religions*, XVII (1977), pp. 121–42; H. P. Müller, 'Mantischer Weisheit und Apokalyptik', *Vetus Testamentum Supplement* XXII (Leiden, 1972), pp. 268–93.
55 I. Gruenwald, *Apocalyptic and Merkavah Mysticism*, p. 29.
56 See P. D. Hanson, 'Prolegomena' (as in note 2), pp. 400–1, for an expression of a consensus view.
57 Geo Widengren, 'Iran and Israel in Parthian Times with Special Regard to the Ethiopic Book of Enoch', in *Religious Syncretisms* (as in note 19), pp. 85–129.
58 See above, notes 35 and 38, as well as P. D. Hanson, *The Dawn of Apocalyptic*, etc.
59 H.-D. Betz, 'On the Problem of the Religio-Historical Understanding of Apocalypti-

cism', in *Apocalypticism* (as above, note 1), p. 138.

60 E.g., P. D. Hanson, 'Jewish Apocalyptic against its Near Eastern Environment' (see above, note 56); John J. Collins, 'Jewish Apocalyptic against its Hellenistic Near Eastern Environment', *Bulletin of the American Schools of Oriental Research*, CCXX (1975), pp. 27–36; and 'Cosmos and History' (as in note 58 above).

61 J. Z. Smith, 'Wisdom and Apocalyptic', in *Religious Syncretisms in Antiquity* (see note 19), pp. 131–56.

62 The prophetic texts that have a relation to apocalypse as a genre (e.g., Isaiah 56–66, Ezekiel 40–8, and Zechariah 1–6) do not contain apocalyptic eschatology.

63 P. D. Hanson's arguments for a sixth-century dating (see note 57) have not proved convincing to other Intertestamental scholars; see, e.g., M. E. Stone, *Scriptures, Sects and Visions*, p. 46; and J. J. Collins, *The Apocalyptic Vision*, p. xiv.

64 M. E. Stone, *Scriptures, Sects and Visions*, pp. 23–5.

65 J. Collins, *The Apocalyptic Vision*, p. 28.

66 E.g., P. D. Hanson, 'Apocalypticism', in *The Interpreter's Dictionary of the Bible. Supplement* (Abingdon, 1976), p. 33; and A. Lacocque, *The Book of Daniel*, pp. 10–12, 229–30, 244. The best account of the *hasidîm* is in A. Tcherikover, *Hellenistic Civilization and the Jews* (1970), pp. 125–6, 196–8.

67 J. Collins, *The Apocalyptic Vision*, pp. 54–5, 201–14.

68 R. H. Charles, *Apocrypha and Pseudepigrapha*, pp. 170–1.

69 For brief introduction, see M. E. Stone, *Scriptures, Sects and Visions*, ch. 5.

70 See J. Collins, *The Apocalyptic Vision*, pp. 212–14; and B. McGinn, *Visions of the End* (1979), pp. 28–36.

71 See note 30 above for some attempts.

72 On the Testament of Moses, see *Apocalypse: Morphology of a Genre*, pp. 45–6.

73 As in Norman Cohn, *The Pursuit of the Millennium* (Oxford, 1970); and Michael Barkun, *Disaster and the Millennium* (New Haven, 1974).

74 Adela Collins, 'The Political Perspective of the Revelation of John', *Journal of Biblical Literature*, XCVI (1977), pp. 241–56.

75 B. McGinn, *Visions of the End*, pp. 33–6.

76 The term 'apocalyptic community' is that of F. M. Cross, *The Ancient Library of Qumran and Modern Biblical Studies* (1961), pp. 76–8. For a recent review of Qumran's relation to apocalypticism, see John J. Collins, 'Patterns of Eschatology at Qumran', in *Traditions in Transformation*, eds. J. D. Levenson and B. Halpern (Winona Lake, 1981), pp. 351–75. For a bibliographical guide to the extensive literature on Qumran, see Joseph Fitzmyer, *The Dead Sea Scrolls. Major Publications and Tools for Study* (Missoula, 1975).

77 Cross, *Ancient Library of Qumran*, pp. 129–47.

78 See Stone, *Scriptures, Sects and Visions*, p. 68.

79 J. Collins, 'Patterns in Eschatology', p. 373.

80 A more complete account of apocalypticism would need to include a consideration of apocalypses and apocalyptic eschatology in the Hellenistic world, especially the Mesopotamian (e.g., Berossus), Egyptian (e.g., Potter's Oracle) and Persian materials (e.g., Zand-i Vohuman Yasn). Classical literature also includes a number of texts (e.g., the Myth of Er in Plato's *Republic*, and Cicero's Dream of Scipio) which have affinities with otherworldly-journey apocalypses. We have a number of similar texts emanating from Gnostic circles from the second century AD onward. Finally, the phenomenon most closely related to apocalypticism is found in the Sibylline texts, products of Hellenistic Judaism, and later of

Christianity, stretching from the mid-second century BC to the third century AD. For an introduction to the various materials, see *Apocalypse: Morphology of a Genre*.
81 See Norman Perrin, *Rediscovering the Teaching of Jesus* (Philadelphia, 1967), for an account based on this view.
82 The most brilliant statement of this view remains Albert Schweitzer, *Vom Reimarus zu Wrede* (1906), translated into English as *The Quest for the Historical Jesus*.
83 The term was popularized by C. H. Dodd, *The Apostolic Preaching and its Developments* (Chicago, 1937), especially the Appendix, 'Eschatology and History', pp. 135–67.
84 N. Perrin, *Rediscovering the Teaching of Jesus*, p. 203.
85 'The Beginnings of Christian Theology', p. 40 (see note 1).
86 R. W. Funk, 'Apocalypse as an Historical and Theological Problem in Current New Testament Scholarship', in *Apocalypticism* (as above, note 1), pp. 175–91. Compare with N. Perrin, 'Wisdom and Apocalyptic in the Message of Jesus' (as in note 16 above).
87 For a critical survey of their views, see H.-D. Betz, 'The Concept of Apocalyptic in the Theology of the Pannenberg Group', *Apocalypticism* (as in note 1), pp. 192–207.
88 Lars Hartman, *Prophecy Interpreted* (Lund, 1966), pp. 235–6, for a summary.
89 *Prophecy Interpreted*, p. 216.
90 *Prophecy Interpreted*, pp. 245, 247.
91 R. W. Funk, 'Apocalypse as an Historical and Theological Problem' (see note 86), p. 185.
92 H.-D. Betz, 'The Concept of Apocalyptic' (see note 91), p. 206.
93 For a brief treatment, see Norman Perrin, *The New Testament: an Introduction* (1974), ch. 4, 'Apocalyptic Christianity'.
94 E.g., N. Perrin, *The New Testament: an Introduction*, pp. 119–20, sees it as deutero-Pauline and dating from c. 70–90 AD, while W. Kümmel (not a conservative biblical scholar) accepts its authenticity in his *The Theology of the New Testament* (Nashville, 1973), p. 141.
95 The name appears in the New Testament only in I John 2.18 and 22, 4.3; and II John 1.7.
96 Wilhelm Bousset, *The Antichrist Legend* (1896). More recently, see Josef Ernst, *Die eschatologischen Gegenspieler in den Schriften des Neuen Testaments* (Regensburg, 1967).
97 For a study of how some of the scriptural texts were used in the medieval period, see Richard K. Emmerson, *Antichrist in the Middle Ages* (Seattle, 1981), chapters 1–2.
98 N. Perrin, *The New Testament: An Introduction*, pp. 144–5, 162–5.
99 N. Perrin, *The New Testament: An Introduction*, p. 191.
100 For a review of the earlier stages, see G. R. Beaseley-Murray, *Jesus and the Future* (1954).
101 For a summary, see N. Perrin, *The New Testament: An Introduction*, pp. 79, 188, 210. A more detailed treatment may be found in L. Hartman, *Prophecy Interpreted*.
102 Fifty years ago G. B. Shaw dismissed the Apocalypse as '... a curious record of the visions of a drug addict which was absurdly admitted to the canon under the title of Revelation', in *The Adventures of the Black Girl in her Search for God* (1932), p. 73.
103 E.g., B. W. Jones, 'More about the Apocalypse as Apocalyptic', *Journal of Biblical*

Literature, LXXXVII (1968), pp. 325–7.
104 P. Vielhauer, 'Apocalyptic in Early Christianity', in *New Testament Apocrypha*, eds. E. Hennecke and W. Schneemelcher (Philadelphia, 1965), vol. 2, pp. 601–7.
105 See John J. Collins, 'Pseudonymity, Historical Reviews and the Genre of the Revelation of John', *The Catholic Biblical Quarterly*, XXXIX (1977), pp. 329–43.
106 For an analysis of the pattern in John, see Adela Y. Collins, *The Combat Myth in the Book of Revelation* (Missoula, 1976), ch. 1.
107 Adela Collins, 'Early Christian Apocalypses', in *Apocalypse: the Morphology of a Genre*, pp. 70–2, lists it as a Type Ib, i.e., an apocalypse with cosmic and/or political eschatology without either historical review or otherworldly journey.
108 For a brief survey of its reception, see N. B. Stonehouse, *The Apocalypse in the Ancient Church: a Study in the History of the New Testament* (Goes, 1929).
109 The dating depends on internal evidence, as well as the external witness of Irenaeus, *Against Heresies* 5.30.5. A minority view has tried without much success to place the text in the reign of Nero prior to 68 AD.
110 These categories are taken from Elizabeth Schüssler Fiorenza, 'Composition and Structure of the Revelation of John', *The Catholic Biblical Quarterly*, XXXIX (1977), pp. 345–50.
111 M. E. Boismard, 'L'Apocalypse ou les apocalypses de Saint Jean', *Revue Biblique*, LVI (1949), pp. 507–41.
112 The recapitulation theory (first advanced in the fourth century by Victorinus) was revived by G. Bornkamm, 'Die Komposition der apokalyptischen Visionen in her Offenbarung Johannis', *Zeitschrift für die neutestamentliche Wissenschaft*, XXXVI (1937), pp. 132–49. For some recent surveys of the composition question, see E. S. Fiorenza, 'Composition and Structure' (as in note 110); and A. Y. Collins, *The Combat Myth*, ch. 1.
113 This is the outline of A. Y. Collins, *The Combat Myth*, pp. 32 *et seq*. See also her popular introduction, *The Apocalypse* (Wilmington, 1979), pp. xii–xiii.
114 John M. Court, *Myth and History in the Book of Revelation* (Atlanta, 1979), ch. 1. There is still no adequate history of the book's exegesis. The best account remains W. Bousset, *Die Offenbarung Johannis* (Göttingen, 1906; reprint 1966), pp. 49–119.
115 W. G. Kümmel, *Introduction to the New Testament* (Nashville, 1966), p. 332.
116 For the mythic character, see the work of A. Y. Collins, *The Combat Myth* and 'The History-of-Religions Approach to Apocalypticism and "The Angel of the Waters" (Rev. 16.4–7)', *The Catholic Biblical Quarterly*, XXXIX (1977), pp. 367–81. For a political stress, see E. S. Fiorenza, *Invitation to the Book of Revelation* (Garden City, 1981).
117 For some background, see John J. Collins, 'The Mystery of Holy War in Daniel and the Qumran War Scroll', *Vetus Testamentum*, XXV (1975), pp. 596–612.
118 Adela Y. Collins, 'The Political Perspective of the Revelation of John', *Journal of Biblical Literature*, XCVI (1977), p. 256.
119 A point emphasized by E. S. Fiorenza, 'Eschatology and the Composition of the Apocalypse', *The Catholic Biblical Quarterly*, XXX (1968), pp. 537–69.
120 A. Y. Collins, 'The Early Christian Apocalypses', in *Apocalypse: the Morphology of a Genre*, pp. 61–121, discusses twenty-four texts.
121 Aside from A. Y. Collins, 'The Early Christian Apocalypses', the only other survey is Heinrich Weinel, 'Die spätere christliche Apokalyptik', in *EUCHARISTERION: Studien zur Religion und Literatur des Alten und Neuen Testaments: Festschrift*

Hermann Gunkel, ed., H. Schmidt (Göttingen, 1923), pp. 141–73.
122 Only one example exists, a work known as Jacob's Ladder, and this may be Jewish in origin. See *Apocalypse: Morphology of a Genre*, pp. 67, 69–70.
123 These texts would include five or six type Ib apocalypses and four type IIb, see *Apocalypse*, pp. 64–5. Along with Jacob's Ladder, then, we would have ten or eleven out of twenty-four texts displaying a concern for history and the triple pattern.
124 On the apocalyptic character of the work, see R. J. Bauckham, 'The Great Tribulation in the Shepherd of Hermas', *Journal of Theological Studies*, n.s. XXV (1974), pp. 27–40.
125 The closest Hermas comes is in the interpretation of the four colors of the head of the beast of Vision IV (see Vis. IV.i.10 and iii.1–7).
126 A. Collins, 'The Early Christian Apocalypses', pp. 72–3.
127 The work as it now stands is a fifth-century Syriac church order, but embedded in it is an earlier apocalypse (chapters 2–14). On the dating and content, see H. Weinel, 'Die spätere christliche Apokalyptik' (as above in note 129), pp. 143–5. There is an English translation by J. Cooper and A. Maclean, *The Testament of the Lord* (Edinburgh, 1902).
128 Among the apocalypses that can be dated with any certainty, four or five that have a public eschatology can be dated to the first two centuries and only one that has a purely personal eschatology (see A. Collins, 'The Early Christian Apocalypses', p. 66). Thus most of the texts with purely personal eschatology seem to be post-200 AD.
129 A. Collins, 'The Early Christian Apocalypses', pp. 78–83, 89–95.
130 A. Collins, 'The Early Christian Apocalypses', p. 66.
131 I. Gruenwald, *Apocalyptic and Merkavah Mysticism*, pp. 45–6.
132 See B. McGinn, *Visions of the End*, p. 15.
133 The fundamental works on the Latin tradition are by Theodore Silverstein, *Visio Sancti Pauli: Studies and Documents* 4 (1935); and 'The Vision of St. Paul. New Links and Patterns in the Western Tradition', *Archives d'histoire doctrinale et littéraire du moyen âge*, XXXIV (1959), pp. 199–248.
134 From the translation of H. Duensing in *New Testament Apocrypha* (as above in note 104), vol. 2, p. 759.
135 See the discussion by H. Duensing in *New Testament Apocrypha*, vol. 2, p. 755.
136 For some accounts, see F. Macler, 'Les apocalypses apocryphes de Daniel', *Revue de l'histoire des religions*, XXXIII (1896), pp. 37–53, 163–76, 288–319; A. M. Denis, *Introduction aux pseudepigraphes grecs d'Ancien Testament* (Leiden, 1970); P. H. Alexander, 'Medieval Apocalypses as Historical Sources', *American Historical Review*, LXXIII (1968), pp. 1997–2018; and Klaus Berger, *Die Griechische Daniel-Diegese: Eine Altkirchliche Apokalypse* (Leiden, 1976).
137 There are few general studies of patristic eschatology in general and apocalyptic in particular. The most complete is the old work of Leonhard Atzberger, *Geschichte der christlichen Eschatologie innerhalb der vornicänischen Zeit* (Freiburg, 1896).
138 A point emphasized by P. Vielhauer, 'Apocalyptic in Early Christianity', (see above, note 104), p. 629.
139 For literature on the periodization of history in patristic times, see R. Schmidt, '*Aetates mundi*: Die Weltalter als Gliederungsprinzip der Geschichte', *Zeitschrift für Kirchengeschichte*, LXVII (1955–6), pp. 287–317; B. Kötting, 'Endzeitprognossen zwischen Lactantius und Augustinus', *Historisches Jahrbuch*, LXXVII (1957), pp.

125–39; and especially Auguste Luneau, *L'histoire du salut chez les Pères de l'Eglise* (Paris, 1964).
140 W. Bauer, 'Chiliasmus', *Realenzyklopädie für Antike und Christentum* (Stuttgart, 1954), vol. 2, c. 1075, claims that the Samaritans had a concept of the 7000-year course of history; and in the Testament of Abraham, another Jewish text probably from first-century Egypt, Death is said to ravage the world for seven ages (chapter 19). Jean Daniélou, on the other hand, saw the origin of the schema in Jewish Christianity, probably in Syria, in his *The Theology of Jewish Christianity* (Chicago, 1964), pp. 396–403, and 'La typologie millénariste de la semaine', *Vigiliae Christianae*, II (1948), pp. 1–16.
141 E.g., Irenaeus, *Against Heresies* 5.23.2 and 28.3; and possibly in Clement of Alexandria, *Miscellanies* 4.25.
142 *Commentary on Daniel* 4.23–4.
143 E.g., Commodian, *Apologetic Song* 45 and 791; Cyprian, *To Fortunatus* 2; Victorinus of Pettau, *On the Making of the World* 6.
144 See B. McGinn, *Apocalyptic Spirituality* (1979), pp. 17–80, for an introduction to and translation of *Divine Institutes*, Book 7.
145 The two crucial passages are *City of God* 20.7 and 22.30.
146 Among the other important apocalyptic schemes of history that cannot be considered here is the Four Empires pattern from Daniel 2 and 7, also found in the eagle vision of IV Esdras.
147 J. Daniélou, *The Theology of Jewish Christianity*, pp. 390–6.
148 For a survey of background, see D. S. Russell, *The Method and Message of Jewish Apocalyptic*, ch. XI. For treatments, see J. Daniélou, *The Theology of Jewish Christianity*, ch. 14; A. Wikenhauser, 'Die Herkunft der Idee des tausendjährigen Reiches in der Johannes-Apokalypse', *Römische Quartalschrift für christliche Altertumskunde und für Kirchengeschichte*, XLV (1937), pp. 1–24; and H. Bietenhard, 'The Millennial Hope in the Early Church', *The Scottish Journal of Theology*, VI (1953), pp. 12–30.
149 E.g., Apocalypse of Paul 21–2, and the Apocalypse of Elijah 3.99. A reference in the Ascension of Isaiah 4.14–17 is more ambiguous.
150 See the attacks of Gaius and Dionysius reported in Eusebius, *Church History* 3.28.
151 On Nepos, see *Church History* 7.24. See also Commodian, *Institutes* 2.3; and Lactantius, *Divine Institutes* 7.24.
152 J. Daniélou distinguishes three strands in *The Theology of Jewish Christianity*, p. 396.
153 For the evidence on Origen, see N. B. Stonehouse, *The Apocalypse in the Ancient Church* (as in note 108 above), pp. 117–28.
154 See T. Hahn, *Tyconius-Studien* (Leipzig, 1900).
155 *On Church Writers* 18.
156 Both the original and Jerome's edition have been edited by J. Haussleiter, *Victorini Episcopi Petavionensis Opera* (Vienna, 1916).
157 For a summary, see G. Folliet, 'La typologie du sabbat chez saint Augustine: son interpretation millénariste entre 388 et 400', *Revue des études augustiniennes*, II (1956), pp. 371–90.
158 For some discussion, see J. Ernst, *Die eschatologischen Gegenspieler* (as in note 96). Nero Caesar (in Hebrew characters) is still the best candidate for the famous number of the beast as 666 in Apoc. 13.18. Some have interpreted the beast from the abyss who kills the two witnesses (11.7) as Nero killing Peter and Paul.

159 E.g., Ascension of Isaiah 4.1–18; Sibylline Oracles 8.139–41. The Jewish Sibylline Oracle 5.101–7, 137–54 and 361 *et seq.* also paints Nero as the final apocalyptic foe.
160 Commodian, *Apologetic Song*, 933–5.
161 Lactantius, *Divine Institutes* 7.16–17; and Sulpicius Severus, *Dialogues* 1.41.
162 For physical descriptions of the Antichrist, see the Testament of the Lord 11 and the Apocalypse of John the Theologian 7. On the development of these descriptions, see K. Berger, *Die Grieschische Daniel-Diegese*, pp. 115–20 (as above, in note 136). Other early Christian apocalypses that contain important material on the Antichrist are the Apocalypse of Peter 2, the Questions of Bartholomew 4, the Apocalypse of Esdras 4.28–5.1, and the Apocalypse of Sedrach 15.5.
163 For an account of Tyconius's views, see H. D. Rauh, *Das Bild des Antichrist im Mittelalter: Von Tyconius zum deutschen Symbolismus* (Münster, 1973), pp. 98–121.
164 For an introduction to the Montanist movement, see R. M. Grant, *Augustus to Constantine* (1970), pp. 131–44; and for the Donatists, W. H. C. Frend, *The Donatist Church* (Oxford, 1971). More work is needed on the apocalyptic views of both groups.
165 Gerhard Ebeling, 'The Ground of Christian Theology'; and Ernst Fuchs, 'On the Task of a Christian Theology', in *Apocalypticism* (as in note 1), pp. 47–98.
166 E.g., John Gager, *Kingdom and Community. The Social World of Early Christianity* (Englewood Cliffs, 1975). See the justly critical remarks of David Bartlett and Jonathan Z. Smith in *Zygon*, XIII (1978), pp. 109–30.
167 An International Colloquium on Apocalypticism was held at the University of Uppsala in August of 1979. The papers of this Colloquium are soon to be published under the title *Apocalypticism in the Mediterranean World and the Near East*, ed. D. Hellholm, a collection that promises to be of great value for all interested in the history of apocalyptic traditions.

MARJORIE REEVES

2 The development of apocalyptic thought: medieval attitudes

I

Following the original sense of the word, I take 'apocalypse' to mean here the disclosure of hidden divine purpose in history, to which common usage has added the dimension of imminent crisis. Thinking about the time-process in apocalyptic terms at once places it on a different plane of understanding from the physical cosmos. The moving moments of time are no longer felt to be succeeding each other in an endless cycle of birth, maturity and death, but as fulfilling a divine purpose in proceeding towards a fore-ordained conclusion. This relates the present moment to a definite beginning and a definite end; it can give a sense of belonging in time and links the fleeting moment to a transcendent purpose outside time. Thus Judeo-Christian apocalyptic thought moved the idea of the time-process on to a new plane and created the concept of history as the field of God's activity, revealing his hidden purposes as the *saeculum* moved towards its end.[1] This is not to say that elements from older systems of thought did not remain, to be held in tension with this positive idea of history. The cyclical concept continued to appear in various forms while the Platonic affirmation of unchanging reality riding high above the fluctuations of time haunted the medieval mind. Nevertheless, a vital part of the medieval inheritance from early Christian centuries is the lineal concept of time and the meaningfulness of historical moments in the operations of God.

This inheritance was mediated largely through St. Augustine and the ambivalence of his attitude to history is reflected right through the medieval period. For, whilst decisively blocking the way, not only to millennial dreams of the future but also to ideas of secular progress within history, he yet bequeathed to succeeding ages the two great time-patterns which provided the framework to medieval thought on the time-process. Both embodied the idea of the progressive self-revelation of God within history. Both were derived from pre-Augustinian sources. The doctrine of the three stages of salvation derives from St. Paul's teaching in Romans 5.13–14, where he clearly envisaged a stage before Moses (*ante legem*), a stage under the law (*sub lege*) and the culminating stage – in this world – under the grace of Christ (*sub gratia*).[2] With the addition of a fourth stage – *in gloria* – this became standard teaching in the Church Fathers. The other pattern was that of the Six World Ages (with the Seventh located outside of time), based on the Week of Creation in Genesis 1. There were complex roots to this, going back, according to Fr. Luneau, to the cycle of seven million years originating in Iranian sources and widely used by pagan writers.[3] But in transforming this into the World Week of God's purpose in history, Augustine made it a one-directional process. There was no cyclical return, no revival of the age of innocence in the Golden Seventh Age: the final apotheosis in the Seventh Age would be, in Luneau's words, 'irrémédiablement neuf'.[4]

Yet in the same breath Augustine was teaching that the climax of history had already been reached and passed in the life and death of Jesus. God's purpose had been unveiled and there was no room for a new revelation within history. For all future generations what remained of the time-process was a period of waiting until the End was consummated in the Second Coming. The only 'movement' was that of individual souls on their pilgrimage through earthly things to the heavenly City. Peter Brown points out that there are

> no verbs of historical movement in the *City of God*, no sense of progress to aims that may be achieved in history. . . . The most obvious feature of man's life in this *saeculum* is that it is doomed to remain incomplete. No human potentiality can ever reach its fulfillment in it; no human tension can ever be resolved. The fulfillment of human personality lies beyond it; it is infinitely postponed to the end of time, to the Last Day and the glorious resurrection.[5]

The shadow of this negative approach lay heavily on medieval aspirations, discouraging attempts, such as those of Eusebius and Orosius to trace a providential pattern in recent history, whether ecclesiastical or secular.[6] The prevailing mood inherited by medieval people was one of pessimism concerning the future. The world was slipping downhill and the signs of its final degeneration were already present. The only possible attitude was one of repentance and watchfulness for the End. The Middle Ages lived in the consciousness of being in the End-Time. People had no sense of looking ahead through uncounted ages stretching out before them: whether the actual End was imminent or not, they lived close to it, for 'The Lord is at hand' rang in their ears. But, though the Day of the Lord would be terrible, apocalyptic expectation linked time with eternity and nourished the hope of passing from the shifting sands of history to the eternal realm of beatitude.

Thus it was the End which now provided history with meaning and structure, and the greatest remaining event was Last Judgement. This, of course, was constantly represented to the medieval imagination in ecclesiastical art. The practice of depicting the Last Judgement over the chancel arch or on the west wall of a church or in the tympanum of its west door soon became widespread. With its gaping mouth of Hell, awful Judge and saints rising to Heaven, this was a constant and vivid reminder to all.[7]

One of the most powerful elements in the program of Last Things was the expected climax to a cosmic struggle between Good and Evil. This probably had roots far back in ancient mythologies and the concept of Antichrist which was inherited by medieval thinkers through Judeo-Christian sources was therefore multi-dimensional. On the one hand, it could represent the total evil presence in the world, with manifestations in every age; on the other, a single character appearing at a specific moment in the program of Last Things. Sometimes Antichrist was identified with Satan; sometimes he was the Devil's minion. One of the most significant problems in the history of Antichrist was his relationship to the Roman Empire. The bitter, if spasmodic, persecution of early Christians naturally led to the identification of Antichrist with a Roman Emperor, and in particular with Nero. Hence arose the later legend of *Nero redivivus* as the expected Antichrist. But already, in Paul's second letter to the Thessalonians, had appeared the belief – which Bousset believed to derive from an older tradition – that so long as the Roman Empire survived Antichrist would not appear.[8] This conviction was, of course, strengthened by the conversion of Constantine. Hence the most common medieval view was that the survival of the Roman Empire postponed the dreaded day of Antichrist. Both terrors aroused by successive barbarian invasions, presaging its break-up, and valiant attempts to believe in its continued existence – whether in Byzantium, in Charlemagne's Empire or the Germanic Holy Roman Empire – must therefore be viewed against the back-cloth of Last Things. Thus Jordanes the Goth holds that the end is not yet because Theodoric, King of the Goths, has received a legitimate title from the Emperor Zeno, while both Cassiodorus and Boethius in the sixth century cling to the belief that the Roman Empire has not yet fallen. When the Lombards destroyed this continuing Roman dream Gregory the Great became obsessed with the imminence of the End and, since the conversion of the world must precede it, saw his mission to convert Ethelbert of Kent as a step towards Last Things.[9] Yet hope perpetually revives: for Isidore of Seville in the seventh century the Visigoths have taken on the role of the Romans, although their conversion is also a sign that the end of the Sixth Age will not be long.[10] Gregory of Tours eagerly installs Clovis as the new Constantine, yet cannot leave the fascinating subject of Antichrist alone and, quoting Matthew 24 on pestilence, famine and false prophets to come, sees the *initia dolorum* in his own time, *sicut praesenti gestum est tempore* ('as manifested in this present time').[11] For Haymo of Auxerre, Charlemagne had once more secured hope,[12] but with the break-up of the Carolingian Empire tension mounts again. Hinckmar of Rheims gathers together from the Fathers all he can find on Antichrist.[13] Similarly, Agobard of Lyons exhorts Louis the Pious, in preparation for the *tempus periculosum*, to order the collection of all possible information on Antichrist.[14] The image of *Nero redivivus* survives, however, as the precursor of the real Antichrist, who would destroy him. He then becomes associated with the figure of Simon Magus, the magician who tried to buy spiritual powers from the Apostles.[15] Later, as we shall see, these early legends develop into the concept of the double Antichrist, a wicked tyrant and a pseudo-pope.

The essential nature of Antichrist is that in all things he must be opposite to Christ. The beginnings of this concept can be seen in Jewish tradition, in the 'abomination of desolation' prophesied by Daniel, when the embodiment of evil, the false Messiah, aspires to the seat of God himself in the Temple at Jerusalem. From this it was an obvious step for the Christian legend to develop in terms of a Jewish Antichrist, born of the tribe of Dan, or alternatively in Babylon, matching Christ's miracles by signs and wonders, gathering his disciples, and so on. By the tenth century there is a complete life of Antichrist for the edification of the faithful.[16] The dualism of the whole scheme is pronounced. Whether worked out thus in terms of one life or seen as embodied in the beasts of the Apocalypse, echoes of a primeval dragon myth embodying the cosmic conflict of good and evil reverberate in the medieval imagination. Contemporary political crises did not, according to Bousset, create the myth of Antichrist, but were successively interpreted in terms of these ancient beliefs.[17]

The sense that any elements of stable order that existed must disintegrate at the approach of the End finds vivid expression in the popular legend of Gog and Magog. If the Roman Empire represented a fragile security, successive waves of barbarians breaking in from the East highlighted its vulnerability. The legend of Alexander's visit to the Caucasus, his viewing of the terrible lands and peoples beyond, and his creation of the great iron gates to shut out these tribes of Gog and Magog was the fairy-tale answer of the imagination to grim forebodings.[18] The legend may have been already in existence as early as the time of Julius Caesar and Alexander's Gate receives early description in the writings of Strabo and Pliny. The legend was Christianized in the story that God had provided a special passage in the mountains where Alexander was directed to build the Gate that would hold in the Biblical Gog and Magog (identified with the ten lost tribes of Israel) until God willed the beginning of the End. Then they would burst forth and this would be the signal for Antichrist to appear. It was a splendid subject for fantastic romance and, as long as the Gate was believed to be holding fast, travellers' tales of those menacing, shut-in peoples could be enjoyed, perhaps with a shiver. Men told of the three defences of the Gate: mechanical iron men who continually struck blows to create the illusion of armed guards, an eagle with a warning cry and trumpets through which the wind blew menacing blasts. But as the bulwark of the civilized world the Gate was taken seriously by learned and simple alike. When in Apocalypse

16 the Sixth Angel pours his phial on the river Euphrates which dries up, this was interpreted as the dread moment when the Roman Empire would 'dry up' and the flood of barbarian people would pour in.

But beside the folk lore of expected drama we must set the calm approach to the future of Beatus of Liebana whose apocalypse commentary, written in the second half of the eighth century, became a standard work of reference.[19] One might never guess that he was living in a Spain suffering under Islam conquerors. The dramatic figures of St. John's vision are translated into moralistic and abstract terms and all temptation to allot roles in a specific sense is resisted. Thus he declares firmly:

> it is not, as some think, that Antichrist will persecute the church in one (specific) place, for antichrists are everywhere. Antichrist will be the latest king to reign over the whole world, calling himself God, that is, Christ. But now truly Antichrist is hidden in the church, for as yet power is not given to him openly. Then, when indeed he will appear, he will unite the whole world with his power.[20]

It is astonishing that Beatus does not seek to identify Mahomet and his followers with Antichrist or one of his minions. On the contrary his interpretations are all 'safe': the Dragon is the devil, the Babylonish Whore is the sum of human sins, while the two witnesses of Apocalypse 11 are *Lex* and *Evangelium* and the Seven Seals are stages in the life of Christ. In adopting the six ages of the world from St. Augustine Beatus makes a clear distinction between these and the Seventh, the Sabbath Age.[21] In the same spirit he disassociates himself from any suggestion of millenarianism by interpreting the thousand years of Satan bound as the period from the First to the Second Advent. Then Satan will be released for a space, *quando in Antichristo ingressus erit ille princeps diabolus* ('when that prince, the devil, will be embodied in Antichrist').[22] Antichrist occupies his mind a good deal and he emphasizes the fact that he is *Anti-*, not *Ante-*, that is, in all things contradictory to Christ, not simply his predecessor. Already the Antichrist history is well developed and Beatus goes through the whole thing: born of the tribe of Dan and so on. The cool tones of this influential commentary speak much for the strength of the Augustinian tradition.

Curiously, the Islamic threat did not play much part in the apocalyptic drama until later. It is true that in the ninth century both St. Eulogius and Alvarus of Cordoba saw Mahomet as the precursor of Antichrist and the rule of Islam as preparation for the End. Alvarus calculated that this rule should last 245 years in all and that therefore the End was very near. He also noted with satisfaction that Mahomet had died in 666 – the number of the Beast.[23] But few outside Spain appear to have taken up this theme.

Beatus' type of exegesis reduced human agencies in history to insignificance. But optimistic hopes for a this-worldly future could not be altogether denied. In times of crisis or intolerable pressure men look for a more immediate deliverance and a more proximate Jerusalem than that beyond the confines of time. It was in a remote corner of Syria, under the scourge of Islam, that the expectation of a Last World Emperor seems to have arisen, drawn probably from Jewish messianic sources. Its earliest surviving appearance is in the seventh-century text we call the Pseudo-Methodius.[24] With significant rapidity it reached Byzantium and was translated into Latin in the West by the early eighth century. Its core is the promise of a mighty emperor who will arise to destroy Islam, recover Jerusalem, put down all enemies of Christians and inaugurate a period of peace and plenty. Men will live in this beatitude until Antichrist appears. Then the Emperor will go to Golgotha, hang his insignia on the Cross and resign his power and his person into the hands of God. The reign of Antichrist will then begin and last, with all the expected tribulations of the faithful, until he is destroyed by Christ. Another version of this prophecy appears in the Latin text of the Tiburtine Sibyl, dated to the eleventh century, with twelfth-century additions. It is not clear whether the two texts are independent or related in some way.[25]

Thus another, penultimate act is added to the end-drama. Before the final confrontation of cosmic forces in the conflict of Antichrist with Christ, human achievement will be allowed its brief moment of this-worldly triumph. Though finally dwarfed and crushed by the supernatural powers, a positive meaning is given to secular history. The eagerness with which this expectation was embraced in the West is seen in the way in which the myth of the Last World Emperor was incorporated into Abbot Adso's *Libellus de Antichristo* in the tenth century.[26] The background to this tract illustrates vividly the way people reacted to the threat of political chaos, relating contemporary tribulations to the great end-time crisis. About 950 Queen Gerberga, sister of the future Otto I and wife of the late Carolingian Louis IV, asked Adso to put together all that was known about Antichrist. It was an age of violence and insecurity: Moslems, Magyars and Vikings still threatened from outside, the break-up of the Carolingian Empire brought disorder within, the Ottonian attempt to restore political order was still in the future. In this situation the message that Adso brought was fundamentally pessimistic – men must endure evil and look for the worst since time began – but one ray of light was focused on the revival of Imperial glory before the final onslaught of evil. It provided motivation for an active participation in end-time history and thus became a factor in the great outburst of apocalyptic energy expressed in the crusading movements from the eleventh century onwards.

It might perhaps seem obvious that round the year 1000 apocalyptic expectations would cluster most thickly, but investigations reveal the curious fact that, while there is evidence for such apprehensions in the mid-tenth century and in the early eleventh, the actual millennium passed with little dramatic demonstration.[27] In 960 a hermit, Bernard, announced the end of the world. Abbo of Fleury, writing in 998, recalled that in his youth c. 940 he heard a Paris preacher announcing the end of the world for the year 1000. He also relates that in 970 a rumor was circulating in Lorraine that the world would end in the year in which the Feast of the Annunciation coincided with Good Friday: this happened in 992. But Abbo wrote to refute such rumors, as had Adso in his *Libellus*. Ralph Glaber does indeed start a new book of his chronicle at the millennium, but, whilst collecting portents whenever possible, he does not record anything startling under this actual year. Under the millennium of the Passion in 1033, however, he does describe famine in terms of the natural order returning to chaos preceding the end of the human race.[28] Official documents in preceding and following times often use a phrase such as *mundi termino appropinquante* ('the end of the world drawing close'), but again no examples have come to light around the actual year 1000. Two points seem to emerge from this ambivalent evidence: first, that fear of the approaching end was a constant, coming to the surface in any crisis, such as famine, eclipse, disaster; secondly, that the official policy of the Church was probably to play down these upsurges of emotion and to teach that the times and seasons are known to God alone. It is perhaps significant that in 998 the Council of Rome imposed a seven-year penance on King Robert of France.[29] Certainly neither official documents of the Church nor the majority of chronicles give any particular emphasis to the millennium, yet paradoxically the anxiety is always there, holding people under the shadow of Judgment: *appropinquante etenim mundi termino et ruinis crescentibus* ('the end of the world indeed drawing near and calamities increasing').

In the eleventh century Jerusalem became a focus for apocalyptic expectations and people pressed towards it. Ralph Glaber, relating the journey of Odalric, bishop of Orleans, to Jerusalem in 1028, speaks of the great crowds there expecting the advent of Antichrist, and similarly the life of St. Altmann in 1064 witnesses to the journey of many noblemen to the Holy Sepulchre under the expectation of the Last Day.[30] It is now thought that Urban II's original sermon at Clermont in 1095, which initiated the First Crusade, was not closely focussed on the deliverance of Jerusalem from the infidel.[31] But among those who preached the crusade this objective was soon added and because of its apocalyptic overtones the attainment of Jerusalem became the most powerful form of propaganda. Thus Guibert of Nogent puts words into Urban's mouth arguing that God's plan requires that Antichrist should make war on Christians, not Jews or Gentiles, in Jerusalem and that the faithful must therefore revive the Christian cult in Jerusalem in order that Antichrist shall have someone to fight![32] Even in this context Islam is not identified with Antichrist and indeed a single letter of Innocent III gives the only clear official equation of Mahomet with Antichrist.[33]

The apocalyptic image of Jerusalem was greatly enhanced by the Last World Emperor myth. Charlemagne was expected to come to life and march on

Jerusalem; Benzo of Alba urged this role on the Emperor Henry IV; similarly, Louis VII of France, preparing for the Second Crusade, was hailed as the fulfiller of this prophecy.[34] It was to the Emperor Frederick I, who lost his life on the Third Crusade in 1187, that the *Ludus de Antichristo* was presented *c.* 1160.[35] In this play the Roman emperor brings the whole world under his rule, finally entering Jerusalem in triumph to worship in the Temple. Then he lays down crown and sceptre and resigns his imperial dignity to the King of Kings. Thus the crusade and the recovery of Jerusalem are placed within an apocalyptic context. But, while spurring on the faithful to supreme effort, the further outlook always holds the inevitable Antichrist. Godfrey of Viterbo, writing *c.* 1186–7, gives in full the current version of the Last World Emperor prophecy, mounting to a climax of glory in the conversion of the Jews, but continues immediately: *In illo tempore surget princeps iniquitatis de tribu Dan* . . . ('in that time the prince of iniquity will arise from the tribe of Dan . . .').[36] But Jerusalem remained a focus of dreams. To St. Anselm and St. Bernard Jerusalem might be a spiritual symbol of celestial bliss, leading them to discourage the cult of the earthly Jerusalem through pilgrimages.[37] Nevertheless, simple folk confused the celestial with the terrestrial Jerusalem, knights expected miracles in their holy war and religiously rushed off on pilgrimage, ready for the imminent End.

At a more sophisticated level of theological interpretation, by the twelfth century present history and human action within it were assuming more significance. This can be traced in several trends of thought. At a much earlier date St. Jerome's apocalyptic arithmetic, based on the two end-time figures in the Book of Daniel, 1290 'days' and 1335 'days', had provided the suggestive notion of a forty-five 'day' interval between the destruction of Antichrist and Last Judgment.[38] Theologians fastened on this and in time it developed into the expectation that there would be a space (perhaps of indefinite duration) for the repentance of apostates and the refreshment of the saints. In essence this made little concession to the idea of meaning in human history, but it opened the door slightly to human optimism and in the twelfth century this 'space' provided room for a vision which cast a kind of sunset glow over the end of history. It was most fully developed by Honorius of Autun and Gerhoh of Reichersberg.

Honorius is strictly Augustinian in placing the Sabbath Age outside time, but in expounding the symbolism of Holy Week in terms of Last Things, he interprets the three days before Easter as the reign of Antichrist and the kindling of the new Easter fire as the death of Antichrist.[39] At this time, he believes, the fire of the Holy Spirit will be re-kindled in the Church and a great multitude will be baptized. Although this period of rejoicing only represents a *transitus ad patriam*, it does precede Last Judgment and places a positive emphasis on the end of history. Again, commenting on the text in the Song of Songs which begins: 'Arise, my beloved, let us go into the fields and sojourn in the villages', Honorius expects that in the dawn after the night of Antichrist the Church will go forth into the field of the world to recall lapsed Christians and convert pagans in this *tempus pacis post mortem Antichristi* ('time of peace after the death of Antichrist').[40] Gerhoh uses the symbolism of the night spent by the storm-tossed disciples on the Sea of Galilee to plot the successive tribulations suffered by the Church.[41] It had weathered the storms of persecution, heresy and inner corruption, but now the fourth and greatest storm was rising into the tempest of Antichrist. Only Christ walking on the waters could save his Church from being engulfed. But Gerhoh follows the symbolism further: Christ enters the boat and there ensures a period of great tranquillity before the Church's vessel reaches the haven of eternal rest. Thus, once again, we meet this expectation of a final moment of peace and joy before history is wound up.

Perhaps it was the sense of great happenings in the late eleventh and twelfth centuries – the great Reform Movement, the conflict of Empire and Papacy, the founding of new religious orders – which concentrated the minds of some theologians on the significance of contemporary history. In the great conflict the end-drama seemed to be already beginning and rhetoric on Antichrist was freely exchanged between Imperial and Papal partisans. But a deeper question was coming to the surface. Since the great truths of the faith were timeless and unchanging, how could the events of the present fleeting moments bear eternal meaning? Yet was not the divine purpose even now manifesting itself in new ways which must be marked as steps towards the End? Anselm of Havelberg tackled this question of the relation of unchanging reality to changing modes. It is argued, he says, that in religion the more inconstant something is, the more contemptible it is (*tanto esse contemptibiliorem, quanto mobiliorem*).[42] The vision of God's purpose which he proceeds to expound is of the Church as unchangingly one in essence but multiform in modes of activity and institutions: *De unitate fidei et multiformitate vivendi ab Abel justo ad novissimum electum* ('Concerning the unity of faith and the multiplicity of forms of living from just Abel to the latest elect [person]') is the heading of the first Dialogue. For Anselm church history since the Incarnation is symbolized in the opening of the Seven Seals of the Apocalypse, and in thus 'periodizing' post-Incarnational history he is giving a new meaningfulness to these latter days.[43] But, although he believes that there have been progressive stages in spiritual understanding, no further stages now lie ahead. Under the sixth seal will come the earth-shaking persecution of Antichrist, while the blessedness of 'silence' at the opening of the seventh seal will not follow until after history has finished.[44] A similar concern with the meaning of history and of God's progressive revelation through it was expressed by Rupert of Deutz in his great work *De Trinitate et operibus suis*. But although he saw history in three great stages, each appropriated to one of the Three Persons, he could not conceive of the third part of his work, that is, the work of the Holy Spirit in post-Incarnational history except as a downward trend towards Last Things. In characterizing its periods by the Seven Gifts of the Spirit, he ends with *Timor Dei* ('the fear of God') as appropriate to the last act, while the Seventh World Age, the Sabbath Age, can only be envisaged as outside of history.[45]

Thus we see that it was only within the context of end-time that history since the Incarnation had any significance for medieval people. There was no prospect of endless progressive change, only of the acts of a drama tightly bound to its final climax. The Apocalypse provided a structure for church history in the Seven Seal-Openings and new interest in its periodization is undoubted in the twelfth century. But the dominant influence of Augustinian thought is still seen in the way in which, not only the Seventh World Age, but also the seventh period of church history, when at the opening of the Seventh Seal there is 'silence in heaven', was placed outside the time-process. Men continued to live under the shadow of an imminently expected Antichrist and winding up of history. When Richard I of England asked to meet the great prophet Abbot Joachim of Fiore his first question was where and when will Antichrist be born?, although he also wanted to know the fate of Jerusalem which he was set to rescue.[46] The traditional approach continued to be disseminated, especially through the illustrated Apocalypse-commentaries which delineated the approaching drama in such vivid terms. Some evidence exists for cycles of Apocalypse pictures from the seventh century and from the ninth Beatus' commentary was frequently illustrated, but it was in the thirteenth century that these illustrated Apocalypses proliferated.[47]

II

In the second half of the twelfth century, however, there was a decisive new influence on apocalyptic attitudes in the theology of history developed by the Abbot Joachim in Calabria.[48] From one viewpoint Joachim of Fiore's break with the Augustinian tradition was revolutionary, but it should be emphasized that he thought within the same framework of end-time as his contemporaries. Whatever great new work the Triune God was about to do within history this belonged to the transience of the *saeculum* which must be dissolved at the Second Coming. Joachim's originality lay in his affirmation that the threefold pattern of history was as yet incomplete and that the work of the Holy Spirit, the Third Person, must shortly be made manifest in a further stage of spiritual illumination. Recasting the traditional Pauline pattern he expounded his famous doctrine of the three *status* in history: the first, beginning in Adam and ending with the Incarnation, has been characterized by the work of the Father; the second, beginning back in the Old Testament (to overlap with the first) and continuing until Joachim's own day, belonged to the Son; the third, with a double origin in the Old Dispensation and the New and about to come to fruition in the near future, would see the full work of the Holy Spirit completed.[49] Here was a magnificent programme of progress which offered an advance still to come within history. Its novelty is well illustrated by the fact that Joachim departs decisively from the Augustinian tradition by placing the Sabbath Age of the World and the opening of the Seventh Seal of the Church clearly within history and identifying them with his third *status*. The Age of the Father had been lived under Law and the Age of the Son under Grace, but the Age of the Spirit would be lived in the liberty of full illumination. There were many Scriptural figures under which Joachim wrote of that blessed time, including the silence of the seventh seal-opening which symbolized the silence of joyful contemplation. But although Joachim could describe it in lyrical terms this was no millennial dream of a supra-natural regime descending from heaven. It was to be the completion of the work of the Trinity within history, set within the framework of end-time. The cosmic conflict between good and evil remains the great historical constraint.

Joachim saw the history of Israel in the Old Dispensation as punctuated by seven tribulations which rose to a climax in the seventh, that of Antiochus Epiphanes, 'the root of sin' (*radix peccati*).[50] This was to be paralleled by the seventh tribulation of the Church, reaching its climax in the persecution of the Seventh Head of the Dragon, the *Antichristus pessimus*.[51] In order to introduce his Age of the Spirit at the Seventh Seal Joachim found Biblical grounds for doubling the last two persecutions under the sixth seal. Into this period he believed the Church was now entering. When these tribulations had been passed the pilgrim Church would enter the Promised Land of the Sabbath Age (third *status*). But this would still be within the imperfections of the time-process and subject to deterioration. According to the concords it must end in the final persecution of Gog and Magog immediately preceding the Last Judgment:

> as at the end of the first *status* the last king, named Antiochus, was more monstrous than others, so at the end of the second *status*, which is close, that seventh king will appear of whom John said 'And one has not yet come and he will be worse than all who were before him . . .'. Truly, at the end of the third, will come another whose name is God: and he will be the last tyrant and the last Antichrist.[52]

There are, indeed, many Antichrists, says Joachim, but these three symbols of evil stand out because of their position in relation to the three *status*.

It is interesting that Joachim, following tradition, does not see the Roman Empire as a direct manifestation of Antichrist. It is certainly New Babylon but in the purposes of God it once served the function of holding back the barbarians. Now it has fornicated with the nations and Joachim sees its doom in the phial poured by the Sixth Angel on the river Euphrates which will dry up and let in the hordes.[53] The Emperor Nero, however, retains his Antichrist role as the second head of the Dragon, and when Joachim turns to the exposition of the two Beasts in Apocalypse 13 – one from the sea and the other from the land – he interprets these as a double Antichrist at the end of the second *status* or sixth seal: a new tyrant and his pseudo-prophet, typified in Nero and Simon Magus. The Beast from the sea (the tyrant) now represents the menace of the Saracens while Simon Magus is a pseudo-pope.[54] To a large extent Joachim worked within the tradition he inherited. His great innovation lay in placing the third *status* of history between the manifestations of Antichrist under the sixth seal and the appearance of Gog and Magog, the final Antichrist, at the close of the seventh.

Joachim's method of concords set a new value on historical events and personages. Old Testament history had always provided types for post-Incarnational history but now the logic of Joachim's pattern of threes suggested parallels extrapolated into the future. Thus, to take a simple example, as there were twelve patriarchs and then twelve apostles, so there would be twelve great leaders in the third *status*. Joachim's detailed concords between the three *status* gave specific happenings a peculiar significance, while the historic structures of the tree-figures he drew emphasized how deeply he felt that the work of the Trinity was to be traced through all the particularities of history. This gave his successors the impetus to fill out the apocalyptic scenario in more detail and to envisage the agencies of the end-time, both good and bad, in more human terms. Thus the agencies to bring in the third *status* are seen as human instruments of the Spirit: St. Benedict and St. Bernard as precursors, two new orders of spiritual men to lead the faithful into the Promised Land and a future 'angelic' pope who would be a second Zerubabbel to rebuild the Temple in Jerusalem. The effects of this new emphasis on those who came under Joachimist influence can hardly be exaggerated. Joachimism gave historical happenings a unique importance, linking past, present and future moments of time with transcendental purpose. It invited the casting of roles in the final acts of the drama. Above all, it opened up the prospect of new human agencies called to participate in the last decisive works of God in history. The backcloth of apocalyptic drama gave enhanced stature to actors in history.

III

Nivissime diebus istis in fine seculorum ('In these latest days at the end of the ages'): this seems to be one of the motifs of the thirteenth century. When in 1255 the two Generals of the Franciscan and Dominican Orders issued the joint encyclical just quoted, their purpose was to proclaim the apocalyptic role of the friars in these last days.[55] The Dominican historian, Vincent of Beauvais, writes of the Fifteen Signs of approaching Judgment and cites a pseudo-Joachimist text: *Ab anno domini MCC et ultra suspecta sunt mihi tempora et momenta* . . . ('From the year of our Lord 1200 and onwards every hour and moment is suspect to me . . .').[56] A Master of Paris, William of St. Amour, seeing in the friars the pseudo-apostles of Antichrist, also quotes the same Joachimist text and declares:

> It seems probable, therefore, that we are near the end of the world and closer to the perils of the latest times which will be before the coming of Antichrist.[57]

Adventuring friars who claim to have penetrated into those terrible regions behind Alexander's Gate bring back rumors of Tartar hordes mustering there which the Franciscan, Roger Bacon, reports with a shiver of apprehension. To him it is so important that intelligent men should be apprised of all the portents and signs which should alert them to the approach of Antichrist that he begs the Pope to institute a study of prophecies:

> I know that if the Church were willing to study again the sacred text and prophecies, as well as the prophecies of the Sibyl, Merlin and Aquila, Sesto, Joachim and many others, and in addition histories and philosophers' books, and would order the ways of astronomy to be considered, then a sufficient inkling or even certitude concerning the time of Antichrist would be discovered.[58]

In 1256 the chronicler, Mathew Paris records in his volume of *Additamenta* a little verse which was flying around:

> Also in these days, on account of such terrible rumours, these (celebrated) verses announcing the advent of Antichrist were on men's lips:
> > When a thousand, two hundred and fifty years
> > have passed since the gracious Virgin gave birth,
> > then Antichrist will be born, full of the devil.[59]

This turns up with varying dates scribbled in a number of manuscripts of this period. In 1260 a mood of mass hysteria, starting in Italy, sweeps through many parts of Europe. This was the Flagellant movement in which crowds of men and women marched through cities tormenting their flesh in an ecstasy of repentance against the coming Judgment Day.[60] The most powerful expression of this mood is embodied in the great poem *Dies Irae* which voices popular terror so dramatically:

> Dies irae, dies illa,
> solvet saeclum in favilla,
> teste David cum Sibylla.
> Quantus tremor est futurus
> quando iudex est venturus,

> Cuncta, stricte discussurus!
> Tuba, mirum spargens sonum
> per sepulchra regionum
> coget omnes ante thronum.[61]

> [Day of anger, Day of terror,
> All shall crumble into ashes,
> Witness David and the Sibyl,
> What a tremor will assail them
> When the Judge shall come to judgement
> Shattering all at once asunder!
> Sounds the Trump with awful note
> Through the tombs of (deathly) regions,
> Summoning all before the throne.]

The most popular figure in the Joachimist series was that of the Dragon with Seven Heads. This is found in the middle and later thirteenth century in a number of manuscripts, always with the heads named down to the seventh which is either the Hohenstaufen Emperor Frederick II or Antichrist.[62] This figure is discussed in his *Distinctiones* by a Franciscan, Thomas of Pavia, who had evidently seen it. He writes of the great debate on when Antichrist will appear, citing Joachim's calculations which were popularly supposed to point to the year 1260: *Utrum autem verum vel falsum dixerit, cito apparebit* ('Whether he spoke truly or falsely will quickly appear').[63] But, though apparently detached, he quotes substantially from Joachim's *Expositio* on the two manifestations of Antichrist, the beast from the sea and that from the land, whom Joachim had paralleled with Nero and Simon Magus. Thomas reserves judgement but cannot refrain from citing the vision of a 'religious' who dreamt that the Lateran Palace in Rome collapsed and a great voice cried: '*Ecce Nero resuscitatus est et ipse est Antichristus*' ('Behold Nero has come to life again and he himself is Antichrist'). The conversations recorded by the Franciscan Friar, Salimbene, turn a good deal on Antichrist and particularly on whether Frederick II was Antichrist.[64] The earliest of the pseudo-Joachimist works, the *Super Hieremiam*, written in the early 1240s, sets the Imperial-Papal struggle firmly in an apocalyptic framework. The cosmic evil is the German *Imperium*, for *ab aquilone pandetur omne malum* ('from the north all evil will spread'), and this work, purporting to be by Joachim, points forward to a 'future' Frederick II who will embody the sixth or seventh head of the Dragon, as well as other sinister portents in the Bible.[65] The apocalyptic imagery even invades Papal pronouncements, as in Gregory IX's Letter of 1239, beginning: *Ascendit de mari bestia* (see Apoc. 13.1–2).[66] Countering this, Frederick promoted propaganda which hailed him in messianic terms.[67] McGinn calls this 'a prime example of the peculiar force that apocalypticism could give to current events by placing them within the sphere of history at its most universal and critical moment'.[68]

When Frederick died in 1250 without a cataclysm having taken place, Salimbene said he gave up such speculations, yet years later he was still willing to hold a clandestine conversation 'behind the dorter' with a disgraced Joachite which began: 'My question is of Antichrist, when and where will he be born.'[69]

Remote from this political apocalypticism but hardly less heated, an academic debate was going on *c.* 1300 in the universities of Paris and Oxford as to the legitimacy of speculating on the advent of Antichrist. The argument was sparked off by the *De Tempore Adventus Antichristi* of Arnold of Villanova, a Spanish Joachite.[70] The scholastics, led by Henry of Harclay, Chancellor of Oxford University, vigorously opposed his speculations. Henry's *Quaestio: Utrum Astrologi vel Quicumque Calculatores possint probare Secundum Adventum Christi* was a weighty and serious treatment of an important subject.[71] The issue was still a live one when, in 1310, Nicholas of Lyra devoted a *Quodlibeta* to the question: *Utrum possimus scire an Antichristus sit natus vel non natus adhuc* ('Whether we can know if Antichrist is already born or not').[72] In a middle position stood the Dominican John Quidort or John of Paris. He began his *Tractatus de Antichristo* conventionally – 'It is not for you to know the times and seasons . . .' – but could not resist gathering prophecies, speculations, visions, calculations, which pointed to the conclusion that the world was nearing its end.[73]

Thus there is evidence to show that there was a general mood of eschatological expectation in the thirteenth century. Professor Daniel has argued that this was especially so in the Franciscan Order[74] and it is within this setting that a more specifically Joachimist outlook on the immediate future can be placed. This came to a focal point in the person of St. Francis. It seems that the identification of St. Francis as the Angel of the Sixth Seal in the Apocalypse, who ascends from the rising of the sun, was first made by Franciscans who were acknowledged as 'Joachites'.[75] This identification was accepted by Bonaventure and incorporated into the official legend but it has clear Joachimist overtones. The Opening of the Sixth Seal for Joachim represented the beginning of the crucial time for the Church. It would see the climax of the conflict between good and evil in the 'double tribulation' and it would culminate in the great *transitus* from the second to the third *status*. The Angel of the Sixth Seal symbolically 'seals' the 144 000 of the faithful: St. Francis and his disciples must save the Church in the day of trial and lead it into the Promised Land. Joachim's prophecy of the two new orders of spiritual men was applied to the two new mendicant orders of Friars Preacher and Friars Minor from about the middle of the century,[76] but it was chiefly in the latter order (though not exclusively) that this apocalyptic role was taken most seriously.

The earliest and most dramatic appropriation of this Joachimist future by a Franciscan was made in 1254 by Gerard of Borgo San Donnino when the whole university of Paris was put in an uproar by his proclamation of the

Eternal Evangel.[77] The third *status* was beginning, the Eternal Evangel was about to supersede the two Testaments of the earlier *status* and authority and leadership in the Church would pass to the 'bare-footed men' of poverty. The Eternal Evangel consisted of extracts from the Abbot Joachim's writings, introduced and glossed by Gerard, while the new order was clearly that of St. Francis. Thus the hidden revolutionary implications of Joachim's system were brought into the open and the rage with which the 'Evangile pardurable'[78] was greeted was partly outrage at the sheer audacity of this claim. The secular Masters of the University used it as a stick with which to beat the hated Mendicant interlopers, while their chief spokesman, William of St. Amour, as we have seen, reversed the eschatological roles by branding the Mendicants agents of Antichrist. When the Eternal Evangel was condemned in 1255 by a papal Commission of Anagni[79] emphasis was laid on this arrogant claim to supersede in these Last Days the sacred authorities of Church and Scriptures.

In his downfall Gerard brought down the General of the Franciscan Order, John of Parma. This placed the new General, Bonaventure, in a delicate position. Whether or not consciously aware of his debt,[80] Bonaventure not only shared the general mood of apocalyptic expectancy but clearly owed much to Joachim's vision of the future. While repudiating with horror any suggestion that the authority of the two Testaments could be abrogated,[81] he believed that the Church was moving into a period when the full illumination of spiritual understanding would bring out the meanings hidden like seeds in the Scriptures. In his theology of history he placed the Church at the crisis of the sixth age and he clearly looked for the time of beatitude, the seventh age of the Church, within history.[82] He adopted the identification of St. Francis as the Angel of the Sixth Seal because he believed that Francis was indeed the harbinger of the new age. In a fascinating scheme of orders symbolized in the hierarchies of angels, Bonaventure salutes St. Francis as the only man yet to have made the *transitus* to the highest, the Seraphic Order, which will characterize the seventh age of the Church.[83] Unwilling to arrogate to his own order any final role, he sees it as having reached the Cherubic stage but falling short of the final contemplative purity. It would seem that this theology of history represented the final stage of Bonaventure's thought, for it was only fully expressed in the *Collationes in Hexaemeron*, a last set of lectures given in Paris in 1273 and known only to us from notes.

Bonaventure's influence was probably decisive for the Franciscan extremists, often called Spirituals, who emerge in the second half of the thirteenth century as those who embrace the apocalyptic role of St. Francis and his order to the extent of believing that, because they hold the key to the future, not one jot or tittle of St. Francis' Rule and Testament must be relaxed or modified. Common sense views on the practical property needs of a great institution collapsed before the burning sense of eschatological mission which led the *zelanti* to endure persecution and imprisonment for the sake of evangelical poverty. Among their leaders the Provençal Petrus Johannis Olivi and through him the Italian Ubertino da Casale, drew a good deal on Bonaventure.

Olivi was an astonishing mixture of scholastic philosopher, theologian, prophet and mystic. It has often been suggested that there was an element of schizophrenia in the apparent sharp divide between his earlier works for the Schools and his final Apocalypse-commentary, but Professor Burr has demonstrated the continuity of his thought by showing, for instance, the apocalyptic elements in his early critique of Aristotle.[84] All his scholastic thinking is done, it would seem, within the framework of a periodization of history which sees his own time poised between the second and third *status* and between the fifth and sixth periods of church history. While drawing directly on Joachim, Olivi modifies the Abbot's scheme, seeing the crucial turning point as between the fifth and sixth, rather than the sixth and seventh, times of the Church. In the fifth age the true faith has been under threat, not only from laxity of life, but from heresies which spring from the false views of pagan philosophers. Whilst ready to use Aristotle at the purely intellectual level, at a higher level of spiritual understanding Olivi actually links him with Antichrist. Thus the final round in the age-long conflict between good and evil which Olivi sketches is now reaching its climax in the precursors of Antichrist: false philosophers and betrayers of true evangelical poverty, 'for nothing so prepares the way for the final Antichrist as the destruction of highest poverty'.[85] But in St. Francis the true evangelical life has already been reborn and his disciples too must pass through tribulation to spiritual understanding and pure living. Olivi expects the conflict to be sharp. In his Apocalypse commentary he writes much of the carnal church: as the synagogue was rejected at the end of the first *status*, so must the carnal church be rejected at the transition from the second to third.[86] This was dangerous language. Olivi never directly identified the carnal church with the Roman Church, using this term symbolically for all the reprobate. But he clearly expected a crisis in high places. There must be a mystic Antichrist, probably a pseudo-pope, as well as an open tyrant. Professor Tierney has argued that one of the things Olivi feared was a papal attack on the doctrine of evangelical poverty and that because Olivi believed that the Bull *Exiit qui seminat* protected this doctrine, he wrote his *Quaestiones* on papal infallibility to render it immutable.[87] However this may be, Olivi came close to maintaining that all who did not defend the life of 'highest poverty' were limbs of Antichrist.

It was the power of this concept which drove groups of Olivi's disciples, the Beguins of south France and Spain, as well as disciples of Angelo Clareno and Ubertino da Casale, the Fraticelli of Italy, into persecuted isolation. Their fanatical adherence to the Rule and Testament of Francis led them finally to regard themselves as the only true Church – the saving remnant. Some Provençals held that only one-third of the Franciscan Order would come purified through the fiery furnace of persecution.[88] Some of the Fraticelli believed that from the time of the fatal Donation of Constantine which endowed the Church with lands and power, the official Church had ceased to be the true one which had been hidden away down the centuries and was now to be found only in their little flock. They were the inhabitants of Noah's Ark which alone would survive the tempest of Antichrist; their navigators were the Abbot Joachim, St. Francis and Olivi.[89] Sporadically throughout the fourteenth century these pathetic groups reappear, usually clashing with authority. The 'saving remnant' mentality belongs essentially to the apocalyptic scene.

The question of authority and spiritual revolution now becomes an urgent one. In Joachim's program the *transitus* to the third *status* had been seen in terms of spiritual tribulation and refinement and the question of how the institutional authority of the Church would survive was never directly tackled. It would become the *ecclesia spiritualis* or *contemplativa*, but – although historians are not agreed about this[90] – a case can be made for the view that Joachim's church of the third *status* was essentially the Roman Church renewed. Before the end of the thirteenth century, however, the contrast between actuality and vision was becoming so sharp that a new figure had to be evolved to satisfy apocalyptic expectation: the Angelic Pope. The origin of this image lies in Joachim's rather sparse prophecies of a new Joseph or David or Zorobabel or Mordecai who represents the final domination of a purified Papacy, but the stages by which the new image of the Angelic Pope developed are obscure.[91] One of the most enigmatic episodes in medieval history is the election of the hermit pope, Celestine V, in 1294.[92] Should he be seen in an apocalyptic setting as the prototype of the Angelic Pope? Certainly when he vanishes from history in 1295 Celestine assumes a prophetic role in the scenario of Last Things.

It was probably within a Spiritual Franciscan group that one of the most astonishing and widely disseminated series of prophecies was produced. The *Vaticinia de summis pontificibus* (Prophecies of the Popes) are usually ascribed to Clareno's circle *c.* 1304.[93] They consist of fifteen prophecies of successive popes, each represented by a picture, a caption and a short text. They are, in fact, an adaptation of a Byzantine sequence of prophecies on the emperors known as the Oracles of Leo the Wise. The western version was in its earliest form ascribed to the Abbot Joachim, thus making possible a telling indictment of actual popes under the guise of *post-eventum* prophecy. The first one can be easily identified as the Orsini Pope Nicholas III[94] and the following portraits stress the corruption of the Papacy, with the exception of an 'angelic' one for Celestine V. But in both the original and the western versions there comes a break and this would seem to be the main point of the series. The 'electors', seeking a new emperor/pope, are directed by the voice of God to go to the most westerly of the seven hills (in Constantinople/Rome) and seek out the hermit among the rocks.[95] In the case of the Pope Prophecies this choice is probably intended to inaugurate the series of Angelic Popes and represents the point at which real prophecy begins. Thus the authors expect very soon a revolutionary moment when a radical change will take place in the Papacy. Only the direct intervention of God can bring about the *transitus* to the Papacy of the third *status*. Yet the Angelic Popes still stand in the historical sequence: it is the Church of Peter transformed which provides the leadership of the new age.

The Pope Prophecies had an immense vogue right down to the seventeenth century. In the mid-fourteenth century a second sequence of fifteen was produced and then joined to the original one to make the thirty of the sixteenth-century printed editions. In many interpretations the apocalyptic purpose was lost but in various forms, visual and literary, the image of the Angelic Pope remained a powerful figure in the apocalyptic scene throughout the Renaissance period. At an early stage it became partnered by that ancient figure, the Last World Emperor, resurrected in a new form.[96] Joachim, of course, had had no place for a political saviour: New Babylon must go down in destruction before Antichrist. But a 'good' as well as a 'bad' emperor had formed part of the political apocalypticism in the thirteenth century and perhaps the use of the Leo Oracles brought a renewed emphasis on the imperial role. In a companion text to the *Vaticinia*, the *Liber de Flore*, a prophetic partnership is developed between the Angelic Pope and a revived Carolingian emperor in which political unification, recovery of Jerusalem and Church renewal are joined to form a vision of a world Christendom in an age of beatitude.[97]

This program was soon taken up and the particular contribution of the fourteenth century to apocalyptic views is the development of a full political scenario for the future. On the stage were now gathered two pairs of partners: the double Antichrist, represented by a great political tyrant and his pseudo-pope, and the twin saviours, the Last World Emperor and the Angelic Pope. The cosmic stature of the Hohenstaufen finds an echo in the wicked future Frederick III, countered by a prophecy of a 'good' Frederick to come. Apocalypse attitudes are becoming national, for there is a recrudescence of belief in the apocalyptic role of the sacred French Monarchy, as we see, for instance, in Pierre Dubois's programme for a crusade to recover the Holy Land.[98] For either side the essential outline is the same: the wicked tyrant will take to himself a pseudo-pope and other allies; together they will make schism, persecuting the true pope and emperor; finally God will give the forces of good victory over evil. In the mid-century a Franciscan Joachite, Jean de Roquetaillade, worked out a full French version of this prophetic future in a series of tracts he was allowed to produce, although imprisoned at Avignon.[99] For Roquetaillade the source of all political evil still lay in the accursed seed of the *serpens antiquus*, Frederick II, from whom had sprung a multiple Antichrist. In contrast, the French princes are the new Maccabees, sent to defend the Church. In his *Liber Secretorum eventuum*[100] the world is lined up in two camps:

Antichrist and his allies, i.e. Italian Ghibellines, the Spanish kings and German tyrants, against the true pope, the King of France and Charles IV of Bohemia. Evil will mount to a climax, with plague and famine – this in 1349 – but finally the holy alliance will triumph. In his latest version of the future c. 1356 – when French fortunes were at their nadir in the Hundred Years War – Roquetaillade exalts the French king 'from the race of Pepin' into the World Emperor who will 'repair the whole globe'.[101]

Schism was an essential part of this program and thus the Great Schism which began in 1377 was at once seen as confirming all the fears and hopes of the apocalyptists. This theme was taken up by another Francophile Joachite, a mysterious Telesphorus of Cosenza (Calabria), who put his prophecies into final shape in a *libellus* written between 1378 and 1390.[102] The chief agents of destruction will be a future Frederick III and a German pseudo-pope who will crown the diabolical emperor. The *nova religio sanctissma* will be championed by the French king, whose name will be Charles, and the Angelic Pope. In the vivid little pictures with which this popular work was illustrated we see the whole drama portrayed: the wicked tyrant rides to battle with his forces, he is crowned emperor by his pseudo-pope, the French king is imprisoned, the faithful seek the angelic pope among the rocks and he is crowned by an angel, the French king is released and the forces of good are led to victory.[103] Then in a holy partnership Emperor and Pope reform the Church and recover the Holy Land in the seventh and last crusade. Then will be the millennium when Satan will be bound for a thousand years. A separate little text, written apparently in 1380 for the young Charles VI, soon becomes associated with Telesphorus' work.[104] He is hailed as 'Charles, the son of Charles, from the nation of the most illustrious Lily'. A victorious program is laid down for him to which a Joachimist conclusion is added. This text had a great vogue in the following centuries, turning up in all sorts of places and applied to a variety of rulers. The French version of the future seems to dominate the scene but some turned to the Holy Roman Empire for their hope. Dante, in the early years of the century, was a notable example,[105] while later Cola di Rienzo tried to persuade the Emperor Charles IV to take up the prophetic role.[106] During the Great Schism a prophet called Gamaleon again tried to proclaim a German future.[107]

It must not be thought, however, that the pessimism of the Augustinian view did not still find many supporters. Jacobus de Paradiso, to take an early fifteenth-century example, concluded that no future renovation of the world was possible: *Aestimo igitur mundum dietum descrescere in pravis moribus* ('I estimate therefore that the world is day by day declining into depraved habits').[108] A little earlier Henry of Langenstein, Vice-Chancellor of Vienna University, had been tempted by the prophecies of Hildegard, Joachim and Telesphorus but had eventually turned against them. In 1385 he launched a bitter attack on these recent prophets: the Church, he believed, was growing old and Christian people at the end of the Age were declining in love and faith.[109] Yet, with other theologians, he still saw the possibility of reform after the death of Antichrist. Similarly, in the mid-fifteenth century, Nicholas of Cusa held that after Antichrist there would be a final revival of the Church before the End.[110]

English apocalypticism in the fourteenth century took its own forms. Professor Bloomfield, in presenting the case for viewing *Piers Plowman* as a fourteenth-century apocalypse, gives many examples to show the prevalence of a 'sense of an ending'.[111] Miss Smalley remarks that this was a good time for 'persons who liked apocalyptic visions and prophecies'.[112] The context of her remark is the lectures of John Lathbury, a Franciscan Regent at Oxford c. 1352. He quotes a lost work, *De Visionibus Sibyllae*, attributed to Flaccianus. Like the citations he makes from Joachim's *Expositio in Apocalypsim*, his material from pseudo-Flaccianus was probably carefully edited to tone it down but the evidence suggests that it was apocalyptic in character, probably speculating on the advent of Antichrist. In the same period a vernacular work, *The Last Age of the Church*, which was formerly attributed to Wycliffe, states that in the year of writing, that is, 1365, there are but forty-four years left before the darkness of Antichrist comes.[113] In 1388 Thomas of Wimbledon preached a famous vernacular sermon at Paul's Cross for which it has been claimed that no other single sermon of the fourteenth and fifteenth centuries has been found in so many manuscripts and printed copies.[114] In the second part the preacher solemnly tolls the warning bell in the three signs of the Last Judgment: the world's sickness, its feebleness or 'charyte acoldyng' and the approach of Antichrist whom Thomas expects in 1400. At the end of the *Chronicon* finished by Galfridus le Baker in 1347 someone, quoting from a work attributed to Joachim, states that humanity is now in the last century *usque adventum Christi*.[115] Of a Malmesbury chronicle, the *Eulogium historiarum sive temporis*, Bloomfield writes that it represents excellently the apocalyptic monastic view: 'History is moving towards a renewal and the social and natural orders give all the evidence needed to the perceptive man. The whole world is agonizing towards a new birth.'[116] Here again we touch the Joachimist theme of *renovatio* and although there may not be direct Joachimist influence, recent research suggests that in the fourteenth century there was an upsurge of belief that the highest perfection to be realized in the end-time was the prerogative of monks. An early fifteenth-century sermon preached before a General Chapter of Black Monks after a Mass of the Holy Ghost, affirms that monks will endure to the end of time to preserve their high role. A remnant will save the monks as a remnant once saved Israel.[117]

Where apocalyptic expectation ran high the theme of the saving remnant or the hidden true church was at once enhanced. We have seen this outlook among Beguin and Fraticelli groups; now, in the late fourteenth and fifteenth centuries we meet Lollards in England and Hussites in Bohemia placing themselves against the backcloth of Last Things. Wycliffe had finally come to the clear-cut and extreme view that the Papacy, the ecclesiastical hierarchy and the religious orders belonged to the congregation of the damned, the members of Antichrist who stood in eternal opposition to the true Church of the redeemed. Because he insisted that the members of the true Church were known only to God, Lollard tended to lack the fanaticism of those who believed that they alone embodied the hidden future. Nonetheless, it was Antichrist and all his members whom they confronted in the final conflict of the last age and when Purvey asserted that Rome was the Great Whore of Babylon the apocalyptic context was obvious.[118]

Elements among the Hussites moved into a much more overtly revolutionary position but the groundwork of Hussitism in the late fourteenth century was similar to, and drew upon, Wycliffism. Among other reforming voices Mathias of Janov, in his *Tractatus de Antichristo*, had proclaimed that Antichrist was already reigning in the Church: *nunc est tempus proprium Antichristi* ('now is the time peculiar to Antichrist').[119] But it is in the radical wing of the Hussite movement that we find the most complete expression of apocalyptic revolution. This is seen at an early stage in the propaganda of Jakoubek of Stříbro and Nicholas of Dresden. In a public determination on 'whether Antichrist had already come in person' Jakoubek answered affirmatively while Nicholas's picture of Antichrist in papal regalia surrounded by whores made the answer explicit.[120] The drive towards a break with the Roman Church found its justification in this apocalyptic outlook which sprang from a conviction about the whole history of the Church: from the days of the fatal Donation of Constantine the official church had belonged to Antichrist. The true church, which Jakoubek saw as the remnant of holy men persecuted by the majority, had its secret source in the Church of Christ and the Apostles. Let us, as the remnant, now return to the primitive church, he preached. By 1419 this message had been appropriated by the Taborites, left-wing groups who called their mountain retreats Mount Tabor, for the place of Christ's transfiguration was a symbol of renewal. At this time, says a contemporary chronicler, 'Taborite priests were preaching to the people a new coming of Christ in which all evil men and enemies of the Truth would be exterminated while the good would be preserved in five cities.'[121] Letters circulated announcing that the time of greatest suffering was at hand: 'it has begun; it stands at the gates'.[122] They called on God's elect to flee from the midst of the evil ones. The Taborites encapsulated the whole idea of the apocalyptic church: saved from Sodom, they expected God's wrath to be poured on all other creatures as limbs of Antichrist. But for the elect the Day of Judgment was the transition to the new age when Christ would appear openly and prepare the Supper of the Lamb. So, in their intensely concentrated fortress, the elect practised their communism, issued forth to destroy enemies of Christ and awaited His Coming, until they were isolated and destroyed by moderate Hussitism in 1434.

It is now generally recognized that, whilst Renaissance scholars were rediscovering the glories of the classical inheritance, their perspective was still in large measure governed by the Christian concept of end-time, with all the traditions of Last Things built up in the Middle Ages. Antichrist was still expected imminently and at intervals through the fifteenth century wild prophets cried Woe! in the streets of the great Renaissance cities.[123] Alongside this fear the Joachimist hope of a new age after Antichrist was also powerful. There was a strange fusion between expectation of the returning classical golden age and the final reign of the Spirit in the end-time, for the further spiritual illumination prophesied by Joachim chimed with the new learning and especially with the forms of secret and mystical knowledge pursued by some of the Platonists. Fears of the worst tribulation and hopes of the new golden age were juxtaposed in 15th-century Italy in a way which make the explosion of Savonarola in Florence, not a strange throw-back to medieval superstition from an enlightened age, but a dramatic expression of fifteenth-century apocalypticism.

Savonarola's message had its roots in Joachimist prophecy:[124] Florence, together with the rest of Italy, must suffer a crisis of great tribulation as punishment for sin, but after chastisement would come beatitude in an age of peace when Florence would lead the nations in righteousness. The convergence of prophecies at this point is astonishing. At the court of the young Charles VIII of France there were poets and prophets urging him to take up the role of the Second Charlemagne prophecy.[125] The programme laid down for him included the chastisement of Florence and Rome, to be followed by the expedition to recover Jerusalem and the inauguration of the age of peace. It seems almost certain that when Charles set out on his expedition in 1494 he saw himself in this apocalyptic role. As such he was certainly hailed by Savonarola in his autumn preaching of 1494: Charles is the new Cyrus, the *flagellum Dei*, 'the scourge of God'. The Deluge is coming upon the peoples, but God has singled out Florence and if the city builds the Ark of repentance under its new Noah, it will ride out the Flood. Professor Weinstein has shown that, as Florence passed unscathed through the crisis of Charles' invasion, Savonarola began to emphasize a more positive role for Florence as the New Jerusalem, destined to become the focus of a new and glorious age. In a sermon of December, 1494, he promises Florence a glorious future, in the eyes of God, in innumerable riches, in power spiritual and temporal: 'You, O Florence, will be the reformation of all Italy, and from here the renewal will begin to spread everywhere.'[126] In his later utterances Savonarola, whilst still expecting an Antichrist, focused a good deal on the Angelic Pope to come and the Sabbath Age when 'the Church will be so full of love that angels will converse with men'. In a sermon of 13 March, 1496, he proclaims that this will come *cito et velociter* ('quickly and swiftly').[127]

Savonarola's preaching fell on ears attuned to this type of message. Members of Marsilio Ficino's Platonic Academy, including both Giovanni Pico della Mirandola and his nephew, Gianfrancesco, become *Piagnone*, disciples of Savonarola, while Marsilio himself – though later disillusioned – elevated Charles into his role as Second Charlemagne in his oration on 17 November 1494, welcoming the King into the city.[128] The most eloquent spokesman of the Platonist *Piagnoni* was Giovanni Nesi who, in his *Oraculum de novo saeculo*, gathered together a strange mixture of Neoplatonism, occult mysteries and Christian prophecy.[129] Another Ficinian who joined Savonarola was Girolamo Benivieni, a friend of Giovanni Pico. He expressed his vision of the *renovatio* which would centre on Florence in a poem on the building of the New Jerusalem written for Palm Sunday:[130]

> In those days of bliss
> You will see all the world come to you,
> Devoted and faithful folk,
> Drawn by the odor of your holy lily. (trs. Weinstein)

In his commentary Benivieni declares that the odour of her sanctity will spread throughout the world, so that people, seeing the felicity of Florence, will seek to share her government and laws, and – placing themselves within the paws of the Florentine lion – will be blessed with temporal and spiritual rewards.[131]

Most striking was the translation of this apocalyptic message into art by Botticelli. His famous eschatological Nativity represents the Incarnation as the symbol of a future divine event when 'angels will converse with men'. The inscription tells us that Botticelli believed himself to be painting at the time of the second Woe of Apocalypse 11, but after the loosing of the devil for $3\frac{1}{2}$ years he will be chained 'and we shall see him trodden down as in this picture' – and we see a little beaten devil crawling away out of the ecstasy of joy.[132] Professor Weinstein has interpreted another of Botticelli's pictures in apocalyptic terms, a Crucifixion probably painted in 1502. The Cross divides the picture in two: the right hand side depicts a scene of wrath and punishment, where an angel whips the Florentine marzocco (lion); on the left the city of Florence appears bathed in light; in the middle a woman embraces the Cross. Here, according to Weinstein's interpretation Florence appears three times: chastised, repentant, glorious.[133]

Savonarola's movement collapsed but its prophetic categories remained valid for many serious-minded humanists. Benivieni continued to look for the *renovatio mundi*. The figure of the Angelic Pope appeared persistently on the road to the future. A succession of preaching friars kept Savonarola's message alive. A particularly interesting figure is Francesco da Meleto who tried to harmonize all prophecies, including Jewish, to show that Savonarola's three-fold scourge was still to be expected, but that by 1530 the universal *renovatio mundi* will have been consummated.[134] In 1536 a Dominican, Luca Bettini, still expected Savonarola's programme to be fulfilled.[135]

Two final examples may be given of the influence which medieval apocalypticism still exercised in the Renaissance period. In the first part of the sixteenth century Giles of Viterbo, Cardinal and General of the Augustinian hermits, was an influential figure in the court of the Medicean Popes at Rome.[136] He had been a disciple of Marsilio Ficino, combining in a peculiarly Renaissance manner the attitudes of the Renaissance scholar and the seeker after mystical and prophetic modes of knowledge. His philosophy of history, embodied in his *De Historia Viginti Saeculorum*,[137] was an attempt to harmonize classical and Christian culture by finding concords between ten periods of history before Christ and ten afterwards. As humanity had moved towards a first climax in the coming of Christianity, so now it was moving towards a second great spiritual unfolding. His twin stars of destiny were the Medici, especially the Medicean popes Leo X and later Clement VII, and the Emperor Charles V. When in 1530 he poured out his prophetic hopes in a mystical little tract entitled *Schechina*,[138] it was to the apocalyptic partnership of Angelic Pope and Last World Emperor that he appealed. Now is the *decimum saeculum*, 'the tenth age'; now all the signs – the new learning, the expanding world of newly discovered lands – point to the great *renovatio mundi*, the last act of history. So he summons Pope and Emperor to the great cosmic task of converting, reforming and uniting the whole world, bringing the peoples into one sheepfold under one shepherd.

Whatever the force of other motivations, there is an apocalyptic strain running even through the movement to explore the new worlds. The Bible taught that one of the signs of the approaching End would be the conversion of all peoples to the true faith and thus the expanding world of the Renaissance challenged men to this great cosmic task. Christopher Columbus collected prophecies in a book which he called the *Libro de las profecías*.[139] He believed himself to have been inspired by the Holy Spirit in his explorations and saw the three climactic events of the Last Age as the discovery of the Indies, the conversion of the Gentiles and the recovery of the Holy City. The chief political agency in executing this divine program was to be the Spanish monarchy. In the next generation the apocalyptic role was taken up by some at least of the missionaries to the New World. Mendieta, a Franciscan missionary to Mexico, saw the whole progress of the Spanish Empire in the New World as following the providential pattern of the Last Age.[140] Cortes was the new Moses, calling the enslaved Indians out of bondage into the Promised Land. The twelve first Franciscan 'apostles' to reach Mexico City in 1524 carry overtones of Joachim's twelve spiritual leaders to usher in the new age, and Mendieta believed that Cortes had been inspired by the Holy Spirit when, on their entry he took off his cape for them to walk over, signifying – in concord with Christ's entry into Jerusalem – the transformation of Mexico City into the New Jerusalem.

Mendieta and others of his Order may well have inherited an apocalyptic strain from the Spiritual Franciscan tradition which probably remained alive in Spain. In the case of the other great missionary order, the Society of Jesus, we know certainly that some members specifically claimed that theirs fulfilled one of Joachim's prophecies of new orders: the society, he had said, which would be 'designated in the name of Jesus'.[141] In other orders there were those who saw their role in terms of the last great conflict with evil and the last great triumph of the faith. The early Jesuits saw the world as the battlefield of two mighty opposites under whose banners of good and evil the whole of mankind was encamped. The final stage of the battle is now approaching and the Jesuits' own eschatological role is emerging.[142] J. Osorius, preaching on the death of St. Ignatius Loyola, hails him as the Fifth Angel of the Apocalypse at the sound of whose trumpet there fell a great star from heaven. The star is Luther and his army of locusts the pernicious sect of Protestants.[143] But the Jesuit role is twofold, for balancing conflict with the heretic in the Old World must be set the marvels of universal preaching to the millions of a New World.

The triumphs of Christ in the New World were redressing the balance in the Old. An idealized picture of Indian tribal societies as innocent and unacquisitive inspired Mendieta and others to believe that a 'golden age' – or perhaps a Joachimist third age – was about to dawn across the Atlantic. The cosmic figure of the Woman clothed with the Sun and Stars and standing on the Moon whom St. John in his vision saw fleeing into the wilderness to escape the Dragon and giving birth to her child there was interpreted by Joachim as a symbol of the *Ecclesia Spiritualis* in the third age. Is there significance, perhaps, in the fact that the figure of the Woman of the Apocalypse is often found in early Spanish missions in America?

The blending of Renaissance motifs – enthusiasm for new critical scholarship, upsurge of curiosity in the exploration of Man and his universe, *realpolitik* in statecraft – with the medieval themes of cosmic conflict between Good and Evil now reaching its climax, of a final age of illumination and beatitude, and of the whole world gathered into one sheepfold before the End, made a paradoxical compound. Scholars studied prophecies. Pico della Mirandola who wrote an essay on the Dignity of Man accepted the coming Day of Judgment as a fact, like most of his contemporaries. While so-called Machiavellian politics were tearing Europe apart, many rulers still believed – or half-believed – in the ecumenical dream of one shepherd and one sheepfold. In the seventeenth century the figures of Antichrist, Angelic Pope and Last World Emperor are still on the stage.[144]

NOTES

1 On the idea that history only became comprehensible in the light of its End, see K. Koch, *The Rediscovery of Apocalypse* (1972), pp. 101–2.

2 A. Luneau, *L'Histoire du Salut chez les Pères de l'Eglise. La doctrine des âges du monde* (Paris, 1964), pp. 45–7, 357–79.
3 Ibid., pp. 37–45, 51–2.
4 Ibid., p. 75.
5 P. Brown, 'Saint Augustine', *Trends in Medieval Political Thought*, ed. B. Smalley (Oxford, 1965), pp. 11–12.
6 Bede, in his *Liber de temporibus* (AD 703) and his later *De Temporum Ratione* (AD 725), follows St. Augustine in his interpretation of the World Week, but surely reveals in his great *Historia Ecclesiastica* a sense of providential meaning in recent Anglo-Saxon history which his Augustinianism could not suppress.
7 For examples, see H. Focillon, *Art d'Occident: le moyen âge roman et gothique* (Paris, 1938), I, pp. 102–11, II, 26–30; idem, *L'An Mil* (Paris, 1952), pp. 46–9; J. Evans, *Art in Medieval France* (Oxford, 1948), see index under *Judgement, Last*; E. Mâle, *L'Art religieux au XIIe siècle* (Paris, 1925), pp. 370–87.
8 2 Thess. 2.3–7; W. Bousset, *The Antichrist Legend*, trans. A. Keane (1896).
9 D. Verhelst, 'La préhistoire des conceptions d'Adson concernant l'Antichrist', *Recherches de Théologie ancienne et médiévale*, XXXIX–XL (1973), 52–103. For Gregory the Great, see Sixth Homily on Ezechiel, *PL*, LXXVI, col. 1010 and *Gregorii I Papae Registrum Epistolarum, Monumenta Germaniae Historica. Epist. Sel.*, I, 2, pp. 309–10. See also *PL*, LXXVI, cols 484–5, 652 ff. At an earlier date St Jerome had reacted similarly; see Epistola CXXIII, *PL*, XXII, col. 1057. [The abbreviation *PL* refers throughout to *Patrologia*, Series latina, ed. J.-P. Migne (Paris, 1844 ff.)].
10 Verhelst (as in previous Note), pp. 80–1.
11 Gregory of Tours, *Historia Ecclesiastica Francorum*, II, 21, *PL*, LXXI, cols 226–7, 556.
12 Haymo of Halberstadt (Auxerre), *In Epistolam II ad Thessalonicenses*, *PL*, CXVIII, col. 777, 780–1.
13 Verhelst (as above, Note 9), p. 92.
14 Agobard of Lyons, *Ad Eundem Imperatorem, De Insolentia Judaeorum*, *PL*, CIV, col. 69.
15 Gregory the Great, *Moralium Lib. XXVIII*, *PL*, LXXVI, col. 484; Haymo of Halberstadt, *PL*, CXVII, cols 780–1; Bousset (as above, Note 8), pp. 79–84, 123, 147–50, 175–90.
16 See, for example, Haymo of Halberstadt, *PL*, CXVII, cols 780–1.
17 Bousset (as above, Note 8), pp. 143, 160. An important survey of early texts concerning Antichrist will be found in P. Alexander, 'The Diffusion of Byzantine Apocalypses in the Medieval West and the Beginnings of Joachimism', in *Prophecy and Millenarianism*, ed. A. Williams (1980), pp. 57–71.
18 A. Anderson, *Alexander's Gate. Gog and Magog and the Inclosed Nations* (Cambridge, Mass., 1932).
19 Beatus of Liebana, *In Apocalypsim Libri Duodecim*, ed. H. Sanders (Rome, 1930).
20 Ibid., p. 243.
21 Ibid., pp. 367–406.
22 Ibid., p. 40.
23 Alvarus of Cordoba, *Iudiculus Luminosus*, *PL*, CXXI, cols 536–6. See also R. Southern, *Western Views of Islam in the Middle Ages* (Cambridge, Mass., 1932).
24 The origins and history of this text were unravelled by P. Alexander, 'Byzantium and the Migration of Literary Works and Motifs', *Medievalia et Humanistica*, N.S. II (1971), pp. 47–68; 'The Medieval Legend of the Last Roman Emperor and its Messianic Origin', *Journal of the Warburg and Courtauld Institutes*, XLI (1978),

1–15. Alexander's final conclusions on the Last World Emperor prophecy, both in Pseudo-Methodius and the Tiburtine Sibyl, are to be found in his latest essay (as above, Note 17), pp. 53–106.
25 Alexander at first thought that the Tiburtine version of the Last World Emperor prophecy derived from the Pseudo-Methodius text. This was questioned by M. Rangheri, 'La "Epistola ad Gerbergam Reginam de Ortu et Tempore Antichrist" di Adsone de Montier-en-Der e le sue fonti', *Studi Medievali*, 3rd ser., XIV (ii) (1973), pp. 708–12. Alexander was not wholly convinced by Rangheri but in his final judgment acknowledged the probability of two separate versions, while leaving open the problem of how they might be related (see above, Note 17: pp. 56–9, 63–5, n. 9).
26 Adso, *De Ortu et Tempore Antichrist*, ed. D. Verhelst, *Corpus Christianorum. Continuatio Medievalis*, XLV (Turnhout: Brepols, 1976), pp. 20–30. See E. Konrad, *De ortu et tempore Antichristi. Antichrist vorstellung u. Geschichtsbild des Abtes Adso v. Montier-in-Der* (Munich, 1964); Verhelst (as above, Note 9), pp. 52–102; Rangheri (above, Note 25), pp. 672–732.
27 H. Focillon (as above, Note 7), especially pp. 50–63.
28 Abbo of Fleury, *Liber Apologeticus*, PL, CXXXIX, cols 471–2. For R. Glaber, see references in Focillon (as above, Note 7), pp. 50–4.
29 E. Gebhart, 'L'Etat D'Ame d'un Moine de L'An 1000', *Révue des Deux Mondes*, LXI Année (1891), p. 601.
30 R. Glaber, *Historiarum sui temporis libri quinque*, trans. E. Pognon, *L'An Mille* (Paris, 1947), pp. 81–93, 110–24; Adémar de Chabannes, *Chronique*, trans. Pognon, p. 185; Sigebert of Gemblours, *Chronographia, Monumenta Germaniae Historica. Scriptores*, VI, p. 339; *Vita Altmanni Episcopi Pataviensis*, ibid., XII, p. 230.
31 A. Bredero, 'Jerusalem dans l'Occident médiéval', *Mélanges offerts à René Crozet*, ed. P. Gallais and Y.-J. Riou (Poitiers, 1966), I, pp. 259–60.
32 Guibert of Nogent, *Gesta Dei per Francos. Receuil des Historiens des Croisades. Historiens Occidentaux*, IV, pp. 138–9.
33 Innocent III, *Regestorum . . . Liber Decimus Sextus*, PL, CCVI, col. 818. See P. Alphandéry, 'Mahomet – Antichrist dans le moyen âge latin', *Mélanges Hartwig Derenbourg*, ed. E. Leroux (Paris, 1909), pp. 261–77.
34 Benzo of Alba, *Ad Heinricum IV Imperatorem Libri VII, Monumenta Germaniae Historica. Scriptores*, XI, pp. 605, 617, 623; Ekkehard of Aura, *Chronicon Universale*, ibid., VI, p. 215.
35 *The Play of Antichrist*, trans. J. Wright (Toronto, 1967).
36 Godfrey of Viterbo, *Pantheon, Monumenta Germaniae Historica, Scriptores*, XII, pp. 145–7.
37 Bredero (as above, Note 31), p. 270. See also the hymn attributed to Abelard: 'O quanta qualia'.
38 Book of Daniel, 12: 11 and 12; St. Jerome, *Commentarii in Danielem*, PL, XXV, col. 579; R. Lerner, 'Refreshment of the Saints: the Time after Antichrist as a Station for Earthly Progress in Medieval Thought', *Traditio*, XXXII (1976), pp. 97–144.
39 Honorius of Autun, *Gemma Animae*, PL, CLXXII, col. 679.
40 Honorius of Autun, *Expositio in Cantica Canticorum*, ibid., cols 471–2.
41 Gerhoh of Reichersberg, *De Quarta Vigilia Noctis, Monumenta Germaniae Historica. Libelli de Lite*, III, pp. 508–25.
42 Anselm of Havelberg, *Dialogi*, PL, CLXXXVIII, cols 1141–4. See W. Kamlah (see below, Note 45), pp. 64–8.
43 Among earliest commentators, Primasius, Bede and Haymo of Halberstadt

(Auxerre) had approached the concept of the opening of the Seven Seals as periods in Church History, but in general, moralistic terms rather than historical.
44 Anselm of Havelberg (as above, Note 42), col. 1159.
45 Rupert of Deutz, *De Trinitate et operibus ejus Libri XLII*, PL, CLXVII, cols 198–9, 1567. See W. Kamlah, *Apokalypse u. Geschichtstheologie* (Berlin, 1935), pp. 75–105.
46 'Benedict of Peterborough', *Gesta Henrici II et Ricardi I*, Rolls Series, II, pp. 151–5; Roger Howden, *Cronica*, Rolls Series, III, pp. 75–9.
47 See M. James, *The Apocalypse in Art* (1931), pp. 34–71; H. Focillon, *Art d'Occident* (as above, Note 7), p. 45. A few examples of illustrated Apocalypses may be cited: *The Apocalypse in Latin and French (Bodleian MS. Douce 180)*, ed. M. James (Oxford, 1922); *The Douce Apocalypse*, with introduction and notes by A. G. and W. O. Hassall (1961); *The Dublin Apocalypse*, ed. M. James (Oxford, 1932); *Die Bamberger Apokalypse*, ed. H. Wölfflin (Munich, 1918). See also R. Freyhan, 'Joachism and the British Apocalypse', *Journal of the Warburg and Courtauld Institutes*, XVIII (1955), pp. 211–44.
48 For a fuller account of Joachim's theology of history, see Marjorie Reeves, *The Influence of Prophecy in the Later Middle Ages* (Oxford, 1969), pp. 16–27, and *Joachim of Fiore and the Prophetic Future* (1976), pp. 1–28.
49 See *Liber Concordie* (Venice, 1519), ff. 9^v seq., for a characteristic statement of Joachim's Trinitarian pattern of history.
50 *Lib. Conc.*, ff. 56^v, 129^r; *Expositio in Apocalypsim* (Venice, 1527), ff. 9^r, 10^v–11^r, 212^v seq.
51 *Expos.*, ff. 10^r, 196^v seq. For a discussion of the problem of the double Antichrist, see R. Manselli, 'Il problema del Doppio Antichristo in Gioacchino da Fioré', *Geschichtsscheibung u. Geistiges Leben im Mittelalter. Festschrift für Heinz Löwe zum 65 Geburtstag* (Köln/Wien, 1978), pp. 427–49.
52 *Expos.*, ff. 9^v–10^r.
53 Apocalypse, 16: 12; *Expos.*, ff. 190^r–2^r, 134^{r-v}.
54 Ibid., ff. 5^r, 8^r, 24^v, 166^v–8^r.
55 L. Wadding, *Annales Minorum* (Rome, 1731), III, p. 380.
56 Vincent of Beauvais, *Speculum Historiale* (Venice, 1591), f. 488^v.
57 William of St. Amour, *De periculis novissimis temporum*, ed. E. Brown, Appendix, *Fasciculus Rerum Expetendarum et Fugiendarum* . . . (London, 1690), p. 27.
58 Roger Bacon, *Opus Major*, ed. J. Bridges (1900), I, pp. 268–9.
59 Matthew Paris, *Chronica Majora. Additamenta*, Rolls Series, VI, 80. See Marjorie Reeves, *The Influence of Prophecy in the Later Middle Ages* (Oxford, 1969), pp. 49, nn.2, 3, 4; 50, nn. 1, 2, 3 for further references to this verse.
60 The main sources for this are listed in Reeves (as in previous Note), p. 54, n. 3. See also 'Il movimento del disciplinati nel settimo centario dal suo inizio', *Convegno internazionale Perugia 1960* (Perugia, 1962); J. Henderson, 'The Flagellant Movement and Flagellant Confraternities in Central Italy, 1260–1400', *Studies in Church History*, XV, ed. D. Baker (Oxford, 1978), pp. 147–60.
61 F. Ermini, 'Il "Dies Irae"', *Biblioteca dell' Archivium Romanicum*, ser. I, X–XII (1928–9), pp. 1–158, argues that the author was the Franciscan, Thomas of Celano, and that it was composed *c*. 1250 (p. 57). For the poem, see 141 seq.
62 L. Tondelli, M. Reeves, B. Hirsch-Reich, *Il Libro delle Figure dell' abate Gioacchino da Fiore*, 2nd ed., II (Turin, 1953), p. 32 for the table of MSS. and Pl. XIV for the figure; M. Reeves, B. Hirsch-Reich, *The Figurae of Joachim of Fiore* (Oxford, 1972),

pp. 146–52 and other references in the index.
63 Thomas of Pavia, *Distinctiones, Archivum Franciscanum Historicum*, XVI, pp. 25–7.
64 Salimbene, *Cronica, Monumenta Germaniae Historica. Scriptores*, XXXII, pp. 238 seq., 302–3.
65 *Super Hieremiam* (Venice, 1516), ff. 3^v, 4^v, 10^v, 11^v, 12^r, 14^r, 15^v, 18^r, 20^v, 45^r–6^v, 58^v, 62^r. See Reeves (as above, Note 59), pp. 307–8, for the development of this political outlook in some later pseudo-Joachimist writings.
66 J. Huillard-Bréholles, *Diplomatica Friderici Secundi* (Paris/Plon, 1857), V, i, p. 327, partly trans. Bernard McGinn, *Visions of the End* (1979), p. 173. For the polemical warfare, see E. Kantorowicz, *Frederick II 1191–1250*, trans. E. Lorimer (1931), pp. 495–508; McGinn, as above, pp. 168–79.
67 In addition to references in Note 66, see Reeves (as above, Note 59), pp. 308–12, for pro-Hohenstaufen propaganda.
68 McGinn (as above, Note 66), p. 172.
69 Salimbene (as above, Note 64), p. 456.
70 The *De tempore* was probably written 1288–90 but was publicly presented to the Masters of the Sorbonne in 1299. For a recent bibliography on Arnold, see E. Cánovas and F. Piñero, *Escritas Condenados por la Inquisicion* (Madrid, 1976), pp. 47–52. See also H. Finke, *Aus den Tagen Bonifaz VIII* (Münster, 1902), II, pp. 210 seq., cxvii–ccxi; Pou y Marti, *Visionarios, Beguinos y Fratecelos Catalanes (Siglos XIII–XV)*, (Vich, 1930), pp. 36 seq.; R. Manselli, *La Religiosità d'Arnaldo di Villanova* (Rome, 1951); H. Lee, 'Scrutamini Scripturas: Joachimist Themes and Figurae in the Early Religious Writings of Arnold of Villanova', *Journal of the Warburg and Courtauld Institutes*, XXXVII (1974), pp. 33–56.
71 F. Pelster, 'Die Quaestio Heinrichs v. Harclay ueber die Zweite Ankunft Christi u. die Erwartung des Baldigen Weltendes zu Anfang des XIV Jahrhunderts', *Archivio italiano per la storia della pietà* (Rome, 1948), pp. 28–78.
72 Pelster, ibid., p. 44. See *Liber apocalipsis ... cum glosis Nicholai de lire ordinis fratrum Minorum* (no place of pub. or date) for his interpretation of Last Things.
73 John of Paris (Quidort), *Tractatus de Antichristo*, published in a group of works attributed to Joachim (Venice, 1516), ff. 44^r–9^v.
74 R. Daniel, *The Franciscan Concept of Mission in the High Middle Ages* (Lexington, 1975).
75 Ubertino da Casale, *Arbor Vitae Crucifixae* (Venice, 1485), f. ccvi^v asserts that this identification was first made by John of Parma. The first certain reference occurs in the excerpts made by the Commissioners of Anagni from the lost *Liber Introductorius* of Gerard of Borgo San Donnino, *Archiv für Literatur u. Kirchengeschichte des Mittelalters*, I (1885), p. 101. See S. Bihel, 'S. Franciscus Fuitne Angelus Sixto Sigilli (Apoc. 7:2)?', *Antonianum*, II (1927), pp. 59–90, for a full list of references to this identification.
76 See references in Reeves (as above, Note 59), pp. 147 seq.
77 Ibid., pp. 58–70, on the scandal of the Eternal Evangel.
78 Jean de Meung, *Roman de la Rose, Société des Anciens Textes Francais*, III (Paris, 1921), 216, l. 11801:
        Uns livres de par le diable
        C'est l'Evangile pardurable.
79 Ed. H. Denifle (as above, Note 75), pp. 99–142.
80 For a discussion of this question, see J. Ratzinger, *Bonaventure* (Munich/Zurich, 1959), pp. 16–96, 106–20; trans. Z. Hayes, *The Theology of History in St.*

Bonaventure (Chicago, 1971), pp. 7–24, 30–49, 82–93, 105–17; Reeves (as above, Note 59), pp. 179–81; B. McGinn, 'The Abbot and the Doctors: Scholastic Reactions to the Radical Eschatology of Joachim of Fiore', *Church History*, XL (1971), pp. 41–5.

81 Bonaventura, *Collationes in Hexaemeron*, ed. F. Delorme (Florence, 1934), p. 180.
82 Ibid., pp. 185, 192–3, 265; ed. Quaracchi, *Omnia Opera*, V, pp. 408–9.
83 Ibid., ed. Delorme, p. 256. See Ratzinger (as above, Note 80 (German ed.)), p. 49.
84 D. Burr, 'The Apocalyptic Elements in Olivi's Critique of Aristotle', *Church History*, XL (1971), pp. 15–29.
85 Ibid., p. 22.
86 D. Burr, 'The Persecution of Peter Olivi', *Transactions of the American Philosophical Society*, NS. LXVI, 5 (1976), pp. 17–24.
87 B. Tierney, *Origins of Papal Infallibility* (Leiden, 1972), pp. 115–30.
88 B. Gui, *Manuel de l'Inquisiteur*, ed. G. Mollat (Paris, 1926), pp. 146–8; P. a Limborch, *Historia Inquisitionis, cui subjungitur Liber Sententiarum Inquisitionis Tholosanae 1307–23* (Amsterdam, 1692), pp. 299, 303, 306, 308.
89 F. Tocco, *Studii Francescani*, III (Naples, 1909), pp. 502–4, 506, 515; quotations in Reeves (as above, Note 59), pp. 213–14.
90 See Reeves (as in Note 59), pp. 395–7. For a more radical interpretation, see McGinn (as above, Note 80), pp. 34–5; H. Mottu, *La manifestation de l'Esprit selon Joachim de Flore* (Neuchatel/Paris, 1977), especially pp. 129–46.
91 See references in Reeves (as in Note 59), pp. 396–400; also Bernard McGinn, 'Angel Pope and Papal "Antichrist"', *Church History*, XLVII (1980), 157–64.
92 See F. Baethgen, *Der Engelpapst. Idee u. Erscheinung* (Leipzig, 1943), pp. 54–184; A. Frugoni, *Celestiana* (Rome, 1954).
93 The pioneer work on these prophecies was done by H. Grundmann, 'Die Papstprophetien des Mittelalters', *Archiv für Kulturgeschichte*, XIX (1929), pp. 77–159. See also Reeves [*vide* Bibl.], (c), pp. 107–34; McGinn [*vide* Bibl.], (b), pp. 164–5.
94 In most versions the picture represents a bear or bears with the Pope, while the earliest literary reference (F. Pipini, *Chronica, Rerurm Italicarum Scriptores*, O.S. IX (Milan, 1721), col. 724), written before 1314, makes this identification.
95 On the hermit among the rocks, see Reeves, 'Some Popular Prophecies from the Fourteenth to the Seventeenth Centuries', in *Popular Belief and Practice*, ed. G. Cumming and D. Baker (Cambridge, 1972), pp. 131–4; McGinn (as above, Note 91), pp. 162, n. 24.
96 For references, see Reeves (as above, Note 59), pp. 311–14, 317–31.
97 On the *Liber de Flore*, see H. Grundmann, 'Die Liber de Flore', *Historisches Jahrbuch*, XLIX (1929), pp. 33–91; Reeves (as above, Note 95), pp. 115–16.
98 P. Dubois, *De recuperatione Terre Sancte*, ed. C. Langlois (Paris, 1891), pp. 98–9.
99 The essential work is J. Bignami-Odier, *Études sur Jean de Roquetaillade* (Paris, 1952).
100 Ibid., pp. 113–29, for a summary.
101 Ibid., pp. 157–72. This work – *Vade mecum in tribulatione* – was printed by E. Brown (as above, Note 57), pp. 496–507.
102 Variously titled *Expositio magni Joachim in librum beati Cyrilli; Liber de magnis tribulationibus . . . compilatus a . . . Theolosphoro; Incipit libellus fratris Theolosphori de Cusentia*, and published in Venice in 1516. The basic study on Telesphorus is E. Donckel's 'Die Prophezeiung des Telesforus', *Archivum Franciscanum Historicum*,

XXVI (1933), pp. 29–104. See also Reeves (as above, Note 59), pp. 325–8, 343–6, 423–4.
103 See especially the 1516 edition, where a number of pictures were added.
104 See Reeves (as above, Note 59), pp. 328–31.
105 See K. Morawski, 'Le Mythe de l'Empereur chez Dante', *Révue des études italiennes*, XII (1965), pp. 280–301; C. Davis, 'Dante's Vision of History', *Dante Studies*, XCIII (1975), pp. 143–60; M. Reeves, 'Dante and the Prophetic View of History', *The World of Dante*, ed. C. Grayson (Oxford, 1980), pp. 44–60.
106 See K. Burdach, *Vom Mittelalter Zur Reformation*, II, 3 (Berlin, 1912), pp. 191–213; 5 (Berlin, 1929), p. 295.
107 See Reeves (as above, Note 59), pp. 332–3.
108 Jacobus de Paradiso, *De Septem Statibus Ecclesiae in Apocalipsi mystice descriptis . . .*, published E. Brown (as above, Note 57), II, pp. 110–11.
109 Henry of Langenstein (Hassia), *Tractus . . . contra quendam Eremitam de ultimis temporibus vaticinantem nomine Theolophorum*, ed. B. Pez, *Thesaurus Anecdotorum Novissimus* (Augsburg, 1721), I, 2, cols 507–64.
110 Nicholas of Cusa, *Conjectura de Novissimis Diebus* (Padua, 1514), f. 1^v.
111 Morton Bloomfield, *Piers Plowman as a Fourteenth-Century Apocalypse* (New Brunswick, N.J., 1961), pp. 91–7.
112 B. Smalley, 'Flaccianus De Visionibus Sibyllae', *Mélanges offerts à Etienne Gilson* (no editor), (Toronto/Paris, 1959), p. 551.
113 ed. J. Todd (Dublin, 1840), pp. xxx–xxxi.
114 K. Sundén, *A famous Middle English Sermon* (Göteborg, 1925). See Bloomfield (as above, Note 111), p. 87.
115 Galfridus Le Baker de Swynebroke, *Chronicon*, ed. E. Thompson (Oxford, 1889), p. 174.
116 Bloomfield (as above, Note 111), p. 87.
117 Ibid., p. 84. See Bloomfield's whole chapter on Monastic Philosophy in Fourteenth-Century England, pp. 68–97.
118 G. Leff, *Heresy in the Later Middle Ages* (Manchester, 1967), II, p. 580.
119 Matthias de Janov, *Regulae Veteris et Novi Testamenti*, ed. V. Kybal (Oeniponte, 1911), Vol. III. *Tractatus de Antichristo*, p. 32.
120 H. Kaminsky, *A History of the Hussite Revolution* (Berkeley and Los Angeles, 1967), pp. 47–52.
121 Ibid., pp. 77–8, 311.
122 Ibid., p. 312. See also E. Werner, 'Popular Ideologies in Late Medieval Europe: Taborite Chiliasm and its Antecedents', *Comparative Studies in Society and History*, II (1959–60), pp. 344–63.
123 See A. Chastel, 'Antechrist à la Renaissance', *Cristianesimo e Ragioni di Stato*, ed. E. Castelli (Rome, 1952), pp. 177–86; Reeves (as above, Note 59), pp. 429–31.
124 For much of the material in this paragraph, see D. Weinstein, *Savonarola and Prophecy: Prophecy and Patriotism in the Renaissance* (Princeton, 1970).
125 Reeves (as in Note 59), pp. 354–8.
126 Weinstein (as in Note 124), p. 143.
127 Ibid., p. 159.
128 Ibid., p. 166.
129 Ibid., p. 31.
130 Ibid., p. 216.

131 Ibid., p. 219.
132 Ibid., p. 334.
133 Ibid., pp. 336–7.
134 Reeves (as above, Note 59), pp. 437–8.
135 Ibid., pp. 439–40.
136 On Giles of Viterbo, see F. Martin, *The Problem of Giles of Viterbo* (Louvain, 1960); Reeves (as above, Note 59), pp. 268–71, 364–6.
137 Unpublished. Two Mss. are in the Biblioteca Angelica, Rome. See L. Pelissier, *De 'Historia Viginti Saeculorum' Aegidi Viterbiensis* (Montpellier, 1896); E. Massa, 'Egidio da Viterbo e la metodologia del sapere nel Cinquecento', *Pensée humaniste e tradition chrétienne aux XVe et XVIe siècles*, ed. H. Bédarida (Paris, 1950), pp. 185–239.
138 *Scechina e Libellus de Litteris Hebraicis*, ed. F. Secret (Rome, 1959).
139 *Raccolta di documenti e studi pubblicati della R. Commissione Columbiana* . . . (Rome, 1894), I, 2, *Scritti di Cristoforo Columbo*, ed. C. de Lollis, 'Libro de las profeciás', pp. 76–160.
140 J. Phelan, *The Millennial Kingdom of the Franciscans in the New World. A Study of the Writings of Geronimo de Mendieta (1525–1604)* (Berkeley/Los Angeles, 1956). On Cortes, see pp. 23–36.
141 *Expos.*, ff. 83[v], 175[v]–6[r]. On Jesuit claims, see Reeves (as in Note 59), pp. 143–4, 274–90.
142 Reeves (as in Note 59), pp. 274–6.
143 Ibid., p. 276.
144 See Reeves, *Joachim of Fiore and the Prophetic Future* (1976), pp. 157–60.

II
The Apocalypse in Renaissance England and Europe

JAROSLAV PELIKAN

3 Some uses of Apocalypse in the magisterial Reformers

On 22 February 1546, at the funeral of Martin Luther in the castle church of Wittenberg, his pastor, colleague, and friend, Johann Bugenhagen (whom he often affectionately called 'Pomeranus') delivered the sermon.[1] His text was Revelation 14.6: 'And I saw another angel fly in the midst of heaven, having the everlasting gospel to preach unto them that dwell on the earth.'[2] Martin Luther had been that angel; and in imitation of Bugenhagen, the hagiography of Luther's followers during the centuries that followed was to see him as such.[3] Especially influential in this regard were the biographical sermons of Johann Mathesius, who had been Luther's student and amanuensis and had been ordained by him.[4] The Lutheran dogmatic theology of the sixteenth and seventeenth centuries gradually evolved a special *locus*, 'De vocatione beati Lutheri', in which this passage from the Apocalypse became part of a total apologia for the unique place of Luther in the history of the church.[5]

Luther was not, of course, either the first or the last figure in the history of Christianity to be recognized as the angel with the everlasting gospel prophesied in Revelation 14.6. The passage was regularly applied to Saint Francis of Assisi, as for example when the Spanish Franciscan and the author of *De planctu ecclesiae*, Alvaro Pelayo (d. 1349) spoke of Francis as the 'signed angel' of God, who 'had in his hand "the everlasting gospel" in the holy church of God and in his Order'.[6] But the Dominicans did not have to yield to the Franciscans on this score, since they could also find a prophecy of one of their own saints in these words. The canonization of Saint Vincent Ferrer (1350–1419), which Pope Callistus III had intended to promulgate but was forced to leave to his successor, Pius II, to carry out, awarded the title 'angel with the everlasting gospel' to Vincent, as did his later disciples.[7] Other, more recent figures, such as John Milton, have also come in for a claim to the title, 'angel of Apocalypse'.[8] But Luther's followers have been perhaps more persistent than most other groups in asserting their claim: the church magazine *Der Lutheraner*, founded in Saint Louis, Missouri, in 1844 by the Reverend Carl Ferdinand Wilhelm Walther (1811–87), continued into the twentieth century to carry on its masthead a pictorial representation of the angel with the everlasting gospel in Revelation 14, referring of course to Martin Luther the Reformer of the church.[9]

The employment of a symbol from the Apocalypse to specify the place of Luther's Reformation within the overall history of the church was not without a certain irony. For Luther himself was quite ambivalent about the status of the Book of Revelation in the canon of the New Testament.[10] Although his derogatory statements about the Epistle of James are better known, he did in fact harbour a lifelong suspicion that the Apocalypse did not come from the same hand as the Gospel of John, which was his favourite among the Gospels,[11] and that it did not really belong in the Bible. In his Preface to the Book of Revelation in the *September Testament* of 1522 he expressed his judgment that it was 'neither apostolic nor prophetic' and acknowledged that, for his part, his 'spirit cannot accommodate itself to this book', because 'Christ is neither taught nor known in it'.[12] To the end of his life, in successive versions of the Preface included in the various revisions of his translation of the Bible, he went on having 'doubt'[13] about the book, citing the views of the early church as presented in Eusebius.[14] Nor were Luther's doubts an isolated phenomenon in the period of the Reformation. John Calvin – who did not share Luther's attitude toward the Epistle of James and who attempted to harmonize its doctrine of justification by faith and works with the doctrine of justification by faith in the Epistle to the Romans, just as Philip Melanchthon did[15] – did refer to the authority of the Book of Revelation even in a context in which he at the same time rejected the authority of Second Maccabees as not a part of 'the canon of the sacred books'.[16] But it is significant that in Calvin's commentaries on the Old and the New Testament, which are in the judgment of many scholars the finest products of Reformation exegesis, there is none on the Apocalypse of John. Moreover, as becomes evident from an examination of the indexes to the monumental twelve-volume translation of Calvin's *New Testament Commentaries*, recently edited by David W. Torrance and Thomas F. Torrance,[17] he did not even refer to it very often to help explain other parts of the New Testament.

Yet it would be an oversimplification to conclude from this that the Apocalypse did not play a part in the thought of the 'magisterial Reformers'[18] or that it became in practice one of the Apocrypha. For whatever its formal status within the biblical canon may or may not have been, the Book of Revelation did contribute significantly to their thought. Thus the very Preface to Revelation in which Luther expressed his unallayed 'doubt' about its right to be part of the New Testament became, in the course of its growth during the 1520s, a miniature commentary on Revelation, chapter by chapter, or, as Luther himself described it in a letter of 25 February 1530, a 'thorough exposition with an extensive preface and glosses'.[19] And while Calvin may not have composed a proper commentary on Revelation, he did, for example, think highly enough of it to conclude his *De sacerdotio papali abiiciendo*, the second of the *Epistolae duae de rebus hoc saeculo cognitu apprime necessariis* of 1537, with verses 1–2 and verses 15–16 of Revelation 3: 'I know thy works.'[20] All of this suggests that the most reliable guide to the place of the Apocalypse in the theology of the Reformation is not the question of its 'canonicity', but the uses to which the various Reformers put it. These uses are by no means the same in the various Reformation thinkers and groups; indeed, it might be possible to construct a taxonomy, particularly of the radical Reformation, on the basis of the functions fulfilled by apocalypse in their systems.[21] What follows here is something far less ambitious, but none the less potentially useful, both for the theme of this volume as a whole and for the understanding of the Reformation: a review and catalogue of some of the principal uses of apocalypse in the thought of the magisterial Reformers, Luther and Calvin.

I APOCALYPSE AS PARAENESIS

'Blessed are the dead which die in the Lord from henceforth. Yea, saith the Spirit, that they may rest from their labours; and their works do follow them' (Revelation 14.13).

It is in keeping with the emphasis of the Reformation on the proclamation of the word of God as constitutive of the Christian life, whether individual or collective, to begin with the function of the Apocalypse in its preaching and biblical exposition. Although Luther was not convinced of the authorship and therefore of the authority of the Book of Revelation, that did not prevent him from using it for his sermons. Near the end of his life, on 29 September 1544, he devoted a lengthy exposition to Revelation 12.7–12, explaining his use of the passage on the grounds that it had been a long-established custom to read this text on the Feast of Saint Michael and All Angels, but never the less going on to find in it, as he said, 'both instruction and consolation'.[22] Instruction and consolation were repeatedly with the paraenesis of the Reformers found in the Apocalypse, especially, of course, in their treatment of death, immortality, and other themes of eschatology.

Thus when Calvin, in his maiden effort in the field of theology, the *Psychopannychia*, composed in 1534, wanted to prove that after death the soul does not sleep, but lives in God, he drew upon the words of Revelation 14.13: 'Blessed are the dead which die in the Lord from henceforth. Yea, saith the Spirit, that they may rest from their labours; and their works do follow them.' This verse proved to him that the peace enjoyed by the blessed dead in 'the bosom of Abraham' was not an unconscious state, but 'the peace of conscience which the Lord bestows upon his followers in the abode of peace'.[23] Some years later – I have surmised elsewhere that it must have been in the first half of 1542[24] – Luther was lecturing on the Book of Genesis. Throughout the lectures he was repeatedly at pains to demonstrate that, despite the apparent similarities between the patriarchal narratives and various pagan histories, the chosen of God were unique. Jacob, for example, 'is described so simply and meagrely that he does not differ in any respect from the lowest and most worthless man among the heathen'. But this was deceptive; for 'the works of the godless and of the heathen are not pleasing to God', while those of true believers, whether in the Old Testament or in the New, 'have the glory and the inspection of God and of his angels'. The clue to this distinction was provided by the words of the Book of Revelation, 'Their works do follow them', which, Luther added, pertained not only to works of a churchly sort but to those in the political and social order as well.[25]

Despite Calvin's extensive argument in support of the notion of the immortality of the soul, in which he employed many of the traditional proofs from reason as well as from revelation,[26] the status of this notion in the thought of the magisterial Reformation remains somewhat ambiguous. It should be noted that the passage just cited from Luther appears in his *Enarratio in Genesin*, the massive printed version of the lectures that he gave on Genesis, beginning probably on 1 June 1535 and concluding on 17 November 1545, just three months before his death.[27] The authenticity of this version has come into question, particularly through the careful researches of Peter Meinhold; for when we do have notes that are one or more stages closer to Luther's own oral presentation, there are some striking discrepancies.[28] For our purposes here it is important to point out that some of the most glaring of such discrepancies involve eschatology. Luther's editors, presumably under the influence of the philosophical theology of Philip Melanchthon, had a tendency to substitute the immortality of the soul for 'eternal life' or for the idea of the resurrection of the body.[29] From other statements of Luther in his unquestionably authentic works it is evident that resurrection, which embodies his soteriological emphasis on the primary of the divine initiative and applies it also the area of the 'life everlasting', was a far more congenial concept to Luther's thought than was the conventional idea of the natural immortality of the human soul, which tended to make eternal life a possession of man rather than a special gift of God.[30] Some scholars have gone so far as to attribute to Luther an even more radical disjunction between resurrection and immortality.[31] Nevertheless there remain many statements of Luther, also in writings that have not been bowdlerized by his Melanchthonian epigones, that put him on the side of universal and in that sense 'natural' immortality – 'natural' meaning here 'concreated', so that immortality and rationality belong together, as indeed they had in the medieval intellectual tradition.[32]

The words of Revelation 14.13 contributed to the thought of the magisterial

Reformers about death and immortality in other ways as well. Beginning with the edition of 1543, Calvin's *Institutes*, in the discussion of prayers for the dead, contained the following passage: 'But Scripture supplies another far better and more perfect solace when it testifies: "Blessed are the dead which die in the Lord." And it adds the reason: "Henceforth they rest from their labours."'[33] The context of the passage is an examination of the claim that the example of the early church supported the practice of praying for the dead, and therefore the supposition that such prayers contributed to the improvement of their condition in the afterlife.[34] The evidence of the writings of the church fathers indicates that the practice of praying for the dead, and in particular of offering the sacrifice of the Eucharist on their behalf, truly was an early one, and that it came much earlier than did any consistent schema of a purgatorial middle state between heaven and hell.[35] Much of this schema did not develop until after the separation of Eastern and Western Christianity, with the result that it became a point of controversy at the Council of Florence in the fifteenth century, between the traditionalism of the Greeks and the scholasticism of the Latins.[36] East and West shared the *lex orandi* of prayers and eucharistic sacrifices for the blessed departed, but they diverged on the *lex credendi* of a full-blown doctrine of purgatory.

It was only gradually that the Reformers themselves surrendered the idea of purgatory. The early Roman Catholic critics of the Reformation pointed out that even after his break with Rome had become fairly evident, Luther went on accepting it.[37] He himself acknowledged that purgatory was one of the last remnants of medieval doctrine to disappear from his theological system.[38] Such a timetable may seem puzzling, above all if one remembers that the principal biblical proof text traditionally cited in support of the practice of prayer for the dead, 2 Maccabees 12.43–5, the account of the 'sin offering' taken up by Judas Maccabaeus as 'atonement for the dead',[39] was unacceptable to the Reformers on the grounds of questionable authority of the Books of the Maccabees, which belonged to the Apocrypha of the Old Testament rather than to the canonical Scriptures, having been included in the Septuagint but not in the Hebrew Bible.[40] But such ideas died hard, chiefly because of the 'solace' to which Calvin refers. Melanchthon, in the *Apology of the Augsburg Confession*, dismissed the arguments from 2 Maccabees as a 'dream [*somnium*]' and declared that, except for this 'dream', there was no testimony in the Scriptures to support such notions as either prayers by the dead or prayers for the dead. Yet in the very same sentence he could say: 'We also grant that the saints in heaven pray for the church in general, as they prayed for the church universal while they were on earth',[41] although apparently they did not pray for any particular needs of particular members of the church. Once again here, it was the 'solace' and pastoral value that gave these ideas such durability. Therefore the availability of the 'far better and more perfect solace' of the testimony in Revelation 14.13 enabled the

Reformers to counter the illusory 'solace' provided by the doctrine of purgatory with a view of death that comported with the evangelical faith and a depiction of the life eternal that stood on (relatively) firmer canonical ground.

Such an emphasis on the 'solace' of Christian faith and life was an echo of a central theme in Reformation thought. As Calvin noted in his usual careful manner, the reference of the apostle Paul to 'patience' and to 'the consolation of the Scriptures' in Romans 15.4 'does not include the whole of that benefit which is to be derived from the word of God, but briefly points to its main object [*praecipuum finem*]'; and in the following verse 'God is designated from the effect which he produces' as 'the God of patience and comfort'.[42] If the 'main object' of the Scriptures truly was to provide consolation, and through consolation to nourish patience, that applied above all to the believer's contemplation of the reality of death. Luther's preoccupation with this reality was sufficient to be regarded by some of his interpreters as obsessive,[43] and it permeated many of his writings. His personal motto was taken from Psalm 118.17: 'I shall not die, but live, and declare the works of the Lord.'[44] Of the relatively few writings that were devoted explicitly to the theme of death, two stand out: the *Sermon von der Bereitung zum Sterben* of 1519; and the *Enarratio psalmi XC per D. M. Lutherum in schola Wittenbergensi anno 1534 publice absoluta*, published in 1541.[45]

In spite of its having been written in the midst of the turbulent events of 1519, as Luther, in the aftermath of the Leipzig Debate of July 1519, was engaged in acrimonious controversies with Johann Eck, his adversary at Leipzig, with Hieronymus Emser, and with other opponents, the *Sermon* (which in this context means not 'sermon' but 'tract') bears virtually no scars from the controversies surrounding its author at the time. It also combines themes from medieval piety with the motifs of the new evangelical faith, urging the believer in the hour of death to call upon the Virgin Mary and the saints for their aid and yet at the same time assuring anyone who did not have access to the sacraments that 'the sacraments are nothing else than signs which help and incite us to faith',[46] which was all-important. Appel's examination of Luther's relation to the *ars moriendi* literature of the fourteenth and fifteenth centuries has also noted some of these contrasts.[47] The full contours of Luther's interpretation of the death of Christ as victory over the enemies of man – sin, death, the devil, and the law – did not develop until later,[48] but they are presaged in this tract. Instead of looking at those 'who were killed by God's wrath and were overcome by death', one was to look at 'those who have overcome death', above all at Christ, through whose cross death 'will seem contemptible and dead, slain and overcome in life'. And that, according to Luther, was the consolation that would enable one 'to die calmly in Christ and with Christ, as we read in Revelation [14.13], "Blessed are they who die in Jesus Christ"'.[49] Although Luther's other great 'Christian thanatopsis',[50] the *Commentary on Psalm 90*, in which he described the existential pathos of the human situation with what Werner Elert has called 'a melancholy without peer',[51] does not quote the *ipsissima verba* of Revelation 14.13, it does set forth a similar contrast between contemplating death and the wrath of God apart from Christ and contemplating Christ, in whom 'we see God clothed in his glorious and gracious works'.[52]

It would, however, be a mistake to conclude from such language that the paraenetic function of apocalypse in the writings of the magisterial Reformers was confined to its significance for the individual and for his private expectation of life eternal after death. As Karl Holl has pointed out, Luther recognized in himself 'a tendency towards melancholy and also toward privacy' and saw in his Christian faith a means of overcoming it.[53] Similarly, a myopic concentration of the individual on his own salvation was one of the very emphases for which Calvin reproved Cardinal Sadoleto. 'It is not very good theology [*parum est theologicum*]', he declared, 'to confine a man's thoughts so much to himself, and not to set before him, as the prime motive of his existence [*principium vitae formandae*], zeal to adorn the glory of God.'[54] In his explanations elsewhere of what it meant to make the glory of God resplendent, Calvin kept in view both the individual and the corporate dimensions.[55] One of his favorite texts for this also came from the Apocalypse. In a catalog of biblical texts dealing with the sacrifices of praise in both the Old and the New Testament,[56] he concluded with Revelation 1.6, which, following both the Greek original and the Latin Vulgate, he rendered, 'hath made us *a kingdom* and priests unto the Father', rather than '*kings* and priests', as both Luther's German Bible and the King James version did. This translation was not only more literal; it also suited his emphasis on the corporate character of the universal priesthood of believers. Conflated with 1 Peter 2.9, in which believers were called not 'priests' but 'a royal priesthood',[57] the passage from Revelation 1 located the Protestant doctrine of the priesthood of all believers in the setting of the doctrine of the church. Eventually, to be sure, the priesthood of all believers was to become instead, in the thought of Pietism, a bulwark of Protestant individualism.[58]

The stress of the Apocalypse on the corporate makes itself evident in the paraenesis of the Reformers above all in their interpretation of history.[59] Luther's Preface to Revelation is instructive here. After explaining the doubtful authorship of the book and disavowing any claim to a definitive interpretation – 'We will', he said, 'give other and higher minds something to think about by stating our own views' – he went on to characterize as 'the first and surest step toward finding its interpretation' the historical one: 'to take from history the events and disasters that have come upon Christendom till now, and hold them up alongside of these images, and so compare them very carefully'. Although the prophecy and the history that fulfilled it had much more of the bad than of the good in them, the message of the book remained one of comfort in the sure knowledge 'that Christendom is to endure in spite of the plagues that are going to come'. For the confession, 'I believe in the holy catholic [or, as Luther preferred to translate,[60] Christian] church', was as much an article of faith, rather than an empirical observation, as was any other statement in the creed: it must be believed, not seen; but once believed, it also became discernible in the historical process.[61]

It would be illuminating to compare Luther's historical identifications, image by image, with the late medieval apocalyptic on which he draws, but a detailed analysis of that sort must await treatment elsewhere.[62] It is clear that much of the specific historical fulfillment in Luther's Preface is the conventional recital of persecutions, heresies, and schisms. But it is a distinctive Reformation emphasis when Luther labels the first angel of Revelation 8.7, whose trumpet blast called forth 'hail and fire mingled with blood', as the doctrine of works-righteousness, which, he adds in reference to Tatian, 'had to be the first doctrine in opposition to the gospel, and it also remains the last, except that it is always getting new teachers and new names, such as the Pelagians, etc'.[63] The phrase 'Pelagians, etc.', like the phrase of the *Augsburg Confession*, 'the Pelagians and others',[64] was directed against late medieval theologians who, in Luther's judgment, glorified human powers at the expense of divine grace. Similarly, the third angel in Revelation 8.10–11, whose trumpet caused a great star to fall, stood for Origen, 'who embittered and corrupted the Scriptures with the philosophy of reason';[65] but this, too, was not a phenomenon confined to the early centuries of the church, since that was likewise what 'the universities have hitherto done among us'. The Preface closes with a typical Reformation paraenesis: 'Therefore let there be offenses, divisions, heresies, and faults; let them do what they can! If only the word of the gospel remains pure among us, and we love and cherish it, we shall not doubt that Christ is with us, even when things are at their worst.'[66]

II APOCALYPSE AS POLEMICS

'And the beast was taken, and with him the false prophet that wrought miracles before him, with which he deceived them that had received the mark of the beast, and them that worshipped his image. These both were cast alive into a lake of fire burning with brimstone. And the remnant were slain with the sword of him that sat upon the horse, which sword proceeded out of his mouth (Revelation 19.20–1).

It is obvious from Luther's Preface to Revelation that paraenesis in the teaching and preaching of the magisterial Reformers is often indistinguishable from polemics. This is true above all of their exegesis of the Apocalypse, a book that was polemical in its original intent and that throughout Christian history has been a kaleidoscope in which successive generations have recognized the heresies and schisms of their own time. Even the most 'spiritual' of commentaries on it have included an attack on contemporary aberrations, if only in the form of a critique of distorted interpretations. Thus Augustine, in the famous exposition of the twentieth chapter of Revelation in the twentieth book [67] of his *City of God*, where the paraenesis of Revelation 14.13 serves to provide the consolation of a 'reign with Christ now in the living and in the dead',[68] nevertheless concludes with a denunciation of those interpreters who, 'blinded by contentious opinionativeness', fail to interpret the obscure portions of the book in the light of the clear ones.[69] Immediately following his own explanation of Revelation 20, Augustine proceeds to an examination of some 'conjectural explanations' of the New Testament prophecies concerning the coming of Antichrist.[70] The *locus classicus* on the Antichrist was 2 Thessalonians 2.3–12, rather than any one chapter of the Apocalypse itself. Now it should be kept in mind that this chapter of 2 Thessalonians does not actually use the word 'Antichrist', for that appears in the New Testament only five times: 1 John 2.18 (twice); 1 John 2.22, 1 John 4.3, and 2 John 7.[71] But the equation of the Johannine 'Antichrist' with the Pauline 'man of sin, son of perdition' began in the early church[72] and would seem to be almost unavoidable; it was also continued by the Reformers.[73] Moreover, the attribution of the Fourth Gospel, the Apocalypse, and the three Catholic Epistles to John 'the beloved disciple'[74] meant that the composite portrait of the 'man of sin' in 2 Thessalonians and the 'Antichrist' in the Catholic Epistles of John would be fleshed out with the aid of the images of the Book of Revelation.

The consensus of the Reformers that the Roman Papacy was the fulfilment of this composite portrait means, for our purposes here, that in the writings of the Reformers we are to look for 'apocalypse' even where there is not a specific allusion to chapter and verse of the Apocalypse. A good example appears as a parenthetical remark in Calvin's graphic denunciation of the 'robbery' perpetrated by the 'Roman archpirate', near the conclusion of the attack on the Roman Catholic definition of priesthood, which is the second of his *Duae epistolae* of 1537. The remark is a verbatim quotation (following the Fulda text of the Vulgate[75]) of 1 Timothy 6.10: 'O Roma (ut uno verbo Radicem Omnium Malorum Avaritiam complectar).'[76] Although the editors of Calvin, whether in the *Corpus Reformatorum* edition of the nineteenth century or the *Opera selecta* edition of the twentieth, failed to identify the quotation as having come from 1 Timothy, much less as imitating a genre employed by the Book of Revelation, the acronym clearly stands in that apocalyptic tradition. Or when Luther, in the hymn, 'Erhalt uns, Herr bei deinem Wort', written probably in 1541, went on to pray, 'Und steur des Papsts und Türken Mord' (mollified by more squeamish later generations to read 'Und steure deiner Feinde Mord'),[77] he was, as the parallels in the Preface to the Book of Revelation show,[78] alluding to the prophecies of the Apocalypse.

An especially intriguing documentation of Luther's interpretation of the

Apocalypse as a prophecy of the Papal Antichrist appears in the book of cartoons with captions that he published in 1521 under the title *Passional Christi und Antichristi*.[79] Just how much of the iconography in the book was actually the work of Lucas Cranach the Elder has continued to be a matter of debate and surmise among art historians, but the solution of that question does not affect the point at issue here.[80] As Georg Kawerau has pointed out, the use of a graphic depiction to draw the contrast between Christ and the Pope was a device that went back to Hussite placards, on which the humble entry of Christ into Jerusalem on an ass was counterposed to the pomp of a triumphal procession by which the Pope and his cardinals entered Rome.[81] The work of 1521 may well have been an adaptation of such Hussite depictions, or it may even have arisen independently of them. Our interest here, of course, is chiefly in the captions. As could be anticipated, the standard proof text for the contention of the Reformers that the Antichrist would not be a foreign intruder, but a 'prelate',[82] 2 Thessalonians 2.4, 'Who opposeth and exalteth himself above all that is called God', appears prominently. It is the explanation for a pair of cartoons in which Christ is depicted as driving the money changers from the temple and the Pope is depicted as bringing them back in.[83] The non-biblical quotations under other cartoons come from the Canon Law; for, as Luther's conclusion puts it, 'Everything that is written here can be found in the papal Canon Law, not only as something fitting but as something legally required.'[84] The ominous prediction of 2 Thessalonians 2.8, 'And then shall that Wicked be revealed, whom the Lord shall consume with the spirit of his mouth, and shall destroy with the brightness of his coming', is the final caption in the book, under a picture showing the Pope being hurled into the abyss.[85]

But under that same concluding cartoon there also appear the words of Revelation 19.20–1: 'And the beast was taken, and with him the false prophet that wrought miracles before him, with which he deceived them that had received the mark of the beast, and them that worshipped his image. These both were cast alive into a lake of fire burning with brimstone. And the remnant were slain with the sword of him that sat upon the horse, which sword proceeded out of his mouth.' The parallel drawn here by Luther between the words of 2 Thessalonians 2, 'shall consume with the spirit of his mouth', and the words of Revelation 19, 'which sword proceedeth out of his mouth', as the weapon by which the consummation and the expulsion of the Antichrist into the abyss would be accomplished, also seems to be at work in Calvin's interpretation of the words of the Lord's Prayer, 'Thy kingdom come', as being finally and totally fulfilled only with the destruction of the kingdom of Antichrist in the brightness of the Second Coming of Christ,[86] although there were also anticipations of it 'daily', whenever the power of the voice of Christ struck down his enemies even before the end of time.[87] The apocalyptic import of these prophecies becomes all the more dramatic in the light of the companion picture in the *Passional*, in which the glorious ascension of Christ is portrayed, together with the prophecy of Luke 1.33 (echoed in the phrase of the Nicene Creed, 'of whose kingdom there shall be no end'), 'And of his kingdom there shall be no end.'[88] In addition to the other passages appearing there, Acts 1.9–11 and John 12.26, it might have contained, though in fact it did not, the words of Revelation 11.15: 'The kingdoms of this world are become the kingdoms of our Lord, and of his Christ: and he shall reign for ever and ever'; for both Luke 1.33 (as Calvin observes in his comment on it[89]) and Revelation 11.15 are a quotation from Daniel 7.14.

The theme of Antichrist as the object of a false worship, sounded here in the final caption with the use of Revelation 19.20–1, was anticipated earlier in the *Passional*, also with a passage from the Apocalypse.[90] The picture of Christ shows him washing the feet of his disciples and contains as an inscription the words of institution of the *mandatum*, John 13.14–17.[91] Then – almost as if in anticipation of Calvin's statement that the obedience to that *mandatum* by the bishops and the Pope on Maundy Thursday is a 'ceremonial comedy' and 'a shameful mockery of Christ'[92] – the opposite picture represents the Pope allowing his feet to be kissed by secular rulers. The caption cites the Canon Law on the kissing of the Pope's feet, and explains: 'The Pope takes it upon himself to imitate certain tyrants and heathen princes, who offered their feet to be kissed by the people. This he does to fulfill what is written: "As many as would not worship the image of the beast shall be killed" (Rev. 13.15).'[93] Both Luther and Calvin quoted the biblical prohibitions of idolatry against the forms of worship that had developed during the Middle Ages, but Calvin was even more consistent and even more vehement than Luther in the specific attack on 'images'. In the first of the *Duae epistolae* of 1537 he rejected the argumentation (developed most fully in the treatises of Byzantine theologians against iconoclasm during the eighth and ninth centuries and in the decrees of the Second Council of Nicaea in 787[94]) that the Old Testament had equated all image-worship with idolatry only because the people of Israel were surrounded by ignorant and idolatrous nations, whereas the church could tolerate and even encourage the worship of the images of Christ, Mary, and the saints because the coming of the Son of God in the flesh had made this permissible.[95] A few years later, in his *Antidote* to the decrees of the Council of Trent, he subjected the exegetical ground of that argumentation at Second Nicaea to a blistering refutation.[96]

The *Passional Christi und Antichristi*, with its apocalyptic portrayals of the antithesis between Christ and his alleged Vicar, was published in May 1521, scarcely three and a half years after the posting of the Ninety-Five Theses. In that short time Luther's thought had evolved on many issues, but perhaps on none so drastically as on the status of the Pope, as he himself acknowledged in the nearest he ever came to an *apologia pro vita sua*, the Preface of 1545 to the first volume of his Latin writings, where he described his early attitude of deference towards the Pope and how it had changed.[97] It was an early expression of the denunciation of the Canon Law as a mark of papal corruption when Luther, with the caution that he was 'whispering this in your ear', expressed in a letter to a friend his growing sense that the Pope was either himself the Antichrist or in any case the apostle of the Antichrist, so miserably was Christ being crucified in the Decretals.[98] But less than a year later, having just read Lorenzo Valla's exposé of the 'Donation of Constantine' as a forgery, he was much more definite, in a letter of 24 February 1520 to the same friend: 'I am so oppressed that I have virtually no doubt that the Pope is really and truly that Antichrist for whom, by the commonly accepted view, the world is waiting. His way of life, his actions, his statements, and his ordinances fit all of this so well'; he promised that he would amplify these ideas in personal conversation.[99] And later in the same year he was openly contrasting Christ and his alleged Vicar, declaring: 'See how different Christ is from his successors, although they all would wish to be his vicars!' And he added: 'Indeed, what is such a "Vicar" but an Antichrist and an idol?' This he did in an open letter addressed to none other than Pope Leo X himself.[100]

When Pope Leo condemned him in the Bull *Exsurge Domine*, dated 15 June 1520,[101] Luther saw his worst suspicions confirmed; and in a treatise that appeared in both Latin and German he attacked 'the Bull of the Antichrist'.[102] He was convinced now that 'all those who support this Bull and follow it should deny God and his word and should be teaching nothing other than error and heresy', and he saw this as the nadir that would in turn become the beginning of the process by which 'Christ is to overthrow the Antichrist',[103] evidently referring to the same conflation of Revelation 19.21 and 2 Thessalonians 2 examined earlier. From this point on the identification of the Pope as the Antichrist becomes a commonplace in his thought, repeated so often that it would be wearisome to recite all the polemics.[104] In many ways the polemics reached its climax in 1537, in events surrounding the gathering of the Schmalkaldic League in February of that year. Luther did not go to Schmalkalden, but he did summarize his identification of the Pope as Antichrist in the second of two sermons delivered for Invocavit, the First Sunday in Lent, 18 February 1537.[105] Taking as his text the Gospel for Invocavit Sunday, the narrative of the temptation of Christ in Matthew 4.1–11, he used the words, 'Get thee hence, Satan!' in Matthew 4.10 as the basis for a discourse that began with the theme: 'The third period in [the history of] Christendom has been called the period of the Antichrist.' Most of the standard polemics came to voice in the sermon. The prophecy of the rise of Antichrist in 2 Thessalonians 2.4 appeared in the very first paragraph; the prophecy of the downfall of Antichrist in 2 Thessalonians 2.8 was applied specifically to the contemporary events of the Reformation, during which the mask of the devil was being torn off. Once again, however, it was not only 2 Thessalonians, but the Apocalypse that provided the imagery for Luther's polemics. 'The gospel', he declared, 'is exposing the shame of the harlot of

Babylon'; and, quoting Revelation 13.2, 'And the dragon gave [the beast] his power, and his seat, and great authority', he interpreted these words as having been fulfilled in the subjection of Charlemagne and later kings and emperors to the authority of the Pope – a process to which the Reformation was now putting an end. Soon, he hoped, the unmasking of the Babylonian harlot would be complete, and, in the words of 2 Thessalonians 2.8, Christ the Lord would destroy the Antichrist with the brightness of his coming.

Also at Schmalkalden in 1537, another event took place that was to be decisive for the polemical use of apocalypse ever after. At the end of 1536 Luther had drafted a series of doctrinal articles, in preparation for a general council that had been summoned for May 1537 (although in fact there would not be a general council until Trent in 1545). Those doctrinal articles were proposed for ratification by the League; and although they failed of official adoption there, they did receive the endorsement of a large number of Luther's followers.[106] Eventually, therefore, they were incorporated into the *Book of Concord* of 1580 as one of the normative Lutheran Confessions, under the title *Articuli Smalcaldici*.[107] Luther's dogmatic and polemical affirmations in the *Smalcald Articles* include the statement: 'This is a powerful demonstration that the Pope is the real Antichrist [*papam esse ipsum verum Antichristum*].'[108] And the biblical proof texts quoted against the Pope are, as should not be surprising, 2 Thessalonians 2 and the Book of Revelation. In both the German and the Latin text of the *Smalcald Articles*, as well as in his treaties of 1539, *Von den Konziliis und Kirchen*,[109] Luther referred to 'Revelation 12' when he clearly meant Revelation 10.3, 'And cried with a loud voice as when a lion roareth.'[110] The mistake in the citation of the Apocalypse was trivial, but the labeling of the Pope as the Antichrist of the Apocalypse was fateful. For as a consequence of their normative standing as part of the official collection of Lutheran Confessions in the *Book of Concord*, the *Smalcald Articles* were taken to be binding. And for centuries to come, adherence to the identification of the Pope as the Antichrist was one of the distinguishing marks of orthodox Lutheranism.[111]

Measured by this criterion (though not, to be sure, by the other criteria applied in orthodox Lutheranism), John Calvin had a right to be called a Lutheran. For he had received the polemical characterization of the Pope as the Antichrist of the Apocalypse, together with most of Luther's other polemics against Rome, as part of his heritage from Luther, whose follower he believed himself to be.[112] Yet it bears mentioning that in their uses of apocalypse, as we have seen, Luther and Calvin were in basic agreement. To Calvin, too, it was as obvious as it was to Luther that the various prophecies of 2 Thessalonians and the Book of Revelation had come true in the Roman Papacy, as is evident from the repeated parallels that we have been able to draw between them. But to those parallels between Luther and Calvin we should add at least two additional passages from Calvin's works. One is a further refinement of the antithesis in Luther's *Passional Christi und Antichristi*. Instead of merely noting how striking the contrasts were between Christ and his supposed Vicar, Calvin went on to draw a historical analogy between the failure of Roman Catholicism to recognize the predicted Antichrist when he stood before them in the flesh and the failure of first-century Judaism to recognize the predicted Christ when he stood before them in the flesh. An imaginary Antichrist, whom they thought to be still in the future, prevented 'the foolish Papists' from seeing that all the marks by which the Spirit of God – in such places as 2 Thessalonians 2, 1 John 2, and the Book of Revelation – had pointed out the Antichrist were now clearly visible in the Pope.[113] The other passage from Calvin that deserves repeating here appeared in one of his ablest summations of the case for the Reformation, the treatise of 1544 usually bearing the title *De necessitate reformandae ecclesiae*.[114] It was addressed to Emperor Charles V, before whom Luther had stood almost twenty-five years earlier at the Diet of Worms and to whom Luther's followers had presented the *Augsburg Confession* at the Diet of Augsburg in 1530. Now it was yet another Imperial Diet, being held at Speyer, to which Calvin sought to explain the Reformation.[115]

Speaking not only for himself, but for Luther and for the entire Protestant movement, or at any rate for the 'magisterial Reformation', Calvin declared:

> I deny that See to be Apostolical, wherein nought is seen but a shocking apostacy – I deny him to be the vicar of Christ, who, in furiously persecuting the gospel, demonstrates by his conduct that he is Antichrist – I deny him to be the successor of Peter, who is doing his utmost to demolish every edifice that Peter built – and I deny him to be the head of the Church, who by his tyranny lacerates and dismembers the Church, after dissevering her from Christ, her true and only Head.[116]

Apocalyptic though such statements by Luther and Calvin patently are, they were apparently not sufficient to dispel the doubts of both magisterial Reformers about the appropriateness of including the Apocalypse of John in the list of books on which they would comment verse by verse. That task they left to others, their opponents and eventually their pupils, as the Bibliography appended to this volume shows. In this sense the magisterial Reformers do not belong, strictly speaking, to the history of the exegesis of the Apocalypse. But as this essay has sought to document, they definitely do belong to the history of the use of apocalypse, and even of the Apocalypse. Moreover, only by a consideration also of their uses of apocalypse can historical scholarship hope to understand the full range of their thought and work, as well as their contributions, direct and indirect, to the thought and work of others, to whom other chapters of this book are devoted.

NOTES

1 Johannes Bugenhagen, *Eine christliche Predigt, uber den Leich und begrebnis, des ehrwirdigen D. Martini Luthers* (Wittenberg, 1546). I have used the copy in the Beinecke Rare Book and Manuscript Library of Yale University.
2 See also Matthias Flacius Illyricus, *Eine erschreckliche Historia von einem, den die Feinde des Evangelii inn welsch Land gezwungen haben, den erkanntnen Christum zuvorleugnen* (Magdeburg, 1549), p. Alr. I have used the copy in the library of the University of Pennsylvania.
3 Ernst Walter Zeeden, *The Legacy of Luther: Martin Luther and the Reformation in the Estimation of the German Lutherans from Luther's Death to the Beginning of the Age of Goethe*, translated by Ruth Mary Bethell (Westminster, Maryland, 1954).
4 Hans Volz, *Die Lutherpredigten des Johannes Mathesius: Kritische Untersuchungen zur Geschichtsschreibung im Zeitalter der Reformation* (Halle, 1929).
5 Johann Gerhard, *Loci theologici* (1609-22), ed. Edward Preuss (9 vols; Berlin and Leipzig, 1863-73), 6.83-90.
6 Alvarus Pelagius (Alvaro Pelayo), *Epistolae*, ed. Vittorino Meneghin, *Scritti inediti di Fra Álvaro Pais* (Lisbon, 1969), p. 122. For another Franciscan statement, see Ubertino de Casale, *Arbor vitae crucifixae Jesu*, 5.3 (Venice, 1485), pp. 421-34. (I have used the edition of 1485 in the Beinecke Rare Book and Manuscript Library, but have added, for the sake of convenience, the pagination supplied in the photocopy published at Turin in 1961).
7 Cf. M. Catherine, *Angel of the Judgment: Life of Vincent Ferrer* (Notre Dame, Indiana, 1954).
8 Joseph A. Wittreich, *Angel of Apocalypse: Blake's Idea of Milton* (Madison, Wisconsin, 1975), esp. pp. 226-7 on Milton as 'eighth angel'.
9 See Walther's Reformation sermon of 1845 on the text, Rev. 14.6-12, *Casual-Predigten und -Reden* (Saint Louis, 1889), pp. 40-54. (This volume of sermons and addresses was published posthumously.)
10 For a brief summary, see Michael Reu, *Luther's German Bible: An Historical Presentation Together with a Collection of Sources* (Columbus, Ohio, 1934), pp. 171-6.
11 Luther, 'Vorrede auf das Neue Testament', *WA DB* 6.10 (*LW* 35.361-2). *WA* designates throughout *D. Martin Luthers Werke: Kritische Gesamtausgabe* (Weimar, 1883 ff.); *Br: Briefe*; *DB: Deutsche Bibel*; and *LW: Luther's Works: The American Edition*, ed. Jaroslav Pelikan and Helmut T. Lehmann (Saint Louis and Philadelphia, 1955 ff.).
12 Luther, 'Vorrede auf die Offenbarung S. Johannis' (1522), *WA DB* 7.404 (*LW* 35.398-9).
13 Luther, 'Vorrede auf die Offenbarung S. Johannis' (1530), *WA DB* 7.408; (1546), *WA DB* 7.409 (*LW* 35.400).
14 Eusebius, *Ecclesiastical History*, III.25, ed. Edward Schwartz, 5th ed. (Leipzig, 1955), p. 104.
15 Calvin, 'Commentarius in Iacobi epistolam', *CR* 55: 405-7; 'Commentarius in Epistolam Pauli ad Romanos', Parker 77 (Torrance 8.79); Melanchthon, 'Apologia Confessionis Augustanae', IV.244-53, *Bekenntnisschriften* 207-10 (Tappert 141-3). The abbreviations used designate here and throughout: *CR: Corpus Reformatorum: Johannis Calvini Opera quae supersunt omnia* (Brunswick, 1863-1900); Parker: *Iohannis Calvini Commentarius in Epistolam Pauli ad*

16 'Institutio religionis christianae' (1559), III.5.8, *CR* 2.497 (McNeill 678–9). McNeill designates throughout *Calvin: Institutes of the Christian Religion*, ed. John T. McNeill (Philadelphia, 1960).
17 It is perhaps in keeping with that neglect when Rudolf Bultmann, in his *Theologie des Neuen Testaments* (Tübingen, 1953), cites the Book of Revelation a total of two times; see the 'Stellenverzeichnis', p. 602.
18 I have taken over this designation of Luther and Calvin from the work of my friend and colleague, George Huntston Williams, *The Radical Reformation* (Philadelphia, 1962), p. xxiv.
19 Luther to Nikolaus Hausmann, 25.ii.1530, *WA Br* 5.242.
20 Calvin, 'Epistolae duae de rebus hoc saeculo cognitu apprime necessariis', *CR* 5.311–12.
21 Cf. Williams, op. cit., pp. 857–61.
22 *WA* 49.570, 582.
23 'Vivere apud Christum non dormire animis sanctos qui in fide Christi decedunt, quae vulgo Psychopannychia dicitur', *CR* 5.189.
24 In my 'Introduction' to *LW* 5.ix–xii.
25 *WA* 43.616 (*LW* 5.271–2).
26 Edward A. Dowey, Jr, *The Knowledge of God in Calvin's Theology* (New York, 1952), p. 79.
27 *WA* 42–4 (*LW* 1–8).
28 Peter Meinhold, *Die Genesisvorlesung Luthers und ihre Herausgeber* (Stuttgart, 1936).
29 See my 'Introduction' to *LW* 1.xi–xii.
30 Luther, 'Das 15. Kapitel der 1. Epistel S. Pauli an die Korinther. Von der Auferstehung der Toten', *WA* 36: 478–696 (*LW* 28.54–213).
31 Carl Stange, *Luthers Gedanken über die Todesfurcht* (Berlin, 1932), and in his subsequent studies.
32 Brian A. Gerrish, *Grace and Reason: A Study in the Theology of Luther* (Oxford, 1962).
33 'Institutio religionis christianae', III.5.10, *CR* 2.500 (McNeill 682).
34 See the notes in McNeill 681–4 on this claim.
35 Cf. Jaroslav Pelikan, *The Christian Tradition: A History of the Development of Doctrine* (Chicago, 1971 ff.), 1.355–6; 3.32–3.
36 *Ibid.*, 2.279–80.
37 Johann Eck, *Enchiridion locorum communium adversus Lutherum et alios hostes ecclesiae* (1525–43), *Corpus Catholicorum*, 34 (Münster, 1979), 262, and parallels cited there.
38 Luther, 'Ein Widerruf vom Fegfeuer', *WA* 30–II.367–90.
39 The passage reads, in the Revised Standard Version: 'In doing this [providing for a sin offering] he acted very well and honorably, taking account of the resurrection. . . . Therefore he made atonement for the dead, that they might be delivered from their sin.'
40 'Institutio religionis christianae', III.5.8, *CR* 2.497 (McNeill 678–79).
41 'Apologia', XXI.9, *Bekenntnisschriften* 318 (Tappert 230).

42 Calvin, 'Commentarius in Epistolam Pauli ad Romanos', Parker 307 (Torrance 8.305).
43 See the work of Stange cited in note 31 above.
44 Luther, 'Das schöne Confitemini, an der Zahl der 118. Psalm', *WA* 31–I.65–182 (*LW* 14.41–106).
45 'Sermon von der Bereitung zum Sterben', *WA* 2.685–97 (*LW* 42.99–115); 'Enarratio psalmi XC', *WA* 40–III.476–594 (*LW* 13.73–141).
46 *WA* 2.692–5 (*LW* 42.108–11).
47 Helmut Appel, *Anfechtung und Trost im Spätmittelalter und bei Luther* (Leipzig, 1938).
48 Gustaf Aulén, *Christus Victor: An Historical Study of the Three Main Types of the Idea of Atonement*, trans. A. G. Hebert, foreword by Jaroslav Pelikan (New York, 1969), pp. 101–22.
49 *WA* 2.689 (*LW* 42.104).
50 As I have called it in my 'Introduction' to *LW* 13.xii.
51 Werner Elert, *Morphologie des Luthertums* (2 vols; Munich, 1931–2), 1.16.
52 *Ibid.*
53 Karl Holl, 'Martin Luther on Luther', trans. H. C. Erik Midelfort, in *Interpreters of Luther: Essays in Honor of Wilhelm Pauck*, ed. Jaroslav Pelikan (Philadelphia, 1968), p. 14.
54 Calvin, 'Responsio ad Sadoleti epistolam', *CR* 5.391 (*Tracts* 1.33).
55 See John T. McNeill, *The History and Character of Calvinism* (New York, 1954), pp. 214–17, for a fine summary.
56 'Institutio religionis christianae', IV.18.17, *CR* 2.1063 (McNeill 1445).
57 Ibid., IV.19.28, *CR* 2.1086 (McNeill 1476, identifying the passages).
58 Cf. Albrecht Ritschl, *Three Essays*, trans. Philip Hefner (Philadelphia, 1972), pp. 53–147, for one analysis.
59 Hanns Lilje, *Luthers Geschichtsanschauung* (Berlin, 1932).
60 Cf. *Bekenntnisschriften* 556, note 2.
61 Ernst Rietschel, *Das Problem der sichtbar-unsichtbaren Kirche bei Luther* (Leipzig, 1932).
62 Hans Preusz, *Die Vorstellungen vom Antichrist* (Leipzig, 1906), was an early attempt to place Luther's apocalyptic into a late medieval, especially a Hussite, context.
63 Luther, 'Vorrede auf die Offenbarung S. Johannis' (1530 and 1546), *WA DB* 7.410–11 (*LW* 35.402).
64 'Confessio Augustana', II.3, *Bekenntnisschriften* 53 (Tappert 29).
65 Luther, 'Vorrede auf die Offenbarung S. Johannis' (1530 and 1546), *WA DB* 7.410–11 (*LW* 35.402).
66 Ibid., *WA DB* 7.420–1 (*LW* 35.411).
67 Augustine, 'De civitate Dei', XX, 7–16, *CCSL* 48.708–27. *CCSL* designates throughout *Corpus christianorum. Series latina* (Turnhout, Belgium, 1953 ff.).
68 Ibid., XX, 9, *CCSL* 48.717.
69 Ibid., XX, 17, *CCSL* 48.728.
70 Ibid., XX, 19, *CCSL* 48.731.
71 Gerhard Kittel, ed., *Theological Dictionary of the New Testament*, edited and translated by Geoffrey W. Bromiley (10 vols; Grand Rapids, Michigan, 1964–76), 9.571–2.
72 Wilhelm Bousset, *Der Antichrist in der Überlieferung des Judentums, des neuen*

Testaments und der alten Kirche (Göttingen, 1895), pp. 88–99.
73 Luther, 'Vorlesung über den 1. Johannesbrief', *WA* 20.669 (*LW* 287–8); Calvin, 'Commentarius in Iohannis apostoli epistolam', *CR* 55.321 (Torrance 5.256).
74 See note 14 above.
75 Eberhard Nestle, ed., *Novum Testamentum Latine* (Stuttgart, 1906), p.534.
76 Cf. Paul Lehmann, *Die Parodie im Mittelalter* (Munich, 1922), p. 66.
77 *WA* 35.467–8.
78 See notes 11–13 and 65 above.
79 *WA* 9.701–15, plus the 'Beilage' of cartoons.
80 See George Kawerau, 'Cranachs Passional', *WA* 9.687–90.
81 Ibid., pp. 678–84.
82 Calvin, 'Vera christianae et ecclesiae reformandae ratio', *CR* 7.610–11 (*Tracts* 3.264). *Tracts* designates throughout *John Calvin's Tracts and Treatises*, trans. Henry Beveridge, notes and introductions by Thomas F. Torrance (Grand Rapids, Michigan, 1958).
83 *WA* 9, 'Beilage', 23–4.
84 *WA* 9.715.
85 *WA* 9, 'Beilage', 26.
86 'Institutio religionis christianae', III.20.42, *CR* 2.667 (McNeill 906).
87 Calvin, 'Commentarius in Evangelium Ioannis', *CR* 47.392 (Torrance 5.154).
88 *WA* 9, 'Beilage', 25.
89 Calvin, 'Commentarius in Harmoniam evangelicam', *CR* 45.29 (Torrance 1.26).
90 *WA* 9, 'Beilage', 5–6.
91 A. Malvy, 'Lavement des pieds', *Dictionnaire de théologie catholique* (15 vols; Paris, 1903–50), 9.16–36.
92 Calvin, 'Commentarius in Evangelium Ioannis', *CR* 47.309–10 (Torrance 5.60).
93 *WA* 9.703.
94 Pelikan, *The Christian Tradition*, 2.117–33.
95 Barth-Niesel 1.295 (*Tracts* 3.368).
96 Calvin, 'Acta Synodi Tridentinae cum Antidoto', *CR* 7.417–18 (*Tracts* 3.75).
97 Luther, 'Vorrede zum ersten Bande der Gesamtausgabe seiner lateinischen Schriften', *WA* 54.184 (*LW* 34.334).
98 Luther to Spalatin, 13.iii.1519, *WA Br* 1.359.
99 Luther to Spalatin, 24.ii.1520, *WA Br* 2.48–9.
100 'Epistola Lutheriana ad Leonem Decimum summum pontificem', *WA* 7.48 (*LW* 31.342).
101 Hubert Jedin, *Geschichte des Konzils von Trient* (4 vols; Freiburg, 1951 ff.), 1.142–58.
102 Luther, 'Adversus execrabilem Antichristi bullam', *WA* 6.597–612; 'Wider die Bulle des Endchrists', *WA* 6.614–29.
103 *WA* 6.620.
104 See the monograph of Hans Preusz cited in note 62 above.
105 Luther, 'Eine predigt uber das Evangelium am ersten Sontage jnn der Fasten, zu Smalkalden getan, im jar 1537', *WA* 45.25–47.
106 *Bekenntnisschriften* 463–8, with identifications (Tappert 316–18).
107 'Vorrede zum Konkordienbuche', *Bekenntnisschriften* 14 (Tappert 13–14).
108 Luther, 'Articuli Smalcaldici', *Bekenntnisschriften* 430 (Tappert 300).
109 *WA* 50.578.
110 'Articuli Smalcaldici', *Bekenntnisschriften* 428 (Tappert 298–9).

111 See the passages collected from various theologians in C. F. W. Walther, ed., *Joh. Guilielmi Baieri Compendium Theologiae Positivae* (3 vols; Saint Louis, 1879), 3.672–83.
112 Calvin, 'De necessitate reformandae ecclesiae', CR 6.473.
113 Calvin, 'Commentarius in Iohannis apostoli epistolam', CR 55.321 (Torrance 5.256).
114 CR 6.453–534 (*Tracts* 1.125–253).
115 Jedin, *op. cit.*, 1.396 ff.
116 CR 6.524 (*Tracts* 1.219).

BERNARD CAPP

4 The political dimension of apocalyptic thought

Politics and apocalyptic thought were bound closely together in early modern Europe, and each influenced the other. The close link was natural: the continental Reformation soon involved the princes while in England the crown itself initiated the break with Rome. In the age of religious warfare which followed, Protestants could rarely ignore the political dimension of the struggle against Catholicism.

For the early English Reformers the appeal of the Apocalypse was as much emotional as intellectual. Many of the early commentators were exiles, among them John Bale and John Foxe. Bale indeed noted the parallel between his situation and that of St. John on Patmos.[1] Exile brought these writers into closer contact with continental thought, which was to influence English commentaries throughout the period.[2] The experience also made them highly susceptible to the story of suffering and eventual triumph set out in Revelation in vivid and emotional language. The dramatic imagery of the Apocalypse made a powerful impact on most commentators. The symbol of the evil, seductive Whore of Babylon (Rev. xvii) sometimes stirred darker, subconscious passions. They are all too clear, for example, in Thomas Brightman's wish to 'see this impudent harlot at length slit in the nostrils, stripped of her garments and tires [attire], besmeared with dirt and rotten eggs, and at last burnt up and consumed with fire'.[3]

For sixteenth-century Reformers the Apocalypse was a key to the past and present; few thought the world had any future. Protestants felt a need to explain the upheavals of the Reformation and justify their rejection of Catholicism. They were vulnerable to the obvious Catholic taunts: why would God have allowed the Roman Church to flourish for centuries, unless true? Where was Protestantism before Luther? The Reformers found satisfying answers in the Apocalypse, which they interpreted historically as a prophecy of God's plan for the world. Revelation foretold the persecution of the godly by

Antichrist, who would be exposed at the last, paving the way for the Second Coming and triumph of the saints. John Bale and his successors elaborated a theory of two churches running parallel throughout history, one persecuted yet true, the other false but powerful. The concept, derived partly from Augustine's two cities, was extremely popular among Tudor writers.[4] John Philpott, the Marian martyr, assured his interrogators that Protestantism was a thousand years older than its rival, and traced the two churches back to Cain and Abel.[5] The emotional support offered by apocalyptic faith is obvious. Latimer, facing the stake, found 'great consolation and comfort' in the firm belief that Christ was about to return 'to keep his great Parliament to the redress of all things that be amiss'.[6]

The polemical value of Revelation was also grasped quickly for, as a later writer remarked, 'if the Pope of Rome be Antichrist, what need shall we have to contend any longer about the Church of Rome, and about the seven sacraments thereof, to make any more disputes touching free-will, justification, good works' or all the other doctrinal points in dispute?'[7] Revelation was a matchless quarry for propagandists. Of course Protestants needed clear proof that the papacy was indeed Antichrist. They found it in the scandalous lives and false doctrines of popes through the centuries, and most of all in papal ambition for worldly power in defiance of Christ's teaching. Bale's play *King John* portrayed a just ruler beaten down by a papal tyrant.[8] Bishop Jewel's apologia for the Elizabethan Church contained a long and fierce attack on the pope's lust for power. Jewel concluded that Catholicism was incompatible with the proper authority of the secular ruler: papists like Anabaptists were subversive by nature.[9] John Foxe's *Acts and Monuments* supplied numerous examples from history to prove the point. 'What kings have been deposed, and emperors stripped from their imperial seat', he declaimed, 'and all because they would not stoop and bend to the image of the beast, that is, to the majesty and title of Rome.'[10] Catholic rebellions against Henry VIII, Edward and Elizabeth showed that papal sedition continued still.[11]

Protestant writers were less sure whether the leading part in resisting Antichrist belonged to magistrates or to preachers and martyrs. The choice could be significant. Pushed to its limit, the cult of the godly prince led to theories of a messianic 'Emperor of the Last Days', familiar in mediaeval Europe.[12] The martyr-tradition, by contrast, was largely passive. But when the magistrate was placed on the side of evil it could produce revolutionary apocalyptic upheavals such as the Anabaptist seizure of Münster in 1534.[13] Mid-Tudor writers, convinced of Christ's imminent return, felt able to straddle both positions. Even so, changing political circumstances produced striking differences of emphasis, well illustrated in the career of John Bale. In the 1530s Bale was an enthusiastic polemicist working for Thomas Cromwell and hopeful that the government would build a better, even millennial future. But by the time he had completed his commentary, *The Image of Both Churches*,

Cromwell had fallen and Henry VIII had turned against reform. Bale lamented this setback as the recovery of the wounded Beast (Rev. xiii.3), and bitterly condemned the behavior of kings as 'childish or else tyrannous'. Henry had usurped Christ's place, and the church was still full of popish remnants. The 1550 edition of *The Image* showed yet another change of attitude. The young Protestant Edward VI was now king, and Bale found renewed enthusiasm for the godly prince. And, after the death of the Catholic Mary, he was willing to heap praise on the new Queen Elizabeth as Christ's champion.[14]

Henry VIII was no Protestant, but it was natural that he should become the focus of Protestant hopes after the break with Rome. Thomas Becon expected the king to press on until, 'all abuses plucked away, the true godliness may reign'. And, citing Virgil's famous lines prophesying the return of a perfect age, Becon added: 'Who shall not justly think, that the golden age is come again . . .?'[15] Nicholas Udall hailed Henry as the 'English David' who had crushed the popish Goliath. The young King Edward, he hoped, would build an 'English Israel' and continue the struggle against Antichrist.[16] In the event, Edward's reign was brief and was followed by fierce persecution under Mary. Bale's despair of monarchy was appropriate once more. Bishop Ridley, facing trial and execution as a heretic, observed bitterly that nobles and magistrates who had favored the Gospel under Edward had now deserted it. The Marian government was 'deceived and bewitched'. The godly could hope for nothing from the magistrate: their choice was simply death or flight.[17]

I THE ELIZABETHAN APOCALYPSE

Succeeding to the throne in 1558, Elizabeth ended persecution and restored the Protestant Church. The importance of the martyrs' testimony was preserved for future generations in Foxe's *Acts and Monuments*, but many writers understandably began to stress once again the role of the godly prince. Foxe himself dedicated his massive work to Elizabeth, comparing her to the Emperor Constantine, who had also ended persecution and brought peace to the church.[18] For Bishop Jewel, Elizabeth was 'the only nurse and mother of the Church of God' in England. For Sandys she was 'God's own elect, . . . the restorer of our religion'. Aylmer called her 'God's chosen instrument' against the power of Antichrist.[19] The role of the godly prince in protecting religious truth was central to Elizabethan thought.

Professor William Haller saw in these works the idea of England as God's elect nation, guided by Elizabeth towards a millennial golden age.[20] It is accepted now that Foxe anticipated the world's imminent end, not a future age of peace. He saw the bitter wars in continental Europe as proof that Satan would continue to rage until the last, and as a reminder that the Apocalypse could not be understood in merely English terms. His study of Revelation, *Eicasmi*, was written in Latin for a European audience and made only passing reference to Elizabeth. Like Bale, Foxe believed that Christ's church was universal, 'dispersed through all nations'.[21] The origins of the apocalyptic nationalism which emerged at the close of the century can nevertheless be traced back to the earlier part of the reign. England was the only major Protestant power and Elizabeth's role as the protector – however reluctant – of foreign Calvinists led naturally to a belief in England's central role. Most of the material was English in Bale's *The Image* and Foxe's *Acts and Monuments*. Both authors explained that this was to capture the interest of English readers,[22] but the effect was that the books appeared to confirm England's importance. Foxe did indeed share the sense of national pride apparent in much Tudor historical writing. He claimed that the English Church stretched back to the Apostles and so owed nothing to Rome. Lucius was a Christian English king in AD 180 while Roman Emperors were still infidels. Constantine, the first Christian Emperor, was born in England of a British mother and used his British army to win power in Rome. His reign brought peace to the Church and marked the binding of Satan for a thousand years (Rev. xx.2), and Foxe drew the reader's attention to England's part in these great events.[23] John Aylmer, later bishop of London, argued in 1559 that the Reformation too had English roots, in the life and work of Wyclif. For 'what greater honour could you or I have, than that it pleased Christ as it were in a second birth to be born again' in England? Aylmer's work was not a scholarly treatise but a polemical tract, occasioned in part by Elizabeth's war against 'Antichrist's friends', Scotland and France. It had a militant, jingoistic tone characteristic of a later period. Assuring his readers that they had 'God and all his army of angels on your side', Aylmer was confident that 'We live in paradise' and that 'God is English'.[24]

Most Protestant writers saw Elizabeth as having a major, distinctive or even unique position in the Church's history, though they stopped short of ascribing a messianic role to her.[25] Aylmer hoped she would destroy Antichrist in England for ever. Thomas Becon hailed her as a 'noble conqueror of Antichrist.'[26] The translators of the Geneva Bible told Elizabeth in 1560 that all the godly were looking to England, expecting that 'God should bring to pass some wonderful work by your grace to the universal comfort of his church'. Sandys asked rhetorically, 'Hath the like ever been heard of in any nation to that which in ours is seen?'[27] Only one writer, James Sandford, was prepared to go still further and give Elizabeth an openly messianic significance. He declared roundly that there was 'some diviner thing in her Majesty, than in the Kings and Queens of other countries', and looked towards a golden age which she would help to inaugurate. Sandford however was outside the mainstream of Elizabethan thought. His belief in a millennial age or 'status' reflected the influence of the Italian Reformer, Giacopo Brocardo, and derived ultimately from the ideas of Joachim of Fiore.[28]

During the first half of Elizabeth's reign there developed a general consensus that the pope was Antichrist and that the end of the world was at hand.[29] Commentators listed the signs of its approach: wars, the decay of nature and of morality, and more specific events such as the '*nova*' of 1572 and the great conjunction of Saturn and Jupiter in 1583. It was interest in such non-biblical forms of divination which helped to shift attention to the time of Christ's return. Most writers in the 1560s and 1570s discussed the signs of the End, not its date. The astrological significance of 1583 led to a new interest in precise dating, which was reinforced by a widely-circulated prophecy of Regiomontanus predicting major upheavals in 1588, possibly even the world's end. These ideas reached a wide public in pamphlets and almanacs, and aroused great excitement – understandably, given Richard Harvey's prophecy that the Beginning of the End would be at noon on 28 April 1583.[30]

Though nothing dramatic occurred in 1583, a sense of crisis persisted as the nation drifted into war with Catholic Spain. Propaganda on both sides stressed the religious, crusading character of the conflict, and the effect was to politicize apocalyptic thought in England. Clearly Antichrist was not destined to fall by the preaching of the Word alone, which had traditionally been given the central role. Consequently the prince must not merely protect the Gospel, but be ready to take up arms against the power of the Beast.

Signs of this change are few before 1588. It was the defeat of the Armada in that year which fused apocalyptic excitement and patriotic fervor. What emerged was a belief in England's unique role as God's elect nation, with Spain portrayed as the epitome of evil. A pamphleteer told his readers in 1588 that the invaders sought 'their vile pleasure of your wives, your sons and daughters, they will utterly destroy you, that the name of our nation shall be no more remembered upon the earth'.[31] Commentators made the point that bloodthirstiness and lust were notoriously the marks of Antichrist and the Babylonian Whore. The Puritan minister Thomas Rogers showed that Spain was the greatest protector of the Roman 'brothel house'. Rogers' avowed aim was to make the Roman Whore so notorious that 'even the very boys and mothers in the streets may never hear Popery named but they may hiss at it, as they do at the sight of known bawds and naughty-packs [strumpets]'.[32] Spain remained a formidable threat even after the Armada's defeat, but the great deliverance was seen as proof that God would intervene to save his chosen people. Edward Hellwis could feel sure that God would always enable his favored nation to the 'overthrow of an hundred thousand of his enemies upon land: and to confound a thousand sail of ships if they arrive within a mile of any shore of England'.[33] Inevitably hopes sprang up of further and still greater successes. In a public sermon at Paul's Cross, Laurence Deios looked towards the future collapse of Antichrist when 'victory followeth upon victory, triumph upon triumph'.[34] While the Armada had been only a defensive victory, Anthony Marten declared that England could also if necessary take the offensive 'for the better safety of our Christian brethren dispersed abroad in the world'. Elizabeth and England, 'the most Christian kingdom of all other', were God's chosen instruments in the international struggle against Rome.[35]

In the post-Armada years commentators on the Apocalypse adopted an aggressive and military style remote from that of Foxe or Jewel. English Protestants were no longer merely preachers spreading the Gospel or martyrs suffering patiently but 'a wing, or an old trained band of that army' which would throw down Babylon.[36] Princes and people, taught the Puritan George Gifford, must join to 'execute the vengeance of God upon this filthy harlot'.[37] Arthur Dent's influential book, *The Ruine of Rome* (1603), discussed the respective roles of the Word and the Sword in the overthrow of Antichrist. Preaching was vital in winning princes to the truth, but Dent's stress was clearly on military force. Kings must lead an armed struggle against Rome and 'slay in the field thousand thousands' of its soldiers. The defeat of the Armada was the first skirmish of Armageddon. Spanish and French Catholics, the great upholders of Rome, would be slaughtered and 'the fowls of the air shall come to their great supper'. The papal Antichrist would be left impotent and derided: 'a poor Pope, a naked Pope, a desolate Pope. . . . He shall be such a pope, as the king of Portugal is a king'. This was not far off. Of the ten horns of the Beast (Rev. xiii and xvii), held to represent ten European kingdoms, Dent thought that seven had already fallen away while the eighth, France, 'beginneth to be somewhat loose'. France, Spain and Italy would soon turn against the Roman Beast and 'the Protestants shall have the day'. Antichrist would fall within a lifetime. Though Dent repudiated the heresy of Christ's millennial reign, his theory, focussing on Antichrist's ruin, was colored by an optimism bordering on relish.[38]

This confident mood coincided with the peak of the cult of Elizabeth in court circles. The image of Elizabeth as the goddess Astraea, returning to bring a new golden age on earth, enjoyed its greatest vogue in the years after the Armada. Sometimes it merged with astrological speculation, the Virgin Queen being identified with Virgo, 'the Zodiac's joy'.[39] These dreams of a golden age derived from pagan classical myth, but they harmonized well with Protestant hopes that Elizabeth would deliver England from Antichrist and bring peace to the church. It was in this period that a minor courtier, Edward Hellwis, published the most extravagant of all the eulogies on the queen. Elizabeth, he suggested, was not merely a woman 'beyond all others, that have lived upon earth'. She was no other than the Woman of Rev. xii who gave birth in the Wilderness, a figure traditionally interpreted as the Christian Church or the Virgin Mary.[40]

Praise of Queen Elizabeth was always commonplace but it was never universal. The Puritans criticized the forms and tone of the Established Church and their dissatisfaction grew over the years. Their early complaints about antichristian survivals in the church were shared by a number of bishops, but some later writers went considerably further. *An admonition to the Parliament* (1572), by Field and Wilcox, suggested that the episcopal system was antichristian by definition, implicitly criticizing Elizabeth for maintaining it. The last of the satirical Marprelate tracts openly rejected the Elizabethan Church because it retained bishops, 'the seats of Antichrist'. Only a small minority of Puritans, however, went so far. Even within the radical Presbyterian wing most stopped short of outright condemnation of the Established Church, and they remained within it. The authorities were inaccurate when they labelled the Puritans as subversives who rejected the Church established by law. The charge was certainly effective as propaganda but was true only of the small separatist groups.[41] Propagandists found another effective weapon with the appearance of fanatical self-appointed messiahs, such as William Hacket and Ralph Durden, who were presented to the public as the natural culmination of Puritan tendencies.[42]

Puritan dislike of popish 'antichristian' relics was only part of a wider disagreement over the Apocalypse. The general consensus that the Pope was Antichrist concealed important differences.[43] For the more traditional wing of the Church, the exposure of Antichrist served primarily to prove the validity of the Protestant settlement of 1559. The Puritan response was far more dynamic. England must champion the international Protestant cause, helping the victims of foreign persecution and giving active support. Puritans consistently pressed for an interventionist foreign policy, and found Elizabeth's caution highly unsatisfactory.[44] In the later 1580s the Spanish war brought at last the policies they had wished. Even so some Puritan commentators doubted Elizabeth's commitment to the role of crusading prince. George Gifford had relatively little to say about her in his sermons on Revelation. Henry VIII, Edward and Elizabeth had 'pulled him [the Beast] down what they can,' he remarked, 'and so have divers kings of other lands done'. He found a far more promising hero in his patron, the earl of Essex. In the 1590s the earl was the leader of the court party which desired 'to war in the Lord'. Gifford argued that Essex and other nobles had a major part to play in this struggle, and that the Apocalypse should be their constant study. He delivered an emotional appeal to Essex to become Christ's champion: 'Put on that fine white linen and pure, ride upon that white horse among his blessed company, and follow this high captain.'[45] Several commentators dedicated their works to Puritan magnates such as Leicester, Warwick and Robert, Lord Rich, urging them to take the lead in the struggle against Antichrist.[46] At the end of the century there was at least a possibility that the nobleman with Puritan leanings and military ambition might oust the godly prince from the central role. Some years later Sir Christopher Heydon, a protégé of Essex, prophesied a future millennial age dominated by the aristocracy.[47] But the accession of James I in 1603 and the return of peace served to check this line of development, at least for a time.

II THE EMERGENCE OF MILLENARIANISM

Scholarly interpretations of Revelation at the time of Elizabeth's death differed radically from those current at her accession. The generation which lived through the traumatic upheavals of the Reformation understandably regarded it as the immediate precursor of Judgment Day. By the end of the century Protestant theologians saw the need for a far longer perspective. And if the End was still some way off, there was greater incentive to study the prophetic numerology to find an approximate date. Stuart commentators were far more concerned with mathematical calculations than were their predecessors, and more sophisticated in handling the arithmetic.[48]

Mid-Tudor writers would have been dismayed at the postponement of the Second Coming. Their successors reacted differently. The defeat of the Armada and Calvinist successes in France and the Netherlands led them to emphasize the eventual triumph of the saints rather than the prolonged sufferings of the martyrs. Dent's book, confidently prophesying the fall of Rome, remained a bestseller throughout the century. Even more influential was the commentary on Revelation by the Scottish mathematician John Napier, first published in 1593. In a systematic and comprehensive analysis, Napier identified and dated the seven vials of God's wrath (Rev. xvi); the seventh and last had already begun, in 1541. The fall of the Roman Antichrist would follow in 1639 and Christ would return to judgment somewhere between 1688 and 1700.[49] Thomas Brightman, a Bedfordshire minister, offered a still more dramatic interpretation. His work was written about 1602 but was too radical to be published in England, and first appeared posthumously in a Latin edition at Frankfurt in 1609. Several foreign editions followed quickly, and English readers were soon able to find his main views summarized in the works of more moderate writers. Brightman prophesied 'a most grievous trial ... straightways to come upon the whole Christian world' but promised that after it would follow 'a most delightful spectacle of perpetual peace, joined with abundance of all good things'. The fall of Rome and conversion of the Jews would occur about 1650, and the final ruin of Antichrist in 1686. Brightman's most novel contribution was the promise of a glorious future age, stretching ahead many centuries. Satan's binding for a thousand years (Rev. xx.2) he dated conventionally as 300–1300 AD, but the thousand years of the saints' reign with Christ (verse 4) was interpreted as a separate period beginning in 1300 with the first dawn of the Reformation, and with its greatest glories yet to come. Christ would 'advance his Church unto the highest honour that can be, even above all Empire that is'. And though the chiliasts had exaggerated the worldly pleasures of the millennium, Brightman was sure there would be 'exceeding great felicity pertaining to this life, ... abundance of this kind of delights', so that the Early Fathers 'did not wander much from the truth'.[50]

Brightman's work also became notorious for his fierce criticism of the

Elizabethan Church, pilloried as 'luke-warm Laodicea'. He condemned the worldliness of the episcopal hierarchy, the lack of pastoral discipline, the persecution of Puritans and the spread of new and dangerous heresies. His ideal was the Calvinist church of Geneva and its offshoots, which he identified as 'godly Philadelphia'.[51] Brightman's attack on the Established Church, going well beyond mainstream Puritan opinion, may at first have reduced his acceptability, though in the reign of Charles I Puritan thought moved steadily towards his position. Brightman never pressed his complaints to the point of separatism, which he denounced as evil and blasphemous, and he stressed that the Elizabethan system was a true church despite its shortcomings.[52] He also irritated some scholars by his very specific and patriotic exposition of the text of Revelation, where he found references to Thomas Cromwell, Cranmer, Elizabeth and Cecil. But this was admitted to be very popular among ordinary English readers.[53]

Not long after Brightman's work appeared, fully millenarian theories were put forward by scholars of unimpeachable respectability. The German encyclopaedist and theologian, Johannes Alsted, argued in 1627 that a thousand-year reign of the saints would begin with the fall of Rome in 1694. Though clearly influenced by the upheavals of the Thirty Years War, Alsted argued that his theory was in line with the teaching of the early fathers and of the best recent scholars, citing a number who had written in favor of an approaching period of 'latter-day glory'. Alsted's work became well known in England, and helped to spread knowledge of these continental developments.[54] The popularity of millenarianism among English Puritan refugees in the Netherlands in the 1630s may well have been encouraged by closer contact with these trends.[55] The most influential expression within England of the millennial creed was the work of the Cambridge scholar, Joseph Mede, first published in 1627 (and discussed later in this chapter).[56] While never accepted universally, millenarian ideas won widespread support in England, especially in the period of the civil wars.

The switch from expectation of the imminent end of the world to belief in a future golden age appears a dramatic reversal, but the change was in fact probably evolutionary. Political successes in the later sixteenth century encouraged Protestants to place more emphasis on the eventual overthrow of Antichrist, which in turn aroused interest in the triumphant period between Rome's fall and Christ's return to Judgment. This 'latter-day glory' could lead quite naturally to the idea of a full millennial age. The writings of Napier, Dent and Brightman were major stepping-stones along the path that led to the theories of Mede, and Alsted's work was the culmination of similar developments on the continent.

III THE FAILING OF THE GODLY PRINCE, 1603-40

Writers on the Apocalypse in the early seventeenth century continued to focus their political hopes on the monarch. Even Brightman wrote of Elizabeth with deep respect, though saddened to see her misled by the bishops. He gave a central role in the overthrow of Antichrist to the Protestant rulers of Europe, calling on them to launch a crusade against Rome. 'Now therefore o you holy and Christian Princes, set upon this worthy and heroical exploit at length. It will not be so hard and troublesome a business as you take it perhaps.' The Spaniards, French and Poles would lament the fall of the Babylonian Whore, but Brightman ridiculed fears that they would raise any considerable forces to defend 'an old withered harlot'. As further inducement he hinted at the prizes to be won by a policy of apocalyptic imperialism: Protestant conquerors would not merely liberate the Catholic nations, they would annex 'a part of those dominions subdued unto them' in the course of the crusade.[57]

Brightman was probably aiming his appeal at the German princes, and perhaps also at King James of Scotland, who succeeded to the English throne in 1603. The new monarch quickly replaced Elizabeth as the subject of apocalyptic hopes. Brought up as a Calvinist, James had published in 1588 (the Armada year) a treatise on the papal Antichrist in which he promised the sudden overthrow of the Catholic states at the very height of their power. He returned to these themes in *A Premonition* (1609), offering elaborate proof that the pope was Antichrist, and seeking to persuade the kings of Europe that the papacy was a deadly threat to all royal authority.[58] It was a major step for a reigning monarch to give public endorsement to Protestant apocalyptic teaching. James's works were naturally cited and praised by numerous later commentators, who felt a new sense of authority in finding a king in their ranks. George Downham, future bishop of Derry, hailed the king as 'the chief patron and defender of the faith and Gospel of Christ (upon earth) against Antichrist', and anticipated the day when godly princes would join to burn and destroy Rome.[59] 'King David against the Philistims, King James against the Antichristians', wrote the Puritan, John Vicars.[60] James's writings underlined the special role of kings in God's work. It was for this reason, argued another Puritan, Richard Bernard, that God had saved James and earlier English monarchs from the hand of the assassin when so many continental princes had been struck down. The English monarchy and nation were God's chosen instruments. James's 'learned pen hath proclaimed open war to Antichrist', and his people must be ready to draw their swords in support of 'Christ, our King and Country'.[61] The king also figured prominently in the writings of James Maxwell, a Scottish antiquarian steeped in miscellaneous biblical, mediaeval, astrological and sibylline prophecy. Maxwell belonged to the Joachimite tradition, looking for a messianic emperor of the last days and a reforming pope, 'Pastor Angelicus'. He hoped to find both in England: James's writings could persuade the kings of Europe to reform the Catholic Church and reunite Christendom, while Prince Charles might perhaps be the long-awaited Emperor Charles, destined to destroy the Turks and recapture Constantinople.[62]

James alas did little to satisfy the hopes placed in him. He made peace and friendship with Spain instead of intensifying Elizabeth's war. He refused to intervene in the Thirty Years War on the Protestant side, preferring – more like Maxwell – to seek harmony through peaceful persuasion. The king ignored Puritan pressure to suppress recusants and his *Premonition* indeed attacked Puritans almost as fiercely as papists. A measure of disillusion among the Puritans was the inevitable consequence. Doubts over James's credentials as godly prince went back to Napier's treatise of 1593. Napier had praised the king's recent work on Antichrist but knew the Scottish court well enough to distinguish between the king and his writings. For could a prince be 'a purger of the world from Antichristianism, who purgeth not his own country? shall he purge his own country, who purgeth not his own house? and shall he purge his house, who is not purged himself?'[63] Many Puritans in England gradually came to share these doubts. James's interest in the exposure of Antichrist was perhaps dampened when a Catholic reply to his treatise was discovered at Whitehall in 1613, allegedly claiming that Britain was the seat of Antichrist and that James was Antichrist in person. The author, a Hampshire recusant squire named John Cotton, was arrested on a charge of treason.[64]

Belief in the godly prince was strong enough to survive James's limitations. In the middle years of the reign, militant Puritans found a more promising champion in Prince Henry, the king's elder son. The young prince was the reverse of his father: athletic, austere and addicted to war-like pursuits and dreams of military glory. He responded eagerly to suggestions that he would one day lead a crusade against Rome. James's 'pen hath made way for your sword', Sampson Lennard told the prince in 1612, dedicating to him a French treatise on the Apocalypse. 'Glorious be his peace, and your wars'. Lennard, an old soldier, hoped to 'live to march over the Alps, and to trail a pike before the walls of Rome, under your Highness' standard'.[65] Instead Henry died that very year. Apocalyptic hopes then shifted to his sister Elizabeth, who in 1613 married Frederick, Elector Palatine. Elizabeth was second in line to the English throne and aroused some dreams of a new Elizabethan age. Primarily, though, she and her husband were supported by Puritans at court and elsewhere as the champions of Calvinist internationalism. In 1619 Frederick accepted the offer of the Bohemian crown after a revolt there against Habsburg rule. This move, which triggered off the Thirty Years War, was welcomed by many in England as opening a way to the ruin of Catholicism in Germany and perhaps ultimately to the fall of Rome. Archbishop Abbot, who was strongly swayed by apocalyptic hopes, supported Frederick's decision as fulfilling Revelation's prophecy that the kings of the earth would turn against the Whore and destroy her. England and other Protestant states should join Frederick in a crusade against Rome.[66] James however had no desire to be a crusader and the Continental princes gave no help. Frederick and Elizabeth, driven out of Bohemia and the Palatinate by Habsburg armies, entered the Calvinist pantheon as martyrs instead of conquerors.

James's surviving son, Prince Charles, became the next focal point for apocalyptic hopes, if only for lack of alternatives. He was clearly less promising than his elder brother. He aroused deep suspicion by his quest for a Spanish bride, and his marriage to a French Catholic princess. Hopes did grow in 1624 when he was pressing for war against Spain and his favorite, Buckingham, was wooing Puritans at court who pursued the same objective. When Charles became king in 1625 he and 'brave Buckingham' could appear as Protestant champions.[67] But this image faded quickly. Buckingham's alliance with the Puritans was only tactical, and it was short lived. Charles leaned to the Arminian party in the Church, the supporters of 'popish' ceremony and episcopal authority. The Arminians were scornful of Calvinist dogma and hostile to Puritan ambitions at home and abroad. They felt no call to battle against Rome, and appeared to Puritan opponents as Catholics in disguise, or at best fellow-travellers. Unsympathetic towards traditional apocalyptic thought, Arminian leaders questioned whether the papacy was Antichrist and discouraged speculation on the subject. Bishop Corbet, in a satirical poem, mocked Puritan interest in Revelation as symptomatic of a comically deranged mind. Arminianism became the dominant wing of the Established Church under Charles I, and its leader William Laud succeeded as primate in 1633. The Elizabethan Protestant consensus, much of which had survived under James, was now lost and indeed repudiated.[68] Thomas Beard, formerly schoolmaster to Oliver Cromwell, was no longer repeating a stale truism when he set out in 1625 to prove that the pope was Antichrist. It was now, as he remarked, 'a point undecided in our church', and he prudently dedicated his book to an anti-Laudian bishop, John Williams.[69] The growing polarization of thought was well illustrated shortly before James's death when Robert Sheldon, a convert from Rome, preached against the papal Antichrist and its Arminian friends. Sheldon claimed provocatively that the king and Prince Charles were far too intelligent to be misled by Arminian falsehoods, and predictably aroused the extreme displeasure of officialdom.[70]

Charles and Laud utterly destroyed traditional confidence in the monarchy and the Established Church. Charles was inadequate as godly prince, and the Arminians devalued the role by stressing instead the importance of divine-right episcopacy.[71] The writings of the Scottish Presbyterian, Alexander Leighton, show the process of disillusion in stark form. In 1624 Leighton addressed his vision of a holy crusade to Prince Charles, 'the Hope of Great Britain'. 'Charles the great made Rome great,' he observed, 'and may not a greater Charles raze Rome's greatness?' He was relieved to see Charles's escape from a 'beastly, greasy' Spanish bride, and pressed for war against Spain. But by 1628, after witnessing the dismal failure of Charles's foreign policy and his attachment to the Laudians, Leighton was taking as his major theme the failure of princes to perform their duty. Henry VIII, Elizabeth, James and Charles had each been led astray by grasping bishops. The remedy lay with Parliament. Its Members, 'the Elders of Israel', must compel the king to abandon his dangerous policies, just as mediaeval Parliaments had intervened in the reigns of weak or misguided rulers. If the monarch reneged on his duty, Parliament must fill the breach, and Leighton made a direct appeal: 'It were happy for our King and us, if you knew your power practically'. The government naturally disagreed; Leighton was arrested, fined, mutilated and imprisoned for life.[72] His fate aroused little interest, for his extreme language and total rejection of the episcopal church alienated most contemporaries. But a similar if slower process of disillusion is visible among more moderate Puritans, such as the London minister Henry Burton. Until 1625 Burton held minor positions under Prince Henry and then Charles. His subsequent pamphlets reveal a growing tension between deep faith in the apocalyptic role of the prince, and awareness of Charles's failings. Eager to win the king back to his rightful course, Burton bombarded him with exhortations. *The Baiting of the Pope's Bull* (1627) contained a woodcut showing the king wounding the papal Antichrist with a lance (Rev. xiii.3), and verses hailing Charles's love of truth and recognition of the Roman menace. In *The Seven Vials* (on Rev. xvi) Burton assured Charles that 'the accomplishment of this prophecy is like to fall in your glorious reign' and that the king must play a major role in it. Elizabeth and James had been instruments of the Lord, and surely Charles's zeal and wisdom 'were not planted in your noble breast for nothing'. Through Burton repeatedly put hope before experience, his doubts grew steadily. In 1628 he warned Charles not to slide from godly rule into tyranny. And, like Leighton, he turned to Parliament, assuring MPs that there were sound precedents for them to intervene to defend true faith 'in these deplored times'.[73] By 1636 Burton's faith was lost. He reproached Charles for succumbing to flattery and breaking promises by introducing Arminian falsehood. With heavy irony he hoped that the people would not think 'This King had no regard to sacred vows.'[74] As a result of these outspoken attacks Burton became in 1637 one of the martyrs of Laudianism, placed in the stocks, mutilated and imprisoned. With his fellow victims, the lawyer William Prynne and the physician John Bastwick, he became a symbol of defiance to Laudian oppression.

Many of those dismayed by Charles's policies shared Burton's reluctance to abandon the godly prince. Some turned back to the king's sister, Elizabeth of Bohemia. Though now a widowed refugee, she remained the symbol of a very different kind of monarchy, the dynamic Calvinism promised by Prince Henry. One extremist allegedly wished to see Charles and Buckingham killed, and Elizabeth invited back to ascend the throne. The king and Laud were uneasily aware of her popularity in England, and its implicit reflection on their own standing. Their response was to treat Elizabeth with a cold reserve.[75] Early in the 1630s a more satisfactory champion emerged in Gustavus Adolphus, king of Sweden. Gustavus led his armies deep into Germany, rescuing German Protestantism from the threat of extinction by the Catholic Habsburgs. A wave of excited anticipation passed through England: would he go on to destroy Habsburg power, or even Rome itself? Many saw him as a deliverer, and the true inheritor of the Elizabethan tradition. The Puritan William Gouge made the link explicit, noting that Gustavus's great victory at Leipzig was won on the anniversary of Queen Elizabeth's birth. Gouge dreamed that the Swedish king would root out Catholicism from central Europe and even beyond. 'A way is hereby opened to the very gates of Rome: whereby the threatening against the seven-headed beast may in the Lord's appointed time be accomplished.'[76] For many years Protestant scholars, including the celebrated Mede, speculated on whether the Swedish campaign had been the fourth vial of divine vengeance (Rev. xvi.8–9).[77] Hopes of still greater triumphs were quickly dashed, however, when Gustavus died in battle in 1632. The lawyer John Bradshaw described the deaths of Prince Henry and Gustavus Adolphus as the two great tragedies of his age. In 1649 the same Bradshaw was to preside over the court which sentenced Charles I to death. There could hardly be more striking testimony to the strength of belief in the godly prince, and Charles's total failure to sustain it.[78]

The cult of Gustavus reflected the fading of belief in England's role as the elect nation, a faith difficult to preserve under Charles I. Even at the time of the Armada the English were warned that God would turn elsewhere if they neglected their duty.[79] Brightman too had coupled his stress on England's special role with the threat that God would 'translate his Court and Palace to some other place' unless the antichristian episcopal hierarchy was thrown down. Brightman indeed saw himself as the mouthpiece of God's final warning: 'What wilt thou say if this admonition of mine be the last watchword and warning-piece thou shalt have?'[80] Under James there was just enough to sustain a faith, if perhaps a diminished faith, in England's elect role. It was vividly expressed, for example, by the Puritan Richard Bernard in 1617.[81] But James's failure, in the following years, to intervene effectively in the Thirty Years War was a severe blow to Calvinist and apocalyptic hopes. His lethargy seemed to repudiate the monarchy's traditional role, as seen by Puritan pamphleteers. The charge of apostasy was explicit in Thomas Scott's *Vox Coeli, or News from Heaven* (1624), which described a discussion between the spirits of England's former rulers. Edward VI, Elizabeth and Prince Henry expressed their amazement at James's inertia, and their alarm at Prince Charles's attempt to secure a Spanish bride; better that he should marry an English milkmaid, growled Elizabeth's ghost. Scott turned to Parliament and to Frederick and Elizabeth of Bohemia as the only hopes for a better future.[82]

Under Charles and Laud it was clear that warnings and exhortations had been in vain. Puritans saw the Laudian church turning from Christ to Antichrist, and concluded that God would accordingly withdraw from the land. Alexander Leighton saw England's humiliation in the wars of the mid-1620s as a sign of that retreat.[83] Many felt they could remain no longer within the church or the land. One solution was to join the growing exodus to New England. The notion that 'the Gospel's fleeing westward' was commonplace in the 1630s, and naturally prompted the thought: 'Why may that not be the place of New Jerusalem?'[84] Abandoning England was a sign of despair, but the Puritan emigration contained a defiant apocalyptic hope. In spreading the Gospel to new lands and establishing new bastions of truth, the settlers felt they were preparing the way for Christ's coming. Apocalyptic expectations, and sometimes hopes of a millennial age, were widespread and deeply held among the New Englanders.[85] Other refugees from Laudian England found shelter in the Netherlands. These too found apocalyptic significance in their flight. The Congregational churches they gathered, more refined and exclusive than earlier Calvinist churches, could in themselves be the new heaven and earth prophesied in scripture. The most celebrated of the English Puritans in the Netherlands, William Ames, disliked apocalyptic speculation but inclined to the idea that the thousand years of Rev. xx represented 'the Church raised from its dead condition, and so continued for that space'. Some of the exiles adopted more radical theories. John Archer and Thomas Goodwin, pastors of the English church at Arnhem, defended belief in a literal future millennium and their church became famous for this doctrine. Goodwin wrote a treatise on Revelation in 1639 in which he anticipated 'a glorious visible Kingdom which Christ sets up on Earth and peaceably possesseth together with his saints'. Though an exile, Goodwin clung defiantly to belief in England as the elect nation, and identified the Laudians as the followers of the Beast who slaughter the witnesses, shortly before the Beast's own downfall.[86]

Among the Puritans remaining in England there was a growing conviction that the Laudian Church was antichristian. Henry Burton, one of the most outspoken critics, moved slowly and reluctantly during the later 1630s to a separatist position. He saw his mutilation and banishment in 1637 as part of the killing of the witnesses, an image which was naturally popular in those dark days.[87] John Lilburne, the future Leveller, was flogged in 1638 for distributing anti-Laudian pamphlets and similarly regarded his punishment as 'a work of the Beast'. In his account of the episode he called on his readers to separate from the Church, study Revelation and prepare for the spiritual battle ahead.[88] As separatists, Burton and Lilburne had moved outside the Puritan mainstream. But many more representative figures felt driven by the end of the 1630s to adopt their conclusion that the Laudian church, and perhaps episcopacy itself, were antichristian. Hatred traditionally directed outwards towards the pope or Habsburgs was now turned inwards. At the same time

Laudian attitudes helped to make apocalyptic beliefs a more exclusively Puritan characteristic than ever before. Interest in the apocalypse had earlier been commonplace among all strands of opinion in the Established Church (though as already seen supporters of an apocalyptic crusade had tended to come from the Puritan camp). Laud was hostile both to Puritans and to apocalyptic speculation, and his effect was to drive the two together. This development is clear in reactions to the work of Joseph Mede. In 1627 Mede, a Cambridge scholar, published the most important English millenarian treatise of the century. He wrote with great learning, modesty and moderation. Mede followed tradition in identifying Antichrist as the papacy but wisely set out no dates for the fall of Rome and, unlike many Puritan firebrands, he hoped its end would be without bloodshed. Mede was indeed no Puritan. He disliked rigorous predestinarian theology, and was a warm advocate of church ceremonial well before the rise of the Laudians. His taste for ceremony, Mede noted wryly, would have made 'another man a Dean or Prebend or something else ere this. But the point of the Pope's being Antichrist, as a dead fly, marred the savour of that ointment'. He found his *Clavis Apocalyptica* coldly received in Laudian Cambridge. His most likely champion in the episcopal hierarchy was Archbishop Ussher of Armagh, who admired Mede's learning and probably accepted his millenarian theories. But Mede was disappointed to find that Ussher, as a man of the world, would give no public endorsement in such unfavorable times.[89] Only the Puritans gave open support. Mede's most enthusiastic disciple over many years was the Puritan divine, William Twisse. 'O Mr Mede!' Twisse wrote in 1636 after a brief visit to Cambridge. 'I could willingly spend my days in hanging upon your ears, while you discourse of Antichrist' (though, he added, he wished to hear no more of Mede's perverse ideas on ceremony).[90]

Twisse was a respected figure, and his enthusiasm was of especial importance because of his close ties with Lord Saye and Sele and other leading members of the Puritan aristocratic opposition to Charles I. Apocalyptic interests were indeed a feature of the group. In 1636 Lord Saye was 'much taken with Mr Brightman', according to Twisse, who was at that time passing on Mede's newer theories on the millennium. Sir Nathaniel Rich, a close ally of Saye in the Commons, was familiar with the minutiae of Mede's analysis.[91] Lord Brooke, the most extreme of the aristocratic critics, was the author of a treatise on Revelation xx (which describes the thousand years reign) and was derided later by his opponents as an open millenarian.[92] His interest reached back many years. In the early 1630s Brooke was greatly impressed by a treatise on Daniel by the Warwickshire preacher, Ephraim Huit. Its theme was the imminent rise of a Fifth Monarchy of the Jews, converted and restored to Israel, and allied to the godly Gentiles of all nations. Such a work could not be published at that time, and Huit later sought refuge in New England. When the book eventually appeared in 1643 Brooke was dead, but the dedication was fittingly given to his widow.[93] The earl of Warwick, perhaps the most influential of the dissident Puritan peers, numbered among his many clerical proteges Jeremiah Burroughes, John Stoughton and William Twisse, all of whom held millenarian beliefs before the civil war.[94]

IV THE REVOLUTIONARY ERA, 1640-60

Charles I's regime collapsed in the late 1630s when Archbishop Laud attempted to extend his program to Scotland. The Scots' resistance revealed the isolation of the king, and when their army entered England in 1640 Charles had no choice but to call Parliament and submit to its demands. Puritan preachers naturally emphasized the religious aspects of the crisis. Convinced that the Laudian bishops were 'limbs of Antichrist', many of them analysed the situation in apocalyptic terms. As early as September 1640 Henry Wilkinson preached in Laudian Oxford on Rev. iii.16 – God's threat to spew out luke-warm Laodicea, identified as Laudian England. Wilkinson declared it needless to explain this divine judgment, for 'this part of my text is taken out of my hands, and is already begun to be put in execution' by the Scots. He was suspended for these words, but when the Long Parliament assembled in November it restored his freedom and invited him to publish the sermon.[95]

During the following months there was a mood of euphoria among Puritan preachers and pamphleteers. Not long since, Jeremiah Burroughes told his Parliamentary audience, we were lamenting that 'our peace is gone, the Gospel is gone, even our God is gone'. Now all should join in a 'joyful song of praise' to the Lord for this miraculous deliverance.[96] But the preachers who addressed Parliament in a series of Fast Day sermons stressed that much remained to be done. Parliament was to be God's instrument in rooting out Antichrist, preparing the way for the final overthrow of Romish Babylon. The 'heavenly Parliament' must destroy the episcopal church, that 'Hierarchical National Whore'.[97] God was planning Babylon's downfall, said William Bridge, and the Commons were 'a quiver . . . full of choice and polished shafts for the Lords work'.[98] Several preachers, perhaps fearing complacency among their auditors, warned that God's will would be done, however Parliament responded.[99] But the fact that the Commons repeatedly thanked preachers for sermons on apocalyptic themes and recommended publication suggests that very many members welcomed the role offered them.

The widespread dream of building a new Israel in England took a variety of forms which fall into three main groups. The most restrained approach was to call on Parliament to 'perfect that new Reformation' begun by Elizabeth and left incomplete.[100] The most radical was the belief that the present upheaval would usher in the millennium. The ideas of Brightman, Mede and Alsted were now circulating freely. Across the Atlantic the influential minister, John Cotton, preached a series of sermons on Revelation at Boston between 1639 and 1641, arguing that episcopacy was the 'kingdom of the Beast' and was visibly collapsing in England. Though he denied a physical return and reign of Christ, Cotton was confident that Antichrist's fall would be followed by the binding of the devil and the triumph of the church for a thousand years.[101] John Archer, pastor of the church at Arnhem, presented in 1641 a more extreme form of millenarianism, predicting the fall of Rome and conversion of the Jews by 1666, and Christ's return to inaugurate his kingdom by the year 1700. Archer made no direct reference to events in England and the tract may indeed have appeared posthumously. But the drama of its message made an immediate impact and several editions followed rapidly. Christ had 'a purpose to swallow up all kingly power', Archer wrote, 'and when all the world groans under tyranny and oppression of kings, then will he come and throw down all their thrones'.[102] This was the true revolutionary voice, and there is a clear link between Archer and the militant Fifth Monarchists of the 1650s.[103] *A Glimpse of Sions Glory* (1641), another radical tract originating in the Netherlands, related millenarian ideas more closely to the English political situation. Its author, probably Jeremiah Burroughes, believed that the Scottish crisis would swell irresistibly into the millennial reign of Christ. He promised an age of spiritual purity, with the union of Protestant churches, the calling of the Jews, and the long-delayed reward of the suffering Puritans: 'the World shall be theirs'.[104]

Between the cautious and the extreme positions outlined above was a broad 'middle path' consciously chosen by Nathaniel Holmes, and probably the most common approach between 1640 and the outbreak of war in 1642. Holmes rejected a future millennium but his vision of a purified church and godly society had a strongly apocalyptic element. Many preachers looked for such a period of 'latter-day glory' about to dawn. 'By new heavens and a new earth,' Holmes explained, we 'understand a new form of worship; religion in the expression thereof reformed, brought more close to the rule of the Gospel, made more spiritual and heavenlike; and earthly men made new, changed, and turned into new creatures by the power of religion so reformed.'[105] A purified church was at the heart of this vision, as it had been for pioneering Congregationalists before 1640. What Holmes and his colleagues added was a clear political dimension: kings and magistrates would honor and protect the godly, and destroy their enemies. William Sedgwick prophesied that 'Kings shall contribute the life and sweetness of their royalties to the help of the Church'. Henry Burton hoped that Charles I would belatedly preside over the fall of Babylon in England.[106] Many preachers, rightly suspicious of the king, stressed instead the role of Parliament in establishing the 'latter-day glory'. Some singled out the Puritan magnates who had protected the godly in the dark Laudian years. A poem in praise of Philip Herbert, earl of Pembroke, contained the bold claim that 'The Pope doth tremble at our Herbert's name', and reflected that if only 'more such peers in England (God) would send, / So should all taxes cease, and schisms end'.[107] Burroughes dedicated to Warwick a work promising a glorious, perhaps millennial future age. The earl, he wrote, had protected the truth in the past and must now shoulder his present duty, 'to set up Jerusalem as the praise of the earth'.[108] In *A Glimpse* Burroughes recognized the role of the poor and obscure who had first called for Christ's reign but added, 'How gladly would we hear this voice come from our nobles, and the King himself, and the great ones of the kingdom' who must perfect the work.[109]

It is difficult to know how far the 'great ones' shared these apocalyptic hopes, though Parliament's taste for sermons on the theme is suggestive. Mede's *Clavis* was translated into English by a M.P. and published with official approval.[110] The millennial-utopian visions of Comenius, Hartlib and Dury won the active support of a wide cross-section of Parliamentary leaders, including Pym, the earls of Warwick and Pembroke, and Lord Brooke. Comenius and his circle looked for social reforms, the spread of learning on 'pansophic' and Baconian lines, and the downfall of Antichrist. All seemed possible in 1640–1.[111] Milton's *Of Reformation* (1641) was shot through with a millennial euphoria, and he expounded his millenarian creed in detail in his later work, *Of Christian Doctrine*.[112]

The growing political divisions of 1641 shook this confident mood, and it was shattered by the king's breach with Parliament in January 1642. During the following summer civil war broke out. Comenius left England, disappointed, and the preachers had to find a new interpretation of events. Though the issues involved in the war were complex, many ministers were quick to offer an analysis in starkly apocalyptic terms. They presented the war as a defence of religious truth against the popish Laudians supported by a misguided king. At the same time the conflict was a crusade to build New Jerusalem after the fall of Babylon. Political and constitutional issues were often brushed aside. Addressing Parliament in May 1643, the Presbyterian Francis Cheynell demanded, 'To what end should we waste time about a discourse of Hull, and the militia? Come speak to the point.' For Cheynell the point was simple. Charles I had handed over power to the Roman Beast, and 'We are engaged to fight against the anti-christian faction.'[113] Similarly the defence of liberty was a minor issue for Stephen Marshall, the most celebrated of the Parliamentary preachers. The only significant 'question is, whether Christ or Antichrist shall be Lord or King, . . . the Protestants owning the one, and the papists and popish-affected the other, as their cause'. Marshall found it exhilarating to live in the age of God's judgments, secure in the knowledge that 'Antichrist shall lose, and Christ shall gain.'[114] Henry Wilkinson thought that 'mighty commotions' must be expected when Christ did battle against the ten-horned Beast (symbolizing ten kings, among them the English). 'What ever horns stand in the way, smite them, till you have knocked them off', Wilkinson urged his auditors. 'There is a stigma and a brand of infamy set upon those kings, that did not go through with the business of Reformation.'[115] Such sermons helped to create a widespread apocalyptic view of the war. Cheap propaganda tracts reached a wider audience, encapsulating the message in vivid titles such as *England's Alarm to War against the Beast*.[116]

Though Parliament was God's main instrument, the army was seen as a close second. In 1643 William Prynne hailed its commander, the earl of Essex, as 'the General of the Lord of Hosts'. According to an army chaplain, God had chosen Essex 'to be his General, and the champion of Jesus Christ to fight the great and last battle with Antichrist'.[117] These ideas filtered down to the common soldiers, some of whom were encountered in 1643 discussing Essex in the role of John the Baptist, preparing the way for Christ to throw down the king.[118]

Preachers and pamphleteers were perhaps too successful in spreading their apocalyptic enthusiasm. Presbyterians and most moderate Puritans envisaged a national, authoritarian and hierarchical church at the centre of the new Israel. They were alarmed by the Independent clergy's plea for a measure of toleration and autonomy, and by the idea of a new religious enlightenment dawning in these latter days – a notion which struck at the roots of discipline.[119] They were still more alarmed by the radical millenarian ideas circulating in the New Model Army from 1645, encouraged by some of the army chaplains. It was allegedly being taught that in the New Jerusalem there would be total religious freedom. Christ was about to throw down monarchy and aristocracy. In Christ's kingdom there would be no private property, and the godly would seize the estates of the wicked and take power from the magistrate. As a final insult Paul Hobson, officer and Baptist preacher, had claimed that Presbyterianism was the Beast of the Apocalypse.[120] Many of these reports came from a group of Presbyterians who in 1645–6 launched a fierce attack on the millenarian 'heresy'. The Presbyterians' own dream of a New Jerusalem quickly faded from their sermons and tracts. Political extremism, social upheaval and spreading heresy had discredited the vision. Those few Presbyterians who clung to it were careful in future to separate their faith from current political events. When Thomas Gataker edited an old apocalyptic tract in 1650, for example, he sternly warned enthusiasts against the delusion 'that it doth belong to them to execute the wrath of God'.[121]

The developments which alarmed the Presbyterians served to stimulate the Independents and radicals. They saw in the Independent party at Westminster, and still more in the New Model, a real chance to secure religious freedom and reform and the sweeping social and economic changes which some expected in the millennium. One of the few female commentators, Mary Cary, even saw the creation of the New Model Army in 1645 as the rising of the witnesses from the dead (Rev. xi.11).[122] Thomas Collier, an army chaplain, preached on Christ's kingdom to the soldiers at Putney in September 1647. He anticipated an approaching age of religious freedom and enlightenment, but also promised that God would give power to the saints to reform the law, end oppression and throw down tithes. He ended by assuring the soldiers that they were chosen by God to create this new world.[123]

The millennial confidence of the Independents and army radicals easily survived the second civil war of 1648. Charles allied with the Scots and many former moderate Parliamentarians, but Cromwell routed the army of the invading 'Scottish Antichrist' at the battle of Preston. The victory destroyed the Presbyterian as well as the royalist cause, and was hailed as conclusive vindication by the army millenarians. William Sancroft, a royalist observer and later archbishop of Canterbury, told with black humor how the radical preacher 'cries aloud from the pulpit, "Babylon is fallen", and having transmuted his quondam brethren into Gog and Magog, he is now puzzling his geography to find Armageddon about Preston and Warrington Bridge'.[124]

After this second war the army and its political allies (the Independent MPs) lost patience with Parliament's continuing and futile attempts to make peace with the king. The army officers' decision late in 1648 to purge Parliament and put Charles on trial was welcomed by most religious radicals, whose concept of the reign of the saints had gone far beyond the ideas current in 1640. As John Simpson wrote in 1648 with obvious relish, 'God hath not only delivered us from the hands of our enemies; but hath given us the necks of our enemies likewise'; the godly would now reign as kings.[125] George Cockayne praised God's intention to drive out evil magistrates in a sermon delivered to Parliament only a week before the army's purge.[126] The king's execution, which followed in January 1649, appeared to the Independent minister John Owen as part of the remoulding of the world's kingdoms into the kingdom of Christ.[127] A pamphleteer who saw the military coup as inaugurating Christ's rule dedicated his tract to John Bradshaw, president of the court which had condemned the king.[128] Another preacher, Thomas Banaster, prophesied an 'earth watered with . . . the blood of kings, princes and mighty ones'. 'Yet further Christ will proceed in blood, even to the horse bridles'. Though few writers matched this crude blood lust, many of them emphasized England's role as the elect nation preparing the way for the downfall of monarchy throughout Europe.[129]

The surviving portion of the Long Parliament, known as the Rump, was now pressed to set up the rule of Christ.[130] Military triumphs in Ireland and Scotland seemed to justify hopes that the millennium was indeed approaching, and army chaplains and pamphleteers stressed the crucial importance of the soldiers' role. The army, said Joseph Salmon, was God's instrument to 'strike through king, gentry and nobility'. God had migrated from Parliament to the army in order to kill the Beast (Monarchy: Rev. xiii.3) 'which they had formerly wounded, and whose wound the Parliament had healed and salved over by a corrupt and rotten treaty.'[131] Millenarian ideas were widespread among the troops. Cromwell's army invading Scotland in 1650 declared its zeal for 'the advancement of the kingdom of Jesus Christ'. King Charles had been killed as one of the ten horns of the Beast, and the Scots should recognize the folly of resisting 'God's executioners'. The officers and soldiers of the distant garrison of Pendennis Castle, Cornwall, had similar views and 'long debated every day for sundry months . . . their present expected personal reign of Christ on earth'.[132]

Charles' sudden overthrow after the uncertainties of 1648 stimulated new and still more radical variations on the millennial theme. A manifesto from separatist churches in East Anglia urged the army to hand over power to novel 'church-parliaments' from which 'mere natural and worldly men' would be excluded.[133] The Ranter Abiezer Coppe saw the king's death as heralding a new age of total equality, liberty and communism. He spoke as God's mouthpiece: 'I the eternal God, the Lord of Hosts, who am that mighty Leveller, am coming . . . to level in good earnest'.[134] Similarly Gerrard Winstanley, the Digger, urged Parliament to destroy kingly power in all its forms by sweeping away private property and social hierarchy. Such a program, he urged, would 'prove England to be the first of nations, or the tenth part of the city Babylon, that falls off from the Beast first, and that sets the Crown upon Christ's head, to govern the world in righteousness'.[135] But Coppe, Winstanley and other perceptive radicals were aware that the Rumpers had been very reluctant revolutionaries, so that future prospects were uncertain. An army chaplain, William Dell, offered only barbed praise to the nation's rulers for at last 'doing that work of God, which once you had little mind to'. Petitioners from Norfolk early in 1649 feared that the army planned a secular republic modelled on Rome rather than Christ's kingdom.[136] Millenarian reformers were quickly disillusioned with the Rump. In 1651 several pamphleteers returned to the idea of a government drawn exclusively from the gathered churches.[137] Some radicals looked to Cromwell, while others found a new champion in Major-General Harrison, the most committed millenarian among the senior officers. Harrison used his position to create a new militia force recruited partly from the separatists, and the 'New Church Regiments' marched to his assistance when the Scots invaded England in 1651.[138] Later that year a number of London congregations turned to direct political action. Unable to persuade Cromwell to act against the Rump, they organized a pressure group agitating for its dissolution. This campaign, the origin of the Fifth Monarchist movement, was resented as subversive and anarchic by Cromwell and leading Independent ministers such as John Owen and Thomas Goodwin.[139] But the separatists' bitter hostility towards the Rump was shared by many others and was impossible to suppress. Urged on by Harrison, Cromwell eventually staged a military coup in April 1653. He was hailed by admirers as a new Moses leading his people from bondage to the promised land, and some were indeed willing to give him total freedom in choosing a new government. Others wanted a franchise based on the churches. In the event Cromwell and other senior officers selected the members of the new assembly, which met in July 1653 and became known as the Barebones Parliament.[140]

Cromwell shared the millennial euphoria of the moment, seeing in the new assembly the fulfillment of apocalyptic promises. 'Truly,' he told the members, 'you are called by God to rule with him and for him'.[141] Though only a small group within the House were Fifth Monarchists (among them Harrison), there were many other radicals present. There were also members of moderate, even conservative views, and the assembly was deeply split on almost every issue. The Fifth Monarchists hoped to abolish tithes and transform the legal system. Meeting strong opposition, they quickly became sceptical and even hostile towards Barebones. Fifth Monarchy preachers denounced Cromwell and spurned his attempts at conciliation. Moderate Members shared with Cromwell a fear of social revolution unleashed in the name of Christ's kingdom. When conciliation failed, a group of moderate M.P.s accordingly contrived the resignation of Barebones in December, a move which Cromwell accepted gratefully.

In the regime which followed, Cromwell ruled directly as Protector. His stated goals were stability and order; the millennial excitement was gone. Christ may come to rule, he declared later, but only 'to set up His reign in our hearts'. He saw the Fifth Monarchists as standing for anarchy and revolution.[142] Many Independent church leaders shared this view and similarly backed away from the political aspects of millenarianism. Only a few years earlier Thomas Goodwin had prophesied the rule of ordinary church-members in the coming millennium. 'The persons that are made kings and priests,' he had promised, would be 'US, the generality of saints'. After the rise of the Fifth Monarchists, Goodwin and others preferred to stress the spiritual nature of Christ's kingdom. Many Independents remained millenarians but began to separate this faith from the contemporary political circumstances.[143] In the army too millenarian hopes underwent change. Many officers held Independent rather than Fifth Monarchist conceptions of Christ's kingdom. Colonel Goffe, who had preached at Putney on the Apocalypse, was in command of the troops who expelled the Fifth Monarchists left in Barebones after the moderates had resigned. There was considerable unrest in the army at the establishment of the Protectorate, but no millenarian mutiny. Harrison laid down his commission, and some other officers resigned or were dismissed.[144]

To the Fifth Monarchists Cromwell was no longer a second Moses but the little horn, Beast, Dragon or some other monster from the apocalyptic menagerie. He had betrayed the Israelites at the very threshold of the promised land. John Tillinghast, the movement's most able theologian, admitted that Christ's cause had lost its 'fresh and amiable countenance' and 'begins now to appear wan with Death in the face of it'. He felt able to prove that the millennium would still arrive by the close of the century, but played down the significance of England's recent history as its harbinger.[145]

In the following years the Fifth Monarchists elaborated their ideas on Christ's kingdom. They envisaged a Parliament of saints chosen by the churches; the establishment of the Mosaic laws; a new social hierarchy which would give proper status to the godly; and a social program to end poverty and oppression. But the chances of implementing these changes were small. A few days after the fall of Barebones, Vavasor Powell posed the stark question, 'Lord, wilt thou have Oliver Cromwell or Jesus Christ to reign over us?' God's will seemed clear but impossible to fulfil. The violence of the Fifth Monarchists' language was a measure of their frustration. They launched propaganda campaigns to coincide with the Protectorate Parliaments, attempted to subvert the army and navy and sought alliances with republicans, Baptists and other opponents of the regime. All these methods failed. Most Fifth Monarchy leaders felt that rebellion, while justifiable, was unlikely to succeed and would play into the hands of the Cavaliers. Among the London artisans there were however some militants prepared to turn violent rhetoric into action. A preacher in 1656 taught that it would be a godly duty to assassinate Cromwell. The following year Thomas Venner, a cooper and former emigrant to New England, led an attempted rising in the capital. It failed totally, and served merely to discredit still further the cause of revolutionary millenarianism.[146]

The propaganda of the Quakers, the other major radical movement of the 1650s, had a similar effect. Though they saw Christ's kingdom primarily as an inward, spiritual transformation, they also looked for the downfall of false churches, worldly rulers and antichristian Rome. Their language was violent and apocalyptic. 'A day of howling is coming', George Fox promised. 'The glittering sword is drawn, it is furbished for the slaughter'. The early Quakers were not pacifists and were in any case often misunderstood. It is not surprising that their promise of 'The Lamb's War against the Man of Sin' was sometimes taken literally.[147]

The Fifth Monarchists were the high-water mark of the revolutionary, 'centrifugal' tide of apocalyptic thought which flowed from disillusion with Charles I as godly prince. During the revolutionary years there was little scope for pro-government, 'centripetal' forms of the faith.[148] The Long Parliament was only temporarily satisfactory as a substitute for monarchy, and Cromwell soon abandoned his role as second Moses. A link between the government's policies and the apocalypse survived during the Protectorate only in foreign affairs. While ignoring the Fifth Monarchists' call for a millenarian crusade, Cromwell did inject an apocalyptic note into his war against Spain. He told Parliament that 'The Lord Himself hath a controversy . . . with that Roman Babylon, of which the Spaniard is the great underpropper. In that respect we fight the Lord's battles'. This view found a number of supporters, among them some officers in the navy.[149]

Cromwell's death in 1658 led rapidly to the collapse of the regime. The unsettled year 1659 was a time of renewed radical hopes, quickly disappointed. Divisions within the army threatened the total breakdown of order and paved the way for the return of Charles II in 1660. A second Fifth Monarchist rising in 1661 could expect success only on the desperate grounds that God would be discredited if He allowed the 'profane, drunken, damning, swearing, idolatrous, adulterous, wicked and ungodly' Stuarts to triumph.[150] Providence was clearly spurning the revolutionaries and, by the same token, breathing new life into royalist dreams. Cavalier, episcopalian interpretations of the Apocalypse had appeared sporadically throughout the Interregnum, usually the work of lay writers and self-styled prophets rather than theologians. In 1651, for example, Edmund Hall had argued that Charles I was not Antichrist, 'as 'tis commonly taught', but one of the Witnesses slain for the truth; after $3\frac{1}{2}$ years, according to prophecy, he would rise again in the person of Charles II.[151] But until 1660 political circumstances did not encourage such interpretations.

The Restoration in 1660 produced a flood of royalist poems and pamphlets hailing Charles II as a messianic king whose miraculous return heralded the golden age. During the second Dutch War in 1664–6 patriotic and millennial fervor combined to reach new heights, stimulated by the approach of the fateful year 1666.[152] Throughout the rest of the century popular writers continued the themes of England's elect role, and looked for a royal conqueror to throw down the Roman Antichrist. By the 1680s internal political divisions were once again becoming a feature of apocalyptic speculation: the reign of the Catholic James II revived the fear that monarchy could side with Antichrist instead of crusading against it. The Ottoman siege of Vienna and Louis XIV's suppression of the French Huguenots intensified this alarm.[153] But the predominant characteristic of Restoration millenarianism was its link with the crown and the Established Church. Archbishops Sancroft and Tillotson and Bishop Lloyd were among the prominent Anglican churchmen expecting a millennial age. Lay believers included such contrasting figures as Isaac Newton and John Evelyn. All of them regarded the approaching millennium in terms of stability and order. The behavior of James II only briefly disturbed progress towards this goal; William and Mary ('two angels in human shape', according to Tillotson) quickly restored England to its course.[154]

The millennium would be a world purified and transformed, but it would definitely not be a world turned upside down. The earlier crusading militancy of Thomas Brightman seemed equally outmoded. Of the earlier writers, it was Joseph Mede whose reputation now stood highest. Mede had once remarked that it was his fate to fall between the stools of Puritanism and Laudianism and be distrusted by both.[155] After his death his writings inspired first the revolutionaries and then the leaders of the Anglican establishment. His ideas were borrowed for the manifesto of the bloody Fifth Monarchist rising of 1661, and yet were also warmly admired by Sancroft and his circle (whose approach was certainly far closer to Mede's own).[156] This small irony is a useful reminder of the infinite variety of seventeenth-century millenarianism. It also points to the continuity of the tradition. The millennial excitement of the civil wars marked the end of a chapter, not of the story. Apocalyptic belief with a clear political dimension was to remain part of the mainstream of thought down to the very end of the Stuart age.

NOTES

1 J. Bale, *Select Works*, ed. H. Christmas (Parker Society, Cambridge, 1849), p. 494.
2 R. Bauckham, *Tudor Apocalypse* (Appleford, 1978), ch. 2. Bauckham's work is the most scholarly study of Tudor apocalyptic thought; P. Christianson, *Reformers and Babylon* (Toronto, 1978) gives most stress to the political dimension.
3 T. Brightman, *The Revelation of St. John Illustrated*, in *Works* (1644), sig. A2v.
4 Bauckham, *Tudor Apocalypse*, ch. 4; K. Firth, *The Apocalyptic Tradition in Reformation Britain 1530–1645* (Oxford, 1979), ch. 2.
5 J. Foxe, *The Acts and Monuments*, ed. J. Pratt (1877), vii, p. 664.
6 Foxe, *Acts and Monuments*, vii, p. 423.
7 Brightman, *Works*, p. 611.
8 John became a popular example: C. Levin, 'A Good Prince: King John and Early Tudor Propaganda', in *The Sixteenth Century Journal*, xi (1980), pp. 23–32.
9 J. Jewel, *An Apology for the Church of England*, and *A Defence of the Apologie* in *Works*, ed. J. Ayre (Parker Society, Cambridge, 1845–50), iii, pp. 75 ff.; iv, pp. 627 ff., 671 ff.; Jewel, *A View of a Seditious Bull*, in *Works*, iv, pp. 1128–60; F. Yates, *Astraea: the Imperial Theme in the Sixteenth Century* (Harmondsworth, 1977), pp. 39–42.
10 Foxe, *Acts and Monuments*, iv, p. 106.
11 (J. Old), *A short description of Antichrist* (no place, 1557?), fol. 18; A. Marten, *An Exhortation* (1588), sig. B–v.
12 See M. Reeves, *The Influence of Prophecy in the Later Middle Ages* (Oxford, 1969).
13 N. Cohn, *The Pursuit of the Millennium* (2nd ed., 1970).
14 Bale, *Select Works*, pp. 309, 341, 427, 431, 443, 485, 640; Bale, *A Comedy concerning Three Laws* (1538) in *The Dramatic Writings of John Bale*, ed. J. S. Farmer (1907, reprinted 1966), pp. 78, 79; Bauckham, *Tudor Apocalypse*, pp. 129, 216–18; Christianson, *Reformers*, pp. 19, 21–2.
15 T. Becon, *The Early Works*, ed. J. Ayre (Parker Society, Cambridge, 1843), pp. 181–2 (citing Virgil's *Eclogue IV*, lines 4–5).
16 *The first tome or volume of the Paraphrase of Erasmus upon the newe testamente* (1548), Udall's epistle, sigs. aiii, iii[v] and *passim*.
17 N. Ridley, *Works*, ed. H. Christmas (Parker Society, Cambridge, 1841), pp. 58–9, 61, 62 ff.; (Old,) *Short Description*, fol. 3; J. Aylmer, *An Harborowe For Faith-full and Trewe Subiectes* (Strasburg, 1559), sig. D3v.
18 Foxe, *Acts and Monuments*, i, epistle dedicatory to the 1563 edition.
19 Jewel, *Works*, iii, p. 118; E. Sandys, *Sermons*, ed. J. Ayre (Parker Society, Cambridge, 1841), p. 56; Aylmer, *An Harborowe*, sig. O2.

20 W. Haller, *Foxe's Book of Martyrs and the Elect Nation* (1963), ch. 7.
21 Foxe, *Acts and Monuments*, i, pp. xvi, 5; viii, p. 754; Bauckham, *Tudor Apocalypse*, pp. 73, 83–8. Firth, Christianson and V. G. Olsen, *John Foxe and the Elizabethan Church* (Berkeley, 1973), also refute Haller's view.
22 Bauckham, *Tudor Apocalypse*, p. 73; Foxe, *Acts and Monuments*, i, p. 5.
23 Foxe, *Acts and Monuments*, i, pp. 306–7, 312.
24 Aylmer, *An Harborowe*, sigs. P4, P4^v, R^v, R3.
25 Bauckham, *Tudor Apocalypse*, 128–30; Christianson, *Reformers*, pp. 29–36.
26 Aylmer, *An Harborowe*, sig. R3; Becon, *Early Works*, p. 29.
27 *The Bible and Holy Scriptures* (Geneva, 1560), sig. ***iii^v; Sandys, *Sermons*, pp. 80–1.
28 (L. Guiccardini,) *Hours of Recreation* (1576), epistle by Sandford, sigs. Aiv^v, Av and *passim*; see Bauckham, *Tudor Apocalypse*, pp. 218–21.
29 Bauckham, *Tudor Apocalypse*, ch. 8; B. W. Ball, *A Great Expectation: Eschatological Thought in English Protestantism to 1660* (Leiden, 1975), chs 1–3.
30 W. B. Stone, 'Shakespeare and the Sad Augurs', in *Journal of English and Germanic Philology*, lii (1953), pp. 457–79.
31 Marten, *An Exhortation*, sig. A2v. On the apocalyptic character of the war see Bauckham, *Tudor Apocalypse*, pp. 173–80; C. Hill, *Antichrist in Seventeenth-Century England* (1971), pp. 14–15.
32 T. Rogers, *An Historical Dialogue touching Antichrist* (1589), sigs. Aiii, iv^v.
33 E. Hellwis, *A Marvell, Deciphered* (1589), sig. B3.
34 L. Deios, *That the Pope is that Antichrist* (1590), pp. 183–4.
35 Marten, *An Exhortation*, sigs. C2, F^v and *passim*.
36 Deios, *That the Pope*, p. 3.
37 G. Gifford, *Sermons upon the whole Book of the Revelation* (1599), p. 348.
38 A. Dent, *The Ruine of Rome* (1607 edition; first published 1603), pp. 217–18, 234–6, 254, 256, 268. Spain had annexed Portugal in 1580.
39 Yates, *Astraea*, pp. 159–87.
40 Hellwis, *A Marvell*, p. 12 and *passim*; Bauckham, *Tudor Apocalypse*, pp. 179–80.
41 This paragraph is based largely on Christianson, *Reformers*, ch. 2 (esp. pp. 54–8) and Hill, *Antichrist*, ch. 2.
42 Both are discussed in full by Bauckham, *Tudor Apocalypse*, ch. 10.
43 P. Lake, 'The Significance of the Elizabethan Identification of the Pope as Antichrist', *Journal of Ecclesiastical History*, xxxi (1980), pp. 161–78.
44 S. L. Adams, 'The Protestant Cause: Religious Alliance with the West European Calvinist Communities as a Political Issue in England, 1585–1630', Oxford D.Phil. thesis, 1973.
45 Gifford, *Sermons*, sigs. A3, A3^v, A4, A5^v, p. 339. (The dedication to Essex is reprinted in Bauckham, *Tudor Apocalypse*, pp. 353–8.)
46 See for example J. Brocardo, *The Revelation* (1582), dedicated to Leicester by the translator, John Field; P. de Mornay, *A Notable Treatise of the Church* (1579) (Leicester); Aylmer, *An Harborowe* (Leicester and the earl of Bedford); Dent, *Ruine of Rome* (Lord Rich); W. Fulke, *Praelections* (1573), trans. G. Gifford (Ambrose Dudley, earl of Warwick); A. Marlorat, *A Catholike Exposition* (1572) (Sir Walter Mildmay).
47 B. S. Capp, *Astrology and the Popular Press* (1979), pp. 168–9.
48 Foxe and George Joye (editor and translator of A. Osiander, *The coniectures of the ende of the world* (1548)) were unusual among Tudor writers in their interest in

numerology. Foxe needed professional help in checking his simple arithmetic (*Acts and Monuments*, i, p. 290). Compare the expertise shown by Napier and F. Potter, *An Interpretation of the Number 666* (1642).

49 J. Napier, *A Plain Discovery of the whole Revelation* (1593). For detailed studies see Firth, *Apocalypse Tradition*, ch. 4; Christianson, *Reformers*, pp. 97–100; R. G. Clouse, 'John Napier and Apocalyptic Thought', *The Sixteenth Century Journal*, v (1974), pp. 101–14; A. Williamson, *Scottish National Consciousness in the Age of James VI* (Edinburgh, 1979), esp. pp. 21–30.

50 Brightman, *Works*, sigs. A2, A2^v, pp. 440, 784, 820–1, 824–5. The work was composed around 1602: see p. 126. For accounts see Christianson, *Reformers*, pp. 100–6; Firth, *Apocalyptic Tradition*, pp. 164–76; P. Toon (ed.), *Puritans, the Millennium and the Future of Israel* (Cambridge, 1970), pp. 26–32.

51 Brightman, *Works*, pp. 109–62. The new heresies probably referred to the ideas of Baro and his group at Cambridge.

52 Brightman, *Works*, pp. 156, 159. Cf. W. Lamont, *Godly Rule* (1969), p. 51.

53 Brightman, *Works*, pp. 510, 524–5, 532; R. Bernard, *A Key of Knowledge* (1617), sig. D4–^{v}.

54 Alsted, *Diatribe de Mille Annis* (Frankfurt, 1627); Toon (ed.), *Puritans*, pp. 42–56; R. G. Clouse, 'Johann Heinrich Alsted and English Millenarianism', *Harvard Theological Review*, lxii (1969), pp. 189–207.

55 See p. 107.

56 See p. 108.

57 Brightman, *Works*, pp. 126, 156, 382, 761–2, 807.

58 James I, *A Fruitefull Meditation* (1603; first published 1588); *A Premonition*, in *The Political Works of James I*, ed. C. H. McIlwain (1918, reprinted 1965), pp. 110–68.

59 G. Downham, *A Treatise concerning Anti-christ* (1603), sigs. A2^v, A3.

60 I.V. (John Vicars), *Englands Hallelu-jah* (1631), sig. F2v.

61 Bernard, *Key of Knowledge*, sigs. C5, C6^v, p. 16.

62 J. Maxwell, *Admirable and Notable Prophesies* (1615), esp. pp. 28, 35–6, 85; Maxwell, *The Laudable Life, and Deplorable Death, of the late peerless Prince Henry* (1612), sig. Fv. On Maxwell see Williamson, *Scottish National Consciousness*, pp. 103–6; Reeves, *Influence of Prophecy*, pp. 499–500.

63 Napier, *Plaine Discovery*, sig. A3^v–4; Clouse, 'John Napier', esp. pp. 104–5.

64 Historical Manuscripts Commission, lxvi, *Ancaster MSS*, pp. 362–85, especially p. 369. The treatise was 'Balaam's Ass', the alleged author John Cotton of Warblington.

65 J. W. Williamson, *The Myth of the Conqueror: Prince Henry Stuart* (1978); P. Mornay, *The Mysterie of Iniquitie*, trans. S. Lennard (1612), sigs. 9I, iii, iii^v.

66 S. L. Adams, 'Foreign Policy and the Parliaments of 1621 and 1624' in *Faction and Parliament*, ed. K. Sharpe (Oxford, 1978), esp. pp. 146–7 (see also his thesis cited above, note 44); F. Yates, *The Rosicrucian Enlightenment* (1972), chs 2, 4; M. A. Breslow, *A Mirror of England: English Puritan Views of Foreign Nations 1618–1640* (Cambridge, Massachusetts, 1970), ch. 2.

67 J. F. Maclear, 'Puritan relations with Buckingham', *Huntington Library Quarterly*, xxi (1957–8), pp. 111–32. The quotation is from (T. Scott), *Vox Coeli, or Newes from Heaven* ('Elisium', 1624), p. 37.

68 R. Corbet, *Poems*, ed. J. A. W. Bennett and H. R. Trevor-Roper (Oxford, 1955), pp. 57–8. On the apocalyptic aspects of Laudianism see Hill, *Antichrist*, pp. 36–40, 69–70; Lamont, *Godly Rule*, ch. 3; Christianson, *Reformers*, esp. pp. 133–5.

69 T. Beard, *Antichrist the Pope of Rome* (1625), sig. A2ᵛ.
70 R. Sheldon, *A Sermon preached at Paules Crosse* (1625), esp. pp. 49–50.
71 Lamont, *Godly Rule*, ch. 3.
72 A. Leighton, *Speculum Belli Sacri* (1624), sig. B–ᵛ, pp. 182, 194; Leighton, *An Appeal to the Parliament* (1628), pp. 68, 72, 74, 174, 208; Christianson, *Reformers*, pp. 116–24.
73 H. Burton, *The Baiting*, frontispiece; *The Seven Vials* (1628), sigs. 13, 442 ff., pp. 68, 75, 77; Burton, *Israels Fast* (1628), sig. A2, pp. 14–15 (misprint for 30–1); Burton, *Babel no Bethel* (1629), sig. 412. See Christianson, *Reformers*, pp. 138–51.
74 Burton, *For God, and the King* (1636), sig. a4 and *passim*; Burton, *An Apology of an Appeale* (1636).
75 Breslow, *Mirror*, pp. 38–42.
76 W. Gouge, *The Saints Sacrifice* (1632), pp. 284–91; Breslow, *Mirror*, ch. 6; M. Roberts, *Gustavus Adolphus* (1953, 1958), i, pp. 522–6, ii, p. 406.
77 J. Mede, *Works*, ed. J. Worthington (1677), p. 822; Mede, *The Key of the Revelation* (1643), p. 117; T. Goodwin, *Works*, ii (1683), p. 100; J. F. Maclear, 'New England and the Fifth Monarchy', *William and Mary Quarterly*, 3rd series, xxxii (1975), pp. 227n–8n.
78 C. Hill, *Puritanism and Revolution* (1962 ed.), p. 129; Breslow, *Mirror*, p. 134; F. Schloer, *The Death of the Two Renowned Kings of Sweden and Bohemia* (1633).
79 Marten, *An Exhortation*, sig. F2.
80 Brightman, *Works*, pp. 162, 382.
81 Bernard, *Key of Knowledge*, pp. 127–9.
82 Hill, *Puritanism and Revolution*, pp. 125–9; Breslow, *Mirror*, *passim*; Adams, 'Foreign Policy', *passim*; Scott, *Vox Coeli*, esp. p. 46.
83 Leighton, *An Appeal*, sig. A5.
84 William Twisse, in Mede, *Works*, p. 799.
85 Maclear, 'New England', and references cited there.
86 Ames, in Mede, *Works*, p. 782; J. Archer, *The Personall Reigne of Christ upon Earth* (1642); T. Goodwin, *An Exposition of the Revelation*, in *Works*, ii (1683), esp. pp. 126, 166, 176–8; G. F. Nuttall, *Visible Saints* (Oxford, 1957), p. 148; J. F. Wilson, *Pulpit in Parliament* (Princeton, 1969), pp. 224–5, 229; Christianson, *Reformers*, pp. 209–16.
87 Burton, *The Sounding of the Two Last Trumpets* (1641), p. 70; Christianson, *Reformers*, pp. 145–51.
88 J. Lilburne, *A Worke of the Beast* (1638), pp. 17–19 (reprinted in W. Haller, *Tracts on Liberty* (1965), vol. ii; W. Haller, *The Rise of Puritanism* (1957), pp. 278–87; Christianson, *Reformers*, pp. 168–77.
89 Mede, *Works*, pp. xviii, 815, 818, 829, 851; Mede, *Key*, part ii, pp. 28–9; Firth, *Apocalyptic Tradition*, pp. 213–28.
90 Mede, *Works*, p. 845.
91 Mede, *Works*, pp. 810, 822; H. R. Trevor-Roper, *Religion, the Reformation and Social Change* (1972 edn.), p. 248; *Dictionary of National Biography*, under William Twisse.
92 *Dictionary of National Biography*, under Robert Greville, Lord Brooke; *Persecutio Undecima* (1648), p. 56; A. Wood, *Athenae Oxonienses*, ed. P. Bliss (Oxford, 1813–20), ii, column 434.
93 E. Huit, *The whole Prophecie of Daniel Explained* (1644; first published 1643), sig. A2–ᵛ and *passim*.

94 J. Burroughes, *Moses his Choice* (1641), dedicatory epistle; Trevor-Roper, *Religion*, p. 259n.; *Dictionary of National Biography*, under William Twisse.
95 H. Wilkinson, *A Sermon against Lukewarmenesse* (1641), sig. A3, p. 37.
96 J. Burroughes, *Sions Joy* (1641), pp. 2, 3.
97 J. de la March, *The Complaint of the False Prophet's Mariners* (1641), pp. 40, 49. March was not preaching to Parliament, but expressed views typical of those in the Fast Day sermons; see Wilson, *Pulpit*; Christianson, *Reformers*, ch. 5; Trevor-Roper, *Religion*, ch. 6.
98 W. Bridge, *Babylons Downfall* (1614), p. 21; similar phrases were used by Burton, N. Holmes, R. Byfield, W. Sedgwick and others.
99 Lamont, *Godly Rule*, p. 82.
100 C. Burges, *The First Sermon* (1641), p. 66.
101 J. Cotton, *The Powring out of the Seven Vials* (1642), vial v, p. 5; vial vi, p. 42; Cotton, *The Churches Resurrection* (1642); Maclear, 'New England', pp. 231–4.
102 Archer, *Personall Reigne*, p. 53.
103 B. S. Capp, *The Fifth Monarchy Men* (1972), p. 46.
104 (J. Burroughes), *A Glimpse*, p. 28 and *passim*. This tract is often attributed to Thomas Goodwin; for Burroughes' authorship see Christianson, *Reformers*, pp. 217n, 251–2, and N. Holmes, *The Resurrection Revealed* (1654), p. 53.
105 N. Holmes, *The New World* (1641), p. 7; Christianson, *Reformers*, pp. 206–9.
106 W. Sedgwick, *Zions Deliverance* (1642), p. 15; Burton, *Sounding*, p. 43 (and for his doubts, born of long experience, p. 91).
107 T. Herbert, *Vox Secunda Populi* (1641), pp. 4, 5.
108 Burroughes, *Moses*, sigs. A2^v, A4^v–5, pp. 485–7.
109 (Burroughes), *A Glimpse*, p. 8.
110 Mede, *The Key of the Revelation* (1643), translated by Richard More, M.P., with a preface by William Twisse.
111 Trevor-Roper, *Religion*, ch. 5, esp. p. 256; see further C. Webster, *The Great Instauration* (1975).
112 Milton, *Of Christian Doctrine*, in *Complete Prose Works*, Yale edition, vol. vi, ed. M. Kelley (1973), esp. pp. 623–5; see further below, pp. 207–37.
113 F. Cheynell, *Sions Memento, And God's Alarum* (1643), p. 10; Hill, *Antichrist*, pp. 79–98; Wilson, *Pulpit*, pp. 189–214.
114 S. Marshall, *A Sacred Panegyrick* (1643), p. 21; Marshall, *The Song of Moses* (1643), p. 45.
115 H. Wilkinson, *Babylons Ruine, Jerusalems Rising* (1643), pp. 16, 26.
116 *England's Alarm* (1643); *The Camp of Christ and the Camp of Antichrist* (1642, with two sequels).
117 W. Prynne, *The Popish Royall Favourite* (1643), epistle dedicatory; T. Palmer, *The Saints Support* (1644), sig. A2.
118 *The Journal of Sir Samuel Luke*, ed. I. G. Philip (Oxfordshire Record Society, 1947–53), i, p. 76.
119 Tai Liu, *Discord in Zion* (The Hague, 1973), esp. pp. 43–51.
120 T. Edwards, *Gangraena* (1646), esp. i, p. 32, iii, p. 148; E. Pagitt, *Heresiography* (6th edn., 1662); J. Graunt, *Truths Victory against Heresie* (1645).
121 R. Parker, *An Exposition of the Powring out of the Fourth Vial*, ed. T. Gataker (1650); Liu, *Discord*, ch. 2; J. Durham, *A Commentarie Upon the Book of Revelation* (3rd edn, Amsterdam, 1660), pp. 707–12.
122 M. Cary, *The Resurrection of the Witness* (1648), pp. 98–9.

123 T. Collier, *A Discovery*, reprinted in A. S. P. Woodhouse, ed., *Puritanism and Liberty* (2nd edn, 1974), pp. 390–6.
124 H. Cary, *Memorials of the Great Civil War* (1842), ii, p. 42.
125 J. Simpson, *The Perfection of Justification* (1648), pp. 118, 133.
126 G. Cockayne, *Flesh Expiring, and the Spirit Inspiring* (1648), *passim*; Liu, *Discord*, pp. 60–1.
127 J. Owen, *The Shaking and Translation of Heaven and Earth* (1649), pp. 18–19.
128 F. Lisle, *The Kingdomes Divisions Anatomized* (1649), pp. 1, 11 and *passim*.
129 T. Banaster, *An Alarm to the World* (1649), sig. A2; Hill, *Puritanism and Revolution*, ch. 4; Capp, *Fifth Monarchy*, pp. 53, 151–3.
130 N. Holmes, *A Sermon, Preached before . . . Thomas Foote* (1650), p. 17; Owen, *Shaking*, pp. 39–42; Liu, *Discord*, pp. 62–8.
131 J. Salmon, *A Rout, A Rout* (1649), pp. 4, 13.
132 *A Declaration of the English Army Now in Scotland* (1650), reprinted in Woodhouse, *Puritanism*, pp. 474–8; W. Prynne, *A True and perfect Narrative* (1659), p. 77; Capp, *Fifth Monarchy*, pp. 54–5.
133 *Certain Queries*, in Woodhouse, *Puritanism*, pp. 242, 244, 246.
134 A. Coppe, *A Fiery Flying Roll* (1649), p. 2.
135 G. Winstanley, *A New-year's Gift* (1650), title-page (reprinted in C. Hill, ed., *Winstanley: The Law of Freedom* (Harmondsworth, 1973)).
136 W. Dell, *The Way of True Peace and Unity* (1649), sig. A3^v; *Certain Queries*, in Woodhouse, *Puritanism*, p. 242.
137 Liu, *Discord*, p. 71 and note.
138 Liu, *Discord*, pp. 68–70; Capp, *Fifth Monarchy*, pp. 54–5, 56–8.
139 Liu, *Discord*, pp. 70–4; Capp, *Fifth Monarchy*, pp. 58–62.
140 Liu, *Discord*, pp. 80–5; Capp, *Fifth Monarchy*, pp. 62–5. For the Barebones experiment see A. Woolrych, 'The Calling of Barebones Parliament', *English Historical Review*, lxxx (1965), pp. 492–513; Liu, *Discord*, ch. 4.
141 Speech of 4 July 1653, in *Oliver Cromwell's Letters and Speeches*, ed. T. Carlyle (1907 edn), iii, p. 218.
142 Speech of 4 September 1654, in *Letters and Speeches*, ed. Carlyle, iv, p. 28.
143 T. Goodwin, *A Sermon of the Fifth Monarchy* (1654), p. 3; Liu, *Discord*, pp. 119–27.
144 Capp, *Fifth Monarchy*, pp. 99–100; Liu, *Discord*, pp. 115–16.
145 J. Tillinghast, *Knowledge of the Times* (1654), sig. a3–^{v}, pp. 77–8.
146 *Calendar of State Papers, Domestic*, 1653–4, p. 306. See Capp, *Fifth Monarchy* chs. 5–8, for the movement's programme and history.
147 G. Fox, *The Vials of the Wrath of God* (1655), p. 8; J. Nayler, *The Lamb's War against the Man of Sin* (1658); Toon, *Puritans*, pp. 99–103; H. Barbour, *The Quakers in Puritan England* (1964), pp. 182–8.
148 The terms are Lamont's: *Godly Rule*, p. 25.
149 Cromwell to Goodson, October 1655, in *Letters and Speeches*, ed. Carlyle, iv, pp. 143–4; Capp, *Astrology*, p. 84.
150 *A Door of Hope* (1661), p. 8.
151 E. Hall, *Lingua Testium* (1651), title page and p. 43; Capp, *Fifth Monarchy*, p. 41.
152 M. McKeon, *Politics and Poetry in Restoration England* (1975), esp. ch. 8.
153 Capp, *Astrology*, pp. 174–9, and cf. pp. 251–3; W. Lamont, *Richard Baxter and the Millennium* (1979), ch. 1.
154 M. C. Jacob, *The Newtonians and the English Revolution 1689–1720* (Hassocks, Sussex, 1976), ch. 3 (Tillotson's comment is at p. 124); F. E. Manuel, *The Religion*

of Isaac Newton (Oxford, 1974), ch. 4.
155 Mede, *Works*, p. 829.
156 *A Door of Hope*, pp. 1, 13, 16; Jacob, *Newtonians*, p. 121.

MICHAEL MURRIN

5 Revelation and two seventeenth century commentators

In the early seventeenth century two prominent Protestant commentators analyzed the structure of Revelation. They were David Pareus and Joseph Mede. Both have been associated with Milton, who quoted and argued with Pareus, especially in the Divorce Tracts, and studied at Christ's when Mede was a fellow. Pareus and Mede have, however, an importance beyond Milton. Pareus was well-known in Calvinist circles; Mede, through his synchronisms and millenarianism, had a major influence on English thought, both during the Revolution and afterwards, in part because of the numerous publications of his student, Henry More (1614–87).[1] I will cite More, therefore, where he speaks for his teacher as well as himself. All three commentators pose questions interesting for literary criticism, questions of structure and imagery and of their interrelation.

One generation separated the work of Pareus and Mede. David Pareus (1548–1622) became Professor of Old Testament at Heidelberg in 1591, of the New Testament in 1602. He gave lectures on Revelation in 1609 and revised and published them in 1618, shortly before his death. Since he regularly cited other critics, his *Commentary* became a massive variorum which ran to nearly 600 pages in its English translation. Joseph Mede (1586–1638) became a fellow at Christ's College in 1613 and a lecturer in Greek. He then devoted most of his study to Revelation. He began with *Clavis apocalyptica* (1627), a table of synchronisms, and afterwards added commentaries to Revelation 4–14 (1632) and notes to the rest. Besides these publications, much of his correspondence and minor work concerned Revelation. In all his criticism equalled that of Pareus in bulk.[2]

The structure and imagery of Revelation caused problems for these commentators. The problems are extrinsic insofar as they involve the commentators' search for historical events which might correspond to the images of Revelation, intrinsic insofar as they concern the structure of the text itself. Mede and Pareus shared certain assumptions about patterns and imagery in Revelation, and about Protestant history and its relation to the prophecies in the text. The two critics, however, each manifest different interplay between ideology and method: Pareus tried to account for apocalyptic patterns aesthetically; Mede turned to philological study and from this deduced his structural system. I will try to indicate both the limits and the advantages of each commentator's approach in order to make it possible for the literary historian to assess clearly what Pareus and Mede achieved. I will make negative judgments on the basis of the critical method of the commentator, not on the basis of modern standards.

I STRUCTURAL PROBLEMS

I EXTRINSIC

Revelation both calls for structural analysis and at the same time tends to impede it. Extrinsically, this analysis concerns the relation of its prophecies to history. Revelation requires a reader to relate an oracle or an image to a set of historical particulars. It explicitly encourages this search by the angel's gloss in chapter 17, the chapter which provided Mede with a key to the whole book. John described the whore on the scarlet, seven-headed Beast; an angel explicates the image, part by part. The seven heads of the Beast are seven kings, five of whom are past, one present, and one to come. Its ten horns are likewise kings, who will reign one hour with the Beast (17.9–12). The manner of the gloss is traditional. In Daniel 2, Nebuchadnezzar dreams that he sees an idol made of various metals; the prophet explains the image part by part with a historical analysis similar to that which the angel uses in Revelation. Such oracles demand an extrinsic criticism.

At the same time Revelation poses two difficulties for this kind of analysis. After the manner of Daniel, many of the oracles are sequences. The seven seals, trumpets, and vials make a commentator relate these visions not to a particular historical situation or event but to sequences of events. He must ask what temporal series corresponds to the order and imagery of the seven seals. Such a procedure encourages even more disagreement than does the identification of a single prophecy with a particular historical event, and hence produces greater variety of interpretations. The commentator juxtaposes two series, one internal to the text, the other extrinsic and historical. He is liable to criticism both in his two series and in their juxtaposition. There are always weak links which betray the limits of his approach and justify yet another interpretative effort; hence, Revelation has one of the richest and most varied critical traditions in the West.

Revelation itself makes no specific applications of its sequences. The visions are timed with respect to one another, many specific numbers are given, but there are no references to historical time.[3] Daniel provides a contrast. The prophet tells Nebuchadnezzar that he is the gold head of the statue (2.38), and the commentator thus has a clear historical application, a point from which he can interpret the rest of the image. Revelation makes no such clear applications. The seven kings of 17.9–11 could be any kings. The Roman emperors of the first century AD would be the obvious choice, but even so the identification could vary. If the commentator began with Julius Caesar, the sixth ruler, the one contemporary with the prophecy, would be Nero. If the commentator started with Augustus, the sixth might be Galba or Vespasian, depending on his count. He might or might not include the generals who claimed the throne in the civil war which followed Nero's suicide. Revelation asks for a historical reading but gives no sure indications where the applications should be made, and readers have responded with many different answers. The spokesmen for Cromwell's army declared that Charles I was one of the ten horns of the Beast.[4]

The internal evidence suggests contrary historical directions. More remarks that interpreters agree that Revelation concerns both the early Church and the end of the world (*Ratio.* 40). The angel's gloss in 17 suggests the former. If five kings are past, then the sequence which the angel unravels for John must be contemporary with him. The frame of the book strengthens this sense. It begins with epistles to local churches and prefaces these with phrases intimating that its prophecies will be accomplished soon:

>Things which must shortly come to pass (1.1)
>
>For the time is at hand (1.3)
>
>I will come unto thee quickly (2.16)

The concluding chapter repeats all these phrases.[5] On the other hand, the book presents the grandest images from the Old Testament, images which could be literally fulfilled only at the end of time. All interpreters applied the concluding chapters to the end of the world. The Renaissance commentator had somehow to reconcile these two different times, and he also had to explain the vast period in between, by then fifteen centuries long. This middle time and the end became the focus of Protestant criticism.

For Protestants, Revelation had an immediate historical relevance. On the one hand, it served a polemical purpose; and on the other, it placed them in a historical situation close to the phenomena of the last times. The angel's gloss of chapter 17 encouraged the polemics, while the sense of urgency in the frame of the book persuaded interpreters that the last times were upon them. We will discuss each in turn.

The angel identifies the seven heads of the Beast spatially as well as temporally (17.9–10). They are seven hills or Rome, and Protestants had long applied this identification not to pagan but to papal Rome. Pareus and More gave the historical rationale. The conversion of the Roman Empire under Constantine turned the garden of the Church into a wilderness because the pagans simply transferred their customs to the new religion, especially polytheism with its many statues, chapels, and holy days (Pareus, 193; More, MG. 168–9; SP. 322–35). What More called 'pagano-Christianity' resulted, and the many satiric allusions to idolatry in Revelation referred to this period of ecclesiastical history.[6] The identification of the Beast with Rome served more than polemical purposes, however, and was so important that our commentators never considered changing it.

By this equation Protestants indicated that their situation recapitulated that of the original audience of Revelation, the Christians under the threat of persecution in the Roman Empire. Protestants generally felt menaced by the Catholic powers, a sense exaggerated during the Thirty Years' War, the period when Mede was writing. Apocalypse as a genre serves such crises. It suggests that friendly powers from another world will intervene in this one and solve its seemingly irremediable problems. Or, as Richard Bauckham explains, 'The apocalyptist looked to the future for a satisfying end to a half-told story. Only by seeing past and present in the light of the End did he find it possible to justify the ways of God to men.'[7] More argued that God wants his people to see the future, so that they do not suffer blindly (*Ratio.* 43). Protestants felt that the prophecies were directed at them, and the repetition of the historical situation allowed them to take the apocalyptic sense of urgency literally.

Both commentators assumed that history was nearing its end. Pareus thought his own were the last times (479); Mede considered England to be Laodicea, the last of the seven churches in historical time (*Works.* 1.296), and wondered whether Gustavus Adolphus was the fourth vial (*Works.* 3.483–4, 528–9). In the first half of the seventeenth century many Englishmen felt that history was near its end.

This sense of the book exaggerated the problems of its time being both early and late. In Revelation, short measurements apply to future time. In 17, the angel gives two: the seventh king will come but for a little while (10); and the ten kings will reign with the Beast but one hour (12). In the next chapter we learn that Babylon was destroyed in one hour (18.10, 19), and an angel emphasizes the suddenness of this execution with a gesture. He throws a millstone into the sea, saying: 'As with the millstone, so will Babylon be thrown' (18.21)[8] The story of the two witnesses is more explicit. The Gentiles will tread the outer court forty-two months (11.2); the bodies of the witnesses will lie unburied $3\frac{1}{2}$ days (11.9). All these references involve the Beast, which overthrows the whore and wars with the witnesses. If the Beast and the whore referred to Papal Rome, however, the brief time spans did not apply. Pareus struggled to explain how the Beast could reign briefly in Revelation and a millenium in history (433). Mede and More had the same problem. Moreover, the Catholic revival made it difficult to explain how Babylon would fall suddenly.

The postulated historical pattern did not fit the internal one. The seemingly evident equation of the whore and Beast with Papal Rome made it difficult to understand the rest. The dissonance between the patterns accounts for most of the aberrant interpretations made by our commentators; it generated a pressure to rearrange the internal structure of Revelation in accordance with the preconceived historical model. This most evident source of confusion, however, is not the most instructive for a literary critic. The internal structures of Revelation pose difficulties which any commentator must consider, whether he concerns himself with historical application or not.

2 INTRINSIC

Besides the problem of historical application, Revelation poses another difficulty, that of its own structure. Daniel, Enoch, and Isaiah were collections of diverse oracles, but John links his together, makes of them a kind of 'plot'. With the exception of the epistles (Revelation 2-3) it is difficult to detach individual oracles from the rest of the book, and even the epistles share phrases and images.[9] This system creates a critical dilemma unlike those in Isaiah or Daniel. Pareus' outline illustrates the problem:

Section	Chapter	Content
1	1-3	epistles
2	4-7	seals
3	8-11	trumpets
4	12-14	beasts
5	15-16	vials
6	17-19	Babylon
7	20-22	New Jerusalem

A seven-fold division had been popular since Bede, yet a critic could question many of Pareus' division. First, certain images recur. The heavens, for example, darken at the sixth seal and at the fourth trumpet. Secondly, the same figures appear in more than one sequence. Pareus himself argued that the trumpeter angels take part in all the later visions. They pour out the vials, and one of their number both introduces the final visions and talks to John at the end (96, 406, 580). The Beast similarly appears in Sections 3 to 6. Most difficult of all, the sequences overlap. The trumpets are the most evident example. After the sixth trumpet, John tells of the opened scroll and the two witnesses. Two chapters, therefore, separate the sixth from the seventh trumpet. Further, a numerical scheme of three woes links the story of the witnesses to the trumpets. The earthquake which destroys part of Jerusalem is the Second Woe, and the seventh trumpet itself the Third. Pareus classed all this diverse material under Section Three, but Mede started a new division where the new matter is introduced (chapter 10).

The system of links affects both meaning and structure. It affects meaning directly by simple repetition. Does the darkened sky or the Beast in its various appearances signify the same thing? Or do they have different meanings because of different oracular contexts? Mede and More normally assumed that a symbol always signifies the same thing, while Pareus allowed it to mean different things at different times.[10]

The system likewise affects hypotheses about structure. Mede, for example, divided Revelation at the scenes where a heavenly figure commands John to go forth and prophesy. He thus divided the book at chapters 4 and 10. The latter division, however, cuts across the trumpet sequence. More defended this choice by the claim that the seventh trumpet is itself the opened book which John eats (*MG*. 176–7). Here, however, he assumed what he had to prove. Pareus in contrast had put all the trumpets in one section – although this in turn ignored the scenes in which John is ordered to prophesy. Such hypothetical structures affect interpretation. For example, despite the fact that Mede normally required an image to have a single meaning, he assumed that the trumpets follow the seals chronologically, and so a repeated image, like the darkened sky, had different applications. Here structure clearly controls meaning.[11]

The interlinked system of Revelation requires a commentator to formulate some kind of structural hypothesis *before* he turns to history. While it is difficult to relate a system of sevens to a historical series, it is much more difficult if the pattern of sevens interrelates with other patterns, perhaps with the whole book. In this sense all interpretation is structural and the source of confusion is double. It comes either from the juxtaposition of oracular and historical sequences or from hypotheses about internal structure. We shall see examples of both.

II COMMON ASSUMPTIONS

1 INTRINSIC CRITERIA

Our two commentators agreed generally on the structure of Revelation and on its methods of signification. They further shared a polemical historical pattern which they set parallel to the internal structure. They related each part of the internal pattern directly to a part in the extrinsic pattern and thus made a set of one-to-one correspondences.

For them Revelation had a discontinuous structure. Pareus was the most extreme, as we can see from his outline. He assumed the book to be a collection of seven visions which occurred at different times and which presupposed different scenes, now a wilderness, now a seashore (20, 364). Mede's editor argued that the same assumption underlay Mede's synchronisms:

> His observing things in distant places of the *Apocalypse* to *Synchronize* and belong to the same time: whence he was well assured That it was a false *Hypothesis* and a fundamental Error in any Commentators to think That all the *Prophecies* and *Visions* in this Mysterious Book are placed in such an order as is agreeable to the order of time wherein they were fulfill'd, or That the *Events* succeeded one another in the same *Series* and order as the *Visions* do. (General Preface 3.1.)

Mede, however, accommodated the 'plot' of the book much more than Pareus did. He divided Revelation 4–22 into the sealed and opened books (4–10, 10–22), each part of which covered the same chronology, the sealed from a political viewpoint, the opened from an ecclesiastical one. He thus made two divisions, in each of which he followed the order of the plot.[12]

Pareus and Mede did agree, however, that the symbols were collective. Pareus said that the dragon of Revelation 12 is a type for all tyrants who persecute the Church (256–7), and he regularly assumed that the Beast signified any Pope after the sixth century. Mede read the seven heads of the Beast not as kings but as types of Roman government (*Works*. 3.524–5). More called this symbolism *henopoeia*: 'The collection of a multitude of individuals into the show of one standing Individual.' More cited Daniel 7, where the four Beasts are kingdoms, and inferred that, if a beast symbolizes a whole people over a period of time, its head or horns refer to a succession of individuals (*SP*. 218–19). The story of the witnesses exemplified this theory of symbols: for Pareus the two witnesses were all who opposed Rome; for Mede they were churches.[13]

This approach to symbols was common among Protestants[14] and had a previous history as old as Christianity. Paul provided the scriptural basis when he equated Hagar and Sarah with Jews and Christians (Galatians 4.21–31) and buildings with Christian communities (2 Corinthians 6.16–18; Ephesians 2.19–22). Tyconius applied this method to Revelation, and his influence, most potent in the early Middle Ages, never died out. There is a tension, as we shall see, between Tyconian exegesis and the normal type of gloss in apocalyptic. More, for example, misread Daniel, who equates the beasts and horns with kings,[15] and the angel of Revelation 17 makes the kind of equations which Daniel made. The Tyconian reading is, however, a logical development from apocalyptic in that Daniel has angels preside over nations (Michael over the Jews, an angel over the Persians, another over the Greeks 10.13, 21). Here an executive function becomes a literary equation: an angel signifies a community.

2 EXTRINSIC CRITERIA

The extrinsic criteria which these commentators shared concerned history and its relation to Revelation. They assumed roughly the same historical pattern, though they saw this pattern symbolized differently in Revelation. For Pareus the millenium began after the fall of Jerusalem and ended with Gregory VII (73-1073). During this time the countermovements were the Imperial persecutions (64-313) and the rise of Antichrist east and west (Mohammed and Pope Boniface III in 606).[16] The High Middle Ages corresponded with the reign of Antichrist, while the Church hid in the wilderness. The Beast received its wound at the Protestant Reformation (Revelation 13.3) and will be destroyed in the near future. All seven sections of Revelation referred to this same scheme, whatever the narrative methods or symbols. Like Pareus, Mede contrasted the period of the primitive Church, which worshipped God without idolatry, with the reversion to idol worship in the Middle Ages, but he assumed that the change occurred in the fifth century. Mede compared the former period to the inner court of the Temple which John is told to measure, while the outer court, unmeasured and given over to the Gentiles, symbolized the period of idolatry (11.1-2; *Works* 3.478-9). Mede's student More, therefore, often talked of the 'symmetral' and 'asymmetral' times. Teacher and pupil both emphasized the Protestant Reformation, when the two witnesses put away their mourning garments and began to rejoice only to provoke a new attack by the Beast (*Works* 4.765-6; Letter 17). Pareus differed in details from the other two, but the general pattern was the same and was traditional.[17] Essential variation came rather through the equation between symbol and event, since the commentators related the historical patterns differently to Revelation.

The historical schema manifests an iconoclastic attitude. More here was the most explicit, for he made the concept part of his definition of the Church (*Dialogues* 40). He and Mede both interpreted the three angels of Revelation 14 as signifying protests against idolatry. As Mede explained, the first angel makes image worship a crime, the second damns the author (Rome), and the third the followers.[18] The strength of this pattern is that it responds to the many attacks on idolatry in Revelation, especially in the episodes of the Beast's image (13-14) and the whore (17-18).

This pattern is likewise polemical.[19] Revelation justified the break with Rome, giving divine authority to the Reformation. Polemics accounted for the popularity of the book and for a certain conservatism in its interpretation. Once

Protestants had re-evaluated ecclesiastical history, the new version became a fixed pattern. A truly different historical reading, like that of Grotius, would have destroyed its popularity.[20] The extrinsic pattern, therefore, had more importance than any internal structure which a commentator might find. The story of the witnesses provides an example. The setting for the story is Jerusalem, where the Temple stood and where Jesus was crucified (11.8), but Pareus and Mede read it as applying to Rome, despite John's equation of Rome with Babylon elsewhere.[21]

This kind of interpretation presupposed an innate link between prophecy and history. Commentators found the fulfillment of prophecy in chronicle history, and some, like Ralegh and More, argued that prophecy itself was but history of the future. It followed that the historical should parallel the internal pattern of Revelation. After Foxe, morever, the commentator expected each image in Revelation to have a single, specific fulfillment.[22] The Beast symbolized Papal Rome, not two or three things at once. Pareus regularly read a single extrinsic sense of the text, though in places he grudgingly allowed for alternate points of view (165). Mede made the same choice for philological reasons. He could recover the meaning of a symbol provided that he assumed a uniform signification in different writers. Then he could compare the several uses and discover the sense (*Works* 4.759: Letter 14). If an earthquake symbolizes a political event in Isaiah, it cannot be eschatological in Revelation. Polyvalency would have made his philological method inoperative. His student More, however, had to retreat from this position. He found polyvalency in the text and tried to accommodate it. Here More differed from the others, for whom the suggestion of more than one meaning normally indicated critical uncertainty.

The extrinsic criteria fit together. Criticism of Revelation served Protestant polemic; it validated a historical pattern. Univocality was necessary and desirable, since polyvalency would point to more than one place in the pattern or to more than one pattern and, therefore, confuse the debate. The whore could not be pagan as well as Christian Rome or some future entity. Nor could she, like Duessa in *The Faerie Queene*, signify a philosophical as well as a historical reality. There was a single extrinsic pattern, and this was the history of the Church and her war with Antichrist.

III DAVID PAREUS OR THE AESTHETIC APPROACH

Pareus applied literary categories to the text of Revelation. He thought that the book had a dramatic structure. He considered it a tragedy, which, like other tragedies, mingled feigned with serious matter for delight. The fictive material set up the dramatic form and included all the choruses (26).

Pareus pointed to Origen, who had read the Song of Songs as an interlude acted by four persons (453). Pareus similarly explained biblical literature through Greek generic categories. He deduced the literary model for Revelation from Greek tragedy but derived the mechanics of his theory from comedy, as was common in the period.[23] Comic phrases, therefore, signal the end of single plays (86, 398–9), and the performers conclude each act with song, to refresh the minds of the beholders (366). John imagines the performance as it occurs on stage. He describes a heavenly stage in Chapter 4 (86), and like the presenters in Renaissance drama, angels introduce each new play (371).

Pareus assumed that the whole consists of seven little plays. Section 6 provides an example. It is the tragedy of Antichrist:

Act	Chapter	Topic
1	17	The whore and the Beast
2	18	The burning of the whore
3	19.1–1–11	The marriage of the Lamb
4	19.12–21	Armageddon

Each play has the same subject matter and ends with the Final Judgment, but the focus varies. Playlets 1 and 2 concern the seven Churches, 5 and 6 the reign of Antichrist (84).

The aesthetic model was attractive, and others used it. Among the English there were Foxe, Broughton, and Brightman before Pareus, and there were Mede and Milton among others after. Mede called the setting a stage, especially the vision of Revelation 4 (*Works* 4.791: Letter 34). He had once thought of the sealed book (Revelation 4–10) as a picture book, but decided that not all the visions could be visualized. The seventh seal was a sequence not visible all at once, nor could John see into the book. Mede concluded that the visions described in the book were performed as drama for John and the other heavenly spectators. He drew an analogy from academic drama, where there were advisors with books for the actors. Revelation was thus a play and the sealed book a prompter's text (*Works* 3.574). Milton twice cited Pareus directly, when he talked of biblical tragedy in *Reason of Church Government* and when he justified *Samson Agonistes*. Nor was this aesthetic concern limited to the English. A decade after Pareus John Alsted talked of protasis, epitasis, and catastrophe for the drama of Antichrist.[24]

Pareus' analogy was attractive because Revelation does affect us dramatically, as much through the overall 'plot', however, as through the individual visions. The ending of each series is delayed. The Lamb opens the seventh seal only after a chapter of suspense (7), during which angels seal the servants of

God and there is celebration in heaven. Two chapters intervene between the sixth and the seventh trumpet. Moreover, each series or story closes inconclusively; the seals in silence, the trumpets in a proclamation, the story of the Beasts (Revelation 12–14) parabolically. The story of the witnesses and the seven vials stops with partial destruction of the enemy, and after a great battle of Chapter 19, the dragon is bound, though not eliminated. And there is a pattern of escalation in the sevens. The fourth seal brings death to a *quarter* of the land; the first four trumpets to a *third* of land, sea, rivers, and stars; the second and third vials turn *all* water into blood, and every living thing in the sea perishes. In this sense the whole book is dramatic, since each of its sections forces us to look to the end, which is the end of all things, constantly suggested to us by grandiose imagery and constantly delayed.

Pareus did not consider the structure of the whole. He perceived the dramatic quality of the 'plot' but read it discontinuously. Pareus' notion of playlets, therefore, distorted the text. He made strained act divisions, as with the seals (106):

Act	Topic
1	The four horsemen
2	The fifth seal, where the martyrs under the altar are comforted
3	The sixth seal, when Antichrist darkens the sky
4	The seventh seal, when Antichrist is contained and Final Judgment comes

To maintain this plot he had to assume an alternating order for Acts 3 and 4. Act 3 was 6.12–14, where the sky darkens, and 7.2–8, where the saved are sealed. Act 4 was 6.15–17, where the damned suffer punishment on earth, and 7.9 ff., where the good receive their reward in heaven. Pareus assumed that the visions corresponded to stage performances but had to rearrange the order to achieve his four act structure, or condense drastically. In chapter 20 he crammed three acts into nine verses (499).

This imposed structure in turn determined interpretation. Pareus was an allegorical structuralist: order determined meaning. The second in a sequence had the same signification regardless of its imagery. The seals and trumpets exemplify this approach most clearly because Pareus constructed an elaborate set of parallels where images clashed. The second trumpet corresponds to the second seal, so both symbolized the Imperial persecutions (160). The two images are disparate – a burning mountain and a rider on a red horse – but share a common color. The third trumpet and the third seal, on the other hand, have nothing in common but position: the star which falls into the rivers and poisons the water, and the man with scales who rides a black horse. The images may differ, but for Pareus they both symbolized heresy. The fourth trumpet and seal clash the most. By its image the fourth trumpet corresponds to the sixth seal, for they both have the sky grow dark. Pareus once more, however, had the fourth trumpet mean the same as the fourth seal, where Death rides his horse. They pointed to the rise of Antichrist.[25]

Pareus' internal criteria worked against each other. On the one hand, order determined meaning. On the other, he had to rearrange the order. His other problems grew out of the imposed extrinsic pattern.

We have already sketched his historical schema, and it is enough here to indicate how it affected the text. First, it clashed with the short time measurements in Revelation. Pareus, therefore, took definite numbers like $3\frac{1}{2}$ and 42 indefinitely.[26] Yet he accepted a literal millennium, fixing 73 rather than 69 for the fall of Jerusalem so that he could make it correspond to the accession of Gregory VII in 1073. This assumption made Pareus read against the text. He had Antichrist or the Beast begin his rise to power in 606 (506–10), but in Revelation the Beast is thrown into the lake of fire before the millennium and the binding of the dragon. The internal structure resisted both his dramatic model and the external historical pattern to which he compared it.

IV JOSEPH MEDE OR THE PHILOLOGICAL APPROACH

In contrast to Pareus, Mede tried to make the internal structure of Revelation the objective basis of his whole interpretation. He began by looking to Israel for help rather than to Greece with its aesthetic traditions. Through philological methods he tried to recover a lost system of symbols. He studied all the uses of a word or phrase in the Bible, as well as the translations in the Targum and the Septuagint. For the New Testament he argued that its Greek recalled either the Septuagint or Semitic usage. He added to this philology a knowledge of ancient history and customs, a familiarity with the rabbinical tradition and with oriental dream lore, which he read to determine how images were interpreted.[27]

His exegesis developed from his philology. The meaning of a term, metaphor, or image was determined by the way in which it was anciently interpreted. The prophets, for example, discussed politics through images of nature. The cosmos symbolized the state (*Works* 3.448–9). Wind storms thus referred to wars (3.454), hail to foreign invasions (3.460), and images of the end signified the ruin of a particular political entity. Isaiah saw in Lucifer's fall that of the King of Babylon (3.465), and a new heaven and a new earth referred to a new kingdom (3.449).

Through these recovered meanings Mede interpreted the setting of Revelation. Its heaven recalls the camp of the Israelites in the desert. God has his 'throne' or tent in the middle. Before it are the seven-branched candelabrum (the seven lamps), the altar of incense, and the ablution basin or sea of glass (3.437–9). Beyond are the tribes, symbolized by the four animals.[28] Action in such a setting is ritualistic, and the vials, for example, recall a dedication ceremony (3.590–1). A cloud fills the building and none can enter, a phenomenon which occurred when Moses first erected the Tent (Exodus 40.34–7) and when Solomon dedicated the First Temple (2 Chronicles 5.13, 7.1–21). Action directed outwards from the 'camp' can likewise be ritualistic. The seven trumpets recall the ritual of war. At Jericho the priests circled the city seven times and blew their trumpets seven times on the seventh day (*Works* 5.910).

Perhaps the most spectacular example of Mede's exegesis was his discussion of the seventh seal. Its silence is that of the incense offering. Afterwards the angel tosses the censer to earth, and voices and thunder proceed from the sanctuary. That is, the oracle replies, since in Hebrew thunder and voice are sometimes synonymous, and thunder alone remained the voice of Yahweh after the exile (3.458–9). God responds favorably to the prayer, and the seven trumpeters come out to execute His vengeance. The seven trumpets are thus part of the seventh seal.

The synchronisms followed logically from a philological definition of symbols. Mede recovered the meaning of a symbol by comparing its various occurrences. To do this he had to assume that the meaning was constant. If a falling star had a political meaning in Isaiah, it would have a political meaning in Revelation, where it lacked a gloss. Hence repetition of an image indicated a return to the same topic. The 144 000 sealed Israelites of Revelation 7 and the 144 000 virgins of 14 had the same application, as did the Beast in its many appearances. This repetition in turn suggested that certain actions were synchronized. The Beast fights the witnesses in chapter 11 and is associated with the whore in 17. Therefore, the whore and the witnesses also had to relate. One set of synchronisms generated another, and ultimately extended to the whole book. The result was an elaborate schema (see plate on p. 138).

The synchronisms are the literal structure of Revelation. They are not an interpretation but the rule and ground for an interpretation (*Works* 3.581–2). They can be refuted only by the letter of the text.[29]

Mede had a consistency and rigor in his method not often found among commentators or literary critics. His philological study of old symbols led by logical stages to the table of synchronisms. The whole complex structure came out of his method; none of it depended on preconceived interpretations. Mede therefore considered his work objective, yet its objectivity was compromised because he did not always follow his method in his practical criticism.

First of all, the new methodology did not produce new results. Mede used it

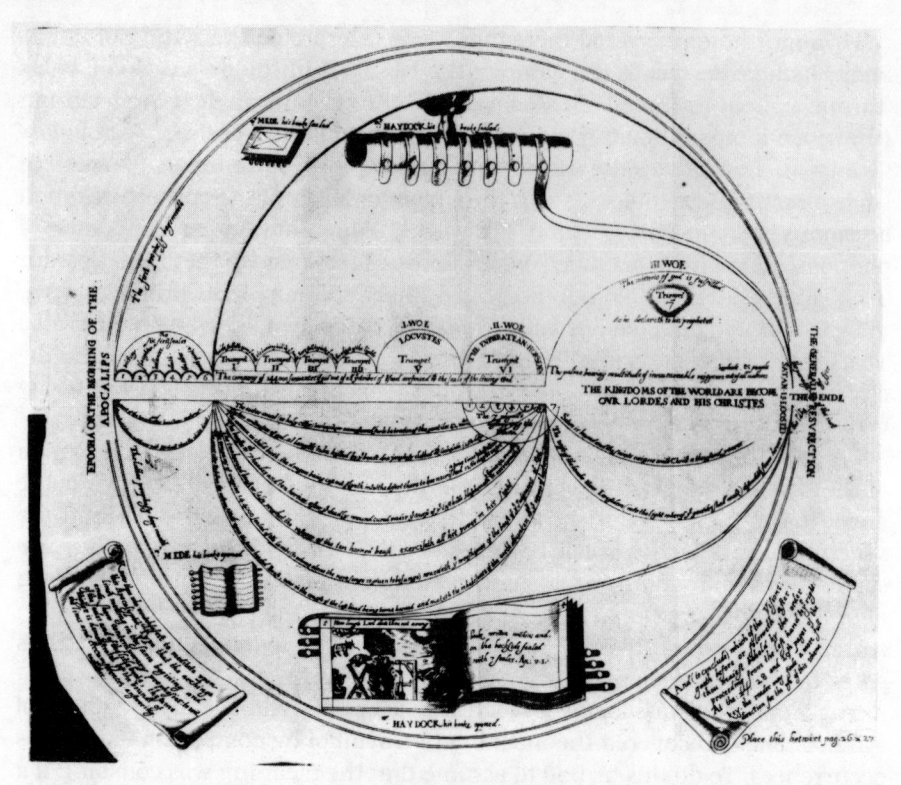

Joseph Mede's Chart of Synchronisms. Reproduced from *The Kitto Bible* by permission of The Huntington Library, San Marino, California

to reinforce standard readings. He acknowledged that earlier commentators had equated the seventh seal with all seven trumpets (*Works* 3.551), and his other specific readings were likewise traditional. Victorinus and Andrew of Caesarea had long ago applied the seals to the history of the Roman Empire; Luther put the Saracens in the sixth trumpet; and Andreas Osiander had equated the five heads of the Scarlet Beast (17.10) with five forms of Roman government.[30] In the specifics of his interpretation Mede differed little from Pareus or other Protestant commentators.

His overall scheme was likewise traditional and approached a chronological sequence. The seals and trumpets concerned mostly early history, the vials the present and future. Chronological readings had been common since Nicholas of Lyra. Luther did such an interpretation of Revelation, and his example encouraged other Protestants. Major critics like Foxe, Brightman, and Alsted all espoused some form of diachronic exegesis,[31] and Mede would be followed by others.

Mede's conservatism helps to explain his influence. Scholars recently have stressed Mede's millenarianism and its effect during the Revolution, a topic too complicated for discussion here.³² Just as important, however, was his justification of the standard reading of Revelation. In the hands of Alcazar and Grotius the new philology was destroying the prophetic status of the book. They applied Revelation to a dim Imperial past, irrelevant for Christians of the seventeenth century. Mede used philological methods but maintained that the book still justified the Reformation and concerned the present and future. He thus preserved Revelation for many diverse thinkers and activists of the 1640s and 1650s, and he did a long range service for Protestant polemic. His pupil More could attack Grotius with the assurance that he argued from an objective basis. Mede's readings remained useful for another century.³³

They also affected Milton. Mede's ritual analysis of Revelation provided a model for the heavenly scenes in *Paradise Lost*. The poet drew on the same book for these scenes, and he understood John the way Mede did. Mede led Milton behind the scenes in Revelation to the ritual of the Tent and the Temple. The poet added to these sources Ezekiel's initial vision and out of the combination made his heaven.

Mede's new methods, however influential, did not always lead to traditional interpretations. Where they clashed, he chose the old readings. This adjustment appears clearly in his discussion of the Beast and the other monsters of Revelation 12–13, 17–18. These chapters had particularly attracted attention by the late sixteenth century, and More would later do a joint exposition of 13 and 17.³⁴ To understand Mede's reading, we must first review the 'plot'.

These chapters concern the history of the enemy. The dragon, defeated in heaven and foiled in its pursuit of the woman (chapter 12), calls up from the sea a Beast to carry on the struggle. This Beast has seven heads and ten horns, and John associates it with another figure, at one time a two-horned beast, at another a whore or a false prophet. Many Protestants equated the seven-headed Beast with secular power and assumed that the other, whatever its shape, referred to the Papacy. Mede accepted these identifications.³⁵ In chapter 13 one of the heads of the seven-headed Beast is wounded but recovers, a miracle which occasions a cult orchestrated by the two-horned beast, which sets up a statue of the seven-headed Beast (chapter 13). In chapters 17–18 the seven-headed Beast turns on its companion, now pictured as a whore, and destroys her.

Mede read chapters 12–13 sequentially. The dragon signified the pagan Roman Empire, and chapter 13 concerned the persecution of sects which began in the High Middle Ages. So far this reading was traditional, but Mede went on to identify the dragon, the Beast, and its statue. The wounding of the Beast was the dragon's defeat in 12, and the birth of the Beast was the healing of its head, which occurred when the two-horned beast set up the statue. Mede's contemporaries pointed out that such a reading destroyed chronological sequence of the kind that Mede himself assumed, and he admitted the charge.³⁶

On 17 Mede again followed tradition, but the old equation of the heads of the Beast with types of government violated his philological approach (*Works* 3.524–5, 597–8). Mede contended that the Bible must gloss itself. In no other way could its symbols be clarified. For Revelation, chapter 17 provided the necessary gloss, and it was the key to Mede's synchronisms and thus to his whole explication. Yet here he denied the gloss and read against the text, for the interpreter angel identifies the heads with kings, not with types of government. Mede may have sensed his problem. He invariably assumed the angel's gloss of 17 but never gave a formal explication of the chapter. The text might have forced him to change either his interpretation or his principles.

We can see the extrinsic reason for this when we ask why Mede merged dragon, Beast, and image. The blur emphasized the other monster, the two-horned beast which heals the wounded head, makes an image, and establishes a cult. This beast was the Papacy. Similarly, the misreading of the angel's gloss in chapter 17 maintained this equation. If the seven heads are seven kings, there is no allusion to the Pope, but if the seven heads are types of government, then the Papacy could be included. Polemics accounts for Mede's departure from his own method and indicates the limits of his own interpretation.

There is also an intrinsic reason for this blur, and it concerns method. Mede assumed that a symbol had a consistent meaning in the Bible, and he probably considered the dragon and the Beast close enough as images to require the same interpretation. The angel's gloss of chapter 17, however, is polyvalent. The seven heads of the Beast are both hills and kings. Polyvalency strains Mede's method. If a symbol can mean more than one thing, then without further evidence the commentator cannot assume uniformity of meaning. Without such an assumption, it becomes difficult to work out a grammar of symbols. Polyvalency upset Mede's critical approach, and it was this problem which his pupil More tried to answer.

More began with an exegesis of chapter 17 and accepted polyvalency. He called it *henopoeia* of the second kind, where 'things of different natures are comprised under one Type'.[37] The angel interprets the heads of the Beast twice. They symbolize a place and a succession of rulers. More understood this polyvalency by another standard theory, that of type and antitype. He termed the basic figure of Revelation *Israelismus*, or the use of Jewish symbols for Christian events. Its logic depended upon the figural nature of the Old Testament. Where in the Old Testament a type prefigured an event in the New, a type in Revelation anticipated events which occur between the two comings of Christ. The distinction was not chronological, since Old Testament types could prefigure both the New Testament and later ecclesiastical history. The Bondage in Egypt anticipated the Imperial persecutions; the plagues, the sufferings of Christians under an Antichristian government; and the Passage of the Red Sea, the Reformation.[38] More drew no examples from Gospel events. He limited this typology to the Old Testament and to Revelation.

More had a strong case, since Revelation, more than any other book of the New Testament, uses Old Testament imagery. Mede had argued that the setting of Revelation presumed the tent ritual of Exodus, and scholars commonly pointed to the Egyptian plagues as a model for the vials. More added Revelation 15.2–4, where the victors sing the canticle of Moses by the glassy sea. It indicated the escape of the Reformed communities from Rome.[39] Exodus clarified the thinking of Revelation: the repeated series of sevens re-enacted the deliverance from Egypt.

This comparison may further have suggested to More his Pauline reading of the text, for it was Paul who had interpreted the deliverance from Egypt allegorically and had drawn equations between that event and his own day.[40] Two occurrences, widely separated in time, illuminate each other, type to antitype. More guessed that John had done the same in Revelation. Unfortunately, the angel in chapter 17 does not use that kind of interpretation. The image in both its meanings refers to a contemporary reality, the city and government of Rome.

The symbol may be polyvalent, the allegory is not. The angel in both his interpretations points to the same thing, and the two meanings together make that application more specific. Pareus and Mede were faithful to the angel's gloss when they insisted on a single political exegesis. All three commentators disagreed with the angel when they tried to read the symbol in the tradition of Paul and Tyconius. Its heads do not stand for collectives, nor is it a type or antitype.

VI CONCLUSION

Pareus and Mede had two difficulties with Revelation. Their assumptions about its symbolism did not quite apply, and they assumed an extrinsic or historical pattern which controlled their interpretations. On the other hand, they had a clear sense of how the patterns in Revelation relate to history, and Mede discovered that in certain cases symbol and pattern were the same. We can see these relationships best if we begin with the glosses in Revelation itself.

John makes specific equations: seven stars for seven angels, seven candlesticks for seven Asian churches, seven lamps or eyes for the seven spirits of God, an inscribed pillar for a good man, and the dragon for Satan (Revelation 1.20, 4.5, 5.6, 3.12, 12.9). The angel's gloss of 17.9–10 is of the same kind: seven heads for seven hills or seven kings. Two of these glosses presuppose temporal sequence: a good man *will be* a pillar; the sequence of seven kings began in the past and will be completed in the future. Here is the schema:

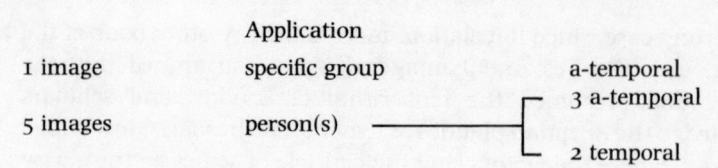

	Application	
1 image	specific group	a-temporal
5 images	person(s)	⎡ 3 a-temporal
		⎣ 2 temporal

Pareus and Mede took part of this system. They assumed that symbols concerned groups in time. They did not follow the normal mode of signification, however, where one star stands for one angel, without any temporal specification; and their precise version had no actual equivalent in the glosses. John never applies a symbol to a group *in time*. Yet the two commentators basically followed the method of the glosses when they insisted that one image have one application. This principle includes even the angel's polyvalent gloss. Pareus and Mede also recognized that John's arrangement of images required patterns. In the seals, trumpets, and vials, our commentators looked for similar sequences in history. In such cases images led directly to structure.

For Mede the angel's gloss of chapter 17 suggested that structure underlay even discrete images. The heads of the Beast made a series of the same kind as the seals or trumpets. Mede then applied this analysis to Chapter 11 and turned the arrangement of the Temple into a historical sequence.[41] Here the two problems which troubled Pareus and Mede became one, and an image resolved itself into a structure.

Pareus and Mede recognized that images in Revelation fit into patterns, and that these image patterns require a one-to-one correlation with an extrinsic historical pattern. Their version of that extrinsic pattern was polemical but correct insofar as it accounted for the iconoclasm in the book. They further perceived that any analysis must be structural, and their hypotheses were influential. Pareus worked out a dramatic pattern, and Mede developed his synchronisms. Both affected Milton, and through him us.

NOTES

1 For their influence see Wilhelm Bousset's 'Einleitung' to his edition, *Die Offenbarung Johannis* (Göttingen, 1966 reprint of the 1906 ed.), pp. 90–1, 100–1, and Joseph Anthony Wittreich, Jr, *Visionary Poetics* (San Marino, 1979), pp. 20–2, 38. For Mede alone see B. S. Capp, *Fifth Monarchy Men* (Totowa, 1972), pp.29, 45–6, 191, 223–4; Katharine R. Firth, *The Apocalyptic Tradition in Reformation Britain 1530–1645* (Oxford, 1979), pp. 203, 233, 245. Henry More's publications on Revelation include parts of *An Explanation of the Grand Mystery of Godliness* (1660), most of the *Synopsis prophetica* (1664), the second volume of the *Divine Dialogues* (1668), the *Illustration of Those Two Abstruse Books in Holy Scripture, the Book of Daniel, and the Revelation of St. John* (1685), and the *Paralipomena prophetica* (1685).

He also wrote three works solely on Revelation: the *Visionum apocalypticarum ratio synchronistica tabulis synchronisticis* (1666), the *Exposition of the Seven Epistles to the Seven Churches* (1669), and the *Apocalypsis apocalypseos; or the Revelation of St. John the Divine Unveiled* (1680). W. Bousset, *Die Offenbarung Johannis*, p. 90, gives 1666 for the *Ratio*. I cite from the Latin text in the *Opera theologica* (1674), where the title page refers to it as a new work. I will use the following abbreviations for More: *MG* (*Mystery of Godliness*), *SP* (*Synopsis prophetica*), *Dialogues*, *Exposition*, *Ratio*, and *Apoc. Apoc.*

2 For Pareus I use *A Commentary upon the Divine Revelation of the Apostle and Evangelist John*, trans. Elias Arnold (Amsterdam, 1644). Mede's *Clavis* and *Commentationes* are Volume 3 of the *Works* (1672), 418–32, 433–537. At pp. 541–79, 581–605 the volume also includes the *Opuscula nonnula* (his controversies over the *Clavis* and *Commentationes*) and the *Remains*, which except for Chapter 9 are the letters he wrote between 1627 and 1632, while he was preparing the *Commentationes*. They were first published posthumously in 1650. Other letters are in *Works*, 4, Letters 3, 5–22, 27–30, 32, 34, 39–40, 44–5, 63–4, 74–5, 89–92, 95. There is also a sermon in *Works* 1.52 and other material in 5.3, 5, 7–8, 10–12. Richard More translated the *Clavis* and *Commentationes* into English in 1634 (the date of his Preface), and Paul Testart did a French translation. Mede had to tell Testart, however, that he was forbidden another edition or any translation of the *Clavis* (*Works*, 4.793–4). He did not explain why. More's English translation did not appear until 1642.

3 This is More's argument (*Ratio*, 34). He points elsewhere to one contemporary allusion (Revelation 2.13), the reference to Antipas, Bishop of Pergamum, who was martyred in the tenth year of Domitian (*SP*, 349–50). More uses this to date the composition of Revelation. He does not suggest that it helps determine the events in the visions. According to Gerhard von Rad the apocalyptic writer normally veils his own standpoint in time (*Old Testament Theology*, trans. D. M. G. Stalker [1965] 2.305).

4 Declaration of 1 August, 1650, cited by William M. Lamont, *Godly Rule* (1969), 136.

5 Revelation, 22.6–7, 10, 20. The references also occur within the visions. At 6.11 the souls under the altar are told to wait a little time, and at 12.12 a voice warns the inhabitants of the earth that the dragon is in rage because he has little time. After the millennium the devil will be loosed only for a short time (20.3).

6 Besides the evident satire of 13–14, there is the whore of 17–18, whom More correctly identifies as an Old Testament image for idolatry (*SP*.256).

7 Richard Bauckham, *Tudor Apocalypse* (Appleford, 1978), 116; John J. Collins, 'The Jewish Apocalypses', in *Semeia*, 14 (1979), 27.

8 My own translation. The Authorized version emphasizes rather the violence of the gesture: 'Thus with violence shall that great city Babylon be thrown down.'

9 Adela Yarbro Collins denies that they were ever independent in 'The Early Christian Apocalypses', *Semeia*, 14 (1979), 71.

10 The seven heads of the Beast are both hills and kings (Pareus 420); the smoke from the bottomless pit signifies the darkness of doctrine in Revelation 9 but hell torment in 13 (353), and the three angels of 14 are evangelical preachers, while they are literally angels in 18 (453). Mede's remark is at *Works*, 4.759. In his second rule for interpretation More requires one sense per word in one vision (*SP*, 259–61).

11 Mede, *Works* 3.447–50, 465–6. The sixth seal symbolizes the conversion of Rome

to Christianity, and the falling stars and the eclipse of the sun and moon indicate the destruction of pagan worship. The fourth trumpet, however, signifies the reduction of Rome to a provincial city, when the Byzantines abolished its magistracies and subordinated the city itself to Ravenna. Pareus argues that the sealed and opened scrolls signify the same thing, the whole book of Revelation (96, 199).

12 R.H. of Salisbury later argued a stricter sequential order and, therefore, attacked Mede's synchronisms. He assumed that each historical sequence must coincide exactly with the visionary sequence. More summarizes his arguments at *Apoc. Apoc.* 261, 265–71, 273–83, 286–7, 289–92, 294–307, 313–14, 332–7, 342.

13 Pareus, 225; Mede, *Works*, 3.482–3. Mede argued through the comparison of the witnesses to candelabra. At the beginning of Revelation candelabra regularly signify churches. His criteria are, therefore, internal.

14 Bale makes the same kind of assumption about the Beast (Bauckham, 60–1); Fulke, Gifford, Marlorat, and Junius about the two witnesses (187 and n.9).

15 In one place, however, the fourth beast is both a king and a kingdom. Von Rad argues that the interpretation of Daniel's night vision (7.17–27) turns the Son of Man into a collective, and his rule becomes that of the saints of the Most High, that is, of the angels (*Old Testament Theology*, 2.313).

16 Englishmen like Ralegh and Milton also stressed the arrival of Roman missionaries in England shortly before 600 AD (Firth, 188, 236). Pareus' reading of the millennium was traditional. (Bousset, *Die Offenbarung*, 87n.). In the Renaissance the linking of Antichrist and Mohammed was likewise standard](Bousset, 84). J. E. Hankins cites Bullinger and Tyndale in *Source and Meaning in Spenser's Allegory* (Oxford, 1971), 220–3. P. Alphandéry gives the medieval background in 'Mahomet-Antichrist dans le Moyen Age latin', *Mélanges Hartwig Derenbourg* (Paris, 1909), 263, 265, 269–70, 273–5. Protestants stressed Boniface III because he assumed the title of universal bishop (Firth, 55, 83, 158; Bauckham, 120–1).

17 Lamont cites Foxe who has five periods: the first 300 years, when the church was pure and suffered persecution; 300 years peace; 400 years, when Rome retarded things; the reign of Antichrist, after Gregory VII became Pope; and the English Reformation (pp. 33–4).

18 The three fly through mid-heaven. The first calls all to worship God; the second proclaims the fall of Babylon; and the third warns against the Beast. The first signified the Byzantine iconoclasts (Mede, *Works*, 3.515–17, More, *Apoc. Apoc.* 140); the second, the Waldensians and Albigensians (Mede, *Works*, 3.517) or the Protestant Reformation (More, *Apoc. Apoc.* 141); and the third, the Reformation (Mede, *Works*, 3.518) or a contemporary warning (More, *Apoc. Apoc.* 142).

19 Paul Christianson, *Reformers and Babylon: English Apocalyptic from the Reformation to the Eve of the Civil War* (Toronto, Buffalo, London, 1978), 5. Mede talked about this least, yet it was the whole import of his interpretation, recorded in his epitaph: 'Quarum praelucente face, / Induit se in abditissimos *Prophetiarum* recessus, et / Spelunca *Apocalyptica* exuit *Romamam Belluam*'. (*Works*, 1.xxxv). (With the torch of his erudition shining ahead, he came into the most remote recesses of prophecies and drew the Roman beast from its apocalyptic cave.) More remarked that his master's teaching implied damnation for all Catholics (*MG*. xxii–xxiii). Pareus was explicit. He published his commentary partially to counter Roman readings of Revelation (*2V).

20 Grotius presented his readings in *Commentatio ad loca quaedam N. Testamenti quae de Antichristo agunt, aut agere putantur* (Amsterdam, 1640) and the *Adnotationes ad*

Novum Testamentum (Paris, 1644).
21 Pareus, 233–5; Mede, *Works*, 3.484. The Catholic commentators whom Pareus cited, Ribera, Alcazar, and Bellarmine, accepted the literal identification with Jerusalem.
22 Bauckham, 87, 96–7, 99, 223 n.74; More, *SP*. 259, 304, 321; *Apoc. Apoc.* 347. Firth cites Bale and Ralegh at 249, 184.
23 Martin Mueller, *The Children of Oedipus* (Toronto, Buffalo, London, 1980), pp. 11–17. Michael Fixler, *Milton and the Kingdoms of God* (Evanston, 1964), p. 118 cites Thomas Goodwin, *The Great Interest of States and Kingdoms* (1646), where Revelation 'is a *Tragy-Comedy*, which begins with a kingdome given to be won by conquest, and ends with a Coronation of a King, and the marriage of his Bride'.
24 Milton, Introduction to Book 2 of *Reason of Church Government* and Preface to *Samson Agonistes*. Wittreich in *Visionary Poetics*, 37–8 and n.100 argues that Pareus and Mede brought about an academic revolution when they turned to aesthetic commentary. He cites among others Richard Bernard, who thought of Revelation as a tragicomedy, and Hezekiah Holland. Firth discusses Alsted at p. 212.
25 Pareus, 164–5. Bousset found this method in Nicolaus Collado (1581), who always linked a seal with a trumpet and a vial (*Die Offenbarung*, 95–6).
26 Pareus argued that John gives definite numbers to indicate divine prescience (219). This assumption is Tyconian, and the Donatist critic likewise assumed that the 'plot' was discontinuous (Bousset, *Die Offenbarung*, 60).
27 He checked chronologies, for example, in Archbishop Ussher's Samaritan Bible (*Works*, 5.896), and Hebraisms in Greek were one of his main concerns. In Letter 17 (*Works*, 4.766) he argued that the Jews in the Greek empire often used Greek words in the full sense of their Semitic equivalents. Mede's editor pointed out his study of history (*Works*, 1, General Preface, 3.1–2). Mede used an anthology of Petrus Galatinus for the rabbinical tradition (*Works*, 3.437, 496, 535–6). On dreams he read the *Oneirocritica* of Achmetes ben Seirim, who collected the prophecies of the Egyptian Tarphan, the Persian Baranus, and the Indian Syrbachamus. Mede was aware that the latter used Christian ideas (*Works*, 3.451–2).
28 He cites Jewish oral tradition via the Talmud (*Works*, 3.437–9, 594). Here is the outline: East, Judah, lion; West, Ephraim, ox; South, Reuben, man; North, Dan, eagle. In Talmudic theory each animal is pre-eminent in its class. Mede actually used Aban Ezra on Numbers 2 and also Bar Nachman and Chazkuni. He has a summary at *Works*, 5.916–17. Psalm 68 has the animals in the wilderness. In Ezekiel they become the cherubim who pull the chariot of God and have four faces to look in the four directions assigned to the ensigns in the desert encampment (*Works*, 3.595).
29 In the construction of his synchronisms Mede abstained from all interpretation except what a grammarian does. The title page (*Works*, 3.419) compares the synchronisms to Ariadne's thread, which brought Theseus through the labyrinth, and to the Lydian stone for tracing out a true interpretation.
30 Bousset surveys Victorinus, Luther, and Osiander (*Die Offenbarung*, 53–5, 84–5). Andrew of Caesarea had equated the seven heads with seven kingdoms (64).
31 Firth stresses the traditional character of Mede's interpretation and illustrates the point with the first six seals (217–19). She also discusses Luther, Brightman, and Alsted (11–12, 168–71, 210–12). Bousset argues that Luther in his *Vorrede* and glosses to the New Testament of 1534 essentially developed Lyra (*Die Offenbarung*,

87–8). Bauckham discusses Foxe (221–2).
32 Capp, for example, shows that Mede, Brightman, and Alsted were major influences on the Fifth Monarchists (29, and the table at 45–6).
33 Bousset discusses Ribera and Alcazar at *Die Offenbarung*, 91–2, 93–4; Capp outlines Mede's influence at 191, 233–4. More complained that a reader of Grotius could never see how Revelation was divinely inspired (*Apoc. Apoc.* xviii). More summarizes and argues with Grotius at *MG.* 173–5, 182–94, 198, 201; *SP.* 220, 229, 242, 253, 270, 278, 281, 306, 311, 342–62, 369, 458; *Apoc. Apoc.* 1.n, 168, 220, 223, 227, 229. This list is not exhaustive.
34 *SP*, 261–316; Firth, 157; Bauckham, 102–3.
35 *Works*, 3.498. Foxe, with his insistence that each image in Revelation have a specific historical fulfilment, had narrowed the meaning of the two-horned beast to the Papacy alone (Firth, 99–100; Bauckham, 86–7, 97, 99). This reading agreed with that in the Geneva Bible (Firth, 123).
36 *Works*, 3.500–1. Mede's opponent, Daniel Lawenus, pointed out that this reading was impossible syntactically, since 13.12 refers to the Beast as the monster cured (*Works*, 3.541–2). R.H.'s objections are at More, *Apoc. Apoc.* 261–9. Mede defended himself with a standard argument. A story must present simultaneous events successively (*Works*, 3.555, 570). Mede identified the Beast with its statue by phraseology. John never links the Beast with its image, though he associates it with the two-horned beast and with the false prophet. He does, however, connect the two-horned beast with the image of the Beast. Since the two-horned is classed both with the Beast and with its image, the Beast is its image (*Works*, 3.421). Again, Lawenus complained that this interpretation confused the plot (*Works*, 3.541–2). Ludovicus de Dieu asked why an image was necessary, since the Beast is the image of the dragon (*Works*, 3.566).
37 *SP*, 219. More cited this example and added Babylon, the two witnesses, and the two-horned beast.
38 *SP*, 221–2, 405–6; *Dialogues*, 102. More read the plagues ironically.
39 *SP*, 188, 222, 399; *Dialogues*, 103–5, 199, 202–4. More assumed the identification of the hyaline sea of 15.2 with the hyaline sea like crystal of 4.6.
40 1 Corinthians 10.1–11. He makes mostly moral applications but does identify the Rock with Jesus.
41 In his fast sermon, *Zerubbabels Encouragement to Finish the Temple* (1642), Thomas Goodwin used the same assumption to get a different sequence for Chapter 11 (Christianson, 229).

III
The Apocalypse in Renaissance English literature

FLORENCE SANDLER

6 *The Faerie Queene*: an Elizabethan Apocalypse

I

Even among contemporaries, Spenser's great poem was recognized as representative of its age. For here was the English vernacular epic, that, in the course of portraying the virtues that 'fashioned the gentleman', as Spenser explained, reflected back to Elizabethan society its own qualities – its nationalism, electicism and adventurousness. Even Spenser's choice of Arthurian material ('The Matter of Britain') turns out to be not eccentric, but part and parcel of the Elizabethans' recovery of their medieval heritage, in poetry as much as in portraiture and court entertainment.

But one of the most noteworthy features of the poem is that among the virtues, priority is given to Holiness. The Legend of the Knight of Holiness, tutored by the three Christian virtues of Faith, Hope and Love, takes narrative and presumably philosophical precedence over the other legends presenting such classical virtues as Temperance and Justice. In the Legend of Holiness, the moral allegory is consistent and predominant. Along with it come not only the traditional typological and anagogical allegories, but also an historical or political allegory concerned with the history and destiny of the Realm of Britain, indicating the nationalistic preoccupation of the new age.

The Legend of Holiness is patterned, however, on the Apocalypse of John and is thus an 'apocalyptic' poem in the only sense borne by that word in Spenser's day. The manner of the literary imitation suggests that Spenser read the Apocalypse itself chiefly as a moral allegory where 'historical' elements were subordinate, and that possibility is all the more interesting if Spenser is as much representative of his time in his handling of apocalyptic as in other matters.

Whatever reservations Luther and Calvin had about the status of the Apocalypse, radical Protestants in later generations came increasingly to read it in a literal or historical sense, as they read the other Biblical texts. It is notorious that the millenarian 'saints' of the New Model Army would take the Apocalypse as a political document and a guide for action in their overthrow of the Stuart King in preparation for the arrival on earth of God's Kingdom and the New Jerusalem. The naïve millenarianism of the 'saints' had been prepared intellectually by the work of Joseph Mede on the Apocalypse and by his two Elizabethan predecessors, Hugh Broughton and Thomas Brightman. Yet orthodox Elizabethan views on the 'historical' content of the Apocalypse are represented not by Brightman and Broughton but by John Foxe, the historian of the *Actes and Monuments*, whose concepts of the Church and the text were more conservative.[1]

Spenser's apocalyptic poem is not detached from history; indeed, it incorporates much of Foxe's own account of Church history to show exactly the apocalyptic significance of the present moment and especially of the Queen herself, to whom *The Faerie Queene* is dedicated. Yet in that very process is seen the predominance of the moral allegory and its ability to contain those elements which, given a literal reading, were capable of assuming autonomy and delivering a predictive account of history. The study of Spenser's apocalyptic poem recalls the other aspect of the orthodox Elizabethan reading of the Apocalypse which followed the moral allegory and balanced the more radical implications of Foxe's apocalyptic history.

The purpose of the present chapter is to delineate the style of the moral allegory to be found in the Legend of Holiness and the way in which it treats the peculiarly apocalyptic theme of the arrival of God's Kingdom. The purpose is best served by studying the poem from the viewpoint of the common reader who came to the text fortified in Tudor patriotism and piety. Significant recent work on *The Faerie Queene* has stressed the problematic nature of the allegory and the way in which the reader's experience in the poem models the difficulty of the epistemological situation in a fallen world.[2] Such an experience the Elizabethan readers surely underwent, though to a lesser degree than their twentieth-century counterparts, especially in the Legend of Holiness where from the outset they could trust the Biblical allusions. God's true word provided, as it were, the providential clues through the labyrinth and anticipated through the woods of Error the perspective to be obtained eventually from the Mount of Contemplation. The recently discovered annotations of *The Faerie Queene* by an Elizabethan reader[3] suggest a habit of mind less like that of the newer Spenser criticism and more in keeping with that of the editors of the Variorum Spenser who glossed the characters and their locales as if the meaning was simple and obvious.

The context for the moral allegory was provided by the Bible itself, by the Book of Common Prayer and by Erasmus's *Paraphrase of the New Testament* which, along with the *Actes and Monuments* and Jewel's *Apologie for the Church of England*, was chained alongside the Bible in the parish church. The influence of Erasmus ran deep. He was the most persuasive spokesman for that early sixteenth-century piety that he shared with John Colet,[4] and his works had been popularized and Protestantized in the reign of Edward VI in the formative phase of the English Reformation. It will not be surprising if Spenser presents to the Elizabethan reader a moral allegory with an Erasmian cast, even in a poem modelled on the Apocalypse, the one New Testament text that Erasmus's *Paraphrase* did not cover.[5]

The Red Cross Knight,[6] the hero of the Legend, is introduced as one 'Faithful and True' (cf. Rev. 19.11), who must yet endure temptations and oppressions, the equivalent of the Apocalypse's plagues and tyrannies that try and winnow the just on this earth. He is deceived at first by the evil ones, in this case Duessa and Archimago who fill roles similar to those of the Apocalyptic Whore and the False Prophet. Yet he perseveres, learning more clearly the character of his enemies and friends. From the time that the Knight has his vision of the New Jerusalem he is charged with new strength and goes forth like St. Michael to fight the Great Dragon; during the three days of battle he is sustained and replenished through the night by the power of the Well of Life and the Tree of Life; finally while the whole city rejoices, the victor becomes also the Bridegroom, betrothed to Una, whose face is now finally unveiled. The Whore of Babylon has been exposed at last, and the True Bride, Jerusalem, revealed. Spenser, reading the Apocalypse as a Quest, has refocussed the story by setting one heroic figure, the Red Cross Knight, firmly in the middle to participate in all actions, while having Una represent throughout the cause for which he fights and the prize he wins after his encounters with the various shapes of evil.

Much of the interest of Spenser's Legend of Holiness lies in the way it revises Romantic literary antecedents, particularly the Matter of Britain as found in Malory's *Le Morte d'arthur*. When Spenser's Knight of Holiness bears the Red Cross upon his shield he thereby proclaims his kinship with the figure of Sir Galahad from Malory (and ultimately from the Cistercian *Queste* which Malory incorporated), and his quest to restore Una's parents to their kingdom, now devastated by the Dragon, bears a resemblance to Galahad's Quest for the Grail kept by the feeble Anfortas whose kingdom is laid waste. Yet Spenser's knight is not, like Malory's, an immaculate prodigy, whose mere appearance fulfills particular prophecies and who proceeds without distraction to the successful completion of his quest. Red Cross is a Knight errant more errant than many.

At the same time Spenser revises Malory's sacramentalism. The radiant object that appears in his poem is not the Grail carried in procession or set upon the altar, but Arthur's shield of faith, the weapon of moral warfare; and the Red Cross Knight may not, like Sir Galahad, disappear from Arthur's court after finding the Grail and be translated to heaven from the Holy City of Sarras; instead he returns to the active and public life in the service of the Faerie Queene.

The biases that Spenser shows here in his transvaluation of Malory are those not simply of Protestantism but of Christian Humanism. There is the Erasmian suspicion of ceremonies and monkery, on the grounds that they obscure the true Christian pursuit, the *philosophia Christi*, which is the finding of self-knowledge in the Spirit of Christ. Indeed, if there is one book which more than others could have provided Spenser with the inspiration for the Legend of Holiness, it is the *Enchiridion Militis Christiani* (1503)[7] in which Erasmus had commended the life of the Christian soldier who maintained his baptismal vow to fight under Christ's captaincy, in the garrison of his own body, against those old enemies, the world, the flesh and the Devil.

The service involves constant vigilance, 'for our vices, our armoured enemies, attack us unceasingly', and we 'are assaulted by their endless deceptions', their 'thousand stratagems'. The warfare is 'anything but simple and straightforward', and can from time to time 'shake the very walls of the mind'.[8] But the resources are reading of Scripture, Prayer and Knowledge (knowledge both of oneself and the enemy: one must confront and analyze one's fears and 'investigate those things which are to be avoided'[9]), and faith in Christ's victory which is also our own. One is helped by other members of the Communion of Saints, as Red Cross is helped by Arthur, and by the examples of great Christian soldiers who have gone before, especially 'St. Paul, the standard-bearer of Christian warfare',[10] that great exponent of the Christian life whom Erasmus revered as much as did John Colet or Martin Luther.

The Arthurean setting of Spenser's poem is apt to obscure the extent to which the Legend of Holiness not only advances the *philosophia Christi* but fulfills the expectations which Erasmus held for Christian composition. Concerned for what was 'vital and dynamic' in sacred doctrine rather than what was 'merely dialectic', Erasmus had deplored the habit of abstraction which he saw as the prevailing disease of contemporary theology and rhetoric, and pointed behind the writings of the schoolmen to those of the Church Fathers and to the Letters of Paul and the Gospels where the life of the Spirit was presented with a vividness that moved the mind and heart. Paul and the Fathers had often found their moving images in the pagan poets, making over the spoils of Egypt for the sake of Israel. Erasmus's preference is for the allegorical style of Augustine and his beloved Origen. Reasonably he saw the allegorical style as belonging with the Platonic tradition, and recommended the Platonic philosophers on the grounds that they not only respected the Delphic injunction, 'Know thyself', but wrote in such a way as to invoke self-knowledge in the reader: 'not only their ideas but their very mode of expression approaches that of the Gospels'.[11] Spenser in his poem has improved upon Erasmus's injunctions: he has read and imitated the pagan poets of Greece and Rome in the light of the Gospel, and by a rectified imagination he has made over more spoils from the Egyptians, that is, the poetry of the age of superstition – not only Chaucer (whom, on John Foxe's evidence, he would have regarded as virtually a Protestant) but also Malory.

The enthusiastic rediscovery of Paul by the first generation of Humanists and Protestant Reformers was part of their effort to recover Apostolic Christianity. Paul was to be rescued from the theologians and dialecticians, and presented afresh as the foremost of the imitators of Christ among the apostles.[12]

For both Humanists and Reformers, the attraction of the Pauline Epistles was their psychology of faith, but there is a difference to be noted. For the Reformers, the central issue in that psychology was Paul's recognition of the law as the power that binds man in sin and the force from which he must be redeemed. For the Humanists, however, the issue was Paul's dichotomy of flesh and spirit, and his understanding of the transforming power of the Spirit. The effect to be observed in the commentaries of Colet and Erasmus is a fusion of what are often regarded as the separate strands of Pauline and Johannine Christianity. The basis of his hermeneutical structure Erasmus derived from passages in the Pauline Epistles (2 Cor. 3.6; 1 Cor. 2.12 ff.) and the Fourth Gospel (John 4.23–4, 6.63). John's 'being born again in the Spirit' who is Love is Paul's 'becoming incorporated into the Body of Christ' and 'transfigured' into the life incorruptible. Taking the transformation in the Spirit as the essential feature of a *theologia vitae*, Erasmus developed in the *Enchiridion*, one of his modern commentators claims, such a 'complete, dynamic, and soteriological explanation of Scripture' as had not been presented since Origen.[13] Paul, Erasmus insisted, was the greatest of the allegorizers, his allegory, like that of the Platonists and the Early Fathers, shadowing forth the mystery of the operation of the Spirit.[14]

The Humanists stressed the active participation of man both in sin and in grace. Each person not only inherited Adam's sin, but personally recapitulated in his own life Adam's sin and disintegration into Death; likewise his 'justification' included a free and loving response to the Divine love (*redamare* is Erasmus's word[15]) along with receptivity to and cooperation with the Spirit. When Erasmus adopts Origen's tripartite division of man in the *Enchiridion*, 'spirit' is that part which unites him to God.[16] 'Taught by God' (John 6.45), loving the image of Christ whom he finds in the Scriptures, the Christian is transfigured into what he loves.

Erasmus' insistence that the saving 'sola fides' is the 'faith which worketh by love' (Galatians 5.6) illuminates Spenser's choice of the Romantic mode and his presentation of the Red Cross Knight accompanied upon his quest by the 'louely Ladie'. Love her well, however, he does not until he has learned from his own misconceptions and betrayals. At length, after their love has shown itself in saving acts, each for the other, they can be 'betrouthed . . . with joy', his heart seeming 'to melt in pleasures manifold' (I.xii.40). That love is necessarily fruitful is presented in the person of Charissa with her children, and in the role of Mercy who, in leading Red Cross to heaven, shows him all the works of charity on the very route to the contemplative vision.

One of the effects of Spenser's writing an Erasmian Legend of Holiness is that actual, not simply imputed, holiness is seen as something to be learned and attained, under the instruction of Dame Caelia and those of her household. The whole process of transformation from sin into grace and the recovery of innocence and immortality Erasmus designated by the name of 'baptism', the ceremony of baptism being at most a sign of the process. Time and again in the *Paraphrase*, even when there was no mention of baptism in the text, Erasmus stated that Christians are joined to Christ through baptism. One notes that Spenser's Knight first appears already bearing on his shield and breast the 'bloudie Crosse', the 'glorious badge' that signifies his baptism in the blood of the Lamb, and his commitment to the Christian virtues – love of God, 'soueraine hope', and faythfulness in deed and work (I.i.2).[17] He is 'manfully to fight under his (Christ's) banner' (in the words of the Public Baptismal Service), '... and to continue Christ's fayth full souldiour and seruaunt unto his lyues end'.

But the fullness, the completion of his baptism will not be seen until the Knight is both victorious over the power of Death and betrothed to Una. Meanwhile he is often led astray by his inexperience in arms and his ignorance of himself and the ways of his enemies, the world, the flesh and the devil. There is at first an unmapped terrain where the Knight errant can stray and indeed err. Not until he is convicted of sin by his confrontation with Despair can he map out the landscape of his own mind, and then he identifies himself, rightly yet partially, as a man of sin, deserving of death. He is impatient for that justice to be rendered. Thereupon Una must remind him both of his baptismal vow ('Is this the battell, which thou vauntst to fight?') and his baptismal heritage, not through the flesh but the spirit:

> Come, come away, fraile, feeble, fleshy wight,
> Ne let vaine words bewitch thy manly hart,
> Ne diuelish thoughts dismay thy constant spright.
> In heauenly mercies hast thou not a part?
>
> (I.ix.53)

Once Una has put him into the hands of Dame Caelia and her daughters, Fidelia, Speranza and Charissa, the Knight is led by clear stages to the perfection of his baptism, through his putting off the body of sin and the Old Adam and his regeneration in grace. In the House of Holiness he is born again in the spirit, and finds his spiritual parents. His godmother is Dame Mercie, the 'godly Matrone' who 'by the hand him beares' (I.x.35) and, in a passage that recalls the phraseology of the Public Baptismal Service, leads him

> aright that he should never fall.
> In all his wayes through this wide worldes waue,
> That Mercy in the end his righteous soule might saue.
>
> (I.x.34)

The 'father' to whom she presents him is the hermit, Contemplation, whose spiritual eye is fixed upon Heaven. His spiritual parentage thus indicates the complementary nature of action and contemplation, of loving works and faith, in the Erasmian description of the Christian life. It is when he looks upon the Celestial City that the Knight learns at one and the same time of his origin, his baptismal name and his 'blessed end', when he shall have reached at last his own essential nature. He is English, and will be enrolled among the saints as Saint George of England. The very name, Saint George, expresses in oxymoron the mystery of membership in Christ, for this is the Man of Earth Sanctified.

Even now the Knight, overwhelmed with the sight of heaven, mistakes himself and is impatient to put off his armour and leave the earth's vain loves and wars, as before he had mistaken himself in the opposite situation in the hands of Despair. He is reprimanded by the hermit who enjoins upon him the patience of the saints; he should not seek to foreshorten the times nor abandon the race that is set before him. In his confrontation with the Dragon, wielding the sword of the Spirit with 'baptized hands' (I.xi.36), Red Cross finds the full invigoration of the Tree and the Well of life (*refocillatio* is Erasmus's word[18]). His victory over the powers of death is concomitant with his incorporation into the Body of Christ. Beyond that again he arrives at the stage of union with the Bride. Even this turns out to be not the final union but rather a sign and promise of that union – the betrothal rather than the wedding – and the Knight must abruptly leave the state in which he would linger. Like the vision of the New Jerusalem, the union with the spiritual Bride is experienced as transitory in the dispensation of time; yet it participates in the eternal reality and shows the end of man.

Spenser has separated into two parallel episodes the implications of the double nature of the New Jerusalem who appears in the Apocalypse as simultaneously City and Bride. In the first episode the Knight's sanctification is made explicit; in the second, his union with God and his Inheritance of the Kingdom. It is well to remember the double nature of the Kingship of Christ (the 'Anointed One') who sits at the right hand of the Father, not only as God but as Man – as the Second Adam or as the 'Son of Man' who receives the Kingdom from the Ancient of Days (Daniel 7.13). Thus the Red Cross Knight, a member of the Body of Christ, is called 'Dear Sonne' and 'heere apparaunt' of the Kingdom by a second father, the 'royall Pere', who is Adam restored: 'Both daughter and eke Kingdome, do I yield to thee' (I.xii.17, 20). One recognizes the essential connection between sanctification and glorification, or to use Paul's terms, putting on the 'body that is incorruptible' and 'obtaining the crown'. Most explicitly the coupling occurs in the prologue of the Apocalypse, addressed to those whom Christ, 'hath made . . . kings and priests unto God and his Father' (Rev. 5.6).

Thus there has emerged in the Legend of Holiness the apocalyptic theme of kingship, or more precisely, the apocalyptic proclamation of the arrival of

God's Kingdom that is without end and the identification of the saints who are to reign with God. In the Legend, however, as in the Pauline Epistles, the context of the kingship of the saints is the Work of the Spirit.

> For as many as are led by the spirit of God, they are the sons of God.
> For ye . . . have received the Spirit of adoption, whereby we cry, Abba, Father.
> The Spirit itself beareth witness with our spirit, that we are children of God.
> And if children, then heirs; heirs of God, and joint-heirs with Christ; if so be that we suffer with him, that we may be also glorified together.
> (Romans 8.14–17)

Nor was it inappropriate that Erasmus had designated the process of coming into the inheritance of the Kingdom as baptism. Historically the rites of baptism practised in the Judean wilderness in the first century may have been a democratization of the kingship rituals of the Ancient Near East. Certainly the New Testament writers present the baptism of Jesus as the 'fulfilment' of the prophecy contained in the Enthronement psalms, having the voice of God recapitulate the adoption formula from the coronation of the Davidic kings: 'This is my beloved Son' (cf. Ps. 2.7). The Christian, baptized into Christ's sonship, shares also in the spiritual Kingdom which is the New Testament fulfilment of the Davidic Kingdom, the Old Testament type. The idea is explicit in the language of the Baptismal Service, where Christians are 'partakers of his (Christ's) everlasting kingdome', and their destiny 'to come to the lande of everlasting lyfe, there to reygne wyth thee, worlde without ende'.

David's own kingship was a symbol of the Kingdom of God. The Christian's attainment of 'Christhood' and spiritual kingship is a further participation in the Kingdom which will be completely realized and apparent at the Eschaton. Meanwhile the human race, and all Creation, groaning and travailing (cf. Romans 8.22) returns to God in Majesty, the Christian already experiencing now a limited version of the eschatological perfection.[19]

The presentation of kingship in terms of moral achievement and spiritual transformation could well have had the effect of dismissing the political realm and emptying the apocalyptic scenario of all political urgency. But Erasmus, like the Reformers, is committed to a *theologia vitae* that is to be lived to the full in the secular world. To die to sin and to be born again in the Spirit, to achieve the contemplative vision, is the high calling not merely of the monk or nun in monastic seclusion but of the Christian in the world, faithfully performing his or her political responsibilities in allegiance to the 'Powers that be' that are 'ordained of God' (Romans 13.1). Erasmus himself gives mutual equality to the realms of Church and State,[20] and appeals to those in political authority to use their office for the regeneration of the Church in their dominions, dedicating his *Paraphrase* of the Four Gospels to four renowned Christian monarchs (Henry VIII of England among them) to whom God has committed the care of good religion.

Spenser is at pains to have Contemplation himself affirm for the benefit of the Red Cross Knight the value of nationhood, and the earthly *polis*, and to commend even the world's 'immortality' of fame, since engagement in earthly wars and loves is to be seen as preliminary (and not, as the Knight at first supposes, merely contrary) to Heaven's love and peace. Particularly he commends Red Cross Knight's service to his earthly queen, whose name is Gloriana. She is the

> soueraigne Dame
> That glorie does to them for guerdon graunt:
> For she is heavenly borne, and heaven may iustly vaunt.
>
> (I.x.59)

Elizabethan readers would have no doubt, even without the benefit of Spenser's 'Letter to Ralegh', that Gloriana is the idealized figure of their own Queen. But when Una herself comes to the Red Cross Knight as his bride, she too recalls that other Queen who was Bride to her realm by virtue of the Coronation ring placed upon her finger. She is a 'goodly maiden Queene', crowned by her maidens with 'a girland greene' (I.xxi.8), like Elizabeth in the pastoral festivities at court. At the same point there appear unmistakable allusions to the Bride of the Apocalypse and the Apocalyptic Woman in the Sun: Una, wearing the virginal garment 'All lily white, withoutten spot' (cf. Rev. 19.8), bears the radiance of the 'morning starre' (cf. Rev. 2.28) and of the sun itself (cf. Rev. 12.1). The poet cannot pen the 'blazing brightnesse of her beauties beame, / And glorious light of her sunshyny face', indeed, all her 'heauenly lineaments' (I.xxi.21-2).

The name Una must from the beginning have suggested the Queen herself. *'Semper Una'* is the title of a poem addressed to her in 1578 on the occasion of her visit to Audley End: *'Una quod es semper, quod semper es Optima Princeps . . .'*, a poem that deals again with her chastity and the love her subjects hold for her; and Una's status as the Princess championed by the Red Cross Knight whose name is Saint George invokes that of the Queen attended, most conspicuously in the Garter Processions, by the illustrious knights of St. George. This is the Queen of the Windsor portrait who wears the Garter Ribbon and holds up the medallion with the device of St. George.[21]

It is to Elizabeth,

> Goddesse heauenly bright,
> Mirrour of grace and Maiestie diuine
>
> (I. Proem. 4)

that Spenser's Legend of Holiness, like the other books of *The Fairie Queene*, is dedicated.

But it is significant that the appearance of a figure who suggests Elizabeth *in majesty* is delayed in the Legend of Holiness until the point at which the Knight, having defeated the powers of Death, enters into the inheritance of the Kingdom of God. The meaning of the appearance is surely given by its context which is the mythos of baptism. To understand the spiritual kingship is to recognize the majesty of Elizabeth, like the majesty of David in his time, as a 'mirrour' reflecting now within the saeculum the Majesty of God which all creatures will reflect in the Eschaton. It is not inappropriate to speak of Elizabeth's majesty in the language by which a sacrament is defined in the Catechism, namely, as an 'outward and visible sign of an inward and spiritual grace'. In the Erasmian scheme, the ceremony of the coronation of the king or queen, like the ceremony of baptism, may be seen as a sacramental sign pointing to the reality which is the Work of the Spirit in bringing the human spirit to its glorification.

But beyond the sacramental significance of the office of any king or queen regnant, there is evidence in Spenser's poem of a particular interest and urgency in the role of the monarch. The Elizabethan poet is heir not only to Christian Humanism but to the Protestant Tudor myth. It is worthwhile to examine the political context of Spenser's poem in order to see the congruence of the political and ecclesiastical myth with the spiritual myth of baptism. For the triumph of Elizabeth as representative of the True Church and the rightful Succession recapitulates in political terms the triumph of the Man of Grace over the Man of Sin in the life of the *miles christianus*.

II

The Reformation under Henry VIII had been originally an Act of State. The British Church had cast off papal jurisdiction, and had necessarily proclaimed that such jurisdiction always had been illegitimate, a matter of the pope's usurpation of the proper authority in ecclesiastical matters of the King in Parliament. The propagandists employed by Thomas Cromwell had refurbished the view of the history of the British Church and State. On the one hand, they denigrated a hero of the past like Thomas a Becket who had supported ecclesiastical autonomy against the State and who had relied upon the papal jurisdiction; and, on the other they rehabilitated those earlier kings, Henry II and John, who had attempted to withstand the papal usurpation.

Inevitably, Britain's extricating herself from the papal authority and discovering her autonomy within her own land found its Biblical analogy in Israel's Exodus from Egypt and entry into the Promised Land. In New Testament terms, it might be found in the Exodus theme of the Apocalypse – under Christ, the New Lamb of the Passover, the elect had departed from Babylon, the City of Death, to reach Eternal Life. John Bale, one of Cromwell's

Protestant propagandists and later, under Edward VI, the Bishop of the Irish diocese of Ossory, had provided in his commentary on the Apocalypse, *The Image of Both Churches* (1548), the basis on which might be built an apocalyptic interpretation of the English Reformation.[22]

Yet the Reformation under Henry and Edward was a relatively easy and superficial matter, exactly because it had occurred as a series of Acts of State. The apocalyptic prophecy of Daniel or John, calling for the divine judgment on the present wicked powers of the world and their overthrow by the heavenly armies that will install on earth the true City of God, is an appropriate rallying cry for the oppressed in the world order. The moment when the English 'saints' felt the oppression of Babylon and the Antichrist and when the apocalyptic scenario took deep root in the English Church did not occur until the reign of Mary Tudor in mid-century, with its attempt to restore the Old Religion. The Protestant Reformation found then its roll of martyrs – the three great bishops, Cranmer, Latimer and Ridley, and the hundreds of otherwise obscure men and women – ploughmen, weavers, young girls – who witnessed to the Protestant faith under imprisonment, torture and death at the stake. Their testimonies were recorded movingly, copiously and definitively, in John Foxe's *Actes and Monuments* (1563), in the context of an apocalyptic history of the universal Church.

Foxe is the English representative of the new Protestant historiography represented on the Continent chiefly by the Magdeburg Centurians – Matthias Flacius, Sleidanus, and others. Luther himself, unimpressed at the outset by the prophecies of the Book of Revelation, had become convinced, as he stated in his preface for Robert Barnes's *Vitae Romanorum Pontificatorum* (1535), that his own moral insight into the corruption of the papal Church, gained by comparing the present institution with the Biblical ideal (a criticism, as it were, '*a priori*'), needed to be supplemented by an historical analysis demonstrating when and how the corruption had set in (a criticism '*a posteriori*').[23] The history of the Church up to his own day was to be read not merely as chronicle but as dynamic revelation.

The methodological innovation of Protestant historiography was to read the Johannine Apocalypse as a protohistorical document, predicting future developments. In *The Image of Both Churches* Bale had presented simultaneously in the text of the Apocalypse and in Christian history a drama of the True Church opposed by the False, Jerusalem by Babylon, the Bride and the Whore. The correlation, as Bale perceived it, was both general and specific. But for Foxe, Bale's friend and successor in the next generation, the prophecy was only specific. The business of Foxe's life was to command the data of fifteen hundred years of Christian history so as to define more precisely the lineaments of the True and False Churches through time and to determine a closer and closer correlation of particular text and particular historical event.

According to Foxe's thesis in the *Actes and Monuments*, the Church had had its first period of triumph in the early centuries, when the blood of the martyrs had been vindicated with the Church's establishment under Constantine. Increasingly thereafter corruption had set in – most particularly when the Popes (through that notorious forgery, the Donation of Constantine) had claimed imperial power for themselves, and oppressed the church with superstitious doctrines and practices that contradicted those of the Primitive Church – clerical celibacy, monkery, transubstantiation, the worship of relics and all 'idle ceremonies'. Even through the ages of papal usurpation, there had been many like Wycliff and Huss to witness for the true faith, though these were miscalled heretics by the papalists. But now the blood of these martyrs and the thousands of Protestant witnesses of the latter age indicated the impending final triumph of the True Church, Christ's Kingdom on earth, and the routing of Popery and the Antichrist.

When in 1558 God spoke by having the papalist Queen Mary die and her Protestant sister Elizabeth succeed her, it was clear that, as in the Apocalypse, the event vindicated the just and faithful ones after their trials and afflictions. The Marian martyrs had joined the 'souls that were slain for the Word of God' beneath the altar in Heaven (Rev. 6.10), and their cry of 'How long, O God?' had been given a timely answer. The application of the Apocalypse was all the more tempting when the careers of the two royal sisters epitomized the struggle between Whore and Bride for the seat of power: Catholic Mary, allied with Spain and Rome, with the blood of the saints upon her skirts; Protestant Elizabeth held in captivity during her sister's reign, but by Mary's demise liberated with her people to be their Queen. The last of Foxe's martyr-histories in the *Actes and Monuments* was that of Elizabeth herself, who now enjoyed her apotheosis as Queen, as Defender of the Faith and as Governor of the Church.

Throughout, the *Actes and Monuments* draws upon the peculiarly Protestant version of the Imperial myth, which laid expectation on the figure of the just Emperor, the Constantine, to reassert control over the Church and revive the true Christian polity obscured through the Middle Ages by the rise of an Imperial Papacy. In England Henry VIII had shown himself to be a true Christian Prince and Emperor by trampling down the arrogant Papacy (the iconography of the 1520s showed Henry seated on his Imperial throne, having made the Pope his footstool), thus reversing the occasions when the Popes had trampled or otherwise humiliated the Holy Roman Emperors, occasions splendidly illustrated in the *Actes and Monuments*. Protestant Elizabeth is presented in an icon similar to her father's within the great initial C that opens the preface to Foxe's book: the C for Constantine in the 1563 edition; for Christ in the edition of 1570.

With Elizabeth's accession, Foxe and the other Marian exiles had come back to England to reestablish the True Church. If this was not as yet the Church perfected, the New Jerusalem of the Apocalypse seen on earth, still it was the representative of the New Jerusalem in its time and place. The English millenarians of the next century, comparing the triumph of God's Kingdom as represented by the saints of the New Model Army with setbacks sustained in Germany and elsewhere, would come to think of their own nation as *the* Elect Nation and their Church as the unique harbinger of the New Jerusalem, reinterpreting Foxe for the purpose. The first such chauvinistic apocalyptic writing in England comes to light precisely in the aftermath of the Armada victory. But Foxe himself was no millenarian, and his eye was on the Church Universal. Installed as a prebend at Salisbury, he refrained from taking a major part in the governance or politics of the Elizabethan Church, and continued beyond the *Actes and Monuments* with his commentary on the Apocalypse, the *Eicasmi*, defining the Signs of the End more and more precisely in the triumphs and catastrophes of the various elect nations of Christendom.[24]

It is generally accepted that Spenser has presented in the Legend of Holiness the 'Image of Both Churches' familiar to Elizabethan readers through the works of Bale and Foxe, and that his story follows loosely the account of universal church history in the *Actes and Monuments*, though without Foxe's concern for specific periodization.[25] When Una appears she is recognizable as the One True Church, whose intention is to restore mankind to its first condition; she has found her champion in the Red Cross Knight, much as the Primitive Church found its champion in the Christian Emperors. Red Cross is always a lay figure, and he despatches the Monster of Error in the first Canto much as Constantine disposed of heresies in his lifetime.

But the Knight is later imposed upon by Archimago, whose conjuring and shapeshifting owes much to the Protestant account of the medieval popes, who were supposed to have included notorious magicians, like Sylvester II, and had in general sponsored the doctrine of transubstantiation with its false mystery and conjuring at the altar. Duessa, the False Church, is Archimago's creation. Derived immediately from the Whore of the Apocalypse who is Babylon, Duessa presents the papalist complex of apostasy and sexual perversion which had obfuscated the True Protestant Faith and the doctrine of Chaste Marriage. No reader of Barnes's *Vitae Romanorum Pontificatorum* would overlook the pernicious innovation of the medieval papacy which consisted in the requirement of clerical celibacy; no reader of Bale's salacious *Actes of the English Votaryes* (1545) would doubt that the monastic system was a cover for sexual perversion!

The Knight acquits himself well in the fights with the Saracen Brothers, as did the Knights of Christendom in the Crusades; nevertheless, he is betrayed by Duessa, who cossets his enemies, as the medieval Papacy was said to have engineered the Crusades for its own purposes and abetted the Turks. Duessa again aids and abets Orgoglio in overthrowing the Knight and keeping him in prison for a period that represents in the historical allegory the triumph of the Imperial Papacy over the Christian Emperors, the period of the Babylonian Captivity of the Church.

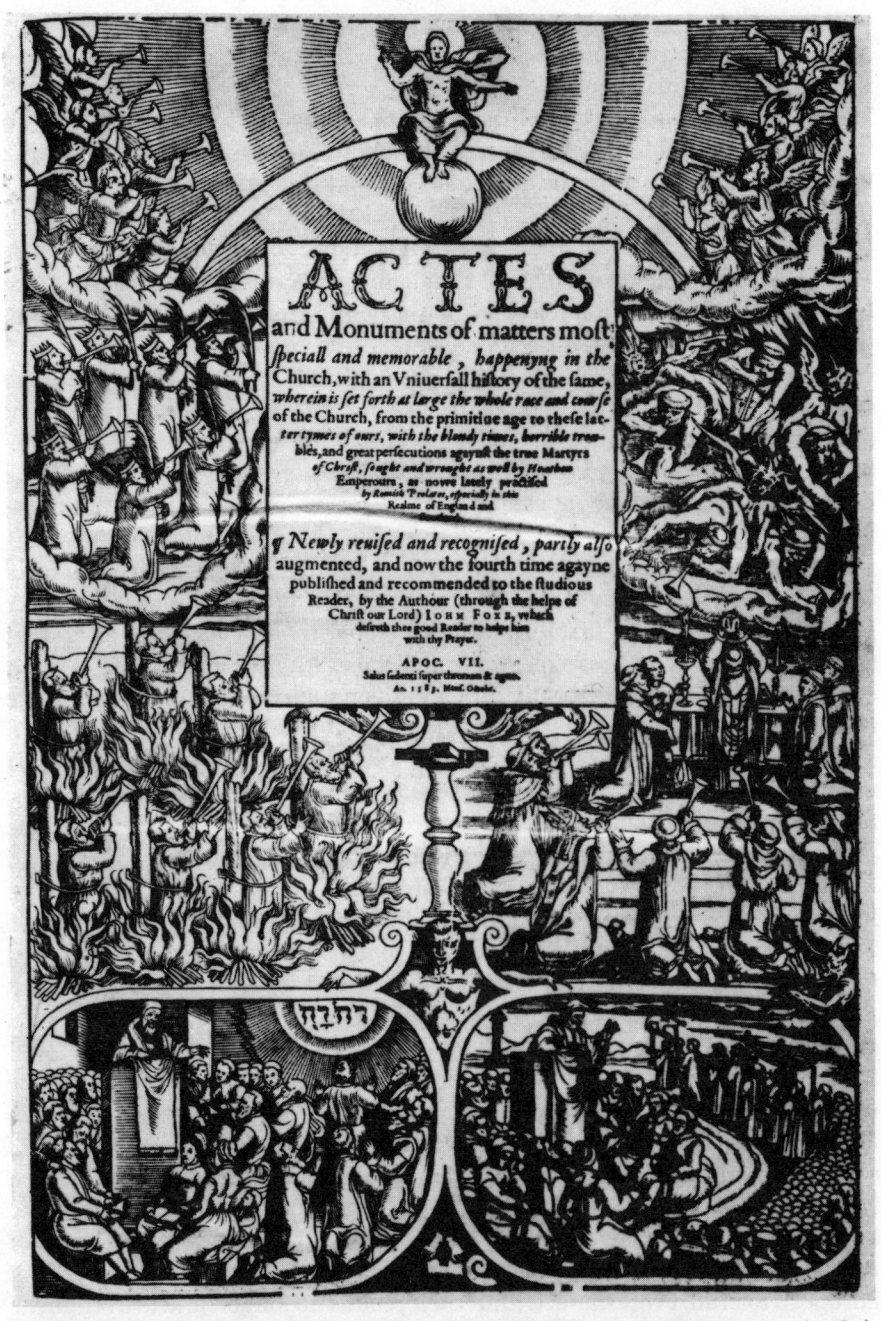

Titlepage from John Foxe's *Actes and Monuments of these latter and perilous days* (1583). Reproduced by permission of The Huntington Library, San Marino, California

The arrival of Arthur, Una's champion, to rescue Red Cross and to fortify him again in his quest, presents the turning point in the Protestant account – the dawn of the Reformation with the appearance of Wycliffe and John Huss. When Red Cross is fortified in Christian Hope against Despair and instructed in the House of Holiness, his return to the basis of the Faith suggests Protestantism's return to the Apostolic religion. But the final appearance of Una in terms that suggest an identification with Elizabeth herself suggests some developments of the Tudor myth that go beyond Foxe's scheme.

It is however not surprising that Elizabeth's subjects had continued to cast her in various apocalyptic roles, particularly in the last decades of her reign, when Rome, Spain and internal enemies appeared to be engaged in a conspiracy against the Queen and the Protestant Succession. The focus of the conspiracy, both in her life and death, was the Catholic Queen of Scots. From the time of her arrival in England in 1568 and her virtual imprisonment by Elizabeth's orders, Mary's claim to succeed to the English throne became increasingly a religious question, and a *cause célèbre* for the Counter Reformation in its drive against Protestantism. Her more impatient followers were not content to let the Protestant Queen live out her reign. The Rebellion of the Northern Earls, with a plan to put the Queen of Scots upon the throne, proved to be only the first of a series of popish plots for insurrection or assassination, and it provoked the papal bull, *Regnans in Excelsis* (1570), excommunicating Elizabeth and absolving her subjects from their allegiance in order to pave the way for Mary's accession.

Whereas Bishop Leslie and other defenders of Mary's claim in the 60s had maintained a courteous tone towards Elizabeth, the pro-Marian propaganda of the 70s and 80s grew more strident towards the English Queen as it exalted the purity and steadfast faith of her prisoner. Nicholas Sanders, the English recusant who worked in Madrid for Elizabeth's dethronement and died in Ireland trying to rouse Irish Catholics against England, had published in 1571 a martyrology to counter the *Actes and Monuments*, showing the imprisoned Queen of Scots as preeminent among the Catholic sufferers. His posthumous *Rise and Growth of the English Anglican Schism* (1585) slandered Elizabeth as the child of a union not only bigamous but incestuous.

More extreme and strident was the propaganda released throughout Europe upon the execution of the Queen of Scots in 1587. To those who extolled Mary's martyrdom for the faith, Elizabeth was 'that inhuman murderess of saints', something rather close to the image of the Whore of the Apocalypse with the blood of the saints upon her skirts. The motive of Adam Blackwood, author of the *De Jezabelis* poem against Elizabeth and of the classic account of the *Martyre de la Royne d'Escosse*, was to persuade the Catholic monarchs of Europe to tolerate Protestants within their realms no longer, and to avenge the blood of this saint by invading England, deposing Elizabeth and restoring the Catholic religion. A host of tragedies, poems and treatises similarly motivated had its effect upon Philip of Spain and the launching of the Armada.[26]

When, in the Legend of Justice, Spenser applauds Elizabeth's execution of the Queen of Scots ('Duessa') as a signal act of justice and mercy, his version of the event accords with that in the officially condoned Protestant literature appearing in the months around the Queen of Scots' death. Elizabeth (as 'Mercilla') is reluctant to punish the royal offender and must be persuaded vigorously by her advisors that it is no part of justice to let such treasons as Mary's go unpunished. And it is for her treason, not her religion, that Mary dies, since she has conspired

>   to depryue
> *Mercilla* of her crowne, by her aspyred,
> That she might it vnto her selfe deryue,
> And tryumph in their blood, whom she to death did dryue.
>
> (V.ix.41)

Yet to use the name 'Duessa' for the Queen of Scots was to refer the reader back to the ominous figure in the Legend of Holiness and to leave no doubt that another manifestation of the Whore of Babylon was engaged in treason against the realm where the True Church was triumphant.[27]

Through the 1580s Elizabeth had been increasingly involved in war with Catholic Spain, both in the Netherlands campaign and in the Armada battle, and had become alarmed at the extent of papalist subversion in Ireland. Spenser's Legend of Justice conveys the embattled situation of Protestant Britain in that decade, its hero, Sir Artegall, being commissioned first to restore peace to Ireland (the land of Irena).[28]

Assaulted by the papal dragon, but triumphant, Elizabeth might be seen as the apocalyptic St. Michael, though, since she was the English Queen and Head of the Order of the Garter, St. George was an alternative comparison. Dressed in pearls and diamonds to receive the homage of her champions, Elizabeth might be the Lady for whom Saint George fought; but dressed in armour at Tilbury she was the champion himself. Roy Strong notes the medal from 1587 which shows on the obverse the Queen enthroned over a seven-headed apocalyptic beast (presumably Rome), attended by the provinces of the Netherlands, while on the reverse Antichrist falls, with his popes and cardinals.[29]

As Protestant Queen and Governor of the Church, Elizabeth might also be seen as the apocalyptic Bride, representing in her virginity the return of the True Church ('A pure virgin, spotted as yet with no idolatry', as John Jewel, following Augustine, described the Primitive Church[30]). Between St. Michael and the Bride, a mediating iconographic term is to be found in the Woman of Revelation 12 who, like her son, is victorious against the threats of the Dragon. This is the Woman 'clothed with the sun and the moon under her feet, and upon her head a crown of twelve stars', who, being with child, is threatened by the Great Red Dragon, yet escapes and delivers the child who is to rule the nations and is caught up to the throne of God. When the Apocalypse was read as a continuing conflict between the forces of the True and the False, and the roles in the drama as complementary manifestations of the one or the other, the Woman in the Sun could be identified with the Bride who descends in Revelation 21. They were the Church as Mother and Bride, both fruitful and chaste; they were the Church in its celestial existence on the one hand, and the Church appearing on earth on the other.

Catholic exegesis had identified the Woman in the Sun with the Virgin Mary, Mother of Christ and of the Church. With her processions and festivals, with her royal coat of arms painted on the tympanums of the parish churches, Elizabeth from the early years of her reign appeared to have replaced the Virgin Mary and the saints in the devotion of Protestant England, 'Viva Eliza! for an Ave Mari!' is the recommendation of an early song in John Dowland's *Second Book of Airs*.[31] Yet this was a matter to be handled cautiously. The obvious charge of a royal idolatry was made both by Jesuit pamphleteers and by radical Protestants. John Milton would follow his tract on the (mere) *Tenure of Kings and Magistrates* with *Eikonoklastes*, aimed to expose the idolatry of the royal image.

The application of the 'Woman in the Sun' allusion to Elizabeth was nevertheless appropriate in the 1560s when she had survived the machinations of Bishop Gardiner and other representatives of the Great Red Dragon of Rome to reach her apotheosis as Queen and 'nursing mother' of the Realm and the Church. The application was reinforced in the 1580s with Elizabeth's survival of various popish assassination plots and her victory over the Armada fleet, when Catholic Spain, attempting, like the Great Red Dragon of Revelation 12, to devour the woman's child as soon as it was born, had been foiled in its attempt, and the woman's issue (i.e., the Protestant dynasty in a Protestant state) was secure. Designs showing the Queen as the Woman in the Sun appear to have circulated in the later decades of the reign. (They must have provided, as the Queen grew older, a rather desperate reassurance against another crisis for the Protestant Succession upon her death, exactly because she had produced no child and heir but an allegorical one.) They were revived again in the years after her death when the Queen could be assumed to have obtained her celestial apotheosis and when popular discontent with the Stuart policies of peace with Spain and toleration for Catholicism invoked the image of the Queen to recall the Protestant state to its apocalyptic role. Yates reproduces in *Astraea* an engraving by Delaram after Hilliard which shows Elizabeth 'clothed with the sun' and 'crowned with the stars' – since the portrait stops below the waist at the point where the clouds envelop her, it is not clear that she has the moon beneath her feet – while the caption hails her in conventional terms as 'Faithes Shield and Queene of State, of Arms and Learning'.[32]

To understand both the force and the limitation of the political allegory in Spenser's apocalyptic poem, it is instructive to refer to the recently discovered annotations in Lord Besborough's copy of the first edition of *The Faerie Queene* (Books I–III), written in an Elizabethan hand, presumably that of the 'John Dixon' who inscribed his name on the title page. Dixon knows his Bible, his Foxe and his British chroniclers. He sees the dependence of Book I on the text of the Apocalypse, he notes the moral allegory, and in some remarkable annotations he uncovers the historical allegory in terms of the Protestant and Elizabethan myth. From the outset, Dixon reads the 'louely Ladie', Una, as 'truth' but also as 'Eliza'. He goes so far as to identify Red Cross, her champion, on his first appearance as Leicester[33] – this exactly at the allusion to the 'Knight faithful and true' of the Apocalypse (I.i.2). The identification is less startling, perhaps, when one remembers that portraits of Leicester and Burghley stood with Elizabeth's in the illustrations of the New Testament of the Bishops' Bible.

Dixon is indignant that Una's status and heritage have been usurped by the daughter of the Emperor of the West enthroned by the Tiber (I.ii.22): 'Antichriste taketh on hir the nam of Truth ... but truth is only ment, to our Soueraigne Eliz. Christe and his gospell'! Without any sense of contradiction, Dixon assumes that Elizabeth is not only Una but also the lion who rushes out of the wood to defend her: 'the Lyon is the tribe of Juda and rote of dauid', he writes (I.iii.5), and, when the lion is mentioned again, 'Eliz: Loue Christe the sone of dauid re: 5:5:' (I.iii.7). Here not only does Dixon invoke the Davidic covenant and the principle of royal legitimacy as applying to England on a par with Israel, but he sees Elizabeth in yet another apocalyptic role. In the text of Revelation 5.5 to which he refers, it is the Lion of the Tribe of Judah who 'hath obtained to open the Booke, and to loose the seven seals thereof'. At the climax of the drama of Book I Dixon is confident that the marriage of Una and the Red Cross Knight is not only as in Revelation the marriage of 'the wyffe of ye Lambe of god' (at I.xii.7) with the victorious Christ (at i.xii.9), but also the Accession, or rather 'the Crownation of or Blessed Eliz:' (at I.xii.40): 'The Church and the Lambe Christe united by god himsellfe. a happy knotte, wherby peace hath beine Continewed 39 yea:' (at I.xii.13).

To Dixon, the Protestant Elizabeth was all along the true heir as against her older Catholic sister, though the Protestant succession, which seemed to have triumphed with Edward, suffered a six-year intermission during Mary's reign. Rome then did her worst, but was unable to prevent the right and godly outcome! He gives a similar interpretation for the motto at the head of Canto XII:

> Fayre *Una* to the *Redcrosse knight*
> betrouthed is with ioy:
> Though false *Duessa* it to barre
> Her false sleightes doe imploy.

The motto presents itself to him as: 'a fiction of or Queene Eliz: the maintainer of the gospell of Christe, to be by god himselfe betrouthed unto Christe, though by k:p: [King Philip] and rc: [Roman Catholics] for: 6:years it was debared'. But in the course of the narrative the Red Cross Knight, betrothing himself to Una, announces that he must leave her for six years and return to the service of the Faerie Queene. Dixon, picking up the clue of the six years, reads that too as 'the time of the raingne of phil: and marye' (at I.xii.18). Eventually there comes the episode mentioned in the Motto, when Duessa sends a message to 'debar' the marriage in view of her prior claim on Red Cross, the messenger discovered to be none other than Archimago himself. Dixon now sees that the Duessa who wants to take Elizabeth's place is not Mary Tudor but Mary Queen of Scots, while the messenger is presumably Pope Pius V, delivering his bull *Regnans in Excelsis*, to excommunicate Elizabeth and support the claim of the Queen of Scots: 'A Fiction of a Challinge by Q: of: s: that the religion by hir maintained to be the truth', he writes at I.xii.26. But if the claim by the Queen of Scots interrupts the betrothal which takes place before the six year separation, while the separation itself represents the reign of Mary and Philip, what has happened to chronology? This is a question that apparently does not concern Dixon when he is reading an allegorical poem. He does not expect the poem to 'follow' history chronologically, but rather to present the basic myth which history also 'follows' in its way, perhaps within individual episodes, perhaps in sequences or duplications of events.

Dixon's readings corroborate one's impression that Spenser has incorporated into the Legend of Holiness much of the political allegory of the Tudor State and Church, and that when he brings his apocalyptic narrative to its culmination in an event which is as much the Accession of Elizabeth as it is the Marriage of the Bride and the Lamb, he has attributed a sanctity to the Elizabethan Church and Succession. Yet clearly Dixon also assumes the predominance of the moral and spiritual allegory over the historical in Spenser's apocalyptic poem. The potency of the images of the rival queens (whether Elizabeth and her half-sister Mary Tudor, or Elizabeth and her cousin the Queen of Scots) derives from their identification as representatives of the 'Both Churches' of Bishop Bale, whether in the Protestant version or in the reversed form to be found in the pro-Marian propaganda, the mythical structure remaining the same though the two Queens change places as Whore and Bride. The dichotomy is the more poignant because it occurs within one royal family.

The ecclesiastical myth of 'Both Churches' derives its potency in turn from representing on another plane the baptismal myth: the struggle between Sin and Grace in the soul where the issue must be the triumph of Grace and the emergence of the true spiritual and glorious identity. The True Queen must triumph and take her place upon the throne and the True Church be vindicated in the world, as Christ who is the Truth triumphs in the human heart. The triumph is not complete within the saeculum, but seen apocalyptically, that is, 'opened' or 'unveiled', it is a sign and promise of the final eschatological triumph when the Kingdom will have come and God will be all in all.

III

It is beyond the scope of this chapter to investigate the relationship of Book I to the other books of *The Fairie Queene*. Suffice it to say that when the Red Cross Knight on the mountaintop can see his life *sub specie aeternitatis* so that his former 'wanderings' and strayings are converted to pilgrimage and he can now cut a clean path through the 'waves' of this world, the same mountaintop perspective will inform the reader's judgment of the wanderings of the Knights subsequently introduced. The 'dilation' of time in which Spenser's heroes move is not merely an extension between the First and Second Comings but, when they come to read it aright, a dynamic dimension in which they work towards their perfection and consummation in that Second Coming.

Spenser intended to end his epic somewhat in the manner of Book I, though on a larger scale, with Arthur's great battle against the Paynim and his marriage with the Faerie Queene. The effect of such an ending would be an enhancement of the apocalypse of Book I. Not only is Arthur, as magnanimity, the sum of all the virtues represented by the other heroes; but his life cycle includes the epicycles of their lives, so that in the action of the epic he assumes the special representativity that comes from his being the first or head of his species – 'Princeps' in more than title. Red Cross's status as heir to God's Kingdom is magnified in Prince Arthur who will come to an earthly crown before a heavenly one and thus reflect God's majesty on earth in a public and overt way.

Though Arthur knows at the outset from Merlin that he is 'sonne and heire unto a King', still his knowledge, like that of Red Cross Knight at a lower level, is imperfect:

> For both the lignage and the certain Sire
> From which I sprong, from me are hidden yit.
>
> (I.ix.3)

Even the British Chronicle he later consults in the House of Alma stops short at the name of King Uther and does not reveal the existence of Uther's son. It is presumably when Arthur too has gained through experience a deeper insight into himself and into the 'secret meaning of th' eternall might, / That rules mens wayes' (I.ix.5) that he will learn of his parentage and his kingdom, and see, by waking sight and face to face, the Faerie Queene his beloved Gloriana, whom now he knows in a dream, and sees as it were in a glass darkly.

But we do not have the projected scene with the apotheosis of King and Queen to close the narrative of the epic in a manner that suggests the historical consummation. Instead we have in the Mutabilitie Cantos the apotheosis of Nature enthroned. Whatever the relationship of the Cantos to the rest of the epic, whether they are to be read as a self-contained piece, a 'parcell' of 'some following Booke . . . under the Legend of Constancie' (as suggested by the 1609 Folio) or a retrospective commentary on the poem as a whole, it is worthwhile in determining the apocalyptic style of *The Faerie Queene* to consider briefly the import of Spenser's image of *Natura naturata* in the Cantos in the light of the New Jerusalem in Book I.

One might begin with the scriptural associations of the Mount of Contemplation and Arlo Hill, the two hills of vision that rise above the plane of mundaneity. The Mount to which Contemplation brings the Red Cross Knight is likened successively to Sinai, to Olivet and to Parnassus. It is the point of revelation first of the Law ('writ in stone / With bloudy letters by the hand of God'), bringing with it the 'bitter doome of death and balefull mone' (I.x.53) but then of the gracious presence of Christ fulfilling the law in love, Olivet being crowned with a 'flowring girland' of 'fruitfull Olives' (I.x.54). It is the mark of the Erasmian not only to assume that the same gracious Presence had been found (or at least adumbrated) in Apollo and sung by the Muses in 'heauenly notes' (I.x.54) but to see the present Christian reality as a grace-filled world. If, in replacing the image of the mountain of the Law with those of fruitful Olivet and the exuberant muses, Spenser has one particular Pauline passage in mind, it is likely to be that in Romans 5:

> Therefore as by the offense of one judgment came upon all men to condemnation; even so by the righteousness of one the free gift came upon all men unto justification of life . . .
> Moreover, the law entered that the offence might abound. But where sin abounded, grace did much more abound.
>
> (Rom. 5: 18–20)

(For that last verb, Erasmus in the *Paraphrases* had found inadequate the Vulgate *superabundavit*, and rendered it instead by *magis exuberavit*. The Greek *hypereperisseusen*, he explained, meant not merely an overflowing but an enlargement *supra modum*.)[34] For the most part the account of the contemplative vision of Red Cross emphasizes the transcendent nature of the New Jerusalem, above and beyond this world, a City that the Knight may glimpse now but not aspire to inhabit until his quest in the world is completed. Yet Olivet remembers endlessly an incarnate Lord who descended into flesh, and still the 'blessed Angels to and fro descend / From highest heauen, in gladsome companne' (I.x.56).

The Incarnational theology is even more explicit in the account of Nature's apotheosis on Arlo Hill where the mountain invoked is not Olivet but Tabor, and the scriptural event the Transfiguration. Nature's garment is 'so bright and wondrous sheene' that the poet finds himself bereft of comparisons:

> As those three sacred *Saints*, though else most wise,
> Yet on mount *Thabor* quite their wits forgat,
> When they their glorious Lord in strange disguise
> Transfigur'd sawe; his garments so did daze their eyes.
>
> (*Mut.* vii.7)

In a linear perspective of history, the Transfiguration episode in the Synoptic Gospels is the event that anticipates the Resurrection and ultimately the Second Coming in Glory. Jesus was seen then in his Glory by the three disciples as he would be seen by all in the Eschaton. Under the aspect of Eternity, however, Jesus was seen then in the temporal world as He Is. The veil which separates the visible from the invisible world, the future from the present, was removed for a moment, and the truth was revealed. There is some irony in Spenser's reference to the Lord 'in strange disguise', since he appears so only to eyes conditioned by temporality.

Moreover, the disciples do not realize that this same glorious state is ultimately their own as 'Sacred Saints'. When the Kingdom comes, the righteous too shall be transformed and 'shine forth like the sun' (Matt. 13.43). The word for Jesus's being changed or transfigured is *mĕtamŏrphŏthĕ* (Mark 9.2), the same word used by Paul in his testimony on the Work of the Spirit within the soul: 'But we all, with open face beholding as in a glass the glory of the Lord, are *changed* into the same image from glory to glory, even as by the Spirit of the Lord' (2 Cor. 3.18); 'The dead shall be raised up incorruptible, and we shall be *changed*' (1 Cor. 15.53).

The adversary in the Cantos who takes the place of Duessa and Archimago in Book I is the Titaness Mutabilitie, advancing her claim against Jove to be autonomous and sovereign. She is, in the psychic drama, the 'earthly' faction which disdains the rule of reason and is unaware of the Work of the Spirit; in the political drama, she is the usurper of the Powers that are ordained of God. But her claim is judged by Nature herself who appears in Glory on Arlo Hill, like Jesus on Mount Tabor. Her presence is a mystery that consists in the reconciliation of opposites. In Jesus the opposites of God and man are reconciled; in Nature, the opposites of male and female, youth and age, terror and beauty. The claims of Mutabilitie cannot impose upon Nature, the unmoved mover, who accommodates all change and mutability within an Order that is sempiternal, and whose appearance brings Arlo Hill and all the world to flower, manifesting the Eternal spring that was seen once in Eden but also in each subsequent springtime.

When Mutabilitie, still obtuse, calls upon the evidence of the world's changes to support her own claim, and Nature's sergeant, Order, leads out the processions of the Seasons, of the Years and the Hours, of Life and Death, the very display of procession disproves Mutabilitie's claim before Nature's verdict is given:

> I well consider all that ye haue sayd,
>   And find that all things stedfastnes doe hate
>   And changed be: yet being rightly wayd
>   They are not changed from their first estate:
>   But by their change their being doe dilate:
>   And turning to themselves at length againe,
>   Doe worke their owne perfection so by fate:
>   Then ouer them Change doth not rule and raigne;
> But they raigne ouer change and doe their states maintaine.
>
> Cease therefore daughter further to aspire,
>   And thee content thus to be rul'd by me:
>   For thy decay thou seekst by thy desire;
>   But time shall come that all shall changed bee,
>   And from thenceforth, none no more change shall see.
>
> (*Mut.* vii. 58–9)

The Christian NeoPlatonic, or more specifically Plotinian, worldview that Spenser here presents sees the phenomenal world, with its ordered cycles, processing from and returning to Eternity. One of its merits is exactly its scope for the resolution of local conflict (ultimately, the conflict between Mutabilitie and Jove, between Change and Order) by their submergence within a larger pattern. The cycles of the NeoPlatonic universe encompass all opposite points: the procession of the hours running from day to night gives the pattern that is repeated in larger form in the procession of the months from March to February and in the procession of the seasons from Spring to Winter. The procession of history is larger still, from the restoration to the ruin of the civic order and then again to restoration; still it follows the same pattern seen in Nature. Yet the ultimate disproof of Mutabilitie's claim is not that changes run in perpetual succession but that at the End change and time itself will be absorbed into eternity, and 'all shall changed bee'. The final meaning of change is not 'mutability' but 'transfiguration', as Spenser had adumbrated by his initial invocation of the Transfiguration upon Mount Tabor.[35]

The effect of the Mutabilitie Cantos is not so much a departure from apocalyptic as an enlargement of it in Biblical as well as philosophical terms. It sets the Biblical genre of apocalyptic, represented in Daniel and the Apocalypse of John and concentrating upon the Vision of Divine Judgment on History, within the larger prophetic tradition from which historically it derived. In the Legend of Holiness Spenser 'unveils' the historical signs, presenting the historical realm of Britain and its Queen transfigured, as the Book of Daniel and the Apocalypse of John present the transfigured kingdom of Israel and the transfigured city of Jerusalem. In the Mutabilitie Cantos he presents the transfigured order of Creation, as Second Isaiah sings the world of Nature restored to its Edenic state with the Lord's return, or the Psalmist of Psalm 104 celebrates the order of Creation which is perpetually radiant in God's sight.

Nevertheless, it is from the Legend of Holiness that there emerges most clearly Spenser's reading of the Johannine Apocalypse. Here he has written a fiction that imitates the fiction of the Apocalypse. That Spenser's Legend proves to be a 'veil' for the mystery of the Spirit suggests that he read the Apocalypse as the supreme example of such a work. Boccaccio, defending the poet's use of fiction, had appealed in the *Genealogy of the Gods* to the authority of the Holy Spirit itself and to 'those parts of the Revelation of John the Evangelist – expressed with amazing majesty of inner sense, though often at first glance quite contrary to the truth – in which he has veiled the great mysteries of God'.[36] To refer to the Humanists' interpretation of the Apocalypse as moral allegory may be to miss the significance of their perspective, if the allegory is seen as merely moral, one among various horizontal levels that might be used. More precisely, the moral or spiritual interpretation the Humanists give to the Apocalypse is a reading in which all events at all levels, whether natural, political or psychological, are seen to be involved in one cosmic process of transformation into Spirit.

Moreover, in John on Patmos the Apocalypse provided the Christian Humanists with the figure of the poet. John speaks as 'your brother and companion in tribulation', and yet also as the man who stands upon the mountaintop of Contemplation, being caught up 'in the Spirit' to hear the voice of God and see the Work of the Spirit in the world. He offers himself as the example of one undergoing the transformation through 'Patience' to the 'Kingdom', within the Body of Christ who has gone before; and when he is caught up in the Spirit *on the Lord's Day*, that prompts recognition of the way in which the day that celebrates the Resurrection (or any day which is the Lord's) anticipates the final Day of the Lord, the Eschaton (Rev. 1.9). The fiction made by John, the man on Patmos, is transparent to that vision; hence, he is saluted by the angel as a 'fellow-servant' and equal (Rev. 22.8–9). The same poet John is the one known as 'the Divine'. In exactly the text that others would use to prove God's inexorable predetermination, the Humanists found the exaltation of poetry and the human spirit.

NOTES

1 William Haller's book, *The Elect Nation: The Meaning and Relevance of Foxe's Book of Martyrs* (1963) opened up the present phase of discussion by reading Foxe's *Actes and Monuments* as a decisive influence on the 'saints' of the English revolution in the mid seventeenth century and assuming that their radical program was to be found in Foxe's book itself. Later commentators have stressed Foxe's conservatism and

seen the turning point in the 1630s and 1640s, when Foxe was subjected to ideological revision. See Peter Toon, ed., *Puritans, The Millennium and the Future of Israel: Puritan Eschatology, 1600 to 1660* (Cambridge, London, 1970); William M. Lamont, *Godly Rule: Politics and Religion, 1603–60* (1969); Katharine R. Firth, *The Apocalyptic Tradition in Reformation Britain: 1530–1645* (Oxford, 1979); Richard Bauckham, *Tudor Apocalypse* (Appleford, Eng., 1978); Paul Christianson, *Reformers and Babylon: English Apocalyptic Visions from the Reformation to the Eve of the Civil War* (Toronto, Buffalo, London, 1978); V. Norskov Olsen, *John Foxe and the Elizabethan Church* (Berkeley, Los Angeles, London, 1973). Foxe's *Actes and Monuments* (1563) has been republished in a full and reliable edition in 8 vols (1965). Many other editions printed in the last three centuries are untrustworthy, since their objective is to update the nefarious activities of the papal Antichrist and the Jesuits, incorporating additional material without notice.

2 See especially Isabel G. MacCaffrey, *Spenser's Allegory: The Anatomy of Imagination* (Princeton, 1976) and Patricia A. Parker, *Inescapable Romance: Studies in the Poetics of a Mode* (Princeton, 1979). Both books have excellent comments on the relationship of Spenser's allegorical style to a Christian worldview. The merits of the old and new traditions in twentieth-century criticism on Spenser are succinctly presented in A. C. Hamilton, 'The Faerie Queene', in *Critical Approaches to Six Major English Works: 'Beowulf' through 'Paradise Lost'*, ed. Robert M. Lumiansky and Herschel Baker (Philadelphia, 1968), ch. IV.

3 Graham Hough, *The First Commentary on 'The Faerie Queene': Being an Analysis of Lord Bessborough's Copy of the First Edition of 'The Faerie Queene'*, (Folcroft, Pennsylvania, 1964).

4 Catherine A. L. Jarrott, 'Erasmus's Annotations and Colet's Commentaries on Paul: A Comparison of Some Theological Themes', in Richard L. DeMolen, ed., *Essays on the Works of Erasmus* (New Haven, 1978), pp. 125–44.

5 Erasmus's collected *Paraphrase of the New Testament* appeared in a two volume edition (1548–9), translated by Nicholas Udall, Thomas Caius, John Old et al. In Edward VI's reign it was ordered to be placed alongside the Bible in every parish church in England.

6 The text of *The Faerie Queene* followed here is the 1596 text, reproduced in J. C. Smith's *Faerie Queene* (Oxford English Texts edition, 1909) and in A. C. Hamilton's *Faerie Queene* (1977).

7 The English translation of the *Enchiridion*, probably by William Tyndale, was published first in 1533 and frequently reprinted through the 1530s and 1540s. Coverdale's abridgement of Tyndale's text was brought out in Antwerp and London in 1548, while further editions of the Tyndale text appeared in 1550 and 1576. Quotations in the present chapter are taken from a translation by John P. Dolan, *The Handbook of the Militant Christian* in *The Essential Erasmus* (1964).

8 *The Handbook of the Militant Christian* (as above, note 7), p. 29.

9 Ibid., p. 52.

10 Ibid., p. 31.

11 Ibid., p. 36.

12 After a dearth of commentaries on the Pauline Epistles through the Middle Ages, many were published over the turn of the century, including those of Colet (1490–9), Lefèvre d'Étaples (1512), Luther (1515–16), Erasmus (1517) and Calvin (1539).

13 Ernst-W. Kohls, 'The Principal Theological Thoughts in the *Enchiridion Militis*

Christiani', in *Essays on the Works of Erasmus* (as above, note 4), p. 70.
14 *Handbook* (as above, note 7), esp. pp. 63–4.
15 'Erasmus's Annotations' (as above, note 4), p. 137.
16 *Handbook* (as above, note 7), p. 50.
17 The significance of baptism in the allegory was first pointed out by A. C. Hamilton in *The Structure of Allegory in the 'Faerie Queene'* (Oxford, 1961). Spenser strikes an Erasmian note in designating the third of the virtues not simply faith but faithfulness. Glossing Romans 4.3, Erasmus in 1521 changed *fides* to *fiducia* as the merit on account of which Abraham was considered justified. For this and other examples, see Albert Rabil, Jr, 'Erasmus's *Paraphrases of the New Testament*', in *Essays on the Works of Erasmus* (as above, note 4), p. 151.
18 Jarrott (as above, note 4), p. 133.
19 Kohls (as above, note 4), p. 77.
20 Kohls (as above, note 4), p. 76.
21 Frances A. Yates, *Astraea: The Imperial Theme in the Sixteenth Century* (1975), p. 65. Yates gives excellent material from contemporary sources on the Elizabethan myth in its various aspects, Protestant and otherwise, relating the English imperial cult to its counterparts in France and Germany.
22 John Bale, *The Image of Both Churches* is reproduced in *Select Works* (Cambridge, 1849). For an account of Bale's role, see Firth, *The Apocalyptic Tradition in Reformation Britain 1530–1645*, and Bauckham, *Tudor Apocalypse* (both as above, note 1). See also Thora Balsbev Blatt, *The Plays of John Bale: A Study of Ideas, Technique and Style* (Copenhagen, 1968).
23 Glanville Williams, *Reformation Views of Church History* (Richmond and London, 1970), p. 8.
24 For Foxe, see especially Firth, *The Apocalyptic Tradition in Reformation Britain: 1530–1645*, Bauckham, *Tudor Apocalypse*, and Olsen, *John Foxe and the Elizabethan Church* (all as above, note 1). Bauckham gives particular attention to the first signs of the chauvinistic 'Elect Nation' mentality in the years of the Armada Victory, stressing the disparity between this and the Elizabethan orthodoxy.
25 For extended comparisons of Spenser's narrative with Foxe's account of Church history, see Frank Kermode, *Shakespeare, Spenser, Donne: Renaissance Essays* (1971) and more especially John Erskine Hankins, *Source and Meaning in Spenser's Allegory: A Study of 'The Faerie Queene'* (Oxford, 1971). (Commentators do not necessarily agree on the historical identifications.) In exile during the Marian years, Foxe himself wrote a dramatic version of ecclesiastical history where the woman who holds Una's place is Ecclesia, the mother of three sons named for the continents where the Church has been established. See *Christus Triumphans*, in *Two Latin Comedies by John Foxe the Martyrologist*, ed. and trans., John Hazel Smith (Ithaca and London, 1973).
26 For the information on the controversy over the Queen of Scots, I am indebted to James Emerson Phillips, *Images of a Queen: Mary Stuart in Sixteenth-Century Literature* (Berkeley and Los Angeles, 1964). Phillips' account of the change of tone as the controversy became an issue of Reformation vs. Counter Reformation is to be found on p. 116 ff. The reference to Elizabeth as 'that inhuman murderess of saints' is Verstegan's (see p. 182).
27 It was about Spenser's account of the guilt of the Queen of Scots that James VI of Scotland complained to the English government on behalf of 'himself and his mother deceased', desiring that the poet be imprisoned. Elizabeth's government

dissociated itself from the poem, explaining that it was printed without privilege. James's concern was to gain reassurance that his own succession in England was not blocked by the 'treason' of which his mother had been found guilty. It is of interest that once he did succeed to the English crown he allowed *The Faerie Queene* to be printed without alteration. Phillips, *Images of a Queen* (as above, note 26), p. 201 ff.

28 As Secretary to Lord Grey on his Irish campaigns, Spenser had first-hand evidence that Smerwick Castle, which Grey captured in 1582, flew the Pope's banner and held foreign soldiers claiming to have been sent by the Pope. See Alexander C. Judson, *The Life of Edmund Spenser*, Vol. 8 of *The Works of Edmund Spenser*, ed. E. Greenlaw, C. S. Osgood, F. M. Padelford (Baltimore, 1945), p. 91.

29 Roy Strong, *Portraits of Queen Elizabeth I* (Oxford, 1963), p. 138, Medal 16. The dating of the medal offers proof that Spenser's poem did not invent the apocalyptic role for Elizabeth, but rather exploited a current myth. See also p. 154 where Strong presents a design by Thomas Cecill (c. 1625) based on an earlier painting. Here Elizabeth, as a St. George figure, is vanquishing the hydra (Rome?) and liberating Truth from her cave. Gerard de Malynes in his *Saint George for England* (1601) alludes to Elizabeth as St. George vanquishing the force of evil by the dissemination of pure doctrine and thus rescuing many from chains of darkness.

30 John Jewel, *An Apology of the Church of England* (Charlottesville, 1963), p. 121.

31 Yates (as above, note 21), p. 78.

32 Yates (as above, note 21), Plate 9b.

33 Dixon writes '*yb:yrfgre*', using a cypher achieved by counting fourteen letters ahead. It reads as '*lo:lester*'. Hough (as above, note 3), p. 2.

34 Jarrott (as above, note 4), p. 131.

35 An account of the NeoPlatonic, worldview and its significance for Spenser's aesthetics is given by S. K. Heninger in *Touches of Sweet Harmony: Pythagorean Cosmology and Renaissance Poetics* (San Marino, 1974). See also Rosalie Colie, 'Being and Becoming in *The Faerie Queene*', *Paradoxia Epidemica: The Renaissance Tradition of Paradox* (Princeton, 1966), Chap. 11.

36 Boccaccio, *On Poetry: Being the Preface and the Fourteenth and Fifteenth Book of Boccaccio's Genealogia Deorum Gentilium*, trs. Charles G. Osgood (1956), p. 64.

JOSEPH WITTREICH

7 'Image of that horror':
the Apocalypse in *King Lear*

> Here is very Night herself. . . . We have heard much and often from the theologians of the light of revelation . . . but the darkness of revelation is here.   A. C. SWINBURNE.

St. John's Apocalypse proved to be a dangerous book during the Renaissance – at least some of the time. Witness the story that John Foxe tells of one Mr Stile who, 'wont to read upon [it]', was burned at Smithfield: 'This good man and the blessed Apocalypse were both together in fire consumed'.[1] At other times the book met with studied indifference, as in the instances of Erasmus, Tyndale, Zwingli, and certainly of Luther and Calvin; or was treated with quiet disdain, as seems to have been the case with those who censured much of it both in the Book of Common Prayer and in their edicts against prophesying. Churchmen and politicians alike ignored John's warning: 'if any men shal diminish of the wordes of . . . the boke . . ., God shal take away his parte out of the boke of life' (20.19). On the other hand, many poets and dramatists heeded these words and so should be numbered among those resisting official efforts to expurgate the book – efforts intended to minimize the attention accorded it. The principal artists of the English Renaissance – Spenser, Shakespeare, Donne and later Herbert, Marvell, and Milton – apparently spurred by a burgeoning number of sermons and commentaries – set for themselves the task of returning the Apocalypse from exile and thrusting it into prominence. Hence the church's, the government's, dislodgement of the Book of Revelation and dismantling of its myth is but one story; another is the resuscitation of the book by religious dissenters and later by secular artists, even by a king. This latter story casts doubt on the widespread supposition that moderates of this period did not often write on the Apocalypse and seldom were inspired by it.

Gabriel Harvey wrote a telling letter to Edmund Spenser: 'I heard once a

Diuine, preferre *Saint Johns Reuelation* before al the veriest Metaphysical Visions, and . . . conceited *Dreames* and *Extasies*, that ever were devised by one or other'. His observation here was but a pretext for instructing Spenser that this 'superexcellent' work – 'the verie notablest, and most wonderful Propheticall, or Poeticall Vision' – was a particularly appropriate model for a poet with Spenser's gifts and concerns.[2] Responsive to the summons, Spenser in *The Faerie Queene* canonizes the apocalyptic myth as a literary convention – makes of it a weapon not for instigating but for averting catastrophe, employs it as a means for scrutinizing the interdependence of self and society and the meaning of history. Spenser's poem is (as so many Renaissance titles proclaimed the Book of Revelation to be) a looking glass on providence, on history, through which we may observe the distance separating the apocalyptic promise from reality. In Spenser's prophetic epic, Nature's concluding words are of apocalypse, though Nature's are not the poem's final words; and even in the first book, the most apocalyptic one in the poem, 'the ending is tentative, a new beginning rather than a determinate conclusion'.[3] To read Spenser's poem within an apocalyptic framework is to behold a gradual withdrawal from the apocalyptic promise – is to witness a distancing of apocalypse into future history and, eventually, a pushing of that promise beyond history into eternity.

Nevertheless, for Spenser the Apocalypse still contains metaphors for history and thus continues to provide it with a structure, to imbue it with meaning; but for John Donne, pondering that book just a few decades later but in another century, the Apocalypse is of minimal use in comprehending history since it cannot be understood until its prophecies are fulfilled – not in the world but in the soul of individual men. Genesis may find its reference points in the history of the world, but Revelation finds them in the spiritual history of everyman. In the former, the danger is in departing from the letter; in the latter, in observing the letter too strictly. If inflections differ in the two testaments, they differ, according to Donne, within the New Testament itself. For 'Christs first tongue was a tongue that might be heard, He spoke to the shepheardes by Angels; His second tongue was a Star, a tongue which might be seene.' It is Christ's second tongue that, for Donne, gives the Apocalypse its distinctive quality as a '*propheticall glasse, . . .* [a] *perspective of visions*'.[4] The special attributes of its expression – the emblematic, hieroglyphic character of the book together with its darkness and obscurity – are but devices for directing attention away from its nominal to its real subject, from its literal to its figurative sense. Donne's interpretation, then, evades the whole notion of a renovated world and envisions, instead, the spiritual resurrection of all men in this life: their resurrection from persecution by deliverance, from sin by grace, and from temptation and other difficulties of human existence by death.

Between *The Faerie Queene* and Donne's few sermons on Revelation stand Shakespeare's history plays and tragedies. In the tragedies especially, the apocalyptic strain becomes increasingly more prominent, with *King Lear*, *Macbeth*, and *Antony and Cleopatra* all harboring the apocalyptic myth. Whether or not these plays countenance the Christian eschatology, their author is clearly cognizant of it, with *Lear* recounting a tragedy of redemption and *Macbeth* one of damnation. In Shakespeare, we find (as M. H. Abrams has found in Donne) 'the root-images of the latter days as described in the Book of Revelation';[5] yet, despite 'the great doom's image' of *Macbeth* (II.iii.83) and 'the promis'd end' of *Lear* (V.iii.264), not to mention the apocalyptic conclusion of *Antony*, Shakespeare has seemed an unlikely quarry for reference to the biblical Apocalypse. Thus Austin Farrer remarks that, while we can 'compare what St. John was doing with what Shakespeare was doing', the comparison 'may have little interest',[6] presumably because of the different character and quality of their respective utterances.

Shakespeare's history plays, nonetheless, are shot through with the prophetic: there is King Henry's prophecy to Prince Hal, as well as Richard's and especially Carlisle's prophecy in *Richard II*; there are Margaret's, Elizabeth's, and Richmond's prophecies in *Richard III*; and even the child Elizabeth serves as her own, and James's, oracle in *Henry VIII*. Within these plays, moreover, the prophetic sometimes modulates into apocalyptic, as in *Henry VI, Part II*:

> ... let the vile world end
> And the promised flames of the last day
> Knit earth and heaven together;
> Now let the general trumpet blast.

(V.ii.40–3)

There are those passages in *Richard III* where the king is perceived as Antichrist; in the same play, Elizabeth sees in 'the downfall of our house / . . . the end of all' (III.i.49, 54), the Prince looks ahead 'to the general all-ending day' (III.i.78), and Richmond proclaims, 'the sun will not be seen today' (V.iii.212). In her dream in *Henry VIII*, Queen Katharine beholds 'a blessed troop', clad in white robes, with palms in their hands and with 'bright faces . . . like the sun', summoning her 'to a banquet' (IV.ii.87–9). Still, there is no easy correlation between the ideology of the Apocalypse and that of the history plays, nor even between history as conceived by Shakespeare and by the Tudor historians who found their providential schemes authorized by the Apocalypse. Shakespeare's great contribution, it has been proposed, was to undo the synthesis of his contemporaries and to neutralize their moralizations. Despite his mocking at drunken and astrological prophecies, Shakespeare introduces into his histories and tragedies an important prophetic component, often with apocalyptic figurations, with no hint of aspersion and with every intention of making functional use of prophecy.[7] These prophetic and apocalyptic elements are, very simply, an aspect of the artist's relationship to his own times.

It is as if 'the mutterings and foreshadowings of doom'[8] in select history plays were intended to find their ultimate expression in *King Lear* whose fidelity to historical truth, if not to chronicle history, has led one critic to conclude: 'there is no play of Shakespeare which reads so much like authentic history'.[9] Apparently the histories led Shakespeare to a set of hypotheses that are consolidated and tested in *Lear*, where the Stuart myth sits as uneasily as the Tudor myth had previously sat in the histories. The history plays, it was once thought, dramatize a carefully selected phase of history through which Shakespeare represents England moving from concord to concord and thereby reveals 'the providential and happy ending of an organic piece of history'.[10] In this scenario, history is a manifestation of God's judgments, a display of his handiwork, with Shakespeare 'cut[ting] his cloth to fit the pattern' and using that pattern to present 'historical mirrors' upon contemporary events.[11] But recent criticism has favored another scenario, which has Shakespeare representing the claims of Tudor historians in order to refute them, along with the providential schemes they would foster.[12] As Shakespeare eyed earlier mythic, artificial shapings of history, he seems to have seen a black cloud emerging and encroaching on history, 'a black death threatening to annihilate history, to return it to primeval horror'; and he expresses this sense 'with all the demonic power of tragedy'[13] in both *Macbeth* and *King Lear*. These tragedies, especially, show Shakepseare subscribing to the idea that history is a 'rehearsal of all the events of human tragedy'.[14]

I 'THE REVERSAL OF ALL HISTORIES'

Consider the title page for the 1608 Quarto edition of *King Lear*:

> M. William Shak-speare: / *HIS* / True Chronicle Historie of the life and / death of King LEAR and his three / Daughters. / *With the unfortunate life of* Edgar ... *and his* / sullen *and assumed humor of* / TOM *of Bedlam:* / *As it was played before the Kings Maiestie at Whitehall upon* / S. Stephans *night in Christmas Hollidayes.* / By His Maiesties seruants. (*Var. Ed.*, p. 354)

The initial words of this title and the text of the play itself pull oppositely, at once joining the play to the tradition of chronicle history and disjoining it from all previous renderings of the Lear story, most notably the anonymous dramatized version published in 1605 but perhaps staged as early as 1594, *The True Chronicle History of King Leir*. The Quarto title provided for Shakespeare's play is a nearly exact redaction of this one, but the play is a topsy-turvy version seeming to paganize a Christian story in much the same way that *Hamlet* had earlier Christianized a pagan story. Through this strategy, as William Elton has observed, Shakespeare blots out 'the patent and ubiquitous Christianity' of his source.[15] The anonymous play occasionally reads like a set of stage directions for Shakespeare's own drama: 'Stand thou up, it is my parte to kneel, / And aske forgiveness for my former faults' (2299–300). But nowhere in Shakespeare's play is there the sentimentalized Christianity so characteristic of its predecessor:

> God forgive both him, and you, and me,
> Even as I doe in perfit charity.
> I will to Church, and pray unto my Saviour,
> That ere I dye, I may obtayne his favour. (1090–3)

Deviations from received historical accounts are common in Shakespeare's histories and can be explained as dramatic necessities in the plays where they occur. But the 'liberties' of the history plays become 'license' in *King Lear* where 'the overwhelming horror of the final scenes becomes immeasurably more significant when we realize', as F. S. Boas does, 'that it did not spring naturally out of the dramatic materials, but that it is the result of a revolutionary alteration of them'.[16] So striking was Shakespeare's revision of history that Nahum Tate altered the ending of the play for performance; and later Dr Johnson complained that he was 'so shocked by Cordelia's death' he could not 'endure to read again the last scenes of the play till . . . [he] undertook to revise them as an editor' (*Var. Ed.*, p. 419). Such a complaint obscures the essential point, however: Shakespeare should be credited 'with a moral and political philosophy which motivated first the choice of story and second the plotting of that story'.[17]

Whether or not the title page refers to the play's first performance, it makes clear that *King Lear* 'was played before the Kings Maiestie at Whitehall upon S. Stephans *night*' during the '*Christmas Hollidayes*' of 1606. The proto-martyr Stephen, within the context of Shakespeare's play, finds a prefiguration in the legendary characters of Cordelia and Lear and, within the context of English history as related by John Foxe, a post-figuration in such a person as the twelfth-century King Stephen who, vexed by wars, managed for a while to achieve peace with David King of Scots, but only for awhile, since that peace was later broken by an obstreperous son who sought vengeance through the massacre of children. As if the antitype of this king, James I would, by intention at least, create a durable peace between England and Scotland that, instead of eventuating in, would evade another catastrophe wherein sons rebel against fathers and perpetuate another massacre of innocents. Here we should remember, as E. W. Heaton urges, that it is not just what the prophet or poet says that counts but, more important, is 'the circumstance in which he says it': 'Because the theology of prophecy is fundamentally a theology of history, it is inescapably "situational".'[18]

Allusion within the play suggests that composition commenced in 1603 and continued until at least 1605. *King Lear* belongs to the initial years of James's reign and contains an element of Stuart propaganda as may be suggested by the emendation of the usual 'I smell the blood of an Englishman' to '*I smell the blood of a British man*' (III.iv.188), as well as by the references to 'The British powers' (IV.v.21) and, only in the 1608 Quarto, to the '*British party*' (IV.vi.252). When it is remembered that James had been 'proclaim'd King of Great Britain . . . that the name of England might be extinct',[19] and that Shakespeare emended his sources so that, instead of France defeating England, France is vanquished by Britain, the possibility emerges that Shakespeare means to acknowledge James's efforts to unite England and Scotland and so to contrast his Britain with Lear's 'scatter'd Kingdom' (III.i.31). Even the omission of the Fool's prophecy regarding disaster befalling Albion (III.ii.91–2) – it appears in the First Folio but not in the 1608 Quarto – has some bearing here. Long ago it was suggested that 'James would not have tolerated even so distant a prospect of a time when "the realm of Albion should come to great confusion"' (*Var. Ed.*, pp. 371–2). In 1606, Shakespeare may not have risked the offense inherent in the Fool's prophecy inasmuch as his intention seems one of touting, not tarnishing, the King's image, though it should not go unnoticed that occasionally in his writings James himself subscribed to a degenerative theory of history as when he speaks of 'the decay of all the Churches, since the beginning of the world'.[20] Nor should it be forgotten that plays and politics had become inextricably intertwined, especially plays such as were performed before the courtly audiences of Whitehall, where, as Stephen Orgel remarks, 'the primary audience was the monarch, and the performance was often directed explicitly at him', even if such political content was conveyed cryptically, through implied analogy and arcane symbolism. To what extent – we must ask of *King Lear* as Orgel asks of Renaissance drama generally – did the central experience of the play, for Shakespeare's contemporaries, involve 'not simply the acting of a play, but the interaction of the play and the monarch'?[21] When we admit that question into criticism of *King Lear*, we must also remember that James was still on the throne when the Fool's prophecy was later incorporated into the play. It may be that Shakespeare introduces the prophecy to accentuate the political content of his play, even to put an edge on it by enlarging the net of reference to implicate the king himself. Surely there was by now an evident discrepancy between what James sought to achieve early in his reign and what by 1623 he had managed to accomplish. If the Quarto text stresses James's good intentions, the Folio text signals a discrepancy between intention and achievement.

In 1603, James had urged that British chronicle history be used as a guide to current history, even if sometimes it provides a negative example and functions as a warning prophecy – one issuing in the reminder that, while disunion sows the seeds of woe, unity is all that is wanting to set men free. 'I would have you to be well versed in authenticke histories and the Chronicles of all Nations; but especially in our owne histories', he tells his son; for 'by reading of authentick histories & chronicles, ye shal learne experience by Theorick, applying the by-past things to the present'. This counsel follows upon these words of warning: '... by diuiding your kingdomes, yee shall leaue the seeds of diuision and discord among your posteritie: as befell to this Ile, by the diuision and assignement therof, to the three sonnes of *Brutu*'.[22] Moreover, as John Draper has demonstrated, between 1604 and 1607, 'in speech after speech, ... [James] was citing the misfortunes that division brought to early Britain'[23] as part of his own effort to establish union in the realm – to join three into one as earlier Brute's survivors, then Lear, had divided one into three. The archetypal division into threes would persist through history as is suggested by the plotting of Mortimer, Glendower, and Hotspur in Act III of *Henry IV, Part I*, where the kingdom, it appears, would again become fragmented. Brute's death instigated the process of fragmentation that Lear and others continued; and Lear's own story, magnifying the evils of disunion, could be taken as a prophecy of history's dissolution which would come in Shakespeare's day and, more, as a warning prophecy to those who would fly in the face of providence, surrendering their appointed status in life. Indeed, Sir Francis Bacon recalls a prophecy he heard in his childhood while Elizabeth was still in her prime: 'When hempe is sponne / England's done'. By that prophecy, Bacon explains, 'it was generally conceived, that after the princes had reigned which had the principal letters of that word *hempe* (... Henry, Edward, Mary, Philip, and Elizabeth), England should come to utter confusion; which, thanks be to God, is verified only in the change of the name; for that the King's style is now no more of England but of Britain'.[24]

Like this and the Fool's prophecy, the Lear story current in Shakespeare's day was thought to prognosticate a disaster that James averts, to project a pattern of history that the new king reverses. The Lear story was also regularly linked to that of Brute and tied into Merlin's prophecy of a second Brute who would return and reunite the kingdom.[25] That figure is identified as James I by Samuel Daniel, Thomas Dekker, Anthony Munday and also by William Harbert who thinks that, with Sidney and Spenser gone, James needs a poet comparable to them. And James finds one of sorts in Harbert who recalls Merlin's prophecy that turmoil abroad and civil war at home will be followed by a new concord: 'Disioynted ... by her first monarches fall', Britain will be restored by a king who 'shall three in one, and one in three unite'. With that king, the golden age will begin anew. James is thereupon heralded apocalyptically, as 'Our second Brute like to the morning starre' who binds war in chains and inaugurates a reign of peace.[26] Britain, apparently, is to be restored from her fall progressively, with Elizabeth uniting the houses of Lancaster and York, thereby repairing the halving of the kingdom by the nephews of Cordelia, and with James now uniting the three kingdoms that Lear, and earlier Brute's survivors, had divided. It may be coincidence that, like Lear, James had three children when *King Lear* was written but is probably no coincidence at all that Shakespeare juxtaposes, however implicitly, the reign of a king charged with restoring paradise with that of a king who, by legend, perpetuated the process of division by which paradise had been lost. Shakespeare thus retells the Lear story in such a way as to elucidate the political doctrine inherent in it and, in the process, accentuates the prophetic element so that in this retelling the story emerges as a warning prophecy.[27] As one popular prophecy dating from 1580 explains, the declaration that the end is at hand, the promise of plagues, wars, disasters of all kinds, 'these are but warnings sent us, to mollifie our harde hearts, and to admonishe us from detestable Pride'; hidden in most such prophecies lies the promise of a good ruler who will restore his kingdom to union and peace.[28] *King Lear* participates in this secular millenialism.

Various elements in the play – its interest in magic, demonology, and astrology, together with its supposed distrust, and occasional deprecations, of prophecies and visions – have been cited as evidence of the extent to which plays were now catering to James's pet attitudes and of the extent, too, to which playwrights like Shakespeare were inclined to represent James's interests, especially his opposition to superstitious excesses. James is even said to authorize the 'Calvinist-inspired views of Deity and related conceptions of providence' that darken the Lear universe.[29]

Just as important is the fact that the Apocalypse, because of the attention James accorded it, acquired a new political identity in the early years of the seventeenth century and, in England, an official respectability. The book obsessed James and was an obsession of England during his reign – in large part because commentators were stressing so insistently the political dimension of the Apocalypse, a dimension that, however muted, was evidence of St. John's own interest in contemporary affairs. The apocalyptic myth, from its very inception, seemed to offer a perspective on contemporary history and to suggest a way of assuming a posture toward it; early Christian apocalyptic, furthermore, seemed to sanction the tendency of supporting the establishment in time of crisis.

As early as 1593, James himself had become enveloped in the apocalyptic myth. John Napier, in a commentary issued six times between 1593 and 1607, explained that, by dedicating his book to James VI of Scotland, he was breaking with the prophetic tradition of 'direct[ing] . . . Admonitions to Kings, Princes, and Governours'. In this instance, Napier allowed, the head of state is a good man, has had ennobling effects on his nation, and hence obliges today's interpreters 'to encourage and inanimate Princes, . . . and also to exhort them generally to remove all such Impediments in their Countreys and Commonwealths, as may hinder that Work, and procure Gods plagues'.[30] In 1599, George Gifford argued that 'while the Kings of England . . . in times past were once horns of the beast, and gave their power to him', recent rulers 'have pulled him downe.... They have... made the Whore desolate and naked'.[31] James's own meditations on the Apocalypse, first published in 1588, were issued again in 1603; and by way of wrapping himself in the cloak of the Apocalypse, the king repeatedly set forth his desire of reunifying a divided kingdom, of consolidating the broken world of which the Lear story had become an emblem. Moreover, a prefatory note, intent upon enveloping James in such a myth, celebrated him for exposing the Whore and binding the beast. Within two years, William Symonds will proclaim that, though the apocalypse may lie in the future, the first resurrection, a prelude to it, commences now.[32] In strikingly particular ways, the Apocalypse seemed to speak to, and of, England with the result that it was appropriated by the king and converted into a national history.

In 1616, remarking of James's *Paraphrase on Revelation*, Isaiah Winton proposed that 'Kings have a kinde of interest in that Book beyond any other: for as the execution of the most part of the *Prophecies* of that Booke is committed unto them; so it may be, that the Interpretation of it, may more happily be made by them'.[33] Promoting the Book of Revelation through two separate commentaries, James not only gave unprecedented official sanction to John's prophecy but, more, used that prophecy as a test of loyalty to him. Enthusiasm for the king might be measured, then, by the extent to which one was engaged with the Apocalypse; and antipathy to him, by a desire 'to assert the limitations – or impropriety – of applying apocalyptic terms to the politics of either of the two kingdoms of "Britain"'.[34] James himself spoke of what would be 'Tragedie to the Traitors, and Tragicomedy to the King and all his true subjects',[35] thereby deploying the Apocalypse as a political weapon and simultaneously emphasizing that history, conceived in terms of the Apocalypse, is at once tragic and tragicomic.

The attention Shakespeare fastens upon the apocalyptic drama in *King Lear* has its political aspect, then, and so may be construed as a part of the compliment playwright pays to king; yet the play, like Napier's popular commentary, contains an anti-apocalyptic component as well or, better, defines apocalypse in terms less of sovereigns than of subjects and in terms less of the history of the world than of the spiritual history of individual men. A prophecy that held no significance for the pre-Incarnational world of *King Lear*, Shakespeare seems to be saying, holds great sway over, has vast implications for the world of King James and his subjects. Yet Shakespeare also withholds from the king the sort of idolatrous flattery that was currently enveloping him in the apocalyptic myth; he casts a dubious eye on apocalyptics and perhaps even on James's declaration that the Book of Revelation pertains to 'this our last age'.[36] For all the adumbrations of end-time that are to be found in *King Lear*, the play does not envision the promised end; indeed, the play resists defiantly the expectations built by its apocalyptic reference, no less than those fostered by its historical sources. The play may appear to be organizing itself around the apocalyptic paradigm: 'the abdication of temporal order, followed by chaos and the reign of Antichrist, culminating in Armageddon and the foundation of a new order, temporal and spiritual';[37] but the last phase of such a pattern is withheld – the new order does not materialize within a play that aggressively denies us what we want.

Shakespeare's strategy here is to use apocalypse against itself, not to deny it as a possibility but to distance the consummation of history into the future. In *King Lear*, apocalypse is not a certainty, nor even a likelihood, but only a *perhaps* dependent not upon a divine hand to alter the course of history but upon individual men to transform themselves and then perhaps history. James may be seen as an agent in the reformation paving the way for an eventual apocalypse, but he is no herald of the apocalypse itself; for that event and the transformation it implies depend not on what kings like James may do for their nations but on what people may do for themselves. The whole process of salvation involves an apocalypse of mind wherein man, instead of transcending his nature, improves himself through spiritual evolution. *King Lear* thus reflects something of the process discovered in it by Christopher Caudwell, 'withdrawal from the Court . . . into oneself', but without the corollary that the Court, 'once the source of health, is now the source of infection'.[38] It is that in Shakespeare's play but presumably not that in Shakespeare's England, James being a measure of how far men and civilizations have thus far evolved and of how far they have yet to go. The Quarto text stresses the former point, while the Folio text advances the latter one.

The apocalypse in *King Lear* is a mind-transforming event that culminates in a King's redemption. As John Napier had argued, even kings require renovation, and with them as with everyman apocalypse begins in the 'inward minde'.[39] 'The weight of this sad time' (V.iii.323) allows for no apocalypse in the present. The play incorporates no messianic vision but does utilize the Lear story in altered form. This fact should remind us that 'much of our difficulty with *King Lear* comes from having read about Shakespeare's sources, instead of having read Shakespeare's sources', or from reading extracts from a source, a habit that 'entirely perverts its draft'.[40] More than simply substituting an unhappy for a happy ending, Shakespeare's revisionism replots the whole course of imagined history, with earlier versions of the Lear story serving here only as a base and point of reference for Shakespeare's symbolic expression.

Viewed in terms of its protagonists, the received story is a conventional tragicomedy wherein disaster is averted by the reunion of Lear and Cordelia and the restoration of their kingdom; but viewed in terms of its true protagonist who is History, the story is a dark tragedy wherein the forces of evil, for awhile restrained, are unleashed again and accomplish the annihilation of all good. The whole world is upset and eventually disintegrates. As Shakespeare retells the story, the personal tragedy is accentuated by irony – there is a reunion without a restoration; but the tragedy of history is alleviated, the possibility for *history* as a tragicomedy is allowed for. For in the universe of this play, evil is self-consuming and goodness triumphant in the calm, if not secured order, at its end. As in *Antony and Cleopatra*, there is 'high order in this . . . solemnity' (V.ii). In *King Lear*, majesty may fall to folly; but the foolish king, persisting in his folly, by the end of the play becomes wise. There is a resurrection; and even if there is death, death is a deliverance from the horrors of this life. All of the evil perish, along with some of the good; but some of the good also survive and, under their aegis, history continues. It is in this sense that we may say with C. J. Sisson: *King Lear* contains 'a happy ending of deeper truth than Tate's'.[41] The play builds up the missing connective tissue between mythology and history: now mythology can become history.

In the Middle Ages, and up to Shakespeare's own day, existence was conceived as a cosmic drama, composed around a central theme and according to a rational plan; and man's duty was to accept the drama as written since he was powerless to alter it. A problem arose, though, when discrete and usually cohesive traditions of prophecy, sacred and secular, were at odds, and in such instances the former took precedence over the latter, becoming the instrument through which the two traditions could be made to mesh. It is not that Shakespeare chooses the occasion of *King Lear* to join a band of prophets; rather, through prophecy and apocalypse he converts legend into myth. Into his new myth, a countermyth, Shakespeare weaves images, ideas, and themes of apocalypse in such a way as to suggest that his play is as much a revision of secular as of sacred history. There is a particular propriety in Shakespeare's joining secular to sacred history through the Book of Revelation; for as Richard Bauckham has documented, in Shakespeare's day it was thought that 'the whole history of the world could be understood if . . . [the Apocalypse] were read alongside the chronicles'.[42] Texts, sacred and secular, were thus bound together on the understanding that Revelation is a light to the chronicles and the chronicles a light to it; Revelation provides *the* framework for a prophetic understanding of history and, says Katharine Firth, was regarded as *the* book through which the English chronicles could be put 'in their right shape'.[43] In this, the heyday of prophetic history, 'the whole structure rested on the conviction that prophecy was the most certain of all sources of historical information and that it could provide an assured framework for the whole course of history'.[44] On suppositions like these, it appears, Shakespeare introduces prophetic and apocalyptic elements into his play and allows them to authorize his astonishing revision of a received tradition whose view of history is grimly pessimistic – indeed to legitimize the claim that *King Lear* is a presentation of *'True* Chronicle Historie' (my italics). Yet even as the play accommodates secular history to the apocalyptic drama, it counters then current views of history, many of which were founded upon John's prophecy. *King Lear* is an emendation of history as it is related by both Renaissance chroniclers and scriptural commentators.

II 'SHATTERING DARKNESS'

King Lear confronts head-on the problem that the Book of Revelation was said to address: the horrors that characterize human existence when the wicked reign and the godly are oppressed. Yet as King James had explained, although God 'suffereth the wicked to runne on while their cup be full: yet in the end he striketh them' – Judgment Day will follow this time of persecution and disaster.[45] The world of the Apocalypse, replicated in the world of *King Lear*, is 'a rack: a scene of suffering' – a world including within itself 'a standing potentiality for progressive transformation into chaos',[46] but the play never lets us forget, either, that Revelation's metaphor of purgation, of suffering to obtain purification and renewal, epitomizes its own idea of transformation, of man's metamorphosis in this life. The Apocalypse is an exhilarating book, but not until its last chapters pertaining to end-time is it a joyful one; it is not a shield from, but an encounter with, the nightmare world of human history. There is consolation here, but only for those who live through the horror and who thereupon can awaken into another reality. The Book of Revelation, then, authorizes in very specific ways the admixture of tragedy and comedy within history and allows for that history to be perceived as prophecy and to be plotted as an apocalypse. Here, as in Shakespeare's play, tragedy and comedy front one another. St. John and Shakespeare alike look horror straight in the face and stare it down. Still, Shakespeare's suppositions about history are different from those that, during the Renaissance, were usually attributed to John.

The apocalyptic element in *King Lear* is therefore ambiguous, so much so that it may be construed as lending all degrees of darkness to the play or, conversely, as shattering that darkness by letting in the light, however scattered, of Revelation itself. In the words of Paul Siegel, 'Shakespeare leaves unresolved whether the darkness of the time will gradually give place to light, as did the darkness of ancient Britain, or whether it will steadily deepen . . . [into] total darkness . . . [and] the extinction of humanity'.[47] This ambiguity, at the heart of the play, is lodged there by its apocalyptic framework, which, though arguably it may not produce Christian sentiments or yield a Christian interpretation, calls into question the conclusion that 'Christian categories never preside over the vision' of the play; that the tragedies 'are not based, as Christian ethics in fact are, upon the eschatology of the Christian system'.[48] On the contrary, if criticism divides sharply over the issue of Christian interpretation, opposing sides unite in the perception that apocalypse is made crucial to the play by the exchange between Kent and Edgar:

> Kent. Is this the promis'd end?
> Edg. Or image of that horror? (V.iii.264–5)

Albany thereupon offers his own comment, 'Fall and cease' (266). The three remarks, taken together, have been described as a 'funeral chorus . . . invoking the Last Judgment'[49] and reminding us that apocalypse and interpretation thereof are particular concerns for those who survive the play's catastrophe.

This glimpsing of end-time in the cataclysm of *King Lear* has always been an obsessive feature of its criticism. Without exception, Shakespeare's early editors found in the last scene of *Lear* 'the horror of the last day, or day of judgment', 'the end of the world', or certainly 'a representation or resemblance of that horror'; they were fond of drawing parallels between *Lear* and *Macbeth* (its image of the great doom) and between *Lear* and, if not always the Apocalypse, at least that apocalyptic passage in Mark, which describes the destruction of Jerusalem (*Var. Ed.*, p. 339). The former parallel suggests that, like *Macbeth*, *King Lear* is 'an imaginative exploration of evil in Biblical terms' and in terms especially of James's 'pessimistic sermon on Revelation';[50] and the latter parallel serves as a reminder that *King Lear* is imaging end-time, not recording it; that in potentiality at least one city, one world, is being destroyed that another may be erected upon its ruins. If, by fixing all meaning in this world, 'Ripeness is All' (V.iii.11) disallows transcendence, a heavenly city, the Christian eternity, it nonetheless allows for a resurrection in time, a new community in history, at least among those who discern Christian elements in the play. Not all do, of course, and even among those who do there is little appreciation of the extent to which such elements are subjected to secularization.

At one extreme are those who believe that, Christian in its essential outlook, *King Lear* records 'the possibilities for human progress under providence' and who thereupon contend that in its final scenes the play 'has passed beyond tragedy to beatitude', that its 'crashing conclusion is aureoled with an angelic sweetness'.[51] At the other extreme are those who perceive a reversal of all religious imagery in the play and who argue that 'from the middle of Act II to the end of Act IV', *Lear* draws upon the Apocalypse for its ambience only to make 'a tragic mockery of all eschatologies':

> of the heaven promised on earth, and the heaven promised after death; in fact, of both Christian and secular theodicies; of cosmogony and of the rational view of history; of the gods and the god nature, of man made in 'image and likeness'. In *King Lear* both the medieval and Renaissance order of established values disintegrate.[52]

Not the play, this argument goes, only its deluded protagonists subscribe to an eschatology that *Lear* itself explodes: here the whole Christian universe tumbles down, collapses, in apocalyptic absurdity. In this terrible unfolding vision, Shakespeare 'offers intimations of Christian apocalypse but frustrates them', allowing reality to declare itself 'in the very revenge it takes upon every belief, upon every expectation or assertion of meaning'.[53] The greatness of the play, for some, resides in its reversal of all affirmations, in the absolute completeness of its negation.

In *King Lear*, it is true, there is all the darkness and fire and whirlwind of the Apocalypse; there is an apocalyptic encroachment on the world of the play, creating that Yeatsian sense of tragedy wrought to the uttermost. Still, the play submits to a middle ground of interpretation: one that sees there, as Grigori Kozintsev has done, 'a whole dead world galloping over the living earth beneath a sky full of stars' and that, sensing an ending in *King Lear*, recognizes the play 'has no end', only a vision of 'life struggling up again from the ruins'.[54] In keeping with its pre-Christian setting, the apocalyptic strain of *King Lear* is primitivistic. The initial suggestion is that 'the world is not to be improved but affirmed' since, according to very early apocalyptic thinking as it is described by Joseph Campbell, 'out of death, decay, violence, and pain come life'.[55] Only at the conclusion of the play is there the further suggestion that those who endure until the end will be saved, and then even this New Testament conception is modified so as to advance the idea that such men, not just saved, will become the saviours of history. In *King Lear*, then, we encounter what Carl Jung calls 'the dark side of the Apocalypse', with Shakespeare, like Jung, seeming to feel that the New Testament Apocalypse, having already produced 'a universal religious nightmare',[56] is an encounter with essential human experience – is as much the province of poets and dramatists as of theologians and historians.

If the whole center of the play creates the ambience of apocalypse and the exchange between Kent and Edgar brings us to its verge, that centre finds it circumference in the apocalyptic trumpets that terminate the play's action. To make a point symbolically, it seems, five trumpets sound in the final act, the last scene, producing the recognition that what occurs with the fifth trumpet, in the centuries preceding the Incarnation, is a scarry overturning of the world's order; that all history is tragedy until the sounding of the seventh trumpet. Only with the trumpet comes the possibility of a renewal of the world, a resurrection after death. Yet before this new theatre of comedy rears itself on the stage of tragedy, all is tragedy – with the Book of Revelation presenting a vision of the world 'overflow[ing] with scourges, slaughters, destructions'.[57] In the words of Bartholomew Traheron, we are given by St. John a universe wherein 'lies, falshod, violence, tyranie, false and franticke opinions, idolatrie and superstition, raigne', while 'truth, righteousness, vertue, and all honestie, is trodden under foote, and lieth wounded, and mangled' in the streets.[58] The world of the Apocalypse anticipates Shakespeare's vision of the world in *King Lear*; and the play's five trumpets may be a way of associating Lear himself with the fifth trumpet, the angel or mighty monarch who falls because of 'spirituall darkness', because of 'great blindnesse and ignorance', and so is himself 'the bringer of this great woe'.[59] In his association with this trumpet, Lear also emblematizes the misery of the human condition from which men cannot, even now, free themselves. Why else is it that 'the Kings in *Tragedies*, are brought in so often lamenting, and calling themselves by the name of wretched men', asks Thomas Brightman, than to figure forth 'this inward grief' that afflicts us all?[60]

Besides the blaring trumpets, the play contains numerous other signatures of apocalypse: the mystery of the seven stars (which the Fool and Lear determine are seven because they are not eight), the cracking thunder and catastrophic earthquakes, the eclipse of sun and moon, the wheel of fire, the lake of darkness, the sulphureous pit, the wrathful dragon, the prince of darkness, the black angel, even the monsters of the deep and the imagery of defiled and fresh garments. The storm on the heath, which Lear refers to as 'this tempest in my mind' (III.iv.12), recalls what the Book of Revelation says of Armageddon: 'And there were . . . thundrings, and lightnings; & there was a great earthquake . . . so mightie an earthquake. And the great citie diuided into thre partes, and the cities . . . fell'; then God pours out 'the fiercenes of his wrath' in the form of 'the plague of haile' (16.18–21). Lear's speech on the heath is apposite:

> Blow, winds, and crack your cheeks! rage! blow!
> You cataracts and hurricanoes, spout
> Till you have drench'd our steeples, drown'd the cocks!
> You sulphu'rous and thought-executing fires,
> Vaunt-couriers of oak-cleaving thunderbolts,
> Singe my white hair! And then, all-shaking thunder
> Strike flat the thick rotundity o' th' world!
> Crack Nature's moulds . . . (III.ii.1–8)

In his first Meditation, John Donne turned Revelation's entire macrocosmic catastrophe back upon the commotion in the microcosm: 'Is this the honour which Man hath by being a little world', he asks, 'that he hath these earthquakes in himself sudden shakings; these lightnings, sudden flashes; these thunders, sudden noises; these eclipses, sudden offuscations, and darkenings of his senses.'[61]

Renaissance commentators generally did not allow one to forget that this is 'a tempest of spiritual haile, . . . and fire that is, of errors, . . . and strong delusions', nor that the falling stars of Revelation are priests and kings drawn mightily down for having been so 'lifted up in pride'.[62] The hail that comes with such tempests, John Napier proposed, is pride – 'selfe-love' – which 'preceeds the day of judgment, but also . . . is the very cause why the day of judgment, shall be hastened'.[63] We should also remember, with William Elton, that in the Venerable Bede 'one version of fifteen doomsday signs predicts, on the fourth day toward the "promised end", monsters of the deep'.[64] In Albany's words, the beast, the end 'will come' (IV.ii.47).

Moreover, Lear's shedding of his garments, his nakedness in the storm scene and subsequent donning of fresh garments, should alert us to the prevailing understanding of Revelation's garment imagery in Shakespeare's day, of the way in which defiled and fresh garments are associated, respectively, with sleeping and waking, blindness and vision – are a covering of error and the cloak of newly acquired illumination. The old garments are cast off in man's period of greatest tribulation, in his time of pilgrimage, and new ones are acquired when man desists from error, experiences transfiguration, comes out of a period of great affliction and commences a new exalted state of existence in this life. The garments of Revelation point 'inwardly', says Heinrich Bullinger, and reveal not just the contrary states of human experience but the spiritual state of their wearer.[65] The extent to which the fresh garments also imply a putting on of Christ and the Gospel is a moot point in *King Lear*, as is the extent to which a resurrection in this life prognosticates a second resurrection into the glory of eternity. But there is no question regarding the prevalence of such imagery in the play and its resonances: 'I do not like the fashion of your garments: . . . let them be changed' (III.vi.81–3); 'in the heaviness of sleep / We put fresh garments on him' (IV.vii.21–2). Or as Cordelia will urge: 'Be better suited: / The weeds are memories of those worser hours: / I prithee, put them off' (IV.vii.7–9).

If no more than this, the garments here signify man's victory over his troubles, his enemies, and, in Lear's case, the royal estate to which he has attained (however reluctantly, he wears regal apparel again). Without his garments, as one seventeenth-century commentator has said, man is 'poor, naked, and blind, poore through the want of . . . Religion within, naked and so deformed through heathen-like conditions'; with his garments, man achieves, at least temporarily in this world, relief from the horrors of existence, deliverance from its miseries.[66]

The Book of Revelation is but one of many possible sources for exposition of the complex of garment imagery in Shakespeare's play, and but one of the scriptural books wherein the image figures prominently. In a meditation on Matthew, King James offers a further gloss on garment imagery, finding in the stripping of Christ and subsequent attiring of him with fresh robes and a crown, 'a paterne for the inauguration of Kings', as well as the paradox of being humbled in order to become exalted.[67] If there is a faint shadowing of his episode in Lear's story – in his being stripped naked only to be dressed again in kingly raiment – there is ironic play as well; for Lear's is a crown of flowers, not of thorns, marking his death out of rather than into glory; and whereas others kneel before Christ to mock him, Lear kneels before Cordelia, in an act of self-humiliation, to ask for her forgiveness.

Characters in Shakespeare's play also exhibit an archetypal connection with figures in the Apocalypse: Gloucester as an adulterous figure of state, Goneril and Regan as a composite image of the Great Whore, Lear as both deposed King and bridegroom, and Cordelia as a suffering saint and soul in bliss. The play is richly allusive; and some of its allusion finds conspicuous reference points in the Apocalypse: the crown of flowers, the tenth day, the wiping of eyes, the wiping away of tears, the persistent concern with the bestial character of man – 'I' th' last night's storm I such a fellow saw, / Which made me think a man a worm' (IV.i.32–3). Indeed, for a long time, the play was said to span ten days (*Var. Ed.*, pp. 408–12), with its tragedy occurring on the tenth day and so playing upon the incongruity of death's coming to Lear and Cordelia on the day that, scripturally, man receives the crown of eternal life. However invalid such calculations may be, the irony still pertains; for early on in the play Lear tells Kent that, 'if on the tenth day' after his banishment he is found in the kingdom, 'The moment is thy death' (I.i. 176–87).

A similar irony is hidden in Lear's appeal to Cordelia, 'Wipe thine eyes' – an appeal that follows upon his assurance of divine justice: 'He that parts us shall bring a brand from heaven'; and that is followed by his particularizing of such justice to Goneril and Regan: 'The good shall devour them, flesh and fill, / Ere they shall make us weep' (V.iii.22–5). The wiping of tears, an event of signal importance in the Apocalypse, was taken as a promise that a time of justice would follow a period of great affliction; that then, as John Donne sermonized, 'all occasions of complaint, and lamentation would be removed'.[68] To some, especially those who read the ending of the play anagogically and thus see in it 'the reawakening of the dead into paradise', there is in Lear's 'mine own tears / Do scald like molten lead' and in his 'weep not' (IV.vii.47–8, 72) an 'astonishing evocation of . . . the supervening state of paradise, which . . . in the words of the Book of Revelation . . . will wipe the tears forever from our eyes'.[69] It is true that this is the promise Lear holds before Cordelia, a promise seemingly fulfilled when the bodies of Goneril and Regan are brought in and the death of Edmund reported – and then seemingly broken as Lear beholds the dead Cordelia and dies himself. There seems to be nothing here, as Coleridge lamented, but 'a world's convention of agonies' (*Var. Ed.*, p. 182). In this world, there may be no divine justice; and there may be no other world where men live after death; so finally all the wiping of tears promises, as John Donne once observed and as Shakespeare may here mean to suggest, is that there is a space in everyman's life for 'establish[ing] the kingdome of heaven upon you, *in this* life'.[70]

In play as in prophecy, man is 'unaccommodated . . . a poor, bare, forked animal' (III.iv.109–10) – is just as St. John describes him: 'wretched . . . miserable . . . poore . . . blinde, and naked' (3.17), and as Lear describes himself: 'poor, infirm, weak, and despis'd' (III.ii.20). In both play and prophecy, such men are tried by fire, a wheel of fire, that they will not appear naked again. The worlds of *King Lear* and the Apocalypse, then, bear a striking similarity – are full of 'Vengeance! plague! death! confusion!' (III.ii.6–7); in both worlds, the 'judgment of the heavens . . . makes us tremble' (V.iii.231), and the time is of general woe. As in the Apocalypse (9.6), here men seek death but death flees from them; and though the plagues come, and with them severe tribulations, not all men perish. Some have in store another plight: as Edgar laments, it is 'our lives' sweetness, / That we the pain of death would hourly die / Rather than die at once!' (V.iii.184–6).

Through such apocalyptic images, themes, and ideas, Shakespeare implies a 'flickering analogy'[71] between secular and sacred history. As in the Book of Revelation so here in Shakespeare's play: even the best are tried and found wanting. Apocalyptic imagery such as the figures of the star and garment and tears, we have seen, place the Lear story within a context provided by the Book of Revelation and act as a guide for correlating the play with the prophecy. And there are other such instances, with the images of the earthquake, the darkened sun and moon, and the falling stars equating the Lear universe with the events that occur under the sixth seal and that cause 'the Kings of the earth ... [to hide] themselues in the dennes, and among the rockes of the mountaines ... For the great day of ... wrath is come' (6.12–17). At this time, the Geneva Bible explains, 'the kingdome of God is hid, and withdrawen from men' (fol. 116ᵛ). There are moments in history (and *Lear* records such a moment) when there is 'no salvation, no revelation, no help for humanity in its fallen condition'.[72] In Shakespeare's words, 'the wrathful skies / Gallow the very wanderers of the dark, / And make them keep their caves' (III.ii.43–5). These are the events under the first woe as well. If certain events of *King Lear* thus correlate with the sixth seal and the first woe, they anticipate, but nonetheless are distanced from, the last trumpet and the third woe when time will reach its period. What characterizes history before the last days is the reign of evil, the tribulation of the saints and the suffering of the martyrs. And there is no visible reward for them, though on 'such sacrifices', Lear says, 'the gods themselves throw incense' (V.iii.20–1). Only during the millennium does the binding of evil produce a reign of peace; and only after all things are made new subsequent to the Last Judgment can man's tears be wiped away. Tragedy is indigenous to history; comedy, to end-time. Apocalyptic reference thus lodges *King Lear* within an historical framework afforded by the Book of Revelation, importantly within an historical phase, the first woe, that for all its adumbrations of last things is but an image of that horror. Apocalyptic reference, besides importing mythic dimensions to this play, also turns the apocalyptic myth against itself in such a way as to challenge received interpretations of it. Like the Lear legend, the myth of apocalypse is first ravaged, then created anew, and this is part of the larger ravaging of Christianity itself.

III 'THE LIGHT OF REVELATION'

Much that militates against the tragedy of history in the Apocalypse is omitted from *King Lear*, or when included by signatures – the tenth day and the song in the cage, for instance – has the effect of intensifying rather than alleviating the tragedy of Lear and Cordelia. But then Shakespeare's point may well be that the tragedy of the pagan world, unlike his own, is that it must endure history without the promises of Revelation; that in his own world, whatever the situation in Lear's, and however agonizing the human condition may be, the redemptive pattern of the Bible, and especially of the Apocalypse, pertains – in the words of Susan Snyder, 'is more or less intact'.[73] The tragedy of *King Lear*, as Northrop Frye explains, should be seen in its historical relations: an old legend in relation to Old Testament history, and both in relation to the current historical moment – the accession of James I. *King Lear* thus achieves its powerfully ironic perspective, as Frye argues is customary in tragedy, by placing its characters in a state (pagan and Old Testament) from which its audience has been theoretically redeemed. 'The events of Geoffrey of Monmouth's British history', Frye reminds us, 'are supposed to be contemporary with those of the Old Testament, and the sense of life under the law is present everywhere in *King Lear*';[74] the audience that receives the play, on the other hand, belongs to another phase of history – exists under a new dispensation.

Finally, it is two worlds that by virtue of the 1608 title page meet and clash – the one pagan, the other Christian. And by virtue of the texture of allusion in the play itself, the darkness of the Lear universe, at first more darkened by contrast with the Revelation prophecy, is shattered in the recognition that what gave no meaning at all to Lear's story now imparts meaning to all men living under the Christian dispensation in Shakespeare's England. The implicit contrast between a king who divides a kingdom and one who restores the kingdom to unity reinforces such a conjecture, as does the fact that, while *King Lear* belongs to a barbarous time, whatever we may think of James's England, Shakespeare believed 'that men are / As the time is' (V.iii.31–2) and so presumably stressed difference rather than similitude between the two kings, using the past to gauge the successes of the present and to accentuate a contrast between pre- and post-Incarnational history. In this way, Shakespeare allows the Book of Revelation to point its beams into the darkness of the world – even the world of *King Lear*. We are thus made to wonder with Battenhouse, 'are not the darkest hours just before dawn', and is not the dark night of the soul a prologue to vision; and then perhaps to give our assent to Edith Sitwell's declaration that, reaching the night of the soul, Lear reaches the light; that here, as in *Hamlet*, is the 'shattering darkness that precedes revelation'.[75]

Still, it is a mistake to suppose with Knight, Battenhouse, and others that

Shakespeare deploys the Apocalypse, as earlier Foxe and Spenser had done, in order to ascribe a traditional meaning to history. This is not the case with his employment of either the Lear legend or the apocalyptic myth. Earth is no paradise yet; and Shakespeare is silent, or virtually so, about the power of poetry, or prophecy, to bring a paradise to earth. On the other hand, history is ongoing at the end of the play, and even if there is no ground for trusting in an apocalyptic present, the play's concluding lines, themselves a prophecy, allow for the efficacy of prophecy in the present and, more, for the possibility of apocalypse in the future. Warwick's lines in *Henry IV, Part II*, have some bearing here:

> ... a man may prophesy,
> With a near aim, of the main chance of things
> As yet not come to life, which in their seeds
> And weak beginnings lie intreasured.
> Such things become the hatch and brood of time ... (III.i.82–6)

The Christian framework provided by the liturgy and the apocalyptic framework supplied by the play itself at once intensify and moderate the tragedy of *King Lear*.

As W. Moelwyn Merchant remarks, 'the tragic end of Lear is given its final import by its setting within a traditional eschatology'.[76] Among the carefully adjusted tensions in *King Lear* is the contrast between Lear and James, the pagan and Christian worlds, the old dispensation and the new. All that the play admits on its surface is what pertains to Lear – pre-Christianity, an old order, a first resurrection but no other. Lear may put off the old and become a new man whose attributes are forebearance, forgiveness, and charity; but Lear's death *is* the end of something. Cordelia may come to embody and emblematize the ideal, even the ideal community; but such a community is never realized in *King Lear*. We can think of her, as John Danby does, in terms of the apocalyptic Jerusalem;[77] but there is no Jerusalem in the world of Shakespeare's play, nor is there even a providential spirit governing its universe. Northrop Frye posits that 'Poor Tom is the providence or guardian spirit' in the play,[78] which is but to remind us of the transference of responsibility from God to man, and not just extraordinary men but every man. The promised end of Revelation is apocalypse; but, as Robert Hunter asks, 'will that horror be the horror of justice, or the horror of the revelation that when the heavens fall and things cease nothing remains?'[79] The play quarrels with all perspectives it countenances, questions a universe that never seems to answer back, and finds its essential meaning therefore in silences, which is to suggest that even if the world is not meaningless its mysteries are beyond man's comprehension – there are seven stars only because there are not eight. Shakespeare's Revelation is not the Revelation of his contemporaries, whether they be churchmen or kings, historians – or even fellow poets. His is much more the Revelation – the sardonic apocalypse – of *Samson Agonistes* and, later, of Blake's *Europe*, Byron's *The Prophecy of Dante*, and Shelley's *The Cenci*.

The apocalyptic framework of *King Lear* neither discredits a non-Christian, nor credits a Christian reading of the play; and rather than lessening, it complicates the problem of perspective in the play. Instead of mediating between opposed interpretations, this framework acts as a mainstay in non-Christian and Christian readings alike, and in such a way as to acknowledge both without affirming either. The apocalyptic elements figure in virtually every mode of criticism the play has elicited; yet every mode of criticism seems to sponsor a decidedly different interpretation of those elements. For some, *King Lear* contains, or at least adumbrates, the promise of a Christian apocalypse; for others, the play envisions a 'naturalistic apocalypse, the metamorphosis of man without heaven's justice' – eludes apocalypse while alluding to it so as to intensify despair, 'implying the disparity between pagan hopelessness and Christian possibility'.[80] Yet there is this further possibility: that within the sardonic or false apocalypse of the play, implying Shakespeare's own 'pessimism about the present and . . . conviction of its imminent crisis' (a common feature of apocalyptic thinking, according to McGinn[81]), lies a prospect for apocalypse in the future, not perhaps in a future eternity but within future history and to be effected not by John of Patmos's God but by man himself.

'As the apocalyptic way of thinking becomes divorced from the underlying theology, the movement of history through wars, slaughters, implacable conflict', says Ernest Tuveson, 'comes to appear simply as the iron law of nature'.[82] So for Shakespeare, the essential task is to rescue the Apocalypse and read it back into the real world; and his way of dealing with that problem is to demystify the Apocalypse and thereby humanize it – is to turn responsibility for the shaping of history over to man and thereby secularize the Christian prophecy. If the orthodox see Christ establishing the ideal world, Shakespeare, from a more radical perspective, sees man himself – at great personal cost and through enormous sacrifice – moving slowly toward a more ideal state. Shakespeare is thus less, not more, apocalyptic than some of his orthodox contemporaries; and yet one finds in *King Lear* what has been called 'the anthropological root of apocalyptic systems of thought': 'a sense of belonging in time, as well as the need to understand the special significance of the present'.[83] Nevertheless, for Shakespeare the present is a time of amelioration, not of history's apocalyptic transformation; it is a time for man's moving toward perfection but not a moment in which perfection is achieved. We are brought to the edge of the world and end of time not because the world is about the end, time about to reach its period, but because, for Shakespeare, from this perspective man can best contemplate the horrors of human existence and negotiate his way around them.

Macbeth makes the point brilliantly. No less strikingly than in *King Lear*, here are the harbingers of apocalypse in the thunder, lightning, and trumpets that commence the play's action. The sun has gone out, scorpions infest the human mind, Judgment summons mankind to heaven and hell. The entire estate of the world is undone, the unity of the earth confounded, the general frame of things disjointed; and the screams of death prophesy, 'with terrible accents / Of dire combustion and confused events / New hatched to the woeful time / . . . Confusion now hath made his masterpiece' (II.ii.62–4; 71; cf. III.ii.16, IV.iii.98–9, V.vi.50). But again, as in *Lear*, apocalypse is forestalled, this time in Macbeth's vision of the kings who seem to stretch out to 'the crack of doom' (IV.i.117). There are the apocalyptic seven but then comes an unexpected eighth king followed by many more with 'treble scepters' (IV.i.121), and with them comes the reminder that a world long ago disjointed is unified again under the rule of James I. What may seem like the end of things is actually an image of that horror; and the horror is mitigated in the realization that the world is healing, that rather than living in the last days Renaissance man occupies a unique place at the beginning of an end indefinitely postposed. Frank Kermode makes the point exactly: 'The millennial ending of *Macbeth*, the broken apocalypse of *Lear*, are false endings, human periods in an eternal world. They are researches into death in an age too late for apocalypse, too critical for prophecy'[84] – or perhaps more simply in an age that became increasingly suspicious of both.

King Lear may therefore eschew the Christian eternity of *The Faerie Queene* and that poem's providential vision of human history; it may also evade the joyous apocalypse of Milton's early prose tracts and the more tentative one of his last poems. Yet subsequent to *King Lear*, Shakespeare writes *Antony and Cleopatra*, which in its final acts registers the immortal longings never felt in *Lear* and provides the sense of exhilaration missing from the earlier play. In both plays, nonetheless, apocalypse marks not the end of history but the termination of a phase of it, with history in *Antony* sitting on the very verge of the Christian dispensation. In both plays, Shakespeare stands between two worlds: the one dead, and the other powerless to be born without man's participation in the historical process. Shakespeare seems to understand the apocalyptic strategy – and to use it himself – of describing a moment of history, of forcing us to view that moment in relationship to the totality, and of thereby calling upon us to make history. In *King Lear* and in *Macbeth* we may – Nietzsche-like – shudder at the sufferings that befall the tragic hero, at the horrors of existence to which he himself is a contributor; yet in *Antony and Cleopatra* – again Nietzsche-like – we are allowed to countenance the possibility that from such sufferings and horrors we may derive a higher, over-mastering joy. The world of tragedy now gives way to, eventually will be supplanted by, the romance world of the late plays. *King Lear* is their stark prologue.

Lear and *Macbeth* and *Antony* collaborate with one another in a single enterprise – in the words of Thomas McFarland, the building up of a 'four-square foundation for a New Jerusalem of the Spirit';[85] they are, in this sense, involved with, and about, the formation of a new religion with *King Lear* projecting a radically new, and newly secularized, version of the myth of apocalypse. There may be more than has met the eye in Lear's plea, drench the steeples and drown the cocks. It is as if Lear – and through him Shakespeare's play – is saying that, 'if it has taken centuries to subdue the human race to the tyrannical yoke of the priests', it may take many more centuries 'to secure its freedom from that yoke';[86] and a part of the new freedom into which man is being led by this play involves the realization that a heavenly city, if it is to exist at all, may have earthly foundations; that the drama of history, far from completed, is still in the making. The apocalyptic myth that *King Lear* fosters anticipates literarily the world of the late romances and, historically, what is said to have come to pass in the eighteenth century when, according to Carl Becker, 'the utopian dream of perfection . . . was at last projected into the life of man on earth and identified with the desired and hoped-for regeneration of society'.[87]

It has been said that 'in the prophetic pattern of . . . [*King Lear*] Shakespeare was alone . . . among his contemporaries', though presumably 'he would not find himself alone today'.[88] There are those who would see the Shakespeare of *King Lear* as a prophet of the collapse of Western civilization and who discovered, subsequent to Shakespeare, the demolition and later remantling of tragicomedy – who thus read Shakespeare and so misread this play by him. We are told that plays continuously tragicomic belong to the post-Enlightenment era and, further, that 'only the traditional and . . . canonical variety of tragedy has disappeared . . . namely that tragedy which presupposes an essentially unshakeable metaphysical world order established by the supreme powers called god, gods, fate, providence, or the like'.[89] We need to be reminded that tragicomedy of this order finds its beginnings in earlier (once eccentric) interpretations of the Apocalypse and its consummation in *King Lear* and that, despite Shakespeare's differences with a modern Revelation commentator like Vasily Rozanov, there is a knit of identity in their thinking about the Apocalypse: St. John and Shakespeare may both be bent upon dismantling the orthodoxies of churchmen, may both chafe against the confines of dogma, and, as consolation, may wish to bring forth something new. Shakespeare may tear God from the firmament in *King Lear* and obliterate the promise of a heavenly city; but he also posits with John of Patmos the possibility of a better life on earth – precisely on earth. He here writes a play that like the Apocalypse, as Rozanov interprets it, 'calls for, and demands a new religion'[90] – a religion with a capacity for organizing life and earthly existence not by God's planning but by man's and that, if rupturing the old alliance between God and man, also makes of man the master of his fate and captain of his destiny. As Iago says in *Othello*, ''Tis in ourselves that we are thus or thus' (I.iii.322–3). Like Rozanov's

Apocalypse, *King Lear* 'shouts . . . "at the end of time" from "the end of time", for "the last age of humanity"'.[91] There is no rejoicing here, and no exhilaration, because both characterize a world of which this play is but the herald – a world in which man creates his own life, shapes his own history, one which may collapse in ruins but from which man may also struggle up again from the wreckage and, through hope, create the very world he contemplates. The Apocalypse is no ordinary book but is, like *King Lear*, written out of a moment of crisis and is typically invoked in such moments of crisis when mankind has reached the nadir of despair. It invades history, as Jacques Ellul remarks, 'at the point of hope' and so 'implies a possible emergence from the present time'. Yet, as Ellul also comprehends, a hope for the future does not provoke the vision, which seems to be provoked instead by 'the apparent impossibility of a future for all mankind'.[92]

In Shakespeare's day, it has been suggested, enthusiasts were already enflaming the ignorant: such elements were 'already working in England which produced the Fifth Monarchy and the Blackfriars' fanatics, Naylor, General Harrison, and the like' (*Var. Ed.*, p. 235). However adverse he may have been to such tendencies, and belittling of them in his plays, Shakespeare evinces in *King Lear* a sensibility like that attributed to Gerrard Winstanley for whom 'the answer to the question of how humanity may find perfection requires the forging of new consciousness and new ways of expressing that consciousness'.[93] In this sense, we may credit Thomas Carlyle's view of Shakespeare as a prophet, or as at least prophetic, and see in *King Lear* a play 'big with destiny'. There is none of the narrow fanaticism, none of the sectarian fierceness or perversion that had curbed lesser prophets – just, as Carlyle might say, 'a Revelation',[94] one of many such produced by the poets of the English Renaissance. However unlike that of some of his contemporaries, Shakespeare's is very much a Revelation like St. John's: one that arises out of the feeling that 'the future of humanity is . . . totally blocked', that 'no explanation concerning the continuity of history can respond to the situation, nor satisfy'.[95] It is then, says Ellul, that the Apocalypse (and we might want to say *King Lear*) delivers its authentic message: 'yes, the future is really blocked; yes, there is no longer any history possible; and in spite of the fact, . . . here is the meaning, here is the break' provided by men like Albany, Kent, and Edgar who will piece together the fragmented world. History is going to be reversed now with men themselves serving as a bridge between the old and new creation. Now we will see the fulfillment of history *in history*, the emergence of a new world that is the work of man – in Ellul's words, 'the sum of his culture . . . *his* creation'.[96]

Renaissance theologians and historians may have been responsible for the enormous proliferation of commentaries on the Apocalypse but not, it may be argued, for that period's richest insights into John's prophecy. The Renaissance also produced a Poet's Revelation; and these poets, like their counterparts in the present age, offer insights that have a depth of meaning, a modernity of attitude, unequalled in 'the anemic and evasive commentaries' offered by orthodoxy which, then as now, attempts to rationalize a discomfiting and, to some, embarrassing book.[77] The Renaissance phase of Revelation commentary, as represented by theologians and historians, may be characterized as a process wherein Catholic readings acquire an overlay of Protestant sentiment. The Poets' Revelation reveals a different development, however, wherein a sacred text becomes secularized and humanized. That process involves, first of all, a gradual synthesis and synchronization of so-called spiritual and historical interpretations of Revelation. In the Poets' Revelation, opposites meet and are reconciled – but over a stretch of time.

Whatever his earlier hopes and enthusiasms, Spenser eventually despairs over the idea of an apocalypse now and so pushes it into a future history and then beyond history into eternity, even as he founds all such hopes on man's renovation in this life. Shakespeare places his hopes there as well and, while he may have despaired over the possibility for an apocalypse in history, never surrenders the possibility itself. Donne withdraws the apocalyptic promise from history altogether, finding all reference points of the Revelation prophecy within the spiritual history of everyman. Milton joins what had become disjointed, but over the course of a lifetime. Initially he invests his faith in apocalypse by revolution and only later, divesting himself of naïve apocalyptics, makes an apocalypse of mind prologue to an apocalypse in history. From the perspective of Milton's last poems, John's prophecy, instead of looking this way or that – inward to the soul of the struggling Christian *or* outward to history – looks both ways simultaneously. Here, an 'either-or' becomes a 'both-and' hermeneutics. As a result of such secularizing tendencies, poets themselves – no longer just national leaders and churchmen – accede to the role of apocalyptic angels; and the whole apocalyptic drama, once regarded as a struggle involving only divine figures, is reconceived to allow for, indeed to require, human participation. That is the premise on which the Poets' Revelation is founded, and it gives to John's prophecy another visage.

A new literature could now emerge out of, and in relation to, the Apocalyptic drama – one in which Revelation's epical dimensions would assert themselves in *The Faerie Queene* and, later, in Milton's epics and one in which history, both in its tragic and comedic aspects, would be scrutinized anew in Shakespeare's history plays and tragedies, especially *King Lear*, and in such another work as *Samson Agonistes*. Resisting the inclination of their age to trust in the imminence of the apocalypse, Spenser, Shakespeare, and the later Milton relegate apocalypse, as popularly understood, to the future (in the case of Spenser, to a future beyond history) and make that event dependent upon an apocalypse of mind in the present age. Each of these poets creates a great prophetic projection through which we can read the Poets' Revelation and which gathers into focus an authentically British tradition of apocalypticism.

The poets, it needs to be recognized, are in an important sense the shapers of that tradition even if, at a glance, their interpretations seem to run on a course parallel with those of theologians and historians.

Theologians and historians of both the sixteenth and seventeenth centuries produce what we might call Tudor, Stuart, and Puritan interpretations of the Apocalypse against which texts the poems of Spenser, Shakespeare, and Milton respectively might be read, always with an eye to the swerve the poems make from such texts and with an eye, too, to the way in which the poets themselves anticipate, even chart the course for, a later phase of commentary. John Bale and John Napier, for example, are nodal points within the Renaissance for moral and historical interpretation respectively, while the Puritan revolution is thought to inaugurate another, spiritual phase of interpretation. Yet before Napier, in Spenser's *Faerie Queene*, the current alters from moral to historical interpretation and, in *King Lear*, from historical to spiritual interpretation, at least in terms of emphasis. In Shakespeare and, more, in Milton are adumbrations of those attitudes that characterize both Henry More and the young Newton's thinking on the Apocalypse – a book, as they read it, that locates the drama of existence in the human psyche and that allows not for immediate transcendence but for betterment through a long process of spiritual evolution. No poet of the Renaissance more fully exploits spiritual interpretation of the Apocalypse than Milton in his epics and tragedy but in such a way as to sanction not subvert moral and historical readings of John's prophecy – in such a way as to manifest not mystify the meaning of John's Revelation. To these three poets, though not necessarily to John's commentators, the cosmic struggle of the Apocalypse was a matter not for scholarly erudition but for human engagement. Here was being played out the great epic of history and the essential drama of human life; here, in the words of Shakespeare's 107th sonnet, was to be found a mirror on 'the prophetic soul / Of the wide world dreaming on things to come'.

NOTES

All quotations from *King Lear* accord with the text of *A New Variorum Edition of Shakespeare: 'King Lear'*, ed. Horace Howard Furness (1880; rpt. New York: Dover, 1963) – hereafter referred to as *Var. Ed.* and cited parenthetically within the text of the essay. Quotations from other of Shakepseare's plays are from *Shakespeare: The Complete Works*, ed. G. B. Harrison (New York: Harcourt, Brace and Co., 1948), and scriptural quotations are from the Geneva Bible (1560).

1 *Acts and Monuments*, ed. Josiah Pratt, 4th edn, 8 vols. (London: Religious Tract Society, n. d.), V, 655.
2 *The Works of Edmund Spenser: A Variorum Edition*, ed. Edwin Greenlaw et al., 10 vols (Baltimore: Johns Hopkins Press, 1943–57), X, 471.

3 See Patricia A. Parker, *Inescapable Romance: Studies in the Poetics of a Mode* (Princeton: Princeton Univ. Press, 1979), pp. 55, 76–7. Speaking of *The Faerie Queene*, Parker says that 'its tendency is "apocalyptic" – but the poem moves away from this clarity as soon as it is introduced': 'the apocalyptic movement towards revelation is countered by a movement towards multiplication and refraction' (pp. 69, 80).
4 *The Sermons of John Donne*, ed. George R. Potter and Evelyn M. Simpson, 10 vols (Berkeley: Univ. of California Press, 1953–62), V, 79, 151; see also X, 59, 60.
5 Abrams finds a complex of such images in 'Batter my heart'; see *Natural Supernaturalism: Tradition and Revolution in Romantic Literature* (New York: W. W. Norton, 1971), p. 50. Frank Kermode discovers a similar system of imagery in *The Faerie Queene*, especially Book I; see *Shakespeare, Spenser, Donne: Renaissance Essays* (New York: Viking Press, 1971), pp. 14–59.
6 *The Glass of Vision* (London: Dacre Press, 1948), p. 128.
7 Henry Ansgar Kelly, *Divine Providence in the England of Shakespeare's Histories* (Cambridge, Mass.: Harvard Univ. Press, 1970), pp. 220, 232, 304.
8 I borrow the phrase from Edith Sitwell, *A Notebook on William Shakespeare* (1948; rpt. Boston: Beacon Press, 1961), p. 166.
9 J. S. H. Bransom, *The Tragedy of 'King Lear'* (Oxford: Basil Blackwell, 1934), p. 183.
10 E. M. W. Tillyard, *Shakespeare's History Plays* (1944; rpt. New York: Collier Books, 1962), p. 40.
11 Lily B. Campbell, *Shakespeare's Histories* (1947; rpt. London: Methuen, 1964), pp. 125, 259.
12 For example, David L. Frey writes: 'I do not think that the plays provide even a modicum of evidence for the view that Shakespeare saw God's guiding hand in the history of England, as did the Tudor historians' (*The First Tetralogy, Shakespeare's Scrutiny of the Tudor Myth: A Dramatic Exploration of Divine Providence* [The Hague and Paris: Mouton, 1976], p. 153). See also C. A. Patrides, *The Grand Design of God: The Literary Form of the Christian View of History* (London: Routledge and Kegan Paul, Toronto: Univ. of Toronto Press, 1972), pp. 79–82; Kelly, *Divine Providence in the England of Shakespeare's Histories*, esp. pp. 300–6; and Robert Ornstein, *A Kingdom for a Stage: The Achievement of Shakespeare's History Plays* (Cambridge, Mass.: Harvard Univ. Press, 1972), esp. pp. 16–31.
13 Grigori Kozintsev, *'King Lear': The Space of Tragedy*, tr. Mary Mackintosh (London: Heinemann, 1977), p. 226.
14 Johann Valentine Andreae quoted by Katharine R. Firth, *The Apocalyptic Tradition in Reformation Britain 1530–1645* (New York: Oxford Univ. Press, 1979), p. 60.
15 *'King Lear' and the Gods* (San Marino, Ca.: Huntington Library, 1966), p. 71.
16 On the liberties Shakespeare has taken in his history plays, see Peter Saccio, *Shakespeare's English Kings: History, Chronicle, and Drama* (New York: Oxford Univ. Press, 1977), p. 14; and on the license he takes with Chronicle history in *King Lear*, see Boas's remarks as quoted by R. W. Chambers, *King Lear* (Glasgow: Jackson, Son, and Co., 1940), p. 11.
17 Campbell, *Shakespeare's Histories*, p. 16.
18 *The Old Testament Prophets* (London: Darton, Longman and Todd, 1977), p. 105.
19 The proclamation is reprinted by John W. Draper, 'The Occasion of *King Lear*', *Studies in Philology*, 34 (1937), 177.
20 *Basilikon Doran. Or His Maiesties Instructions to His Dearest Sonne, Henry the Prince* (London, 1603), p. 31.

21 *The Illusion of Power in Political Theater in the English Renaissance* (Berkeley and Los Angeles: Univ. of California Press, 1975), pp. 9, 14. See also Alvin B. Kernan, '*King Lear* and the Shakespearean Pageant of History' and G. E. Bentley, 'Shakespeare, the King's Company, and *King Lear*', in *On 'King Lear'*, ed. Lawrence Danson (Princeton: Princeton Univ. Press, 1981), ppp. 7–24, 47–60.
22 *Basilikon Doran*, pp. 66, 73–4.
23 'The Occasion of *King Lear*', p. 179.
24 'Of Prophecies', in *Francis Bacon: Selected Writings*, ed. Hugh G. Dick (New York: Modern Library, 1955), pp. 96–7.
25 See Glynne Wickham, 'From Tragedy to Tragi-Comedy: *King Lear* as Prologue', *Shakespeare Survey*, 26 (1973), 35.
26 *A Prophesie of Cadwallader, Last King of the Britaines* (London, 1604), sig. B2–B2^v, H–H^v.
27 Irving Ribner argues that Shakespeare 'changed the story of *King Lear* . . . to better effect his tragic purposes and, in the orthodox tradition of Renaissance historiography, to better effect his political purposes' ('Shakespeare and Legendary History: *Lear* and *Cymbeline*', *Shakespeare Quarterly*, 7 [1956], 51); and Kozintsev confides, 'I wanted to see Lear in the midst of . . . the world of politics' (*'King Lear': The Space of Tragedy*, p. 39). The prophetic element in *King Lear* has been discerned and described rather eccentrically by Abraham Schechter, *'King Lear': Warning or Prophecy* (New York: Privately printed, 1956) and quite aptly by both Benjamin T. Spencer, '*King Lear*: A Prophetic Tragedy', *College English*, 5 (1944), 302–8, and A. C. Harwood, *Shakespeare's Prophetic Mind* (London: Rudolf Steiner Press, 1964). See also G. Wilson Knight, *The Imperial Theme: Further Interpretations of Shakespeare's Tragedies Including the Roman Plays* (1931; rpt. London: Methuen, 1965), p. 361.
28 See Eyriak Schlichtenberger, *A Prophecy Uttered by the Daughter of an Honest Man* (London, 1580), no sigs.
29 Elton, *'King Lear' and the Gods*, p. 35.
30 *A Plaine Discovery of the Whole Revelation of Saint John* (Edinburgh, 1593), sig. A2.
31 *Sermons upon the Whole Booke of the Revelation* (London, 1599), p. 339.
32 *Pisgah Evangelica* (London, 1606), p. 208.
33 James's observation is quoted from LeRoy Edwin Froom, *The Prophetic Faith of Our Fathers: The Historical Development of Prophetic Interpretation*, 4 vols. (Washington, D.C.: Review and Herald, 1945–54), II, 539.
34 Arthur H. Williamson, *Scottish National Consciousness in the Age of James VI: The Apocalypse, the Union and the Shaping of Scotland's Public Culture* (Edinburgh: John Donald, 1979), p. 94.
35 James's words are quoted by Wickham, 'From Tragedy to Tragi-Comedy', p. 36. In the early years of the seventeenth century, it was common to use these generic labels to designate political, as well as religious, allies and opponents. In his 1605 Preface, entitled 'To the Christian Reader', Gabriel Powel, implying that the Apocalypse is a tragicomedy, says that the Catholics 'play all the parts in this Tragedie' while the Protestants, it seems, are the protagonists in this comedy (see Symonds, *Pisgah Evangelica*, no sigs.).
36 *A Fruitefull Meditation; Containing a Plaine and Easie Exposition . . . of the 7. 8. 9. 10. Verses of the 20. Chap. of the Revelation* (London, 1603), no sigs. According to James, the Book of Revelation is 'a Prophesie of the latter time' – the Day of Judgement is near.
37 This is the view of Gary Taylor, 'The War in *King Lear*', *Shakespeare Survey*, 33 (1980), 27.

38 *Romance and Realism: A Study in English Bourgeois Literature*, ed. Samuel Hynes (Princeton Univ. Press, 1970), pp. 43-4.
39 *A Plaine Discovery of the Whole Revelation*, sig. b^v.
40 *King Lear*, pp. 10-11. For another account of Shakespeare's recasting of history, see Thomas P. Roche, Jr., '"Nothing Almost Sees Miracles": Tragic Knowledge in *King Lear*', in *On 'King Lear'*, ed. Danson, pp. 150-7.
41 In *Shakespeare: 'King Lear'*, ed. Frank Kermode (London: Macmillan, 1969), p. 235.
42 *Tudor Apocalypse: Sixteenth-Century Apocalypticism, Millennarianism and the English Reformation* (Appleford, Eng.: Sutton Courtenay Press, 1978), p. 71.
43 *The Apocalyptic Tradition in Reformation Britain*, p. 60; see also Paul Christianson, *Reformers and Babylon: English Apocalyptic Visions from the Reformation to the Eve of the Civil War* (Toronto: Univ. of Toronto Press, 1978), pp. 15-16.
44 Southern, 'Aspects of the European Tradition of Historical Writing', *Transactions of the Royal Historical Society*, 72 (1972), 159.
45 *A Fruitefull Meditation*, no sigs.
46 John Holloway, *The Story of the Night: Studies in Shakespeare's Major Tragedies* (Lincoln: Univ. of Nebraska Press, 1961), pp. 77, 90.
47 *Shakespearean Tragedy and the Elizabethan Compromise* (New York: New York Univ. Press, 1957), p. 188.
48 See Arthur Sewall, 'Tragedy and the "Kingdom of Ends"', in *Shakespeare: Modern Essays in Criticism*, ed. Leonard F. Dean (New York: Oxford Univ. Press, 1961), p. 331; and Sylvan Barnet, 'Some Limitations of a Christian Approach to Shakespeare', in *Approaches to Shakespeare*, ed. Norman Rabkin (New York: McGraw-Hill, 1964), p. 222.
49 Elton, *'King Lear' and the Gods*, pp. 271-2. On Shakespeare's use of the Day of Judgment motif, see Mary Lascelles, '*King Lear* and Doomsday', *Shakespeare Survey*, 26 (1973), 69-79; but also Walter B. Stone, 'Shakespeare and the Sad Augurs', *Journal of English and Germanic Philology*, 52 (1953), 457-79. Roche comments incisively: 'It should also be observed that each half line takes up a dramatically opposed vision of the Last Judgment, the first emphasizing the promise, the second the horror: both together constitute the whole image of that day of conflagration' ('"Nothing Almost Sees Miracles"', in *On 'King Lear'*, ed. Danson, p. 158).
50 Jane H. Jack, '*Macbeth*, King James, and the Bible', *ELH*, 22 (1955), 180. Jack argues persuasively: 'Shakespeare leant heavily on *Revelation* and James's commentary on it for the expression of his imaginative apparition of overwhelming evil' (p. 186).
51 See Roy W. Battenhouse, *Shakespearean Tragedy: Its Art and Its Christian Premises* (Bloomington, Ind.: Indiana Univ. Press, 1969), p. 301; Donald A. Stauffer, *Shakespeare's World of Images: The Development of His Moral Ideas* (1949; rpt. Bloomington, Ind.: Indiana Univ. Press, 1966), p. 207; and G. Wilson Knight, *The Christian Renaissance: The Influence of the Bible and the Dogma of Christianity on the Works of Shakespeare, Dante, Goethe, and Other Poets* (1962; rpt. New York: Norton Library, 1963), p. 51. Viewing the play from this perspective often leads critics to conclude that 'in *King Lear*, as in the earliest Chronicles, God is again working in history . . . Edmund has to give way to Edgar and Cordelia' (John F. Danby, *Shakespeare's Doctrine of Nature: A Study of 'King Lear'* [London: Faber and Faber, 1949], pp. 204-5), or to argue, as does Irving Ribner, that *King Lear* is 'a triumph of dramatic consolation which in its total effect . . . offers justice in the world, which is seen as a harmonious system ruled by a benevolent God' (*Patterns in Shakespearian Tragedy* [New York: Barnes and Noble, 1960], p. 117).

52 Jan Kott, *Shakespeare Our Contemporary*, tr. Boleslaw Taborski (New York: Doubleday, 1966), p. 147. On *Lear* as a sardonic or broken apocalypse, see Frank Kermode, *The Sense of an Ending: Studies in the Theory of Fiction* (New York: Oxford Univ. Press, 1967), pp. 28, 82, 88. Whatever conclusions the play tends to confirm, Kott contends that 'Lear and Glouchester are adherents of eschatology; they desperately believe in the existence of absolutes' (p. 166). See also Battenhouse, *Shakespearean Tragedy*, pp. 176–9; and for discussions of Shakespeare and the Apocalypse generally, see Ethel Seaton, '*Antony and Cleopatra* and the Book of Revelation', *Review of English Studies*, 22 (1946), 219–24; Jack Lindsay, '*Antony and Cleopatra* and the Book of Revelation', *Review of English Studies*, 23 (1947), 66; and Helen Morris, 'Shakespeare and Dürer's Apocalypse', *Shakespeare Studies*, 4 (1968), 252–62.

53 Kermode, 'Introduction', in *Shakespeare: 'King Lear'*, ed. Kermode, p. 19. See also S. L. Goldberg's remarks in *An Essay on 'King Lear'* (Cambridge: Cambridge Univ. Press, 1974), pp. 152, 157–8.

54 Kozintsev, *'King Lear': The Space of Tragedy*, pp. 48, 176.

55 *The Masks of God: Occidental Mythology* (New York: Viking Press, 1969), p. 258.

56 *Psychology and Religion* (New York: Pantheon Books, 1958), p. 736.

57 Thomas Brightman, *The Revelation of S. John* (1611; rpt. Leyden, 1616), p. 178.

58 *An Exposition of the Fourth Chapter of S. Johns Revelation* (London, 1577), sigs. Bv^v–Bvi.

59 See Gifford's *Sermons upon the Whole Booke of the Revelation*, pp. 164–5, and the anon. *A Plaine Explanation of the Whole Revelation of Saint John* (London, 1622), p. 47.

60 *The Revelation of S. John*, p. 178.

61 *Devotions upon Emergent Occasions* (Ann Arbor: Univ. of Michigan Press, 1959), p. 8.

62 Gifford, *Sermons upon the Whole Booke of the Revelation*, p. 162.

63 *A Plaine Discovery of the Whole Revelation*, p. 142.

64 *'King Lear' and the Gods*, p. 299.

65 *A Hundred Sermons upon the Apocalypse*, ed. and tr. John Day (1561; rpt. London, 1573), p. 232.

66 John Mayer, *Ecclesiastica Interpretatio: or the Expositions upon the Difficult and Doubtful Passages of the Seven Epistles Called Catholike, and the Revelation* (London, 1627), p. 295. See also Arthur Dent, *The Ruine of Rome, or an Exposition upon the Whole Revelation* (1607; rpt. London, 1633), p. 243; and for a recent explanation of the image, see Maurice Charney, '"We put fresh garments on him": Nakedness and Clothes in *King Lear*', in *Some Facets of 'King Lear': Essays in Prismatic Criticism*, ed. Rosalie L. Colie and F. T. Flahiff (Toronto: Univ. of Toronto Press, 1974), pp. 87–8.

67 *A Meditation upon the 27, 28, 29 Verses of the XXVII. Chapter of St. Matthew* (London, 1620), pp. 4, 6, 32.

68 *Sermons*, ed. Potter and Simpson, VI, 65.

69 Thomas McFarland, 'The Image of the Family in *King Lear*', in *On 'King Lear'*, ed. Danson, pp. 108–9.

70 *Sermons*, ed. Potter and Simpson, V, 112.

71 Battenhouse, *Shakespearean Tragedy*, p. 131.

72 Roche, '"Nothing Almost Sees Miracles"', in *On 'King Lear'*, ed. Danson, p. 157.

73 *The Comic Matrix of Shakespeare's Tragedies* (Princeton: Princeton Univ. Press, 1979), p. 168.
74 *Anatomy of Criticism: Four Essays* (Princeton: Princeton Univ. Press, 1957), p. 222; but see also p. 221.
75 See Battenhouse, *Shakespearean Tragedy*, p. 288, and Sitwell, *A Notebook on William Shakespeare*, p. 53. See also G. Wilson Knight, *The Christian Renaissance*, p. 56.
76 'Shakespeare's Theology', *Review of English Literature*, 5 (1964), 78.
77 *Shakespeare's Doctrine of Nature*, p. 126; see also Russell Fraser, *Shakespeare's Poetics in Relation to 'King Lear'* (London: Routledge and Kegan Paul, 1962), p. 133.
78 *Fools of Time: Studies in Shakespearean Tragedy* (Toronto: Univ. of Toronto Press, 1967), p. 106.
79 *Shakespeare and the Mystery of God's Judgments*, p. 109; see also Snyder, *The Comic Matrix of Shakespeare's Tragedies*, p. 168.
80 Elton, *'King Lear' and the Gods*, pp. 271–2, 298.
81 *Visions of the End; Apocalyptic Traditions in the Middle Ages* (New York: Columbia Univ. Press, 1979), p. 10. C. A. Patrides reminds us that the *Nürnberger Chonik* contains 'a description of the Last Judgment with appropriately terrifying illustrations ingeniously introduced by six folio pages left totally blank' (*The Grand Design of God*, p. 47). Here may be the best analogue to *King Lear* – an image of the horror yet indetermination about the end itself.
82 *Redeemer Nation: The Idea of America's Millennial Role* (Chicago: Univ. of Chicago Press, 1968), p. 51.
83 McGinn, *Visions of the End*, p. 30.
84 *The Sense of an Ending*, p. 88. The pages that follow in my own essay are, however, a qualification of Kermode's earlier observation: 'The end is now a matter of imminence; tragedy assumes the figurations of apocalypse, of death and judgment, heaven and hell; but the world goes forward in the hands of exhausted survivors. . . . This is the tragedy of sempiternity; apocalypse is translated out of time into the *aevum*' (p. 82). Particularly the last sentence needs revision.
85 *Tragic Meanings in Shakespeare* (New York: Random House, 1966), p. 16.
86 Carl Becker, *The Heavenly City of the Eighteenth-Century Philosophers* (New Haven: Yale Univ. Press, 1932), p. 17.
87 Ibid., p. 139.
88 Spencer, 'King Lear: A Prophetic Tragedy', p. 308.
89 Karl S. Guthke, *Modern Tragicomedy: An Investigation into the Nature of the Genre* (New York: Random House, 1966), p. 97.
90 *The Apocalypse of Our Time and Other Writings*, ed. Robert Payne (New York: Praeger, 1977), p. 236. Snyder makes the identical point about *King Lear* – a play, she says, that is 'about religion in the making. Shakespeare created for it a thoroughly pagan milieu . . . steeped in Christian allusion and assumption' (*The Comic Matrix of Shakespeare's Tragedies*, p. 178).
91 *The Apocalypse of Our Time*, p. 238.
92 *Apocalypse: The Book of Revelation*, tr. George W. Schreiner (New York: Seabury Press, 1977), pp. 26, 27, 61.
93 T. Wilson Hayes, *Winstanley the Digger: A Literary Analysis of Radical Ideas in the English Revolution* (Cambridge, Mass.: Harvard Univ. Press, 1979), p. 121.
94 *On Heroes and Hero-Worship* (New York: Oxford Univ. Press, 1957), pp. 144, 145–6. Carlyle discovers in the *vates* poets such as Shakespeare a 'melodious Apocalypse of Nature' (p. 109).

95 Ellul, *Apocalypse*, p. 62.
96 Ibid., p. 222 (my italics).
97 Guilford Dudley, *The Recovery of Christian Myth* (Philadelphia: Westminster Press, 1967), p. 64.

C. A. PATRIDES

8 'Something like Prophetick strain': apocalyptic configurations in Milton

Qu'est-ce qu'un homme dans l'infinit?   PASCAL

I 'HISTORY AND PROPHECY STRANGELY SHAKE HANDS'

'Creatures of an inferiour nature', said Donne in 1627, 'are possest with the *present*; Man is a *future Creature*.'[1] Donne's immediate reference is to the expressly Christian belief that man journeys along a path that is to terminate beyond the sublunary maze of the phenomenal world, in the world to come. Conscious as man is of the future, however, he tends to enquire into that future habitually and sometimes obsessively. For a committed Christian in the age of Milton, certainly, the focus of such an obsession was the Book of Revelation, its imposing contours studied by major theologians, its manifold complexities examined by formidable mathematicians from Napier to Newton, its arresting visions intoned in the characteristic activity attested by one delighted father: 'John repeated the 12th, Eliezer the 10th of Revelation last night in bed, blessed be God.'[2]

The Apocalypse was widely commended as utterly indispensable. On the popular level, Arthur Dent averred that 'this booke doth not only concerne preachers, and deep diuines; but euen all the Lords people whatsoeuer: for it doth minister great comfort and strength of faith to all the people of God'.[3] But on a higher level, too, it was proclaimed by no less an authority than King James that 'of all the scriptures, the buik of the Reuelatioun is maist meit for this our last age'.[4] The method of approach was deceptively simple. The 'argument' that, inspired by Heinrich Bullinger, was prefixed to the annotated text of the Geneva Bible (1560), urged the faithful to 'Read diligently: iudge soberly, and call earnestly to God for the true vnderstanding hereof'. But 'true vnderstanding' was by no means readily forthcoming. The generalization ventured by Thomas Brightman ('the Reuelation doth still require necessarily a Reuelation')[5] was certainly shared by all commentators, responsible and otherwise. The Apocalypse, after all, is 'carried along by Figurative expressions'; it is 'involved with mystical allegories, and types'; it is 'replenished with great secrets, types, and darke sentences'; it soars – to quote Milton – 'to a Prophetick pitch in types, and Allegories'.[6] The great commentator Joseph Mede called it a 'holy *Labyrinth*' – holy indeed, but a labyrinth all the same.[7] The penetration into its innermost recesses, however, became the ultimate challenge; and George Sandys was not exceptional in his commendation of the ambition involved:

> this booke of the Apocalyps . . . is by all men confessed to be full of mysteries, and that it is by reason thereof verie darke and obscure, is by manie affirmed: yet I see this hath neither disswaded the mindes, nor discouraged the industries of godly men in all ages from searching to find out the true sence and meaning thereof.[8]

Yet the difficulties stalking all explicators of the Book of Revelation did not prevent their unanimous conclusion that it appertains, after one fashion or another, to 'history' past and to 'history' future. Mede, for example, was of the opinion that the Apocalypse delineates 'a certain bare history of things done', while one of his more discriminating successors, William Hicks, thought it adequate enough to call it 'a Book of History of memorable Acts and passages'.[9] The intent is clear: the dimension so manifestly concerned with what Hicks termed 'Prophetical Representations, and Hyerogliphique Figures'[10] had to be firmly connected to the historical process, not severed from it as a mere 'prophecy' of the obscure future. Henry More was later to make the point with admirable clarity. 'History and Prophecy', he wrote, 'strangely shake hands together in these things.'[11]

But the problem persisted stubbornly. In the case of Napier's magnificent effort to comprehend the Book of Revelation (1593), a series of parallel columns neatly place every episode within an immediately intelligible context 'historicallie applyed'. Clearly uneasy over the implications, however, Napier was also obliged to warn that many details are 'not literallie to be takẽ, but after a propheticall and figuratiue maner of speach'.[12] The qualification, of course, militates against the recurrent Protestant declaration that the Bible may be interpreted solely after one sense, the literal. As early as the dawn of Protestantism in England, William Tyndale had defined the standard opposition to the four senses traditionally espoused by Catholicism – the literal, the analogical, the tropological, and the anagogical – by asserting categorically that 'ỹ scripture hath but one sence w̃ is the litterall sence. And the litterall sence is ỹ rote & grounde of all . . .'. However, even Tyndale was obliged to pause, troubled, before the gates to the Book of Revelation. 'The Apocalipse or reuelacions of John', he acknowledged, 'are allegories whose litteral sence is herde to finde in many places.'[13]

Yet the problem was not beyond resolution, however much that resolution required the talents rather of a poet than of a theologian. Tyndale provided the hint when he observed in passing that the spirit that is God discourses in words that are spiritual. 'His litteral sence', in this respect, 'is spiritual.' Later, when the polymath Andrew Willet opposed yet again the Catholic claim that there are 'diuers senses and meanings' to the Bible, he articulated the fully formulated Protestant attitude thus:

> We affirm that of one place of scripture there can bee but one sense, which we call the literall sense, when as the wordes are either taken properly, or figuratiuely to expresse the thing which is meant: as in this place, *The seede of the woman shall breake the Serpents head* [Genesis 3.15]: the literall sense is of Christ, who should triumph oter Sathan, though it be spoken in a borrowed and figuratiue speech. There can be therefore but one sense, which is the literall: as for those three kindes [i.e., the analogical, the tropological, and the anagogical], they are not diuers senses, but diuers applications onely and collections out of one and the same sense.[14]

The sense that is at once literal and figurative can be explicated best – and perhaps solely – by a poet. 'The literall sense', Donne declared conventionally enough, 'is always to be preserved.' 'But,' he added in an arresting display of his poetic sensibility, 'the literall sense of every place, is the principall intention of the Holy Ghost, in that place: And his principall intention in many places, is to expresse things by allegories, by figures; so that in many places in Scripture, the figurative sense is the literall sense.'[15]

For poets in particular, it is evident, the handshake between history and prophecy was prefatory to an imaginative adaptation of the literal to the purposes of the spiritual. But the deployment of materials drawn from the Bible generally, and from the Apocalypse specifically, was not undertaken in a vacuum. It was affected positively no less than negatively by the indefatigable labors of Protestant commentators both before and during the age of Milton.

II MANIFESTATIONS OF ANTICHRIST

The Protestant commentaries on the Apocalypse seem at first glance to partake of the nocturnal demesne of Nerval's *Aurélia*, as if they too inhabit a preternatually dark planet of alarming shapes now stretched and now coiled, and of forms wild and forbidding against a universe of arid rocks. Unlike Nerval's shapes and forms, moreover, the commentaries do not suddenly change into visions of beauty, their erstwhile cacophonous sounds displaced by a celestial melody. Such, no doubt, was the aspiration; but the aridity lingers still, and the harsh sounds persist. In what sense, then, might one claim that commentaries utterly devoid of literary merit had an impact on literature?

We may consider by way of an example – an illuminating example precisely because it is nominally the least promising – the common Protestant identification of Antichrist with the papacy. True, Sir Thomas Browne in *Religio Medici* irenically asserted his total disinclination to bestow on the pope 'the name of Antichrist, Man of sin, or whore of *Babylon*';[16] but Browne is the exception that proves the rule. For endorsed by both Luther and Calvin, codified in the marginal annotations to the Geneva Bible, and monotonously maintained in any number of treatises,[17] the persuasion that the See of Rome is Antichrist's 'chiefe Kennell' – to quote Milton's phrase from *Of Reformation* (1641)[18] – assumed in Protestant commentaries on the Apocalypse proportions one may not unreasonably describe as hysterical. Express Biblical references to Antichrist occur, in fact, solely beyond the Apocalypse, in a diversity of other contexts (1 John 2.18; 2 John 7; cf. Thessalonians 2.3–9 and 1 Timothy 4.1); however, since the Apocalypse was widely regarded as the most sustained chronicle of Antichrist's advent and progress to the end of time, the Protestant case was most often presented within its confines and in terms of its orotund language. That case depended, as one might expect, on interpretations not so much 'historicallie applyed' as phrenetically distorted, the 'proof' often encompassing such ferine expositions as the transposition of '666' – the number of the beast in Revelation 13.18 – into letters that spelled, among other possibilities, ΛΑΤΕΙΝΟΣ (Latinus).[19] Improbabilities masked as the ultimate verities, joined to a tone of virulence unmatched even in that virulent age, finally obliged Catholic spokesmen to mount equally formidable efforts to prove that the pope is *not* Antichrist[20] – itself, perhaps, the most astonishing development of all.

It was in the twilight of such a background that Milton studied, and responded to, the Book of Revelation. The wilder aspects of the polemic exchanges between Protestants and Catholics appear not to have affected him; but the common identification of Antichrist with the pope was voiced in *Of Reformation* as already noted, while later, in *De doctrina christiana*, he affirmed with telling austerity that Antichrist is 'a name given to the pope himself chiefly from his encroachments on the consciences of mankind'.[21] Far more illuminating than these two instances, however, is the way Milton derived from the ongoing exchanges dimensions peculiarly suitable to his purposes both as polemicist in prose and as poet. In his prose, especially the antiprelatical tracts of the early 1640s, he repeatedly deployed the term 'antichristian' not simply to assert the opposition of the episcopalian form of ecclesiastical authority to the actual practice of 'primitive' Christians but, more specifically, to suggest the distinctly apocalyptic notion that the prelates resemble in their 'encroachments on the consciences of mankind' the activities of Antichrist as delineated in the Apocalypse and practised by the pope. The conviction that 'Prelaty is Antichristian' was annotated in *The Reason of Church-Government* (1642):

> if such like practises, and not many worse then these of our Prelats, in that great darknesse of the Roman Church, have not exempted both her and her present members from being judg'd to be Antichristian in all orthodoxall esteeme, I cannot think but that it is the absolute voice of truth and all her children to pronounce this Prelaty, and these her dark deeds in the midst of this great light wherein we live, to be more Antichristian then Antichrist himselfe.[22]

In his poetry, on the other hand, Milton adapted analogous materials after a fashion at once less predictable and more imaginative.

In advance of *Paradise Lost* there is but one poem that partakes of the controverted issues centered on the pope as Antichrist: the sonnet composed in 1655 on the occasion of the massacre of the Piedmontese 'Protestants', the so-called Waldensians, by Italian troops.

> Avenge O Lord thy slaughter'd Saints, whose bones
>   Lie scatter'd on the Alpine mountains cold,
>   Ev'n them who kept thy truth so pure of old
>   When all our Fathers worship't Stocks and Stones,
> Forget not: in thy book record their groanes
>   Who were thy Sheep and in their antient Fold
>   Slayn by the bloody *Piemontese* that roll'd
>   Mother with Infant down the Rocks. Their moans
> The Vales redoubl'd to the Hills, and they
>   To Heav'n. Their martyr'd blood and ashes sow
>   O're all th'*Italian* fields where still doth sway
> The triple Tyrant: that from these may grow
>   A hunderd-fold, who having learnt thy way
>   Early may fly the *Babylonian* woe.

Fully characteristic of the more passionate Protestant condemnations of the Roman Antichrist, the sonnet is a stunning explosion of scorching indignation that reflects the numinous wrath expected to be unsealed during the Second Advent. The language comprehends in the first instance an allusion to the cry of the martyrs in the Apocalypse, 'How long, O Lord, holy and true, dost thou not judge and avenge our blood on them that dwell on the earth?' (6.10). But the language draws to an even more striking degree on the violent denunciation of evil by the great prophets as well as on the terms commonly deployed by Protestant expositors of the Apocalypse, most obviously in the terminal association of the pope – 'the triple Tyrant' who presumes to hold the keys of Heaven, earth, and hell – with the diabolic Babylon in the Book of Revelation. The convulsions within the form that enact the argument would be recalled later, in *Paradise Lost*, when Milton would attribute much the same zeal to the Son of God during the exorcism of the demonic powers from Heaven. The keynote on that occasion would be yet again the apocalyptic wrath of the numen.

Clearly cognizant of the Protestant expositions of the Apocalypse, Milton was also aware that while Catholics expected Antichrist to materialise in a particular individual, Protestants insisted – to quote Willet once more – that 'it is a meere fable, that Antichrist shall be one singular man'.[23] The Protestant view once 'historicallie applyed' tended in effect to regard Antichrist as the cumulative mystery of iniquity rampant in the postlapsarian world, his diverse manifestations collectively encompassing representatives of institutions like the papacy, national entities like the Ottoman Empire, extreme radicals like the millenarians at Münster, and individual persecutors of the elect whether like Antiochus IV Epiphanes – 'he was', said the great Puritan Richard Sibbes, 'a naughty man'[24] – or like Archbishop Laud, Charles I, Cromwell, and whoever was judged by the given partisan to have been guilty of 'encroachments on the consciences of mankind'. The principle was, it appears, flexible.

It was also a principle that Milton used in *Paradise Lost* extensively if discreetly. Where Spenser in the first book of *The Faerie Queene* places the 'antichristian' activities of its demonic anatagonists within a manifest apocalyptic framework, Milton in the first two books of *Paradise Lost* obscures their parallel burden in a premeditated effort to make Satan a nominally credible opponent of the Almighty. Yet Milton's Satan gathers in himself no fewer of the facets of Antichrist that Spenser had diversely apportioned to Archimago or Duessa. For one, the designation of Satan as 'great Sultan' (I, 348) invokes the mediaeval identification of Antichrist with the Ottoman Empire, updated in the sixteenth century when 'the scourge of the East' also became 'the terror of the West' by advancing under Suleiman the Magnificent (1520–66) to the very gates of Vienna.[25] Still another facet, equally indirect but far more eloquent, is that other commonplace Milton deployed, the immemorial tradition of *diabolus simius Dei*.

The tradition in asserting Satan's parody of the activities of God reaches back to the New Testament, partly to St. Paul's prophecy of the advent of Antichrist ('he as God sitteth in the temple of God, shewing himself that he is God' [2 Thessalonians 2.4]), but especially to the series of parodies enacted by the forces of darkness in the Book of Revelation: the dragon's bestowal of 'great authority' in the style appropriate solely to Christ (13.2), the ominous figure seated on a white horse in imitation of Christ similarly astraddle (6.2, 19.11–13), and particularly the congregated essays of the demonic trinity – the dragon, the first beast, and the second beast – to be a false god, a false Christ, and a false prophet.[26] Generously extended thereafter, the tradition was reiterated with undeviating insistence whether by Calvin ('the Diuell is always an Ape of God and a counterfeyter of his woorkes'), Sir Walter Ralegh ('the Diuell changeth himselfe into an *Angell* of light: and imitateth in all he can the waies and workings of the most High'), or the eloquent Thomas Adams ('the Deuill is Gods Ape, and striues to match and parallel him, both in his words and wonders').[27] The designation of Satan as 'Gods Ape' was so common, indeed, as to have been reduced to a cliché;[28] but it was one that Spenser appears to have adapted to his purposes,[29] while Milton embedded it into the very fabric of *Paradise Lost*.

Certainly no reader of Milton's epic has failed to observe either Satan's imitation of the form of angelic address common in Heaven or the way the fallen angels bow 'prone' before Satan in hell as their counterparts do reverently before God in Heaven (II, 477–8; III, 349–50). In fact, however, the principle is operative in the poem at large, each of its revelations marking both the thrust of Satan's imitative ambitions and the impossibility of their realization beyond mere parody. Accordingly, the grandiose prospect of Satan seated on the throne of hell in plain emulation of the Most High – 'shewing himself that he is God' or, in Milton's words, displaying a 'God-like imitated State' (II, 511; cf. VI, 99) – is promptly undercut by its sheer vulgarity as much as by the narrator's massive sarcasm:

> High on a Throne of Royal State, which farr
> Outshon the wealth of *Ormus* and of *Ind*,
> Or where the gorgeous East with richest hand
> Showrs on her Kings *Barbaric* Pearl and Gold,
> Satan exalted sat, by merit rais'd
> To that bad eminence; and from despair
> Thus high uplifted beyond hope, aspires
> Beyond thus high, insatiat to persue
> Vain Warr with Heav'n
>
> (II, 1–0)

The word '*Barbaric*' explicates itself, diagnostic as it is of the nature of both Antichrist and his agents like the Ottoman Empire or the papacy. Even more purposively, terms assertive of self-aggrandisement – 'exalted', 'rais'd', 'high', 'uplifted', 'aspires' – explicate Satan's 'merit' in relation to his misguided 'sense of injur'd merit' that led to the war in Heaven (I, 98), to the same sense as gradually instilled in prelapsarian man (V, 80), and to the correct pattern disclosed through the Son of God's reign 'by Merit more then Birthright' (III, 309; cf. VI, 174–8).

The thematic pattern of 'Gods Ape' also operates within an apocalyptic context in the way that the parallelism between Satan's offer to destroy man, and the Son's to redeem him, is underlined by the moment of silence that precedes each (II, 417–29; III, 217–21). The silence would in both cases have been a nicely theatrical gesture had not the juxtaposed episodes obliged us to recall that sombre occasion in the Apocalypse, just after the opening of the seventh seal, when the 'silence in heaven about the space of half an hour' (8.1) is followed by the blaring of the trumpets and the devastation of the created order. At that moment, in other words, the lines of demarcation between Christ and Antichrist are drawn firmly in the Apocalypse as they are in *Paradise Lost*; and the cosmic battle is joined in the one as it is in the other.

Diabolus simius Dei is no less an elemental aspect of the conception of Satan in *Paradise Lost* than it is of the vision of Antichrist in the Book of Revelation. Placed within a broader context, the tradition also suggests that as the Apocalypse and *Paradise Lost* alike have a Christological dimension, so they also have an antichristological one. Innate to both works, in brief, is a sustained view of history.

III A GESTURE TOWARD THE APOCALYPSE

Milton's response to the Book of Revelation was ample and, because ample, could on occasion tempt us into a number of unwarranted claims. But the limits of his response are clearly drawn and should be heeded. As if inclined to warn us, indeed, he went out of his way to deviate from an express detail within the Apocalypse: the shape of Heaven, conceived as a cube ('The length and the breadth and height of it are equal' [21.16]) in symbolic reflection of the sacrosanct nature not only of the square in prophetic literature (cf. Ezekiel 45.2) but especially of the cube that was the Holy of Holies. Several commentators on the Apocalypse pretended that the shape was 'wonderfull incredible'.[30] Bunyan thought that it represented 'perfection', while Giovanni Diodati – the professor of theology at Geneva who was uncle of Milton's friend Charles Diodati and whom Milton visited in 1639 – decided that as the cube is 'the most stable and equal figure of all', it intimates necessarily 'the perfect and everlasting stability of the Church in heaven'.[31] But conditioned as they all were to favor not the square or the cube but the circle or the sphere, they should have wondered – as Napier was among the very few so to wonder – that the Holy Ghost had failed to resort to 'the round figure, as of all solide bodies the most perfect figure'.[32] Milton's resolution of the problem was to claim in *Paradise Lost* that the shape of Heaven is neither square nor round but 'undetermind square or round' (II, 1048). The authority of the Bible was not thereby denied; but neither was the cumulative witness of traditions beyond the Bible.

The detail is suggestive of Milton's characteristic method of approach. It suggests that what inheres in the Bible and extra-scriptural traditions is jointly central to his poetry at large, but that claims we might advance about the exclusive impact of the Apocalypse on that poetry's structure, language, imagery, or tone, will in the end have to admit of extensive qualifications. The Apocalypse may or may not possess the 'formal pattern' we have attributed to it.³³ But that Milton coincidentally discerned such a pattern and adapted it to his purposes, that his major poems 'take shape, substance, and strategies from the Revelation model',³⁴ or that *Paradise Lost* is 'plainly and most naturally divisible' into the seven sections or visions evidently central to the Apocalypse and that in consequence the latter provided 'the actual inner design, indeed the model for the poem'³⁵ – these are claims we may accept only if we care to credit that any major poet has but a single 'model' of rather remarkable exclusiveness.

Milton was certainly privy to the explication of the Apocalypse by David Pareus in terms of seven visions.³⁶ He mentions the theory twice, first in *The Reason of Church-Government* in 1642 ('the Apocalyps of Saint *John* is the majestick image of a high and stately Tragedy, shutting up and intermingling her Solemn Scenes and Acts with a sevenfold *Chorus* of halleluja's and harping symphonies: and this my opinion the grave authority of *Pareus* commenting that booke is sufficient to confirm') and lastly in the preface to *Samson Agonistes* in 1671 ('*Parœus* commenting on the *Revelation*, divides the whole Book as a Tragedy, into Acts distinguisht each by a Chorus of Heavenly Harpings and Song between').³⁷ The two remarks are necessarily relevant to the 'high and stately Tragedy' that is *Samson Agonistes* and have in fact resulted in a substantive study of its influence by the Apocalypse within the experiential and typological framework elucidated by Pareus and other commentators; but it was a case, we have been sagely assured, of simply 'one influence' upon the play.³⁸ The larger claims involving the Apocalypse as an exclusive 'model' are of a radically different order. Its decisive numerological obsessions centered on seven – 'this number seven', Diodati reasonably enough declared, 'in Scripture signifieth perfection, or a compleat thing'³⁹ – are not in evidence in *Samson Agonistes*, much less in the two epics or the shorter poems. *Paradise Lost*, in particular, is 'plainly and most naturally divisible' into seven visions solely to the extent that it can also be apportioned into six parts in order to reflect the traditional division of universal history into Six Ages.⁴⁰ In short, predetermined theories often yield but predetermined results.

The range of Milton's allusions to the Book of Revelation should likewise not be overestimated. To tabulate his Biblical allusions, indeed, were to make the singularly unsurprising discovery that the Apocalypse is invoked not more often than are the major prophetic utterances, the Pauline epistles, or the synoptic gospels.⁴¹ The apparently authoritative judgment that 'Milton owed his greatest literary debts to the imagery of the Apocalypse' is, alas, an unfortunate misrepresentation of the actual evidence.⁴² *Paradise Lost* may not be treated as if its comprehensive allusiveness coincides with the particularity of apocalyptic concerns so palpably evident in the first book of *The Faerie Queene*, in T. S. Eliot's 'Journey of the Magi', or even in Yeats's 'The Second Coming'. We but confine the epic by describing the Son of God as 'the rider of the white horse' in order to align Milton's vision with that of the Apocalypse.⁴³

The Son of God astraddle a white horse is, in fact, utterly alien to Milton's mode of conceptualisation. But so are nearly all the great individual images of the Apocalypse inclusive of the visions of the seals or of the vials, save only that there are adumbrations of its beasts in the portrayal of both Satan and Sin, and of its great whore in the portrayal again of Sin but also of Dalila in *Samson Agonistes*.

The language of the Apocalypse had no exclusive impact on Milton's poetry possibly because he was cognisant that it is by no means the finest Greek of the New Testament and certainly because its daedalian excesses severely circumscribed their compatibility with his aspirations both linguistic and thematic. Thematically, we should remind ourselves, Milton went out of his way to oppose the relentless emphasis of the Apocalypse on implacable retribution by introducing into all the eschatological visions of *Paradise Lost* (III, 323–38; X, 635–9; XI, 900–1; XII, 458–65 and 545–51) a decisive and recurrent element of lenity. Where the tradition insisted that Christ is to reappear 'not as a Sauiour or Mediator, but as a Iudge',[44] Milton on the contrary urged that Christ at the end of time is to be as much judge as mediator and saviour. This is not to say that *Paradise Lost* minimises the Cimmerian shadow that evil casts on the sum of history. Far from it. The vision of the future that Michael unfolds before the stricken Adam discloses that the world shall go on

> To good malignant, to bad men benigne,
> Under her own waight groaning
>
> (XII, 538–9)

The catalogue of woes that are to befall the human race (XI, 477–90) was grim enough in the first edition of *Paradise Lost*; yet Milton amended it in the second edition by adding to the horrors detailed (ll. 485–7). Even so, the terminal point of history in the epic is not preceded by the massive and devastating calamities set forth in the Apocalypse at such epidemic length and, it should be admitted, ever so lovingly. Not vengeance but the fulfilment of God's promises and the beatific vision beyond history are what appealed to Milton most: the prospect of the Second Advent when the Son of God is to

> raise
> From the conflagrant mass, purg'd and refin'd,
> New Heav'ns, new Earth, Ages of endless date,
> Founded in Righteousness and Peace and Love,
> To bring forth fruits Joy and eternal Bliss.
>
> (XII, 547–51)

Whether in structure, language, imagery, or tone, Milton's response to the Apocalypse is not as if to an exclusive 'model'. It were best to say as has been said with caution due, that many elements in Milton's work 'gesture toward the Book of Revelation'.[45] The gesture, after all, is not insubstantial. It encompasses on the one hand the antichristological dimension already noted and on the other the spacious patterns we are to consider next.

IV UPON ACTION IN THE IMMEDIATE PRESENT

The mighty line of the Nativity Ode, 'The wakefull trump of doom must thunder through the deep' (156), heralds the advent of a major poet with particular interests. Any number of other aspiring poets shared Milton's interests – but not, unfortunately, his talents, witness the versifier who ever so uncertainly looked ahead to

> the last Trump
> That up thou jump
> When all must rise and live again.[46]

Milton's version conflates the past and the future to rest, firmly, on the present:

>   to those ychain'd in sleep,
> The wakefull trump of doom must thunder through the deep,
>
> With such a horrid clang
> As on mount *Sinai* rang
>   While the red fire, and smouldring clouds out brake:
> The aged Earth agast
> With terrour of that blast,
>   Shall from the surface to the center shake;
> When at the worlds last session,
> The dreadfull Judge in middle Air shall spread his throne.
>
> And then at last our bliss
> Full and perfet is,
>   But now begins . . .
>
> (ll. 155–67)

The 'now' marks Milton's primary commitment. However full the eventual bliss, and however perfect, it appertains to the future; and imperative though its study is to our direction and our conduct in the present it should not be so exclusively contemplated as to displace the 'now'. That might partake in form if not in essence of those utopian schemes which in *Areopagitica* are renounced with specific reference to Sir Thomas More's *Utopia* and Bacon's *New Atlantis*:

> To sequester out of the world into *Atlantick* and *Eutopian* polities, which never can be drawn into use, will not mend our condition; but to ordain wisely as in this world of evill, in the midd'st whereof God hath plac't us unavoidably.[47]

Milton would have agreed with the insistence of the Cambridge Platonists that man is acknowledged by God only when he is 'in motion' now, 'upon Action' in the immediate present, so that the Cartesian *cogito ergo sum* should be revised to read – as Benjamin Whichcote did revise it to read – 'I act, therefore I am'.[48] Milton's endorsement of analogous premises is writ large in his early poetry, initially in the Nativity Ode as noted, and finally in both *Comus* and *Lycidas*.

The endorsement is involved with the declared ambition of the narrator in *Il Penseroso* after 'Something like Prophetick strain' (l. 174). In that relatively early poem, probably written when Milton was twenty-three, the aspiration is admittedly voiced by one who is far from identical with the poet and in any case refers to the distant future when 'old experience' could realize the hope expressed. For Milton himself, however, the hope was to be realized all too soon. Once he attained his twenty-fourth year and dedicated himself to the Great Taskmaster in the sonnet beginning 'How soon hath Time the suttle theef of youth', he penned also the exquisitely-modulated poem 'On Time' that wings beyond the 'now' to a prospect of eternity fully anticipatory of the serenely-apprehended beatific visions of *Paradise Lost*:

> Then long Eternity shall greet our bliss
> With an individual kiss;
> And Joy shall overtake us as a flood,
> When every thing that is sincerely good
> And perfetly divine,
> With Truth, and Peace, and Love shall ever shine
> About the supreme Throne
> Of him, t'whose happy-making sight alone,
> When once our heav'nly-guided soul shall clime,
> Then all this Earthy grosnes quit,
> Attir'd with Stars, we shall for ever sit,
>   Triumphing over Death, and Chance, and thee O Time.
>
> (ll. 11–22)

'On Time' is apocalyptic without recourse to the Apocalypse. But in a related poem of the same period, 'At a Solemn Musick', Milton provided the first elaboration of the vision of God enthroned so central to both the Apocalypse and *Paradise Lost*. 'God which sitteth upon the throne' (Revelation 4.2 ff., 20.11 ff., but especially 7.10 ff. in extension of Ezekiel 1.26) is envisaged with an optimum of musical imagery as the poet-prophet hears

> That undisturbed Song of pure concent,
> Ay sung before the saphire-colour'd throne
> To him that sits theron
> With Saintly shout, and solemn Jubily,
> Where the bright Seraphim in burning row

> Their loud up-lifted Angel trumpets blow,
> And the Cherubick host in thousand quires
> Touch their immortal Harps of golden wires,
> With those just Spirits that wear victorious Palms,
> Hymns devout and holy Psalms
> Singing everlastingly;
>
> (ll. 6–16)

'At a Solemn Musick' advances next to the characteristic conflation of the past and the future – the time at the outset of time and the time beyond time – in order to pray for the immediate present: 'O may we soon again renew that Song, / And keep in tune with Heav'n' (ll. 25–6). The prayer with its evident concern for the 'now', and the poem's equally evident musical framework, inform also Milton's ensuing performance in the major achievement that is *Comus* (1634).

Like the poem 'On Time', *Comus* is at once apocalyptic and distant from the Apocalypse. The apocalyptic dimension is measurable in terms of the pattern enacted initially through the mission of the Attendant Spirit to sustain those who 'by due steps aspire / To lay their just hands on that Golden Key / That ope's the Palace of Eternity' (ll. 12–14), next through the expectations of the Lady that 'the Supreme good . . . / Would send a glistring Guardian if need were / To keep my life and honour unassail'd' (ll. 217–20), and lastly though the advent of Sabrina 'To help insnared chastity' (l. 909), in order to suggest that man's ascent through virtue is matched by Heaven's descent through Grace. The distance from the Apocalypse, on the other hand, is measurable in terms first of the antagonist's association with bestial forms to the conspicuous exclusion of the 'antichristian' affinities later to compass Satan in *Paradise Lost*, and secondly of the confinement of the pattern of *diabolus simius Dei* to but a single acknowledgement that Comus and his crew 'Imitate the Starry Quire' (l. 112). Even more striking is the singular lack of interest in the eventual fate of Comus. He is certainly not punished. He simply disappears (l. 814); and the gathered protagonists, contemptuously silent about their antagonist, join by the end in 'victorious dance' (l. 974). The masque's 'resolution', in short, is not deferred to any time or place attainable hereafter. It occurs 'now', in the immediate present and within our own sublunary world. Evil may hover in the background, and does; but its potent weapons have been stilled in demonstration of the infinite capacity of good to overcome evil, precisely as the poem's concluding rhythms assimilate Comus's gay rhythms (ll. 93 ff.) within a distinctly ethical context. The gaiety of Comus's

> Midnight shout, and revelry,
> Tipsie dance, and Jollity,

is merely derivative, a distant echo of the prototypical pattern that emerges with the invocation of Sabrina (ll. 867 ff.) and terminates in the final proclamation of the joy inherent in virtue:

> Mortals that would follow me,
> Love vertue, she alone is free,
> She can teach ye how to clime
> Higher then the Spheary chime;
> Or if Vertue feeble were,
> Heav'n it self would stoop to her.

The orchestration in *Comus* of sounds attesting an ethical orientation became three years later, in *Lycidas*, a triumph of luminous suggestiveness. *Lycidas* is the first of Milton's poems to derive much of its power from a dialogue with the Apocalypse.[49] Most obviously, the final vision of 'the blest Kingdoms meek of joy and love' (ll. 174-81) alludes through 'the unexpressive nuptiall Song' to the marriage of the Lamb in the Apocalypse (19.7-9) and adapts, too, the celebrated promise that God shall eventually wipe away all tears from our eyes (7.17 and 21.4, in extension of Isaiah 25.8). Earlier in the poem, moreover, St. Peter's stern denunciation of corruption within the Church (ll. 113 ff.) is demonstrably responsive to the violent tone that attended similarly apocalyptic warnings in any number of Protestant commentaries. The ominous 'two-handed engine at the door', in particular, is doubtless related to the 'sharp two-edged sword' that, issuing according to the Apocalypse from the mouth of Christ (1.16, 2.12), was habitually interpreted as an image that 'sheweth his wrath and indignation vnto the enemies of his Church, and their destruction'.[50] The position of the engine 'at the door' is an explicit declaration of immediate expectations of Christ's reappearance, as in the ensuing eloquent prayer:

> thy Kingdome is now at hand, and thou standing at the dore. Come forth out of thy Royall Chambers, O Prince of all the Kings of the earth, put on the visible roabes of thy imperiall Majesty, take up that unlimited Scepter which thy Almighty Father hath bequeath'd thee; for now the voice of thy Bride calls thee, and all creatures sigh to bee renew'd.

The prayer is Milton's, part of a sustained plea uttered four years after the composition of *Lycidas*.[51] The poet's response to the Apocalypse and to apocalyptic modes of thought, it is clear, was by the late 1630s quite prominent and by the early 1640s fully conspicuous.

Notwithstanding, Milton's commitment to the 'now' remained constant. The synoptic movement in *Lycidas* is not increasingly toward the vision of 'the blest Kingdoms meek of joy and love'; it is, rather, an obliquation away from that vision toward the time and the place of our recognizable sublunar order:

> And now the Sun had stretch'd out all the hills,
> And now was dropt into the Western bay:
> At last he rose, and twitch'd his Mantle blew:
> To morrow to fresh Woods, and Pastures new.

Within the poem, by the same token, the individual movements whether centered on the reply of Phoebus (ll. 76–84) or the denunciation by St. Peter (ll. 113–31) are so inapposite to the urgent question of the premature death of Lycidas that they are so many retrocessions from that question. The reply of Phoebus, for one, is couched in strictly pagan terms, within an exclusively mythological framework, and as such it 'never can be drawn into use' (as Milton said of utopian schemes). The Petrine denunciation, by contrast, unfolds within a Christian context; yet its temper is so manifestly one-sided, so obsessed solely and merely with justice, that the dire warning about the 'two-handed engine' awaiting to strike constitutes not a 'vindication of God'[52] but – as the narrator expressly states – a 'dread voice' that has 'shrunk' the very streams of Alpheus (ll. 132–3). Significantly, it is at this very point (ll. 134 ff.) that Milton introduces the splendidly orchestrated rhythms of the flower passage. The urgent question at the heart of the poem can be answered, if at all, in terms of the natural order, the world as we know it. The search thus focused within history, the narrator advances expeditiously to the historical reality of Christ who, as both man and God, connects the waves he once walked on and the 'groves and other streams' beyond our planet (ll. 173–4). With supreme confidence, the poem's concluding *ottava rima* returns us to the 'now' that we never really left.

V APOCALYPTIC EXPECTATIONS IN MILTON'S PROSE

Milton's persuasion from the late 1630s through the early 1640s that the Last Judgment was imminent reflects an attitude widespread among his immediate contemporaries. 'I cannot nor dare not prescribe', declared Bishop Godfrey Goodman in 1616, 'the day and houre of that judgement, rather with patience I will waite on Gods leisure.' He added:

> Yet sure I am, that the time cannot bee long absent, for all the signes of his comming doe already appeare: when the hangings and furniture are taken downe, it is a token that the King and the Court are remooving; nature now beginning to decay, seemes to hasten Christs comming.[53]

Nature's decay was in some accounts joined to 'the vanity, decay, mortalitie, and marvellous abuse of the creatures'. According to a lengthy tirade penned by a particularly pessimistic writer,

> The world waxeth old as a garment; it, and all the parts of it, fade, waste, consume, and draw toward their fatall period. All things (by sinfull, licentious, and rebellious man) are abused, perverted, mis-applyed (against the Creators scope, and the creatures desire) to unlawfull, or immoderate profite and pleasure; yea to revenge, and open persecution. The Sunne and Moone, those two great Eyes of heaven, are often darkened, and fearefully eclypsed, and (as learned Astronomers have observed) many thousand miles neerer the earth then in times past. The Planets and the other Starres, like so many Candles and Spangles in the heavens, are much decayed in their vertues and operations. . . . In Plants, Hearbs, Trees, there is not the same vigor, efficacy, feeding, and medicinable vertue, which was in times past. Men are not so tall of stature, not so long lived, not so strong as in the daies of old: They are more fraile, feeble, mortall; and though they are more illumined, more witty, and learned, by many degrees, then in old time; yet they generally are more crafty, wicked, mischeivous: they have science, but not so much conscience.[54]

But the imminence of the Last Judgement could be maintained even by the many who refused to credit the decay of nature and man. These would mount a judicious interpretation of the 'signs' that the Book of Revelation details as prefatory to the end of history. The result was not unpredictable. Everyone in the early seventeenth century had seen 'with open eyes', it was claimed, 'the accomplishment of most of the Prophecies of this booke already'.[55] Could the reappearance of Christ be far off? In vain did some writers invoke in opposition Christ's admonition in Mark 13.32 as in Matthew 24.36 ('of that day and that hour knoweth no man, no, not the angels which are in heaven, neither the Son, but the Father'), and in vain also did Sir Thomas Browne entreat that 'to determine the day and yeare of this inevitable time, is not onely convincible [i.e., convictable] and statute madnesse, but also manifest impiety'.[56] The majority continued adamantly to believe that 'the day draweth neer', that 'this is even the last houre, the world cannot continue long'.[57]

Milton was caught up in the rapture of the moment. He had been often, and was to be even more often, directly involved with partisans of the Apocalypse, among them Joseph Mede, author of the widely-acclaimed *Clavis apocalyptica* (1627, translated into English in 1643), who was Milton's tutor at Cambridge and may have been the 'old Damœtas' of *Lycidas* (l. 36);[58] Stephen Marshall and Edmund Calamy, two of the combatants who comprised the 'Smectymnuus' group defended by Milton in the *Animadversions* of 1642; and Samuel Hartlib, the recipient of Milton's treatise *Of Education* (1644), who was instrumental in securing the translation of Mede's great work. But Milton had in any case already entertained ambitions after 'Something like Prophetick strain'; and as time appeared opportune to assume his prophetic mantle, he joined the embattled Presbyterians in their war against the latest manifestation of Antichrist, the prelates of the established Church. The fourth of the five tracts he wrote to that purpose, *The Reason of Church-Government urg'd against Prelaty* (1642), articulates his ultimate aim, his sense of mission, and his major precedent, in a statement immemorially voiced by all aspirants after the office of the prophet:

> surely to every good and peaceable man it must in nature needs be a hatefull thing to be the displeaser, and molester of thousands; much better would it like him doubtlesse to be the messenger of gladnes and contentment, which is his chief intended busines, to all mankind, but that they resist and oppose their own true happiness. But when God commands to take the trumpet and blow a dolorous or a jarring blast, it lies not in mans will what he shall say or what he shall conceal. If he shall think to be silent, as *Jeremiah* did, because of the reproach and derision he met with daily, and *all his familiar friends watcht for his halting* to be reveng'd on him for speaking the truth, he would be forc't to confesse as he confest, *his word was in my heart as a burning fire shut up in my bones, I was weary with forbearing and could not stay.*[59]

Thus persuaded, Milton descended into battle armed with the prodigal vocabulary and the martial imagery of the great prophets and of St. John in the Apocalypse. The prelates – 'a whippe of Scorpions'[60] – were associated with the dragon from the bottomless pit; but the Presbyterians in Parliament, with 'our old patron Saint *George*':

> if our Princes and Knights will imitate the fame of that old champion, as by their order of Knighthood solemnly taken, they vow, farre be it that they should uphold and side with this English Dragon; but rather to doe as indeed their oath binds them, they should make it their Knightly adventure to pursue & vanquish this mighty saile-wing'd monster that menaces to swallow up the Land, unlesse her bottomlesse gorge may be satisfi'd with the blood of the Kings daughter the Church; and may, as she was wont, fill her dark and infamous den with the bones of the Saints.[61]

'Apocalyptic thought', it has been said, 'rarely throbbed with such baroque splendor.'[62]

Of Milton's five antiprelatical tracts, however, it was the first and the third – *Of Reformation touching Church-Discipline* and *Animadversions*, both published in 1641 – that reveal his apocalyptic predilections most lucidly. The two works contain sustained prayers articulated in unmistakably apocalyptic terms. Part of the prayer in *Animadversions* has been quoted already (above, p. 220); the other, in *Of Reformation*, concludes the tract with a plea to the Trinity that is tantamount to an interpretation of history in full alignment with the common apocalyptic expectations within Protestantism. Accepting the standard view that the defeat of the Spanish Armada and the interception of 'that horrible and damned blast' – the Gunpowder Plot of 1605 – were alike manifestations of Providence, Milton prays for God's intercession yet again, vows himself to celebrate the divine favors hereafter, joys at the prospect of the rewards to be distributed by the 'shortly-expected' Christ, and envisages with considerable pleasure the certain confinement of all 'antichristian' forces within the bottomless pit. The prayer deserves to be quoted in full:

Thou therefore that sits't in light & glory unapprochable, *Parent of Angels* and *Men!* next thee I implore Omnipotent King, Redeemer of that lost remnant whose nature thou didst assume, ineffable and everlasting *Love!* And thou the third subsistence of Divine Infinitude, *illumining Spirit*, the joy and solace of created *Things!* one *Tri-personall* GODHEAD! looke upon this thy poore and almost spent, and expiring *Church*, leave her not thus a prey to these importunate *Wolves*, that wait and thinke long till they devoure thy tender *Flock*, these wilde *Boares* that have broke into thy *Vineyard*, and left the print of thir polluting hoofs on the Soules of thy Servants. O let them not bring about their damned *designes* that stand now at the entrance of the bottomlesse pit expecting the Watch-word to open and let out those dreadfull *Locusts* and *Scorpions*, to *re-involve* us in that pitchy *Cloud* of infernall darknes, where we shall never more see the *Sunne* of thy *Truth* againe, never hope for the cheerfull dawne, never more heare the *Bird* of *Morning* sing. Be mov'd with pitty at the afflicted state of this our shaken *Monarchy*, that now lies labouring under her throwes, and struggling against the grudges of more dreaded Calamities.

O thou that after the impetuous rage of five bloody Inundations, and the succeeding Sword of intestine *Warre*, soaking the Land in her owne gore, didst pity the sad and ceasles revolution of our swift and thick-comming sorrowes when wee were quite breathlesse, of thy *free grace* didst motion *Peace*, and termes of Cov'nant with us, & having first welnigh freed us from *Antichristian* thraldome, didst build up this *Britannick Empire* to a glorious and enviable heighth with all her Daughter Ilands about her, stay us in this felicitie, let not the obstinacy of our halfe Obedience and will-Worship bring forth that *Viper of Sedition*, that for these Fourescore Yeares hath been breeding to eat through the entrals of our *Peace*; but let her cast her Abortive Spawne without the danger of this travailling & throbbing *Kingdome*. That we may still remember in our *solemne Thanksgivings*, how for us the *Northren Ocean* even to the frozen *Thule* was scatter'd with the proud Ship-wracks of the *Spanish Armado*, and the very maw of Hell ransack't, and made to give up her conceal'd destruction, ere shee could vent it in that horrible and damned blast.

O how much more glorious will those former Deliverances appeare, when we shall know them not onely to have sav'd us from greatest miseries past, but to have reserv'd us for greatest happinesse to come. Hitherto thou hast but freed us, and that not fully, from the unjust and Tyrannous Claime of thy Foes, now unite us intirely, and appropriate us to thy selfe, tie us everlastingly in willing Homage to the *Prerogative* of thy eternall *Throne*.

And now wee knowe, O thou our most certain hope and defence, that thine enemies have been consulting all the Sorceries of the *great Whore*, and have joyn'd their Plots with that sad Intelligencing Tyrant that mischiefes the World with his Mines of *Ophir*, and lies thirsting to revenge his Navall ruines that have larded our Seas; but let them all take Counsell together, and let it come to nought, let them Decree, and doe thou Cancell it, let them gather themselves, and bee scatter'd, let them embattell themselves and bee broken, let them imbattell, and be broken, for thou art with us.

Then amidst the *Hymns*, and *Halleluiahs* of *Saints* some one may perhaps bee heard offering at high *strains* in new and lofty *Measures* to sing and celebrate thy *divine Mercies*, and *marvelous Judgements* in this Land throughout all AGES; whereby this great and Warlike Nation instructed and inur'd to the fervent and continuall practice of *Truth* and *Righteousnesse*, and casting farre from her the *rags* of her old *vice* may presse on hard to that *high* and *happy* emulation to be found the *soberest, wisest,* and *most Christian People* at that day when thou the Eternall and shortly-expected King shalt open the Clouds to judge the severall Kingdomes of the World, and distributing *Nationall Honours* and *Rewards* to Religious and just *Common-wealths*, shalt put an end to all Earthly *Tyrannies*, proclaiming thy universal and milde *Monarchy* through Heaven and Earth. Where they undoubtedly that by their *Labours, Counsels*, and *Prayers* have been earnest for the *Common good* of *Religion* and their *Countrey*, shall receive, above the inferiour *Orders* of the *Blessed*, the *Regall* addition of *Principalities, Legions*, and *Thrones* into their glorious Titles, and in supereminence of *beatifick Vision* progressing the *datelesse* and *irrevoluble* Circle of *Eternity* shall clasp inseparable Hands with *joy*, and *blisse* in over measure for ever.

But they contrary that by the impairing and diminution of the true *Faith*, the distresses and servitude of their *Countrey* aspire to high *Dignity, Rule* and *Promotion* here, after a shamefull end in this *Life* (which *God* grant them) shall be thrown downe eternally into the *darkest* and *deepest Gulfe* of HELL, where under the *despightfull controule*, the trample and spurne of all the other *Damned*, that in the anguish of their *Torture* shall have no other ease then to exercise a *Raving* and *Bestiall Tyranny* over them as their *Slaves* and *Negro's*, they shall remaine in that plight for ever, the *basest*, the *lowermost*, the *most dejected*, most underfoot and *downetrodden Vassals* of *Perdition*.[63]

The explicit conviction that God favors England above all nations, while by no means unique to Milton, fired his imagination and sustained his activities all too often. Its finest articulation in prose – the very *locus classicus* of Milton's prophetic vision, we have been told[64] – was ventured on a particularly memorable occasion in *Areopagitica* (1644):

Methinks I see in my mind a noble and puissant Nation rousing herself like a strong man after sleep, and shaking her invincible locks: Methinks I see her as an Eagle muing [i.e., moulting, renewing] her mighty youth, and kindling her undazl'd eyes at the full midday beam; purging and unscaling her long abused sight at the fountain it self of heav'nly radiance; while the whole noise of timorous and flocking birds, with those also that love the twilight, flutter about, amaz'd at what she means, and in their envious gabble would prognosticat a year of sects and schisms.[65]

Yet this conviction, together with every other precept embraced by the magniloquent prayer in *Of Reformation*, was in time to be reconsidered, on occasion drastically.

The reconsideration is in some respects readily to be marked. The prayer's monomaniacal emphasis on judgment, in particular, had been transcended in *Lycidas* before Milton was overwhelmed by the tide of apocalyptic expectations, and would be transcended again in *Paradise Lost* through the superimposed lenity already annotated (above, p. 216). Equally, the nationalistic strain would eventually be qualified – some could justly say metamorphosed – into a cosmic vision distinctly more appropriate to a poet with stated prophetic aspirations. But such developments were in a sense inevitable in that Milton was temperamentally circumspect about the Apocalypse even during his most passionate apocalyptic moments. His disinclination to adapt most of the major images of the Apocalypse, noted earlier, corresponds to his equally evident reluctance to deviate from the mainstream of the Protestant apocalyptic tradition. Averse to the militantly apocalyptic theocracy of the Fifth Monarchists, for example, he was also indisposed even to mention the Joachimist surmises (see Marjorie Reeves, above, pp. 49–51). Only about the vexing issue of the millennium postulated in the Apocalypse (20.1–6) did Milton prevaricate.

It was certainly an issue to prevaricate about. The experience of Luther and Calvin is indicative; for in spite of the Apocalypse's embarrassingly explicit reference to Christ's earth-bound reign of a thousand years, the two Reformers were so appalled by the violent consequences of its literal interpretation at Münster that thereafter they evinced but a 'horror of apocalypticism'.[66] Every form of chiliasm was in consequence condemned by their followers as a 'foolish error' at best or a 'herisie' at worst, [67] while the 'thousand years' specified by the Apocalypse were blandly annotated by Protestants and Catholics alike as 'a long tyme' (thus Erasmus no less than Diodati), 'a long time indefinitely' (Featley), 'time without ende' (Marlorat), 'æternitie' (Napier) – in short, said Diodati, 'the time that it shall please the Lord to suffer his Church to be at rest'.[68]

By the early 1640s, however, presumptions about the imminence of a literally apprehended millennium had risen sharply, endorsed by one of the period's most eminent authorities, the Calvinist Johann Heinrich Alsted, professor of theology and twice rector of the University of Herborn.[69] The continuing opposition should not be underestimated;[70] yet when Milton hoped in *Of Reformation* that the 'shortly-expected' Christ was about to inaugurate his 'universal and milde *Monarchy* through Heaven and Earth', he was very much on the side of the considerable majority of his contemporaries. Nevertheless, given his temperamental circumspectness about the Apocalypse, he failed pointedly to specify Christ's reign as 'a thousand years'. In his vision, indeed, the millennial reign would seem to be the final event within time-bound history and yet coterminous with or protracted into eternity, *id est*, quite unlike the period precisely dated in the Apocalypse as scheduled to be followed by the loosing of Satan (20.7 ff.). So far as the more esoteric aspects of millennial expectations are concerned, Milton appears to have agreed with Cromwell: 'they are things I understand not'.[71]

Milton's qualified response to the millennium was in time qualified further still by a decreasing emphasis on its imminence and an increasing emphasis on its spiritual aspects.[72] Some of the attitudes espoused in the tracts of the early 1640s were in *Paradise Lost* to become explicit, most notably in connection with the transfer of the cosmic battle within the soul of man on the pattern of the 'secret' deeds of Christ in *Paradise Regained* (I, 15). On the other hand, Milton's theological treatise *De doctrina christiana* stands in diametric opposition not only to the two epics but to the antiprelatical tracts and the subsequent prose works. The treatise confirms Milton's ever more marked reluctance to credit the imminence of the Last Judgment, on this occasion with a suitable invocation of Matthew 24.36 as of Mark 13.32 ('The day and hour of Christ's coming are known to the Father only').[73] The millennial reign, however, is conceived literally as destined to occur 'on earth' for 'a thousand years', at the expiration of which Satan is to rage again.[74] The resolution is odd not because Milton could entertain it so late in life and so long after millennial expectations were fashionable but because he should expound it with such astonishing literalism. Unconfirmed as it is by *Paradise Lost*, however, one might argue that its presence in the treatise is further testimony that *De doctrina christiana* is 'prosaic', 'an abortive venture', indeed 'a singularly gross expedition into theology'.[75] Milton's prophetic soul, so often able resonantly to dream on things to come, dreamt in *De doctrina christiana* but vapidly.

VI APOCALYPTIC PATTERNS IN *PARADISE LOST*

Milton's gesture toward the Book of Revelation in *Paradise Lost* is comprised of many elements. There are the numerous echoes of the Apocalypse whether in the fallen Adam's plea to nature to hide him from the face of God[76] or in the association of Uriel with 'the angel standing in the sun' as well as with the seven spirits before the throne of God.[77] There are also the poem's larger components that include the critical invocation of the Apocalypse at the outset of Book IV, the entire account of the war in Heaven as we shall observe presently, and of course the proliferation of woes and the visions of the end in the last two books. There are in addition such comprehensive motifs as the antichristological pattern already noted and, attendant upon that, the bestial imagery that stalks Satan throughout the poem. And there are lastly the diverse general affinities that the poem shares with the Apocalypse, notably the theatrical configurations of their vision, the symmetrical parallelism of their structures, and the historically-oriented burden of their thematic concerns.

The theatrical configurations of the Apocalypse and of *Paradise Lost* revolve about the widely held attitude that the Johannine vision is 'the majestick image of a high and stately Tragedy', to quote Milton's summary statement of the conventional view (above, p. 215). The numerous references in passing to 'the last Act . . . of a most longe & dolefull Tragedy',[78] were not meant only metaphorically, it should be emphasized. They were on the contrary evidential of the persuasion that the Apocalypse constitutes an essentially dramatic form, even a 'celestiall Theater' – to quote Joseph Mede – an 'heavenly Theater' where events unfold 'as upon a Stage'.[79] As Pareus explains in his formulation, that which beginneth at the fourth Chapter (which is the first propheticall Vision) and the following unto the end, if you well observe them, have plainly a *Dramaticall* forme, hence the Revelation may truely be called a *Propheticall Drama*, show, or representation. For as in humane Tragedies, diverse persons one after another come vpon the Theater to represent things done, and so again depart: diverse Cho[i]res also or Companies of Musitians and Harpers distinguish the diversity of the *Acts*, and while the *Actors* hold vp, do with musicall accord sweeten the wearinesse of the Spectators, and keepe them in attention: so verily the thing it self speaketh that in this Heavenly Interlude, by diverse *shewes* and *apparitions*.[80]

If Pareus's division of the Apocalypse into seven visions is not demonstrably applicable to *Paradise Lost*, his claim about its '*Dramaticall* forme' is not irrelevant to the songs of celebration interspersed 'with musicall accord' within the poem's cosmic tableaux. The same 'forme', however, could also be said to have had some influence on the poem's several perspicuously dramatic contours. But perhaps structurally, too, there is a relationship between the poem's tautly constructed parallels and the Apocalypse's predilection for a like symmetry, witness the latter's series of parodies noted earlier (above, p. 212) but also its series of opposed parallels such as the mark by the Lamb and the mark by the beast (14.1, 13.16), the sacrificial mark on the Lamb and the maleficent mark on the beast (5.6, 13.1), or the bride of the Lamb and the whore of Babylon that is but a 'counterfeit Lamb'.[81] Given Milton's respect for Biblical precedents, he would have been sensible of these elements not as 'models' to be followed submissively but as so many stimuli to his own inventiveness.

When all is said, however, it is the attitude of the Apocalypse toward the historical process that is most apposite to *Paradise Lost*. That attitude is a highly particular version of the view of history characteristic of the Christian tradition at large. History, according to the Christian tradition, is essentially a unilinear movement in time distinguished by three interlocked acts – creation, redemption, and judgment – alike presided over by Christ. The central act is also history's central event: the advent of Christ at a specific moment in time, in 'the reign of Tiberius Caesar, Pontius Pilate being governor of Judaea, and Herod being tetrarch of Galilee' (Luke 3.1). Eventually affirmed to have divided history into the periods respectively designated as 'BC' and 'AD', the advent of Christ looks back upon the creation and ahead to its dissolution upon his reappearance at the end of time. In short, history is Christocentric.[82]

Like the tradition at the centre, the Apocalypse is Christocentric, historically minded – 'in the highest degree historically minded'[83] – and teleologically oriented. At the same time, however, the Apocalypse emphasizes eschatology relentlessly, upholds the sharp dichotomy between Christ and Antichrist rigidly, and asserts a fully deterministic viewpoint rigorously. 'We may see by this [book]', wrote Richard Bernard in 1617, 'all things falling out, in, with, or against the Church of Christ, from the day of the reuelation thereof vnto the worlds end, to haue been by God fore-determined.'[84] The pattern of the Apocalypse is begged strictly from above.

Yet it is a pattern that, oddly, delineates the future not at the expense of the past but in terms of that past. Here the fundamental presupposition is that the course of history can be accurately perceived solely from Heaven, for it is only from that vantage point that one can appreciate the eternal nature of God – 'the first and the last' (1.11, 2.8), 'Alpha and Omega, the beginning and the ending' (1.8), 'which was, and is, and is to come' (4.8) – as against the transcience of the future-less demonic powers, 'the beast that was, and is not' (17.11). History's design thus apprehended, it will be recognized not only that the past and the present are anticipatory of the future but that the future is inherent in the past and that both are present in the present. In this respect the numerous allusions within the Apocalypse to times past as if they are times present or times future – the tree of life in Eden (2.7, 22.2), the plagues that befell Egypt (16.2 ff.), the song of Moses (15.3), the manna (2.17), the several earthquakes so clearly reminiscent of the Crucifixion (6.12, 11.19, 16.18) – alike reinforce the Apocalypse's typological framework but proclaim, too, the concurrence of all events in the eyes of God. That 'old Damœtas', Joseph Mede, happily termed this concurrence 'synchronisme', characteristically observing its relevance whether he remarked on the flood caused by the dragon to overwhelm the woman clothed with the sun ([12.15]: 'So also *Pharaoh* persecuted the people of *Israel* marching from under his dominion into the Wilderness, but with another floud') or argued that the mission of the two witnesses (11.13 ff.) is 'according to the pattern of those famous pairs under the Old Testament, *Moses* and *Aaron* in the wildernesse, *Elias* and *Eliseus* [i.e., Elijah and Elisha] under the Baaliticall apostasie, *Zorobabel* and *Iesua* under the Babylonian captivity'.[85] Mede's approach parallels Milton's, certainly in the poet's like-minded preoccupation with typology but equally in his concern with the 'synchronisme' of all events. We might have expected these strains to have been gathered in *Paradise Lost* within Michael's prophecy of the future in Books XI and XII. In the event, however, they are gathered within another episode altogether, the war in Heaven.

The brief account of that war in the Apocalypse appears to be set in the future even though, somehow, it already 'was' (12.7). Milton deliberately transferred it – 'as divers Expositors doe', said Donne[86] – to the remote past, before even the foundation of the world and the outset of history, 'on such day / As Heav'ns great Year brings forth' (V, 582–3). Placed there, however, the war behaves most peculiarly as if it really belongs to the future. It is fraught with allusions to three historical events to come: first, Israel's redemption from Egypt and the annihilation of Pharaoh's might;[87] next, the redemption of the world by Christ and his conquest of death on the third day of his Passion;[88] and finally, the Second Advent, intimated through the conduct of the Son of God when 'full of wrauth bent on his Enemies' (VI, 826) he adopts the style appropriate to the 'wrath of the Lamb' detailed in the Apocalypse (6.16 and *passim*). Milton's vision of the war in Heaven, it has been asserted justly, 'is a shadow of things to come, and more particularly a shadow of this last age of the world and of the Second Coming'.[89]

It is also a war whose Christocentric emphasis is axiomatic. In the Apocalypse the protagonist of the war is, of course, Michael; and the commentators, embarrassed by the relegation of such an important role to a mere archangel, tried ever so valiantly to identify him with Christ ('we affirme Christe to be figured and signified to vs vnder the tipe of Michaell').[90] Milton, on the other hand, allotted the final victory not to Michael but to the Son of God, no doubt on the authority of the Apocalypse that the dragon was ultimately overcome 'by the blood of the Lamb' (12.11). The implications extend far beyond the poem's Christocentric argument. They encompass the suggestion that where anyone but God uses arms to attain a goal, the result will necessarily be the defeat that it is in Satan's case or, at best, the standstill that it is in Michael's. The farcical features of the war in Heaven are in this respect a commentary on the efforts as much of Satan as of Michael. In the light of the Apocalypse's display of the martial implements deployed – on the part of the demonic powers, armed warriors and horsemen and chariots; but on the part of the faithful, 'the blood of the Lamb' and 'the word of their testimony' (12.11) – one may presume that Milton's version was so structured as to commend the paradox and certainly to deride the tactics of the satanic host. The classical allusions that attend those tactics are inverted not because Milton had turned against Graeco-Roman civilization but because the powers of darkness imitate its external form without duplicating its ethical premises. Best expressive of Milton's attitude is that boldest of his gestures, the extension literally of the plea of the mighty of the earth in the Apocalypse that the mountains might fall on them (6.16). We have thought the corresponding episode in *Paradise Lost* to be merely risible when it is pregnant with Milton's contempt:

> [God's] mighty Angels...
> From thir foundation loosning to and fro
> They pluckd the seated Hills with all thir load,
> Rocks, Waters, Woods, and by the shaggie tops
> Up lifting bore them in thir hands: Amaze,
> Be sure, and terrour seis'd the rebel Host,
> When coming towards them so dread they saw
> The bottom of the Mountains upward turnd,
> Till on those cursed Engins triple-row
> They saw them whelmed, and all thir confidence
> Under the weight of Mountains buried deep,
> Themselves invaded next, and on thir heads
> Main Promontories flung, which in the Air
> Came shadowing, and oppressd whole Legions armd...
>
> (VI, 638–55)

Arguably, Milton's gesture toward the Book of Revelation in *Paradise Lost* is but a gesture. The historically-oriented premises of both works, for example, need not argue the exclusive influence of the Apocalypse on the epic, so long as Milton might have been affected – and, demonstrably, was – by the collective interpretations of the historical process by Christian spokesmen. Equally, the manifest commitment of the Apocalypse to typology need not be regarded as the capital precedent for Milton's reading of history in terms of 'types / And shadowes' (XII, 232–3), so long as a similar strategy is common to the Christian tradition at large. All the same, both the Christian view of history and the typological patterns immemorially discerned in its course were materially advanced by the Apocalypse's espousal of the one as of the other. The Johannine vision, as Thomas Brightman summarily observed in 1615, 'sufficiently furnish[es] thee with the Historyes of the world from the first beginning of it to the last end'.[91] Concurrently viewed as 'the majestick image of a high and stately Tragedy', the Apocalypse displays within the context of a 'celestiall Theater' the creative and redemptive thrusts of God in opposition to – and, eventually, in triumph over – the forces of Antichrist defined as 'the cumulative mystery of iniquity rampant in the postlapsarian world' (above, p. 212). Placed centrally upon this mighty stage, man acts after a fashion suggestive of configurations at once literal and figurative: literal in that he adheres to a given mode of conduct, and figurative in that the mode intimates a spiritual reality. The approach is descriptive of the strategy at the heart of *Paradise Lost*, its imposing contours assertive of the epic nature of the engagement, its manifold complexities suggestive of the cosmic dimensions of 'synchronisme', its arresting visions probative of the spiritual orientation characteristic of the sum of Milton's poetry.

The sum of Milton's poetry and, indeed, his prose: the Apocalypse, as we have had occasion to note, attends the ambition after 'Something like Prophetick strain' that informs the Nativity Ode and 'At a Solemn Musick', *Comus* and *Lycidas*, the antiprelatical tracts of the early 1640s, *Areopagitica*, the sonnet on the Piedmontese massacre – and ultimately both *Samson Agonistes* and, however odd its convolutions, *De doctrina christiana*. The impact of the Apocalypse can certainly be exaggerated, and it has been. But it is also possible to underestimate it much.

NOTES

1 *The Sermons of John Donne*, ed. E. M. Simpson and G. R. Potter (Berkeley and Los Angeles, 1953–62), VIII, 75.
2 Quoted by Kenneth Charlton, 'The Educational Background', in *The Age of Milton*, ed. C. A. Patrides and Raymond B. Waddington (Manchester, 1980), p. 128. On Napier, see especially Katharine R. Firth, *The Apocalyptic Tradition in Reformation*

Britain 1530–1645 (Oxford, 1979), pp. 132–49.
3 *The Rvine of Rome: or an Exposition vpon the whole Reuelation* (1603), sig. aa2.
4 *Ane frvitfvll Meditatioun* . . . [*on*] *Reuelation in forme of ane sermone* (Edinburgh, 1588), sig. A3.
5 *A Revelation of the Reuelation* (Amsterdam, 1615), sig. A2.
6 *Seriatim*: William Twisse, in his preface to Mede (see ensuing Note), sig. A4; Mede, I, 27; Pareus (as below, Note 36), p. 5; and Milton in *Animadversions*, C: III, 154, and Y: I, 714. Milton's prose is quoted from two – and, where appropriate, three – editions, abbreviated thus: (1) C: *The Works of John Milton*, gen. ed. Frank A. Patterson (Columbia University Press, 1931–40), 20 vols; (2) Y: *Complete Prose Works of John Milton*, gen. ed. Don M. Wolfe (New Haven: Yale University Press, 1953 ff.), 8 vols [in progress]; and (3) P: *John Milton, Selected Prose*, ed. C. A. Patrides (Penguin Books, 1974). Milton's poetry is quoted from *The Poetical Works of John Milton*, ed. Helen Darbishire (Oxford, 1952–5), 2 vols.
7 *The Key of the Revelation*, trans. Richard More, 2nd ed. (1650), sig. B1.
8 *Sacræ heptades* (1626), p. 2.
9 Mede (as above, Note 7), I, 27, and Hicks, Ἀποκάλυψις Ἀποκαλίψεως *or, The Revelation Revealed* (1659), sig. c1v.
10 *Ibid.*, sig. A2.
11 *The Two Last Dialogues* (1668), p. 148.
12 *A Plaine Discovery of the whole Revelation*, rev. ed. (1611), -. 235.
13 'The iiii. senses of yͤ scripture', in *The Obedience of a Christian Man*, rev. ed. (Marburg, 1535), fols 129–37.
14 *Synopsis Papismi, that is, A Generall Viewe of Papistrie*, 2nd edn (1594), p. 43.
15 *Sermons* (as above, Note 1), VI, 62; quoted, and discussed further, by C. A. Patrides, 'The Experience of Otherness', in *The Age of Milton* (as above, Note 2), p. 181.
16 *Religio Medici*, I, 5; in *The Major Works*, ed. C. A. Patrides (Penguin Books, 1977), p. 65.
17 On Luther, consult Warren A. Quanbeck, 'Luther and Apocalyptic', in *Luther und Melanchthon*, ed. Vilmos Vajta (Göttingen, 1961), pp. 125 f.; and on Calvin: Heinrich Quistorp, *Calvin's Doctrine of the Last Things*, trans. Harold Knight (Richmond, Va., 1955), pp. 118 ff. In England the same cause was first espoused by John Bale, next writ large in the martyrology of his friend John Foxe, and thereafter set forth in sustained treatises such as Thomas Becon's *The Actes of Christe and of Antichriste, concerning both their life and doctrine* (1577) and George Downham's *Papa Antichristo* (1620). On the background, consult Richard Bauckham, *Tudor Apocalypse* (1978), Ch. V.
18 C: III, 55; Y: I, 590.
19 This particular exposition was endorsed by the Geneva Bible. Through even more specious 'proofs', the number of the beast could also be made to yield phrases like 'Ecclesia Italica' and even 'Vicarius generalis dei in terris'. See *inter alia* Henoch Clapham, *A Chronological Discourse* (1609), sig. L1v; John Hull, *Saint Peters Prophesie of these Last Daies* (1610), p. 503; *et al.* Later, Francis Potter penned a treatise devoted entirely to *An Interpretation of the Number 666* (Oxford, 1642). It was commended by Mede, and regarded by Pepys as 'mighty ingenious' (*The Diary of Samuel Pepys*, ed. Henry R. Wheatley [1895], VI, 58).
20 The foremost effort in English was ventured by 'Michael Christopherson' (i.e., Michael Walpole), S.J., *A Treatise of Antichrist. Conteyning the defence of Cardinall Bellarmines Arguments, which inuincibly demonstrate, That the Pope is not Antichrist*

([St Omer], 1613). The treatise is mainly directed against Downham's (above, Note 17).
21 C: XVII, 395; Y: VI, 797–8. Cf. the analogous statement in *Of Civil Power* (1659): 'Chiefly for this cause do all true Protestants account the pope antichrist, for that he assumes to himself this infallibilitie over both the conscience and the scripture' (C: VI, 8; P: p. 301).
22 C: III, 269; Y: I, 850. Thus, in consequence, evocative phrases like 'Antichristian times' (C: IV, 18; Y: II, 439), 'Antichristian rigor' (C: IV, 220; Y: II, 706), 'Antichristian malice' (C: IV, 337; Y: II, 548), and the like.
23 As above, Note 14: p. 252.
24 *Bowels Opened* (1641), p. 408. The persecutions by Antiochus (d. 163 BC) are related in 1 Maccabees 1.11–67, 2, 3, and 6.1–16 (cf. Daniel 11.11–45).
25 See the details I have provided in '"The Bloody and Cruell Turke": The Background of a Renaissance Commonplace', *Studies in the Renaissance*, X (1963), 126–35. See further Samuel C. Chew, *The Crescent and the Rose* (1937), Ch. III; and on Luther's influential views: Dorothy M. Vaughan, *Europe and the Turk* (Liverpool, 1954), pp. 135 ff., and Heinrich Bornkamm, *Luther's World of Thought*, trans. M. H. Bertram (St. Louis, 1958), pp. 195–217.
26 On the 'demonic parody' at the heart of the Apocalypse, consult especially Austin Farrer, *A Rebirth of Images* (1949), Ch. XI.
27 Calvin, *Sermons . . . vpon the Booke of Iob*, trans. Arthur Golding (1574), p. 571; Ralegh, *The History of the World* (1614), I, 321 [Bk. II, Ch. 6, §7]; and Adams, *Workes* (1629), p. 211. On the circumference of this tradition, consult Maximilian Rudwin, *The Devil in Legend and Literature* (Chicago, 1931), ch. XII. Catholics accepted the tradition just as readily. Erasmus, for example, speaks of the devil as 'a counterfetter of gods workes' (as below, Note 68: fol. xi).
28 Thus, for example, Heinrich Bullinger, *A Hvndred Sermons vpō the Apocalips*, trans. John Daws (1561), p. 148; Augustin Marlorat, *A Catholike Exposition vpon the Reuelation*, trans. Arthur Golding (1574), fol. 200; Thomas Lodge, *Wits Miserie* (1596), p. 2; Donne (as above, Note 1), III, 148; William Narne, *Christs Starre* (1625), p. 207; Daniel Dyke, *Two Treatises*, 5th impr. (1631), p. 235; John Swan, *Profano-Mastix* (1639), p. 38; Nicholas Billingsley, *A Treasury of Divine Raptures* (1667), p. 23; et al.
29 See Millar MacLure, 'Nature and Art in *The Faerie Queene*', in *Critical Essays on Spenser from 'ELH'* (Baltimore, 1970), pp. 143 ff., who expands the seminal remarks by C. S. Lewis, *The Allegory of Love* (1936), p. 326.
30 Richard Bernard, *A Key of Knowledge for the opening of. . . Revelation* (1617), p. 330.
31 Bunyan, *The Holy City* (1665), in *Works*, ed. George Offor (Glasgow, 1859), III, 422, and Diodati, *Pious and Learned Annotations vpon the Holy Bible*, 3rd ed. (1651), sig. Yyy3. Milton while in Geneva 'saw Professor Diodati daily' (W. R. Parker, *Milton: A Biography* [Oxford, 1968], I, 181).
32 As above, Note 12: p. 311. On the period's extreme partiality to the circle as reflected in literature, see Marjorie H. Nicolson, *The Breaking of the Circle*, rev. edn (1962), Ch. II, and Frank L. Huntley, 'Sir Thomas Browne and the Metaphor of the Circle', *Journal of the History of Ideas*, XIV (1953), 353–64. On its wider manifestations in literature, consult Georges Poulet, *The Metamorphoses of the Circle*, trans. Carley Dawson and Elliott Coleman (Baltimore, 1966); and on its appearance in other disciplines – e.g., in architecture – observe the circular patterns of Bramante's Tempietto of S. Pietro in Montorio, discussed and illustrated by Paolo

Portoghesi, *Rome of the Renaissance*, trans. Pearl Sanders (1972), pp. 53 ff., and plates 17–20.

33 For a sophisticated endeavour to establish such a pattern, see Farrer (as above, Note 26), ch. II–III.

34 Joseph A. Wittreich, 'A Poet amongst Poets', in *Milton and the Line of Vision*, ed. Wittreich (Madison, 1975), pp. 97–142.

35 Michael Fixler, 'The Apocalypse within *Paradise Lost*', in *New Essays on 'Paradise Lost'*, ed. Thomas Kranidas (Berkeley and Los Angeles, 1966), ch. VII. His theory is endorsed by Wittreich in the study cited in the ensuing note (*'Paradise Lost* is itself a sevenfold vision'). Even more sweepingly, Austin C. Dobbins, *Milton and the Book of Revelation: The Heavenly Cycle* (University, Ala., 1975), p. 62, asserts that 'the structure of *Paradise Lost*' – presumably the entire structure! – 'Milton derived (*sic*) from the Book of Revelation'.

36 *A Commentary upon the Divine Revelation*, trans. Elias Arnold (Amsterdam, 1644); the relevant theory is initially proposed on p. 19 and detailed thereafter *passim*. The commentary was first published, in Latin, in Heidelberg (1618). On Pareus consult Joseph A. Wittreich, *Visionary Poetics: Milton's Tradition and its Legacy* (San Marino, Calif., 1979), pp. 40 f. and *passim*, as well as the discussion by Michael Murrin in the present volume.

37 The former quotation is in *C*: III, 238; *Y*: I, 815; *P*: p. 56. The latter quotation is in *C*: I, 331; *P*: p. 367. Fixler (as above, Note 35), p. 146, rightly observes that the earlier statement represents a careless reading of Pareus who had referred not to 'a sevenfold *Chorus*' but – as the preface to *Samson Agonistes* correctly claims – to choruses in between the acts.

38 Consult Barbara K. Lewalski, '*Samson Agonistes* and the "Tragedy" of the Apocalypse', *PMLA*, LXXXV (1970), 1050–62.

39 As above, Note 31: sig. Xxxl.

40 This equally unlikely theory is argued by George W. Whiting, *Milton and this Pendant World* (Austin, Texas, 1958), ch. VI.

41 Consult *inter alia* the index of Biblical references compiled by James H. Sims, *The Bible in Milton's Epics* (Gainesville, Fla., 1962), pp. 259–78. Professor Sims informs me that in fact 'Milton's allusions to the major prophets and to Paul considerably outnumber his references to the Book of Revelation'.

42 The judgement is ventured by Michael Fixler, *Milton and the Kingdoms of God* (1964), pp. 71–2, who cites in support Theodore H. Banks, *Milton's Imagery* (1950), pp. 176/7. In fact, however, Banks asserts that Milton's most comprehensive debts are to the Apocalypse *and* the synoptic gospels.

43 Thus Dobbins (as above, Note 35), p. 46. Dobbins usefully collects a number of 'parallels' between the apocalyptic tradition and *Paradise Lost*; yet he appears on occasion to be unaware that parallels in poetry have a tendency to look in several directions at once, not solely toward the Apocalypse.

44 Samuel Smith, *The Great Assize . . . foure sermons, vpon the 20th Chap. of the Reuel.*, 4th rev. impr. (1628), p. 16. See further my study of 'Renaissance and Modern Thought on the Last Things', *Harvard Theological Review*, LI (1958), 169–85.

45 Joseph A. Wittreich (as above, Note 36), p. 89.

46 The lines were never published, which is probably just as well. They are quoted here from a manuscript in the Bodleian Library, Edmund Spoure's *A Booke of Poems . . . transcrib'd, Anno Domini 1695* (MS. Eng. poet. f. 52).

47 *C*: IV, 318; *Y*: II, 526; *P*: p. 219.

48 *Several Discourses*, ed. John Jeffery (1701–7), II, 135, and III, 328; quoted in *The Cambridge Platonists*, ed. C. A. Patrides (Cambridge, Mass., 1969), p. 15.
49 Most of its power indeed, according to Wittreich's extended discussion of *Lycidas* in *Visionary Poetics* (as above, Note 36). As much cannot be claimed on behalf of *Comus*: the apocalyptic background sketched by Alice-Lyle Scoufos, 'The Mysteries in Milton's *Masque*', *Milton Studies*, VI (1974), 113–42, is not, I think, manifestly evident in the foreground of the poem itself. On the other hand, the restrained observations of James Holly Hanford on the impact of the Book of Revelation on Milton's shorter poems are entirely acceptable (see his extended essay 'The Youth of Milton: An Interpretation of his Early Literary Development', in his *John Milton: Poet and Humanist* [Cleveland, 1966], especially pp. 59–65).
50 Thomas Mason, *A Revelation of the Revelation* (1619), p. 7. The Geneva Bible provides the equally standard identification of the sword with the word of God on the basis of Hebrews 4.12.
51 In *Animadversions* (1641); in *C*: III, 148, and *Y*: I, 707.
52 Thus Fixler (as above, Note 42), p. 61.
53 *The Fall of Man* (1616), p. 383.
54 Thomas Draxe, *An Alarum to the Last Judgement* (1615), pp. 43–5.
55 Henry Burton, *The Seven Vials* (1628), p. 1.
56 *Religio Medici*, I, 46; in *Works* (as above, Note 16), p. 118. For a typical discourse in agreement with Browne's thesis, see Samuel Gardiner, *Doomes-Day Booke* (1606), pp. 15 ff. Like everyone else, of course, Browne did accept that his age was history's last. 'The great mutations of the world are acted', according to *Hydriotaphia*, 'or time may be too short for our designes' (*Works*, p. 309).
57 Francis Rous, *The Diseases of the Time* (1622), p. 324, and John Andrewes, *A Golden Trumpet* (1648), sig. A5v.
58 As suggested by Marjorie H. Nicolson, 'Milton's "Old Damoetas"', *Modern Language Notes*, XLI (1926), 293–300. On Mede consult especially Wittreich (as above, Note 36), pp. 38–40, but also Firth (above, Note 2), pp. 213–28, as well as Paul Christianson, *Reformers and Babylon* (Toronto, 1978), pp. 124–9, and Ernest L. Tuveson, *Millennium and Utopia* (Berkeley and Los Angeles, 1949), pp. 76–85.
59 *C*: III, 231; *Y*: I, 803; *P*: p. 51. The Biblical reference is Jeremiah 20.8–10. Milton's statement – or indeed Jeremiah's – need not be construed as a negation of the prophet's personality. As John Smith the Cambridge Platonist remarked in his discourse on prophecy, 'It may be considered that God made not use of Idiots or Fools to reveal his Will by, but such whose Intellectuals were entire and perfect' (*Select Discourses* [1660], facsimile ed. C. A. Patrides [Delmar, N.Y., 1979], p. 273).
60 *Of Reformation*, in *C*: III, 49, and *Y*: I, 584.
61 *The Reason* etc., in *C*: III, 275, and *Y*: I, 857.
62 Paul Christianson (as above, Note 58), pp. 194–5.
63 *C*: III, 76–9; *Y*: I, 613–7; *P*: pp. 108–11.
64 By Joseph A. Wittreich (as above, Note 36), p. 84.
65 *C*: IV, 344; *Y*: II, 557–8; *P*: p. 240.
66 Thus Quistorp on Calvin (as above, Note 17), p. 115. On Calvin's rejection of chiliasm, consult his *Institutes of the Christian Religion*, III, xxv, 5 (trans. Henry Beveridge [1957], II, 259 ff.), and Quistorp, pp. 158 ff.
67 Dent (as above Note 3), p. 274, and Napier (Note 12), p. 294. Thus also Pareus (Note 36), pp. 524 ff., and Heinrich Bullinger's Second Helvetic Confession (1566), Ch. XI: 'we condemn the Jewish dreams, that before the day of judgment there shall

be a golden age in the earth' (*The Creeds of Christendom*, ed. Philip Schaff, 3rd edn. [1877], III, 853). The Augsburg Confession has a parallel clause (Appendix VII).

68 *Seriatim: The Second Tome or Volume of the Paraphrase of Erasmus vpon the Newe Testament*, the commentary on the Apocalypse translated by Edmund Allen (1549), fol. xxxii; Diodati (as above, Note 31), sig. Yyy2v; Daniel Featley, *Annotations upon all the Books of the Old and New Testament* (1645), sig. UU4v; Marlorat (as above, Note 28), fol. 276v; and Napier (Note 12), p. 294.

69 On Alsted see especially R. G. Clouse, 'The Rebirth of Millenarianism', in *Puritans, the Millennium and the Future of Israel*, ed. Peter Toon (Cambridge, 1970), pp. 42–56.

70 The opposition was formed in the main by Anglicans like Bishop Joseph Hall but included Presbyterians like Robert Baillie, professor of divinity at Glasgow and one of the Scottish representatives to the Westminster Assembly. See Baillie's *A Dissuasive from the Errours of the Time* (1645), notably its last chapter ('The thousand yeares of Christ his visible Raigne upon earth, is against Scripture'), discussed within a broader context by A. R. Dallison, 'Contemporary Criticism of Millenarianism', in the Toon collection (previous Note), Ch. VI. On the more general developments, consult B. S. Capp, 'The Millennium and Eschatology in England', *Past and Present*, LVII (1972), 156–82, and his chapter in the present volume.

71 Quoted in the anonymous tract *The Faithful Narrative of the Late Testimony* (1655), p. 35; *apud* B. S. Capp, 'Extreme Millenarianism', in the Toon connection (as above, Note 69), p. 71. The present interpretation, it may be noted, departs in fundamental respects from Christopher Hill's *Milton and the English Revolution* (1977). Hill is exclusively concerned to proclaim Milton as a consistent and undeviating 'radical Protestant heretic'. The endeavour is a salutary reminder of Milton's immediately contemporary context; but it is mounted with a commitment that often borders on monomania.

72 See Arthur E. Barker, *Milton and the Puritan Dilemma 1641–1660* (Toronto, 1942), ch. XII. Dobbins and Fixler (as above, Notes 35 and 42) are in essential agreement.

73 C: XVI, 339; Y: VI, 615.

74 C: XVI, 359 ff.; Y: VI, 623 ff.

75 As I have argued in '*Paradise Lost* and the Language of Theology', in *Bright Essence: Studies in Milton's Theology*, by W. B. Hunter, J. H. Adamson, and myself (Salt Lake City, 1971), pp. 159–78.

76 Revelation 6.16 conflated with Hosea 10.8; and *Paradise Lost*, IX, 1088–90, and X, 723–4. The same Biblical verses inform the cry of Marlowe's Faustus, 'Mountains and hills, come, come, and fall on me, / And hide me from the heavy wrath of God' (*Doctor Faustus*, XIX, 152–3).

77 Revelation 19.17 and 1.4, respectively, of which the latter is an extension of Zechariah 4.10; and *Paradise Lost*, III, 648–51. It was even possible, it appears, to regard the seven spirits as a representation of the Holy Ghost. Thus the formidable William Perkins: 'the holy Ghost may be called by the name of the *seuen spirits*' (*A Godly and Learned Exposition or Commentarie vpon the three first Chapters of the Reuelation* [1606], p. 16).

78 Thomas Brightman (as above, Note 5), sig. A3v.

79 As above, Note 7: sig. A8, and I, 30 et seq. On the more 'theatrical' elements in *Paradise Lost*, consult especially F. T. Prince, 'Milton and the Theatrical Sublime', in *Approaches to 'Paradise Lost'*, ed. C. A. Patrides (Toronto, 1968), pp. 53–63, and

John G. Demaray, *Milton's Theatrical Epic* (Cambridge, Mass., 1980).
80 As above, Note 36: p. 20. Pareus is also quoted and discussed by Barbara K. Lewalski (as above, Note 38), who additionally cites Hezekiah Holland, *An Exposition . . . upon the Revelation* (1650), p. 146.
81 Revelation 19.7 and 17.1 ff. The phrase quoted is Richard Bernard's (as above, Note 30), p. 247.
82 For a more detailed exposition and further references, see C. A. Patrides, *'The Grand Design of God': The Literary Form of the Christian View of History* (1972).
83 Walter Schmithals, *The Apocalyptic Movement*, trans. John E. Steely (Nashville, 1975), p. 33.
84 As above, Note 30: p. 12.
85 As above, Note 7: II, 45 and 7, respectively. Mede's basic premise is that 'the interpretation of propheticall Symboles, is not easily to be attained other-where, then from those properties which the Scripture some-where doth warrant' (II, 33).
86 *Sermons* (as above, Note 1), IV, 50.
87 Consult especially Jason P. Rosenblatt, 'Structural Unity and Temporal Concordance: The War in Heaven in *Paradise Lost*', *PMLA*, LXXXVII (1972), 31–41. On the exilic pattern in *Paradise Lost*, see also two other essays by Rosenblatt, of equally capital importance – 'Adam's Pisgah Vision: *Paradise Lost*, Books XI and XII', *ELH: Journal of English Literary History*, XXXIX (1972), 66–86, and 'The Mosaic Voice in *Paradise Lost*', *Milton Studies*, VII (1975), 207–32 – and additionally: Harold Fisch, 'Hebraic Style and Motifs in *Paradise Lost*', in *Language and Style in Milton*, ed. R. D. Emma and J. T. Shawcross (1967), Ch. II, and John T. Shawcross, '*Paradise Lost* and the Theme of Exodus', *Milton Studies*, II (1970), 3–26.
88 Cf. the Father's statement to the Son: 'Two dayes are therefore past, the third is thine; / For thee I have ordained it' (VI, 699–700). Consult especially William B. Hunter, 'The War in Heaven: The Exaltation of the Son', in *Bright Essence: Studies in Milton's Theology*, by W. B. Hunter, C. A. Patrides, and J. H. Adamson (Salt Lake City, 1971), pp. 115–30.
89 William G. Madsen, *From Shadowy Types to Truth: Studies in Milton's Symbolism* (New Haven, 1968), p. 111.
90 Bullinger (as above, Note 28), p. 356. Thus also Pareus (Note 5), p. 266; Diodati (Note 31), sig. Xxx4; Franciscus Junius [François Du Jon] the Elder, *The Apocalyps . . . with a briefe and methodicall Exposition*, trans. Anon. (Cambridge, 1592), p. 148; Thomas Wilson, *A Christian Dictionarie* (1622), sig. Hhh3; *et al.* The ultimate justification offered for the identification of Michael with Christ was: 'the composition of the word of three Hebrew particles, *Mi-ca-el*, who is like or *equall to the Lord*, that is onely Christ' (Edward Leigh, *Annotations upon all the New Testament* [1650], p. 597; thus also Thomas Taylor, *Christs Victorie over the Dragon* [1633], pp. 341–2; *et al.*). So far as I know, only Napier proposed another possibility: '*Michael* meaneth the holie Spirit' (as above, Note 12: p. 205). See further the details provided by Stella Revard, *The War in Heaven: 'Paradise Lost' and the Tradition of Satan's Rebellion* (Ithaca, N.Y., 1980).
91 As above, Note 5: sig. A4.

IV
The aftermath

PAUL J. KORSHIN

9 Queuing and waiting: the Apocalypse in England, 1660–1750

I

The outlines of millenarianism in England during the early Enlightenment are clear. The intense speculation of the late Renaissance about the possible arrival of the apocalypse continued throughout the period, almost a century long, on which this essay will focus. But the character of this speculation differs from that of the sixteenth and early seventeenth centuries, although we will be able to detect some strong continuities with the earlier period. Orthodox Anglican churchmen were involved in millenarian thought – indeed, the pursuit of the Millennium in the age of reason is by no means limited to the contributions of Dissenters or Puritans – but their involvement slowly declined after the onset of the eighteenth century. An important impetus for Anglican discussion of the subject came from the estate of the prominent layman and scientist Robert Boyle, whose will established the annual lectureship known as the Boyle Lectures, which immediately became a rostrum for orthodox Anglican thought. The Lectures began in 1692, and the early lectures often dealt quite thoroughly with expectations of the Millennium, but by the first decade of the new century Anglican clergymen found less and less reason to expect the apocalypse soon.[1] They had no doubt that it would come, and some of them, including most notably William Whiston, fixed firm dates for its advent, but by the end of the period of my focus Anglicanism had turned from effective advocacy of an imminent Millennium to cautious suspicion of self-styled messianic prophecy. The febrile chronological predictions, familiar to generations of readers beginning with the late sixteenth century and fortified in the seventeenth century with elaborate tables and impressive foldouts that purported to intertwine the diverse strains of sacred books and variant chronologies, lost some of their immediacy after 1700. No doubt Whiston's mathematical abstractions contributed to this decline. Whiston's own self-confessed errors in his calculations, moreover, did not enhance the reputation of prophecy or the exegesis of the prophetical books of Scripture as exact sciences. So the Church of England, impelled in part by such forces as its own well-meaning but misdirected clergy, gradually turned from active acceptance of the idea of apocalypse and left the field to the shrill clarion of dissenting millenarian sects.

Of course the signs of the apocalypse, whether embodied in the prophetical books or part of the code of the created world (Jakob Boehme's *signatura rerum*), continued to be available to exegetes of every theological persuasion.[2] And, inevitably, some of these exegetes were Anglicans. However, while orthodox Anglican exegesis gradually grew more conservative in the liberties that it took with existing texts and signs, interpreters with mystical leanings or dissenting attitudes were much less hesitant in the freedom of their interpretations. From the Cambridge Platonists of the 1670s and 1680s to the French Prophets of the first decade of the eighteenth century to John Wesley and his disciples in the second third of the century to the divines and social thinkers whom the American and French Revolutions convinced that the signs of the times spelled apocalypse, the English Enlightenment included many men and women who joined the queue that waited for the Millennium to come. Scholars have already examined the thought and opinions of some of the people and groups in this long and ever-shifting line. While I shall touch on the work of some of these writers, I have no intention of repeating what they have said. I have commented at length myself on the importance of typology to contemporary millenarians, for it helped many visionaries to identify the signs, or types, of the forthcoming apocalypse in familiar texts and landscapes.[3]

One of the consequences of my investigation was an awareness that imaginative millenarian exegesis of Scripture did not die out during the English Enlightenment but rather, abetted by a steady stream of fundamentalist Christian, Jewish, and – in Britain's new empire – Islamic visionaries, flourished throughout the eighteenth and early nineteenth centuries. This millenarianism flourishes still, always taking on new shapes, eternally plastic.[4] What I shall do here is to touch on the highpoints of religious millenarian thought and exegesis, to examine some of the literary texts in which the Millennium is a significant presence, and to study the behavior of some of those in the millenarian queue. In recent years sociologists have become aware that the behavior of those who queue for something – anything – has special characteristics that merit attention and that something may happen to the minds of those who wait for an event that may come soon but that, on the contrary, may not come at all.[5] The Millennium, during the late seventeenth century and the first half of the eighteenth century, is a phenomenon for which many queued. But how many of them waited? And how many of them gave up in their waiting and turned against the notion of their quest or went elsewhere? Not all of those in the queue, to be sure, could have been so astute as Coleridge, who realized, once the excitement of the French Revolution gave way to the imperial struggles of the Napoleonic Wars, that the Millennium was not coming soon, if at all.[6] What, finally, were contemporary attitudes towards millenarian behavior? Let me try to provide some answers to these questions in the following pages.

II

In the last forty years of the seventeenth century, expectations of the Millennium ran high in England. Religious writers of every kind mention the beginning of Christ's thousand-year reign. Acceptance of Joseph Mede's interpretation of Revelation 20, which he had set forth in his *Clavis Apocalyptica* (1627), could not have been greater in this period, but, all the same, millenarianism divides into various camps of believers whose behavior and attitudes differ markedly. The moderate Anglicans who came to dominate the Church of England after the Restoration take the most conservative view of the Millennium of any of the religious groups that speculated on the subject. Even before the Restoration, the leaders of this group realized that millenarianism was a major aspect of the radical political and social thought that characterized the Puritan Interregnum. Hence, while there could be no denying that the Millennium was canonical, there was substantial question about its immediacy. Orthodox Anglicans – their tone is set by influential bishops and archbishops like Edward Stillingfleet, Gilbert Sheldon, John Tillotson, and Thomas Tenison – seldom discuss the Millennium in sermons, for pulpit oratory reached the largest audience of any religious discourse or writing. Anglicans tend to confine their millenarian observations to exegeses of the prophetical books or to elaborate chronological studies of 'prophetic' time harmonized with events in secular history.

A prominent Anglican layman like Isaac Newton, for example, wrote privately about the Millennium, but feared that calendrical predictions were uncertain, and held back his major work on the subject so that it did not appear during his lifetime. When Newton's *Observations upon the Prophecies of Daniel, and the Apocalypse of St. John* finally appeared in 1733, the political impact of his reasonings was blunter than it would have been in the 1690s, and his predictions less relevant to contemporary affairs.[7] And *Observations upon the Prophecies* is only one of a profusion of works, most of them left incomplete and surviving only in manuscript, that Newton wrote about biblical prophecy and the coming of the Millennium. As Frank Manuel has observed, Newton's heirs and the custodians of his papers felt that publishing some of his millenarian speculations might be inappropriate and that the contents of these works would be inconsistent with the prevalent view of Newton as an apostle of 'enlightened' scientific thought.[8] There can be no question that Newton had many associations with dedicated millenarians; one of his protégés, Nicolas Fatio de Duillier, later became active in the movement of the French Prophets, England's chief millenarian sect of the early eighteenth century.[9] But Newton's friendship with Fatio flourished in the 1690s; by the time the young Frenchman joined the French Prophets, their association had ceased or the friendship had cooled.[10] Newton speculated on the apocalypse, then, like so many of his contemporaries; his speculations, unlike those of most, are especially learned and mathematical; his conclusions, again unlike those of the truly committed, are highly circumspect.

Henry More's view of the Millennium – that of a Cambridge Platonist – was even more moderate than Newton's. In his line-by-line exegesis of Revelation, *Apocalypsis Apocalypseos; or the Revelation of St. John the Divine Unveiled* (1680), More undertook to undeceive the Fifth Monarchy men and other extreme millenarian sects by assuring them that the events which the Book of Revelation had prophesied had already taken place 'in the late *Reformation*'.[11] More defended this position five years later in *Paralipomena Prophetica*, where he holds consistently that the typology of Revelation prefigures not the Millennium but rather the state of the Church on earth and the state of the Church triumphant in heaven.[12]

Some Anglican writers with scientific tastes speculated on the nature as well as the time of the Millennium. Thomas Burnet, whose *Sacred Theory of the Earth* (1681–9; Engl. trans. 1684–90) was most influential in the last years of the century, tried to write a further chapter to the Mosaic account of the Creation by giving a scientific account of how the world would end. Despite its geological and cosmological theorizing, Burnet's book had political implications as well, for it tended to give credence to other, more precise predictions about the coming of the Last Days in the final decade of the century. This was the very decade when William III's Protestant government was threatened by Catholic wars and incursions from the Continent and when some writers portrayed William as the Messiah and James II as the Antichrist.[13] And, of course, Burnet's scientific work inspired a number of poetical epics and pindaric odes on the final days, whether on Judgment Day, the last conflagration, or the Creation and its inevitable dissolution.[14] Burnet thought that the earth would split apart in a general display of fireworks, but his follower William Whiston saw dissolution on a more cosmic scale. In a chapter called 'Phaenomena relating to the General Conflagration', he decided that comets would retard the earth's natural motion so that its orbit would touch the sun's perihelion. This contact would last long enough for the earth to be thoroughly scorched. After this purifying fire, Whiston expected the earth to be renewed in a process similar to the Mosaic creation. This new condition of the world, which would consist of eternal day, would be the Millennium, a new Edenic state.[15] With a restraint that he would abandon in later writings,

Whiston refrained from suggesting an exact date for this accomplishment.

The relative moderation of Anglican attitudes toward the Millennium hardly serves as a counterweight to the enthusiastic millenarianism of many Protestant sects and individual dissenting writers. These included former Anglican clergymen whom the Act of Uniformity of 1662 had ousted from their livings, Quakers, Baptists, transplanted French Huguenots, and self-styled prophets and popular messiahs. Some of the more extreme millenarians of this period, finding their reception in England chilly, migrated to North America, where they helped to establish the profound and wide-reaching millennialism of the American colonies. The dissenter William Sherwin is a good example of the millenarian style in the last third of the century. His major works on the apocalypse are *Prodromos* (1674), an analysis of the Millennium based on chronology, and *Irenicon* (1676), a study of prophecy and prophesying. Sherwin is a strongly typological writer who sees the Old Testament as a typological basis proving that God has shadowed forth the Millennium from earliest times. His chronological defense of the Millennium argues that earlier millennia shadow forth the end of the six thousand years and the ensuing of the reign of Christ and the saints. The Book of Revelation is his text, but all Scripture and secular history are the fields from which he culls inspiration for his beliefs.[16] Sherwin's works – he wrote a dozen millenarian books in the 1670s – exemplify much of the enthusiastic apocalypticism of the late seventeenth century. They are a hodge-podge of personal letters, inspired statements, impressionistic exegeses of selected texts, enthusiastic ejaculations, prayers, and witnessings, all purporting to show the uniqueness of his own special revelation. Sherwin is an extreme example of millenarianism, but he is nevertheless fairly moderate compared to some of his colleagues, for he makes no strong prognostications of social or political revolution and does not fix the date of the Second Coming earlier than 1700.[17]

I must also mention two other groups of millenarians, those who are more mystical than former Anglican divines like Sherwin and those whose predictions are mainly political. Among the mystics, the Quaker Jane Lead deserves attention, for her enthusiastic writings are filled with inspired readings of Scripture, personal revelations, and a certainty that the apocalypse was nigh. One of her first books, *The Revelation of Revelations* (1683), contains her record of 'the new raised Life', followed by a Pisgah-sight of the New Jerusalem and other visions derived from the Book of Revelation which, in the manner of such writings, are in biblical style as well. Her inspiration and style strongly suggest two later visionaries, Richard Brothers and Joanna Southcott; all three have a slight touch of mental instability. Lead is uncertain about the commencement of 'the time of the Lord's reign', but she is certain that the current generation will see all millennial prophecies come to pass.[18] As with Bunyan, Benjamin Keach, and other non-Anglican writers on sacred topics, Lead's most profound ejaculations are in verse (in her case, atrocious verse).

And, like other writers whom Jakob Boehme's mysticism inspired, Lead has a quick apprehension of the signs and forerunners of divine things in the created world around her. At the end of the century, after more than twenty years of mystical speculation on the Millennium, Lead – still unbudgingly in the queue – writes, in *The Signs of the Times* (1699), of the certain forerunners of the kingdom of Christ. Her signs are the traditional interpretations of the contemporary world that Revelation had long enforced – voluptuousness, debauchery, the insolence of unbelievers, and so on.[19]

Lead's interpretation of Revelation is neither rare nor surprising for, by the end of the seventeenth century, the exegetes have universally agreed that St. John's witnessing is mainly a symbolical, predictive narration, a series of types whose antitypes can be sought and found in the events of secular history since St. John or which are yet to be fulfilled. The more political readers of the signs of the times justified their views on their belief that the biblical prophecies of dire events to happen in certain Old Testament or Judean kingdoms were, in reality, allegorical predictions that applied equally well to contemporary Europe. Hence the Baptist Benjamin Keach, whose popular writings fall somewhere between Bunyan's and Defoe's in zeal, could assure his readers, in *Antichrist Stormed* (1689), that present-day Rome and the Roman Catholic Church are the antitypes of the typological destructions that Revelation promises.[20] The Huguenot Pierre Jurieu is more successful than most of his contemporaries in demonstrating that the types of Revelation foreshadowed modern European history, especially that of France. Jurieu's works were understandably popular – in English translation – in the last decade of the century, when the fall of Louis XIV and the conquest of Catholic France were desiderata that many in Protestant England longed for.[21] It is difficult to assess the millenarian behavior of writers like Sherwin, Lead, Keach, and Jurieu, for we know little about their personal lives. However, the internal consistency of their writings is exceptionally strong: in the case of the first three of these figures, we have available literary works that span from twelve to twenty-five years, and it is notable that they are millenarian from first to last. Clearly, then, some of the better known millenarians did not at all seem to mind waiting in the queue for the Millennium to come. If it did not come so soon as they expected, they found other things to occupy them, new ways to predict when it would come for sure.

III

The early eighteenth century in England, what some writers have called the dawn of the age of reason, is remarkable in having an outbreak of popular prophecy that would not be surpassed in intensity until the 1790s. The prophetical movements of the last decade of the century would be inspired in part by the French Revolution, and that of the opening of the century also had its French roots, deriving from the Huguenot group known as the Camisards. The immigrant community of French Huguenots in London responsible for this remarkable series of prophecies had already, following the revocation of the Edict of Nantes (1685), shown a tendency to produce popular messianic prophets and leaders. The persecutions to which Louis XIV's absolutist state subjected the Huguenots were often extremely severe and, from Old Testament times, persecution, isolation, captivity, and migration of a group or a people from a beloved homeland have frequently aroused a spirit of enthusiastic hope for a better future. Hence the behavior of the Huguenots in England can be explained, although there was no longer any immediacy of persecution as there had been in France. Hillel Schwartz has told the story of this group and their movement in *The French Prophets: the History of a Millenarian Group in Eighteenth-Century England* (1980).[22] I shall not repeat his well-narrated story here, but will concentrate instead on the leading figure among the French Prophets, the Englishman John Lacy, and reactions to his prophetic message from his contemporaries.

Lacy appeared as the chief apostle of this new millenarian group around 1705, publishing his major work, *The Prophetical Warnings of John Lacy, Esq; Pronounced under the Operation of the Spirit; and Faithfully taken in Writing, when they were spoken*, in 1707. Automatic speech, the principal means by which Lacy claimed to be inspired, was nothing new in the annals of English millenarianism, but Lacy went further than most of his predecessors, for he was able to describe his convulsive fits of inspiration in some detail. 'I am the better assured,' he wrote, '. . . that my Agitations and Words in the Ecstasie, are produced by a Superior Agent, and are independent of me.'[23] Lacy tried to describe his trances and revealed that his prophetic speaking was a form of speaking in tongues, or glossolalia. Lacy's glossolalia – whether real or contrived we cannot know at this distance from the fact – allies his brand of prophecy with pentecostalism. It is also possible that there was a connection between Lacy's singular physical behavior and epilepsy. His 'prophecies' consist of inspired mouthings in English, French, and Latin, all in the form of imprecations, warnings of the coming apocalypse, and visions in the manner of Revelation. Apparently Lacy was accustomed to fall into his prophetical fits at certain times of the day when he could arrange to have a stenographer nearby to record his ejaculations. Thus his prophecies are arranged in diary form, carefully dated with a headnote telling where he was when the spirit took him and who else was present (the presence of witnesses was obviously important for proving the authenticity of Lacy's visions). Here is his prophecy for Friday, 13 June 1707:

> O my dear Babes, shall the Men of the Earth pluck you out of my Hands? O Dust, Dust! What! rebellious Dust contend with Me? Contend with these? O all the Earth, I

will make thee know that I AM. Man shall no longer prevail. Oh no, for I will not have a competitor with me in my Throne. They shall see it's I AM, I AM, I AM. Shall Men overcome me? O Fools, Fools, I sit in the Heavens to laugh at the vain Thoughts and Attempts of Men against my Christ. The Earth make a noise! And the Seas roar! what! against their God! O tremble thou Earth at the Presence of thy God.[24]

All of Lacy's prophecies are pseudo-biblical rant of this sort, carelessly confusing 'biblical' language with unexpected locutions like 'rebellious' and 'competitor'. As Lacy proceeds – *Prophetical Warnings* consists of three volumes – he sometimes speaks in his own voice about the coming apocalypse, but most of his millenarian pronouncements are in the voice of the Holy Spirit. Occasionally the Spirit, apparently anxious to be accepted as authentic, goes so far as to give interpretations of certain difficult passages of Scripture, perhaps not the first time in recorded history that the presumed author of the Bible, speaking through an intermediary, had deigned to assume the role of exegete, but inconsistent with most eighteenth-century apologetics.[25]

Lacy's millenarian warnings provoked a number of attempts at refutation from members of the established church. These refutations – there are several dozen replies to his prophecies – are of two kinds. One group of refuters held that Lacy's prophesyings could not be genuine because, under the dispensation of Christ, true prophecy had ceased a long time ago (if not by the time of the New Testament, as some argued, then surely by the time of primitive Christianity). In terms of revealed religion, this view runs, there was no longer any need for prophecy. The other group of critics was more particular: Lacy was an impostor or a madman. The evidence of fraud was not hard for these critics to assemble, especially with regard to his glossolalia. From the first group of critics, let me select Nathaniel Spinckes who, in *The New Pretenders to Prophecy Examin'd* (1709), linked Lacy and the Camisards with a long tradition of false prophecy. True prophecy of the Millennium is to be found in Scripture, where those who were genuinely inspired have said all that needs to be said on the subject of the apocalypse; hence there is no need for another message on the same subject. The 'sufficiency' of the Bible for mankind's needs, an old Anglican argument, means that Lacy and his fellow 'Pseudoprophets', none of whom has displayed the elements of true prophetical inspiration as the Old and New Testaments describe them, are fraudulent.[26] Spinckes, of course, was not alone in claiming that the spirit of prophecy was no longer necessary and that, consequently, Lacy's prophesying had to be false. The group of particular critics, however, is larger than the body of refuters who depended upon Scripture itself for their condemnations. These writers, again mainly Anglican clergymen, deal with the spirit of prophecy in recent times, with the nature of enthusiasm, with true and false inspiration, and with the behavioral qualities of the falsely inspired. From these works we can extract a brief history of fanaticism in the late seventeenth and early eighteenth centuries and a better understanding of what many moderate Englishmen and women regarded as millenarian behavior.

Some of Lacy's critics, significantly, add enough physiological detail about false prophetic seizures to compare with the techniques of contemporary medical literature. Benjamin Bayly, for instance, in *An Essay on Inspiration* (1708), described the local prophets in the following terms:

> The manner of their Seizure is another strong Ground of Prejudice against this Mission [as authentic]. *The Tremblings, the Gulpings, the Hiccupings, Foamings, Distortions and Convulsions of the Body, the utter Ignorance of what is deliver'd in their Agitations, the Drumming, Whistling, Laughing, Threshing, and many other odd things* with which this Inspiration is attended, represent the men Frantick, rather than Inspir'd, more resemble them to the Heathen Priests than the true Prophets of GOD.[27]

If St. Paul had appeared to the gentiles like one of these modern prophets, Bayly continues, they would have thought him 'a mad Man or *Dæmoniack* instead of an Apostle'. Thus Lacy and his followers are certainly mad, no different from 'persons in Bedlam'.[28] George Hickes, the lexicographer of the northern European languages, had delivered a popular sermon, *The Spirit of Enthusiasm Exorcised*, in 1680; now it reappeared in a new, enlarged edition complete with a *History of Montanism* (a variety of false inspiration from primitive Christianity). Hickes had condemned the millenarian enthusiasts of the last age – Nayler, Venner, and Muggleton – so the reappearance of his work inevitably compared the new enthusiasts with the impostors of thirty years past.[29] For Hickes, 'the Poyson of Enthusiasm, which is the Spiritual Drunkenness, or Lunacy of this Schismatical Age' was a form of mental illness, madness itself. Francis Hutchinson, another critic, noticed that one of Lacy's claims to the genuineness of his inspiration was that, during one of his seizures, his body had slid across the room as if drawn by a supernatural force, which Lacy reasoned to be the Holy Spirit. But Hutchinson had some medical knowledge, and remembered 'that when Persons are fallen into a State of Madness, their Strength, at some critical times, is much greater than it is in its usual Course; and then, if it be imploy'd that way, the Person may very well slide across a Floor with a Motion unusual'.[30] Hutchinson adopts a mocking tone, but Richard Kingston, in *Enthusiastick Impostors No Divinely Inspired Prophets* (1709), is often ironical and satirical. And Swift – another Anglican clergyman – presents a short history of fanaticism in *The Mechanical Operation of the Spirit* (1704) that we must now see, I believe, not simply as one of his greatest satires but also as a response to contemporary millenarianism.

Lacy and his adherents responded to their critics, but they could bring no facts concerning prophecies that had been realized to support them. In fact, Lacy is far less effective in plain expository prose than he is in his effusions. He devotes one part of his *The General Delusion of Christians* (1713) to the proposition that prophecy in modern times may still, under certain circumstances, be genuine. One of Lacy's claims in this work is relevant to my inquiry: 'I shall not offer at any Proof here, of true Prophecy, either precedently to, or attending the Time of the Reformation; because the Principles universally prevailing among Christians, could never by any thing I can find, from the period mention'd above, unto this Day, suffer a true Prophet to pass for other than a Monster, a Heretick, a Fanatick or Madman, an Impostor or Blasphemer.'[31] That Lacy should perceive, as he clearly does, that it is almost impossible for a 'prophet' to be taken seriously shows that, now and then, even well-intentioned pretenders to inspiration may realize that their stories are hard to credit. Of course, when Lacy speaks of a 'prophet', he is certainly referring to a millenarian visionary, for such he was and so all his followers and adversaries acknowledged him to be. During the eight or ten years that the French Prophets, led by John Lacy, engaged the interest of the early eighteenth century, those who wrote to refute them were mainly members of the Anglican clergy, but they were not bishops, archbishops, or the leading controversialists of the established church. The Church establishment stayed aloof from the contemporary debate over millennialism and the genuineness of prophetical inspiration about the apocalypse. After the first decade of the eighteenth century, as I have already noted, the Millennium rapidly declines in popularity as a subject of Anglican discourse. Those who dealt with it were divines with unorthodox views, like the antitrinitarian William Whiston, deists like Anthony Collins who questioned all biblical prophecy, Protestants from the Continent, and dissenting clergymen and ministers. Anglican exegesis of Scripture would continue to acknowledge and interpret the prophets and Revelation, but for the most part this scholarship would be unemotional and lacking in a willingness to assign a date to the Second Coming. After the interlude of the Camisards or the French Prophets, millenarianism would become ever more a subject for popular culture and dissenting religion.

IV

Religious writings on the Millennium during this period, then, show two distinct and different strains. These are the favorable presentation of millenarian ideas, with varying degrees of fervor, and the criticism of expectations of the apocalypse. Such criticism focuses either on the notion of apocalypse as unlikely or on the attitude and credibility of the individual millennialist person or sect. An awareness of millenarian behavior in the early Enlightenment evolves as a result of the carefully reasoned responses by religious thinkers to many writers on the apocalypse. But religious commentaries and apologetics are not the only treatments of millennial ideas and attitudes. It is necessary to consider literary responses as well, for these treatments of the subject represent an important secular trend in contemporary attitudes toward the Millennium and herald the growth of a new and more popular audience for millenarian ideas. It is inevitable that poetry, popular prose literature, and both fictional and non-fictional narrative should reflect millenarianism, since art always imitates reality and the apocalypse was very much a reality in the last half of the seventeenth century. Literary treatments of this subject are important for another reason: they reveal a great deal about contemporary views of the millenarian queue and the people in it.

No seventeenth-century English writer commented more astutely on the varieties of religious fanaticism than Samuel Butler. In his character of 'A Fifth-Monarchy Man' (c. 1663), he writes, 'He interprets Prophesies, as *Whittington* did the Bells, to speak to him, and governs himself accordingly'.[32] To Butler, the millenarian, at least as the extremist Fifth Monarchists personify this character, is a spiritualist and a mystic, one who sees government, indeed all life as 'abstracted from all Matter, and consisting wholly of Revelations, Visions, and Mysteries'. Butler's millenarian is not quite a lunatic, or no more so than are any of his remarkable characters, but his sketch – which he duplicates in many other characters – represents one of the most powerful popular responses to millenarian behavior, ridicule. As literary comments on a widely prevalent millenarianism become more numerous during the 1650s and 1660s, we will notice that the satiric strain in these responses appears long before it becomes common in religious refutations of the same phenomena. Literary men, then, are somewhat ahead of Church controversialists in attacking – often in satiric terms – the excesses of contemporary apocalypticism. Yet the literary response is not all negative, and sometimes we will find that the same author can both favor and criticize those in the millenarian queue. Butler, of course, can only criticize extreme religious behavior – his *Characters* and *Hudibras* have nothing favorable to say about any sectarian behavior whatsoever – but other writers, like Marvell and Dryden, show the ambivalence toward millennialism that is characteristic of the period.

The ambivalence is understandable when one considers the intensity of millenarian activities in the 1650s and 1660s. To many of his followers, Cromwell was a messianic figure whose government was a type on earth of the thousand years' reign, yet extreme sectarian elements regarded Cromwell as insufficiently radical, a mere moderate answer to royalism. Early in 1661, one group of Fifth Monarchists, led by Thomas Venner, set out to establish the reign of King Jesus, and popular prophets throughout the Interregnum and the first half of the 1660s persisted in believing that 1666 (a year that reproduced the numbers, with one more digit, from the head of the beast of Revelation 13.18) would be the year of the Second Coming. Moderate writers responded to the claims of the extremists in various ways. Butler's satiric comments are just one reaction. Other writers adopt one or more styles of response. Marvell, for example, is highly critical of radical millenarianism in the first of his major poems about Cromwell, *The First Anniversary of the Government under O. C.* (1655). He presents 'Angelique *Cromwell*' as a messianic figure responsible for the heavenly harmony, 'the wondrous Order and Consent', of government after the death of Charles I. He is the scourge of the Babylonian whoredom that still afflicts England, truly a composite of the glittering visions of Revelation. But the Canaanite is still in the land in the person of the millenarian sects which believe that the only right road to the New Jerusalem is the total destruction of civil society. Marvell writes:

> Yet such a *Chammish* issue still does rage,
> The Shame and Plague both of the Land and Age,
> Who watch'd thy halting, and thy Fall deride,
> Rejoycing when thy Foot had slipt aside;
> That their new King might the fifth Scepter shake,
> And make the World, by his Example, Quake.[33]

The millenarians are 'Accursed Locusts, whom your King does spit / Out of the Center of th'unbottom'd Pit', and, further, a 'race most hypocritically strict! / Bent to reduce us to the ancient Pict'.[34] It is evident that Marvell's own notion of the Millennium comes close to that of the Anglican moderates of the Restoration and the last decades of the century. A few years later, in *A Poem upon the Death of O. C.* (1658), he marmorealizes Cromwell as a savior in whose short reign England has glimpsed a vision of Christ's Second Coming and the kingdom of the saints. By relating Cromwell to the Old Testament types of Christ – Moses, Joshua, and David – Marvell suggests that the Protector, in life and in death, is a type of the warrior Christ of Revelation 19. His epitaph, 'O *Cromwell, Heavens Favorite!* to none / Have such high honours from above been shown', urges that Cromwell is even more a hero to his people than Moses had been to the Israelites.[35] To outdo the greatest type of the Old Testament is no mean achievement. Thus Cromwell is Marvell's exemplary Messiah.

The millenarian aura that surrounded Cromwell is modest compared to that within which Royalist apologists of the 1660s encapsulated Charles II. Charles's return in 1660 and his coronation the following April led to a great literary outpouring of enthusiastic typology and millennial self-gratulation. Dryden was not alone in regarding the Stuart restoration as a return of the golden age, but his panegyrics of the 1660s have remained as the most famous of the decade. Certain familiar structural features of millennial prophecy recur in Dryden's panegyrics to Stuart rule – the interlude of stillness before an apocalyptic event, the typological allusions to the covenantal figures and events of the Old Testament, the visionary passage that recalls Virgil's fourth *Eclogue*, and the sight of a heavenly city beyond a range of delectable mountains. These literary qualities, which Dryden refined beyond what any of his contemporaries could achieve, are the type-scenes of the Millennium that the later seventeenth century used again and again. But Dryden's greatest vision of the apocalypse does not occur in his poems of praise; rather, it appears in his long stanzaic study of England's future, *Annus Mirabilis* (1667).

It is difficult for us to recall now with what ardor contemporary millenarians awaited 1666 as a year of millennial significance.[36] Nevertheless, as has happened from time to time in the annals of millenarian thought, the numerological significance of 1666 captured popular imagination, and, from 1660 on, there was a spate of fresh speculation on the signs of the times, the arrival of the beast, the coming of Armageddon, and similar events. Against this outpouring of popular nonsense Butler undoubtedly directed some of his satire in the First and Second Parts of *Hudibras* (1663–4), for Hudibras's squire Ralpho has millenarian leanings that Butler ridicules. The orientalist John Spencer wrote his *Discourse concerning Prodigies* and his *Treatise concerning Vulgar Prophecies* (both 1665) to confute some of the superstitious silliness of contemporary Merlins. And Dryden contributed his great poem to the cause of moderation, using it to show that the plague and the Fire of London were indeed millennial experiences of a kind. Dryden's point, however, is that these living types of the apocalypse are prefigurations of events that will occur at an indefinite point in the future; his millennial chronology is always vague, as befits an Anglican moderate. But there can be no question about the fervor of Dryden's vision:

> Me-thinks already, from this Chymick flame,
> I see a City of more precious mold:
> Rich as the Town which gives the *Indies* name,
> With Silver pav'd, and all divine with Gold.[37]

Dryden's new London is undoubtedly the New Jerusalem of Revelation 21.18, and he sees it as a present rather than as a future good. His closing stanzas show that it is a heavenly city of commercial prominence which he depicts, 'New deifi'd' (line 1178), with an eastern, almost Levantine character. Dryden's millenarian vision, then, lacks the political and social immediacy of those that his Fifth Monarchist contemporaries urged; it is the vision of a poet and a moderate who cannot comply with the revolutionary zeal of radical apocalypticism.

Dryden is not always aloof from millenarian politics – in *Absalom and Achitophel* (1681) in particular he satirizes the Duke of Monmouth's extreme Protestant supporters as messianic fundamentalists – but his tendency is to take an irenic view of the Millennium. A famous passage in *Absalom and Achitophel* – the 'Essay on Innovation' (lines 753–810) – opposes radical innovations in government and society: 'All other Errors but disturb a State; / But Innovation is the Blow of Fate' (lines 799–800). Dryden concludes the poem – essentially a satire – with a peaceful view of the Millennium:

> Henceforth a Series of new time began,
> The mighty Years in long Procession ran:
> Once more the Godlike *David* was Restor'd,
> And willing Nations knew their Lawfull Lord.[38]

The 'Series of new Time' is an allusion to the contemporary chronologies whose tables attempted to synchronize the times and duration of different realms and to predict the date of the Second Coming with due attention to the scriptural prophecies. On this context, 'Godlike David['s]' second restoration reminds us that just twenty years before Dryden and many others had greeted Charles II's restoration as if it were a species of peaceful Millennium. Millenarianism would undergo many changes in Dryden's lifetime, but, in the last year of his life, at the end of a decade – the 1690s – of much millenarian zeal, and writing now as a Catholic rather than as an Anglican, his view is much the same. Embodied in his magnificent epistle, 'To the Dutchess of *Ormond*' (in *Fables* [1700]), his prophecy of the thousand years' reign is closer to Shelley's in *Prometheus Unbound* than to the message of the sectarian prophets:

> When at Your second Coming You appear,
> (For I foretell that Millenary Year)
> The sharpen'd Share shall vex the Soil no more,
> But Earth unbidden shall produce her Store:
> The Land shall laugh, the circling Ocean smile,
> And Heav'ns Indulgence bless the Holy Isle.[39]

We can trace Dryden's traditional eschatology from his moderate Anglican (and Royalist) view of the Millennium in the early 1660s. Then he had foreseen a blessed emporium, while now, himself a member of a persecuted minority faith, his vision is Edenic, focused not on a city of 'precious mold' but on the paradise of a 'Holy Isle'. Virgil, whose fourth *Eclogue* Dryden had translated in the late 1690s, is behind this interpretation, but so too is Milton.

A view of late seventeenth-century millenarianism that notices the importance of the 1660s in the development of the concept, as this essay does, must also comment on the role that Milton takes in the molding of contemporary attitudes. Conventional scholarly arguments that *Paradise Lost* had but modest influence in the century in which it appeared have gradually lost credence in recent years; Dryden and Addison, we now agree, were *not* the first English writers to pay attention to Milton's epic. Dryden's view of the apocalypse certainly relates to, if it is not derived from, Milton's, and we must remember that *Paradise Lost* first appeared in 1667, at a historical highpoint of millennial speculation. Milton clearly refers to the Millennium in four books of the poem. The first such allusion is the speech of the Father in Book III.[40] This passage is a conventional view of the Last Judgment (III.323–41), whereas the references to the apocalypse in Books X, XI, and XII repeat some of the ideas about renewal of the earth ('Then Heav'n and Earth renew'd shall be made pure' – X.638; 'New Heav'n and Earth shall to the Ages rise, / Or down from Heav'n descend' – X.647–8; 'Resigns him up with Heav'n and Earth renew'd' – XI.66) that were current topics among millenarians in the last third of the seventeenth century.

Milton does not actually present a *vision* of the Millennium in *Paradise Lost*. Adam's Pisgah-sight would seem the ideal – and traditional – place for it, but Milton does not give Adam such a foresight in Book XI. Instead – and significantly so, I believe – Milton reserves his view of the apocalypse until Book XII, when Michael perceives Adam's mortal sight to fail and says 'Henceforth what is to come I will relate' (XII.11). Contemporary literary recreations of the apocalypse, following the style of Revelation, were common and were – or at least were *meant* to be – frightening in their detail. That Milton elects to present his extended account of the apocalypse as an abstraction through the discourse of Michael rather than in the graphic style of Books I and II shows that he probably wished to avoid imitating the extremism of other contemporary representations. Hence his description of the Millennium (XII.485–551) is long but general, beginning with apostolic times. The first apostles, Milton notes, alluding to the Book of the Acts, will be aided by the Holy Spirit and '[endued] / To speak all Tongues' (XII.500–1). Many millenarians in the 1660s claimed the ability to speak in tongues, and glossolalia is, as I noted with respect to the French Prophets, a usual aspect of millenarian behavior. The apostles, however, are genuinely inspired while, in Milton's account, their followers are 'Wolves . . . grievous Wolves' (XII.508). Now Milton condenses all Christian history since apostolic times into no more than thirty lines, amply showing what the signs of the times will be before the Millennium ensues: greed, false religion enforced by civil laws (Milton is criticizing the concept of an established church), persecution of minority faiths, specious outward forms of worship, slander, lack of faith. 'So shall the World go on, / To good malignant, to bad men benign' until Christ's Second Coming:

> At return
> Of him so lately promis'd to thy aid,
> The Woman's seed, obscurely then foretold,
> Now amplier known thy Saviour and thy Lord,
> Last in the Clouds from Heav'n to be reveal'd
> In glory of the Father, to dissolve
> *Satan* with his perverted World, then raise
> From the conflagrant mass, purg'd and refin'd,
> New Heav'ns, new Earth, Ages of endless date
> Founded in righteousness and peace and love,
> To bring forth fruits Joy and eternal Bliss (XII.541–51).

Milton's account deserves close attention. Nowhere does he mention that there will be a herald of the Millennium in the person of a new prophet or an inspired witness (contemporary millenarianism commonly was associated with a visionary or a 'prophet'). Nowhere does he suggest that the Millennium will be detectable through an interpretation of biblical numerology (a favorite pastime of the millennialists, especially in the years preceding 1666, when Milton could have been writing or revising this very book). And nowhere does he propose that the 'New Heav'ns, new Earth' will last a thousand years; instead, Milton's new model world is a paradisal utopia 'of endless date'. A recent interpreter of *Paradise Lost* has seen in this long account of the apocalypse a 'reference to Restoration England [that] could hardly be more explicit'.[41] Perhaps it *is* correct to see the signs of the times that Milton cites here as direct allusions, or even as vague references, to the intellectual and social milieux of the 1660s. But if such is the case, then it is remarkable to note how restrained is Milton's view of the immediacy of the Millennium, especially in view of his lifelong exposure to the millenarian debate. As a consequence of the references in *Paradise Lost*, I think it is safe to say that Milton was interested in the Millennium without being a millenarian and that his references to Restoration England in his account of the apocalypse are so vague as to suggest his dismissal of contemporary lore on the subject. The restraint of Milton's position would influence many ideas about the apocalypse in the next century.

A final figure from the later seventeenth century whose millenarian ideas deserve attention is Bunyan. The typology of the apocalypse is present in almost all of Bunyan's religious writings, even in his collection of emblems for children, *A Book for Boys and Girls* (1686), which would achieve great popularity in the eighteenth century as a children's book and which is especially significant as a paradigm for Blake's *Songs of Innocence and of Experience*. His most famous work, *The Pilgrim's Progress* 'from this world to that which is to come' presents the devout Christian's life as a pilgrimage to the Heavenly Jerusalem of Revelation. And what Bunyan's text might not make clear the omnipresent marginal glosses gently prod the reader to understand. Bunyan's most elevated literary work, *The Holy War* (1682), is a better place to examine his views of the Millennium than *The Pilgrim's Progress*, for here Bunyan is writing on a different level from his more popular works, creating and sustaining a tremendous allegory that ranks with Spenser's as one of the best in English literature.

The latest editors of *The Holy War* remark 'the vague millenarian thread' present in the work.[42] But the book is more than vaguely millenarian. Indeed, Bunyan evokes the visionary style from the very first paragraph: 'In my travels, as I walked through many Regions and Countries, it was my chance to happen into that famous *Continent* of *Universe*; a very large and spacious

Countrey it is.'⁴³ The style of the Christian visionary could not be lost on Bunyan's original audience, accustomed as it was to reading visionary works. So the saving of Mansoul from Diabolus by Emanuel, acting on orders from his father Shaddai, is simultaneously a transparent allegory and a narrative with only one possible conclusion, eternal salvation in a state of timeless perfection. That perfection, for Bunyan, is the Millennium, but the storyteller in him does not permit him to reveal this (obvious) point during his narrative, except through foreshadowing. Instead, Bunyan reserves his vision of the Millennium until the end of *The Holy War*.

After Emanuel has delivered Mansoul from the armies of Diabolus for the final time, he delivers the longest and most important speech in the book (in fact, it concludes the work), embodying the following vision:

> For yet a little while, O my *Mansoul*, even after a few more times are gone over thy head, I will (but be not thou troubled at what I say) take down this famous town of *Mansoul*, stock and stone, to the ground. And will carry the stones thereof, and the timber thereof, and the walls thereof, and the dust thereof, and the inhabitants thereof, into mine own Country, even unto the Kingdom of my Father; and will there set it up in such strength and glory, as it never did see in the Kingdom where now it is placed. I will even there set it up for my Fathers habitation, for, for that purpose it was at first created in the Kingdom of *Universe*; and there I will make it a spectacle of wonder, a monument of mercy, and the admirer of its own mercy. There shall the natives of *Mansoul* see all that of which they have seen nothing here; there shall they be equal to those unto whom they have been inferiour here. And there shall thou, O my *Mansoul*, have such communion with me, with my Father, and with your Lord *Secretary*, as is not possible here to be enjoyed. Nor ever could be, shouldest thou live in *Universe* the space of a thousand years.⁴⁴

Bunyan's last battle between Emanuel and Diabolus, which precedes this passage, is analogous to the Armageddon of Revelation 19, while Emanuel's speech represents the building of a new heaven and a new earth of Revelation 21. The speech is rich in types of the last things – garments of righteousness, vestments of white, thorny paths replaced by straight ways, shadows yielding to clear gaze. Emanuel refers to Mansoul's seeing 'all that of which they have seen nothing here', as mysteries vanish in the clear light of revelation. Another favorite millenarian theme is that of full equality, as inferior and superior disappear; it is the familiar seventeenth-century concept of levelling that Bunyan introduces here. Bunyan's millenarianism is thus more popular, more populist, than Milton's, closer to the desires of the folk, the mechanics, and the nonconformist multitudes beyond the reach of Anglican preaching. His apocalyptic message, with its seasoning of utopianism, resembles the politicized evangelicism of Wesley and his followers and the principal strains of millenarianism after 1700. There can be little doubt that Bunyan influenced some of those in the millenarian queue in eighteenth-century England.

V

Literary reactions to the Millennium after 1700 continue to show the same ambivalence that I have discussed in the age of Marvell, Milton, Butler, Bunyan, and Dryden. The 'Last Day' poems that I cited earlier (see note 14), for instance, describe the apocalypse with a restraint (and often in a blank verse) that recalls Milton's style in Book XII. Pope's *Messiah* (1712) reflects both Milton and Dryden, closely following Virgil's fourth *Eclogue*, which it sets out to imitate, but also evoking a paradisal vision in the manner of *Paradise Lost* and 'To the Dutchess of *Ormond*'. However, the impression of early eighteenth-century treatments of the apocalypse that lingers longest is one reminiscent of Marvell and Butler, critical and even satirical rather than bland and favorable. This impression receives additional force from the fact that two of the most influential writers of the period, Swift and Pope, satirize millenarian behavior. Since the established church, after the turn of the century, increasingly identified millenarianism with fanaticism, it is hardly surprising that the leading satirists in the golden age of English satire should have looked at those in the queue with such scorn.

Swift's great satire against false religious inspiration, *A Tale of a Tub* (1704), is really a seventeenth-century work, a product of the 1690s. The behavior of some of the fanatical sects that he ridicules in the *Tale* is undoubtedly millennial, although we cannot always tell for certain which millenarian group is his satiric object. Yet the satire is present nonetheless, as a glance at Swift's crowded title page reveals. The title page of the first five editions, all published between 1704 and 1710, contains, about two-thirds of the way down, the following epigraph: 'Basima eacabasa eanaa irraurista, diarba da caeotaba fobor camelanthi. *Iren. Lib.* 1. C. 18.' Those who have troubled to trace this gibberish back to its source, St. Irenaeus' *Adversus Haereses*, have found that it occurs in a passage where Irenaeus describes the initiation rites of the second-century Marcosian heretics. Irenaeus even offers a 'translation', but commentators, noting that the passage is in a language that is otherwise unknown, have wondered how he could have deciphered what the Marcosians actually meant. In fact, the meaning is easier to puzzle out, for Swift has chosen as his epigraph one of the earliest recorded examples of glossolalia. Even in Swift's time students of antiquity knew that the ancient heretics had used glossolalia to predict the end of the world, that is, for apocalyptic purposes (Eusebius makes this observation). By the beginning of the eighteenth century, students of language had noticed that glossolalic speech is a phenomenon without a specific grammar rather than a real language.[45] And Swift would have been aware that contemporary millenarians – among them, John Lacy and the French Prophets – claimed that their speaking in tongues authenticated their prophecies. Since *A Tale of a Tub* is an ironical work, an attack upon fanaticism in the style of a spirited defense of it by a fanatic contemporary writer, a glossolalic utterance on its very title page helps to 'authenticate' the genuineness of the book's fanatical 'defense' of sectarian behavior, biblical exegesis, sexual mores, and millennialism.[46] Had Swift somewhere heard speaking in tongues, so that he could identify Irenaeus' quotation as an example? Could he have been aware that the so-called glossolalia that often appears in collections of prophecies was a sham? My answer to the first question is uncertain. Swift could have visited a dissenting conventicle in London and observed – and heard – speaking in tongues, but there is no evidence that he ever did so. It is much more likely that he knew that Lacy's efforts to speak in tongues were false, for several of Lacy's Anglican critics made this observation. Whatever Swift's knowledge of glossolalia may have been, it is noteworthy that he should have ridiculed such an important aspect of millenarian behavior on the title page of his attack upon fanaticism.

With *A Tale of a Tub* Swift published 'A Fragment' which he entitled *A Discourse concerning the Mechanical Operation of the Spirit*, a condensed history of inspiration as the fanatic sects of Christian history have employed it. It is a study of religious enthusiasm not in its genuine strain, which is '*Prophecy* or *Inspiration*', but as the enthusiasts contrive it, through the phenomena of spiritual mechanism. Of the mechanisms that contemporary fanatics employ to simulate prophetical enthusiasm, 'the Gift of speaking several Languages' or the influence of '*cloven Tongues*' occupies Swift most; glossolalia is evidently at the root of much, if not all, false inspiration.[47] This quality of enthusiastic religion is intimately associated, in the early eighteenth century, with millenarianism. While Swift does not speak of those who waited for or sought the apocalypse as such, the few leaders of sects whom he does mention are well known as millenarians. The 'Visionary or Enthusiastick Preachers' whom *The Mechanical Operation* attacks, with their numerous women disciples and their overtly sexual devotions, again bear resemblance to well known characteristics of contemporary millennialists.[48] The picture that Swift paints of fanatic social and sexual practices may remind us of the signs of the times – idolatry, fornication, corruption, and the like – that perfectly sincere commentators on Revelation and the Millennium urged their audiences to attend to. The behavior of Swift's fanatics, furthermore, closely approximates what Michael describes to Adam in Book XII as the sort of actions that would inevitably lead to Christ's Second Coming. Swift's irony reverses the situation from what the usual millenarian would have expected. Traditionally, the millenarian enthusiast, claiming to speak as an exemplar of virtue, points to the signs of the times – corruption, disease, and so on – as evidence that the Second Coming is at hand. Swift's parodic millenarians *embody* the very sinful behavior that such people usually cite as one of the evidences of the forthcoming apocalypse. However, since his fanatics are impostors who merely work at the *trade* of inspiration, their impostures are signs of either the wickedness of false prophets or of the Millennium as a bad joke. Although the satire of Swift's two works is not directed against Lacy and the French Prophets (it predates their arrival by a year), it does take the Millennium as one of its subjects.

Swift pays special attention to certain aspects of millenarian behavior – sexual licentiousness, glossolalia, visionary experiences, madness. His gaze is almost medical, as if the fanatic were a patient in an asylum (as, no doubt, some of them were) and he were the physician writing a case history. Pope does not quite duplicate this satirical technique, but his scrutiny of millenarianism employs a similar quasi-medical gaze. Pope had written of the Millennium in a straightforward manner in *Messiah* and had hinted at the millennial perfection of England under Stuart rule in *Windsor-Forest* (1713). But the maturing of his apocalyptic vision comes in satiric form, in *The Dunciad* (1728); he repeats and enlarges this vision in his four-book version of the poem (1742). Along the way, Pope adds the extensive mock scholia of *The Dunciad Variorum* (1729). Twentieth-century readers usually see *The Dunciad* as fraught with thickets of impenetrable commentary, but its first eighteenth-century audience read it in three books, with virtually no satiric scholarly apparatus. To its first readers, *The Dunciad* must have seemed especially close to *Paradise Lost* in some of its allusions and in its vatic, prophetic style; Pope's commentary would later underscore the Miltonic echoes and allusions. The apocalypse, which ends the poem, is actually a vision that the dunce, Lewis Theobald, has in a dream; in the shades, the ghost of Elkanah Settle (the father of dunces) gives him a long view of the future from a mount of vision. So Pope's apocalypse is a Pisgah-sight or, as he puts it in his commentary, 'A scene, of which the present action of the Dunciad is but a Type or Foretaste, giving a Glimpse or *Pisgah-sight* of the promis'd Fulness of her Glory; the Accomplishment whereof will, in all probability, hereafter be the Theme of many other and greater Dunciads.'[49]

Yet *The Dunciad* is more than a parody of the Miltonic Pisgah-sight; it is an inversion, for satiric purposes, of a central element of Christian belief. The poem's many religious allusions suggest, moreover, that it is not a parody without a purpose. Since *The Dunciad*, in both the three- and four-book versions, ends with an apocalypse (or a vision of one), the matter that comes *before* this event must function for Pope as a sort of cumulative signs of the times. Hence the action of *The Dunciad*, in this context, is the evidence that, in the world of intellect, some kind of Judgment Day is close at hand. Swift's fanatics, as I said earlier, are madmen. Pope's dunces – and he presents a great many varieties of them – are madmen, too, for the permutations of millenarian behavior are almost infinite, and lunatics may be anywhere. Settle, who pretends to give Theobald a vision of the apocalypse, is a false prophet, a species of madman, and many of the characters whom his vision holds forth are clearly mad as well. Hence *The Dunciad*, in both its forms, is a comment on millenarian behavior. Pope could reasonably have expected that his audience would recognize his mock-epic millennial machinery, for comments on the Millennium were a frequent part of contemporary culture. That he satirizes millenarianism so thoroughly shows that, by the late 1720s, this kind of religious belief furnished material for attack on a broad scale. In other words, the fanatics whom Swift had attacked nearly three decades before in *A Tale of a Tub* had not in the least disappeared by the time Pope wrote. Pope compares his dunces, first Theobald and, in the four-book version of the poem, Colley Cibber with 'the Antichrist of Wit'.[50] The apocalyptic identification is deliberate; it is a frequent embellishment of Pope's poetry in the 1730s and of English political journalism throughout the earlier eighteenth century. Perhaps one of the greatest paradoxes of the Millennium in the early Enlightenment is that, as the notion of the apocalypse diminishes in immediacy for the established church, it grows in importance for minority religions and in popular literature. The millenarian queue, as I have already mentioned, is long and complicated. Most eighteenth-century literary figures end up in it at one time or another or, from alongside, behold its members with amazement or scorn.

VI

Historians and literary scholars involved with the late Renaissance and the seventeenth century have sometimes dealt with the Millennium as if it were a specialty of these chronological periods whose popularity temporarily ceased in the early eighteenth century, the age of reason and of classical revival. Christopher Hill writes on this subject: '"Fanaticism" and "enthusiasm" were the bugbears of polite and scholarly restoration society. The carefully cultivated classicism of the age of Dryden and Pope was . . . the literary form of this social reaction . . . [Royalist intellectuals] saw themselves as preserves of literary culture in a time of barbarism. They deplored excess, emphasized decorum and obedience to the rules, in all walks of life. The classical revival may thus have played its part against the dionysian freedom favored by the Ranters . . .'.[51] Hill appears to believe that neoclassicism, with its insistence upon decorum and rules, put an end to religious and political millenarianism. But I should emphasize that, in fact, millennial speculation never ebbs seriously at any time during the period of my focus in this essay.[52] The *forms* of millenarian thought do change and the output of the printing press changes, too – it increases substantially – but old bogeys like fanaticism and enthusiasm are not the only place to look for this alteration. Post-1700 writers attack fanatics and enthusiasts very severely, but so did solid citizens of the 1650s, 1660s, and 1670s like Meric Casaubon, Henry More, and Samuel Parker.

What, then, makes post-1700 millenarianism different from that of the seventeenth century? The most important new development in the field after

1700, I believe, is the growth of a perception of millenarian behavior, an understanding of the phenomenon in depth and in the contexts of religion, politics, medicine, and human behavior. One might call this development a sociology of millenarianism, in the terms of eighteenth-century study of human attitudes. Henry More had early noted that enthusiasts, especially those who prophesy of the Millennium, were affected by mental instability which threatened to cast doubt on the authenticity of their preachings. He wrote:

> There are certain advantages also that *Enthusiasts* have, which are to be taken notice of, whereby they have imposed upon many; as That they have spoken very *raisedly* and *divinely*, which most certainly has happen'd to sundry persons a little before they have grown stark mad; and that they may hit of something extraordinary is no pledge of the truth of the rest.[53]

Many others, including Samuel Parker, Swift, and the opponents of the French Prophets, would make the association of millennial prophecy and madness as a way of suggesting that those who engage in millenarian activities are untrustworthy or seek some immediate personal advantage. The leaders of millenarian sects, as Kenelm Burridge points out, may vary considerably, but the prophet will always be suspect, whether this person is a half-crazed woman or a dreaming boy, a clever organizer, a visionary who falls into trances, or a saintly man misled by his own piety.[54]

The people who most doubt the sanity and authenticity of self-declared prophets are members of polite society or subscribers to Dryden and Pope's 'carefully cultivated classicism' (to use Christopher Hill's phrase). The doubters are the orthodox Anglican clergy, laymen with a sceptical or scientific turn of mind, or medical practitioners who recognized the similarities between millenarian behavior and what they understood to be mental illness. At the height of the French Prophets' popularity, for example, the physician Thomas Fallowes wrote, in *The Best Method for the Cure of Lunaticks*, of the treatment of those suffering from religious mania:

> But the ordinary Fore-runners of this Malady are, *violent Fears*, a *Tremor* and *Shaking* of the *Nerves*, a new *Turn of the Eye*, *confus'd Thoughts*, *Starts*, *and sudden Fits of speaking*, *and a declination of the Voice*, *amazing Dreams*, *deep Sighs*, *and a continu'd dread of Damnation*, which some *Religious Persons* are frequently disturb'd with, and that which at first appear'd only *Enthusiasm*, by want of proper and judicious instruction, or by the mistaken Representation of *God's Method of Grace*, grown up to be a *proper Madness*, and is the more difficult to cure, because of the habitual Indisposition of the Mind and the strong Impressions that their Principles have made upon it.[55]

Fallowes's description accords closely with contemporary accounts of millenarian behavior and, in the next few decades, other medical writers made similar identifications and comments. The actual examination of a religious fanatic for the purpose of taking a case history, of which Swift attempts a satirical analysis in *A Tale of a Tub*, does not happen until later in the eighteenth century, so the early medical writers who link millenarian inspiration with insanity are themselves speculating. This new kind of speculation does not prevent millennialists from continuing to appear but, by associating their activities with an undesirable level of mental instability, the new attitude tends to make millenarianism socially and intellectually unrespectable.

Waiting for the Millennium never ceases to preoccupy some people, as exegeses of Revelation throughout the first half of the eighteenth century show and as both religious writers stress in a variety of works. A millennial attitude becomes almost a necessary metaphor in certain kinds of books, as we may see from two authors so different as Defoe and Edward Young. In *A Journal of the Plague Year* (1722), Defoe uses a circumstantial account of the plague of 1665 as a particular sort of sign of the times. That the plague finally remitted could be no accident, but was rather a temporary reprieve from destruction. The gradual disappearance of the plague, Defoe writes, 'was evidently from the secret invisible Hand of him, that at first sent this Disease as a Judgment upon us; and let the Atheistic part of Mankind call my Saying this what they please, it is no Enthusiasm'.[56] Those with sound medical training would indeed have called Defoe's statement an 'Enthusiasm', for his narrator does use the language of apocalypse to describe an event for which there was a scientific, medical explanation. And Young, who had written a popular poetic account of the end of the world, employs millennial imagery as a basis for the argument that the modern world would surpass antiquity: '*since*, as the moral world expects its glorious Millenium [*sic*], the world intellectual may hope, by the roles of analogy, for some superior degrees of excellence to crown her later scenes'.[57] Thus millennial thought works itself into the language of intellect in such a way that, during the first half of the eighteenth century, even bystanders who have no real part in the millenarian queue become affected by the behavior of those who wait. The complete story of millennial thought in early Enlightenment England remains to be told, but from the outlines that I have given here, we can see that the millenarians of the end of the eighteenth century did not have to look far for their inspiration.

NOTES

1 The Boyle Lectures for some years do not survive; sometimes not even the lecturer's name is known. For a list of the lectures from 1692 to 1714, see Margaret C. Jacob, *The Newtonians and the English Revolution, 1689–1720* (Ithaca: Cornell Univ. Press, 1976), pp. 273–4. Many lectures appeared as separate works, while all available texts were published as *A Defence of Natural and Revealed Religion: being a Collection of*

the *Sermons preached at the Lecture founded by the Honourable Robert Boyle, Esq.; (from the year 1691 to the year 1732)*, 3 vols (London, 1739).

2 Boehme's *De signatura rerum* (Engl. trans. 1657) is a popular and influential attempt to find natural hieroglyphics of divine things – the 'signatures of things' – in the Creation.

3 See my *Typologies in England, 1650–1820* (Princeton: Princeton Univ. Press, 1982), pp. 328–68.

4 Relevant works are Ernest R. Sandeen, *The Roots of Fundamentalism: British and American Millenarianism, 1800–1930* (Chicago: Univ. of Chicago Press, 1970); Gershom S. Scholem, *Sabbatai Sevi: The Mystical Messiah*, trans. R. J. Zwi Werblowsky (Princeton: Princeton Univ. Press, 1973); and, on Islamic millenarianism, Michael Adas, *Prophets of Rebellion: Millenarian Protest Movements against the European Colonial Order* (Chapel Hill: Univ. of North Carolina Press, 1979).

5 See Barry Schwartz, *Queuing and Waiting: Studies in the Social Organization of Access and Delay* (Chicago: Univ. of Chicago Press, 1975).

6 On Coleridge's millenarianism, see *Typologies in England*, pp. 388–9.

7 The *Observations* are, in fact, the most conservative of Newton's writings on the apocalypse, strictly historical in nature, free from typological figuralism, and very careful to avoid setting a date for the Millennium.

8 *Isaac Newton, Historian* (Cambridge, Mass.: Harvard Univ. Press, 1963), pp. 3–4, and see pp. 1–8 for a discussion of the extent of Newton's unpublished works on prophecy and religion.

9 See Jacob, *The Newtonians and the English Revolution*, pp. 253–4, 257–8, and Hillel Schwartz, *The French Prophets* (Berkeley and Los Angeles: Univ. of California Press, 1980), pp. 268–9, a brief comment on Fatio's friendship with Newton.

10 See Richard S. Westfall, *Never at Rest: A Biography of Isaac Newton* (Cambridge: Cambridge Univ. Press, 1980), pp. 538–9, on this friendship and the likelihood that it was over by 1700. See also Manuel, *A Portrait of Isaac Newton* (Cambridge, Mass.: Harvard Univ. Press, 1968), pp. 361–80 for an assessment of Newton's view of prophecy.

11 *Apocalypsis Apocalypseos* (London, 1680), p. xxv.

12 *Paralipomena Prophetica* (London, 1658), pp. 166–80.

13 See Margaret C. Jacob and W. A. Lockwood, 'Political Millenarianism and Burnet's Sacred Theory', *Science Studies*, 2 (1972), 265–79, for a discussion of Burnet's millennial speculations and their effect in the late 1680s.

14 A sampling of such poems includes the following: Marshall Smith, *The Vision, or a Prospect of Death, Heav'n and Hell. With a Description of the Resurrection and the Day of Judgment* (1702); Edward Young, *The Last Day* (1713; 10 eds. in all); John Bulkeley, *The Last Day. A Poem in XII. Books* (1720); Samuel Catherall, *An Essay on the Conflagration, in blank verse* (1720); Thomas Newcomb, *The Last Judgment of Men and Angels* (1723); and Joseph Trapp, *Thoughts upon the Four Last Things* (1734).

15 See William Whiston, *A New Theory of the Earth, from its Original, to the Consummation of all Things* (London, 1696), pp. 368–78.

16 See his *Prodromos: or the Fore-Runner of the Peaceable Consideration of Christ's Peaceable Kingdom upon Earth* (London, 1674), Part i, p. 39; Part iii, pp. 32–8.

17 See *The Times of Restitution of All Things with their Neer Approach upon the Ruine of the Beast . . .* (London, 1675), pp. 74, 77. See also Michael R. Watts, *The Dissenters*. Vol. I: *From the Reformation to the French Revolution* (Oxford: Clarendon Press, 1978), pp. 129–34 ('A New Heaven and a New Earth: The Coming Millennium').

18 *The Revelation of Revelations* . . . (London, 1683), pp. 28, 129. Lead's later work, *The Ascent to the Mount of Vision* (London, 1699), also argues that the prophecies of the Old and New Testaments will soon be fulfilled.
19 *The Signs of the Times: Forerunning the Kingdom of Christ, and evidencing when it is come* (London, 1699), pp. 6–7, 9.
20 *Antichrist Stormed: or, Mystery Babylon the great Whore and great City, proved to be the present Church of Rome* (London, 1689), pp. 103–16.
21 See Jurieu, *The Accomplishment of the Scripture Prophecies or the Approaching Deliverance of the Church* (London, 1687), Part I, pp. 233–4.
22 See pp. 37–54, on the Millennium in England.
23 *The Prophetical Warnings of John Lacy, Esq.* (London, 1707), p. iii.
24 Ibid., p. 7.
25 Ibid., Part iii, p. 173.
26 *The New Pretenders to Prophecy Examin'd, and their Pretences shewn to be Groundless and False* . . . (London, 1709), pp. 363, 370–9, 421.
27 *An Essay on Inspiration* (London, 1708), p. 398.
28 Ibid., pp. 403, 409.
29 *The Spirit of Enthusiasm Exorcised: In a Sermon Preached Before the University of Oxford* . . ., 4th edn, much enlarged (London, 1709), pp. 2, 63–9.
30 *A Short View of the Pretended State of Prophecy, taken from its First Rise in the Year 1688 to its Present State among us* (London, 1708), p. 19.
31 *The General Delusion of Christians Touching the Ways of God's revealing Himself, To, and By the Prophets, Evinc'd from Scripture and Primitive Antiquity* (London, 1713), p. 366.
32 *Characters*, ed. Charles W. Daves (Cleveland: The Press of Case Western Reserve Univ., 1970), p. 81.
33 *The First Anniversary*, lines 293–8, in *Poems and Letters*, ed. H. M. Margoliouth, 3rd edn, 2 vols (Oxford: Clarendon Press, 1971), I, 116.
34 Ibid., lines 311–12, 317–18.
35 *A Poem upon the Death of O. C.*, lines 157–8; *Poems and Letters*, I, 133.
36 For an account of the speculation about the millenarian significance of the year 1666, see Michael McKeon, *Politics and Poetry in Restoration England: The Case of Dryden's 'Annus Mirabilis'* (Cambridge, Mass.: Harvard Univ. Press, 1975), pp. 190–204.
37 *Annus Mirabilis*, lines 1169–72 (Stanza 293). Dryden adds a note identifying the *'Town'* of the *'Indies'* as *'Mexico'*, itself a contemporary paradise of wealth.
38 *Absalom and Achitophel*, lines 1028–31.
39 'To Her Grace the Dutchess of *Ormond*', lines 80–5.
40 For a concise treatment of Milton's millennial eschatology, see C. A. Patrides, *Milton and the Christian Tradition* (Oxford: Clarendon Press, 1966), pp. 272–8.
41 See Christopher Hill, *Milton and the English Revolution* (Harmondsworth: Penguin Books, 1978), p. 384. Hill does not mention the millenarianism of this passage.
42 Ed. Roger Sharrock and James F. Forrest (Oxford: Clarendon Press, 1980), p. xxxi.
43 Ibid., p. 7.
44 Ibid., p. 247 (italics reversed).
45 On the early heretics' use of glossolalia, and on Eusebius' awareness of it, see Anthony A. Hoekema, *What About Tongue-Speaking?* (London: Paternoster Press, 1966), p. 11, and John P. Kildahl, *The Psychology of Speaking in Tongues* (London: Hodder and Stoughton, 1972), pp. 11, 14, 16, 17.

46 Swift's adversary William Wotton, in *Observations upon The Tale of a Tub* (1705), insisted that the epigraph from Irenaeus was in Syriac. In fact, more recent commentators can find no language that it fits. See *A Tale of a Tub*, ed. A. C. Guthkelch and D. Nichol Smith, 2nd edn (Oxford: Clarendon Press, 1958), pp. 323, 353.
47 *The Mechanical Operation*, in *A Tale of a Tub*, pp. 270, 275.
48 Ibid., p. 288; cf. pp. 285–7.
49 'Argument' to *The Dunciad in Four Books* in *Poems of Alexander Pope*, ed. John Butt et al., 11 vols in 12 (London: Methuen and Co., 1939–69), V, 56.
50 *The Dunciad*, A–II.12; B–II.16; see *Poems*, V, 97, 297.
51 *The World Turned Upside Down: Radical Ideas during the English Revolution* (London: Temple Smith, 1972), p. 287.
52 Watts, *The Dissenters*, pp. 129–34, shows that millenarianism was popular among the sectarians throughout the late seventeenth and eighteenth centuries.
53 *Enthusiasmus Triumphatus; or, A Brief Discourse of the Nature, Causes, Kinds, and Cure of Enthusiasm* (1656), in *A Collection of Several Philosophical Writings of Dr. Henry More* . . . (London, 1712), p. 39; cf. p. 21.
54 *New Heaven, New Earth: A Study of Millenarian Activities* (Oxford: Basil Blackwell, 1969), p. 12. On the mental equipment of the millenarian prophet, see pp. 105–16, 119.
55 *The Best Method for the Cure of Lunaticks* (London, 1705), pp. 8–9.
56 *A Journal of the Plague Year*, ed. Louis Landa (London: Oxford Univ. Press, 1969), pp. 246–7.
57 *Conjectures on Original Composition in a Letter to the Author of Sir Charles Grandison* (London, 1759), p. 73.

STEPHEN J. STEIN

10 Transatlantic extensions: apocalyptic in early New England

In the first book of his ecclesiastical history of New England, Cotton Mather (1663–1728), minister of the Second Church in Boston, objected to the judgment of the learned Cambridge don, Joseph Mede (1586–1638), concerning the role of America in the millennial age. Mede had suggested in his commentary on the Book of Revelation that perhaps the New World would be the location from which the forces of Gog and Magog would arise in assault upon the saints at the end of the thousand-year reign.[1] On the contrary, exclaimed Mather, New England, is 'the Spot of *Earth*, which the God of Heaven *Spied out*' as the center of that future kingdom. Mather believed that the efforts of his Puritan predecessors in the new land, '*feeble*' though they were because of 'the unavoidable *Vanity* of *Humane Affairs*, and *Influence* of *Satan* upon them', anticipated the prophetic New Jerusalem which would someday embrace the '*American Hemisphere*' and find its center and fulfilment there.[2] His confidence rested upon a conviction shared with others that biblical prophecy held the key to such matters. Like counterparts and contemporaries in Old England, Mather and others in New England sought ways to appropriate the visions of the Apocalypse, believing it their responsibility to discover the full meaning – historical, contemporary, and prospective – of the scriptural texts. In pursuit of that goal, New Englanders during the seventeenth and eighteenth centuries manifested a distinctive but changing apocalyptic sense of self, of place, and of time.

It is fitting that attention be given to the transatlantic dimensions of the apocalyptic tradition in English Renaissance thought and literature. During the seventeenth and eighteenth centuries the residents of New England imported elements of the English apocalyptic tradition, transplanting and in some cases transforming them. They added their own interpretations, thereby extending the body of apocalyptic materials. Cotton Mather stands at the center of two centuries of continuing attention to these matters in New

England, building on the work of those who preceded him and influencing the views of others who followed. These two centuries of creative reflection on the Apocalypse are the subject of this essay.

I 'UPON THE WING, FOR A WILDERNESS IN AMERICA'

> Your griefs I pity much, but should do wrong,
> To weep for that we both here pray'd for long,
> To see these latter dayes of hop'd for good,
> That Right may have its right, though 't be with blood;
> After dark Popery the day did clear,
> But now the Sun in's brightnesse shall appear,
> Blest be the Nobles of thy Noble Land,
> With (ventur'd lives) for Truths defence that stand.[3] (Anne Bradstreet)

The abundance of fervent eschatological activity in England during the 1620s and 1630s formed the context for the planting of the colonies in New England. For the settlers of the first generation and others like-minded who stayed behind, the journey across the sea was a significant event in the divine economy. John Winthrop (1588–1648), Governor of Massachusetts Bay, reminded his company, 'Thus stands the cause betweene God and us. We are entered into Covenant with Him for this worke.' Accordingly, 'wee must consider that wee shall be as a citty upon a hill. The eies of all people are uppon us'.[4] The Puritan divines of the first generation regarded their collective undertaking as 'a sign of the approach of the millennium'. This perspective developed into a 'relentless pressure driving some men to New England'.[5] Richard Mather (1596–1669), minister at Dorchester in the New World, spoke of Old England as a place where 'many signs of fearful Desolation' abounded – one of the arguments he marshalled in favor of the 'lawful, but also necessary' move to Massachusetts.[6] Providential deliverance from near shipwreck on the voyage in 1635 persuaded him that the exodus from England was under divine direction and further strengthened his commitment to the endeavor. Flight was a practical response to the apparent success of the antichristian forces of Archbishop Laud (1573–1645) which Mather knew firsthand having been dismissed on two occasions from his pulpit at Toxteth Park for, among other things, failure to wear the surplice.[7] Mather and others fled from the site of the 'beast' to preserve themselves and the truth from impending destruction.

The controversy over ceremonies in the Church of England extended beyond the surplice, kneeling, and the sign of the cross. The struggle over particular liturgical practices had a bearing upon the general understanding of scripture, the nature of Christian worship, the character of ecclesiastical authority, and the question of the unity of a national church. Thomas Hooker (1586–1647), who became the minister at Hartford, recognized this complexity when he wrote a preface to the *Fresh Suit Against Ceremonies* by the English Puritan William Ames (1576–1633). Hooker attacked Anglican ceremonies because they demanded submission to human authority in matters of religion. In this manner 'the determinations and commands of men' detracted from the sovereignty of Christ. Human invention was a mark of false religion identified with the beast or the Roman Catholic Church and its antichristian allies. 'It is the Romish tenet to a hair and one of the most fulsome points and loathsome dregs of the filth of popery', he contended. Hooker wrote his preface in Rotterdam and probably left it unsigned in order not to jeopardize his own safe passage to New England.[8] 'Wherefore, about this time', noted Cotton Mather, 'understanding that many of his friends in *Essex*, were upon the *Wing*, for a *Wilderness* in *America*; where they hoped for an opportunity to enjoy and practise the *Pure Worship* of the Lord Jesus Christ, in Churches gathered according to his Direction, he readily answered their Invitation to accompany them in this Undertaking.'[9]

Hooker and other of the first generation viewed the anti-Puritan party in England as minions of the Antichrist. They interpreted the ecclesiastical struggle in apocalyptic categories, carrying with them to New England an intense hatred of their opponents which was the product of decades of religious conflict. The unrelenting pressure of the bishops upon non-conforming Puritans forced the removal of many to New England. John Wilson (1588–1667), the minister of the First Church in Boston, suffered at the hands of the Anglicans. As a result of his experience, he divided the religious world into opposing forces of good and evil. Once when a parishioner 'who had been absent for some while' among Roman Catholics returned home and presented himself for communion, Wilson admonished him for his relationship 'with the Papists, whose Religion is Antichristian'. Only if he repented properly, warned the minister, could he take part in the ordinance without damnation, which the man did, 'professing his Innocency'. Mather's record of the incident concludes on an ironical note: 'But as if the *Devil had entered into him*, he [i.e. the man] soon went and *hanged* himself' – a fitting end in the eyes of those who viewed the Catholic Church as an engine of evil, the beast of the Apocalypse.[10]

The first New Englanders drew upon the apocalyptic sections of the Bible for their conception of the future. John Davenport (1597–1670), another leading Puritan of the first generation, also came to America as a result of pressures upon the Nonconformists. Davenport, an advocate of strict orthodoxy and a leader in the New Haven colony, first tried the religious climate of Holland as an alternative to England. That proved unacceptable to him, however, because of the liberal practice of administering baptisms to the children of parents who were not church members. In Holland Davenport received word from those already in New England that conditions in the churches and in the commonwealth were so favorable that, according to the *Magnalia*, 'it brought into his Mind the New Heaven, and the New Earth, where in dwells Righteousness'. This apocalyptic vision, according to Mather, became the most distinctive feature of Davenport's life and work. In both Old and New England Davenport preached and wrote 'about the *future state*, and *coming* of the Lord, the *calling* of the Jews, and the first and second *Resurrection* of the dead'. On the basis of his continuing studies of the Scripture he was convinced of a *'Personal, Visible, Powerful, and Glorious Coming of the* Lord Jesus Christ *unto* Judgment, *long before the End of the World*.'[11] Thus for him flight from adversity in England accompanied the hope for a more glorious future.

Among the leaders of the first generation in New England none was more prominently associated with eschatological issues than John Cotton (1584–1652). Cotton gained his reputation as a leading divine in part on the strength of his sermons dealing with these matters. His publications became standard commentaries on apocalyptic texts. His correspondence was filled with observations on the visions. Cotton's interest in apocalyptic began during the years of his ministry at St. Botolph's in Old England. There he preached the sermons that comprised his commentary on the Song of Solomon, an exposition influenced by the work of the English commentator, Thomas Brightman (1562–1607). Cotton did not set aside his interests after arriving in America in 1633. Late in the 1630s he preached a series of sermons on the thirteenth chapter of the Book of Revelation and within the space of a few more years on the topics of the vials (Rev. 16) and the millennial promises (Rev. 20). Although his sermons did not appear in print until later, they are an indication of Cotton's heavy investment in apocalyptic and a measure of the views of 'the acknowledged leader in the acknowledged leading class' of the first generation, one called by his grandson and namesake 'the Father and Glory of *Boston*'.[12]

Mather declared that John Cotton's *'Textual Divinity'* was his most extraordinary accomplishment as a theologian. 'His Abilities to Expound the *Scriptures*, caused him to be Admired by the Ablest of his *Hearers.*'[13] Cotton's sermons on the Apocalypse mirrored a rising optimism within Puritanism during the years 1639–41. He believed that the seven-headed beast (Rev. 13), which he identified with the Catholic Church, was being destroyed by the successes of Protestantism. With the eventual fall of the papacy and the rise of an evangelical ministry, Cotton expected the bondage of Satan for a thousand years. He calculated that the 1260 years of the reign of the beast (Rev. 13.5) would end in 1655.[14] Therefore the years of his own life, according to him, constituted a crucial period of anticipation for the saints.

Cotton's apocalyptic exegesis intersected with his other theological interests. He was certain that the fifth vial (Rev. 16) was being poured out upon 'the whole machinery of authoritarian episcopalian rule'; the sixth vial, in turn, was designed to destroy papal revenues and thus temporal support for Catholicism. These apocalyptic changes, Cotton reckoned, would be accompanied by the conversion of the Jews, an event he identified with the 'first resurrection', and by the destruction of the enemies of Christ in the battle of Armageddon. The contemporary struggles in England and elsewhere were a time of preparation. Although the millennium had not yet arrived, nevertheless, a new light was dawning in New England where the pure gospel was being preached and the true church order was now established. The people of New England were to take full advantage of the times lest through some fault of theirs the reign of the saints fail to materialize.[15]

Cotton's apocalyptic reflections underscored his view of the importance of the times and the fact that the millennium was to be the product of human activity under the guidance of God's spirit. Cotton did not expect the future age to be inaugurated by the physical descent of Christ from heaven. Rather, he looked for the increasing success of the gospel and for the triumph of true over false religion. Christ would return at the end of the glorious age, at the time of the 'second resurrection', to judge the world. In some measure, according to Cotton, New Englanders bore responsibility for the success of God's plan. For example, he agreed with John Winthrop who said that 'if wee shall deale falsely with our God in this worke wee have undertaken, and soe cause him to withdrawe his present help from us, wee shall be made a story and a by-word through the world'.[16] Cotton never wavered in his conviction about the end times nor in his interest in these affairs. In 1651, for example, he preached a sermon on a day of public thanksgiving occasioned by the execution of Charles I. Taking Revelation 15.3 as his text, Cotton justified the regicide, speaking also with confidence about the future millennium.[17] In a letter to Oliver Cromwell (1599–1658) during the same year, he placed the tumultuous events in England into a prophetic context, defending the military actions of the Lord General and speaking of Cromwell and his army as 'chosen and faithfull, Rev. 17. 14'.[18]

In 1653 Edward Johnson (1598–1672) proclaimed the pride that New England felt in Cotton's accomplishments as an apocalyptic commentator: 'Johns Revelation hath/By thee been open'd, as nere was of old.'[19] Not all of Cotton's contemporaries, however, were so positive about his interpretation of the visions. One strident voice of protest belonged to Roger Williams (1603–83), the dissenter who came to New England in 1631 seeking refuge from the evils of England but who found the Puritans in the New World insufficiently pure. He called for total separation from the Church of Rome and from the Church of England because both had forsaken 'apostolic doctrine and discipline'. According to Williams, the desolation of the Antichrist through the ages had destroyed all true religion, even though from time to time small bands of Christians had witnessed against the beast. These faithful few suffered persecution at the hands of established religious and civil authorities – an experience repeated in his own life. Williams believed that only when the authentic church was restored with a repristinated form of 'the doctrine, discipline, and spiritual authority of ancient, apostolic Christianity' would the millennial reign begin and history be carried to its glorious completion. This 'primitivism' contrasted sharply with the views of most ministers in New England.[20]

William's dissent was intertwined in other ways with his views on the Apocalypse. In the seventeenth century it was common for many in both Old and New England to consider the American Indians within the framework of apocalyptic speculation. The spread of the gospel in the latter days was expected to include the Christianization of the natives. These conversions were to signal the approach of the end times. Promotional literature and sermons alike celebrated this interpretation of the conversion of the Indians, thereby encouraging efforts at evangelization.[21] Williams took issue with this line of reasoning and argued against exploitation of the natives. He contended that the churches had become so tainted by antichristian influences that they no longer had authority to convert the Indians, or any one else for that matter. He also attacked the authority of the king to grant title to lands that belonged, in his view, to the natives of America. Williams advocated, by contrast, respect for the cultural, economic, and religious integrity of the Indians.[22]

Many in early New England shared a conviction that the natives in America were the ten lost tribes of Israel, a view that intensified speculation concerning the relationship between their conversion and the beginning of the millennium. One Puritan divine in New England who made his own contribution to the cause of Christianizing the natives was John Eliot (1604–90) of Roxbury, Massachusetts, the leading missionary among the Indians during the first generation. Cotton Mather described Eliot as the hero who '*fought the* Devil in (once) his American *Territories, till he had recovered no small Party of his old Subjects and Vassals* out of his cruel Hands'.[23] Eliot believed that in the future kingdom the principles of scriptural government would rule all things. In his tract on civil order which appeared near mid-century in England written in part as a possible solution to the political chaos at the time, he affirmed, 'The prayers, the expectation, and faith of the Saints, in the Prophecies and Promises of holy Scripture, are daily sounding in the ears of the Lord, for the downfall of Antichrist, and with him all humane Powers, Polities, Dominions, and Governments; and in the room thereof, we wait for the coming of the Kingdom of the Lord Jesus' when all things will be 'done by the direction of the word of his mouth'. Eliot thought that his communities of 'praying Indians' might become models of civil and religious order for the millennial age and for Old England. In his judgment, certain qualities of the Indians – their innocence and lack of sophistication – made them ideal subjects for Christ's kingdom.[24]

The apocalyptic interests of the early settlers also found expression in the works of Anne Bradstreet (1612–72), America's first female poet, who regarded the Old World as the location for the events of the latter days. She was confident that the scenes prophesied in scriptures were 'soon to be revealed in

European history'.[25] Bradstreet addressed England as 'deare Mother, fairest Queen and best,/ With honour, wealth, and peace, happy and blest'. Yet from England the Puritans had fled because of conflict and adversity, religious strife and civil injustice. They sought sanctuary wherever it could be found, in Holland or in America. Nevertheless, those who left did not sever their bonds totally, for both their interests and their affections remained attached to the mother country. But the Puritans demanded reform in England. Bradstreet exclaimed, 'These are the dayes, the Churches foes to crush,/ To root out Prelates, head, tail, branch, and rush./ Let's bring *Baals* vestments out, to make a fire,/ Their Myters, Surplices, and all their tire,/ Copes, Rotchets, Crossiers, and such trash.' The Puritans hated '*Romes* Whore, with all her trumperie'. In civil affairs they demanded the restoration of justice. 'Then bribes shall cease,' Bradstreet wrote, 'and Suits shall not stick long/. . . . Then High Commissions shall fall to decay'. The 'happy Nation' would flourish again and its armies put to flight 'proud *Rome*, and all her vassalls' and Turkey, the seat of Gog. The redemption of '*Abrahams* seed' will follow. 'Then fulness of the Nations in shall flow,/ And Jew and Gentile, to one worship go,/ Then follows dayes of happiness and rest,/ Whose lot doth fall to live therein is blest.'[26] The experiences of the first generation in New England shaped their perspective upon the Apocalypse.

II 'INTO FRUITFULL FIELDS AND GARDENS'

> Ah dear New England! dearest land to me;
> Which unto God hast hitherto been dear,
> And mayest be still more dear than formerlie,
> If to his voice thou wilt incline thine ear.
>
> Consider wel & wisely what the rod,
> Wherewith thou art from yeer to yeer chastized,
> Instructeth thee. Repent, & turn to God,
> Who wil not have his nurture be despized.[27] (Michael Wigglesworth)

The passing of the first generation in New England was marked by the deaths of several notable leaders: Hooker in 1647, Winthrop in 1649, and Cotton in 1652. These deaths not only signaled a change of leadership, but also the beginning of a period of heightened self-consciousness and sense of responsibility. By 1650 the situation in New England was very different from that of the first generation. No longer was survival the preoccupation, for a measure of prosperity appeared within grasp of the colonists. Growing pains became evident throughout society. In these circumstances, the second and third generations 'formulated the idea of the mission of New England'.[28]

Grafting onto the apocalyptic vision of their fathers, they cultivated an increasingly unique sense of self which was highly particularistic in time and place.

Samuel Danforth (1626–74) sounded the dominant themes of this new perspective in his sermon before the General Assembly of the Bay colony in 1670. Danforth, who settled as the colleague of John Eliot at Roxbury, was 'a Notable *Text-Man*', a preacher known for his biblical learning.[29] Using scriptural cues, he intoned a harsh judgment upon New England because it had lost sight of the reason for its establishment, namely, enjoyment of 'the free and clear dispensation of the Gospel and Kingdome of God'. He called on the leaders and others to examine themselves and to renew their commitment to the 'Errand into the Wilderness'. According to Danforth, the indictment against the region was especially damning because New England had been distinguished from 'other Colonies and Plantations in *America*' by the presence of the ministry of God's faithful prophets and pure ordinances. In 1670 there were abundant signs that God was displeased with the region, warned Danforth. Therefore it is time to '*remember whence we are fallen, and repent, and do our first works*' [Rev. 2.5].[30]

The jeremiad, of which Danforth's sermon was a notable example, became the characteristic expression of New England's developing sense of mission. This genre fused secular and sacred history, combining the woeful cries of the lamenter with the forward glances of the visionary. The apocalyptic mode was especially congenial to the preacher of the jeremiad who indicted his audience for their sins and then called them to repentance. The hermeneutical key to this genre was the Puritan disposition toward typology – an interpretive device that allows the exegete to connect the present with either the past or the future through the prism of scripture. Type and antitype state and restate similar themes.[31] Nicholas Noyes (1647–1717) of Salem affirmed this principle in 1698 when he declared, '*Prophesie* is *History antedated*; and *History* is *Post-dated Prophesie*: the same thing is told in both.'[32] He and other divines literally created the myth of the golden age of New England's founders, looking back upon the accomplishments of the first generation. In the words of John Higginson (1616–1708), the plan of God for New England 'would dazle the eyes of Angels, daunt the hearts of devils, ravish and chain fast the Affections of all the Saints'.[33] These same divines looked to the future, toward the prospect of a more glorious age anticipated by the successes of the founding generation. History and Prophecy thus constituted a continuum, the past, present, and future forming a single whole. With the passage of years, this view of New England became the standard orthodoxy.

One Puritan who contributed to the Americanization of the apocalyptic tradition was Increase Mather (1639–1723), minister of the Second Church in Boston. Shaped inexorably by the circumstances of his time, Mather took part in the public affairs of New England at nearly every stage of his career. He was a powerful preacher who lived with the burden of being one of the sons of the founders. The 'central value in Mather's universe' was loyalty to the founding generation.[34] Accordingly, he searched for an understanding of the place of New England in history.

Increase Mather was a master of the jeremiad, as is evident in his response to King Philip's War, a struggle between the colonists and Indians in 1675–6. He regarded the conflict as a righteous punishment meted out by God because the sins of the second generation were 'ripe' for judgment.[35] Among the specific charges Mather lodged against the people were violations of the '*Patterns of Sobriety*', wigs and false locks, '*Ill entertainment*' of the ministers of the land, formalism in religion, sabbath-breaking, and forms of economic exploitation. According to Mather, God was using the scourge of the natives who fought to dispossess them of the land – whom he equated with the apocalyptic 'red horse' (Rev. 6.4) – to bring New England to repentance. He urged his readers to 'receive instruction' from '*the divine Dispensations*'. '*If we be indeed bettered thereby*', he warned, '*we are like to see happy dayes again in* New-England, *but if otherwise*, New-England hath not yet seen its worst dayes'. Mather called for New Englanders to renew the covenant made by the founders, persuaded that renewal would advance 'the Kingdome of the Lord Jesus amongst the *Heathen*'. For Mather these glorious things were 'not far off'. 'The Lord hath a great Interest in this Land', he affirmed, which is a type of the New Jerusalem. His prayer was that God would redeem New England from all troubles.[36]

Late in life, his hopes for an earthly millennium chastened, Increase Mather became preoccupied with the day of judgment and the shortness of the time remaining for those out of grace. In 1702 in a sermon entitled *Ichabod* he sounded the note that the glory of God had departed from New England.[37] During the years that followed he often spoke of Christ as the righteous judge who sentenced those who failed to fulfil their covenant obligations. Mather did not hesitate to use sustained terror to bring sinners to repentance. He described in detail the literal return of Christ to earth and the anguish which would accompany that event. Mather also changed his view on the conversion of the Jews. In 1666 he had denied that it was under way. By 1710, however, he reversed his position and pointed to abundant signs that the world was drawing to a close and that the national conversion of the Jews had begun. Several hundred Jews in Hamburg provided evidence, and he expected a 'greater harvest' to follow 'shortly'. In this change Mather joined his contemporary Samuel Willard (1640–1707), minister of the Third Church in Boston, who had earlier pointed to the contemporary gathering of the Jews.[38]

Another contemporary equally concerned with the day of judgment was Michael Wigglesworth (1631–1705) of Malden, Massachusetts, author of a poetic description of the judgment. In his depiction of the final separation of the sheep and the goats, Wigglesworth included among the latter 'Scoffers at Purity', 'Sabbath-polluters, Saints persecuters', and those who use 'vile wayes themselves to raise/ t'Estates and worldly wealth'. Although they will beg for mercy, the judge will pronounce the sentence: '*Ye sinfull wights, and cursed sprights,/ that work Iniquity,/ Depart together from me for ever/ to endless Misery;/ Your portion take in yonder Lake,/ where Fire and Brimstone flameth:/ Suffer the smart, which your desert/ as it's due wages claimeth*'. The scene might have been different, according to Wigglesworth, if the damned had given credit to their 'faithful Preachers'. The saints, by contrast, ascend to heaven where they sing 'a Song of endless Praise' and enjoy the happiness and the delights of God's grace. The poem closed on a vision of their beatific state: 'Made *Kings* and *Princes* to *God* through *Christs*/ dear loves transcendency,/ There to remain, and there to raign/ with him *Eternally*.' Wigglesworth did not delight in terror for its own ends. Rather, he wrote, 'Awake, awake, O Sinner, and repent,/ And quarrel not, because I thus alarm/ Thy Soul, to save it from eternal harm.'[39]

The writing of history was another means whereby New Englanders interpreted their collective undertaking and buttressed their myth of origins. In 1653 Edward Johnson published the 'first general history of New England' in response to sustained attacks upon the colonies, defending the mission of the region as the cause of God.[40] According to him, Christ created New England in order 'to muster up the first of his Forces' to free 'his people from their long servitude under usurping Prelacy'. The colonial settlements were to be instrumental in the reformation of the world and of Old England in particular where the gospel had not reached fulfillment. Even more, wrote Johnson, New England was 'the place where the Lord will create a new Heaven, and a new Earth in, new Churches, and a new Common-wealth together'. The remarkable acts of God on behalf of the colonies and the churches in the land have turned the wilderness into 'fruitfull Fields and Gardens'. In the future the inhabitants of New England must 'be strong and of a good courage', Johnson wrote, the 'Souldiers of Christ', dedicated to congregational principles and prepared to fight for the gospel as it spreads in triumph over the face of the earth from East to West. The 'blessed dayes' of the millennial age will begin when Christ's 'powerfull Presence' fills the churches and the governments.[41]

The use of biblical commentary was an additional way of expressing the heightened sense of purpose felt in New England. The most prominent commentator on the Apocalypse during the period was Samuel Sewall (1652–1730), a magistrate and man of public affairs. He had been occupied with apocalyptic for years before he published his commentary in 1697. As early as 1684 he had written to Cotton Mather concerning the reasons why 'the Heart of America' might be 'the seat of the New-Jerusalem'.[42] He was persuaded that the 'drying up' of the River Euphrates (Rev. 16.12) referred to the destruction of the Spanish Empire in the Americas. In opposition to Mede, Sewall contended that America would probably be 'the Seat of the Divine Metropolis' and 'a *Coparcener*' with the other three quarters of the world – Asia, Africa, and Europe – in the work of God's grace. In the New World, he wrote, '*in these latter Ages*, GOD *hath begun in a Terrible and Wonderful Way, to form a People for Himself, that they may shew forth his Praise*'. He regarded the first colonists in New England as the 'Forerunners' of the apocalyptic kings of the East, a prophetic indication that God's favor was about to shine '*upon this despised Hemisphere*'.[43] Sewall corresponded with Edward Taylor (1642–1729) of Westfield, Massachusetts, Nicholas Noyes (1647–1717) of Salem, and others about these issues. Although they did not always agree, Sewall did not falter in his conviction. In 1713 he depicted Christ as having one foot on the Old World and another – the right – on the New. The Old World had lost its opportunity, he believed, and now the instrumental role in God's plan had passed to America.[44]

In Cotton Mather the diverse apocalyptic interests of the second and third generations found their fullest expression. Scion of a leading family, heir apparent to a position of influence in both ecclesiastical and civil affairs, Mather seemed positioned for a successful career as a spokesman for the New England way. In point of fact, he never lived up to these expectations. Mather came on the scene at a time when the pace of change in the colonial setting was accelerating. Caught between two centuries, he made a last desperate effort to bolster an ailing theological system and at the same time took the first and sometimes bold steps towards the future. His contemporaries were not ready to follow him in either direction. He had a consuming passion for apocalyptic.[45] The most prolific writer in early America, Mather displayed his apocalyptic preoccupation in his varied productions as diarist, preacher, commentator, speculative thinker, and historian.

The private side of Cotton Mather has attracted fresh attention. Personal reflections recorded in his diary and in his correspondence reveal the centrality of apocalyptic in his life. In 1697, for example, he noted 'Apprehensions' that the kingdom of God was '*at Hand*'. Accordingly, he set aside a private fast day on which he pleaded to God for a 'cure' to the '*Distempers*' that rendered him 'unfit' for the kingdom. On that occasion he spoke of the 'bereaved Condition of some Churches' in the American 'Wilderness' and of the general danger posed by the prospect of a French invasion. As he laid 'prostrate' on the 'Floor, in the Dust, before the Lord', he resolved to spend time 'in Supplications' for 'the Captivity of the Church to bee hastned unto its Period'. He also determined to gather like-minded persons for regular sessions dealing with his 'Researches' into apocalyptic matters.[46] As the years passed Mather became even more persuaded 'that God had given him extraordinary knowledge of the coming Kingdom'. He often spoke of an expectation that 'the Prophetic Spirit' of the primitive Christian church would be revived and that he had been chosen as its special recipient. In 1719 he wrote of the return of that spirit 'unto us'. In 1724 he offered the judgment that the 'Lord has led me into fuller Views than I have ever yett had, and such as I have exceedingly longed for and asked for, of what shall be the true State of Things in His Kingdome'.[47]

As a preacher of jeremiads, Mather had few who were his peer. *Theopolis Americana*, a sermon preached to the elected officials in 1709, is typical. Mather dedicated the published version to Samuel Sewall who, he said, first gave '*Some of the* Hints' developed in it concerning the city with streets of 'pure gold' (Rev. 21.21). Mather believed that the vials were about to be poured on the antichristian world and that the building of the New Jerusalem would follow subsequently. The golden streets were an indication that righteousness will prevail in that city. According to Mather, the '*Golden* Rule' will govern all activity in the marketplace of the New Jerusalem whereas in New England there was an abundance of cheating through short measures on tea, salt, cheese, wood, and hay as well as robbery of the public treasury by deception and false report. In like manner, there will be no room for drunkenness in the holy city whereas the 'Bottel' – a sin he associated with Catholics – exercised widespread dominion in New England. Nevertheless, Mather was confident of 'Better Things to be yet Seen in the American World'. 'Be Awakened, O ye CHURCHES of the LORD', he exhorted, for then this land will be called the 'city of righteousness'. He wrote, 'There are many Arguments to perswade us, That our Glorious LORD, will have an Holy City in AMERICA; a *City*, the Street whereof will be *Pure* Gold'. America, he suggested, was 'Legible' in the prophecies of the Apocalypse as 'Fertile' ground for the work of regeneration. When the New World is filled with the knowledge of the Lord, he opined, then Babylon will fall.[48]

As a biblical commentator, Mather has yet to be fully revealed. Although his works are replete with biblical citations, proof texts, and explanations of particular passages, his self-acknowledged *magnum opus* in the field remains unpublished. The 'Biblia Americana' was the product of many years of study and the object of even more years of frustration as he searched unsuccessfully for a publisher for the 'close and thick amassment' of 'treasures' contained in his translation and commentary on the Bible. The 'Biblia Americana', a sourcebook filled with evidence of his wide reading, comprises six folios running to several thousand pages of manuscript. By 1713 he was at work on the section dealing with the Book of Revelation, a disproportionately long portion documenting his conviction about the importance of apocalyptic.[49] Years earlier in a sermon to an artillery company, Mather had underscored the advantages for those who 'count the numbers'. 'I confess,' he wrote, '*Apocalyptical Studies*, are fittest for those Raised Souls, whose *Heart-strings* are made of a Little *Ficer* Clay, than other mens; and it is to them especially, that I take leave to say, There is a World of *Sweetness* in Diligent and Regular Studies upon the *Kingdom* of our Lord Jesus'. Mather even thought that the study of the prophecies might assist in the fulfilment of those prophecies, an attitude which helps to explain his heavy investment in the Apocalypse.[50]

Mather's apocalyptic interests often led in speculative directions. He believed, for example, that he was living on the edge of history, that the promised millennial age was about to begin – a lifelong view he expressed once more shortly before his death when he wrote, 'Certainly, The *Kingdom of* GOD *is at hand.*'[51] Mather based his conviction on a reading of the contemporary situation. He viewed the 'Disadvantage' being given to the '*Antichristian Interest*' in the Roman Catholic Church and the Catholic nations as evidence that the apocalyptic timetable was speeding towards its conclusion. Mather regarded the missionary successes among the Indians and the rise of a pietistic movement in Europe as encouraging. He pointed to the growth of reformation societies in America and elsewhere – especially in Boston – as an indication that the reign of the Spirit was beginning.[52] As piety and experimental religion spread, Mather's boldness in apocalyptic speculation grew. At one time he looked for the end of the world in 1697. Later he became persuaded by the calculations of the Englishman William Whiston (1667–1752) that the end might come in 1716. That year became a moment of high excitement for him. He spoke with confidence that the 'hideous Wilderness' would be turned into 'a most Pleasant PARADISE'. In this same vein he wrote, 'The MAXIMS of the *Everlasting Gospel*, are the *Plough-shares* and *Pruning-hooks*, to be employ'd for the Cultivation, of the *New Earth* wherein *shall dwell Righteousness*; and we shall see a Restored PARADISE. *Come, Let us Walk in this Light of God!*' With this vision in mind, he affirmed: 'The *Great Trumpet* is now to be Blown.'[53] No matter what the year, Mather was confident that the end was near.

Mather's apocalyptic vision reached its most comprehensive expression in the *Magnalia Christi Americana*, an ecclesiastical history of New England. In the introduction he announced, 'I WRITE the *Wonders* of the CHRISTIAN RELIGION, flying from the Depravations of *Europe*, to the *American Strand*: And, assisted by the Holy Author of that *Religion*, I do, with all Conscience of *Truth*, required therein by Him, who is the *Truth* it self, Report the *Wonderful Displays* of His Infinite Power, Wisdom, Goodness, and Faithfulness, wherewith His Divine Providence hath *Irradiated* an *Indian Wilderness*'. The *Magnalia* was not written merely for provincial readers but for the edification of the '*whole World*'.[54] Called by one critic 'a gigantic pietistic tribute to the founding generation' and by another 'the epitome of the seventeenth-century jeremiad', it both glorified the first settlers and indicated those that followed in its celebration of 'The Great Acts of Christ in America'. Mather wrote, 'The poor Church History of New England was written with no design so much as to serve all interests of real and vital piety, for which it lays hold on all occasions'.[55] In it he fused sacred and secular history so that the history of New England became an important part of the account of redemption. Mather's objective was to demonstrate that New England, like ancient Israel, had enjoyed 'continuous providential guidance' but now was in danger of losing that special position if the sense of mission held by the founders was not recovered. Mather was not a disinterested spectator. In the closing pages of the *Magnalia* he pleaded, 'BUT, Oh, my Dear NEW-ENGLAND, give one of thy

Friends leave to utter the *Fears* of thy best Friends concerning thee; and consider what fearful Cause there may be for thee to expect sad THINGS TO COME? If every *Wise Man* be a *Prophet*, there are some yet in thee that can *Prophesie*.'[56] The *Magnalia* was a foundation document in the prophetic tradition which continued in New England throughout the eighteenth century.

III 'FROM ONE END OF THE EARTH UNTO THE OTHER'

> The SPIRIT takes Delight to view
> The holy Soul he form'd anew;
> And Saints and Angels join to sing
> The growing Empire of their KING.[57] (Isaac Watts)

The close of the first century of colonial experience marked more than merely the maturation of the Puritan experiment. Sometime during the first half of the eighteenth century New England's Puritans became Yankees. The institutions governing life and thought in the region bent before new social and economic pressures.[58] Despite changes, some cultural continuities persisted. The traditional preoccupation with apocalyptic, for example, became a measure of both continuity and discontinuity. The inhabitants of eighteenth-century New England inherited from the preceding century the hope for a time of religious renewal when prophecies of the latter-day would be fulfilled. Yet a new pattern of evangelical spirituality also developed, manifesting itself in religious revivals triggered by a series of events that invited apocalyptic speculation.

One event of signal importance was the earthquake that shook New England on 29 October 1727, producing a 'horrid rumbling like the Noise of many Coaches together, driving on the paved Stones' and 'a most awful *Trembling of the Earth*'. Within the space of a few months more than a score of sermons were published offering interpretations.[59] New Englanders were accustomed to commentary on remarkable providences. Thomas Prince (1687–1758) of Old South Church in Boston described the earth as containing 'a vast and inconceivable number of *Caverns* or hollow Places' where chemicals and minerals combined to cause earthquakes. Others echoed his judgment about subterranean explosions. Nevertheless, wrote Cotton Mather, 'Let the *Natural Causes of Earthquakes* be what the *Wise Men of Enquiry please, They* and their *Causes* are still under the Government of HIM that is the *GOD of Nature*'. Mather suggested that the quake was a sign of the times, an indication that the '*Kingdom of* GOD *is at hand*', and an anticipation of coming terrors.[60] Other ministers declared that God was punishing the sins of society. The most remarkable fact about 1727, according to many, was the absence of any loss of life. Samuel Phillips (1691–1771) of Andover proclaimed that New England *'can't be Thankful eno''* that God did not open the earth 'and swallow us up alive'. God's mercy was 'the Method of Providence, in our *Fathers* Days; and so it has been in *our* Day'. Phillips and others used the occasion to underscore the importance of being in grace at the moment of such terrors. Thus Samuel Wigglesworth (1688–1768) of Malden warned, 'Thunder, Lightning, Storms nor Earthquakes need to be feared by us, if our Sins are repented of, and blotted out thro' the Blood of the Lamb'.[61]

Unfortunately, Cotton Mather noted, the piety and grave impressions produced in times of distress are easily forgotten.[62] By 1730 on the centennial of the arrival of the *Arbella*, Thomas Prince addressed the elected leaders of Massachusetts as a 'backsliding People'. 'Let us cry earnestly for the SPIRIT of Grace to be poured forth on us', he exhorted. 'And being revived our selves, let us labour to revive Religion . . .'. Prince called for repentance as he recalled the remarkable works of God in the past, *'both of Judgment and of Mercy, both to Them and their Fathers'*. He observed 'that there never was any People on Earth, so parallel in their general History to that of the ancient ISRAELITES as this of NEW ENGLAND'. If one changed the names, he wrote, 'one wou'd be ready to think the greater Part of the OLD TESTAMENT were written about *us*, or that *we*, tho' in a lower Degree, were the particular Antitypes of that primitive People'. Therefore New Englanders need to consider 'the great & special Obligations' laid upon the people and 'our Interest and Wisdom for the future'. This region, once *'horrid and dismal'*, was transformed by the founders into a 'fruitful Land'. The 'wilderness and the solitary place' became 'Glad' when the 'Waters of the Divine Influence' were poured out. Similarly, wrote Prince, 'May we be EMMANUEL's Land, the People of the Holy one of ISRAEL; And may the LORD make us an eternal Excellency, a Joy of many Generations'.[63] Thomas Foxcroft (1697–1769) of the First Church in Boston expressed the same sentiment, hoping that the people who had become 'an Harlot' might be inspired by the *'excellent Character and Spirit'* of the founders and by *'their Errand into this Wilderness'* to labor for 'a happy Revival of the Work of God', repairing all 'Defects' and rectifying all 'Mismanagements'.[64]

Another incentive for apocalyptic reflection in the new century was the continuing struggle for control of the Americas. In New England the imperial conflict fuelled a trenchant form of anti-Catholicism. Many New Englanders feared a conspiracy of 'antichristian forces' comprised of the nations of France and Spain, the Jesuit order – the embodiment of evil for Protestants, and surrounding Indian tribes. During Queen Anne's War many volunteered for an expedition to Canada to strike a blow against the 'beast'. In New England the imperial struggle was a religious conflict.[65] One captive in the war described his experience as follows. My captor 'took hold of my hand to force me to *Cross my self*', wrote John Williams (1664–1729) of Deerfield,

Massachusetts, 'but I strugled with him, and would not suffer him to guide my hand; upon this he pulled off a *Crucifix* from his own neck, and bad me *kiss* it; but I refused once and again; he told me *he would dash out my brains with his Hatchet if I refused.* I told him I should sooner chuse death then to Sin against God'.[66] The same anti-Catholicism led Solomon Stoddard (1643-1729) of Northampton to support missionary activity so that the Indians might not 'fall in with the *Papists*' and cause additional bloodshed. He added that if the natives 'be brought to Religion, then there will be Hopes of a Durable Peace'. (Stoddard rejected Mede's suggestion that Christians in America would '*Indianize*' and become Gog and Magog.)[67] Not even an interlude in the conflict removed these fears. When peace was arranged on terms perceived by some to be unfavorable, Cotton Mather opposed the settlement, writing of the 'irresistible torrent of slavery, popery, and confusion' likely to follow. He rejected the peace on prophetic grounds too, noting that 'Her Majesty had not studied the Revelation' as much as those who counselled her to continue the struggle.[68]

Not all apocalyptic reflection was provoked by remarkable providences. Some New Englanders in the eighteenth century continued to be delighted with the sheer pleasure of speculation. Mather, for example, believed that the Holy Spirit had instructed Christians to be at 'pains to *Count* it, & Search out' the proper meaning of the apocalyptic number 666. Samuel Sewall likewise remained fascinated with matters of 'Apocalyptical Chronology'. He calculated that Christ did not set his right foot in the New World (Rev. 10) until the year 1492 when Columbus discovered America – a date that fit well with the chronology of the visions, according to him. Sewall discussed a variety of such issues with his contemporaries including speculation about the slaying of the witnesses (Rev. 11).[69] In 1717 when many in New England were frustrated in their prophetic hopes, Joseph Sewall (1688-1769), the son of Samuel and a minister in Boston, preached about the coming of the millennium; 'though it tarry', the text said, 'wait for it'. William Williams (1665-1741) of Hatfield argued that there were insufficient grounds for proposing that America would be the center for the coming kingdom. On the contrary, he wrote, if 'any particular spot of Earth should be pitch'd upon rather than another', it ought probably to be the 'land of Judea' in accord with the prophecy of Ezekiel. Williams expected the kingdom to be a moment of 'political' glory when the church which suffered under Antichrist would 'be brought into a prosperous and flourishing condition' – not a time when resurrected saints reign on the earth. Benjamin Colman (1673-1747) of the Brattle Street Church in Boston joined the debate, suggesting that many apocalyptic commentators were presumptuous, becoming 'too *Curious* and *Positive*' about particular issues. He preferred less speculation because, he insisted, no man can know the secrets of God.[70]

The prosperity of the churches, once only hoped for, was realized in widely scattered locales throughout New England during the first decades of the eighteenth century. In 1712 and 1718 under the ministerial leadership of Solomon Stoddard, Northampton experienced spiritual 'harvests'. In 1721 congregations at Windham, Windsor, and Norwich, Connecticut, had moments of success. These awakenings were sporadic and scattered, not sustained and widespread. Nevertheless, the hopes of many were buoyed. Small wonder then that the more widespread and sustained outburst of religious activity centering in Northampton and the Connecticut River valley in 1734–5 under the leadership of Jonathan Edwards (1703–58), grandson and successor of Stoddard, gave cause for celebration and reflection on the 'surprising work of God'. In Northampton a change was first apparent among the youth of the town who laid aside their frolicking and began to take religion seriously. By April 1734, Edwards reported, 'a great and earnest concern about the great things of religion and the eternal world became universal in all parts of the town, and among persons of all degrees and all ages; the noise amongst the dry bones waxed louder and louder'. The people became so concerned, Edwards added, that the 'only thing in their view was to get the kingdom of heaven, and everyone appeared pressing into it'.[71] The town was transformed, and the awakening became the talk of the valley.

This 'extraordinary dispensation of providence' which spread to many other towns invited prophetic interpretation. In 1737 when Edwards described the events more fully, he pointed to the 'new sense of things, new apprehensions and views of God, of the divine attributes, and Jesus Christ, and the great things of the Gospel' which were central to the revival. His parishioners possessed a 'burning of heart' never before experienced; 'we are evidently a people blessed of the Lord!' he concluded. 'And here, in this corner of the world, God dwells and manifests his glory.' Despite his excitement, Edwards was more cautious in his interpretation than the Englishmen Isaac Watts (1674–1748) and John Guyse (1680–1761) who wrote a preface to his published account in which they associated these 'astonishing exercises' with the promise of God's presence in the 'latter days'. Four American ministers in Boston – Thomas Prince, Joseph Sewall, John Webb (1687–1750), and William Cooper (1694–1743) – voiced a similar viewpoint in the American edition of Edwards' narrative. 'And as this wonderful work may be considered as an earnest of what God will do towards the close of the Gospel day,' they wrote, 'it affords great encouragement to our faith and prayer in pleading those promises which relate to the glorious extent and flourishing of the kingdom of Christ upon earth, and have not yet had their full and final accomplishment.'[72]

The decline of the awakening in 1735 dashed the hopes of evangelicals waiting for the fulfilment of prophecy. Even so, Edwards 'improved' the very dark times in a series of sermons in mid-1739 addressed to the members of his congregation who were 'neglecting the business of religion and their own souls'. The work of redemption, he asserted, will be accomplished by successive outpourings of the Spirit of God. Moreover, he observed, advances in God's kingdom often follow closely on the heels of hardship; sometimes 'the darkest time with the Christian church [occurs] just before the break of day' – a conclusion he reached on the basis of his studies of the Book of Revelation. The Apocalypse had been the object of Edwards' special attention for many years; he had kept a separate notebook, recording commentary and ruminations on the text. He had tried his own hand, for example, at calculating the time of the fall of the Antichrist, but in 1739 he told his congregation, 'I am far from pretending to determine the time when the reign of Antichrist began, which is a point that has been so much controverted among divines and expositors'. Nevertheless, Edwards was persuaded that the world stood under the sixth vial (Rev. 16.12) and that the beginning of the millennium was not distant. He urged his parishioners to pray for the 'accomplishment of the great and glorious things which yet remain to be fulfilled'.[73] He hoped that his ministry might be a partial means for bringing a return of the Spirit to Northampton.

The hopes of evangelicals were freshly aroused by reports of the successes of George Whitefield (1714–70), an Anglican associated with the fledgling 'methodist' movement in England. In December 1739 *The New England Weekly Journal* described Whitefield's triumph in New York where he addressed large crowds. According to the account, he spoke 'as one having Authority: All he said was *Demonstration, Life* and *Power*!' Among his auditors who numbered in the thousands, many shared the conviction of one who said, '*Surely God is with this Man of a Truth*'. Whitefield proclaimed the necessity of a new birth, urging sinners to look to Christ for salvation. The evangelicals who read of Whitefield's activities hoped he would come to New England, and he did in September 1740. He was greeted by large crowds everywhere, including as many as 8000 at one time in Boston. In Whitefield's own words, 'Wonderful things are doing here. The word runs like lightning. Dagon daily falls before the ark . . .'.[74] All of New England yearned to share in the religious revivals, no one more so than Edwards who followed the news closely and invited Whitefield to visit Northampton. His ultimate hope, he wrote, was that this stirring might prove 'the dawning of a day of Gods mighty Power and glorious grace to the world of mankind'. Edwards encouraged Whitefield to preach in order to shake the 'Kingdom of Satan' and to establish the 'Kingdom of Christ . . . from one end of the Earth unto the other!' Whitefield's visit to Northampton was not disappointing, for Edwards' congregation experienced a revival. Religious contagion swept the population of New England; hundreds, if not thousands, raced to hear Whitefield.[75] The general revival for which Cotton Mather had prayed finally dawned.

The Great Awakening was the formative religious event for the generation of the 1740s in New England, shaping their self-conception and their understanding of history. Edwards emerged as the most articulate spokesman for this new American evangelicalism. The religious successes made him confident, if not euphoric, about the current state of affairs and optimistic about the future. Edwards regarded the 'great and continual commotion, day and night' as evidence that these doings were the 'most remarkable' work of God, and his was not an isolated judgment. Peter Thacher (1688–1744) of Middleborough, Massachusetts, declared that 'the Lord Christ is carrying on his own Work with such a mighty Arm in so many Places. . . . I trust the whole Earth shall soon be filled with the Knowledge of the *Saviour*'. John Moorehead (1703–73) of Boston was even more certain: 'Let the Guardian Angels carry the News to Heaven of the numerous Converts: the *Millennium* is begun, Christ dwells with Men on Earth'.[76] Edwards echoed these sentiments the next year in his published defense of the revivals. ''Tis not unlikely that this work of God's Spirit, that is so extraordinary and wonderful', he wrote, 'is the dawning, or at least a prelude, of that glorious work of God, so often foretold in Scripture, which in the progress and issue of it, shall renew the world of mankind'. He believed that the millennial age was at hand, 'that the beginning of this great work of God must be near'. Furthermore, observing the religious contagion in the land, he added that 'there are many things that make it probable that this work will begin in America'. (Before many years had passed, Edwards had occasion to regret his bold statement concerning the place of America in the divine economy.)[77]

Another spokesman who interpreted the awakening in an apocalyptic mode was Thomas Prince, Jr (1722–48) of Boston, the editor of *The Christian History*, the first religious periodical in America. Prince undertook his publication 'for the Advancement of the Redeemer's Kingdom and Glory'. He stated that the magazine was designed to serve the interests of true religion and to satisfy the curiosity of those who were watching for '*Zion's* KING'. Prince filled its pages with information about revivals in various locations, including 'An Account of the late Revival of Religion in Taunton' which is typical of the apocalyptic construction placed upon events. In it Josiah Crocker (1719–74) described at length the 'marvellous *Effusion* of the Spirit of Grace, in his *awakening, convincing, humbling, converting, sanctifying,* and *comforting Influences*' in Taunton. Before the awakening, the situation had been 'very dark and awful' with little 'Life and Power of Godliness' among the people who had 'degenerated from the primitive Piety of their *Ancestors*'. With the revival, wrote Crocker, a change became apparent as 'religious *Conversation* increased' and a 'solemn and awful Seriousness appear'd' in the town. '*Zion's* KING rode in Triumph upon the Word of Truth', producing a 'wonderful Reformation' throughout the town, even among the young and the Negroes.[78] Similar scenes were repeated throughout New England as a convocation of ministers that met in July 1743 testified. The ministers described the 'plentiful Effusion' of God's Spirit in the awakening and the resultant 'Enlargement of the Kingdom of CHRIST in the World'. They also acknowledged that these remarkable events had raised 'the Hopes, of such as are *waiting for the Kingdom of God*, and the coming on of the Glory of the latter Days' and must be defended against those who '*despise* these Out-pourings of the Spirit'. The clergy urged New Englanders to pray for 'fresh, more plentiful' showers of the Spirit so that 'this Wilderness, in all the Parts of it, may become a fruitful Field' and this awakening may be 'an *Earnest* of the glorious Things promis'd to the Church in the latter Days'.[79]

The fullest defense of the awakening in New England came from the hand of Jonathan Edwards who attempted to place the extraordinary events into an apocalyptic perspective. Edwards regarded the revivals as 'forerunners of those glorious times so often prophesied of in the Scripture, . . . the first dawning of that light, and beginning of that work, which, in the progress and issue of it, would at last bring on the Church's latter day glory'. But as the years passed, he was forced to acknowledge that 'where God of late wonderfully appear'd, he has now in a great Measure withdrawn; and the Consequence is, that *Zion* and the Interest of Religion are involved in innumerable and inextricable Difficulties'. Nevertheless, he remained confident that God would revive his work again.[80] Edwards found encouragement for his view in England, Scotland, and other parts of America. He delighted in the missionary successes among the Indians which, he concluded, 'have a favourable Aspect on the Interest of Religion'. Edwards took heart from the military victories of the English and other Protestant powers, regarding them as evidence that the sixth vial was being poured on the Antichrist and papal revenues were being destroyed. And he searched for ways to renew the ebbing revivals. For example, Edwards supported a proposal for a concert of prayer whereby evangelicals throughout the world would join in prayer at a specified moment, asking for God's Spirit and thereby hastening the advent of the latter days. In 1748 he published an extended apologetic for the concert which drew heavily upon apocalyptic logic.[81]

Not all of Edwards' apocalyptic reflections, however, were the product of pastoral concerns, for he planned to incorporate his lifelong ruminations into a major treatise. Edwards contemplated a 'great work' of divinity in a 'new method' to be entitled a '*History of the Work of Redemption*'. He hoped to write theology from an historical perspective, embracing all of history from the beginning to its consummation. Edwards believed that God controlled the course of events in the world and that the church would finally conquer the forces of evil just as the lamb emerges triumphant in the Apocalypse. In union with Christ, the church will move from times of distress to a moment of victory, a triumph that will become manifest in the millennium and in the new heaven and new earth. The visions of the Seer informed Edwards' theological perspective in essential ways. He wrote, 'In the beginning of this revolution all things come from God, and are formed out of a chaos; and in the end, all things shall return into a chaos again, and shall return to God, so that he that is the *Alpha*, will be the *Omega*'.[82] In this manner the goal of creation, which is the glory of God, will be accomplished.

The apocalyptic perspective formulated by Edwards was shared by a number of his students and evangelical colleagues in America, most notably Joseph Bellamy (1719–90) of Bethlehem, Connecticut, and Samuel Hopkins (1721–1803) of Great Barrington and later Newport, as well as by like-minded correspondents abroad who were also committed to the link between the new birth and the fulfilment of prophecy. The awakenings had the effect of increasing the confidence of those who were watching, even though progress in the work of redemption often seemed slow. The revivals also made evangelicals conscious of their own responsibility for the accomplishment of prophecy. Bellamy and Hopkins alike affirmed the wisdom of God in his scheme of history, a scheme that ultimately will culminate in the millennium.[83] Both spent considerable time speculating about the nature of the millennium, specifically, about the number of those who would be saved during the thousand years – one of the interests shared by their correspondents abroad. John Willison (1680–1750), for example, a Presbyterian in Dundee, Scotland, voiced his deep hostility toward the Roman Catholic Church and his commitment to the concert of prayer. John Erskine (1720–1803), another correspondent in Scotland, agreed that the events in New England and elsewhere were 'a Prelude of greater Things to come', namely, the fulfilment of prophecy at the end of the ages.[84] In sum, the evangelical party which emerged in New England during the first half of the eighteenth century remained preoccupied with the apocalyptic tradition. In that sense they were the heirs of Cotton Mather and other Puritans as well as the progenitors of those who would reshape that tradition in useful ways during the years ahead.

IV 'WITH ALL THE GRACES SPARKLING IN HER TRAIN'

> O Land supremely blest! to thee tis given
> To taste the choicest joys of bounteous heaven;
> Thy rising Glory shall expand its rays,
> And lands and times unknown rehearse thine endless praise.[85]
>
> (Timothy Dwight)

The second half of the eighteenth century proved a momentous time for New England and all of America as the colonists took the decisive steps leading to independence and subsequently to the formation of a new nation. New England played a significant role in these developments, and the apocalyptic vision handed down from generation to generation continued to exercise a formative influence upon many in the region. During the several stages of the conflict and its aftermath, New Englanders drew upon apocalyptic thought and literature as they reflected upon their experience. They also bequeathed to the new nation a portion of their apocalyptic legacy.[86]

The ebbing of the Great Awakening in New England was concurrent with a rising preoccupation with the French and Indian Wars. Again the apocalyptic mode proved congenial for expressing the hopes and fears related to these struggles. Edwards struck a characteristic note in 1745 when he proclaimed the victory at Cape Breton one of 'the late wonderful works of God in America', and evidence of 'a day of great things'. According to him, the whole of the affair was 'a dispensation of providence, the most remarkable in its kind, that has been in many ages'. The spirit of that military expedition was evident in the actions of Samuel Moody (1676–1747), a chaplain from York, Maine. After Louisburg fell, Moody – though nearly eighty years old – 'took an ax went into one of their Churches Cutt downe of their Images or Cross, then preached a Thanksgiving Sermon'.[87] When the campaign on Cape Breton proved to be only one contest in a long series, a siege mentality invaded New England. John Mellen (1723–1807), the minister in Sterling, Massachusetts, sounded a dire note. 'It is possible,' he warned, 'our land may be given to the beast, the inhabitants to the sword, the righteous to the fire of martyrdom, our wives to ravishment, and our sons and our daughters to death & torture!' These fears caused some to suggest that better New England be destroyed than fall to the French whom John Burt (1716–75) of Bristol described as 'the Offspring of that *Scarlet Whore, that Mother of Harlots*, who is justly *the Abomination of the Earth*'.[88]

As the imperial struggles wore on, the preachers of New England continued to make frequent use of the apocalyptic tradition, often in conjunction with political agitation. For many the French were the agents of slavery and the English guardians of liberty. Thus James Cogswell (1720–1807) of Canterbury, Connecticut, addressed colonial soldiers in 1757: 'Fight for Liberty and against Slavery. Endeavour to stand the Guardians of the Religion and Liberties of *America*; to oppose Antichrist, and prevent the barbarous Butchering of your fellow Countrymen'. Some New Englanders integrated traditional apocalyptic with Whig political values and with the myth of the founders. For example, in the election sermon of 1754, Jonathan Mayhew (1720–66) of Boston declared that 'the wisdom & piety' of the forefathers were responsible for the 'many invaluable privileges' enjoyed in the colony. He exhorted the elected officials 'to consult and prosecute the public good', including greater investment in Indian missions in order to keep the natives from 'the religion of Rome'. Mayhew raised the specter of unfriendly tribes on the borders, led by Gallic 'perfidy', intent upon dispossessing 'the free-born subjects of King GEORGE, of the inheritance received from their forefathers, and purchased by them at the expence of their ease, their treasure, their blood!' Mayhew warned that 'an herd of lazy Monks, and Jesuits, and exorcists, and Inquisitors, and cowled and uncowled impostors' would replace the faithful ministers when liberty and property, religion and happiness, are 'transubstantiated, into slavery, poverty, superstition, wretchedness!'[89] When victory came in the conflict, a spate of sermons struck the note that '*Babylon the great is fallen*', to use the words of Samuel Langdon (1723–97), the minister at Portsmouth, New Hampshire, who earlier had been at the battle of Louisberg. The defeat of the 'antichristian' French forces was regarded as a sign of the approach of the latter days. Mayhew expected a 'flourishing kingdom in these parts of America, peopled by our posterity'. Mather Byles (1706–88) of Boston declared, 'And now, what a Scene of Wonder opens to our View!'[90]

The years that followed the French and Indian wars did not bring an end to turmoil in New England or America, for the steady march of events carried the colonies; 'Michael stands ready', Sherwood declared, 'with all the artillery of Independence provoked a variety of apocalyptic justifications for the revolution. Perhaps 'the most popular and most inflammatory sermon of 1776' was preached by Samuel Sherwood (1703–83) in Norfield, Connecticut, who urged a radical response to threats against colonial 'Liberties, Properties, and Priviledges'. He argued that the plight of Americans was the subject of the prophecies of the Apocalypse which had been written 'for the instruction, support, and consolation of God's saints, in the wars and conflicts they might have with their enemies, in every age and period of time'. According to him, the 'great whore of Babylon' – the papacy – had enticed others to join common cause against true religion. Sherwood identified the 'image of the beast' with 'the corrupt system of tyranny and oppression, that has of late been fabricated and adopted by the ministry and parliament of Great-Britain', citing the Quebec Act of 1774 as evidence of an intention to establish Roman Catholicism in the New World. Despite concerted efforts by the forces of evil, Sherwood wrote, 'This American quarter of the globe seemed to be reserved in providence, as a fixed and settled habitation for God's church'. In union with other nations, Americans will destroy the whore and overcome 'by the blood of the Lamb, and by the word of their testimony'. God is on the side of the colonies; 'Michael stands ready,' Sherwood declared, 'with all the artillery of heaven, to encounter the dragon, and to vanquish this black host'.[91]

The sides were drawn clearly in the revolutionary struggle. The patriots in New England had little doubt about the righteousness of their cause. In 1776 Samuel West (1730–1807) of New Bedford, Massachusetts, delivered the annual election sermon in an atmosphere charged with emotion. He declared that the British army was more barbarous than the 'Turks and Mahometan infidels' in the exercise of 'arbitrary power', political tyranny being a mark of the Antichrist. West challenged the population 'to stand fast' in liberty and 'to strive to get the victory over the beast and his image, over every species of tyranny'. Armed revolution was the proper course of action. 'We must *beat our plowshares into swords*', West exclaimed, '*and our pruning hooks into spears.*'[92] Similar sentiments rang from other pulpits as the 'black regiment' sprang into action throughout New England. In the previous year Samuel Langdon, newly installed president of Harvard College, linked the colonists with ancient Israel and England with the enemies of God's people. 'If God be for us', Langdon intoned, 'who can be against us? . . . And may we not be confident that the most High who regards these things will vindicate his own honor, and plead our righteous cause against such enemies to his government as well as our liberties . . .'. Langdon's confidence was unlimited: 'we shall have no reason to be afraid though thousands of enemies set themselves against us round about'.[93] In a similar vein, Nicholas Street (1730–1806) of East Haven, Connecticut, called upon his hearers in 1777 to recognize the signs of the times and to accept the conflict as punishment for sins and to 'repent and turn to God by an universal reformation' so that he may 'restore to us our liberties as at the first, and our privileges as at the beginning'. Thomas Bray (1738–1808) of North Guilford, Connecticut, justified the conflict by arguing that the pouring of the sixth vial pointed to the destruction of all 'civil and ecclesiastical despotism', including the papacy, the Turks, and Islam, all of which he considered antichristian powers. He expected the destruction to occur in 'the appendages of the Roman empire' which for Bray included America. He viewed the revolution as an effort to drive tyranny back to the East from whence it came. (Some Tory sympathizers in the colonies sought to use anti-Catholic sentiments to their advantage against the patriots who favored an alliance with France, a 'popish' nation.)[94]

The successful conclusion of the War of Independence was celebrated by New Englanders with an outpouring of sermons interpreting the victory. For example, Ezra Stiles (1727–95), the president of Yale College, drew a parallel between ancient Israel and the newly independent colonies. He delivered a discourse on 'the political welfare of GOD's American *Israel*', using his text (Deut. 26.19) 'as allusively prophetick of the future prosperity and splendour of the *United States*'. He believed that its 'primary' and 'literal' accomplishment would come with the 'latter day glory of the church'. Exuding confidence, Stiles found cause to compare the victories of George Washington with those of Joshua of old. Washington's military success he attributed to 'the indubitable interposition and energetick influence of Divine Providence in these great and illustrious events'. With the end of the hostilities, he declared, 'Let there be a tranquil period for the unmolested accomplishment of the *Magnalia Dei*'. The new nation – though yet unformed – had a special opportunity and responsibility. It will be watched by all other nations of the world. Here truth and liberty must be perfected, exhorted Stiles. The sense of mission once associated with New England Stiles transferred to the emerging nation which was to be a model in both religion and politics. Certain events were especially significant for the accomplishment of these goals – the annihilation of the papacy, the restoration of the Jews to Palestine, and the conversion of the Gentiles. The spread of Christianity in America, assisted by the revolution, was setting the stage for the latter-day events. Accordingly, he wrote, 'we have reason to think, that the *United States* may be of no small influence and consideration'.[95] In 1783 David Tappan (1752–1803) suggested that the 'grand chain of Providence – in which the American revolution is a principal link ... is hastening on the accomplishment of the Scripture prophecies relative to the millennial state, the golden age of the church and the world in the latter days'.[96]

The apocalyptic interests of the late eighteenth century found representative expression in the writings of Timothy Dwight (1752–1817), the grandson of Jonathan Edwards, a chaplain during the War of Independence, and the eventual successor of Ezra Stiles as president of Yale College. In his diverse roles as preacher, poet, theologian, and social critic, Dwight reflected the character of his age and its use of the century and a half of apocalyptic tradition in New England. His preoccupation with the Apocalypse, similar to that of his grandfather and many others, was evident at an early age. In a 'Valedictory Address' delivered in 1776 while a tutor at Yale College, Dwight displayed the way in which his vision for America was informed by apocalyptic ideas. The progress of knowledge and liberty in the world, he observed, had been in a westwardly direction. Therefore the course of history will culminate in America, he judged, for 'the Empire of North-America will be the last on earth' and it will be the 'most glorious'. In America, Dwight affirmed, 'will be accomplished that remarkable Jewish tradition that the last thousand years of the reign of time would, in imitation of the conclusion of the first week [of creation], become a glorious Sabbath of peace, purity and felicity'. Confident that America would be the seat of the last kingdom, 'the last retreat of science, of freedom and of glory', he urged his hearers to rise to the challenge of the future and participate wholeheartedly in 'laying the foundations of American greatness'. Some of you, he warned his youthful audience, may even be required to fight for the freedom and glory of this future empire.[97]

In some measure Dwight himself accepted the challenge laid down for his youthful listeners in the 1776 address. Despite a 'personal and lifelong abhorrence of war', in 1777 and 1778 he served as a chaplain in General Parsons' brigade which gave occasion for reflection upon the prophetic dimensions of the revolutionary situation. In 1777 when General Burgoyne was defeated at Saratoga, New York, Dwight drew a parallel between the patriotic victory and the success of King Hezekiah over his Assyrian enemies. He wrote, 'The cause of both was the same. HEZEKIAH paid a tribute to SENNACHERIB, and these States to GEORGE the third; but in both instances insatiable tyranny demanded more than the tributaries were willing or able to pay; this was the cause.'[98] As the conflict continued, in 1780 Dwight published his poem *America* which he had written as many as ten years earlier as a 'tribute' to his 'native Land'. According to Dwight, America was glorious in its millennial splendor. 'Celestial science, raptur'd we descry/ Refulgent beaming o'er the western sky;/ Bright Liberty extends her blissful reign,/ With all the graces sparkling in her train:/ Religion shines with a superiour blaze,/

And heaven-born virtue beams diviner rays;/ Justice enthron'd maintains an equal sway,/ The poor dwell safely, and the proud obey'.[99] A more ideal situation would be impossible to imagine, according to the young poet. In 1781 when Lord Cornwallis surrendered at Yorktown, Dwight placed an apocalyptic perspective upon events in a sermon based on a text from the prophecy of Isaiah (Is. 19) which he regarded as emblematic of the role of America in the work of redemption. America was to provide instruction for the nations of Europe, and especially for Britain. The military victory was a 'preparation' and an anticipation of events of equal or greater importance which would occur at the beginning of the millennium around the year 2000. For Dwight the American revolution marked a watershed in human history, and future possibilities appeared infinite. Despite the intoxication of his vision, Dwight also sounded a note of warning that all progress might not be glorious – a theme which later became a fixation with him. 'This very war, a judgment which ought to awaken repentance and humiliation, hath produced a dissipation of thought, a prostitution of reason, a contempt of religion, a disdain of virtue, a deliberation in vice, and an universal levity and corruption of soul, before unseen and unimagined'. Dwight became especially hostile to skeptics who trusted in progress but wanted, in his view, 'to destroy the kingdom of God'.[100]

Dwight's apocalyptic vision may have reached its fullest expression in his lengthy poem, *The Conquest of Canaan*, published in 1785, called by one critic 'an epic jeremiad that builds on constant crises (rebellion, backsliding, treachery, holy war) toward a celebration of the New World republic – America, the second "blissful Eden bright," "by heaven design'd"'.[101] The opening lines read, 'The Chief, whose arm to Israel's chosen band/ Gave the fair empire of the promis'd land,/ Ordain'd by Heaven to hold the sacred sway,/ Demands my voice and animates the lay'. Dedicated to George Washington, 'Commander in chief of the American Armies, The Saviour of his Country, The Supporter of Freedom, And the Benefactor of Mankind', the poem tells how Joshua led the people of Israel to victory. For Dwight the historical parallels were overwhelming between the situation of ancient Israel and the new society in America. God determined to give the land to the new nation just as the promised land was bestowed upon the Jews of old. On the shores of this new Canaan will be erected a new society. 'Here Empire's last, and brightest throne shall rise;/ And Peace, and Right, and Freedom, greet the skies'. The hero Joshua is a prefiguration of a greater dispensation to come with the advent of the millennial age.[102] In this manner Washington and America both fulfill the original mission of Joshua and ancient Israel and also anticipate the future triumph of the church. Dwight wrote history in the manner of Cotton Mather's *Magnalia Christi Americana*, tying together past, present, and future.

The years following the War for Independence – the Critical Period in American history – witnessed continuing controversy in New England. The republican ideals which had guided the colonies through the conflict with England became themselves the source of debate as factions favoring liberty with order contended against others wanting freedom without restraints. As political parties became more clearly defined, the conflict heightened. For staunch Federalists the French Revolution became a symbol of the threat being made against civil and religious liberty, a threat embodied in the rumored plot of the Bavarian Illuminati. The response of many New Englanders was predictable. Again the clergy stepped into their pulpits to meet the challenge by arguing for 'Christian republicanism'.[103] Jeremy Belknap (1744–98) of Boston affirmed in 1798, 'It is curious and amusing, as well as instructive, to observe, how nearly the conduct of France toward us, in the present controversy, resembles that of Britain in a former controversy'. Nathan Strong (1748–1816) of the First Church in Hartford denounced French infidelity as the culmination of antichristianism. A year later the Congregational clergy of Massachusetts issued a similar call for withdrawal from the influences of 'the infidel, antichristian world'.[104] Perhaps no more forceful voice for the Federalist view spoke than Timothy Dwight. When word of the Bavarian Illuminati spread across New England, Dwight preached a sermon to warn the citizens of New Haven of the approach of the terrors of the end times. He also spoke of the infidels as part of one unified antichristian cause, a concerted movement against liberty and order. In particular he attacked the publications which spread these views, most notably, Tom Paine's *The Age of Reason*, equating them with the prophetic 'frogs coming out of the mouth of the beast to gather Satan's forces for the final struggle at Armageddon'.[105] Ten years earlier Dwight had published a poem entitled *The Triumph of Infidelity* narrated by the devil himself who dedicated his creation to Voltaire. According to Dwight, Voltaire and others taught that 'the chief end of man was, to slander his God, and abuse him forever'. In 1801 in a sermon looking back on the preceding century, Dwight spoke of 'rising periods of order, peace, and safety', when 'general happiness and universal virtue' will prevail in the same breath that he warned about the 'troublous times' in which he was living.[106] Like so many others before him, Dwight found apocalyptic an effective device for both celebration and condemnation.

V 'SOME OBSERVABLE THINGS'

Cotton Mather closed the *Magnalia* with some reflections that included a 'prognostication'. 'But, oh, my dear NEW-ENGLAND', he wrote, 'give one of thy friends leave to utter the *fears* of thy best friends concerning thee; and consider what fearful cause there may be for thee to expect sad THINGS TO COME/ If every *wise man* be a prophet, there are some yet in thee that can *prophesie*'.[107] During the first two centuries of experience in New England many in the land were given to prophecy. New England proved a fertile field for the transplanted English apocalyptic tradition. The seventeenth and eighteenth centuries reveal the presence of a diverse apocalyptic tradition in New England with certain fundamental continuities and discontinuities. Throughout the period the Apocalypse proved a rich source of ideas and symbols. The visions of the Seer never ceased to attract the curious, encourage the faithful, or mystify the commentator. From the coming of the first settlers until the founding of the new nation, the Book of Revelation remained a constant point of reference as New Englanders struggled to understand themselves, their responsibilities, and their place in history.

NOTES

1 Joseph Mede, 'A Conjecture concerning GOG and MAGOG', in *The Key of the Revelation* (1650), n.p.
2 Cotton Mather, *Magnalia Christi Americana: Or, the Ecclesiastical History of New-England* (1702), Bk. I, pp. 4–5.
3 Anne Bradstreet, 'A Dialogue between Old England and New, concerning their present troubles Anno 1642', in *The Tenth Muse Lately Sprung Up in America* (1650), pp. 187–8.
4 John Winthrop, *A Modell of Christian Charity*, in *Collections of the Massachusetts Historical Society*, 3rd ser., VII (1838), 46, 47.
5 J. F. Maclear, 'New England and the Fifth Monarchy: The Quest for the Millennium in Early American Puritanism', *The William and Mary Quarterly*, 3rd ser., XXXII (1975), 229–30.
6 Increase Mather, *The Life and Death of That Reverend Man of GOD, Mr. Richard Mather* (Cambridge, Mass., 1670), pp. 12, 17.
7 Robert Middlekauff, *The Mathers: Three Generations of Puritan Intellectuals 1596–1728* (1971), pp. 19–21. See also B. R. Burg, *Richard Mather of Dorchester* (Lexington, Ky., 1976).
8 George H. Williams, Norman Pettit, Winfried Herget, and Sargent Bush, Jr, eds, *Thomas Hooker: Writings in England and Holland, 1626–1633* (Cambridge, Mass., 1975), pp. 300–1, 327–8.
9 C. Mather, *Magnalia*, Bk. III, p. 62.
10 Ibid., p. 48.
11 Ibid., pp. 53, 57.
12 Maclear, 'New England', p. 232; Larzer Ziff, *The Career of John Cotton: Puritanism and the American Experience* (Princeton, 1962), p. vii; C. Mather, *Magnalia*, Bk. III, p. 14. See Cotton's *A Brief Exposition of the Whole Book of Canticles, or Song of Solomon* (1642); *The Churches Resurrection, or the Opening of the Fift and Sixt verses of the 20th Chap. of the Revelation* (1642); *The Powring Out of the Seven Vials: or an Exposition of the 16. Chapter of the Revelation* (1642); and *An Exposition upon the Thirteenth Chapter of the Revelation* (London, 1655).
13 C. Mather, *Magnalia*, Bk. III, p. 25.

14 Peter Toon, 'The Latter-Day Glory', in *The Puritans, the Millennium and the Future of Israel: Puritan Eschatology 1600 to 1660* (Cambridge, Eng., 1970), p. 34.
15 Ibid., pp. 34–6; Maclear, 'New England', pp. 233–4.
16 Winthrop, *Modell*, p. 47.
17 Francis J. Bremer, 'In Defense of Regicide: John Cotton on the Execution of Charles I', *The William and Mary Quarterly*, 3rd ser., XXXVII (1980), 110–24.
18 Thomas Hutchinson, ed., *A Collection of Original Papers Relative to the History of the Colony of Massachusetts-Bay* (Boston, 1769), p. 235.
19 Edward Johnson, *Wonder-Working Providence of Sions Saviour in New England* (1654), p. 89.
20 W. Clark Gilpin, *The Millenarian Piety of Roger Williams* (Chicago, 1979), pp. 56, 59.
21 See Maclear, 'New England', pp. 243–8.
22 Gilpin, *Millenarian Piety*, pp. 133–4; Edmund S. Morgan, *Roger Williams: The Church and the State* (1967); and Sacvan Bercovitch, 'Typology in Puritan New England: The Williams-Cotton Controversy Reassessed', *American Quarterly*, XIX (1967), 166–91.
23 C. Mather, *Magnalia*, Bk. III, p. 172.
24 John Eliot, *The Christian Commonwealth: Or, The Civil Policy of the Rising Kingdom of Jesus Christ* (1659), preface; Gilpin, *Millenarian Piety*, p. 130.
25 Maclear, 'New England', p. 248.
26 Bradstreet, *Tenth Muse*, pp. 180, 188–90.
27 Michael Wigglesworth, 'God's Controversy with New England', in *Proceedings of the Massachusetts Historical Society*, XII (1873), 93.
28 Middlekauff, *The Mathers*, p. 99.
29 C. Mather, *Magnalia*, Bk. IV, p. 154.
30 Samuel Danforth, *A Brief Recognition of New-Englands Errand into the Wilderness* (Cambridge, Mass., 1671), pp. 8, 16, 18–19.
31 Concerning typology in New England, see Sacvan Bercovitch, ed., *Typology and Early American Literature* (Amherst, Mass., 1972); Earl R. Miner, ed., *Literary Uses of Typology: From the Late Middle Ages to the Present* (Princeton, 1977); Bercovitch, *The American Jeremiad* (Madison, Wisc., 1978); Barbara K. Lewalski, *Protestant Poetics and the Seventeenth-Century Religious Lyric* (Princeton, N.J., 1979), especially pp. 388–426; and Mason I. Lowance, Jr., *The Language of Canaan: Metaphor and Symbol in New England from the Puritans to the Transcendentalists* (Cambridge, Mass., 1980).
32 Nicholas Noyes, *New-Englands Duty and Interest* (Boston, 1698), p. 43.
33 John Higginson, *The Cause of God and His People in New-England* (Cambridge, Mass., 1663), p. 12.
34 Richard Slotkin and James K. Folsom, eds, *So Dreadfull A Judgment: Puritan Responses to King Philip's War, 1676–1677* (Middletown, Conn., 1978), p. 65; Middlekauff, *The Mathers*, p. 93. See also Mason I. Lowance, Jr., *Increase Mather* (1974).
35 Increase Mather, *A Brief History of the Warr with the Indians in New-England* (Boston, 1676), pp. 1–2.
36 Increase Mather, *An Earnest Exhortation to the Inhabitants of New-England* (Boston, 1676), pp. ii, 2, 7–10, 17, 26
37 Middlekauff, *The Mathers*, pp. 173–4; I. Mather, *Ichabod, or a Discourse, Shewing*

What Cause there is to Fear that the Glory of the Lord, is Departing from New-England (Boston, 1702).

38 Increase Mather, *A Discourse Concerning Faith and Fervency in Prayer* (Boston, 1710), p. 99; I. Mather, *The Mystery of Israel's Salvation Explained and Applyed* (1669); I. Mather, *A Dissertation Concerning the Future Conversion of the Jewish Nation* (1709); and Samuel Willard, *The Fountain Opened* (Boston, 1700).

39 Michael Wigglesworth, *The Day of Doom* (Cambridge, Mass., 1666), pp. 31, 68, 73–5, 90.

40 Edward J. Gallagher, 'An Overview of Edward Johnson's *Wonder-Working Providence*', *Early American Literature*, V (1970–1), 30. See also Cecelia Tichi, *New World, New Earth: Environmental Reform in American Literature from the Puritans through Whitman* (New Haven, 1979), pp. 37–66.

41 Johnson, *Wonder-Working Providence*, pp. 1, 3, 10–11, 71–2, 236.

42 Mukhtar Ali Isani, 'The Growth of Sewall's *Phaenomena Quaedam Apocalyptica*', *Early American Literature*, VII (1972), 64–75.

43 Samuel Sewall, *Phaenomena Quaedam Apocalyptica Ad Aspectum Novi Orbis Configurata; Or, Some few Lines towards a description of the New Heaven As It makes to those who stand upon the New Earth* (Boston, 1697), Dedication, preface.

44 M. Halsey Thomas, ed., *The Diary of Samuel Sewall 1674–1729* (2 vols, 1973), I, p. 501; Isani, 'Growth', pp. 70–1. See also Mukhtar Ali Isani, ed., 'The Pouring of the Sixth Vial: A Letter in the Taylor-Sewall Debate', *Proceedings of the Massachusetts Historical Society*, LXXXIII (1971), 123–9.

45 Middlekauff, *The Mathers*, pp. 189–367; Sacvan Bercovitch, *The Puritan Origins of the American Self* (New Haven, 1975); David Levin, *Cotton Mather: The Young Life of the Lord's Remembrancer 1663–1703* (Cambridge, Mass., 1978); Richard F. Lovelace, *The American Pietism of Cotton Mather: Origins of American Evangelicalism* (Grand Rapids, Mich., 1979).

46 Worthington Chauncey Ford, ed., *Diary of Cotton Mather* (2 vols, Boston, 1911–12), I, pp. 224–6.

47 Middlekauff, *The Mathers*, p. 316; Ford, ed., *Diary*, II, pp. 387, 733; and Kenneth Silverman, ed., *Selected Letters of Cotton Mather* (Baton Rouge, La., 1971), p. 270.

48 Cotton Mather, *Theopolis Americana: An Essay on the Golden Street of the Holy City* (Boston, 1710), pp. Dedication, 4–5, 19–20, 31–6, 39, 41, 43–4, 46–7. See also Emory Elliott, *Power and the Pulpit in Puritan New England* (Princeton, 1975).

49 Silverman, ed., *Selected Letters*, p. 189; Lovelace, *American Pietism*, p. 67; 'Biblia Americana', MSS in The Papers of Cotton Mather, 6 fols., Massachusetts Historical Society.

50 Cotton Mather, *Things to be Look'd For* (Boston, 1691), pp. 46–7.

51 Cotton Mather, *Boanerges. A Short Essay to Preserve and strengthen the Good Impressions Produced by Earthquakes* (Boston, 1727), p. 44.

52 Cotton Mather, *Shaking Dispensations. An Essay Upon the Mighty Shakes, which the Hand of Heaven hath given, and is giving, to the World* (Boston, 1715), p. 45. See also Middlekauff, *The Mathers*, pp. 262–78.

53 Cotton Mather, *The Stone Cut out of the Mountain* (Boston, 1716), pp. 7, 13; Middlekauff, *The Mathers*, pp. 320–49.

54 C. Mather, *Magnalia*, Intro., p. i.

55 Richard S. Dunn, 'Sixteenth-Century English Historians of America', in *Seventeenth-Century America: Essays in Colonial History*, ed. James Morton Smith

(Chapel Hill, N.C., 1959), p. 218; Bercovitch, *American Jeremiad*, p. 87; and Silverman, ed., *Selected Letters*, p. 313. See also Peter Gay, *A Loss of Mastery: Puritan Historians in Colonial America* (Berkeley, Ca., 1966); and Kenneth B. Murdock, 'Clio in the Wilderness: History and Biography in Puritan New England', *Early American Literatire*, VI (1971–2), 201–19.

56 Lowance, *Language of Canaan*, p. 168; C. Mather, *Magnalia*, Bk. VII, p. 103.
57 Thomas Prince, ed., *The Christian History, Containing Accounts of the Revival and Propagation of Religion in Great-Britain and America* (2 vols., Boston, 1744–5), I, p. 416.
58 Richard Bushman, *From Puritan to Yankee: Character and the Social Order in Connecticut, 1690–1765* (Cambridge, Mass., 1967), p. ix.
59 Cotton Mather, *The Terror of the Lord* (Boston, 1727), p. 1. See William D. Andrews, 'The Literature of the 1727 New England Earthquake., *Early American Literature*, V (1973), 281–94.
60 Thomas Prince, *Earthquakes the Works of GOD and Tokens of His Just Displeasure* (Boston, 1727), p. 9; C. Mather, *Terror*, p. 11; C. Mather, *Boanerges*, p. 44.
61 Samuel Phillips, *Three Plain Practical Discourses* (Boston, 1728), pp. 51, 153; Samuel Wigglesworth, *A Religious Fear of God's Tokens Explained and Urged* (Boston, 1728), p. 34.
62 C. Mather, *Boanerges*, p. 5.
63 Thomas Prince, *The People of New-England Put in Mind of the Righteous Acts of the Lord to Them and their Fathers* (Boston, 1730), pp. 17, 21–2, 25, 28, 38–9, 48.
64 Thomas Foxcroft, *Observations Historical and Practical on the Rise and Primitive State of New-England* (Boston, 1730), pp. vi, 39, 44–5.
65 See Douglas Edward Leach, *Arms for Empire: A Military History of the British Colonies in North America, 1607–1763* (1973), chs 4–7; Mary Augustina Ray, *American Opinion of Roman Catholicism in the Eighteenth Century* (1936).
66 John Williams, *The Redeemed Captive Returning to Zion* (Boston, 1707), p. 25.
67 Solomon Stoddard, *Whether God is not Angry with the Country for doing So little towards the Conversion of the Indians?* (Boston, 1723), p. 11. See Ralph J. Coffman, *Solomon Stoddard* (Boston, 1978).
68 Silverman, ed., *Selected Letters*, p. 106.
69 Cotton Mather, 'Biblia Americana' at Rev. 13.18, cited in Stephen J. Stein, 'Cotton Mather and Jonathan Edwards on the Number of the Beast: Eighteenth-Century Speculation about the Antichrist', *Proceedings of the American Antiquarian Society*, LXXXIV (1975), 299; *Letter-Book of Samuel Sewall*, in *Collections of the Massachusetts Historical Society*, 6th ser., I (1886), 289–90, II (1888), 64.
70 *Letter-Book*, II, pp. 251–2; James West Davidson, *The Logic of Millennial Thought: Eighteenth-Century New England* (New Haven, 1977), pp. 69–72.
71 Jonathan Edwards, *A Faithful Narrative of the Surprizing Work of God*, in *The Great Awakening*, ed. C. C. Goen, vol. 4 in *The Works of Jonathan Edwards* (New Haven, 1972), pp. 149–50. See also Perry Miller, *Jonathan Edwards* (1949); and Conrad Cherry, *The Theology of Jonathan Edwards: A Reappraisal* (1966).
72 Goen, ed., *Great Awakening*, pp. 131–2, 141, 208, 210.
73 Jonathan Edwards, *A History of the Work of Redemption*, in *The Works of President Edwards* (4 vols, 1843), I, pp. 420, 449, 457, 480; Edwards, *Notes on the Apocalypse*, in *Apocalyptic Writings*, ed., Stephen J. Stein, vol. 5 in *The Works of Jonathan Edwards* (New Haven, 1977), pp. 95–305.
74 *The New England Weekly Journal*, No. 659, Dec. 4, 1739, p. 1, col. 3; Edwin S.

Gaustad, *The Great Awakening in New England* (Chicago, 1968), pp. 26–7; *The Works of the Reverend George Whitefield* (7 vols, 1771–2), I, p. 216.
75 Henry Abelove, 'Jonathan Edwards's Letter of Invitation to George Whitefield', *The William and Mary Quarterly*, 3rd ser., XXIX (1972), 488–9. See Michael J. Crawford, 'The Spiritual Travels of Nathan Cole', *The William and Mary Quarterly*, 3rd ser., XXXIII (1976), 89–126.
76 Goen, ed., *Great Awakening*, pp. 547–50; Prince, ed., *Christian History*, II, p. 95; Jules H. Tuttle, 'The Glasgow-Weekly-History, 1743', *Proceedings of the Massachusetts Historical Society*, LIII (1919–20), 213.
77 Goen, ed., *Great Awakening*, p. 353; Stein, ed., *Apocalyptic Writings*, pp. 27–9. See also Alan Heimert, *Religion and the American Mind from the Great Awakening to the Revolution* (Cambridge, Mass., 1966), chs 1–2.
78 Prince, ed., *Christian History*, I, pp. 2, 16; II, pp. 321, 323, 325–6, 328–9, 340.
79 *The Testimony and Advice of an Assembly of Pastors of Churches in New-England* (Boston, 1743), pp. 5–6, 12.
80 Sereno E. Dwight, ed., *The Works of President Edwards* (10 vols, 1829–30), I, p. 213; James Robe, ed., *The Christian Monthly History* (2 vols, Edinburgh, 1743–6), no. 8 (Nov. 1745), p. 235.
81 Ibid., p. 240. See Jonathan Edwards, *An Humble Attempt to Promote Explicit Agreement and Visible Union of God's People in Extraordinary Prayer* (Boston, 1748), in *Apocalyptic Writings*, ed. Stein, pp. 253–97.
82 Dwight, ed., *Works*, I, pp. 569–70; IX, p. 402. See C. C. Goen, 'Jonathan Edwards: A New Departure in Eschatology', *Church History*, XXVIII (1959), 25–40; William J. Scheick, 'The Grand Design: Jonathan Edwards' *History of the Work of Redemption*', *Eighteenth-Century Studies*, VIII (1975), 300–14; and John F. Wilson, 'Jonathan Edwards as Historian', *Church History*, XLVI (1977), 5–18.
83 Joseph Bellamy, *Sermons upon the Following Subjects* (Boston, 1758); Samuel Hopkins, *A Treatise on the Millennium* (Boston, 1793); Heimert, *Religion*, pp. 113–14, 340–6.
84 John Willison, *Popery Another Gospel* (Edinburgh, 1745); John Erskine, *The Signs of the Times Consider'd* (Edinburgh, 1742), p. 8. See Iain H. Murray, *The Puritan Hope: A Study in Revival and the Interpretation of Prophecy* (1971); Arthur Fawcett, *The Cambuslang Revival: The Scottish Evangelical Revival of the Eighteenth Century* (1971).
85 Timothy Dwight, *America: or, a Poem on the Settlement of the British Colonies* (New Haven, 1780), p. 9.
86 See Nathan O. Hatch, *The Sacred Cause of Liberty: Republican Thought and the Millennium in Revolutionary New England* (New Haven, 1977); Davidson, *The Logic*; Heimert, *Religion*.
87 Stein, ed., *Apocalyptic Writings*, pp. 33, 449, 459.
88 John Mellen, *The Duty of All to be Ready for Future Impending Events* (Boston, 1756), pp. 19–20; John Burt, *The Mercy of God to His People* (Newport, R.I., 1759), p. 4.
89 James Cogswell, *GOD, the Pious Soldier's Strength & Instructor* (Boston, 1757), p. 26; Jonathan Mayhew, *A Sermon Preach'd in the Audience of His Excellency William Shirley* (Boston, 1754), pp. 23, 25, 31, 36–8.
90 Samuel Langdon, *Joy and Gratitude to God* (Portsmouth, N.H., 1760), p. 43; Jonathan Mayhew, *Two Discourses Delivered October 25th. 1759* (Boston, 1759), p. 61; Mather Byles, *A Sermon Delivered March 6th 1760* (New London, Conn., 1760), p. 13.

91 Bercovitch, *American Jeremiad*, p. 125; Samuel Sherwood, *The Church's Flight into the Wilderness* (1776), pp. 8, 11, 14–15, 24, 37, 46. See Stephen J. Stein, 'An Apocalyptic Rationale for the American Revolution', *Early American Literature*, IX (1975), 211–25.
92 Samuel West, *A Sermon Preached before the Honorable Council* (Boston, 1776), pp. 53–4, 67.
93 Samuel Langdon, *Government Corrupted by Vice, and Recovered by Righteousness* (Watertown, Mass., 1775), cited in *The Wall and the Garden: Selected Massachusetts Election Sermons 1670–1775*, ed. A. W. Plumstead (Minneapolis, 1968), pp. 372–3.
94 Nicholas Street, *The American States Acting Over the Part of the Children of Israel in the Wilderness* (New Haven, 1777), cited in *God's New Israel: Religious Interpretations of American Destiny*, ed., Conrad Cherry (Englewood Cliffs, N. J., 1971): Thomas Bray, *A Dissertation on the Sixth Vial* (Hartford, 1780), p. vii; Davidson, *The Logic*, p. 247; Lowance, *Language of Canaan*, p. 186; Heimert, *Religion*, p. 394.
95 Ezra Stiles, *The United States Elevated to Glory and Honour* (New Haven, 1783), pp. 8–9, 66, 70, 96–8.
96 David Tappan, *A Discourse Delivered at the Third Parish in Newbury* (Boston, 1783), cited in Catherine L. Albanese, *Sons of the Fathers: The Civil Religion of the American Revolution* (Philadelphia, 1976), pp. 300–1.
97 Timothy Dwight, *A Valedictory Address . . . At Yale College* (New Haven, 1776), pp. 13–14, 16. See Kenneth Silverman, *Timothy Dwight* (1969).
98 Silverman, *Dwight*, p. 38; Timothy Dwight, *A Sermon, Preached at Stamford . . . upon the General Thanksgiving* (Hartford, 1778), p. 9.
99 Timothy Dwight, *America*, pp. 3, 9.
100 Timothy Dwight, *Sermon Preached at Northampton . . . Occasioned by the Capture of British Army* (Hartford, 1781), pp. 19, 27.
101 Bercovitch, *American Jeremiad*, p. 130.
102 Timothy Dwight, *The Conquest of Canaan* (Hartford, 1785), pp. 1, 255. See also Ernest Lee Tuveson, *Redeemer Nation: The Idea of America's Millennial Role* (Chicago, 1968), pp. 106–8; and J. F. Maclear, 'The Republic and the Millennium', in *The Religion of the Republic*, ed., Elwyn A. Smith (Philadelphia, 1971), pp. 183–216.
103 Hatch, *Sacred Cause*, p. 130.
104 Jeremy Belknap, *A Sermon Delivered on the 9th of May, 1798* (Boston, 1798), pp. 19–20; Nathan Strong, *Political Instruction from the Prophecies of God's Word* (Hartford, 1798); *Independent Chronicle*, 1–4 July, 1799, p. 1, col. 4.
105 Timothy Dwight, *The Nature and Danger of Infidel Philosophy* (New Haven, 1798); Dwight, *The Duty of Americans, at the Present Crisis* (New Haven, 1798); Davidson, *The Logic*, p. 290.
106 Timothy Dwight, *The Triumph of Infidelity* (n.p., 1788), p. iii; Dwight, *A Discourse on Some Events of the Last Century* (New Haven, 1801), p. 41.
107 C. Mather, *Magnalia*, Bk. VII, p. 103.

MARY WILSON CARPENTER
GEORGE P. LANDOW

11 Ambiguous revelations: the Apocalypse and Victorian literature

I

Victorian literature presents an interesting case to those concerned with the influence of the Bible and biblical tradition upon secular culture. M. H. Abrams and other critics have clearly demonstrated the major extent to which Wordsworth, Blake, and the other Romantics employed secularized extensions of Christian thought, of which the apocalyptic themes of the marriage of heaven and earth and the end of the world figured importantly.[1] Nonetheless, critics of the Romantics have so accustomed us to thinking of nineteenth-century British culture as essentially humanistic, rather than Christian, that students of the later nineteenth century too easily assume that any reference to Apocalypse after 1800 can only take the form of loose analogy. Of course, British art and literature, like that throughout the West since the 1790s, displays many more situations, metaphors, and images of crisis analogous to the Apocalypse than detailed allusions to it.[2] One unfortunate corollary of the false assumption that English Romanticism and Post-Romanticism relate only distantly to contemporary religion is that their students do not have to acquaint themselves with either the Bible or the interpretive traditions according to which it was commonly understood.

Even were such an interpretation of Romanticism correct, Victorian studies would have to follow a different path. The situation in Victorian literature differs profoundly from that created by the first Romantic generation because of a dramatic – and until recently, almost completely unnoticed – revival of biblical prophecy, typology, and apocalyptics. This return to prominence of older exegetic practice, which often took on specifically Victorian intonations, means that the student of the age must know well both the Bible and contemporary attitudes towards its interpretation. Victorian uses of the Apocalypse in secular literature, for example, take far more elaborate forms than mere distant echoes of archetypal structures drawn from it.

The great Evangelical revival of the early nineteenth century produced a religious situation at mid-century which differed radically from what had obtained at 1800, for by the third decade at least two thirds of British Protestants within and without the established church practised some form of Evangelical religion. Evangelicalism, which thus shaped most people's attitudes towards reading and interpretation, taught countless nineteenth-century readers sophisticated approaches to typology and biblical prophecy, both of which they often found in rather surprising portions of Holy Scripture.[3] Therefore, a precise knowledge of the Bible and its associated interpretive traditions formed a crucial element in the intellectual heritage (or intellectual baggage) of nineteenth-century readers, who possessed a rich repertoire of forms, codes, and symbols derived from the Book of Revelation and other books of the Bible.

The cultural accessibility of complex allusions to the Apocalypse in the Victorian age perhaps best appears in the fact that so many popular works made use of them. One finds little surprising in the fact that Edward Bickersteth, an Evangelical clergyman, wrote a popular visionary epic, *Yesterday, Today, and For-Ever* (1866), which tries to outdo Milton both by casting away all allusions to pagan literature and by furnishing a poetic redaction of the Apocalypse.[4] Similarly, William Holman Hunt's *The Light of the World* (1853), which was probably the most popular British religious painting of the nineteenth century, illustrates a verse from the Book of Revelation, and the artist's very popular *Triumph of the Innocents* (versions 1884, 1887), which he painted many years later, parallels – and possibly derives from – John Keble's 'The Holy Innocents', which takes as its text Revelation 14.4. Keble's extraordinarily popular *The Christian Year* also makes half a dozen other references to the Apocalypse.

Given a large contemporary audience capable of responding to the kind of allusions made by these religious works, Victorian authors like Carlyle and Ruskin frequently salt their prose with heavy allusion to the Apocalypse. Tennyson's 'The Holy Grail', which makes several crucial allusions to Revelation, employs them differently than did either of these two previous groups of literary and pictorial artists. Whereas Bickersteth, Hunt, and Keble represent those who convey essentially religious themes by means of orthodox allusions, Carlyle and Ruskin, both of whom at one time or another abandoned orthodox Christianity, represent those many authors who employ specific allusions to the Apocalypse in extended and usually secularized forms. In contrast, Tennyson, who writes as a Christian, employs his allusions to the Book of Revelation to call into question the entire notion of revelation itself. Tennyson, we recall, began *The Idylls of the King* with 'The Coming of Arthur', in which he dramatizes the essentially subjective means by which men and women attain to belief. After questioning others about their reasons for accepting Arthur's authenticity, King Leodogrand, Guinevere's father, falls asleep and has an ambiguous dream which presents Arthur's kingship in apocalyptic terms, for it includes both a joining of heaven and earth and the end of a world. He awakens and decides to give his daughter, his faith, and his allegiance to the young, untested monarch. Later in *The Idylls*, Tennyson presents such essentially subjective decisions far more darkly, since in 'The Holy Grail' the grail vision comes to almost every knight as a disruptive force which leads him to break faith with his king and seek salvation for himself. At the close of the idyll, Tennyson has Arthur, who had been away from Camelot on a mission of justice and mercy when the vision appeared, tell how he, like the ploughman, must first do his task and not chase after ambiguous revelations. Using allusions from the Gospels and contemporary prophetic readings of the Psalms, Tennyson thus strongly suggests that one should avoid immersing oneself in apocalyptics and instead confine oneself to the clearer portions of scripture as guides for living on this earth. The poet's closing allusions, like those to the Book of Revelation in the visions of Percival, Bors, and Launcelot, display a detailed knowledge of apocalyptics being used, at least in part, to attack what he believes to be an excessive concentration upon them.

II

As a way of suggesting the almost astonishing popularity of both commentaries on the Apocalypse and speculations about its contemporary relevance, we shall look in detail at George Eliot's *Romola*. George Eliot provides a particularly interesting test case. Although she wrote her novels as a non-religious, self-consciously humanistic author, she had earlier been a devout Evangelical and, like so many other major writers of the age, including Carlyle and Ruskin, she retained Evangelical attitudes towards symbolism, meaning, and interpretation long after she relinquished her religious belief. *Romola*, Eliot's historical novel set in fifteenth-century Florence, thus offers the intriguing example of a secular author's employing detailed allusions to the Apocalypse in a work of popular fiction.

Critics who have perceived that a concern with the Apocalypse informs the subject and theme of her final novel, *Daniel Deronda*, have mistaken the presence of such a concern and have taken it to be a surprising development in Eliot's art and thought. Indeed, they have seen it as a radical departure from her earlier writing.[5] In fact, *Romola* and the novels which follow it – *Felix Holt*, *Middlemarch*, and *Daniel Deronda* – all employ such apocalyptic materials. Like *Romola*, each employs as a structural device a central change or personal reformation, and, as the following pages will demonstrate, precisely such reformation played a major part in those apocalyptic schemes familiar to Eliot.

Thus, the novels which U. C. Knoepflmacher has well characterized as centering on the 'historical life of man' all employ apocalyptic schemes in one way or another.[6]

Daniel Deronda thus tells the story of how a young Jew named Daniel discovers both his prophetic vocation and his mission to gentile society. In *Middlemarch*, on the other hand, apocalyptic imagery provides a kind of metaphorical drama or apocalyptic myth, which adds another dimension to the novel's complex web.[7] In *Felix Holt*, Rufus Lyon's interest in 'those painstaking interpretations of the Book of Daniel', which the narrator describes as 'mistaken criticism', nevertheless constitute an important strand in the little minister's characterization.[8] All three of Eliot's novels following *Romola*, then, reveal obvious indications of her continuing interest in both the Book of Revelation and the various traditional modes of interpreting it.

Each of these novels is apocalyptic in another sense: each exhibits a structure based on a central turning point which functions as an analogy for the Protestant Reformation. Henry Alley postulates that chapters 35 and 36, which occur precisely midway through the book's 70 chapters, provide a crucial 'turning point' in the action, for both Daniel and Gwendolyn experience dramatic changes of perspective which constitute reformations of their views of themselves.[9] Similarly, a central reformation divides *Middlemarch*, for at the end of the fourth of eight books Dorothea achieves that first great renovation of fellow-feeling for her husband and walks down the corridor with him, hand in hand. A similar division of the novel into two eras of political reform parallels Dorothea's personal change, for the Reform Bill struggle echoes only faintly in the town of Middlemarch during the first four books of the novel, but in the second four it becomes active in the town.[10] In *Felix Holt* the Reform Bill has already become the law of the land but the elections based on it have not yet taken place. Therefore, the political life in Treby Magna is divided by the election held on 15 December. The election also divides Esther's spiritual or visionary growth, for Felix is imprisoned after it, and she must proceed independently to her declaration to reject Transome Court. Again, a division into pre- and post-Reform periods parallels the beginning of a personal reformation.

Belief in a central division symbolizing both personal and political reformation characterized the expositors who made up the continuous historical school of apocalyptics. *Romola* exhibits not only that division, but a complex poetic scheme which imitates the Apocalypse in detail. In addition, the novel, which centers upon the problems of an ordinary person following a prophet during a time of shaken religious belief and political turmoil, exemplifies another common Victorian practice – the detailed use of allusion to the Apocalypse to call it into question.

Clearly, the kind of sophisticated, ironic, and often subversive application of this specific portion of scripture to a work of secular art could only appear at a particular stage in the history of Western culture. Such sophisticated allusion requires that a sufficiently large portion of the author's intended audience have the knowledge of hermeneutic traditions necessary to understand such allusions and yet have relinquished literal belief in them sufficiently to be willing to see such matters treated in what are ultimately non-religious and, to some, even blasphemous ways. Such literary applications, in other words, can only arise at the end of a tradition, at a time when considerable numbers of a work's potential audience possess detailed knowledge of some system of belief and its associated cultural codes but no longer feels willing or able to give allegiance to it.

George Eliot's Florentine novel, *Romola*, takes the form of a symbolic narrative in which elaborate patterns of myth and metaphor inform her characteristic realism, and the model for such a reading of history is to be found primarily not in classical mythology or other sources proposed by recent critics but in the Book of Revelation, which she had learned to read as a symbolic history of the Western world.[11] As Eliot's struggles with the scheme of her novel attest, she was unable to employ that design without a great deal of ambivalence. Long before she began *Romola* Eliot had abandoned her earlier Evangelical Anglican religious belief but not its associated attitudes towards history, time, and interpretation, for like so many other lapsed Evangelicals, such as Ruskin and Carlyle, she long retained the impress of her former faith. In particular, after she had lost the belief that served as the basis for certain basic Evangelical attitudes, she still felt drawn to the Apocalyptic scheme as an imaginative structure.

A second major reason for the influence of Evangelical interpretation of the Book of Revelation upon *Romola* appears in the fact that public interest in prophetic exposition reached an unprecedented peak of popularity by 1860, when Eliot decided to write her 'historical romance' based on the life of Savonarola. She thus conceived, wrote, and published her novel in the context of what Robert Mackay in 1854 had termed 'a crazy infatuation about prophecies'.[12] Eliot's portrait of a problematic prophet is, then, a critical response to a wave of mid-Victorian apocalypticism which attempts not only to offer a valid interpretation of the Book of Revelation for her own time but also comment upon the basic nature of prophetic inspiration itself. *Romola* represents the crucial question of the prophet's authenticity – and also Eliot's solutions to this problem.

Prophecy 'fulfilled and unfulfilled' had been a burning issue in the Evangelicalism of Eliot's youth,[13] and her letters show her fully caught up in expectations of a coming Apocalypse. For example, in October 1840 she described waiting for the great changes to come:

> Events are so momentous, and the elements of society in so chemically critical a state that a drop seems enough to change its whole form. After expanding the

imagination in questions as to the mode in which the great transmutations of the kingdoms of the world into the kingdoms of our Lord will be effected we are reduced to the state of pausation in which the inhabitants of heaven are described to be held, before the outpourings of the Vials.[14]

In a letter written two years before, in November 1838, she had looked askance at the 'vagaries of the Irvingites and the blasphemies of Joanna Southcote' and similar 'fanciful interpretations', which erroneously convinced many sober people to take

> any diving into the future plans of Providence as the boldest presumption; but I do think that a sober and prayerful consideration of the mighty revolutions ere long to take place in our world by God's blessing serve to make us less grovelling, more devoted and energetic in the service of God. Of course I mean only such study as pigmies like myself in intellect and acquirement are able to persecute; the perusal and comparison of Scripture and the works of pious and judicious men on the subject. (GEL, I, 11)

This widespread fascination with applying the apocalyptic predictions to contemporary nineteenth-century events clearly violated the spirit of the more conservative approaches that had dominated English scriptural studies a short time before. For example, Bishop Thomas Hartwell Horne, whose *An Introduction to the Critical Study and Knowledge of the Holy Scriptures* was a standard work for clerical students of many denominations, specifically warned: 'We are not to attempt the particular explanation of those prophecies which remain to be fulfilled'.[15] According to Horne, who advocated elaborate typological interpretation (and hence was hardly against elaborate interpretations per se), the subject of the Book of Revelation

> is not a temporal but a spiritual kingdom ... governing the inward man, by possession of the ruling principles: *the kingdom of God*, says our Lord, *is within you.* (Luke xvii. 21). The predictions relative to this kingdom, therefore, are to be spiritually interpreted. Wars, conquests, and revolutions, of vast extent and great political import, are not the object of apocalyptical prophecies; unless they appear to have promoted or retarded in considerable degree the *real* progress of the religion of Jesus Christ, whose proper reign is in the hearts and consciences of his subjects.

The kind of fascination with an external, historical fulfilment of the prophecies in the Apocalypse displayed by the young Eliot and so many of her contemporaries, then, clearly marks a change in attitude from views just a few decades earlier. The significance of such changed attitudes towards the Book of Revelation for the student of Victorian literature appears in the fact that many major writers came to maturity during the period when such renewed fascination with the subject of Apocalypse was at its height.

References to prophecy and to the Millennium long filled the pages of the

Christian Observer, the periodical which published Mary Ann Evans's first poem and which the religious historian Owen Chadwick describes as 'the focus and arbiter of instructed evangelical opinion'.[16] For example, in 1825, when Eliot was still a child, two lengthy articles reviewed a dozen recent English works on prophecy, and their author remarked upon 'the present revivification' of the Millennial question.[17] A decade later James H. Frere, himself an expositor of the Apocalypse, commented that 'the inundation of prophetic writings with which the church has been deluged for the past 10 years having in some measure passed away . . . I am observing with some anxiety what form the inquiry into the meaning of the Prophetic Scriptures will now assume'.[18] The lull he observed was only temporary, for by 1839 this great concern with the millennial question produced an acrimonious debate about missionary work. The debate began when a Rev. Goode announced that he expected no great results from proselytizing since these were not pre-millennial times but rather the 'times of the Gentiles' when the Church could expect only persecution and inevitable diminishment.[19] The conservative editors of the *Observer* did their best to damp down the resulting flames of controversy, noting that 'In reply to several correspondents who take different views of the Pre-Millenarian question upon Missionary Societies, we think enough has been said on both sides for the purposes of truth, and that more might not promote love'.[20] Evangelical interest in the Millennium – as this interchange suggests – was not characterized by radicalism in either theology or politics. As Owen Chadwick has observed, the Evangelicals were 'prayer-book men, establishment men, Tories', who believed that 'reform was of the heart', not of the institution.[21]

Eliot, who accepted the historical interpretation of the Book of Revelation, assumed that its images and symbols accurately prophesied the events of world history. This assumption appears in her intended 'Ecclesiastic Chart', a project which occupied her during 1840. As she wrote to Maria Lewis, she intended the chart, which she wished to sell to raise money for church charities, to correlate ecclesiastical and political history and to include 'possibly an application of the Apocalyptic prophecies, which would merely require a few figures and not take up room' (GEL, I, 44). Although Eliot subscribed to two series of religious books and received encouragement to use the Arbury Hall library at this time, she seems to have been unaware of the existence of other, historico–prophetic charts. This fact suggests that she was largely unacquainted with interpretations of prophecy written in the early decades of the nineteenth century, since many such works contained detailed charts correlating historical events with 'figures' – that is, with chapter and verse numbers – for prophecies from Revelation and Daniel.[22] Eliot's letters suggest that she saw such charts for the first time in March and April 1840 when Maria Lewis and Martha Jackson each sent her one (GEL, I, 44, 48), and apparently only then did she learn that her scheme was not original but a common presentation of history in her time.

E. B. Elliott's Chart of Synchronisms. Reproduced from *Horae Apocalypticae* (1862) by permission of the Widener Library, Harvard University

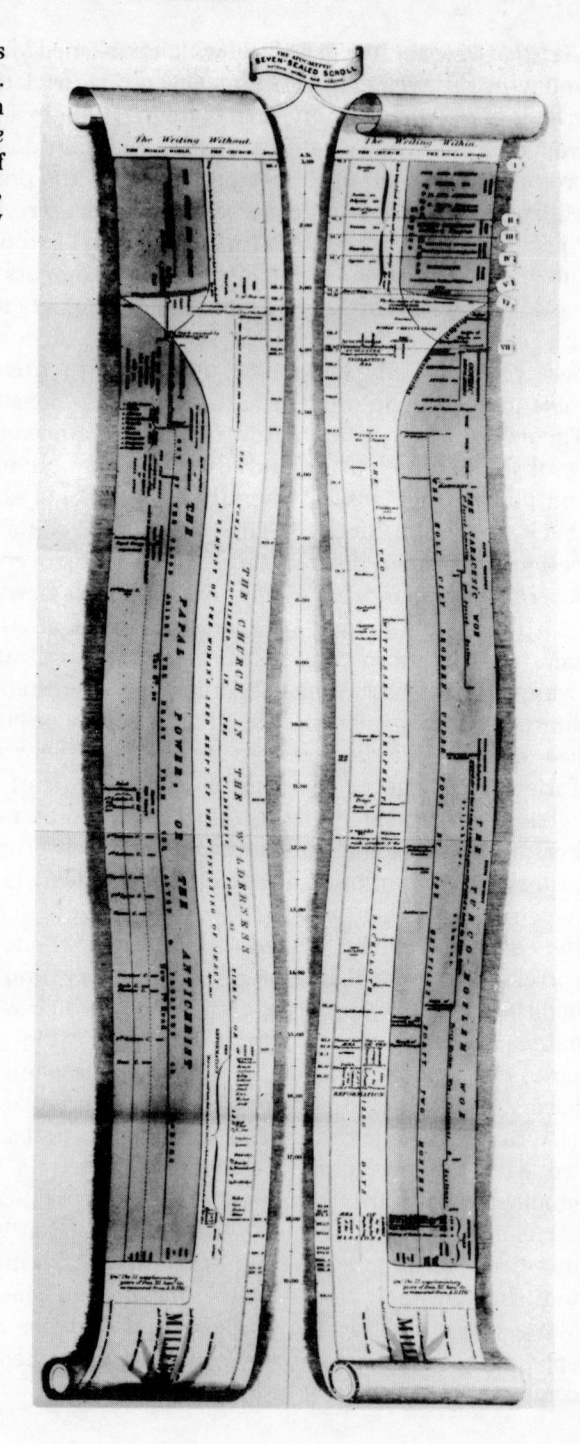

The great, perhaps astonishing, fascination with such prophetic exegesis that pervaded mid-Victorian England appears with clarity in the sympathetic article that the *Times* accorded to the subject on 9 November 1859. As the writer correctly pointed out,

> There has arisen during the stirring years which still run their course a very widespread attention to the study of unfulfilled prophecy. Books on the subject are in great demand, and the supply apparently meets the demand. It is not unnatural to expect this. The last 10 years, dating their beginning at the great European convulsion of 1848, have, without doubt, witnessed so many national complications, social changes, and individual sufferings – event has so rapidly thundered on event, and scene flashed on scene – so altered have the face of Europe and the relations of Cabinets become, and so unsettled is the European sky at this hour, that intelligent and sober-minded men, with no spice of fanaticism in their nature, have begun to conclude that the sublime predictions uttered on the Mount 1800 years ago are being daily translated into modern history. Students of prophecy allege that they see the apocalyptic 'vials' pouring out, and hear the 'seven trumpets' uttering their voices and pealing in reverberation through Christendom.

The Times writer describes three main schools of apocalyptic exposition in contemporary England: first, those 'very few and feeble' writers, known as the Praeterist School, who believed that the prophecies in Daniel and Revelation had all met fulfillment in the distant past; the second group, 'far more numerous, learned, and intelligent', who believed that nothing of the Apocalypse had yet been fulfilled and were accordingly called the Futurist School; and the third 'most able and laborious school' whose members held that 'the Apocalypse is a continuous prospective history of Christendom'. According to this last group, 'the continuous historical school', the seals, trumpets, and vials of the Apocalypse accurately predicted the history of the Roman Empire and the barbarian invasions as well as the course of the French Revolution and the decay of the Ottoman Empire. Such a reading of the Book of Revelation so convinced the writer for *The Times* that he found himself 'almost driven to accept the interpretation'.

This 'continuous historical school' formed a distinctively Protestant exegetic tradition which identified the Pope as Antichrist and read the Apocalypse as a symbolic history whose principal event was the Reformation.[23] E. B. Elliott, the leading exponent of this school in England during the 1850s and 1860s, first published his four-volume commentary on Revelation, *Horae Apocalypticae*, in 1844, and other editions appeared in 1846, 1847, 1850, and 1862. The third and later ones included a detailed 'Sketch of the History of Apocalyptic Interpretation', which summarized the subject from the earliest known to the most recent commentators. Elliott's 'Sketch' is of particular interest to the student concerned with the influence of such scriptural exegesis upon secular literature because it reveals the overwhelming interest in narrative structure which characterizes his school. Despite Elliott's erudition, he – like so many others who accepted the historical interpretation of apocalyptic prophecy – could not himself resist donning the mantle of prophecy and predicted the Millennium would begin sometime in 1866.[24]

Although Elliott and other members of the continuous historical school looked upon Joseph Mede as the 'father of English apocalyptics', their readings of the Book of Revelation differed fundamentally from those of many seventeenth-century exegetes who followed Mede but were far more politically radical than he. In fact, the apocalyptic interpretations which characterized the seventeenth-century adherents of this exegetical school found themselves transformed in the nineteenth century into defences of politically conservative and even reactionary positions. In other words, the Apocalypse justified throwing off the papal yoke, but it did not justify either enfranchising Roman Catholics or granting civil rights to the Jews.

The essential conservatism of this continuous historical school also appears in its expectable opposition to the largely German hermeneutic approaches of the Praeterists, who were unwilling to ascribe supernatural inspiration to the literary structures and symbols in the Apocalypse.[25] Instead, Praeterist critics emphasized the historical situation of the prophet, his audience, and message, and they therefore attempted to explain apocalyptic images by reference to the events of the prophet's own time.

The twenty-two year old Eliot broke decisively with Evangelical Christianity in January 1842, when the tide of millenarianism in England was continuing its rapid rise. By 1855 Eliot, who had herself once asserted that one could look 'into the future plans of Providence' (GEL, I, 11) without presumption, attacked the kind of prophetic interpretation epitomized by Dr Cumming, the popular Evangelical preacher whose lectures on the Apocalypse had packed Exeter Hall. The central problem with such 'Evangelical teaching', she protested, was its 'net moral effect', for Cumming was more concerned with encouraging the believer to look for 'the visible advent of Christ in 1864' than with encouraging the believer to look for the kingdom of God within.[26] Granted, Eliot had long looked askance at Cumming's extravagant prophetic exegesis, but now that she abandoned her own faith she was attacking him for attempting to make even the kind of interpretation she once thought entirely possible and appropriate. Not surprisingly, an article which appeared in the sceptical *Westminster Review* did little to dampen the mid-Victorian rage for prophecy, which became even more heated.

Of course, Eliot hardly opposed the mushrooming school of historical interpretation alone. In fact, three of her acquaintances published works criticizing this approach in 1860 and 1861. Of these, the most conservative was the Broad Churchman, F. D. Maurice, whose warm response to *Romola* deeply touched her.[27] In 1861 he published his *Lectures on the Apocalypse*, which argues that since the author of the Book of Revelation actually described the fall of Jerusalem and other first-century events, his visions have met fulfillment and do not constitute a supernatural vision of events far in the future. They can therefore have no predictive value for Victorian England. Maurice none the less defends the essential value of the Apocalypse and all biblical prophecy, which according to him, is not 'a mere announcement of future events' but 'the utterance of the mind of Him who is and was and is to come.... The seer was to explain the past and present; only in connexion with these did he speak of the future.... This is Prophecy.'[28]

In contrast to Maurice's approach to the Apocalypse, that taken by Sara Hennell, one of Eliot's oldest friends and her most faithful correspondent, essentially abandons any belief in divine inspiration of such prophetic works. Her pamphlet on New Testament prophecy, which emphasized the Apocalypse, was reviewed quite favorably in the *Westminster Review* and won the Baillie Prize.[29] Hennell's essay, which expresses admiration for the Apocalypse as a literary work, presents a profoundly Romantic conception of prophecy, for it holds that the divine order depicted in the prophet's 'glowing colours' and 'gorgeous imagery' will be realized, not by '*sudden violent interposition*' but by '*the gradual unfolding of the human mind*' and spirit.[30] She holds that although Christ and his apostles mistakenly believed that the world would end in their generation, the author of the Book of Revelation nevertheless had envisioned an eternal truth. But this truth takes the form of a poetic, rather than an historical one. Thus, while corroborating the sceptical findings of German High Criticism, Hennell still manages to defend the essential truth of the Apocalypse by interpreting it as a work of poetic truth.

Both Hennell's and Maurice's books appear on the heading list of an essay about the Apocalypse which appeared in the October 1861 *Westminster Review*. W. M. W. Call, the author of this study, was also known to Eliot, who had first recommended him as a contributor to the journal.[31] Call, who cites prominent German as well as English students of the Apocalypse, presents an admittedly 'secular exposition' of the matter. To begin with, he identifies the Apocalypse as partaking of a distinct and distinctive literary genre. First describing the 'cycle' or literary tradition of Judaeo–Christian apocalyptic works from which the Book of Revelation emerged – Daniel, the Jewish Sibyl, Enoch, and the fourth book of Esdras – he then analyzes the apocalyptic structure, style, and theme which characterize the tradition. Call clearly does not accept historical interpretation to be literally true, and he describes prophecy as 'a dim outline of an imagined history of the immediate future of the world'.

The chief significance of Call's essay lies in its detailed examination of the Apocalypse as a literary work which remained profoundly relevant (he claimed) to his own time. Call's analysis of the structure of the Apocalypse rests on its division into two great 'series', the second of which begins with the woman clothed with the sun. He also describes the prophet's use of numbers, not as either mystical symbols or as historical facts, but as an indication of the 'artificial and imaginary character of the whole work'. According to Call, the author of the Book of Revelation invoked the 'septenary principle', or the repeated use of the number seven, because 'Seven is a symbol of perfection or entireness', and he similarly employed the number four because it symbolizes unity:

> We thus see a reason for the septenary arrangement of the Apocalyptic vision, and are perfectly convinced that there could not be more than seven trumpets, seven vials, and seven seals, or fewer than three woes, or more than four cherubim. Does not Irenaeus assure us, on the authority of a somewhat different though equally cogent logic, that there could not be more than four Gospels, because there were not more than four winds, and was not Irenaeus right? (p. 470)

Call even makes a playful sally at the symbolism of 666, the number of the beast, when he provides his own arithmetical computation for the consideration of Cumming and his fellow 'mystagogues'.

In his closing paragraph, Call, who eloquently expresses the same belief in the apocalyptic nature of the present age found in *The Times* article, argues in terms clearly reminiscent of Carlyle that despite the failure of the Apocalypse's multiple predictions it nonetheless possesses 'an element of truth and reality':

> Our own times, since, at least the French Revolution, have been stormy, turbulent, explosive, minatory as his. Old creeds are dying out; a new faith slowly and simply growing up; social and national change advancing or impending. In the midst of the wreck of the past the prophetic soul that is in man reawakens.... Our ideal is not a celestial but an earthly ideal. We ask for no millennial resurrection, and for no impossible theocracy. . . . But not the less does 'the hope that springs eternal' connect us with the future of the world: not the less do we look for some proximate realization of our dream of terrestrial justice, wisdom, and love; . . . not the less do the bells of our English towns and villages seem . . . to 'ring out the darkness of the land; to ring in the Christ that is to be'. (pp. 486–7)

Call here goes beyond the usual office of the apocalyptic expositor, and, like Tennyson (whose *In Memoriam* he quotes), dons the mantle of prophecy. Instead of merely explaining the scheme of prophecy as it exists in history or Apocalypse, he proclaims a 'new faith' and looks at an 'earthly ideal'.

III

At the time she wrote *Romola* George Eliot held views closer to the Praeterists than to any other school of prophetic interpretation, and in *Felix Holt* she had her narrator consign the continuous historical school to 'the limbo of mistaken criticism'. Nonetheless, when she came to write her novel, she still chose to draw heavily upon Evangelical Anglican interpretive approaches. One reason that she continued to draw upon a body of thought that she had apparently outgrown and then abandoned appears in the imaginative power, coherence, and fascinating structures with which it endows apocalyptics. As Bernard McGinn has correctly pointed out in his study of mediaeval thought, the fundamental impulse underlying apocalyptics is 'the desire to understand history – its unity, its structure, its goal, the future hope which it promises'.[32] In other words, the apocalyptic expositor, like the historical novelist, seeks to give history a meaningful form. The continuous historical school's attempts to map the landscape of time, which Eliot learned as a young woman, first shaped her conceptions of human history, and in her later years she reinterpreted the apocalyptic map rather than casting it away and drawing an entirely new one.

Schooled in the continuous historical critic's interpretation of the Book of Revelation, George Eliot had available to her a model of complexity and richness to impose upon (or discover in) history. She was thoroughly familiar with what Samuel Davidson would later protest was 'the fatal error of converting apocalyptic poetry into historical prose, and of making all symbols significant'.[33] But for her as for Call the apocalyptic model cried out to be translated into an earthly ideal: what had become a closed pattern in the English school of continuous historical interpretation demanded to be turned into an open one – one prophesying the new faith which would transform visions of past, present, and future.[34]

After many abortive attempts, Eliot finally succeeded in drafting a 'scheme' for the plot of *Romola* in December 1861, and on the first day of the new year she noted in her journal that she had begun the novel. The scheme which finally satisfied her was in fact a reinterpretation of the traditional scheme of apocalyptics. Like the members of the continuous historical school, she accepted that history could be found mirrored in the symbols and structure of the Book of Revelation. Unlike her orthodox predecessors, however, Eliot conceived that these apocalyptic forms and structures should culminate not in an imminent Second Coming but in a second Reformation of Christianity itself.

Eliot thus organizes the narrative around a reformation which serves as a landmark both in her protagonist's spiritual journey and in the historical Reformation, for the historical school considered Savonarola an 'early Protestant'. Reform, which occurs twice in Romola's story, becomes a structural metaphor that signifies the means by which the past is brought into meaningful relationship with the present. *Romola* thus interprets both the life of the individual and the history of Western civilization, then, as a series of such prophetic reforms in which prophetic vision transforms the religious and philosophical traditions into new, higher laws. In fifteenth-century Florence, Eliot found the same conflict between classical philosophy and Christianity – that is, between reason and spirit – which she believed characterized her own time. *Romola* gives this clash between what Arnold termed 'Hellenism' and 'Hebraism' the dramatic form of an apocalypse.[35]

Although *Romola* employs several apocalyptic historical structures to endow time and history with form, this essay will deal with but two of them: the bipartite division into two 'principal prophecies' and the septenary structure, in which the progress of the Church of Christ and its battle with Antichrist takes the form of seven stages or sections. These two narrative structures clearly reveal the influence of an apocalyptic vision of history which finds its center in reformation.

Precisely in the novel's center – in the thirty-sixth of seventy-two chapters – Romola is struck by 'a vague but arresting sense that she was somehow violently rending her life in two'.[36] Eliot accompanies her main character's recognition with an extensive symbolization of division into two parts. For example, Romola prepares to seal forever the chest containing her wedding clothes and puts on, instead of them, a monastic garment, and her wedding circlet of pearls is contrasted to the dark veil she will now assume; she takes out the little cross given to her by Savonarola from the tabernacle – painted, we remember, with a Bacchic scene – that her husband presented to her; the sweetness of the sugar-plum remaining from the wedding feast is contrasted with the bitterness of Romola's present feeling towards Tito. The novel's iconological patterns, which thus underline the significance of this dividing point in Romola's life, imitate the central division of the Apocalypse.

Although it had long been an interpretative commonplace to note that both the Apocalypse and the Book of Daniel divide into two roughly equal halves, post-Reformation historical interpretation endowed this division with a major new meaning. According to Protestant expositors, the command in Revelation 10.8–11 to the prophet to take the 'little open book', eat it, and 'prophesy again' functioned as a divinely ordained prophetic image of the Protestant Reformation, which opened the Bible to all men. Victorian expositors of the historical school merged this interpretation of history with Joseph Mede's division of the Apocalypse into 'two principal prophecies' and interpreted all history as dividing into two eras – those of the Pre- and Post-Reformation world.[37]

Romola's division of her own life into two parts resembles this apocalyptic division symbolically as well as numerologically. Just as the prophet finds the 'little open book' sweet in the mouth but bitter in the belly, so the 'sugar-plum' of Romola's wedding has turned to bitterness after initial sweetness; and, similarly, the first great prophecy of her life has also turned to bitterness, just as it has for the prophet of the Apocalypse. Furthermore, the painted tabernacle or triptych which has been 'sealed' is now opened, and from it Romola takes the little cross, which functions as a prophetic symbol of her 'reformation' into a Christian under the inspiration and guidance of Savonarola's 'higher law'.

In addition, the second great prophecy of Romola's life – like that in the Book of Revelation – signifies the historical Reformation. One contemporary critic finds it surprising Eliot devoted so little space in the novel to the 'Protestant era' and suggests she chose Savonarola as her prophetic figure because of a supposed Victorian fascination with Roman Catholicism, but the English school of historical interpretation characteristically took Savonarola as a proto-Protestant – a voice of the Reformation *before* the Reformation itself. According to this school, the 'two witnesses' of Revelation 11.3 should be interpreted as *voices* from within the Roman Catholic Church who prophesied or witnessed the Reformation before it took place. Bishop Newton, for example, describes Savonarola as one of the 'good men, who called aloud for a reformation in faith as well as in morals, in doctrine as well as in discipline' while yet in 'the bosom of the church of Rome'.[38] The biographies of Savonarola which Eliot read in preparation for *Romola* also emphasized such a Protestant view of him. Pasquale Villari described Savonarola, for instance, as a 'Martyr of Protestantism' and Karl Meier praised him as an 'evangelical prophet' who stood 'at the head of a new era'.[39]

The fact that it is Savonarola who now calls Romola to 'a higher law than any she had yet obeyed' thus conforms precisely to the apocalyptic scheme of history. Savonarola's teaching not only reforms or renovates her spiritually but also gives her the philosophical means to unite both halves of her life, and her marriage bond to Tito, which she had been on the point of breaking, is now strengthened in the context of a larger duty to the citizens of Florence. Moreover, under his direction Christianity reforms the pagan traditions of classical Stoicism and Bacchic hedonism, for charity, one's love of God in His creatures and creation, gives higher meaning to self-denial and romantic love.

Savonarola's call to Romola, which provides the second 'principal prophecy' of her life, thus serves as the heart of Eliot's narrative and presents the central meaning of Romola's entire history. The group of seven chapters beginning with chapter 42, all of which take place on 30 and 31 October 1496, depict Romola's 'Reformation' by means of an astonishingly complex web of poetic allusion to the Book of Revelation and the exegetical traditions by which it was most commonly understood. In these chapters, Romola's new law of charity first appears when she offers bread and wine to Baldassare – a symbolic eucharist which not only restores life to a dying man but simultaneously revives the past as well. The two succeeding chapters – 'The Unseen Madonna' and 'The Visible Madonna' – present Romola as the visible embodiment of that charitable love symbolized by the hidden madonna carried in a 'painted tabernacle'. The novel's movement from tabernacle to visible embodiment of Christianity and true Christian love obviously recalls the sequence created by the movement from Romola's little triptych, which is also called a 'painted tabernacle', to the cross which she takes from it. Both sequences suggest a typological interpretation of Revelation 7, the 'harvest of the Church', as the fulfillment or antitype of the Old Testament feast of tabernacles. According to the elder Edward Bickersteth, many of whose works were published in the Christian Family Library to which Eliot subscribed as a young woman, the Hebrew festival of the harvest was a type of the 'harvest of the Church' depicted in the 144 000 sealed 'in the forehead' and standing before the throne.[40]

The feast of tabernacles was believed by apocalyptic interpreters to have taken place sometime in the month of October, but this belief provides only one reason Eliot chose to set these crucial chapters on 30 and 31 October. Another reason appears in the fact that they enact not only the law of charity but also that of rebellion – or Protestantism. Suspecting Tito of a plan to betray Savonarola, she publicly compromises him in such a way that he dares not carry it out, and she then privately challenges him to 'begin a new life'. These acts of protest, which take place on 31 October, perhaps serve as a type, a prophetic embodiment, of Luther's nailing his 95 theses to the door, which took place on 31 October 1517. It is surely not coincidence either that Tito calls Romola 'my angry saint' on this Eve of All Saints Day, which in Keble's *The Christian Year* is commemorated by a poem on Revelation 7 and the 'unseen armies' of the servants of God.[41]

Eliot's uses of apocalyptic symbolism in this historical novel go even further. We have already observed that chapter 42 is the first of the seven chapters which portray Romola's spiritual renovation and rebellion. The forty-two months are, of course, the prophetic period of time assigned to the struggle between the woman 'clothed with the sun' who is menaced by the dragon as she struggles to bring forth a child.[42] Like the woman in the Apocalypse, Romola appears 'clothed' in the sun of righteousness in this section of the novel, and she also brings forth a spiritual 'child' in response to the prophesying of the witness Savonarola, even as she is also menaced by Tito's deceptions and betrayals. The seven chapters in which all this action takes place appropriately begins with the forty-second – in other words, with the prophetic number signifying all the major prophecies of the 'little open book'. Eliot's secularized applications of apocalyptic symbolic patterns imply that the Book of Revelation chiefly foretells spiritual reformations which occur in the life of each individual.

This group of seven chapters so laden with apocalyptic symbolism also plays a part in a larger septenary structure which divides Romola's story into seven stages that correspond to the 'stages of the Church' in the Apocalypse. In addition, this crucial gathering of chapters also incorporates allusions to two other parallel prophetic structures – the seven days of creation and the seven ages of time. The first four of these stages consist of clearly demarcated chronological periods consisting of groups of seven or fourteen chapters, each of which begins with a chapter whose number is a multiple of seven. The last three stages, which are less clearly demarcated, do not seem to follow an exact numerological pattern of chapters, but they nevertheless continue to mirror apocalyptic scheme and prophetic pattern. This division between four and three, the four being exact and the three less precise, resembles Savonarola's analysis of the stages of the Church.[43]

The first stage of the septenary structure, which can be only briefly summarized here, begins with the Feast of St. John the Baptist in chapter seven and ends in the twentieth with the carnival or pre-Lenten season of 1493, during which Tito and Romola are betrothed. These fourteen chapters cohere as an 'Age of Creation', a period of innocence and illusion for both Romola and Tessa. Light, the creation of the first day, is emphasized by the Feast of John the Baptist, which takes place on the summer solstice. Keble's poem for the feast suggests another, even more important symbolic association, since it develops the lectionary text from Malachi 5.5–6 – 'and he shall turn the hearts of the fathers to the children, and the heart of the children to their fathers' – into a type of returning to the past in order to prepare for the future. Keble's poem thus reminds us that Tito's deliberate decision to betray his foster-father breaks several divine commandments just as it attempts what no human being can do – to deny the reality and force of the past.

The next section, chapters twenty-one to thirty-four, take place during the month of November 1494. Savonarola's Advent sermons clearly identify this group of chapters with the Age of the Flood, for the preacher prophesies that the arrival of the French King in Florence will be a purifying scourge like that of the Deluge. In accordance with the traditional association of the Flood with the Fall, Romola experiences a fall from innocence when she discovers that her husband has sold her father's library. This section also subtly – and ironically – invokes a lectionary theme for the liturgical season when Tito dons an 'armour of fear' in sharp contrast with the 'armour of light' theme of the Advent collect.

The narrative moves to a third, distinct chronological period with chapters thirty-five through forty-one, which are set just before Christmas on 23 and 24 December 1494 (a flashback to Tito's affairs seems to include 22 December). In this section, which centres on the winter solstice or darkest time of the year, Romola feels she is tearing her life in two as she sets out to leave Tito, and during her flight she encounters Savonarola and his new spiritual light. Fittingly, the third age of time is that one in which Abraham leaves the land of his fathers and receives a new covenant; the parallel to Romola's case is clear, as is the symbolic appropriateness of the Christmas Collect, which petitions for regeneration and renewal. Tito, meanwhile, who denies Baldassare again at the Ruccellai supper and becomes deeply involved in political conspiracy, exemplies the work of darkness, whereas Romola embodies light beginning to shine in darkness.

The fourth section, which is set on 30 and 31 October 1495, corresponds to the fourth day of creation during which the sun, moon, and stars are created. During this period Romola's shining with the light of charity makes her seem a 'visible madonna'. This fourth age, or Age of David, serves as a type of Christ's kingdom, and his 'bride' Israel thus serves as a type of the bride of Christ, or the

Church. In this scheme Romola has now become the 'bride' or true church, for it is in such individual, personal form that Eliot holds that true religion must embody itself. As a harvest period, this section suggests a spiritual birth or Christ child. For the first time, however, Eliot's narrative deviates from the liturgical sequence of John the Baptist, Advent and Christmas Eve to an All Saints Eve rather than the expected Christmas season which follows in the liturgical year. Romola's journey, which has so far taken her through stages of innocence, a fall, and a darkest moment that is also an epiphany, culminates here in a universalized reformation and spiritual harvest rather than adhering strictly to the liturgical sequence. Eliot's modification suggests that she interprets Western history as a movement from self-directed forms of religion and philosophy to the Protestant Reformation, which purifies both Christianity and 'Hellenism' (Neo-Platonism).

The remainder of *Romola* continues to parallel this apocalyptic scheme of history, although it no longer does so with a precise septenary chapter structure. The flaming pyramid in chapter forty-nine symbolizes the beginning of a period of painful illumination for Eliot's protagonist, for she experiences a fiery baptism or Pentecost which begins a new epoch in her life. Both Camilla Ruccellai's dangerous fanaticism and Savonarola's increasingly political motivation force Romola to recognize the limitations of prophet and prophecy. As a division of the narrative, chapters forty-nine through fifty-four correspond to the schemes exegetes traditionally associated with the days and ages of creation: scriptural expositors associated the fifth day, on which birds and fishes were created, with the 'fishing' or judgment of men, and some also interpreted the fifth epoch, the Age of Exile or Captivity, as a period of painful education. In the Apocalypse, the pouring out of the vials of Revelation 16 and 17 similarly signifies a day of judgment.

Beginning in chapter fifty-six, 'the Other Wife', Romola enters a sixth stage which is, in many ways, a culmination of her old life, for with the seventh and last stage she begins a new life. Her discovery of Tessa, Tito's mistress, and the execution of her godfather Bernardo Del Nero, which takes place despite her attempts to intervene with Savonarola, complete her disillusionment with both Tito and Savanarola. 'All clinging' to the past ends, for she no longer feels any viable ties to her father's house, her husband, or the prophet who had directed the course of her life. Now her first creation is finished, and she stands on the eve of a new vision. Like the sixth age in human history, which takes man from the birth of Christ to His Second Coming, Romola's sixth age is apocalyptic, since it stands poised on the eve of a new dispensation and second great remaking and re-formation.

In chapter sixty-one, 'Drifting Away', Romola sets out to sea in a small boat, an action which critics from Sara Hennell on have judged to be inappropriately unrealistic but which Eliot defended as part of the 'romantic and symbolical elements' (GEL, IV, 104) planned from her earliest version of the story. Having already observed the elaborate applications of apocalyptic symbol and structure that Eliot made in the earlier portions of her novel, we can now perceive that she chose this action because it parallels the woman in Revelation 12.13–17 who takes refuge in the wilderness when the serpent sends forth a flood to carry her away. The boat perhaps also suggests a third tabernacle or ark from which Romola will emerge once again as a living symbol of charitable love. This time, however, that love takes on even greater breadth, for Romola experiences a 'new baptism' or new perspective on life during her period in the village.

A proof of the artfully intricate planning of Eliot's scheme for *Romola* appears when one counts the days in the narrative. Only then can one discover – as has Bonaparte – that the day Romola leaves bears symbolic significance, for it is 29 August, the day commemorating the martyrdom of John the Baptist. Here, as in Romola's earlier reform, the old prophet must be martyred before the 'new baptism' can occur. During her stay in the little village, Romola once again re-enacts the law of charity, but her rescue and baptism of the Jewish child seems intended to symbolize a reform of Christianity itself into a Religion of Humanity, one which will encompass all the children of the earth.[44]

At the end of chapter sixty-one, Romola's story temporarily disappears from the narrative, but this structural hiatus is filled by equally apocalyptic events in the lives of Tito and Savonarola. Like the 'beast' and the 'false prophet', the pair are taken, the one to be cast into the river and the other into prison. In chapter sixty-eight, or the seventh chapter after 'Drifting Away', the narrative returns to Romola and describes her 'new baptism', suggesting that the hiatus is another septenary structure which appropriates the 'artificial and imaginary character' of the Apocalypse. Romola then re-enters Florence, not only on Easter Eve, as Bonaparte has pointed out, but in the seventieth chapter. Her rediscovery of Tessa and the adoption of her children in this chapter suggests a humanistic 'New Jerusalem' which takes the poetic form of a fulfilment of Daniel's seventy weeks as well as that of the prophesied resurrection of the Messiah. Romola's narrative has reached its appropriate culmination, proceeding from the first feast of John the Baptist to the fulfilment of prophecy in a new reformation. From seven to seventy, the narrative proceeds from the prophetic reform of Hellenism by Hebraism to a reform of Hebraism by a new prophetic vision of humanism.

IV

But outside the straightforward progress of Romola's own narrative there remains a circle of ambiguity concerning the nature of the prophet. Tito, the 'prophet' of the first six chapters (which all take place on the day he arrives in

Florence) is 'killed off', as Eliot wrote when she arrived at the end of her manuscript. But Savonarola, who taught Romola how to reform egoistic into altruistic love, remains something of an enigma. The final two chapters of the novel describe his recantation and execution, but to the end Romola remains uncertain whether ambition or a true spirit of prophecy dominated in him. In the epilogue she characterizes him as one whom she loved because he helped her when she was in great need – a resolution which tells us much about Eliot's views of prophets of both fifteenth and nineteenth centuries. For Eliot it was possible to 'prophesy again' and thus interpret the Apocalypse anew, but she could grant prophets – herself included – only a qualified authenticity. Romola's tale, which has so many parallels in the lives of Eliot's Victorian contemporaries, many of whom found the same guidance in Carlyle or Ruskin that Romola found in Savonarola, suggests that in the novel Eliot instructs her readers how to take the apocalyptic prophecying of those who preached as modern analogues to her Florentine prophet. Such an identification would have seemed quite appropriate for Eliot's contemporary readers, since even in their own time it was commonplace to identify Carlyle, Ruskin, and similar writers as 'Victorian prophets'. In fact, the kind of non-fiction they invent not only self-consciously draws upon the prophetic books for image, diction, and literary structures, it also attempts to borrow the prophet's mantle to convey a visionary rebuke and call for reformation.[45] Although Eliot might approve of their prophet-like warnings to a society which had apparently fallen away from the laws of God and nature, and although she might also grant the essential value of their inspiration and guidance in a time of waning faith, she nonetheless remains fully aware that no human being truly possesses the old prophetic stature. According to her, one must take the modern prophet (as indeed one must now take the ancient ones) as men and not mouthpieces of a personal deity.

Of course, Eliot herself is the prophet who reinterprets the Apocalypse for her contemporaries, for when she reinterprets and reapplies its symbols and patterns within her fiction she not only shapes a narrative that contains her attitudes towards religion and human development, she also challenges traditional Christian expositors (and readers). *Romola* in others words directly instructs her contemporaries how to take such apocalyptic materials and also, one must emphasize, how to regard the means by which they are usually interpreted. At the same time, Eliot inevitably places herself in the same relation to her public as Savonarola had to his, since, like him, she becomes preacher, prophet, and sage. However, she has warned us with the example of Savonarola himself that, although an individual can inspire others to change their lives for the better and may even speak as if inspired, no individual can be fully accepted as a prophet with direct access to God. George Eliot, like Savonarola and like other Victorian prophets, such as Carlyle, Arnold, and Ruskin, could inspirit men and women and help them see their lives as the true setting of Apocalypse. But, as the sceptical Eliot warns us by the example of her narrative, she, no more than her fellow Victorian sages, can be taken as anything but a fellow interpreter of the real.

NOTES

1 *Natural Supernaturalism: Tradition and Revolution in Romantic Literature* (New York, 1971).
2 George P. Landow, *Images of Crisis: Literary Iconology, 1750 to the Present* (Boston and London, 1981), examines such analogous materials as well as paintings by John Martin and similar painters of apocalyptic and other forms of prophecy.
3 George P. Landow, *Victorian Types, Victorian Shadows: Biblical Typology in Victorian Literature, Art, and Thought* (Boston and London, 1980), ch. 1, offers a detailed examination of the kinds of typological exegesis practiced by the parties within the Anglican Church as well as by various denominations outside it.
4 Edward Henry Bickersteth (1825–1906), Bishop of Exeter, was the son of the prominent Evangelical clergyman and prophetic expositor, Edward Bickersteth (1786–1850).
5 U. C. Knoepflmacher makes this distinction in *Religious Humanism and the Victorian Novel* (Princeton, 1965), p. 116.
6 *George Eliot's Early Novels: the Limits of Realism* (Berkeley and Los Angeles, 1968), p. 5.
7 Mark Schorer points out the 'apocalyptic drama' in 'Fiction and the "Matrix of Analogy"', in George Eliot, *Middlemarch*, ed. Bert G. Hornback (New York, 1977), pp. 706–14.
8 *Felix Holt, The Radical*, ed. Peter Coveney (Harmondsworth, 1972), [ch. 41], p. 503.
9 'New Year's at the Abbey: Point of View in the Pivotal Chapters of *Daniel Deronda*', *Journal of Narrative Technique*, 9 (1979), 147–59.
10 *Middlemarch*, [ch. 42], p. 296 and [ch. 56], p. 317.
11 Felicia Bonaparte, *The Triptych and the Cross: The Central Myths of George Eliot's Imagination* (New York, 1979), pp. 13 and 18, takes the rather extreme position that the novel is 'a symbolic narrative in which every character, every event, every detail – every word, in fact – is an image in an intricate symbolic pattern'. Although we are indebted to Bonaparte's convincing demonstration that *Romola* is a 'symbolic history of Western civilization', her discussion refers to a more general conception of Christian myth than the so-called historical apocalyptic tradition we describe.
12 *The Rise and Progress of Christianity* (London, 1854), p. vi.
13 Ernest R. Sandeen, *The Roots of Fundamentalism: British and American Millenarianism, 1800–1932* (Chicago, 1970), provides the most complete survey available of the Anglican millennarian tradition in Britain during the period of Eliot's youth. Elisabeth Jay, *The Religion of the Heart, Anglican Evangelicalism and the Nineteenth-Century Novel* (Oxford, 1979), pp. 88–97, discusses millenarianism as a 'non-essential' doctrine of Evangelicalism. J. F. C. Harrison, *The Second Coming: Popular Millennarianism, 1780–1850* (New Brunswick, N.J., 1979), is concerned primarily with popular millenarianism which flourished outside the established church but

does admit its existence among leading divines. Owen Chadwick, *The Victorian Church. Part 1* (New York, 1966), p. 451, touches briefly but illuminatingly upon Evangelical 'visions of a millennium'.

14 *George Eliot Letters*, ed. Gordon S. Haight (New Haven, 1954), I, 72. Hereafter cited parenthetically in text as 'GEL'.
15 4 vols, 7th edn (London, 1834), IV, 491. The passage quoted below appears on this same page.
16 *The Victorian Church*, p. 451. Jay, *The Religion of the Heart*, p. 23, however, places this periodical midway between two other Evangelical organs, the *Christian Guardian* (which reflected the views of conservative clergy) and the *Record* (which devoted itself to 'apocalyptic fervour and zealous espousal of premillennialist doctrine').
17 *Christian Observer*, July 1825, pp. 422–34 and August 1825, pp. 489–520.
18 'On the Expectation of an Individual Antichrist', *Christian Observer*, November 1835, p. 658. Frere was the author of *A Combined View of the Prophecies of Daniel, Esdras, and St. John* (London, 1815) and *On the General Structure of the Apocalypse* (London, 1826).
19 See 'On the Influence of Certain Doctrines Upon Missionary Exertions', *Christian Observer*, October 1839, pp. 598–603, and 'The Rev. Mr. Goode on His Missionary Sermon: – With Remarks on His Letter', *Christian Observer*, December 1839, pp. 722–45.
20 *Christian Observer*, January 1840, p. 63.
21 *Victorian Church*, p. 442.
22 (Plates 1 and 2) For example, William Cuninghame, *A Dissertation on the Seals and Trumphets of the Apocalypse, and the Prophetical Period of 1260 Years* (London, 1813); George Stanley Faber, *The Sacred Calendar of Prophecy* (London, 1828); and Edward Eicksteth, *Scripture Help* (New York, 1832) and *Practical Guide to the Prophecies* (Philadelphia, 1841).
23 Not surprisingly, when Isaac Williams, a leading Tractarian, preaches on the Antichrist, he makes no mention of this favorite Evangelical reading of the Reformation. See Williams's 'The Antichrist', which is appended to *The Characters of the Old Testament in a Series of Sermons* (Oxford, 1870), pp. 323–38.
24 'The Time of the End' . . . *by a Congregationalist* (Boston, 1856), which reprints the last chapter of *Horae Apocalypticae*, offers 'about 1865', but the 1862 edition of the commentary revises the expected date of the Millennium to 1866 (IV, 237).
25 According to Dean Henry Alford, *Greek Testament* (London, 1861), p. 246, the most prominent members of this interpretative school were German: Ewald, Lucke, De Wette, and Dusterdieck, He names only a single Englishman, Samuel Davidson, and an American, Moses Stuart, as members of this school.
26 *Essays of George Eliot*, ed. Thomas Pinney (New York, 1963), p. 165.
27 Although Eliot once described Maurice's thought as 'muddy rather than "profound"', in 1861 she mentioned going to hear him preach, and she was deeply touched by his response to her novel. See GEL II, 125; III, 381 and n; IV, 104.
28 *Lectures on the Apocalypse* (London, 1861), pp. 10–11. Thus, although this liberal churchman retains a belief in the authenticity of biblical prophecy, he emphasizes both that this major instance of it has already met reached fulfilment long ago and that, at any rate, the essential religious truths embodied in any prophecy always have more importance than mere historical prediction. The effect of such an approach, of course, is to move the realm of wonder into the distant past while

simultaneously emphasizing broad religious doctrine.
29 *Westminster Review*, V (January 1861), 247. Hennell presented Eliot with a copy of the essay, upon which she later commented (GEL, III, 329).
30 *The Early Christian Anticipation of an Approaching End of the World* ... (London, 1860), pp. 88 and 33–4.
31 'The Apocalypse', *Westminster Review*, LXXVI (October 1861), 448–87. Hereafter cited parenthetically by page number in text. For Eliot's acquaintance with Call, see Gordon S. Haight, *George Eliot* (New York, 1968), p. 242. Eliot noted in her journal that she had read this issue of the *Westminster*, and since she was at this time reading 'Savonarola's Prophecy' and 'Tiraboschi on Abate Gioachimo' (Joachim of Fiore) and specifically mentions an article in the *Westminster* discussing Joseph Smith, the Mormon 'Prophet', she almost certainly read Call's piece with great attention (George Eliot's Journal for July 1861–December 1877, p. 13; Yale University Manuscript IV.3). We would like to thank Yale University for granting permission to publish extracts from unpublished materials in its possession.
32 *Visions of the End: Apocalyptic Traditions in the Middle Ages* (New York, 1979), p. 30.
33 'The Apocalypse of St. John', *National Review*, April 1864, p. 351.
34 Joseph A. Wittreich, Jr, *Visionary Poetics: Milton's Tradition and His Legacy* (San Marino, California, 1979), p. 52, has suggested that 'Epic poets and prophets alike impose historical pattern upon historical pattern; but, whereas the epic poet translates pattern into model, the prophet searches beyond pattern for a new model, his search causing him to turn closed patterns into open ones, which become not emblems of perfection but gateways leading toward it'.
35 Eliot's division of the ideological traditions of British culture into Hellenism and puritan Protestantism anticipates Matthew Arnold's *Culture and Anarchy* but also looks back to Robert Mackay's *The Progress of the Intellect* (London, 1850), which she reviewed enthusiastically in January 1851; her review is reprinted in *Essays of George Eliot*, pp. 27–45.
36 *Romola* (New York, 1873), p. 288. All quotations from the novel are taken from this edition.
37 According to E. B. Elliott, *Horae Apocalypticae* (London, 1862), several sixteenth-century expositors interpreted Revelation 10 to refer to the Reformation, although Joseph Mede and all those followed his lead did not. Elliott himself adopts this interpretation, and John Cumming, whose *Lectures on the Apocalypse* follows Elliott's interpretation closely, emphasizes it.
38 Thomas Newton, *Dissertations on the Prophecies* (London, 1832), p. 525.
39 Pasquale Villari, *The History of Girolamo Savonarola* (London, 1863), I, 315, and F. Karl Meier, *Girolamo Savonarola aus grossen Theils handschriften Quellen dargestellt von Fr. Karl Meier* (Berlin, 1836), which last volume is no. 1430 in the Garland *George Eliot–George Henry Lewes Library*, ed. William Baker (New York, 1977).
40 *Practical Guide to the Prophecies*, Ch. 16.
41 Eliot, who had purchased a copy of Keble's immensely popular volume in March 1840 (GEL, I, 46), was as familiar with it as with her Bible and her prayerbook, and she continued to refer to it in both letters and fiction. G. E. Tennyson, *Victorian Devotional Poetry: The Tractarian Mode* (Cambridge, Mass., 1980), pp. 72–113, provides a valuable discussion of both Keble's poetry and some of the reasons for its enormous popularity.
42 Expositors consider the 1260 days during which the woman remains in the wilderness identical to the forty-two months and three and a half years referred to

elsewhere in the Apocalypse.
43 See *Apocalyptic Spirituality*, trans. and ed. Bernard McGinn (New York, 1979), pp. 190–1. McGinn translates Savonarola's *Compendium of Revelations* in its entirety, pp. 192–275.
44 U. C. Knoepflmacher, *Religious Humanism and the Victorian Novel* (Princeton, 1965), p. 40, points out the resemblance between Romola carrying the child in her arms and the Comtean banner of a religion of humanity.
45 George P. Landow, 'Ruskin as a Victorian Sage: the Example of "Traffic"', in *New Essays on Ruskin*, ed. Robert Hewison (London, 1981), which proposes that the writings of what Holloway termed the 'Victorian Sage' form a definable genre, analyzes Ruskin's use of technique drawn from biblical prophecy, contemporary homiletics, neoclassical satire, and classical rhetoric.

ERNEST L. TUVESON

12 The millenarian structure of *The Communist Manifesto*

Millenarianism in its various forms, as will appear later in this essay, provides a kind of scenario for great change in society; in a large sense, it might be called a scenario for revolution. The change may be seen as inaugurated by violent conflict between the forces of good and those of evil, or those of oppression and those of 'liberation'; or the great, transforming change may come about by peaceful, evolving movement, according to a program established in the nature of things. The opposition of these two ideas, and the place of Marxist revolutionary ideology with relation to them, is the subject of this paper.

But first we should see the situation in the early nineteenth century in broad perspective. Most of the eighteenth century had been permeated by a ferment of social change, of utopian and literally revolutionary expectation. The question was the method and form of change. Originally, there was what might be called an 'open-ended' and unstructured concept of reform. The philosophers and their followers saw the ideal society as one comparatively static in nature, ruled by persons who were perfectly 'rational' and benevolent. The irrationality and selfish exploitation of human beings arose in a dark night of ignorance and superstitions – literally, the 'dark age'. All this would be ended by education, by the creation of a class of enlightened philosophers who would gain control of society, replacing the selfish and ignorant, particularly the priests and their tools the feudal aristocracy. Theoretically, all this change could be effectuated at any time, through the propagandizing and educating by enlightened teachers and popular authors who would demonstrate conclusively the folly and vice of the old order. The planned establishment of a rational society, so organized that the citizens had always before them, in every aspect of their lives, a perfectly ordered, sensible and fair social order, would prevent falling back into chaos. Hence the revolutionary calendar, for instance, which abandons all the superstitious saints' days, etc., and sets nature forth, in the progression of the seasons, in a truly rational way, with realistic, scientific names, such as 'Brumaire'.

This kind of revolutionary ideology I call 'open-ended' and unstructured. It is open because there is no absolute beginning and no fixed destination. Ignorance and exploitation have long prevailed, but, with education and strong leadership by an enlightened class, there can be a dramatic transformation; this event is not predestined, and there is no real certainty that, even if the great reform takes place, it will endure. There is no pre-appointed shape and sequence to the changes, and there is no doctrine of 'progress'.[1]

W. H. Auden, towards the end of his Communist period, observed that:

> The keynote of Marxism is surely that history has moved and is moving in a certain direction despite the efforts of individuals or classes to stop or deflect it: in other words that life is working out. Perfection is certainly, if you like, a nonexistent mystical absolute, but Marxism teaches that historical development is asymptotic to perfection. Its line isn't straight: it wiggles and makes spirals, but its general direction is perfectly clear.[2]

This definition is characteristic of an apocalyptic view of history. During Marx's time, there were two versions of the attitude of 'chiliastic utopianism'. In the early decades of the century, German 'conservative millenarianism', drawing from both the Judaic–Christian apocalyptic and hermeticism, envisioned a spiritual progression, in history, through definite stages, culminating in a 'perpetual theocracy'.[3] History they saw as process which causes social and intellectual and cultural changes, rather than, as in Voltaire, for instance, the other way round.[4] The corollary of such an attitude is that the workings of the process are fixed and predictable; the 'ages' of world history are stages in the working out of the realization of perfection. History, it has been truly observed, replaced philosophy as the supreme and essential fact; in this point lies the difference between the philosophers' revolution and that of the apocalypticists.

It has been suggested that Marxism derived from the romantic apocalypticism. In a way, a paradoxical way, it did. For romantic theories of history lie in the background of Hegel's view that history is the process whereby the world spirit realizes itself; like the romantic theories, Hegelianism sees a fixed progression of ages, leading to a kind of perfect state. A characteristic of these theories is that they see the advance of history as essentially harmonious and peaceful, even if violent confrontations may occur incidentally. Ultimately, there is one reconciliation of conflicts after another, until the final stage is reached. Auden's image of the asymptote applies to this kind of thinking; for as a curve moves in regular patterns towards the line with which it is asymptotic ('perfection'), so history moves in regular, progressive stages to realize or restore the perfect harmony.

That Marxism derived from this kind of theory is, I said, paradoxical – for, although the Communist doctrine shared the romantics' belief in history as process, and in a relatively perfect state as the determined end, it reacted against the concept of progressive, regular advances. And therein lies the real contribution of Marx and Engels. For them, as we shall see, history does indeed have stages, but each one is not an advance, or a resolution of opposites, leading to a higher level. On the contrary, the series of historical ages is a long preparation for the ultimate Armageddon, the one great conflict in which the opposition of classes is violently solved.

The apocalyptic interpretation of revolution gave the practical revolutionary a number of advantages over the other prophets. Revolution came to seem inevitable; success was certain; the nature of things, the being of creation guaranteed it. The God who was seen as ruling the world became immanent; God, as well as history, became a kind of process. It became immaterial whether the power behind the process was envisioned as a Self, or merely the 'laws of science'. A second advantage of apocalypticism was that the revolutionary act was given a definite shape; the destruction, not only conversion or education, of the ruling powers was the modus operandi. Finally, the revolutionary program became closed rather than open. If at first this fact seems a handicap rather than asset, further reflection will demonstrate its value. The revolutionary act is not merely a reform, an improving change, no matter how far-reaching, as in the French Revolution; it is the final solution, the absolute answer to human problems. How exciting, how challenging, how totally wonderful to participate in this Armageddon – to bring in the predestined era, the true millennial age, which will last not only a thousand years, but during the rest of the existence of human society!

Of the two revered founding fathers of 'Marxism', Friedrich Engels appears to have been consistently slighted. It is true that Marx was by far the more profound thinker, the major economist. Yet what Engels probably contributed was of crucial importance. He was the theologian, the prophet, the rhetorician, and his presence is felt everywhere in the *Manifesto of the Communist Party*. However much philosophers and historians as well as economists may stress *Das Kapital*, it is certainly the *Manifesto*, with its ringing phrases, its conception of a righteous party and class, of revolution sure to succeed, that has rallied and carried the Communist forces. Few of the 'workers of the world', many of whom have been illiterate, could understand Marx's lucubrations about the value of labor, but the call to action in the *Manifesto* brings it into the class of the great converting documents of world religions – the Gospels and the Koran, for examples.

The nineteenth century, as we have seen, was a time when apocalyptic notions sprouted in great numbers.[5] And these ideas reached their height just when the *Manifesto* appeared (1848). The two facts are not coincidental; the *Manifesto* in fact was a version of the ancient prophecy, and it carried much of the force that apocalyptic prophecy has had throughout the history of Judaism and Christianity. Thus it gave to revolution a power much greater than aspiration and idealism alone; as indicated above, the millenarian format added to hope the irresistible force of destiny.

The intellectual world, to which Marx and Engels emphatically belonged, was then intoxicated by the millennialist kind of hope: the conviction that by a series of peaceful and decisive events, coming to a climax probably in the nineteenth century, the ancient wrongs and injustices would be forever eliminated. What were in effect hymns ardently referred to the 'millennial dawn'. Whitman and Tennyson were among those who saw in the advances in knowledge and technology the harbingers of Utopia Unlimited. Political and economic changes, even though radical, would come about. 'Progress' would take place in every aspect of life, for there was an assumption that spiritually as well as intellectually the human race would advance. Such optimism permeated the abortive revolutions of 1848. Although this failure was certainly disappointing, it is at least arguable that the millennialist type of optimism and faith in progress dominated reform thought until the First World War.

Marx and Engels, however, had become disillusioned with traditional reform before the events of 1848. 'Practical' reformers were busy planning new institutions and arrangements of society and economics. New constitutions and laws, bureaucratic direction, etc., would produce the secular version of the millennium. All this Marx-Engels rejected. In *The German Ideology* (1846), they repudiated the whole conception of upward movement that had been epitomized in the magic word 'evolution'; an ideal 'Man', Marx-Engels said, had been invented, a creature abstracted from real persons in real periods, and an imaginary process had been constructed – 'it was possible to transform the whole of history into an evolutionary process of consciousness'.[6]

All this is a dream, and previous attempts at radical change have consequently failed. The stage-by-stage upward movement will not and cannot occur. Only a pure class, pure because exiled from the corruption of the ruling orders, can create a 'communist consciousness'. This is the true new order of society. It can come about only through violent upheaval, a real revolution – because, realistically, the ruling class will not give up for any other reason, and because 'the class overthrowing it can only in a revolution succeed in ridding itself of all the muck of ages and become fitted to found society anew'.

The feeling that the peaceful ascent to the utopian age was somehow unrealistic was not altogether new; Friedrich Schlegel, in his *Concordia*, for example had envisioned a short period of divinely imposed destruction, after which the glorious reborn age would emerge. Here is essentially the pattern of the old millenarianism, in contrast with millennial hopes. The evil of the world must proceed to its height before, in one great complete root-and-branch upheaval, it would be swept away. But vague notions of some kind of divine intervention were hopeless dreams. In the process which is history itself there must be found the forces, moving inexorably and according to an internally established plan, which would result in the final solution. It was the contribution of Marx–Engels to revive the old millenarian pattern in the forms of modern social and economic thought.

It has been observed as a curious fact that the Marxists Gyorgy Lukács and Ernst Bloch 'spent much of their youths studying ancient and medieval eschatologies ...'.[7] The fact is however susceptible of logical explanation; for these eschatologies were, of course, millenarian and likely to be radically revolutionary in purpose. The eschatology of Marxism, which is kin to them, might learn from their experience. And we can, I suggest, learn much about Marxist eschatology, too, from looking back on the development of Judaic–Christian apocalyptic.

Millenarian pessimism about the perfectibility of the existing world is crossed by a supreme optimism. History, the millenarian believes, so operates that, when evil has reached its height, the hopeless situation will be reversed. The original, the true harmonious state of society, in some kind of egalitarian order, will be re-established. It was easy enough for a realist in 1848 to see in the new, dark industrial age just this time of the ultimate in evil which would give, paradoxically, the real hope for redemption.

The Biblical account of the history of the chosen people gives from the beginning the impression that they are outsiders, like the redemptive class Marx–Engels described. Their lapses were those into participation in the doings of the great world, symbolized by their worship of the false gods which the world served. But throughout there is the messianic expectation – under the leadership of a great captain sent by God, the armies of the chosen people will overcome the alien nations; and the later prophets more and more saw this triumph as not merely the victory of the Jewish tribes but the means of universal salvation. The stone that the builder rejected will become the cornerstone of the temple.

With the Captivity, Israel became a subject nation, and there were further developments in the conception of the messianic mission. In the later prophetic texts we can see an increasing identification of the chosen people as not only separated in their special integrity from the sinful great world but also as subject to oppression by hopelessly superior forces. Their enemies are the rich, the mighty, the proud – the enduring ruling class, in fact. We sense that the war between the chosen people and their enemies is a struggle between the oppressive, powerful segment of the human race, and those victimized by conquerors. Thus in Ezek. 39, the vision of the Great Day of the Lord, the true God tells the prophet to call on the birds and the beasts to eat 'the flesh of the mighty, and drink the blood of the princes of the earth . . .' that 'ye shall be filled at my table with horses and chariots, with mighty men, and with all men of war'. (39.18, 20) Isaiah 49 describes a vision of universal redemption through the sufferings of Israel, with the significant phrase 'to restore the preserved of Israel' (49.6). Here are combined two key words of millenarianism in any form – redemption and restoration. The prophet, who complains that he has 'laboured in vain', is promised ultimate triumph – 'that thou mayest say to the prisoners, Go forth; to them that are in darkness, Shew yourselves. They shall feed in the ways, and their pastures shall be in all high places' (49.9). So another key element of millenarianism appears – the reversal of status. There is the famous first verse of Isaiah 24: 'Behold, the Lord maketh the earth empty, and maketh it waste, and turneth it upside down' – going on, in the next verse, 'And it shall be, as with the people, so with the priest; as with the servant, so with his master . . . as with the taker of usury, so with the giver of usury to him'. The image of a great earthquake in nature is the symbol of a great and levelling revolution in society, the sacrosanct distinctions of class being abolished. The Lord tells the prophet to call on the birds and beasts to 'drink the blood of the princes of the earth', of *all*, not merely of the special enemies of Israel.

Opposed to God's people is 'Babylon'. Originally the actual conqueror of Israel, this state came to symbolize the whole succession of oppressors. In the revelation of John, a pastiche of apocalyptic imagery, set forth in a Christian interpretation, 'Babylon' looms over the world. 'Israel' is now composed of the whole body of the redeemed, innocent people. The predicted fall of Babylon is the crucial moment of history; not until it is razed can the series of oppressions and limited judgments, on this or that nation, be ended once for all. Probably the immediate significance of Babylon is the Roman empire, but clearly this state is the last and the culminating in the successive tyrannical powers. The people of the promise are humble, innocent, and, it may be presumed, mostly poor. The Book of Revelation brings to its climax the implied association in later Jewish prophecy between tyrants and exploitation of all kinds. Babylon is not only a political power, but it comprehends all the rich, grasping, insatiable. When, after supreme struggles, the great city is overthrown, in her is found the blood not only of saints, but of all 'that were slain upon the earth'. (Revelation 18.24). The incendiary potential of this passage is obvious. For 'Babylon' has not yet been destroyed. Through the centuries, it has remained the symbol of hated rulers and possessors. The Black Panthers in the 1960s customarily referred to the United States as 'Babylon', but in its full significance the image was clearly universal in meaning.[8]

Revelation describes individual, limited 'judgments' on various nations. The first six are limited in scope, and without final importance. Apparently history could go on indefinitely, with 'bowls of wrath' being inflicted periodically. But the seventh is different. This judgment is 'upon the air' – signifying that it is effective everywhere; only this one is on the 'air'. What accomplishes this universal judgment of the evil powers? There is no part for the Messiah. An angel will destroy the woman mounted on a scarlet beast. There will be a kind of short counter-revolution, represented by ten 'kings' who however will reign but a short time, being in the end decisively defeated by the Lamb, the Messiah, and his followers. (Revelation 17).

In Revelation there is, then, a plan or scenario for the drama of millenarian redemption. The plot may be summarized as follows. The original, innocent people of God, who live in a harmonious world, first are conquered and oppressed by evil, aggressive enemies, both internal and external. The avaricious rulers, 'Babylon', then war with one another, this one winning and then being conquered by another, but without changing the real situation of the subject class, who are destined for a time to be oppressed. After a long series of power transfers, at a fore-ordained point the unrepentant rulers will be destroyed by a cataclysmic revolution, and Babylon will be destroyed, the place where it was laid waste. In this, the 'millennial' age, the righteous will rule; God's people will be on top at last. To put the situation in modern terms, the whole system is in crisis and approaching its breakdown.

It may seem strange to say that the Book of Revelation is both materialistic and this-worldly, but so in effect it is. The great day of God is a metaphor for a period of earthly happiness, for earth does not become heaven, but heaven becomes earthly. Throughout the history of Christianity, this fact has been implicitly recognized by the vision of a very substantial paradise, a utopia – the millennium denounced by many Christian preachers, including Augustine, as 'carnal'. A life on this earth according to heart's desire – that is the goal of the Christian prophetic vision.

It is not difficult to see how the millenarian dream could serve as a pattern for a great economic revolution in which the workers (the good people of the prophets) would become the rulers and all things would be made new. I shall trace, necessarily here only in general outline, how this came to be. Marx and Engels lived, as we have seen, at a time when millenarian ideas were pervasive. There have been many peaks of millenarian excitement. It may be said in general that each occurs at a time when big changes in the structure of social and political power are occurring. There was, for example, the millenarian interpretation of the American revolution.[9] It is characteristic of these agitations that a class comes to see itself as unjustly treated and feels in itself a strength that should elevate it to a position of leadership; originally, the middle class undoubtedly saw in millennial prophecies a forecast of the reduction of aristocratic power and leadership.

It is not strange, therefore, that in the dark days of the beginning Industrial Revolution, millenarian speculation became common. Much of this foresaw the kind of peaceful change, by enlightenment, that I have described. Here for instance is the 'Rational Religionist's Advent Hymn':

> Brothers, arise behold the dawn appear
> Of Truth's bright day, and Love's Millennial Year . . .

> The midnight gloom of Ignorance retires;
> And fast are fading Error's fatual (sic) fires . . .[10]

Here is true 'secular millennialism'; the ancient prophecies set forth an ideal, certain to be achieved some day, towards which it is the Christian's duty to work. There is an assumption that advances in knowledge and technology have made it possible for modern Christians to understand fully just what the Scriptures had meant. Thus the 'social Gospel' movement proclaimed that a Kingdom of God of this world, of living people in the true millennial state, is the real end of Christianity – not an immaterial heaven. In the realization of the Kingdom, there is no inevitable pattern of events, no fixed timetable. It implies universal harmony, reconciliation of classes, or peaceful abolition of such distinctions, in a form of socialist state.

The great English reformer Robert Owen has a special place in the history of Marxism, for Engels contributed (1842–4) to perhaps the most important of the many journals through which Owen advanced his ideas – *The New Moral World*. An irony of history is that Owen, not Marx–Engels, might have created the concept of militant Communism. Owen took the final step of interpreting the prophecies in terms of the industrial age. His position was that the message is true, but that its real meaning has been concealed and distorted. (I am not concerned here with Owen's attempts to establish advanced millennialist communities. One lesson that Marx–Engels learned, quite likely from such efforts as Owen's, was that these little utopias accomplished nothing; but Owen himself came around to the opinion that society must be regenerated as a whole, and that model communities were not the way to do this.)

Christianity, Owen's own prophecy announced, is a religion of social and economic salvation. This alone is salvation. The preoccupation with visionary notions of individual immortality and redemption has come from misunderstanding, not altogether honestly motivated, of the Biblical message. This misunderstanding was predicted. But the moment of enlightenment, also predicted for a definite time, is near at hand. As he explains in *The Book of the New Moral World* (1836):

> The time approaches, when, in the course of nature, the evil spirit of the world, engendered by ignorance and selfishness, will cease to exist, and when another spirit will arise, emanating from facts and experience, which will give a new direction to all the thoughts, feelings and actions of men, and which will create a new character of wisdom and benevolence for the whole human race. This is the 'NEW MORAL WORLD' in which evil, except as it will be recorded in the past sufferings of mankind, will be unknown.[11]

The moment of epiphany has come. We now know 'that truth is nature, and nature God'.[12] God is truly 'immanentized'. The old idea of the divine has been transferred to nature. The other of things, the workings of that deity of the scientific age, 'natural law', performs the judgments, brings about the ultimate moral triumph.

Owen set forth a simplistic and naive theory of a pleasure–pain psychology, combined with a primitive behaviorism. The human being, he asserts, is shaped by his training; with correct educational formation, he will become a superior being. What has been thought to be an innate strain of evil – the kind of taint, in fact, the millenarian finds in the rulers of the earth – is really, for Owen, the product of bad education, setting up of bad incentives for the child. These determine 'whether the prevailing will of the individual shall be essentially good or bad, superior or inferior; also whether the stimuli to act shall be strong, or weak . . .' (p. 19). This element in Owen's doctrine has had a long and vigorous life; we can see how it is kin to Marxist teaching. We can see why Communist nations have tended to envision a 'new Man', totally shaped by a new kind of education. We can see also how the individual, in Communist thought, is seen to be totally a creature of his (or her) class. How, for example, can Marx–Engels assume, as we shall see, that the new workers' class, the 'proletariat', will be innocent and uncorrupted, rightly guided where all others are tainted? Because the experience, the education, of these workers has not exposed them to the corrupting influence which hopelessly ruins members of the other classes. Hence the necessity for a root-and-branch extirpation of other classes.

Owen was given to sensational public debates with orthodox believers, of which the most famous was with the Rev. J. H. Roebuck (1837). In it he uttered this impassioned apostrophe to the coming 'moral world', which, as Roebuck correctly pointed out, clearly recalls 'Isaiah's sublime description of the kingdom of Messias':

> Oh . . . that the time may now commence when men shall become rational, and, in consequence, turn their spears into pruning hooks, and their swords into ploughshares; when each man shall sit under any vine, or any fig tree, and there shall be none to make him afraid; . . .[13]

Owen's vision of the transformed society would be that of Communism, but his confidence that by some kind of unexplained miraculous change mankind would become so completely reformed is hardly in keeping with his own opinion of the completely determining effect of education and environment. Even he, however, possibly taking up a suggestion of Saint Simon, saw the need for a transition period between the present state of things and the destined millennium; descending into the Marx–Engels prophetic, the suggestion was to have a long and sinister life. Eventually the transformed society would be composed of a 'federative system' of independent townships (an anticipation of the Marxist solution); but –

> Until the characters of men can be new-created by society, from their birth, so as to form them into rational beings who will act wisely and consistently through life, *an intermediate or preparatory government* must be made to govern those townships, while the new characters are in progress of formation from birth. When these new characters have come to maturity, then will each township be well and rationally governed, by its own population, without any elections and selections.[14]

Of course this is the 'rule of the proletariat' in embryo. But typical of Owen is his idealistic inability to see that 'government' cannot accomplish this and many other great things; is not 'government' the very agency of the old rulers? This kind of confidence demonstrates that Owen was an ancestor of the Fabian socialists. It demonstrates his real lack of realization of the radical evil in society which he recognized abstractly. Marx–Engels saw the true nature of the problem, and provided a solution.

Owen for this reason was characterised, by Engels, as 'utopian'. This statement has been misunderstood in two ways. The first is the implication that Owen was never more than a minor crank, of little importance. In fact Owen, to his contemporaries of the 1840s, was the dominant figure in reform agitation. As Harrison says:

> By 1840 socialism was virtually synonymous with Owenism; so much so that when Marx and Engels came to write their *Manifesto* in 1847 they could not call it a Socialist Manifesto but had to resort to the alternative title of Communist.[15]

A second error is the impression that Marx–Engels contemptuously rejected Owenism and were uninfluenced by it. A recent editor of the *Manifesto* states, however: 'Engels contributed to Owen's *New Moral World*. Marx was even more strongly influenced by Owen's ideas'.[16] The true difference between Owens and Marx–Engels consists in the fact that the latter returned to true millenarianism. Far from rejecting the ancient faith, they provided a version in modern terms; there is reason to think of them as the last great prophets of the Judaic apocalyptic tradition. The *Manifesto*, dropping the outdated symbolism, speaking in the terms of the industrial age, trumpets forth the old certainty that 'The history of all hitherto existing society is the history of class struggles', but that the historical process is to produce the Armageddon.[17]

Marx–Engels took over the conception of rigidly defined 'stages of the evolution of society' which was common among social philosophers. But, where the conventional opinion saw advance from one stage to the next, Marx–Engels – like the apocalyptic prophets – see the evils of oppression becoming more and more intense.

> Freeman and slave, patrician and plebian, lord and serf, guildmaster and journeyman, in a word, oppressor and oppressed, stood in constant opposition to one another, carried on an uninterrupted, now hidden, now open fight, a fight that

each time ended, either in a revolutionary reconstruction of society at large, or in the common ruin of the contending classes. (p. 474)

These contentions, like the pouring out of the first six 'bowls of wrath', leave the situation essentially unchanged. In time the 'bourgeoisie' – the modern version of the ancient Babylon–Rome – emerges in force: 'each step in the development of the bourgeoisie was accompanied by a corresponding political advance of that class'. As Babylon–Rome carried the power of evil to all parts of the world, so the modern oppressive class has extended its grasp until the final, all-encompassing corruption has taken command, expressed as 'that single, unconscionable freedom – Free Trade'. The *Manifesto* in its description of the situation in its time has plenty of company. In fact, both Marx–Engels and Carlyle see the essential evils symbolized by the Four Horsemen of the Apocalypse dominating their age.

But to Carlyle the evils of industrialism and laissez-faire were the darkest of omens; to Marx–Engels, in the true spirit of millenarianism, these same horrors seemed harbingers of the real, the universal judgment. The fact that they are the very worst of the evils humanity has known is evidence that, as in Revelation, the reversal is being prepared. This point is made in Marx's tract *The Poverty of Philosophy*, just before the *Manifesto*:

> It is only in an order of things in which there are no more classes and class antagonisms that *social evolutions* will cease to be *social revolutions*. Till then, on the eve of every general reshuffling of society, the last word of social science will always be: Combat or death; bloody struggle or extinction. It is thus that the question is inexorably put. (p. 219)

The *Manifesto* proclaims that, at last, the final extinction is to occur soon with the triumph of the proletariat, as John saw the ending of history with the reign of the people of God.

Such thinking seems to be the reverse of any kind of evolutionary philosophy. As I indicated earlier, the conception of incessant struggles and pointless defeats and victories is quite out of harmony with Hegelianism. Marx–Engels see history as process and judgment – the judgment of the 'determinism' of nature, which, however, as Owen pointed out 'proceed(s) solely from a cause unknown and mysterious . . .'. In saying this, I of course recognize that Marx–Engels take great pains to set forth the cause-and-effect system, the process, of 'historical dialectic', eliminating any kind of supernatural intervention. But consideration will show that all this theorising merely pushes the ultimate source back beyond empirical knowledge. What set in motion this sequence of events? Why does there seem to be a built-in time scheme? In the end, when God is 'immanentized' into historical process, the question of a personal, decreeing deity becomes moot. One may or may not envision a bearded divine patriarch, like the deity in Blake's illustrations for Job; 'nature', the creation (if one likes to think of it in that way) of the deity, is all in all.

The new class, once it has gained dominance, is radically different from all others. Like Owen, Marx–Engels see environment as all-important. It follows, therefore, that members of the bourgeoisie, whatever their personal characters, share the radical evil of the class. A few exceptions there may be to this iron rule (Marx and Engels themselves?) – but they are truly the exceptions who prove the rule. Figures such as John Reed take on then, for the orthodox Marxists, a peculiar glamor and pose difficult questions. But the Communist society is to be a world inhabited by a whole new race, in effect, in all of whom there will be 'altered consciousness' (old apocalyptic style, 'spiritualized') – altered in that what have appeared the deepest drives in human nature have been transformed. The intense desire to gain wealth and power, to dominate, to 'succeed', will be quite eliminated.

It follows therefore that the new society will be self-perpetuating and self-correcting. In this fact lies the great break between Communist theory and all other forms of utopianism, except for apocalyptic. Writers of utopias have exercised great ingenuity in devising social arrangements, schools, laws, etc., that would get around the problems of recalcitrant human nature. The danger that the good society, once well established, is always subject to corruption has been evident from Plato to the philosophes. Despite the constantly repeated assertions of Communist theorists that their conclusions are reached only by rigidly objective observation, it is difficult to see how any truly objective study of human behavior could arrive at such a statement of faith in a wholly 'innocent' class. Only a descendant of the apocalyptic prophets could see the proletariat, or any other group of people, as perpetually innocent and untouched by selfishness and greed; and, even more remarkable, believe that, if this class gains power, it will certainly remain forever pure and undefiled in a kind of world that certainly has not been known in historical times, and that it will 'abolish its own supremacy as a class' (p. 491). But in the millennial age, and when the New Jerusalem descends to earth, just such a world is expected. Even Laski had to admit that Marx 'was wrong in his belief that the breakdown of capitalism would give place to a comparatively simple society'.[18] But a millennial order must be simple. Marx–Engels perceived this fact; their romantic visions of small, nonpolitical communities are not merely desiderata; these, or something like them, *must* be the end form of human society if the doctrine is true.

The claim of Marx–Engels to have discovered the real nature of history by 'scientific' observation is not unique in this century. In an earlier period religious teachers would have claimed some kind of supernatural inspiration, but in the age of 'science' it was logical that some would 'discover' their doctrines. There is Mary Baker Eddy, officially described as 'discoverer and founder' of Christian Science. Members of this church are officially known as 'scientists'. Analogy of this 'discovery' with the work of Newton is suggested by the fact that Mrs Eddy named her college 'Principia'. Even Swedenborg, who did claim to have supernatural visions, set his teaching in a 'scientific' form, and he himself was a respected scientific investigator in the Newtonian tradition. In his tribute at the grave of Marx, Engels stated that 'just as Darwin discovered the law of development of organic nature, so Marx discovered the law of development of human history' (p. 684). (It is interesting to recall that what Marx discovered is the reverse of what Darwin found: Marx discovered that history is to end with the end of the struggle for survival, in the human species.) Yet, Engels said in 'Socialism: Utopian and Scientific', the emergence of this scientific revelator 'is not an inevitable event, following of necessity in the chain of historical development, but a mere happy accident. He might just as well have been born 500 years earlier, and might then have spared humanity 500 years of error, strife, and suffering' (p. 685). This, from a firm believer in historical determinism, is startling. Its implication is that history is redeemed by a superman. For how, if the proletariat had not, could not have emerged in the fourteenth century, could the final age begin?

The *Manifesto* warns that 'utopian' socialists – the progressivists, of whatever form – 'want to improve the condition of every member of society, even that of the most favored'. Marx–Engels are associated with Owen on this point. Only after a completely new generation, with a new education, has taken over control, can there be a new world. Neither Owen nor Marx–Engels would agree with the 'utopians' in asking 'how can people, when once they understand their system, fail to see in it the best possible plan of the best possible state of society?' (p. 498). This 'new social Gospel' is mere fantasy, which deadens the 'class struggle'. Like many radical teachings, this one carried implications that would go far beyond the intentions of their founders. In some Communist societies – modern China and Cambodia come to mind – it has been assumed that the purge of the old bourgeoisie must be extended to the descendants of property-owners. The burning of Babylon must be complete, and none of its inhabitants may be left. When, in the Amsterdam address of 1872, Marx made his famous concession that in America, England, Holland, 'the workers may not need to resort to violence', he roused strong opposition from his most devoted followers (p. 523). The statement seemed to Lenin 'revisionist'; and the history of conflicts within Communist parties over this point is a large part of the history of Communist dissensions of the past century. What would John have said to a suggestion that in Babylon the great some virtuous merchants might be worth saving from the fire and sword?

The final state of mankind is a kind of amalgamation of the millennium and the New Jerusalem; but just this kind of conflation had already occurred in most Christian churches. Yet there is in Marxism a recollection of the temporary, thousand-year reign of Christ and the saints and the eternal New

Jerusalem which is to succeed the last, great battle. In the millennium, proper, there is to be a virtuous dictatorship; needless to say, both Owen's and Marx–Engels' ideas about the transition period recall this concept. In one respect Marx–Engels are in fact more idealistic than Owen himself. The former strictly limited the transitional period, and specifically set forth the kind of changes which must occur before the new moral society can be established. Marx–Engels, in contrast, are indefinite about what actually is to occur in the dictatorship of the proletariat and beyond. The 'new consciousness' as in Owen's scheme will of itself take care of all problems. The old evils will disappear, like fog before the sun, in a purified community:

> When, in the course of development, class distinctions have disappeared, and all production has been concentrated in the hands of a vast association of the whole nation, the public power will lose its political character. Political power, properly so called, is merely the organized power of one class for oppressing another. (p. 490)

A question that must arise is: where, in all this action, is the Messiah? Can a millenarian doctrine exist without this figure? First, we may recall that in Revelation the great climactic event of the fall of Babylon occurs, apparently, as a mass movement in which we hear nothing about leadership. His function is to lead and to inspire the saints in the subsequent events – the intermediate holy dictatorship, and in the battle of Armaggedon. Second, the Messiah in Revelation is not a 'personal savior'. The individual saint participates only as one of an army, one is tempted to say 'class'. There are many martyrs, but we never have any sense of knowing or identifying with any individual among them. After the Four Horsemen have appeared, the fifth 'seal' – one of the preparatory revelations – is opened, and John sees beneath the altar the souls of 'those who had been slaughtered for God's word and for the testimony they bore'; they cry out for vengeance, but they receive white robes, and they are told 'to rest a little while longer' until the tally of martyrs, the fore-ordained tally, is complete. So the 'workers' of the proletariat must endure the fore-ordained oppressions, and redemption must not take place until the 'historically determined' time.

Is there, then, any place for a Messiah in the Marxist prophecy? I suggest one solution. It may be significant that, after a series of false messiahs, the Jewish messianic hope by the nineteenth century had 'declined and become moribund'.[19] For young thinkers of the Jewish tradition, with 'advanced' ideas about philosophy, it would seem logical that disillusionment would be not with the concept of some messianic function, but with placing all the hope and functions in one person – who, experience had so often shown, was likely to be an impostor. And, of course, after Waterloo – in the youth of Marx–Engels – there was a reaction against the romantic personality cult epitomized by Napoleon.

Would it not then seem possible that a *group* might fulfill at least some messianic functions – leading, inspiring, sustaining the masses? This group, who of course would come principally from the proletariat, are called, simply, 'the Communists', and are defined in the *Manifesto* as 'practically, the most advanced and resolute section of the working-class parties of every country, that section which pushes forward all others' (p. 484). (Interestingly, nothing is said about their possessing superior ability and intelligence: egalitarianism of the proletariat must be assumed. One suspects, also, that this conception is partly a reply to the contemporary theory of 'Young England', that a benevolent aristocracy might lead and protect the workers against the rapacity of the bourgeoisie.)

This plan of modern millenarian salvation, however, still lacked one element to make it complete. Just as Darwin's evolutionary hypothesis was not finished without the laws of Mendelian heredity, so Marx–Engels needed some *evidence* that there had been a primal, egalitarian, harmonious society which was corrupted and which is to be restored. Marx–Engels proclaimed the 'scientific' basis of their theory; but without empirical support for the proposition that the original state of mankind was a utopian, egalitarian community, Communism would seem, as indeed it did to most people of the time, a mere utopia seated in the brain. What really *was* the original state? Marx was testy on the subject. In the 'Critique of Hegel's *Philosophy of Right*' he speaks contemptuously of 'easygoing enthusiasts' who look for the origin of freedom in the 'primeval Teutonic forests'; but 'how is the history of our freedom different from the history of the wild boar's freedom if it is only to be found in the forests?'[20] In *The German Ideology*, Marx–Engels hypothesized a tribal ownership, during the 'hunting and fishing', 'pastoral', and early agricultural stages of culture (p. 151). Original sin – the rise of a different and corrupt consciousness – begins when 'the ancient communal and State ownership', along with slavery, develops. Class relations between citizens and slaves now begin. The reason for this momentous change is pressure of increasing population. But of course all of this is speculation, in a category with that of the philosophes (whose successors, in many ways, Marx and Engels were). It was unsatisfactory in another, supremely important way. There is about this postulated degeneration a strong suggestion that greed and aggression are innate qualities which will out. Whence came this change of consciousness, before a ruling class had been established? And population pressure is a continuing fact; why, then, should not slavery be established again, even after the triumph of the proletariat?

Not until many years later – ironically, after Marx had pretty much finished his work – did what seemed confirmation and explanation of the theory of the origin of social evil become available. Several pioneer anthropologists, after field investigations of 'primitive' peoples, had advanced accounts of an original non-monogamous, matrilineal constitution of society. The most important seemed to be that of the eccentric lawyer Lewis Morgan, who derived social evolution

> from the mother-right *gens* to the father-right *gens* and patriarchal family current in ancient Greek and Roman societies. The change in the nature of economic activity and production bringing in their wake greater accumulation of wealth, and engendering male dominance inter alia, was the prepotent cause of the change.[21]

The Morgan book was the most valuable because its author was not known as a socialist.

Morgan's notions formed the basis for what was in effect a 'prolegomenon' to the Marxist philosophy. Engels' *On the Origin of the Family, Private Property and the State* (first edition, 1884) contributed the missing element. For now, it appeared, there was apodictic proof that the original egalitarian community was a historical fact; and now appeared a satisfactory explanation for the origin of possessive 'consciousness'. The change to patriarchal monogamy produced in the small child this change of consciousness. This evidence seemed to justify what had all along been the most controversial part of the *Manifesto* – its rejection of traditional marriage and monogamy. From exclusive marriage and possession of women resulted the

> epoch, lasting until today, in which every advance is likewise a relative regression, in which the well-being and development of the one group are attained by the misery and repression of the other. It is the cellular form of civilised society, in which we can already study the nature of the antagonisms and contradictions which develop fully in the latter. . . . Everything engendered by civilization is double-sided, double-tongued, self-contradictory and antagonistic.[22]

In this Rousseauistic denunciation Engels is at his most prophetic:

> Since the exploitation of one class by another is the basis of civilization, its whole development moves in a continuous contradiction. Every advance in production is at the same time a retrogression in the condition of the oppressive class, that is, of the great majority. What is a boon for the one is necessarily a bane for the other; each new emancipation of one class always means a new oppression of another class.[23]

If this sounds like Rousseau, writing for the Dijon Academy, the pattern of history recalls the Revelation.

We can now understand what Marx–Engels mean by 'democracy'. Like Owen, they insist that the great age would be democratic – a point which presents difficulties to comprehend. For how can the 'dictatorship' of the proletariat, guided by the Communist group, be other than wholly authoritarian? (And is not the Biblical millennium also authoritarian?) How can the elimination of large numbers of people, even if afflicted by corrupt consciousness, be in any way democratic? To Marx–Engels these problems are really illusory. In the virtuous, spontaneous society, democracy – the making of necessary decisions by consensus – will occur as naturally and instinctively as breathing. As for the purges, Marx–Engels, like the Hebrew prophets, see the enemies of righteousness, or of 'the people', as simply not deserving of existence. The process of history must produce the destruction of Babylon.

For Marx–Engels the sacred words 'democracy' and 'religion' have become irreparably associates with ideas that provide powerful support for the 'oppressors'. Paramount among them is religion. They all assume one great falsehood, thus defined in the 'Theses on Feuerbach': 'To abstract from the historical process and to fix the religious sentiment as something by itself and to presuppose an abstract – *isolated* – human individual'. From this foundation of the whole oppressive system came the world religions, specifically the Judaeo–Christian and Islamic. These are concerned with an illusory notion of personal salvation; they set up a great number of sanctions designed to separate the individual from the natural social group, and hold out a deceptive hope for immortality to the oppressed. In the early essay 'On the Jewish Question' Marx associates this kind of religious perversity with Judaism especially. 'What was, in itself, the basis of the Jewish religion? Practical need, egoism' (p. 50).

Christianity is the sublime thought of Judaism; Judaism is

> the vulgar practical application of Christianity. But this practical application could only become universal when Christianity as perfected religion had accomplished, in a *theoretical* fashion, the alienation of man from himself and from nature. (p. 25)

Owen believed that the apocalyptic prophecies of the Old and New Testament, if rightly understood, are true. False impressions of their true meaning had arisen, however, doing much to produce the false ideas which govern society. In the Last Judgment, for instance, the emphasis is on the separated individual. It is well to remember that Augustine, Luther, and Calvin never were enthusiastic about Revelation. Its emphasis on mass salvation, on a very material utopia, etc., was not really consonant with their concern for the religious experience of the individual soul.

Several characteristics of historical Communist movements recall millenarian agitations. There is, for one, the well-known fanaticism of millenarian believers. This is a rather curious fact. The firm conviction that a sequence of events, leading to universal redemption, is ordained (or 'determined') would seem to lead to passivity on the part of an individual; one must only wait for the predicted events to occur. But, characteristically, there is a vitally important qualification. Although the series of events is prophesied, their *timing* may be retarded by the failure of mankind. To delay the coming of redemption, then, is a great sin, against one's fellow beings, against posterity, against the power that has ordained events. But whole-hearted, zealous participation in the historically determined duties, doing what the old millenarians would call 'doing God's will', gives special *éclat*. In most millenarian groups there is something corresponding to the 'Communist party'. In Revelation itself there are the hundred and forty-four thousand, 'the first fruits unto God and to the Lamb', who are without guile, for they are without fault before the throne of God' (Revelation 14.4–5). Thus the whole proletariat, like the whole body of the saved, is without damning fault, but the specially distinguished group – like those who teach the 'new song' to the rest of the redeemed – are chosen from the chosen.

And so we come to the last version of the great apocalyptic tradition, which has truly spread over the earth. No history could more clearly demonstrate the enormous explosive power of ideology. Any attempt to imagine world history of recent centuries without the presence of apocalyptic boggles the imagination. And, while the past two centuries would no doubt in any case have been a time of revolution, the direction and effect of these movements would certainly have been different if Owen, Marx, Engels – and before them, the prophets – had never existed. Accounts of revolutionary manifestations at the present time almost always are characterized as 'Marxist'. Much of the power of the great religions, especially Christianity, has been transferred to this Marxist faith. For indeed the modernized apocalyptic has the effect and nature of religion; it is essentially a religious doctrine, even if not so rich and varied as the usual religions. But perhaps this simplicity, this concentration on mass salvation narrowly conceived has added to its strength. Faith does not require depth.

NOTES

1. See, for example, Eric Voegelin, *The New Science of Politics* (Chicago, 1952), p. 124.
2. W. H. Auden, 'The Prolific and the Devourer' (1939), in *Antaeus*, No. 42 (1981), p. 59.
3. Paul Gottfried, *Conservative Millenarians: The Romantic Experience in Bavaria* (New York, 1979), p. 146. On hermetic influence, I refer to my book *The Avatars of Thrice Great Hermes* (New York, 1981).
4. Gottfried, op. cit., p. 148.
5. The *Manifesto*, of course, was written in England. The British at this time were especially excited about millenarian expectations, as will appear later. For a survey of orthodox millenarianism, see Ernest Sandeen, *The Roots of Fundamentalism* (Chicago, 1970).
6. *The German Ideology*, translated and edited by Robert Tucker, in *The Marx–Engels Reader* (2nd edn, New York, 1978), p. 192. All quotations from Marx and Engels are from this collection, unless otherwise indicated.
7. Gottfried, op. cit., p. 145 and footnote references.
8. E.g.: 'The cardinal rule of the Black Panther Party says: Have faith in the People,

Have faith in the party. This principle is not to be applied just in Babylon, but around the world'. (The Black Panther; quoted in Philip Foner, ed., *The Black Panthers Speak* [Philadelphia, 1970], p. 38. See also G. Louis Heath, ed., *Off the Pigs* [Meutchen, N. M., 1976], p. 279).

9 There have been several recent studies of millennialist influence on both the Revolution and the Civil War. See my *Redeemer Nation: The Idea of America's Millennial Role* (Chicago, 1968); Nathan Hatch, *The Sacred Cause of Liberty* (New Haven, 1977); Sacvan Bercovich, *The Puritan Origins of the American Self* (New Haven, 1975); James W. Davidson, *The Logic of Millennial Thought* (New Haven, 1977); and James Moorhead, *American Apocalypse, Yankee Protestants and the Civil War 1860–1869* (New Haven, 1978).

10 Reprinted in John F. C. Harrison, *Quest for the New Moral World: Robert Owen and the Owenites in Britain and America* (New York, 1969), p. 100.

11 *The Book of the New Moral World* (London, 1836), p. xv.

12 *Letters to the Human Race . . .* (London, 1850), p. 120.

13 *Public Discussion between Robert Owen and the Rev. J. H. Roebuck* (Manchester, 1837), p. 97. I have discussed the celebrated debate of Owen and Alexander Campbell (1829, in Cincinnati), in *Redeemer Nation*, pp. 79–82.

14 *Letters to the Human Race . . .*, op. cit., p. 127.

15 *Quest for the New Moral World*, p. 45.

16 D. Ryazonoff, ed., *The Communist Manifesto* (New York, 1967), p. 236.

17 From the 1888 text. *The Marx–Engels Reader*, p. 473.

18 J. H. Laski, *Communism* (London, 1927), p. 121.

19 Raphael Patai, *The Messiah Texts* (New York, 1979), p. lii.

20 Marx, *Selected Writings*, ed. D. McLellan (Oxford, 1977), p. 65.

21 G. S. Gheerye, *Family and Kin in Indo-European Culture* (University of Bombay Publications, Sociology Series No. 4, 1955), p. 203. This author goes on to say that Morgan's hypothesis now has little scholarly reputation, and that he (Gheerye) mentions it only because of its influence on Engels. The theory has, however, had a substantial revival in the 1970s. See, e.g. the introduction to a reprint of Engels' *On the Origin of the Family*, ed. Eleanor Leacock (New York, 1972).

22 Engels, *On the Origin of the Family, Private Property, and the State* (Moscow, 1959); no translator identified.

23 Ibid., p. 58.

M. H. ABRAMS

13 Apocalypse: theme and variations

Near the end of his life D. H. Lawrence wrote an extended interpretation of the Book of Revelation. 'From earliest years right into manhood', he said by way of introduction, 'like any other nonconformist child I had the Bible poured every day into my helpless consciousness, till there came almost a saturation point'. In the Bible its concluding book was the most emphasized and had the greatest effect:

> By the time I was ten, I am sure I had heard, and read, that book ten times over.... Down among the uneducated people, you will still find Revelation rampant. I think it has had, and perhaps still has more influence, actually, than the Gospels or the great Epistles.[1]

In some aspects Lawrence under-assesses both the prominence and influence of Revelation in England. As the essays in this volume show, the book has attracted the devoted attention, within as well as outside the established Church, of some of the greatest English scholars, and of the greatest scientists as well; both Newton, for example, and Joseph Priestley wrote more extensively on the prophecies of Revelation than on the physical sciences.[2] The influence of Revelation also extends far beyond 'uneducated people' who believe in the literal truth of its apocalyptic predictions. For whether we are believers or unbelievers, uneducated or learned, we, like our Western ancestors over the last two millennia, continue to live in a pervasively biblical culture, in which theological formulas are implicated in our ordinary language and we tend to mistake our inherited categories for the constitution of the world and the universal forms of thought. A century and one-half ago Pierre Proudhon, the radical economic and social theorist, and himself an advocate of 'humanitarian atheism', acknowledged the inescapability of religious concepts and patterns of thinking. I am, he said, forced to proceed like the materialist – that is, by observation and experience – and to conclude in the language of the believer, because there is no other; not knowing whether my formulas, theological in spite of me, would be taken literally or figuratively. ... We are full of Divinity, *Jovis omnia plena*; our monuments, our traditions, our laws, our ideas, our languages, and our sciences, all are infected by this indelible superstition, outside of which we can neither speak nor act, and without which we do not even think.[3]

Many of the schemes and ruling concepts of *les sciences humaines*, as well as the plotting and representation of character in much of our literature,[4] have been shaped by the historical design and theological ideas derived from the Bible and from biblical exegesis. Especially prominent in this biblical culture has been the imprint, in narrative plot, characters, and imagery, of the Revelation of St. John the Divine. In a number of Western philosophers, historians, political and social theorists, and poets, the thinking and imagination has been apocalyptic thinking and imagination; sometimes directly so, at other times by the deliberate enterprise of an author to translate the biblical myth into abstract concepts and a non-supernatural design, but increasingly during the last century by a transposition of the theological model into secular terms, in a process of which the author himself has remained largely unaware.

I THE SHAPE AND CONTENT OF HISTORY

Revelation (or in the Greek derivative, Apocalypse) is the concluding book of the biblical canon which presents, in the mode of symbolic visions, a series of events, even now beginning, which will culminate in the abrupt end of the present, evil world-order and its replacement by a regenerate mankind in a new and perfected condition of life. The wisdom of historical hindsight makes it possible to discriminate features of Revelation which have been especially potent in forming Western conceptions of the human past, present, and future.

Most important is the conception of the nature of history itself. Like preceding books in the Bible, but more thoroughly than any of them, Revelation is recursive in its procedure; that is, it represents the present and future by replicating or alluding to passages in earlier biblical texts, especially in Genesis, Exodus, the Old Testament prophets, and the apocalyptic visions in Daniel. The Book of Revelation thus incorporates and confirms an implicit design of the course and prime cause of earthly affairs which was soon made explicit by Christian exegetes – a paradigm of history which is radically distinctive. As against Greek and Roman primitivism and cyclism (the theory of eternal recurrence), the biblical paradigm attributes to earthly history a single and sharply defined plot, with a beginning (the *fiat* of creation), a catastrophe (the fall of man), a crisis (the Incarnation and Resurrection of

Christ), and a coming end (the abrupt Second Advent of Christ as King, followed by the replacement of the old world by 'a new heaven and a new earth') which will convert the tragedy of human history into a cosmic comedy. This historical plot, furthermore, has a divine Author, who planned its middle and end before the beginning, created the great stage and agents of history, infallibly controls all its events, and guarantees its ultimate consummation. As the Voice declared to John after his vision of the last things: 'I am the Alpha and Omega, the beginning and the end, the first and the last' (22.13).

This biblical paradigm has survived the biblical myth in which it was incorporated and has deeply informed Western views of the shape of history and the destiny of mankind and the world, whether in simple or sophisticated, in religious or secular renderings. History, it is said, 'has meaning'; by this is signified that it is not a play of blind contingencies but that it has a plot, and that this plot has a controller who orders it towards its outcome. Increasingly since the eighteenth century, however, the function of the controller of history and the guarantor of its consummation has been shifted from an external and supervisory Providence to forces which, though immanent within history itself, are no less infallible: an inherent teleology, or dialectical necessity, or set of causal laws which compel the course of events. But the prototype of the Western concept that history has an intelligible and end-determined order, whether fideistic or naturalistic, is the scheme of the course of earthly affairs from genesis to apocalypse which is underwritten by a sacred text.

Within this overall scheme the Book of Revelation envisions the agents and events of the latter and last days in ways which have strongly imprinted Western intellect and imagination; although because of the equivocal composition of Revelation itself, and the flexibility of the interpretive schemes that have been applied to its elucidation, the influence of apocalypse has manifested itself in diverse, and even in contrary forms.

I THE EARTHLY AND TRANSCENDENTAL KINGDOM

In Old Testament prophecy and apocalyptic, the ultimate peaceable Kingdom under divine dominion is to be a perfected condition of mankind on this earth which will endure forever. So in the dream of Daniel 'one like the Son of man', though descended from heaven, is given dominion over the earth that 'is an everlasting dominion, which shall not pass away' (Daniel 7.14). In Revelation, however, the binding of the Dragon and the restoration of earthly felicity under the dominion of Christ and his resurrected Saints will last only a millennium, one thousand years. The Dragon will then be loosed again, to be defeated in a final battle at Armageddon, after which will occur a general resurrection and the last judgment. The earthly stage of the cosmic drama, its function in the divine plot completed, will then be replaced by 'a new heaven and a new earth', while a 'new Jerusalem' will come down 'from God out of heaven' to be married to the Lamb in an eternal union.

Believers who are fundamentalists continue to interpret this promise of the felicity of the redeemed as applying only to a supramundane existence in a heavenly Jerusalem, after our bodily life and this temporal world shall have been abolished. Since the Reformation, however, there has been an increasing tendency to assimilate the prophecy of eternal felicity to the enduring state of this world, after it shall have been purged and renovated. Milton, for one, dismissed the problem of the location of the ultimate human blessedness as insoluble, and of no great consequence. Whether by

> *its final conflagration* . . . is meant the destruction of the substance of the world itself, or only a change in the nature of its constituent parts, is uncertain, and of no importance to determine. . . . Our glorification will be accompanied by the renovation of heaven and earth, and of all things therein adapted to our service and delight, to be possessed by us in perpetuity.[5]

In the secularized renderings of apocalyptic prophecy during the last two centuries, the felicitous outcome of history is of course held to take place on the stage of the existing earth, with the timelessness of eternity translated into perpetuity – or at least indefinite duration – in this-worldly time.

2 POLARITY

Apocalyptic narrative and prophecy is a chiaroscuro history, in which the agencies are the opponent forces of light and of darkness and there is no middle-ground between the totally good and the absolutely evil. On the negative side are ranged Satan, the Beast, and the Great Whore, 'Babylon the Great, the Mother of Harlots and Abominations of the Earth', together with the earthly agents of iniquity ('the kings of the earth, and their armies'), to whom exegetes soon applied the collective term 'Antichrist'. Opposed to them are God, Christ, the 'new Jerusalem . . . prepared as a bride adorned for her husband', and the company of earthly Saints. The consummation of history will occur, not by mediation between these polar opposites, but only after the extirpation of the forces of evil by the forces of good.

This aspect of the Book of Revelation has fostered a dubious heritage of reductive historical thinking in terms of absolute antitheses without the possibility of nuance, distinction, or mediation. Complex social, political, and moral issues are reduced to the two available categories of good and bad, right and wrong, the righteous and the wicked. Those who are not totally for are totally against; if you are not part of the solution you are part of the problem; and the problem can only be resolved by liquidating the opposition. In the popular mind – especially in countries such as America where there is a long and deep millenarian tradition – Revelation has also fostered a conspiracy-view of history in which all reverses or disasters are attributed to the machinations of Satan or Antichrist, or else of human agencies, whether individuals or classes or races, who are demoniac or (in the secular rendering) are motivated by the negative forces in the historical process. In times of extreme stress such thinking has helped engender a collective paranoia, religious or racial or national, which has manifested itself in Crusades, sacred wars, pogroms, witch-hunts, or other attempts to achieve, by annihilating the massed forces of evil, a final solution.

On a sophisticated and abstract level, which is not morally pernicious, the apocalyptic paradigm has also contributed toward a mode of thinking in which all process, whether historical, logical, or empirical, is attributed to the dynamic generated by polar opposites. The translation of apocalyptic dualism into a polar logic of process is especially patent in William Blake, who told H. C. Robinson, without inordinate exaggeration, that 'all he knew was in the Bible'. Blake had no patience for middling positions, for temporizing, and for what he called 'Negations', which are 'Exceptions & Objections & Unbeliefs' that, lacking a true opposite, are inert. What he sought was a consolidation of opponent-forces into genuine 'Contraries', for 'Without Contraries is no progression'; and 'From these contraries spring what the religious call Good and Evil'.[6] It is the energy generated by the tension between contraries which impels all development, organization, and creativity. The biblical opposition of absolute contraries and its destined outcome was also one among diverse sources of the dialectic of post-Kantian German philosophy, as adumbrated by Fichte, developed by Schelling, and given its final form by Hegel. The driving force of all process – including generic and individual history, logic, and the self-generative, automotive, self-sufficient system of philosophy itself – is the compulsion within any element to pose, or else to pass over into, its opposite, or contrary, or antithesis, which in turn generates its own opponent, in a ceaseless movement toward a consummation which is the annulment, or else the stable equilibrium, of all oppositions.

3 THE END IN THE BEGINNING

The shape of history implied by Revelation is a circular one which constitutes, as Karl Löwith has put it, 'one great detour to reach in the end the beginning'.[7] 'And he that sat upon the throne said, Behold, I make all things new.' But the new is represented as a renewal, and the *Endzeit* as a recovery of the *Urzeit*. The heaven and earth that God in the beginning had created he ends by re-creating; Adam and Eve, who have fallen, are replaced by the Lamb and his redeemed Bride; the paradise which has been lost recurs in an equivalent state which includes the Edenic properties of the 'river of water of life' and 'the tree of life'; and men and women shall in the end regain their original innocence and its attendant felicity, for 'there shall be no more curse', hence 'no more death, neither sorrow, nor crying [nor] any more pain'.

In a number of Church Fathers the biblical pattern of a Paradise-to-be-regained was assimilated to the neo-Platonic paradigm of an emanation from, division, and return to the Absolute One, and gave rise to the persistent concept that the temporal process – both in the history of mankind and in the life of each individual – is a circular movement from a unitary felicity, through self-division, sin, exile, and suffering, back to the initial felicity. This circular course was often figured according to the biblical (and Plotinian) metaphor of the *peregrinatio vitae*, and to it was adapted Christ's parable of the Prodigal Son who leaves home, journeys 'into a far country' where he wastes 'his substance with riotous living', and, penitent, returns home to a rejoicing father.

In a consequential variant of this figure of history as a great-circle route back to the origin, the blessedness at the end is conceived not simply to equal, but to exceed the innocence and happiness at the beginning. To John Milton, for example, a Puritan exponent of the strenuous moral life, the fall of man was a fortunate fall, not only because it gave us Christ, but because the ultimate paradise will have been earned, whereas the initial paradise was merely inherited. Thus when Christ shall receive his faithful into bliss, the earth

> Shall all be Paradise, far happier place
> Than this of *Eden*, and far happier days.
> (*Paradise Lost*, XII.461–5)

A century or so later philosophers and poets translated this myth of man's circuitous course from Eden to a far happier paradise into the distinctive Romantic figure of development – whether in history, the individual life, intellection, or the realm of morality, culture, and art – as a spiral: all process departs from an undifferentiated unity into sequential self-divisions, to close in an organized unity which has a much higher status than the original unity because it incorporates all the intervening divisions and oppositions. As Hugo von Hoffmannsthal later epitomized the Romantic concept: 'Every development moves in a spiral line, leaves nothing behind, reverts to the same point on a higher turning'.

The recurrent plot of Blake's prophetic poems, as he describes it at the opening of *The Four Zoas*, concerns 'a Perfect Unity . . . of Eden', figured as a single Primal Man, followed by 'His fall into Division & His Resurrection to Unity'. This course of events, as Blake describes it elsewhere, is a spiral progress from simple innocence up and back to an 'organized innocence'; or in an alternative description, it is mankind's loss of Eden and his struggle to achieve, by 'mental fight', the New Jerusalem, which is not simply the garden of the origin but the great city of civilization, intellection, and the arts. No less explicitly Friedrich Schelling adverts to the language of the Book of Revelation as the ground for his spiral view of intellectual and historical process. 'I posit God as the first and the last, as Alpha and Omega, but as Alpha he is not what he is as Omega'. For at the beginning he is merely '*Deus implicitus*', and only 'as Omega is he *Deus explicitus*'.[8] Translated into conceptual terms, this theological representation yields Schelling's philosophic method. 'Philosophy', he declares, 'opens with the Absolute and with the absence of all oppositions', and its 'ultimate destination' is 'to bring about a higher, truly all-encompassing unity' – the 'perfect inclusion of all-in-one' that is 'the one truly absolute knowledge, which is also . . . a knowledge of the Absolute'. And this process, Schelling adds, 'applies just as much to the sciences as to art'.[9]

We recognize a similar provenience and pattern in Hegel's dialectic. As he says at the conclusion of his shorter *Logic*: 'We have now returned to the notion of the Idea with which we began', but 'the return to the beginning is also an advance'.[10] And so in the self-compelled movement of Spirit in all its manifestations, whether in history, logic, metaphysics, science, or art, the consummation, or 'Absolute', having overcome yet preserved all intervening self-alienations, is that 'Truth' which includes in an organized form not less than everything. As Hegel puts it – in an explicit parallel of his conceptual scheme to the 'life of God and divine cognition' – the True is 'not an *original* or *immediate* unity as such', for which 'otherness and alienation, and the overcoming of alienation are not serious matters'. Instead, it is a circuitous progression –

> the process of its own becoming, the circle that presupposes the end as its goal, having its end also as its beginning; and only by being worked out to its end, is it actual.[11]

II TWO WAYS TO THE MILLENNIUM

The plot of biblical history is sharply discontinuous. Each of its crucial events is abrupt, cataclysmic, and inaugurates a drastic change: the creation, the fall, the Incarnation and Resurrection, and the advent of what Rufus Jones has called 'the fierce comfort of an apocalyptic relief expedition from the sky'[12] to establish the millennium. Revelation represents all present-day rulers and institutions as radically evil, and promises that these will be annihilated and replaced by the millennial kingdom. After the triumph of Christianity this millennial component posed an obvious threat to the Church and the established social order – a threat the more obvious because the seat of the Western Church was the very Rome which in Revelation had been figured as unholy Babylon, the Great Whore. Repeated attempts were made in the early Christian centuries to delete this threat by eliminating Revelation from the biblical canon. Much more effectively and enduringly, however, Augustine succeeded in saving yet denaturing Revelation by proposing the allegorical interpretation that the millennium signifies the present, but invisible, spiritual kingdom that has in fact been inaugurated at the Resurrection of Christ. Although Augustine's view became authoritative for the Church, belief in a literal millennium remained alive in the Middle Ages, and was widely revived after the Reformation.

As a consequence, Christianity has through the centuries harbored a strong historical prospectivism – the certainty that, though mankind is radically corrupt and inhabits a vale of tears, the best is inevitably about to be, in this life and this world. This millennial expectation has helped engender Western convictions about the future of mankind which have no close parallels in civilizations that developed outside the Hebrai–Christian orbit.

I MILLENNIALISM, MELIORISM, AND THE IDEA OF PROGRESS

One such conviction is that the human race is gradually progressing toward a much better, or even perfect, condition in the material, intellectual, moral, and social realms. So early as the twelfth century the Cistercian monk, Joachim of Fiore, reinterpreted Revelation in accordance with a Trinitarian conception of history, dividing the course of events into three great eras: the initial age of the Old Testament Father, the present age of the Son, and the coming age of the Holy Spirit when, by the joint agencies of God and men, all the world will achieve a state of perfect spiritual liberty. Joachim thus transformed the single-fall, single-redemption shape of biblical history into a sequence of three upward quantum-leaps and levellings-off, ending in an earthly perfection. After Joachim's death some of his followers, especially the Spiritual Franciscans, converted his prophecy of a Third Age into a militant program of radical political, as well as moral and religious, reform which has had a recurrent influence on revolutionary thinking, especially in Catholic countries.

The modern form of the idea of progress, however, has been mainly a product of Protestant Christianity. Recent researches have shown that this idea was not, as it was once represented by historians, simply an optimistic extrapolation into the future of the conspicuous advances in Europe, during and after the Renaissance, in science, technology, geographical exploration, and the arts. Instead, these advances in the sciences and the practical arts were assimilated into the inherited theological scheme of historical prospectivism, but in a way that drastically altered both the shape and dynamics of the scheme. For beginning with the Renaissance, mankind seemed to have developed the human means to achieve the promised state of felicity gradually and peacefully instead of by an abrupt and destructive intervention; and in the course of centuries, progress was increasingly conceived to be attainable by purely human agency, and to be guaranteed by the operation of purely natural causes, without the need for an apocalyptic relief expedition from the sky.

Francis Bacon, for example, was one of the earliest proponents of the idea of historical progress, as a destined consequence of the use of experimental science to increase man's control over the material conditions of his well-being. He presents this view, however, within the express context of the Christian pattern of providential history, and with persistent allusion to apocalyptic prophecy. He thus reads the assertion in Daniel concerning 'the last ages', that 'many shall go to and fro, and knowledge shall be increased', to signify that geographical exploration 'and advancement of the sciences, are destined by fate, that is, by Divine Providence, to meet in the same age'.[13] In Bacon's interpretation of the first and last things, man's fall, in its moral aspect, was a fall from innocence, but in its cognitive aspect, it was a divorce of mind from nature, hence of man's original dominion over the creation. Experimental science, however, promises to restore the 'commerce between the mind of man and the nature of things . . . to its perfect and original condition'. The end of human progress on earth will thus be a return to the condition of Eden, which Bacon equates with the heavenly Kingdom of the latter days: 'the entrance into the kingdom of man, founded on the sciences', is 'not much other than the entrance into the kingdom of heaven, whereinto none may enter except as a little child'. And he celebrates the anticipated consummation in the great apocalyptic figure of a marriage, although not between Christ and the renovated Jerusalem, but between

> the mind and the universe, the divine goodness assisting, out of which marriage let us hope (and be this the prayer of the bridal song) there may spring . . . a line and race of inventions that may in some degree subdue and overcome the necessities and miseries of humanity.[14]

Even in the heyday of the idea of progress in the nineteenth century, when the sanction of its inevitability was asserted to be the inherent laws of social development, many proponents of social reforms to expedite a perfected society continued to use the language of biblical prophecy. In some part, of course, the biblical allusions were merely metaphors for secular convictions, designed to make new concepts and programs intelligible and acceptable to a traditionalist public and to endow new ideas with the potency of an existing religious faith. The biblical language, however, manifests an unbroken continuity with the origin of the concept of inevitable progress in millennial prophecy. As Coleridge said of classical myths, 'The fair humanities of old religion',

> They live no longer in the faith of reason!
> But still the heart doth need a language, still
> Doth the old instinct bring back the old names.[15]

The socialist and industrial reformer, Robert Owen, for example, even though he repudiated all religious creeds, repeatedly expressed his conviction about the peaceful evolution to a 'New Moral World' in terms of the new heaven and new earth prophesied in Isaiah and Revelation. On his trip to America in 1824–5 Owen declared, in an address about his social schemes to the President and Congress, that 'the time is now come, when the principle of good is about to . . . reign triumphant over the principle of evil. . . . Old things shall pass away and all shall become new'. Later he declared to the population of the Owenite community, New Harmony:

> The day of your deliverance is come, and let us join heart and hand in extending that deliverance . . . until it shall pass to all people, even unto the uttermost parts of the earth. Then will be the full time of that universal sabbath, or reign of happiness, which is about to commence here, and which I trust you who are ready to put on the wedding garment will long live to enjoy.

Followers of Owen hailed him as the Messiah who, in the fullness of time, has now appeared; and just before his death Owen himself soberly declared that, in 'a calm retrospect of my life . . . there appears to me to have been a succession of extraordinary or out-of-the-usual-way events . . . to compel me to proceed onward to complete a mission, of which I have been an impelled agent'.[16]

II MILLENARIANISM AND REVOLUTION

Another historical concept which, in its original development, was unique to Western culture, is both more primitive than gradual progress (in that it is much closer to the apocalyptic prototype) and more sophisticated (in that it has in the last century and one-half been sanctioned by a complex structure of economic and social theory). This concept is that both the institutional and moral evils of the present world will, by an inner necessity, be abolished once for all by a sudden, violent, and all-inclusive political and social revolution.

The millenarian feature of Revelation, as Ernest Tuveson remarks in this volume, provides a scenario for revolution. And recurrently in Protestant Europe the Book of Revelation, together with the apocalypse in Daniel, has inspired revolutionary uprisings against the institutional powers of evil. In the sixteenth century the Anabaptists in nothern Europe, under such leaders as Thomas Müntzer and John of Leyden, 'The Messiah of the Last Days', initiated violent movements against the established powers in order to prepare the way for the divine Kingdom. In the English civil wars of the next century, radical sects such as the Fifth Monarchy men and the Diggers were possessed by the fervent belief that the conflict was the inauguration of the Second Coming and millennium – a belief that for an interval was shared by Oliver Cromwell and John Milton. In the latter eighteenth century the American Revolution evoked millenarian excitement among some adherents; while the early period of the French Revolution was widely interpreted as the glorious prelude to the universal felicity prophesied in Apocalypse – in Catholic France only by a few fringe-groups, but in Protestant England and Germany by many of the major intellectuals of the 1790s.[17]

The event of the French Revolution and its European after-waves precipitated the development, in the course of the nineteenth century, of the theory of absolute revolution, which is best known in the version of Marx and Engels. In its distinctive features, an absolute revolution is conceived to be: (1) inevitable, because compelled by iron laws, or by a dialectical teleology, operative within the historical process itself; (2) abrupt and relatively imminent; (3) effected through the radical and irreconcilable opposition between institutions, races, or economic classes, in which one side (fated to prevail) embodies the historical right and good and its opponent (fated to be defeated and annihilated) embodies historical wrong and evil; (4) led by a militant élite, who recognize, cooperate with, and so expedite the irresistible process of history; (5) violent, because destined to be achieved by a fierce but purifying destruction of the forces of historical evil; (6) absolute, in that instead of gradual improvement or reform, there will be a rapid transformation of the very foundations of society and its institutions so as to effect a state of peace, community, justice, and the optimal conditions for human well-being; (7) universal – though it is to be initiated at a critical time and place, the revolution will, by irresistible contagion, spread to encompass all the inhabited world; and (8) ultimate and irrevocable, in that the transformation of society will also transform those attributes of human nature which have brought us to our present plight, restore man to his original humanity, and thus ensure the perpetuation of the new era.[18]

The certainty that the future will culminate in such a radical transformation, it is claimed, is based on valid induction from the historical past. But in its salient features we recognize in the theory of absolute revolution the stark outline of the apocalyptic prophecy, guaranteed by omnipotence, that history, after an imminent and violent victory of a messianic leader and his forces of good over the consolidated forces of evil, will eventuate in an abrupt and total alteration of the conditions of mankind into a state which is figured as a redeemed City that will recuperate the felicity of the aboriginal garden.

III THE APOCALYPSE WITHIN

The Apocalypse, as Milton remarked, rises 'to a Prophetick pitch in types, and Allegories'. The symbolic and typological mode in which it is set forth has made Revelation a very flexible text for historical application. The antitype of the Beast, or of Antichrist, in accordance with the time, place, and persuasion of the interpreter, has been variously identified as the Jews, the Ottomans, the Pope, France, Charles I, Cromwell, priestcraft, the alliance against revolutionary France, the landholding aristocracy, capitalists, the American slaveholder, and Hitler; while in the same interpreter, the antitype has sometimes shifted drastically, in consonance with a shift in the interpreter's outlook and preoccupations. This flexibility has also served to make predictions based on Revelation invulnerable to disconfirmation. In the demotic type of prediction – in which a group, having computed the precise date, dispose of their worldly goods, don white robes, and ascend a hill to await the relief expedition from the sky – the failure of the event to happen on schedule usually results, not in a rejection of the prediction, but in a recalculation of the prophetic arithmetic. In the derivative, secular mode of prediction, the failure of a revolution to effect the predicted transformation in the nature and well-being of mankind has led to the postponement of the change to a secular second advent after an ever-extending period of the dictatorship of the proletariat, or to its reformulation as the emergent product of an indefinitely continuing revolution. In both instances, religious or secular, the capacity of the predictive scheme to survive all counter-evidence rests on faith in an infallible but equivocal charter which allows broad play to the force of human desire.

The freedom of interpretive manoeuvre was greatly increased by the early application to Revelation of an allegorical mode of reading, either as an overlay or as a total displacement of its 'literal' – that is, historical – reference, and especially by the interpretation of its 'carnal sense' as encoding an inner 'spiritual sense'. The tendency to internalize apocalypse by a spiritual reading began in the Gospels themselves: 'For, behold, the kingdom of God is within you' (Luke, 17.20–1). Paul, the first exemplar of the distinctively Christian experience of conversion, enlarged the analogy to include an equivalent, in the spirit of the individual convert, of a second creation, of a new heaven and new earth, and of the marriage between the Lamb and the New Jerusalem: 'Therefore if any man be in Christ, he is a new creature: old things are passed away; behold all things are become new' (2 Corinthians 5.17). 'Wherefore, my brethren, ye also are become dead to the law . . . that ye should be married to another . . . who is raised from the dead' (Romans 7.1–4). In his *Confessions* St. Augustine, who rejected the literal reading of the millennial promise, effected instead the full transfer of apocalyptic prophecy from the outer world to the theater of the individual spirit, where one experiences the pre-enactment, in this life, of the historical events of the latter days. Building, as he himself indicates, on the established pattern of Christian conversion from St Paul to Athanasius' recent *Life of St Anthony*, Augustine describes in detail the sustained and anguished conflict between his 'two wills' (the inner equivalent of the forces of Christ and Antichrist), culminating in a spiritual Armageddon in the garden at Milan, the final triumph of the good will, and the abrupt interposition of grace to effect the annihilation of the old creature and the birth of the new: 'dying unto death and living into life' (*Confessions*, Book VIII).

By completing the process of psycho-historical parallelism, Augustine established the distinctive Christian paradigm of the interior life as one of polar self-division, internecine self-conflict, crisis, abrupt rebirth, and the consequent renovation of the way we experience the world; at the same time, by his detailed narration of these events in the course of his own life, he established the enduring literary genre of the spiritual autobiography. We recognize the mode, for example, on the moral level of its multiple significations, in Dante's account of his toilsome spiritual journey through hell and purgatory to the vision of paradise – a personal, inner experience which is proleptic of what will happen, historically, to all those who shall be redeemed *all'ultima giustizzia* to dwell in that 'true kingdom' which is 'our city', where at the appointed time Dante too shall attend the wedding feast as a member of the Spouse (*Paradiso*, XXX). In *The Faerie Queene* Spenser converted the chivalric quest-romance of the Middle Ages into his 'continued Allegory, or darke conceit', of which the chief prototype was the Book of Revelation. The narrative signifies, in its reference to the historical future, the events preparatory to the Second Advent of Christ, His ultimate victory over the dragon, and the apocalyptic marriage which will inaugurate the restoration of Eden; at the same time it signifies, spiritually, the question for redemption, the fights against the agents and deceptions of evil, the triumph, and the spiritual marriage which is enacted in this present life within the soul of each wayfaring Christian, including Spenser himself. Augustine's *Confessions* has also engendered numerous spiritual autobiographies in prose; most of these writings are Protestant, and many represent a working-class pilgrim who makes his laborious interior way past the pitfalls of Satan toward the celestial city and the apocalyptic marriage of the Lamb. John Bunyan, who wrote a proletarian form of the Augustinian autobiography, *Grace Abounding*, also wrote in *Pilgrim's Progress* the immortal allegory of the proletarian spiritual journey – a pedestrian equivalent to the quest for an inner apocalypse by Spenser's courtly knight on horseback.

In the central tradition of Christian, and especially of Protestant exegesis, the spiritual sense is justified as an over-reading of the basic sense of Scripture, which is literal and historical. Some radical inner-light Protestants, however, proposed a mode of interpretation which regarded the spiritual meaning not as supplementing, but as totally displacing the literal sense. Gerrard Winstanley, leader of the sect of 'Diggers' – that is, Christian Communists – during the

Puritan Revolution in England, proclaimed that any reading of the Bible which substitutes 'bare letters, words, and histories for spirit' is the work of the 'great Dragon', for 'all that which you call history . . . is all to be seen and felt within you'. Not only the places, events, and doctrines, but all the human and supernatural protagonists in the Bible, including Jehovah and Jesus, are nothing more than figurative vehicles for the powers and processes of individual minds in mundane experience. Anyone who worships an external God 'in the heavens' in fact worships the Devil; also, not 'Jesus Christ at a distance from thee . . . but a Christ within is thy Saviour. . . . *And besides him there is no Saviour*'. By the same token the events of the last days in Revelation signify solely a personal and internal experience: 'Now the second *Adam* Christ hath taken the Kingdom my body, and rules in it; *He makes it a new heaven, and a new earth, wherein dwells Righteousness*'. 'And this is to be made a new creature . . .'. The new heaven and new earth, it thus turns out, instead of a transcendant habitat that is 'not to be known and seen, till the body is laid in the dust', is simply our present world, perceived in a new way by our redeemed and glorified senses:

> I tel you, this great mystery is begun to appear, and it must be seen by the material eyes of the flesh: And those five senses that is in man, shall partake of this glory.[19]

A century and one-half later William Blake told H. C. Robinson that 'all he knew was in the Bible', but added the crucial proviso that 'he understands by the Bible the spiritual sense'. Blake's 'spiritual sense' is very like Winstanley's, in that it invalidates the literal sense as a fiction propagated by 'Priesthood' and internalizes both the divine and human agents and events of the biblical narrative. 'All deities reside in the human breast'; all powers to effect drastic change in the perceived world are mental powers; and heaven, hell, and paradise are states of mind.

> I know of no other . . . Gospel than the liberty both of body & mind to exercise the Divine Arts of Imagination. . . . What is the Joy of Heaven but Improvement in the things of the Spirit? What are the Pains of Hell but Ignorance, Bodily Lust, Idleness & devastation of the things of the Spirit? . . . To labour in Knowledge is to Build up Jerusalem.

Blake identifies Christ the Redeemer with the human imagination, therefore conceives the apocalyptic new earth to be this world, when it is perceived imaginatively – that is, through our redeemed and liberated senses. 'The ancient tradition that the world will be consumed in fire is true', but in the spiritual sense that 'this will come to pass by an improvement of sensual enjoyment'; for 'if the doors of perception were cleansed everything would appear to man as it is, infinite'. It is in this radical sense that 'the Eye altering, alters all'.[20]

Blake probably derived his version of biblical hermeneutics from left-wing dissenting sects in late-eighteenth-century England. To spiritualize biblical history and prophecy, however, was a common poetic procedure among Blake's younger contemporaries. Wordsworth, for example, proclaimed that the theme of his poetic autobiography concerned divine powers and actions, internalized as processes of his own mind –

> Of genius, power,
> Creation, and divinity itself,
> I have been speaking, for my theme has been
> What passed within me. . . .
> This is in truth heroic argument,
> And genuine prowess. . . .
>
> (*Prelude*, 1805, III.171–83)

And in the verse 'Prospectus' to his overall poetic enterprise, which resonates with echoes of Revelation, Wordsworth announces that his poetic journey must ascend beyond 'the heaven of heavens' past 'Jehovah, with his thunder, and the choir of shouting Angels', and must also sink deeper than the lowest hell; all this, however, without leaving the confines of

> the Mind of Man,
> My haunt, and the main region of my Song.

The conclusion of his 'high argument' is the recovery of a lost Paradise, but a Paradise which is the very world of all of us, to be achieved by a consummation figured as an apocalyptic marriage between the prime Romantic opposites of subject and object, Spirit and its alienated other – or in the English terms, between mind and nature: 'Paradise, and groves/ Elysian, Fortunate Fields',

> why should they be
> A history only of departed things,
> Or a mere fiction of what never was?
> For the discerning intellect of Man
> When wedded to this goodly universe
> In love and holy passion, shall find these
> A simple produce of the common day.
> . . . This is our high argument.[21]

IV AMERICAN MILLENNIALISM

Writers in diverse times and places have claimed that their nation is the typological 'New Israel', divinely chosen to play the leading role in initiating the earthly Kingdom. The nation possessed of the most thoroughly and enduringly millennial ideology, however, is America, in a tradition that began even before it was settled by Europeans. Columbus himself suggested that the New World he had discovered was to be the locale of the new earth prophesied in Revelation. This belief was brought to American by the early Franciscan missionaries (heirs to the preachings of Joachim of Fiore), and entrenched by the fervent iteration of America's millennial destiny by the Puritan settlers of New England. 'For your full assurance,' Edward Johnson reminded his fellow New-Englanders in 1653, 'know this is the place where the Lord will create a new Heaven and a new earth . . . new Churches and a new Commonwealth together'. A century later Jonathan Edwards viewed the Great Awakening as the initial stage in fulfilling the New World's apocalyptic destiny, interpreted in the spiritual sense: 'This new world is probably now discovered . . . that God might in it begin a new world in a spiritual respect, when he creates the *new heavens* and *new earth*'.[22] Even in our time the American one-dollar bill echoes the persistent expectation, in its motto from Virgil's prophecy of a new age of gold: *Novus ordo Seclorum*.

Belief in the providential role of the New World helped form the concept of the American's identity as a new Adam, freed from the corruptions of the Old World. In its secularized form this view fostered the stress, especially prominent among the Transcendentalists, on the American as one who is uniquely able to reachieve the innocent vision of a child, and so to experience the unspoiled American world as a pristine Eden. The militant application of millennial prophecy emerged in the American Revolution, in the Civil War (which produced the greatest of all hymns on the imminent Second Advent, 'Mine eyes have seen the glory of the coming of the Lord'), and again in the First World War. In an alternative form the indurate myth of a millennial America resulted in the imperialist doctrines of the American Mission and of Manifest Destiny. We recognize, in William Gilpin's proclamation of 1846, the ancient faith in America as the divine agency and initial theater of the world-wide consummation of history:

> The untransacted destiny of the American poeple is to subdue the continent . . . to regenerate superannuated nations . . . to carry the career of mankind to its culminating point . . . to absolve the curse that weighs down humanity, and to shed blessings around the world![23]

This awesome mission, however, entailed corresponding responsibilities and dire penalties for failure, as native prophets have persistently warned in American jeremiads that have preempted the imagery of the *dies irae*; it has also fostered a paranoid tendency to blame historical setbacks on diverse baleful conspirators, determined to frustrate the divine intention. And the investment of inordinate hope in the American promise has effected, in times of disillusion, an equal but opposite reaction of unqualified despair. Herman Melville in 1850 had shared the ardent belief that 'We Americans are the peculiar, chosen people – the Israel of our time. . . . God has predestined, mankind expects great things from our race'. In this 'New World', the 'political Messiah . . . has come in *us*'. A quarter-century later Melville voiced the depressive other-side of America's manic millennialism. Beyond all the saddest thought of old Europe, he lamented in *Clarel*,

> Might be the New World's sudden brought . . .
> To feel the arrest of hope's advance,
> And squandered last inheritance;
> And cry – 'To Terminus build fanes!
> Columbus ended earth's romance:
> No New World to mankind remains![24]

V ROMANTIC APOCALYPTICISM: POLITICAL, COGNITIVE, IMAGINATIVE

In its founding and continuing ideology, America is the most millennial of nations, but the period of English and German Romanticism, in its preoccupation with the philosophic, social, or poetic seer who demonstrates the way to a secular redemption, is the most apocalyptic of cultural eras.[25] In England, with its inheritance of Puritan millenarianism during the Civil Wars, and in Germany, with its even older chiliastic tradition and the emphasis on eschatological renewal in Pietist theology, the outbreak of the French Revolution revived the ancient hope. In both countries a chorus of preachers, poets, and young intellectuals endowed the Revolution with the myth of apocalypse, in the excited expectation that this local event heralded a renovated world for a regenerate mankind. As Robert Southey said, in retrospect from his conservative middle age, few persons who have not lived through the bright initial period of the French Revolution 'can conceive or comprehend . . . what a visionary world' it seemed to open: 'Old things seemed passing away, and nothing was dreamt of but the regeneration of the human race'.[26] 'Bliss was it in that dawn to be alive', Wordsworth recalled those years in *The Prelude*, with

> France standing on the top of golden hours,
> And human nature seeming born again.
>
> (X, 692; VI, 353–4)

Hegel, Schelling, and Hölderlin, while fellow-students at Tübingen Seminary, all shared this perfervid millenarian enthusiasm. Looking back, like Southey and Wordsworth, from the standpoint of his later conservatism, Hegel described the effect of this 'world-historical' event of his youth in theological terms similar to theirs:

> It was a glorious dawn. All thinking beings shared in the jubilation of the epoch. . . . An enthusiasm of the spirit thrilled through the world, as though the time were now come of the actual reconciliation of God with the world.[27]

Through the mid-1790s the poets Blake, Wordsworth, Coleridge, Southey, like Hölderlin in Germany, responded to the great events of the time by writing visionary epics, verse-narratives, or Pindaric odes which, with a lavish use of apocalyptic symbols, depicted the dark and violent past and present of mankind, then hailed the outbreak of the French Revolution as the critical event which will usher in a new world combining the features of the biblical paradise and the pagan age of gold. The conclusion of Coleridge's prose 'Argument' for his extended poetic vision, *Religious Musings*, written in 1794, laconically summarizes this prophetic reading of current events: 'The present State of Society. The French Revolution. Millenium. Universal Redemption. Conclusion.'

At the French excesses that began with the Reign of Terror, English and German commentators abandoned hope in the imminence of a literal millennium. But as in earlier ages, the paradigm demonstrated its capacity to survive discomfirmation by the course of events. The scientist and Unitarian preacher, Joseph Priestley, despite some wavering, insisted near the end of his life in 1804 that the mistake was merely in computing the Second Coming, and that the 'greatest of all events is not less certain for being delayed beyond our expectations'.[28] Much more representative, however, was the view of S. T. Coleridge, who wrote to Wordsworth in 1799 that there had been a 'complete failure of the French Revolution', but exhorted his friend to write a poem designed to banish the despair of those who, in consequence of that failure, 'have thrown up all hopes for the amelioration of mankind'.[29] So late as the second decade of the nineteenth century Shelley wrote that the French Revolution continues to be 'the master theme of the epoch in which we live', and that this theme is a central element in what he, like many English and German contemporaries, called 'the spirit of the age' with its great 'new birth' in poetry and philosophy. But as Shelley also recognized, this theme was that of a failed Revolution, the resulting collapse of millenarian expectation, and the need to salvage hopes for the amelioration of mankind.[30] Writing in 1815 Thomas Noon Talfourd observed – and his opinion has many contemporary parallels – that this crisis, which was intellectual and moral no less than political, interpenetrated and inspired the great new literature of the age. In the early days of the Revolution, 'all was hope and joy and rapture; the corruption and iniquity of ages seemed to vanish like a dream; the unclouded heavens seemed once more to ring with the exulting chorus of peace on earth and goodwill to men'. But suddenly these 'sublime expectations were swept away' by 'the terrible changes of this august spectacle'. And one effect 'of this moral hurricane . . . this rending of the general heart', was 'to raise and darken the imagination', hence to help 'form that great age of poetry which is flourishing around us'.[31]

'The Revolution', Talfourd added, 'completed the regeneration of our poetry'. This remark applies to Germany as well as England, and to post-Kantian philosophy as well as literature. In both countries, and in both the cognitive and imaginative realms, the apocalyptic design survived, but was given a spiritual interpretation – a new kind of spiritual interpretation, adapted to the social and intellectual conditions of the times. In what Wordsworth in 1805 called 'This melancholy waste of hopes o'erthrown . . . this time/ Of dereliction and dismay' (*Prelude*, II, 447–57), he and other vanguard writers undertook to reconstitute the grounds of hope, in a way that would be not only pertinent to post-Revolutionary despair but acceptable to post-Enlightenment thinking. For an apocalypse by revelation, or an apocalypse by revolution, they substituted an apocalypse of consciousness: the mind of man possesses the power, by an interior revolution, to transform his intellect and imagination, and by so doing to transform his perception of the everyday world into a new earth in which he will be thoroughly at home.

I PHILOSOPHIC CHILIASM AND POETIC CHILIASM

Romantic philosophers and poets were steeped in the Bible and in biblical exegesis. Schiller assiduously read theology in his early youth, and Fichte, Schelling, and Hegel, as well as the poet Hölderlin, had all been university students of theology. Wordsworth and Coleridge narrowly escaped becoming preachers; for Novalis, as for Blake, the Bible was 'the great code of art'; and Shelley, although an uncompromising agnostic, studied the Bible constantly and listed it as 'last, yet first' among fifteen books adequate to constitute a good library.[32]

A distinctive feature shared by the new philosophy and new poetry of the Romantic era is that it was an innovation by deliberate reversion to the biblical paradigm of Paradise, the fall, the redemption, and Paradise-to-be-regained. Herder, Kant, Schiller, Fichte, Schelling, and Hegel (following the precedent of Lessing's *The Education of the Human Race*, 1780) all undertook, as they expressly asserted, to translate the conceptual truth incorporated in biblical myth into the secular mode that the Germans call *Universalgeschichte*. In this historical genre, the vanguard of human consciousness, represented as a single character called 'Mankind', falls from the paradisal unit of a purely instinctual life into the 'evil' of having to make moral choice, as well as other kinds of self-division and conflicts which, by their internal energy, compel him along the journey back toward the unity and felicity of his origin. To such a rational transposition of the biblical millennium by himself and other writers, Kant applied the term *der philosophische Chiliasmus*; 'One sees', he also remarks, 'that philosophy too can have its chiliasm . . . which is nothing less than visionary'.[33] In the 1790s the frustrated promise of the French Revolution became for philosophers (including the elderly Kant)[34] a crucial event in this progressive educational journey of Mankind. In addition it was increasingly stressed that man's fall from instinctual self-unity into dispersion and self-conflict was a *felix culpa*, because the way back is also a way up, from a simplex unity to the complex integrity of a superior Mankind inhabiting a Paradise happier far than the distant and undivided original. In parallel with this *Universalgeschichte* was the Romantic *Bildungsgeschichte*, narrating, in the vehicle of a life-journey, the educational growth of a single mind; among its instances are Hölderlin's *Hyperion* (1797–9), Wordsworth's *Prelude* (1805), and Carlyle's *Sartor Resartus* (1833–4). This latter genre, constituting a theodicy of the individual life, was a secular revision of the Christian spiritual autobiography. In the Romantic mode the fragmented consciousness reaches a crisis, or spiritual breakdown, immediately followed by a breakthrough to a higher integrity, from which vantage the individual finally is able to discern the implicit teleology that governs, and justifies, his painful educational journey – that is, the achievement of his mature identity and the recognition of his predestined vocation as public spokesman in his time of troubles.

What is less obvious – though the fact was expressly asserted by the philosophers themselves, and reiteratively implied by the design, imagery, and allusions in their writings – was that the great post-Kantian philosophical systems, no less than the 'universal history' these thinkers expounded, were secularized versions of the Christian paradigm of the creation, fall, and apocalyptic consummation of history. What Novalis said of Fichte's philosophy, that it is 'perhaps nothing else than applied Christianity',[35] can be even more emphatically claimed for the speculative systems of Fichte's younger contemporaries, Schelling and Hegel. As Hegel repeatedly said, while philosophy 'must not allow herself to be overawed by religion', it cannot neglect, but must translate into its own non-supernatural terms 'the tales and allegories of religion'.[36]

In Hegel's *Phenomenology of Spirit* the emergence of 'the Revealed Religion', with what he calls its 'picture-thinking' in 'the form of objectivity', is the penultimate stage of the Spirit's process of self-education toward a consummation in philosophical *Wissenschaft*. In his narration of this process Hegel systematically translates the crucial occurrences and concepts of biblical history into the conceptual mode of genuine philosophy, which transcends, while preserving its truth-content, the mythical representations of revealed

Christianity.[37] Carlyle's German philosopher, Professor Teufelsdroeckh, speaks for his major contemporaries when he asserts that 'the Mythus of the Christian Religion looks not in the eighteenth century as it did in the eighth', then sets himself the task 'to embody the divine Spirit of that Religion in a new Mythus, in a new vehicle and vesture . . .'.[38]

The overall plot and critical events of biblical history, conceptualized, thus reappear as the constitutive paradigm in the systems of Romantic philosophy, however diverse the details in each system. These philosophies, unlike most traditional systems, are not static structures of truth, but are constantly on the move, and their movement is end-oriented. In the beginning is the creation, at the timeless 'moment' when the unitary Absolute, or universal Ego, or Spirit sets itself off as object to itself as subject. 'Thus,' in Hegel's version, 'the merely eternal or abstract Spirit becomes an "other" to itself, or enters into existence. Accordingly' – in the language that is, of picture-thinking – 'it *creates* a world'. This primal self-division inaugurates a process of ever-renewing others, or oppositions, or antitheses which impel a movement, through a crisis, toward that last, far-off, divine event toward which both speculative thinking and the universe inevitably move. In the *Phenomenology* the Armageddon, or *crise de conscience*, of the self-alienated Spirit manifests itself, historically, in the French Revolution and the Reign of Terror. And the goal-event of the process, which Hegel calls 'Absolute Knowledge' or the self-reunited 'Spirit that knows itself as Spirit', is presented, in Hegel's persistent use of *double entendres*, as the cognitive translation both of the human restoration of its original mode of existence and of the new heaven and new earth prophesied in the picture-thinking of Revelation. As Hegel puts it in the concluding page of the *Phenomenology*: 'This transformed existence – the former one, but now reborn of the Spirit's knowledge – is the new existence, a new world and a new shape of Spirit'.[39]

Hegel's *das neue Dasein* which is *eine neue Welt* – the 'goal' and 'fulfillment', as he calls it, both of consciousness and history that will justify their agonized evolution – has its equivalent in his fellow-philosophers. In Schiller's *Aesthetic Education of Man* (1795), the equivalent is the 'aesthetic state'; this state replaces what Schiller describes as the 'vain hope' invested in political revolution by 'a complete revolution' of consciousness which will yield – although, for the time being, only in the realm of 'aesthetic semblance' – a condition of genuine liberty, fraternity, and equality.[40] In Fichte's version of 1806, this ultimate state is the life of 'Blessedness' which Fichte substitutes for his earlier millenarian hope in the French Revolution; this 'Doctrine of Blessedness', he now asserts, 'can be nothing else than a Doctrine of Knowledge', by means of which we will achieve 'the new world which rises before us' and 'the new life which begins within us'.[41] To Schelling, writing in 1804, the consummation of philosophy will be a 'golden age, of an eternal peace'; this is to be reached, however, not by 'external activity' but by a cognitive turn-around, back to the lost 'inner identity with the Absolute' which 'will be the true revolution [*Revolution*], the idea of which is utterly different from that which has been called by that name'.[42]

Kant's 'philosophical chiliasm' has its literary parallel in the imaginative chiliasm espoused by Romantic writers in verse and prose. In *The Prelude* Wordsworth narrates the spiritual crisis consequent on the failure of his revolutionary millenarianism, followed by his recovery and a recognition of his mature identity which is also the discovery of his poetic vocation. Attendant upon this discovery is his vision of the world transformed by imagination, which it is his poetic mission to make public:

> And I remember well
> That in life's every-day appearances
> I seemed about this period to have sight
> Of a new world – a world, too, that was fit
> To be transmitted and made visible
> To other eyes –

a new world which is to be achieved, not by political activity, but by an 'ennobling interchange/ Of action from within and from without' (XII, 368–771). A similar new world, brought about by a spiritual revolution which yields an apocalypse of imagination, is the end-state in many other Romantic writings, whether in the form of autobiography, epic, prose-romance, or drama. These include Blake's prophetic poems, Shelley's *Prometheus Unbound* and other visionary works, Carlyle's *Sartor Resartus*, Hölderlin's *Hyperion*, as well as Novalis' *Heinrich von Ofterdingen* and the literary genre he called the *Märchen*, with its fusion of classical, scientific, occult, and especially eschatological elements. What Novalis says in his cryptic notes on the *Märchen* is relevant to the vatic literary works of his age. 'It is at the end the primal world, the golden age'. But this end is to be achieved by 'Man' himself as 'the Messiah of nature', and the event is told in the form of a 'New Testament – and new nature – as New Jerusalem'.[43] In *Sartor Resartus* Carlyle echoes Novalis on man as 'the Messias of Nature', and his Teufelsdroeckh says that, after his agonized mental crisis, he 'awoke to a new Heaven and a new Earth'; this, however, was the old earth, seen anew because 'my mind's eyes were now unsealed'. And he exhorts the reader that if his 'eyesight' were to become 'unsealed', he would also see 'that this fair universe, were it in the meanest province thereof, is in very deed the star-domed City of God'. In the early 1830s Carlyle thus summarized the endeavor of the preceding generation to achieve a New Jerusalem not by changing the world, but by changing the way we see the world, through an exchange of what he calls the 'Imaginative' faculty for the 'Understanding' and the merely physical eye.[44]

2 THE SEER AND THE BARD

Throughout the altering interpretations and applications of the apocalyptic theme, a persistent element is the interpreter's representation of himself as a philosopher-seer or poet-prophet – in the British version, a 'Bard' – in the lineage of the biblical prophets of apocalypse. At the height of his millenarian expectations in 1641, Milton had celebrated the coming of 'the Eternal and shortly-expected King' to proclaim 'thy universal and milde Monarchy through Heaven and Earth'. At that time 'some one' (patently Milton himself)

> may perhaps bee heard offering at high *strains* in new and lofty *Measures* to sing and celebrate thy . . . *marvelous Judgments* in this Land throughout all ages.[45]

Two centuries later, in *The Ages of the World* (1811), Friedrich Schelling announced the approaching culmination of philosophy in a renewal of the primordial union between mind and nature which will effect a paradisal world: 'There will be one world, and the peace of the golden age will make itself known for the first time in the harmonious union of all sciences'. Like Milton, Schelling (who had himself once undertaken an epic poem) heralds the seer who will chant this ultimate state of consciousness:

> Perhaps he will yet come who is to sing the greatest heroic poem, comprehending in spirit what was, what is, what will be, the kind of poem attributed to the seers of yore.[46]

Hegel in his *Phenomenology of Spirit* (1807) had already assumed the office of a seer who, as the qualified spokesman for, as well as participant in, the Spirit is able to recapitulate its long evolution in human consciousness and history; in the final paragraph he represents the consummation of the Spirit's development in 'Absolute Knowing' as an event that takes place in the consciousness of Hegel himself, in the very act of writing that conclusion. Schelling's seer who comprehends 'what was, what is, what will be' coincides exactly with William Blake's prophetic persona as 'the Bard/ Who Present, Past & Future sees'. This role is assumed also by Novalis, as well as by Carlyle, who is the transitional figure between the Romantic seer and the Victorian prophet.[47] In the original introduction to the Prospectus for his high poetic argument, Wordsworth claimed that he has been granted 'an internal brightness' that 'is shared by none', which both qualifies and compels him, 'divinely taught', to speak 'Of what in man is human and divine'. He proceeded to announce the paradise which will be regained by the wedding of mind to nature, and his office as the poet-prophet who

> long before the blissful hour arrives,
> Would chant in lonely peace the spousal verse
> Of this great consummation.[48]

Hölderlin had also assumed the stance of elected prophet in his odes of the early 1790s which proclaimed that 'zur Vollendung geht die Menschheit ein',[49] and again, late in the 1790s, in the visionary passages of his prose *Hyperion*.

More than two decades later Shelley announced, in the final chorus of *Hellas* (1821),

> The world's great age begins anew
> The golden years return.

In a note appended to this chorus Shelley reveals that, in the course of his poetic life, he has become a touch ironic about assuming the role of 'bard', and much less assured about the validity of bardic prophecy. But with that combination of empirical scepticism and indefeasible idealism characteristic of his poetic maturity, Shelley pleads as his exemplars Isaiah, the Old Testament prophet of an enduring earthly millennium, and Virgil, whose 'messianic' fourth Eclogue, interpreted as an approximation to revealed truth, had over the Christian centuries motivated the conflation of the return of the pagan golden age with the restoration of Paradise prophesied in Revelation:

> ... to anticipate however darkly a period of regeneration and happiness is a ... hazardous exercise of the faculty which bards possess or feign. It will remind the reader ... of Isaiah and Virgil, whose ardent spirits overleaping the actual reign of evil which we endure and bewail, already saw the possible and perhaps approaching state of society in which the *"lion shall lie down with the lamb,"* and *"Omnis feret omnia tellus."* Let these great names be my authority and my excuse.

NOTES

1. D. H. Lawrence, *Apocalypse* (1931), London, 1972, pp. 3, 5–6.
2. See Frank E. Manuel, *The Religion of Isaac Newton* (Oxford, 1974); and, on Priestley's writings on Revelation, Clarke Garrett, *Respectable Folly: Millenarians and the French Revolution in England* (Baltimore, 1975), ch. 6.
3. P. J. Proudhon, *System of Economical Contradictions* (1846), translated by Benjamin R. Tucker (Boston, 1888), I, 27, 30–1.
4. On biblical patterns in Western fiction see Frank Kermode, *The Sense of an Ending: Studies in the Theory of Fiction* (New York, 1967).
5. Milton, *The Christian Doctrine*, I, xxxiii. See also *Paradise Lost*, XII, 463–4: 'Whether in Heav'n or Earth, for then the Earth/Shall all be Paradise ....'.
6. H. C. Robinson, *Blake, Coleridge, Wordsworth, Lamb, Etc.*, ed. Edith J. Morley (Manchester, 1922), p. 12; Blake, *Jerusalem*, 17.33–5, and *The Marriage of Heaven and Hell*, Plate 3.
7. Karl Löwith, *Meaning in History* (Chicago, 1949), p. 183.
8. F. W. J. von Schelling, *Denkmal der Schrift ... des Herrn F. H. Jacobi, Sämtliche Werke*, Pt. I, Vol. VIII, 81.

The aftermath

9 Schelling, *Vorlesungen über die Methode des Akademischen Studiums*, *Sämtlichte Werke*, Pt. I, Vol. V, 275.
10 *The Logic of Hegel*, trans. William Wallace (2nd edn; Oxford, 1892), p. 379.
11 Hegel's *Phenomenology of Spirit*, trans. A. V. Miller (Oxford, 1977), pp. 10–11.
12 Rufus M. Jones, *The Eternal Gospel* (New York, 1938), p. 5.
13 Francis Bacon, *The New Organon and Related Writings*, ed. Fulton H. Anderson (New York, 1960), pp. 90–2. As Lord Acton, late in the nineteenth century, put the relation between Providence and what Bacon called 'fate' in history: 'Progress was Providence: unless there was progress there could be no God in history.' (Cited by H. Butterfield, *Man on His Past*, Cambridge, 1955, p. 130).
14 *The New Organon and Related Writings*, pp. 3, 14, 15, 22–3, 66.
15 Coleridge's interpolation in his translation of Schiller's drama, *The Piccolomini*, II, iv, 123 ff.
16 J. F. C. Harrison, *Robert Owen and the Owenites in Britain and America* (London, 1969), pp. 106, 126, 134.
17 The rationale and practice of absolute revolution in non-European civilizations has either been taken over from Western theorists or else has been exported to underdeveloped countries by the indefatigable Christian missionaries who, preaching the religion of peace, unwittingly brought a sword – the apocalyptic faith in a divine, or divinely appointed, champion who would reverse the local status of oppressor and oppressed, to inaugurate a world of universal abundance and happiness. See Vittorio Lanternari, *The Religions of the Oppressed: A Study of Modern Messianic Cults*, translated Lisa Sergio (New York, 1963).
18 Marx, especially in his earlier writings, incorporated the theory of absolute revolution into the Romantic pattern of history as a spiral movement. The ultimate state of mankind will be a return to the primitive state of communal unity, but on a higher level because, as Marx puts it, it will be 'a return which assimilates all the wealth of previous development'. See M. H. Abrams, *Natural Supernaturalism: Tradition and Revolution in Romantic Literature* (New York, 1971), pp. 313–16.
19 *The New Law of Righteousness* (1648), in *The Works of Gerrard Winstanley*, ed. George H. Sabine (Ithaca, N.Y., 1941).
20 *The Marriage of Heaven and Hell*, 11, 14; *Jerusalem*, 77; 'The Mental Traveller', I, 62.
21 This vatic passage, originally used at the end of *Home at Grasmere* to announce the 'theme' of the new poetry Wordsworth felt that it was his special mission to sing, was reprinted as 'a kind of *Prospectus*' to his projected masterpiece, *The Recluse*, in his Preface to *The Excursion* (1814).
22 Edward Johnson, *Wonder-Working Providence*, ed. J. Franklin Jameson (New York, 1910), p. 25. Jonathan Edwards, *Thoughts on the Revival of Religion in New England*, *Works of Jonathan Edwards* (New York, 1881), III, 314.
23 As quoted by Henry Nash Smith, *Virgin Land* (New York, 1957), p. 40.
24 Melville, *White Jacket* (1850), ch. 36, cited in Ernest Lee Tuveson, *Redeemer Nation* (Chicago, 1968), pp. 156–7; *Clarel* (1876), in *The Works of Herman Melville* (New York, 1958), XV, 250.
25 For a detailed discussion of the pervasive apocalyptic design and imagery in Romantic thought and literature see M. H. Abrams, *Natural Supernaturalism*, especially Chapters III–VII; also 'English Romanticism: The Spirit of the Age', in *Romanticism Reconsidered*, ed. Northrop Frye (New York, 1963).
26 *The Correspondence of Robert Southey with Caroline Bowles*, ed. Edward Dowden (Dublin, 1881), p. 52.

27 Hegel, *Vorlesungen über die Philosophie der Weltgeschichte*, ed. Georg Lasson (Leipzig, 1919), II, 926.
28 Joseph Priestley, cited by Clarke Garrett, *Respectable Folly: Millenarians and the French Revolution in France and England* (Baltimore, 1975), pp. 142–3.
29 *Collected Letters of S. T. Coleridge*, ed. E. L. Griggs (Oxford, 1956 ff.), I, 527.
30 E.g., Shelley to Byron, *The Letters of P. B. Shelley*, ed. F. L. Jones (Oxford, 1964), I, 361; *Shelley's Prose*, ed. David Lee Clark (Albuquerque, 1954), pp. 239–40, 296–7.
31 T. N. Talfourd, 'An Attempt to Estimate the Poetical Talent of the Present Age', *The Pamphleteer*, V (1815), 432–3.
32 Mary Shelley, notes in *The Complete Poetical Works of Shelley*, ed. Thomas Hutchinson (London, 1948), pp. 156, 551; Thomas Medwin, *Life of Shelley*, ed. H. B. Forman (Oxford, 1913), p. 255.
33 *Kant's gesammelte Schriften* (Akademie Ausgabe, Berlin, 1902 ff.), VIII, 109–10, 27; see also VI, 34, 134–6.
34 On the role of the French Revolution in man's progress toward a secular millennium, see Kant's 'The Victory of the Good Principle over the Evil One and the Establishment of the Kingdom of God on Earth' (1792), and 'Whether the Human Race is continually advancing toward the Better' (1792).
35 Novalis, *Briefe und Werke* (Berlin, 1943), III, 702.
36 *The Logic of Hegel*, translated William Wallace (2nd edn, Oxford, 1892), p. 54.
37 Hegel, *Phenomenology of Spirit*, translated A. V. Miller (Oxford, 1977), p. 479. For Hegel's systematic translation of the Christian history and creed into his philosophical equivalents, see especially the section, 'The Revealed Religion', pp. 453–78.
38 Carlyle, *Sartor Resartus*, ed. C. F. Harrold (New York, 1937), p. 194.
39 *The Phenomenology of Spirit*, p. 492. In his Preface Hegel represents the imminence, and abruptness, of the coming of the apocalyptic new world, spiritually interpreted, in his own post-Revolutionary age: 'It is not difficult to see that ours is . . a period of transition to a new era. Spirit has broken with the world it has hitherto inhabited and imagined. . . . The Spirit . . . [is] dissolving bit by bit the structure of its previous world. . . . The gradual crumbling . . . is cut short by a sunburst which, in one flash, illuminates the features of the new world.' (Ibid., pp. 6–7).
40 Schiller, *On the Aesthetic Education of Man*, translated and ed. Elizabeth M. Wilkinson and L. A. Willoughby (Oxford, 1967), pp. 25, 205, 215–19.
41 *The Way towards the Blessed Life*, in *The Popular Works of J. G. Fichte*, translated William Smith (London, 1889), II, 306–9. In 1795 Fichte had said that the French Revolution inspired his first major work, the *Wissenschaftslehre*, and that this work is the equivalent in philosophy of the political revolution in history. To Baggesen, April, 1795, in Fichte's *Briefwechsel*, ed. Hans Schulz (Leipzig, 1925), I, 449–50.
42 Schelling, *System der gesammten Philosophie* (1804), *Sämtliche Werke*, Pt. I, Vol. VI, 562–4. For Schelling's description, in 1795, of his philosophy as a 'revolution of knowledge' which will re-establish the original conditions of intellectual life, see *Sämtliche Werke*, Pt. I, Vol. I, 156–9.
43 Novalis, *Schriften*, ed. Paul Kluckhohn and others (Stuttgart, 1960), I, 347, 110–11.
44 *Sartor Resartus*, pp. 186, 264, 222.
45 *Of Reformation*, in *Complete Prose Works of John Milton* (New Haven, 1953), I, 615–16. Bacon, it will be recalled, had also represented himself as intoning 'the bridal song' of the millennial state to be achieved by natural science; see above.

46 Schelling, *The Ages of the World*, ed. and translated by F. DeWolfe Bolman, Jr. (New York, 1942), pp. 90–1. On Schelling's uncompleted epic poem, see Fritz Strich, *Die Mythologie in der deutschen Literatur* (Halle, 1910), II, 31–9. As early as 1795 the young Schelling had proclaimed himself a prophetic herald of a messianic philosopher who will bring about the liberation and reintegration of the enslaved and divided human intellect – 'a deed reserved . . . perhaps only for one man – but may it nonetheless be granted to the individual, who has a presentiment of the coming day, to rejoice in it by anticipation'. *Von Ichals Princip der Philosophie, Sämtliche Werke* (Stuttgart, 1856–61), Pt. I, Vol. I, 156–9.
47 See John Holloway, *The Victorian Sage* (London, 1953).
48 Wordsworth, MS.D, 11, 686 ff., in *Home at Grasmere*, ed. Beth Darlington (Ithaca, 1977). In the passage excerpted from this poem that he later called his 'Prospectus', Wordsworth indicates that he is emulating Milton, whom he denominates 'the Bard,/ Holiest of Men'. In the great ode 'To William Wordsworth' that Coleridge wrote in 1807, after hearing the author read *The Prelude* aloud, he repeatedly hailed Wordsworth as a 'Bard', singer of that 'More than historic, that prophetic Lay'.
49 Hölderlin, 'Hymne an die Menschheit'.

JOSEPH WITTREICH

The Apocalypse:
a Bibliography

I COMMENTARY ON / INTERPRETATION OF THE BOOK OF REVELATION
  1 ORIGIN [FL. 217–35) TO DÜRER (1498)
  2 THE SIXTEENTH AND SEVENTEENTH CENTURIES
  3 1700 TO THE PRESENT

II ANCILLARY READING ON PROPHECY AND THE BOOK OF REVELATION
  1 LITERATURE ON PROPHECY, ESPECIALLY WITH REFERENCE TO THE BOOK OF REVELATION
  2 LITERATURE AS PROPHECY, ESPECIALLY LITERATURE AND THE BOOK OF REVELATION

Except for its representation of Renaissance commentary and interpretation (where it strives for completeness), this bibliography is selective, especially so in its reference to Medieval materials. Here particularly the principles for inclusion are not only that a work be representative of its period and influential therein but that it deal prominently with the aesthetic dimension of the Book of Revelation and that its influence be felt, demonstrably so, upon Renaissance thought and literature. Accordingly, the first commentary ever penned on Revelation—the lost treatise of Melito, Bishop of Sardis (165)—is not included here. Most of the commentaries that are, on the other hand, are cited in Section I, Part 1, only by title with a full bibliographical citation provided in Section II, Part I, by way of acknowledging the first Renaissance printing of a text. The Renaissance printings of Medieval texts are indicated by an asterisk (*). Because of the general inaccessibility of many of these volumes, modern editions when they exist have also been noted; and in the few instances where there are neither Renaissance nor modern printings of a text, citations are to the *Patrolgiae*. Together, the *Patrolgiae Cursus Completus . . . Series Latina*, ed. J.-P. Migne, 221 vols (Paris, 1844–64), see esp. vol. 219, col. 114, 122, and the *Patrologiae Cursus Completus . . . Series Graeca*, ed. J.-P. Migne, 162 vols (Paris, 1857–1912), contain most of this commentary; and the recent volume, *Apocalyptic Spirituality*, with a Preface by Marjorie Reeves and Introductions by

Bernard McGinn (London, 1980), makes some Medieval texts available in translation for the first time. Other useful guides to the vast body of Medieval commentary are provided by Eligius Dekkers and Aemilius Gaar, *Clavis Patrum Latinorum*, 2nd ed (Steenbrugis, 1961), esp. p. 550; P. C. Spicq, *Esquisse d'un histoire de l'exégèse . . . du moyen age* (Paris, 1944), esp. p. 400; and Friedrich Stegmüller, *Repertorium biblicum medii aevi* (Madrid, 1950–61).

In the past two centuries, at roughly fifty-year intervals, there have been three monumental efforts to organize and systematize the literature that has accrued to the Book of Revelation over the centuries: E. B. Elliott's *Horae Apocalypticae* (see [1237]), R. H. Charles' *Studies in the Apocalypse* (see [1272]), and LeRoy Edwin Froom's *The Prophetic Faith of Our Fathers* (see [1395]). These large-scale efforts should be supplemented with the period refinements provided by Bernard McGinn's *Visions of the End: Apocalyptic Traditions in the Middle Ages* (see [1472]), Marjorie Reeves' *The Influence of Prophecy in the Later Middle Ages* (see [1509]), Craig Harbison's *The Last Judgment in Sixteenth-Century Northern Europe* (see [1408]), Richard Bauckham's *Tudor Apocalypse* (see [1322]), Katharine Firth's *The Apocalyptic Tradition in Reformation Britain* (see [1394]), Paul Christianson's *Reformers and Babylon* (see [1354]), Christopher Hill's *Antichrist in Seventeenth-Century England* (see [1421]), and T. Wilson Hayes' *Winstanley the Digger* (see [1650]). Bauckham prints selected passages from numerous Renaissance commentators, and each of these volumes provides essential bibliography. But so too do Ferdinand Stosch, *Catalogus variorum in Apocalypsin Johannis commentariorum*, in *Symbolae Literarine* (Brenne, 1745), I, iv, 560–88; J. George Watchii, *Bibliotheca Theologica Selecta* (Geneva, 1765), IV, 769ff.; and especially the anonymous *Dictionary of Writers on Prophecy*, the only copy of which I have seen is in the Philadelphia Bible College Library. The recent bibliography by Richard M. Tresley, included as an appendix to his fine dissertation (see [1739]), is essential, as is the work of Otto Böcher, *Die Johannesapokalypse* (Darmstadt, 1975).

Entries on 'Apocalypse', 'Prophecy', etc. in the following sources are also useful: *Encyclopedia of Religion and Ethics*, ed. James Hastings, 13 vols (New York, 1913–27); *Interpreter's Dictionary of the Bible*, ed. George Arthur Buttrick *et al.*, 4 vols (Nashville, 1957–62); *New Catholic Encyclopedia*, ed. William J. MacDonald *et al.*, 16 vols (New York, 1967–74); *Journal for Theology and Church*, vol. 6 (New York, 1969). Any study of John's Apocalypse eventually must be supplemented by commentaries on other apocalyptic passages in Scripture, especially the Book of Daniel, 2 Thessalonians, and parts of the Gospels such as Matthew 24, Mark 13, and Luke 21. It might be supplemented too by a systematic listing of Bibles too numerous to mention here, or by the citation of almanacs, especially of the seventeenth century, and of secular political prophecies particularly popular in the Renaissance. This task of supplementation, for the most part, I have left to others. In Section I, Part 2, I have listed original titles and those for English translations and have supplied dates of later printings so as to indicate availability and popularity of individual titles. In the final stages of preparing this bibliography, welcome assistance came from Richard Tresley. When I have appropriated an item from the bibliography in Tresley's dissertation I have indicated so by 'Tresley', followed by a page number, at the conclusion of the entry. Items in the bibliography are numbered consecutively. Throughout the bibliography it should be assumed that the initial place of publication is London unless otherwise indicated.

The following bibliography has been compiled from the resources of the Berg Library at New York University, the Columbia University Libraries, the New York Public Library, the Library of the Union Theological Seminary, the Houghton, Andover, and

Widener Libraries of Harvard University, the Bieneke Library of Yale University, the Library Company of Philadelphia, the Philadelphia Free Library, the Library of the Philadelphia Bible College, the University of Pennsylvania Library, the Milton S. Eisenhower Library of Johns Hopkins University, the Folger Shakespeare Library, the Library of Congress, the University of Michigan Library, the University of Wisconsin Library, the Newberry Library in Chicago, the Henry E. Huntington Library, the William Andrews Clark Memorial Library, the Library of the University of California at Los Angeles, the Princeton University Library, the British Library, the Libraries of Cambridge University, the Bodleian Library of Oxford University, and the National Library of Scotland. This bibliography could not have approached completeness without the resources of these libraries, nor without the resourcefulness of the following: Morton Bloomfield, Stuart Curran, Horton Davies, Carol Herron, Carolyn Hill, Christopher Hill, Karl Josef Höltgen, Carol Kaaske, Sheila Spector, Leslie Tannenbaum, Richard Tresley, Raymond Waddington, and Hyatt Waggoner. All the contributors to this volume have come forth with valuable assistance, especially my co-editor, C. A. Patrides, as well as Bernard Capp, Mary Carpenter, Paul Korshin, Bernard McGinn, and Michael Murrin.

1 COMMENTARY ON / INTERPRETATION OF THE BOOK OF REVELATION

1 ORIGEN (FL. 217–35) TO DÜRER (1498)

[1] Origen (fl. 217–35). *Der Scholien-Kommentar des Origenes zur Apocalypse Johannis* (Leipzig, 1911).
[2] Victorinus (fl. 284–305). *Scholia in Apocalypsin*. See [384].
[3] Jerome (340–420). *In Apocalypsim*. See [106], [195].
[4] Augustine (345–430). *The City of God*, tr. Gerald G. Walsh and Daniel J. Honson, 3 vols (New York, 1954). See [79].
[5] Tyconius (4th c.). *The Turin Fragments of Tyconius's Commentary on Revelation*, ed. Francesco LoBue (Cambridge, 1963).
[6] Oecumenius. *The Complete Commentary on the Apocalypse* (c. 500), ed. H. C. Hoskier (Ann Arbor, 1928). See [138].
[7] Prismasius, Bishop (d. 560). *Commentarium libri quinque in Apocalypsim Ioannis Evangelistae*. See [114].
[8] Andreas of Caesarea. *Apocalypsin commentarius* (c. 632). See [271].
[9] Bede, Venerable (c. 673–735). *Bedae Commentarius in Apocalypsin*, Modern Language Association Photo Facsimiles, no. 222 (New York, 1932). See [100].
[10] Ambrosius Ansbertus [Autpertus]. *In Apocalypsin* (778 or 781), in *Opera*, ed. R. Weber (Turnholt, 1975). See [115].
[11] Beatus of Liebana (730–98). *Beati Apocalypsin libri duodecim*, ed. Henry A. Sanders (Rome, 1930).
[12] Alcuin (735–804). *Commentariorum in Apocalypsin*, in *Patrologiae Latina*, vol. 100, col. 1085–156.
[13] Haymo, Bishop of Halberstadt (fl. 840–70). *In Apocalypsim*. See [97].
[14] Arethas, Archbishop (c. 914). *In Apocalypsim*. See [107], [138].

[15] Adso. *Libellus de Antichristo* (954). See [158].
[16] Berengaudus (c. 11th or 12th c.). *Expositio super septem visiones libri Apocalypsis.* See [149].
[17] Bruno of Segni (1049–123). *Expositio in Apocalypsim.* See [742].
[18] Theophylactus, Archbishop (fl. 1078). *In qvatvor prophetas enarrationes.*
[19] Otto of Freising (1114?–58). *Chronica sive Historia de Duabus Civitatibus. The Two Cities,* tr. Charles Mierow (New York, 1928). See [71].
[20] Rupert of Deutz. *Commentariorum in Apocalypsim* (1117–126). See [91], [213].
[21] Rupertus Tuitiensis. *In Apocalypsim libri 12* (c. 1120–9).
[22] Joachim of Fiore (1132–202). *Apocalypsis nova* (exists in manuscript version only).
[23] ——, *De Ultimis Tribulationibus,* ed. E. R. Daniel, in *Prophecy and Millenarianism,* ed. Ann Williams (1980), pp. 167–89.
[24] ——, *Enchiridion in Apocalypsim,* in *Joachim von Floris und die joachitische Literatur* (Frieburg, 1938), pp. 287–305.
[25] ——, *Enchiridion super Apocalypsim* (exists in manuscript version only).
[26] ——, *Expositio in Apocalypsim.* See [93].
[27] Alufus de Tornaco (d. 1141). *Expositiones in Apocalypsim.* See [73].
[28] Anselm of Havelberg (d. 1158). *Dialoges,* ed. G. Salet (Paris, 1966).
[29] Richard of St. Victor (d. 1173). *In Apocalypsim.* See [238].
[30] Alexander de Villa Dei (1170–250). *Summarium Biblicum.* See [67].
[31] Hugo de S. Caro (1190–263). *In Apocalypsim.* See [457].
[32] Alexander of Bremen. *Expositio in Apocalypsim* (1235), ed. A. Wachtel (Weimar, 1955).
[33] Thomas Aquinas (1225?–74). *In Apocalypsim.* See [157].
[34] Ubertinus de Casali (1259–329). *Arbor vitae crucifixae Jesu.* See [78], [214].
[35] Albertus Magnus (d. 1280). *In Apocalypsin.* N.B. This commentary is no longer extant; see Tresley, p. 124.
[36] Gorrannus, Nicolaus (d. 1298). *Commentarius in Apocalypsin.* See [452].
[37] Parisiensis, Joannes. *Tractatus de Antichristo* (c. 1300). See [75].
[38] Berchorius Pictaviensis, Petrus (c. 1290–362). *Reductorium Morale super totam Bibliam . . . Genesis-Apocalypsis.* See [70].
[39] Aureoli, Petrus. *Commendium sensus litteralis totius sacra Scripturae* (1319). See [64].
[40] Nicholaus de Lyra. *Postilla in Apocalypsim* (c. 1329). See [59], [522].
[41] ——, *In Apocalypsim* (c. 1339). See [429].
[42] Johannes de Ruprescissa. *Visiones seu Revelationes* (1349). See [1011].
[43] ——, *Vademecum in tribulatione* (1356).
[44] Telesphorus of Cosenza (c. 1356–86). *Item explanatio Figurata and pulchra in Apochalypsim.* See [77].
[45] Huss, John (1369–415). *De Anatomia Antichristi.* See [87].
[46] Wimbledon, Ralph. *A Sermon . . . Preached at Pauls Cross* (1388). See [160].
[47] Purvey, John. *Commentarius in Apocalypsin* (1390). See [96].
[48] Bernardinus de Siena. *Commentaria in Apocalypsim* (c. 1420). See [57].
[49] Dionysius de Leuwis (1402–72). *Eiusdem in Apocalypsim Joannis.* See [102].
[50] Didacus de Deza (1444–523). *Commentarium in Apocalypsim.* See [245].
[51] Veneto, Federico. *Apocalipsis Iesu Christi, hoc est reuelatione fatta a Sancto Giohanni Euangelista* (1470). See [72].
[52] Annius, Joannes (Nannio de Viterbo, Giovanni). *Glossa super Apocalypsim* (1481). See [63].

[53] Savonarola, Girolamo. *Compendio di revelatione* (Florence, 1495).
[54] ———, *Lezioni sull' Apocalisse* (exists in manuscript only).
[55] ———, *Trattato della revelatione* (1495). See [116], [118].
[56] Dürer, Albrecht. *Apocalypsis cū Figuris* (1498). See [68].

2 THE SIXTEENTH AND SEVENTEENTH CENTURIES

1501
[*57] Bernardinus de Siena. *Commentaria in Apocalypsim*, in *Opera omnia* (Lyon). Other editions: 1591, 1636. Tresley, p. 153.

1502
[58] Greff, Hieronymous. *Die heimliche offenbarung Johannis* (Strassburg).
[*59] Nicolaus de Lyra. *Postilla in Apocalypsim*, in *Postilla litteralis in Vetus et Novum Testamentum* (Basel, 1498–1502). Other editions: 1507–8, 1519, 1520, 1524, 1528, 1545, 1588, 1590, 1600, 1603, 1617, 1634, 1660. Tresley, p. 210.

1505
[60] Valla, Lorenzo. *Adnotationes in Novum Testamentum* (Paris). Tresley, p. 234.

1506
[*61] Albertus Magnus, Bishop of Ratisbon. *Postillatio in Apocalypsim* (n. p.). But see [35].
[62] Anon. *Sermones super Apocalipsim* (Lyon). Another edition: 1512.

1507
[*63] Annius, Joannes (Nannio de Viterbo, Giovanni). *Glosa siue Expositio super Apocalypsim* (Cologne). Another edition: 1536.
[*64] Aureoli, Petrus. *Compendium sensus litteralis totius sacra Scripturae* (Venice). Other editions: 1508, 1514, 1565, 1571, 1581, 1585, 1596, 1610, 1613, 1647, 1896. Tresley, p. 149.

1508
[65] Petit, John. *Apocalypsis idest reuelatio Iesu Christi: quam tota trinitas reulauit christo secundum humanitartem* (Paris). Another edition: 1515.

1510
[66] Anon. *Hier behint dat were der apostelen met veel schoone prophetien ende Apocalipsis* (Amsterdam).

1511
[*67] Alexander de Villa Dei. *Summarium Biblicum*. Other editions: 1519, 1526, 1545, 1660. Tresley, p. 126.
[*68] Dürer, Albrecht. *Apocalypsis cū Figuris*. Numerous subsequent editions.

1512
[69] Pseudo-Melito of Sardis. *In Apocalypsim sacratissimarum . . . revelationum melliflua explanatio* (Paris). N. B. This commentary was initially confused with the lost commentary of Melito. Tresley, p. 205.

1515

[*70] Berchorius Pictaviensis, Petrus. *Reductorium Morale super totam Bibliam . . . Genesis-Apocalypsis* (Basel). Other editions: 1583, 1609. Tresley, p. 152.

[*71] Otto of Friesing. *Chronica sive Historia de Duabus Civitatibus* (Strassburg). Other editions: 1569, 1669, 1670, 1868, 1928.

[*72] Veneto, Federico. *Apocalypsis Iesu Christi, hoc est reulatione fatta a Sancto Giohanni Euangelista* (Venice, 1515–16). Another edition: 1519.

1516

[*73] Alufus de Toranco. *Expositiones in Apocalypsim* (Strassburg).

[74] Andrea, Zovan. *Apochalypsis Ihesu Christi cum quindecim figuris* (Venice).

[*75] Parisiensis, Joannes. *Tractatus de Antichristo* (Venice).

[76] Phillippus de Mantua. *Lectura perlucida in Apocalypsim* (Padua). Another edition: 1527. Tresley, p. 217.

[*77] Telesphorus of Cosenza. *Item explanatio figurata et pulchra in Apochalypsim*, ed. Silvestro Meuccio (Venice). Another edition: 1565.

[*78] Ubertinus de Casali. *De septem statibus ecclesiae iuxta septem visiones Apocalypseos* (Venice). Another edition: 1525. Tresley, p. 234.

1520

[*79] Augustine. *De Civitate dei*. English translation: *Of the Citie of God*, tr. John Healy (1610). Numerous other editions.

[80] Gilbertus. *Commentarius in Apocalypsim* (Milan). Tresley, p. 179.

[81] Anon. *Catena moralis in Genesim-Apocalypsim* (Paris). Other editions: 1550, 1574.

[82] Anon. *Here Begynneth the byrth and lyfe of the most false and deceytfull Antechryst*.

1522

[83] Luther, Martin. *Das Newe Testament Deutzsch* (Wittenberg). N. B. This volume contains Luther's first preface to the Book of Revelation. See [96].

1523

[84] Columna, Pietro. *In Apocalypsim . . . Commentaria* (Vatican MS. Lat. 5567).

[85] Anon. *Das gantz neuw Testament . . . auch die Offenbarung Joannis mit hüpschen Figuren* (Basel). Another edition: 1524. N. B. The illustrations are by Hans Holbein. Tresley, p. 142.

1524

[86] Purstinger, Bertold (?). *Onus Ecclesiae temporibus hisce deplorandis Apocalypseos* (Ausburg). Other editions: 1531, 1532.

1525

[*87] Huss, John. *De Anatomia Antichristi . . . Commentarii in loca aliquot Apocalypsin*, in *Opera*, ed. Otto Brunfels, 3 vols (Strassburg, 1525?).

[88] Theodorius Andreas. *Expositio in Apocalypsim* (c. 1525). Tresley, p. 231.

[89] Tyndale, William. *The Boke off the Revelacion off Sainct Ihon the Devine Done into Englysshe*.

[90] Anon. *Les choses contenu en ceste partie du nouveau testament*, tr. Le Fèbvre (Basel). Tresley, p. 142.

1526
[*91] Rupert of Deutz. *Commentariorum, in Apocalypsim Johannis libri XII* (Cologne).

1527
[92] Emser, Hieronymous. *Das new testament* (Dresden). Another edition: 1528.

[*93] Joachim of Fiore. *Expositio magni prophete Abbatis Joachim in Apocalypsim*, ed. Silvestro Meuccio (Venice). N. B. A much abbreviated version of this commentary is appended to Joachim's *Concordia Novi et Veteris Testamenti*, ed. Silvestro Meuccio (Venice, 1519).

1528
[94] Jacobus de Lausanne. *Opus Moralitatum* [Genesis . . . Revelation] (Limoges). Tresley, p. 192.

[95] Lambert, Francois. *Exegeseos in sanctam Divi Joannis Apocalypsim Libri VII* (Marburg). Another edition: 1539.

[*96] Purvey, John. *Commentarivs in Apocalypsin ante centum annos aeditus* (Wittenberg). N. B. This commentary, sometimes misattributed to John Huss, is introduced by Luther's preface of 1522; he wrote another in 1530, which represents a significant revision of his earlier, more hostile views. Both these prefaces are conveniently reprinted in *Works of Martin Luther* (Philadelphia, 1922), vol. 6.

1529
[*97] Haymo, Bishop of Halberstadt. *Commentariorum in Apocalypsim beati Iohan. libri VII* (Cologne). Other editions: 1531, 1534, 1540, 1629.

[98] Luther, Martin. *The Revelation of Antichrist*, tr. John Firth (Antwerp).

1530
[99] Angelo, Paolo. *Profetie certissime, stupende et admirabili dell' Antichristo et innumerabili al mondo* (Venice).

[*100] Bede, Venerable. *Eximie uenerandi patris Bedae presbyteri* (Vienna).

[101] Hoffmann, Melchoir. *Auslegung der heimlichen offenbarung Ioannis* (Strassburg).

[*102] Dionysus de Leuwis. *Eiusdem in Apocalypsim Joannis* (Cologne). Other editions: 1537, 1541, 1542.

[103] Luther, Martin. *Das Newe Testament Deutzsch* (Wittenberg). N. B. This volume contains Luther's second preface for the Book of Revelation. See [96].

[104] Titelman, Franciscus. *Libri duo de authoritate Libri Apocalypsis Beati Joannis Apostoli* (Antwerp).

1531
[105] Cajetan, Thomas. *Epistolae Pauli et aliorum apostolorum ad. Graec. veritatem castigatae* (Venice). Other editions: 1532, 1534, 1540, 1546, 1556, 1558, 1571, 1611. Tresley, p. 160.

[*106] St Jerome. *Was geheimnaus die vier Thiern Apocaly. am IIII beschriehen* (n.p.).

1532
[*107] Arethas, Caesareae Cappadociae. *Explicatio Apocalypseos* (Verona). Other editions: 1545, 1547, 1618, 1630, 1631, 1677. N. B. The 1547 edition carries a new preface by Jean Henten.

[108] Carion, Johann. *Chronica durch Magistru Johan Carion* (Wittenberg). N. B. Carion's *Chronicles* is translated into English by Walter Lynne in 1550 and, in 1560, is edited and enlarged by Philipp Melanchthon.

[109] Luther, Martin. *A Very Comfortable, and Necessary Sermon . . . Concerning the Coming of Our Savior Christ to Judgment* (n. p.). Other editions: 1570, 1578.

[110] Stifel, Michael. *Ein Rechen Büchlin vom End Christ. Apocalypsis in Apocalypsim* (n. p.). Another edition: 1553.

1534

[111] Meyer, Sebastian. *In Apocalypsim Iohannis . . . Commentarius* (Zurich). Other editions: 1539, 1554, 1584, 1603.

1535

[112] Barnes, Robert. *Vitae Romanorum Pontificum* (Basel).

[113] Notalius, Gregorius. *In Apocalypsim* (c. 1535). Tresley, p. 211.

[*114] Prismasius, Bishop. *Commentarium libri quinque in Apocalypsim Ioannis Evangelistae*, ed. Robert Winter (Cologne). Other editions: 1544, 1545, 1550, 1618, 1654, 1677.

1536

[*115] Ambrosius Ansbertus [Autpertus]. *Apocalypsim libri decem* (Cologne). Other editions: 1618, 1677.

[*116] Savonarola, Girolamo. *Trattato delle revelatione* (Venice). Another edition: 1674.

[117] Anon. *The Popish Kingdom or Reign of Antichrist.*

1537

[*118] Savonarola, Girolamo. *Lamentatio sponsae christae adversus tepidos* (Venice).

1539

[119] Beham, Hans Sebald. *Typi in Apocalypsi Ioannis depicti vt clarivs vaticinia Ioannis intelligi possint* (Frankfurt). Other editions: 1540, 1584.

[120] Bèze, Théodore de. *Descriptio Supremi Judicii* (n. p.).

[121] Bullinger, Heinrich. *De omnibus sanctae scripturae libris Expositio* (Zurich).

[122] Franck, Sebastian. *Verpitschietes mit sieben siegeln verschlossenes buch.* Tresley, p. 175.

[123] Anon. *Familiere et briefve exposition sur l'Apocalypse de Sainct Jehan l'Apostre* (Geneva). Tresley, p. 173.

1540

[124] Aemilius, Georgius. *Imaginum in Apocalypsi Ioannis descriptio* (Frankfurt). N. B. The figures are by Hans Sebald Beham.

[125] Clarius, Isidorus. *Scholia in Novum Testamentum* (Venice). Other editions: 1544, 1557, 1564.

1541

[126] Choquet, Louis. *Lapocalypse sainct Jehan Zebedee* (Paris). Tresley, p. 162.

[127] Gregorio, Francesco (Coelius Ponnonius). *Collectonea in sacram Apocalypsim* (Venice). Other editions: 1547, 1571.

[128] Pagninus, Sanctes. *Sermones quamplurimi in . . . Apocalypsim* (c. 1541). Tresley, p. 213.

1543

[129] Bale, John. *Yet a course at the Romysh foxe compyled by J. Harryson* (Zurich).
[130] Gagny, Jean de. *Itidem in septem canonicas epistolas, & D. Ioannis Apocalypsin* (Paris). Other editions: 1547, 1550, 1624, 1629, 1630, 1633.
[131] Melanchthon, Philipp. *In Danielem prophetam Commentarius* (Wittenberg).
[132] Pinet, Antoine du. *Exposition sur l'Apocalypse* (Geneva). Tresley, p. 218.

1544

[133] Bale, John. *A Brefe Chronycle concernynge the Examynacion and death of the blessed martyr of Christ, Syr Johan Oldecastell* (Antwerp). Other editions: 1545, 1548.
[134] Osiander, Andreas. *Conjecturae de ultimis temporibus, ac de Fine Mundo*. English translation: *The Conjectures of the ende of the worlde*, tr. George Joye (1548). N. B. This revised and expanded edition contains a number of Joye's own observations.
[135] Vannius, Theodoricus. *Commentarius in Apocalypsim* (c. 1544). Tresley, p. 234.

1545

[136] Bibliander, Theodorus. *Ad Omnium Ordinum Reipublicae Christianae Principes Viros, Papulumque Christionum Relatio Fidelis* (Basel). Other editions: 1549, 1569. N. B. This commentary derives from Bibliander's Zurich lectures of 1544.
[137] Cochlaeus, Johannes. *In quattour Andraeae Osiander Conjecturas de fine Mundi velitatio* (Ingolstadt).
[*138] Henten, Jean. *Enarrationes vetustissimorum theologorum . . . in Apocalypsim* (Antwerp). Another edition: 1547, N. B. Commentaries by Arethas and Oecumenius are reprinted here.
[139] Hoffmann, Christopher. *De Christiana religione, et de regno Antichristi* (Frankfurt).
[140] Joye, George. *The exposicion of Daniel the Prophete* (Geneva).

1546

[141] Antonio, Nicolás. *Yu Tria Priora Capita Apocalypsis* (Hispali).
[142] Anon. *Wycklyffes Wycket*.

1547

[143] Henten, Jean. *Sacra Biblia, ad vetvstissima exemplaria castigata* (Frankfurt). Other editions: 1571, 1572.
[144] Hoffmeister, Johann. *Enarrationes . . . in Apocalypsim* (c. 1547). Tresley, p. 189.
[145] LaRue, François. *De gemmis aliquot, iis praesertim quarum divis Joannes apostolus in sua Apocalypsi neminit* (Paris). Other editions: 1565, 1588, 1595, 1596. Tresley, p. 199.
[146] Maugin, Jean. *Les figures de l'Apocalipse de Saint Ian* (Paris).
[147] Selneccer, Nicolaus. *Erklärung der offenbarung Ioannis und des propheten Daniels* (Geneva). Other editions: 1567, 1568, 1608.

1548

[148] Bale, John. *The Image of Both Churches* (Antwerp?). Other editions: 1550, 1555, 1570, 1849, 1973. According to Richard Bauckham, Bale probably began his commentary in 1540 and completed most of it by 1542, but 'the process of publication is somewhat unclear. The three parts were evidently published successively, Part 1 first before 1545. Parts 1 and 2 were published together, probably at Antwerp, in 1545, and Part 3 also appeared before Henry VIII's death,

for all three parts appeared on lists of proscribed books in his reign and were burned at Paul's Cross by bishop Bonner' (see [1322], p. 22). Matthew's Bible of 1551, which provides copious annotation for Revelation, draws that annotation wholly from Bale. Here for the first time an English Bible, hitherto reticent to interpret Revelation, offers substantial guidance for its understanding.

[*149] Berengaudus. *Expositio super septem visiones libri Apocalypsis*, ed. Cuthbert Tunstall.

[150] Judah, Leo. *A Paraphrase or Commentarie upon the Revelacion of S. Iohn*, tr. Edmund Allen (1548–49).

[151] Anon. *Eine Weissagung und ein schöner herrlicher Trost . . . aus dem 14 cap. der Offenbahrung Johannis* (n. p.).

1549

[152] Artopoeus, Petrus (Peter Becker). *Pro consolatione afflictae nostrae Ecclesiae, Apocalypseos i sagoge, et Propheticae imaginis nostri temporis explicatio* (Frankfurt). Tresley, p. 151.

[153] Claude de Montmarte. *In Apocalypsim enarrationes* (Paris). Another edition: 1550. Tresley, p. 163.

[154] Crowley, Robert. *The Voyce of the Laste Trumpet Blowen bi the Seventh Angel*.

[155] Erasmus, Desiderius. *The Paraphrase of the New Testament . . . The Second tome . . . a paraphrase upon the Revelation.* These notes are the source for those appearing in Richard Jugge's 1552 revised edition of Tyndale's New Testament. Moreover, they are not the work of Erasmus but of Leo Judah and are Englished by Edmund Allen. Erasmus's *Novum Testamentum, cum adnotationibus* was first published in Basel (1516).

[156] Ochino, Bernardino. *A Tragoedie or Dialoge of the unjuste usurped Primacie of the Bishop of Rome.*

[157] Pseudo-Aquinas. *In beati Joannis Apocalypsim expositio* (Florence). Other editions: 1570, 1642.

1550

[*158] Adso. 'A Papistes Account of Antichrist', tr. anon. BM MS. Harleian 422. fols 102ff.

[159] Tyroboschi, Lucrezio. *Commentarius in Apocalypsim* (c. 1550). Tresley, p. 223.

[*160] Wimbledon, Ralph. *A Sermon . . . Preached at Pauls Cross*. Other editions: 1573, 1575, 1578, 1579, 1582, 1584, 1588, 1593, 1617. For a manuscript version different from the published versions, see Bodleian MS. Hatton 57.

1551

[161] Brosamer, Hans. *Apocalypsis S. Ioannis* (Frankfurt).

[162] Foxe, John. *Christus triumphans, comoedia Apocalyptica*. Other editions: 1556, 1579, 1607. English translation: *Christ Jesus Triumphant*, ed. R. Daye (1579). N. B. This work is a dramatization of the Book of Revelation.

[163] Leonardi, Giovanni. *Commentarius in Apocalypsin* (Basel). Tresley, p. 200.

1552

[164] Esquillus, Publius. *Wonderful News of the Death of Paule III*, tr. William Baldwin. Tresley, p. 172.

1553

[165] Bibliander, Theodorus. *De fatis monarchiae romanae* (Basel).
[166] ——, *Sonanium vaticinium Esdrae* (Basel).
[167] Oecolampadius, Johannes. *Commentarium in Danielem* (Geneva).
[168] Politi, Ambrosius Catharinus. *In Apocalypsim secundum literalem sensum* (c. 1553). Tresley, p. 218.
[169] Servetus, Michael. *Christianismi Restitutio* (Vienne-en-Dauphiné).
[170] Zegerus, Tacitus-Nicolaus Oesa. *Scholion in omnes Novi Testamenti libros* (Cologne).

1554

[171] Curione, Coelio Secondo. *De amplitudine beati regni Dei, dialogi sive libri duo* (Basel).
[172] Foxe, John. *Comentarii rerum in ecclesia gestarum* (Strassburg). Other editions: 1559, 1570, 1576, 1583, and many others. English edition: *Actes and Monuments of these latter and perilous days*. See esp. the edition of 1583 revised by Josiah Pratt, which, with its some 2314 pages, 'was ordered to be made available in churches and other public places. By the end of the century', says T. Wilson Hayes, 'approximately 10 000 copies were in circulation—more than any other book except the Bible' (see [1750], p. 43).
[173] Anon. *A Short Description of Antichrist*.

1555

[174] Jacobus de Paradiso. *De Septem Statibus Ecclesie in Apocalipsi mystice de scriptis, in Antilogia Papae* (Basel). Another edition: 1690.
[175] Nauseas, F. *De Consummatione mundi* (Cologne).
[176] Sascerides, Johannes. *Ausslegunge ser Sieben zeiten in der Heiligen kirche auss der offenbarung Johannis* (n. p.). Other editions: 1684, 1699.

1556

[177] Artopaeus, Petrus (Peter Becker). *Vaticinium sacrum de Ecclesia . . . ex Apocalypsi capite XI* (Basel).
[178] Bèze, Théodore de. *Novum D. N. Jesu Christi testamentum* (Geneva).
[179] Camerarius, Joachim. *Notatio figurarum orationis et mutatae simplicis elocutionis in Apostolicis Scriptis* (Leipzig). Another edition: 1572.
[180] Chateillon, Sebastien. *Biblia . . . vna cvm eivsdem annotationibus* (Basel). Other editions: 1573, 1697, 1726, 1735.
[181] Gualter, Rudolph. *Antichrist, That Is to Say . . . Antichrist Is Come*, tr. John Old (Zurich).
[182] ——, *Sententiae in Apocalypsim* (n. p., c. 1556?).

1557

[183] Bale, John. *Scriptorum Illustrium Majoris Brytannie . . . Catalogus*, 2 vols (Basel, 1557–9).
[184] Bucer, Martin. *De Regno Christi*.
[185] Bullinger, Heinrich. *Deux sermons de la Fin dv Siecle* (Geneva). English translation: *Of the End of the World*, tr. T. Potter (1580).
[186] ——, *In Apocalypsim . . . Conciones centum* (Basel). Other editions: 1558, 1559, 1560, 1561, 1564, 1565, 1570, 1573, 1587, 1589, 1590, 1597, 1599, 1609, 1677. English translation: *A Hundred Sermons upon the Apocalips*, ed. and tr. John Day

(1561). The annotations for the Book of Revelation in the 1560 Geneva Bible rely heavily upon Bullinger.

[187] Fulke, William. *Praelectiones in Apocalypsin*. English translation: *Praelections upon the Sacred and Holy Revelation of S. John*, tr. George Gifford (1573). For a copy of the 1573 edition with manuscript notes, see Bodleian 10199. e. 3.

[188] Pseudo-Hippolytus. *Oratio de Consummatione mundi ac de Antichristo*, tr. Johannes Picus (Paris).

[189] Machabaeus, Johannes. *Commentarius in Apocalypsim* (c. 1557). Tresley, p. 202.

[190] Old, John(?). *A Short Description of Antichrist* (n. p., 1557?).

[191] Traheron, Bartholomew. *An Exposition of the 4. chap. of S. Joans Revelation* (Wesel, 1557–8). Other editions: 1573, 1577, 1583.

1558

[192] Bibliander, Theodorus. *Temporum a condito mondo usque ad ultimam ipsius aetataem supputatio partitioque exactior* (Basel). Tresley, p. 156.

[193] Funck, Johann. *Apocalypse. Der Offenbarung Künsstiger geschect Johannis . . . Auslegung* (Wittenberg). Other editions: 1586, 1596. English translation: *A Complete Exposition of the Revelation of St John*, ed. Michael Sachsen (1596). N. B. The first edition has a preface by Melanchthon.

[194] Knox, John. *The First Blast of the Trumpet against the Monstrous Regiment of Women* (Geneva).

[195] Pseudo-Jerome. *Victorini Pettaviensis Apocalypsis*, ed. B. Millanius (Bologne). Tresley, p. 193.

[196] Anon. *A Treatise on the Principles of Christ's Doctrine, and the Antichrist's Doctrine*.

1559

[197] Borrhaus, Martin. *Commentarius in Apocalypsin* (Basel). Other editions: 1561, 1600.

[198] Brice, Thomas. *A Compendious Register in Metre* [Rev. 6 and 7].

1560

[199] Corrado, Alphonso. *In Apocalypsim D. Joan* (Basel). Other editions: 1570, 1574.

[200] Cyprianus de la Huerga. *Commentarius in D. Joannis Apocalypsim* (c. 1560). Tresley, p. 166.

[201] 'The Revelation of John the Divine', in *The Geneva Bible* (Geneva). N. B. The argument, headnotes, and marginal glosses rely heavily upon Bullinger.

1561

[202] Calvin, John. *Praelectiones in librum prophetiarum Danielis* (Geneva). Other editions: 1563, 1570, 1591. English translation: *Commentaries on the Prophet Daniel*, tr. Arthur Golding (London, 1570). Bale believed that Calvin had written a commentary on the Book of Revelation. Allegedly, Calvin observed that 'he was not able to understand anything in so obscure a Writer, whose Name and History were not yet settled among the learned'—an observation that Richard Bauckham finds 'almost certainly apocryphal and not representative of his [Calvin's] real attitude to the Apocalypse' (see [1322], p. 51). Whether or not he wrote such a commentary, Calvin did quote from the Apocalypse in his other writings. See both H. Quistorp, *Calvin's Doctrine of Last Things* (1955), esp. pp. 11–13, and T. H. L. Parker, *Calvin's New Testament Commentaries* (Grand Rapids, Mich., 1971), esp. pp. 75–8.

[203] Duvet, Jean. *L'apocalypse figuree* (Lyon).
[204] Marlorat, Augustin. *Novi Testamenti catholica expositio ecclesiastica*, 2 vols (Geneva). Other editions: 1564, 1574. English translation: *A Catholike exposition vpon the Reuelation of Sainct John*, tr. Arthur Golding (1574).

1562
[205] Doni, Antonio Frencesco. *Dichiaratione del Doni, sopa il XIII. cap. dell'Apocalisse* (Venice).

1563
[206] Artopoeus, Petrus (Peter Becker). *Apocalypsis Sancti Johannis* (Basel).
[207] Chytraeus, David. *Explicatio Apocalypsis Ioannis perspicua et breuis* (Wittenberg). Other editions: 1564, 1568, 1571, 1572, 1575, 1581, 1584.
[208] Scaliger, Paul. *Aeroama in caput primum Apocalypseos* (Royaumont). Tresley, p. 226.
[209] Serrano, Pedro. *Commentaria in Apocalypsim* (Alcalà de Henares). Tresley, p. 227.

1564
[210] Becon, Thomas. *The Summary of the New Testament*, in *Works*.
[211] Benoist, Jean. *Biblia sacra vetus et Novum Testamentum* (Paris). Tresley, p. 152.
[212] Dee, John, *Mona Hieroglyphica* (Antwerp). Tresley, p. 166.
[*213] Rupert of Deutz. *Commentariorum in Evangolium Ioannis, libri XIIII* (Louvain).
[*214] Ubertinus de Casali. *Arbor vitae crucifixae Jesu* (Venice). Tresley, p. 234.

1565
[215] Crespin, Jean. *Actes des Martyrs* (Geneva).
[216] Rej, Mikolaj. *Apocalypsis* (Krakow).
[217] Striegel, Victorinus. *Hypomnemata in omnes Libros Novi Testamenti* (Leipzig).

1566
[218] Agnello, Giovanni Battista. *Epositione . . . sopra un libro intitolato Apocalypsis spiritus secreti*.
[219] Bodin, Jean. *Methodus, ad facilem historiarum cognitionem* (Paris).
[220] Harpsfield, Nicolas. *Dialogi Sex* (Antwerp).
[221] Whitgift, John. 'Lectures on the Apocalypse'. Cambridge University Library MS. Ff. 2.36.
[222] ———, 'Theses or Determinations'. Cambridge University Library MS. Ff. 1.19.

1568
[223] Berus, Oswaldus. *Commentaria in Apocalypsim* (c. 1568). Tresley, p. 154.
[224] Noot, Jan Baptista van der. *Het theatre oft Toon-neel*. English translation: *Theatre for Worldlings*, tr. T. Roest [and Edmund Spenser] (1569).
[225] Anon. *Az Szent Ianosnac tött ielenesnec igaz es iras szerint valo magyarazasa predikatioc szerint* (Varadon). Another edition: 1579.

1569
[226] Bateman, Stephen. *A Christall Glasse of Christian Reformation*.
[227] Serafino da Fermo. *Sopra l'Apocalisse* (Piacenza). Other editions: 1570, 1581.

1570

[228] Flacius Illyricus, Matthias. *Novum Testamentum Jesu Christi felii Dei* (Basel). Another edition: 1659.

[229] Fulke, William. *A Sermon . . . Wherein is playnly proved Babilon to be Rome* [on Rev. 17]. Other editions: 1571, 1572, 1574, 1579, 1580.

[230] Kirchenmeyer, Thomas, *The Popish Kingdome, or reigne of Antichrist*, tr. B. Googe. Tresley, p. 197.

[231] Scaliger, Paul. *Primi tomi Miscellaneorum, de rerum causis et successibus atque secretori methodo ibidem expressa, effigies ac exemplar, nimirum vaticinorum et imaginum Joachimi* (Cologne). Tresley, p. 226.

1571

[232] Fulke, William. *A Sermon on Rev. XIV.*

1572

[233] Caponsacchi, Pietro. *In Iohannis Apostoli Apocalypsim observatio* (Florence). Another edition: 1586.

[234] Faso, Antonio. *Commentaria in Danielem & Apocalypsim* (c. 1572). Tresley, p. 173.

[235] Field, John. *An Admonition to the Parliament.*

[236] Anon. *An Admonition to the Parliament.* N. B. A separate, different tract from the one listed above.

1573

[237] Nigrinus, Georgius (George Schwartz). *Apocalypsis, Die Offenbraunge Sanct Johannis* (Orsel). Other editions: 1586, 1593.

[*238] Richard of St. Victor. *In S. Joannis apocalypsim libri septem* (Louvain).

1574

[239] Buckley Francis. *Note on Marlorat's Exposition of the Revelation.*

[240] Studley, John. *The Pageant of Popes . . . according to the Prophecye of John in the Apocalips.*

1575

[241] LeRoy, Louis. *De la Vicissitude, ou Variete des Choses en l'Univers* (Paris). Other editions: 1576, 1579, 1583, 1584, 1585, 1592, 1594. English translation: *Of the Interchangeable Course, or Variety of Things in the World*, tr. Robert Ashley (1594). Tresley, p. 200.

[242] Montano, Benito Arias. *Eiusdem in S. Ioannis apostoli et evangelistae apocalypsin significationes* (Antwerp). Another edition: 1588.

1576

[243] Curteys, Richard. *Two Semons . . . Apoc. XII. 1–9.*

[244] Daneau, Lambert. *Tractatus de Antichristo* (Geneva). Other editions: 1577, 1582, 1589, 1590. English translation: *A Treatise Touching Antichrist*, tr. John Swan (1589).

[*245] Didacus de Deza. *Commentarium in Apocalypsim*, in *Opera* (Madrid).

[246] Petrus de Uzeda Oesa. *Sylva lectionum super Apocalypsim* (c. 1576). Tresley, p. 217.

[247] Sanford, James. *Dedication to Sir Christopher Hutton's Houres of Recreation.*

[248] Wigandus, Joan. *Synopsis Antichrist Romani Spiritu oris Christi relevati* (n. p.).

1577
[249] Becon, Thomas. *The Actes of Christe and Antichrist.*
[250] Geveren, Sheltco à. *Of the Ende of This World, and the Second Coming of Christ*, tr. Thomas Rogers. Other editions: 1578, 1582, 1589.

1578
[251] Heunisch, Caspar. *Synopsis chronotaxeos apocalypticae* (Jena).

1579
[252] Dyos, John. *A Sermon Preached at Paules Cross* [on Rev. 17].
[253] Anon. *A Szent Ianos Latasanac 12. reszeböl valo Enek* (Debreczen).

1580
[254] Brocardus, Jacobus. *Interpretatio et paraphrasis libri Apocalypseos* (Leiden). Other editions: 1582, 1584, 1610. English translation: *The Revelation of S. John Reveled*, tr. James Sanford (1582).
[255] Cartigni, Jean de. *In D. Johannis Apocalypsim* (c. 1580). Tresley, p. 161.
[256] Chardon, John. *A Sermon . . . of the Second Comming of Christ unto Judgement, and of the End of the World.*
[257] Edwards, Roger. 'A Phantastical Booke Made by One Roger Edwards'. BM MS Landsdowne 353. fols. 192–230.
[258] Fleming, Abraham. *A Bright Burning Beacon.*
[259] Gregorius Ragusaeus. *Super Apocalypsim* (c. 1580). Tresley, p. 180.
[260] Harrison, Robert. 'A Treatise of the Church and Kingdome of Christ', in *The Writings of Robert Harrison and Robert Browne*, ed. Arthur Peel and Leland Carlson (1953).
[261] Harvey, Gabriel. *Three Proper, and wittie familiar Letters: . . . touching the Earthquake in Aprill late.* N. B. These letters are from Harvey to Edmund Spenser.
[262] Lucas, François. *Annotationes in Biblia* (Antwerp). Other editions: 1583, 1660.
[263] Schlichtenberger, Eyriak. *A Prophecy Uttered by a Daughter of an Honest Man.*

1581
[264] Aretius, Benedictus. *Commentarii . . . in Apocalypsim* (Berne). Another edition: 1583.
[265] Bateman, Stephen. *The Doome Warning All Men to the Judgemente.*
[266] Chassanion de Monistrol. *Des grands et redoutables jugement et punitions de Dieu* (Morges). Tresley, p. 162.
[267] Colladon, Nicolas. *Methodus facillima ad explicationem sacrosantes Apocalypseos Joannis* (Morges). Another edition: 1584.
[268] Rogers, Thomas. *The General Session, conteining an Apologie . . . Concerning the Ende of the World, and Seconde Coming of Christ.*
[269] Marcellinus, Evangelista. *In Apocalypsim* (Camerino). Tresley, p. 202.

1583
[270] Frisius, Matthias. *Tabula Synopticae Apocaltptiae Novi Testamenti* (Luneberg).

1584

[*271] Andreas of Caesarae. *Apocalypsin commnetarius*, tr. Theorodus Peltanus, ed. Fridericus Sylbergius (Ingolstatt). Other editions: 1596, 1609, 1618, 1677.

[272] Browne, Robert. 'A True and Short Declaration', in *The Writings of Robert Harrison and Robert Browne*, ed. Arthur Peel and Leland Carlson (1953).

[273] Fulke, William. *De successione ecclesiastica et latente ab Antichristi tyrannide*.

[274] Heunisch, Caspar. *Hauptschlüssel der offenbarung Ioannis* (Schleusingen). Other editions: 1684, 1698.

1585

[275] Durden, Ralph. 'A Writing of one Durden who called Himself Elias'. BM MS. Landsdowne 101 na 49.

[276] Keff, Francis. *The Glorious and Beautiful Garland of Man's Glorification*.

[277] ——. *An Epistle . . . Proving the Pope to Be the Beast*.

[278] Sandys, Edwin. *Sermons*.

1586

[279] Harbert, William. *A Letter Written by a True Christian Catholike, to a Romaine Pretended Catholike: Wherein . . . the 12. 13. and 14. Chap. of the Reuelations Are Briefly and Trulie Expounded*.

[280] Tymme, Thomas. *The Figure of Antichriste Disciphered by a Catholike*.

1587

[281] Bacci, Andrea. *Discorso dell' alicorno e della gran bestia* (Rome).

[282] Barrow, Henry. *The Writings* (1587–93), ed. Leland Carlson (1962–70).

[283] Foxe, John. *Eicasmi, seu meditationes in sacram Apocalypsin*. Another edition: 1596.

[284] Perkins, William. *A Fruitfull Dialogue Concerning the Ende of the Worlde*.

1588

[285] Browne, Robert. *A Treatise on the Book of Revelation*. N. B. According to Paul Christianson, Browne wrote this treatise which, 'if printed, . . . has not survived' (see [1354], p. 64).

[286] Drusius, Joannes. *Parallela sacra, hoc est locorum Veteris Testamenti cum iis quae in Novo citantur conjuncta commemoratio* (Franeker).

[287] James VI of Scotland and I of England. *A Fruitfull Meditation, Containing a Plaine and Easie Exposition . . . of the 7. 8. 9. and 10. Verses of the 20. Chap. of the Revelation* (Edinburgh). Another edition: 1603.

[288] Marten, Anthony. *An Exhortation, to Stirre up the Mindes to Defend Their Countrey*.

[289] Whitaker, William. *Disputatio de sacra scriptura contra hujus temporis papista* (Cambridge). Tresley, p. 237.

[290] Wither, George. *A View of the Marginal Notes of the Popish Testament*.

1589

[291] Bellarmine, Robert, S. J. *De Translatione Imperii Romani a Graecis ad Francos* (Antwerp).

[292] Bridgewater, John. *Confutatio virulentae disputationis theologicae . . . conatus est docere Pontificem Romanum esse Antichristum* (Triers).

[293] Bellengerus, Petrus. *In Apocalypsim D. Ioannis Apostoli* (Paris).

[294] DuJon, François (Junius). *Notae in Apocalypsim*. Other editions: 1599, 1602. English translation: *Annotations upon the Revelation* (1599).
[295] Gaspar de Melo Oesa. *Commentaria in Apocalypsin* (Valladolid).
[296] Hellwis, Edward. *A Marvell, Deciphered* [on Rev. 12].
[297] Marten, Anthony. *The Second Sound, or Warning of the Trumpet unto Judgement.*
[298] Mazerus, Baptista. *In divi Johannis cap. XII Apocalypsis* (Turin).
[299] Morel, Jean Baptiste. *De Ecclesia Dei ab Antichristo*. Other editions: 1590, 1594.
[300] Poyssel, Eustachius. *Das Dreyzehende Capitel der Offenbarung Ioannis, mit kurtzer Ausslegung* (n. p.).
[301] Ockland, Christopher. *The Fountain and Welspring of All Variance: . . . the Name of Babylon in the Revelation of St. John.*
[302] Rogers, Thomas. *An Historical Dialogue Touching Antichrist and Poperie.*
[303] Wright, Leonard. *The Hunting of Antichrist.*

1590
[304] Broughton, Hugh. *A concent of scripture*. Other editions: 1602, 1606.
[305] Deios, Laurence. *That the Pope Is That Antichrist: and an Answer to the Objections of Sectaries, Which Condemne This Church of England.*
[306] Erasmi, Johannes. *Commentarius in Apocalypsim* (c. 1590). Tresley, p. 172.
[307] Fontana, Johannes. *Commentaria in Apocalypsim* (c. 1590). Tresley, p. 174.
[308] Höe von Höenegg, Matthias. *Commentarius in Apocalypsin Libri I, II, III* (Leipzig). Other editions: 1610–11, 1640, 1671. N. B. This volume carries a preface by Martin Geler.
[309] Lindt, Willem von der. *Glaphyra in Christi Domini Apocalypticas ad episcopos epistolas*, ed. J. Malderus (Louvain). Another edition: 1602. Tresley, p. 201.
[310] Nicolai, Philipp. *De duobus Antichristis, Mahumete et Pontifice Romano* (n. p.). Another edition: 1609.
[311] Trigge, Francis. *Noctes sacrae, seu lucubrationes in primam partem Apocalypseos* (Oxford).
[312] Willet, Andrew. *De universali et novissima Judaeorum vocatione* (Cambridge).
[313] Winckelmann, Johann. *Commentarius in Apocalypsim* (Frankfurt). Other editions: 1600, 1609, 1615.
[314] Anon. 'The Twelfthe and Thirteenthe Chapiters of the Revelation Expounded'. BM MS. Harleian 6660 and Lambeth Palace MS. 488. I, fols 1–39.

1591
[315] DuJon, François (Junius). *Apocalypsis Joannis Apostoli et Evangeliste* (Heidelberg). Other editions: 1592, 1594, 1596, 1598, 1599, 1600, 1606, 1608, 1616. English translation: *Apocalypsis: A Briefe and Learned Commentarie upon the Revelation of Saint John* (1591). N. B. Richard Bauckham explains that 'Junius's commentary was available in two forms' with this shorter version being 'very popular and probably second only to Bullinger's commentary in its general influence in England' (see [1322], p. 138). The 1602 Geneva Bible draws heavily upon Junius in supplementing the earlier notes provided by Bullinger.
[316] Ludovicus Legionensis. *Commentarius in Apocalypsim* (c. 1591). Tresley, pp. 201–2.
[317] Ribeira, Francisco. *Commentarius in Apocalypsin* (Salamanca). Other editions: 1592, 1593, 1603. N. B. This commentary was apparently written about 1578.

1592

[318] Gallus, Carolus. *Clavis prophetica nova Apocalypseos* (Antwerp).
[319] Sohn, George. *A Treatise Containing a True Description of Antichrist*, tr. Nicholas Grimoald (Cambridge).

1593

[320] Bartholomaeus. *Commentarius in Apocalypsim* (c. 1593). Tresley, p. 150.
[321] LeBuy, Jonas (Pierre de Launay). *Commentarium quoque in Danielem et Apocalypsim* (Geneva). Other editions: 1600, 1651.
[322] Loyerts, Petrus. *Commentarius in Apocalypsim* (c. 1593). Tresley, p. 201.
[323] Mercator, Gerard. *Commentarius . . . in Apocalypsim* (c. 1593). Tresley, p. 205.
[324] Napier, John. *A Plaine Discovery of the Whole Revelation of Saint John* (Edinburgh). Other editions: 1594, 1600, 1603, 1605, 1607, 1611, 1615, 1627, 1642, 1645.

1594

[325] Broughton, Hugh. *A sedem olam, that is, order of the worlde; or yeares from the fall to the restoring.*
[326] Desportes, Philippe. 'Plainte II', in *Premieres Oeuvres* (Rouen).
[327] Dove, John. *A Sermon . . . of the Second Comming of Christ . . . and the Disclosing of Antichrist* (1594?).
[328] Morel, Jean Baptiste. *Explicatio Apocalypseos* (Basel).

1595

[329] Clapham, Enoch. *Sermons to Doomsday* (Amsterdam). Tresley, p. 163. N. B. Clapham sets out to refute Napier.
[330] L., T. *Babilon Is Fallen. Wherein Briefly Is Unfolded All the Matters of Greatest Moment* (n. p.). Other editions: 1597, 1610, 1614, 1620, 1651.
[331] Webb, Jessop. *A Sermon Preach'd at the Funeral of Mrs Costivell.*

1596

[332] DuJon, François (Junius). *The Apocalyps, or Revelation of S. John*, tr. Thomas Barbar (Cambridge). N. B. This is a greatly expanded version of Junius's 1591 commentary (now some 286 pp. in comparison with the earlier 88 pp.).
[333] Gifford, George. *Sermons upon the Whole Booke of the Revelation*. Another edition: 1599.
[334] Nicolai, Philipp. *Commentariorum de regno Christi* (Frankfurt). Other editions: 1630, 1631, 1659. English translation: *Chronologica sacra*, tr. D. Forbes (1630). Tresley, p. 209.

1597

[335] Foord, John. *Apocalypsis Iesu Christi.*
[336] Williams, Erasmus. 'Expositio, Revelationis Sancti Joannis Theologi'. Bodleian MS. Rawlinson A. 439. N. B. Williams was a friend of Richard Haydock, a correspondent of Joseph Mede and a contributor of the illustration visualizing the Book of Revelation that is published in many editions of Mede's commentary (see fig. on p. 138).

1598

[337] Eglinus Iconius, Raphael. *Prophetia Halieutica nova et admiranda, ad Danielis et*

sacrae Apocalypseos calculum chronographicum (Zurich).

[338] Gualter, Rudolph, and Bullinger, Heinrich. *Archetypi homeliarum . . . in Apocalypsin Divi Johannis*, ed. Heinrich Wolphius and Heinrich Bullinger the younger (Zurich). N. B. Here printed for the first time are the outlines for Bullinger's previous commentary.

[339] Pont, Robert. *A newe treatise of the right reckoning of the yeares, and ages of the world, and mens lives and of the estate of the last decaying age thereof the 1600 year of Christ* (Edinburgh).

[340] Suarez, Jacques. *Conciones viginti tres in tria prima capita Apocalypsis* (Lyon). Another edition: 1608.

[341] Viegas, Basius. *Commentarii Exegetici in Apocalypsin Ioannis apotoli* (Eborae). Other editions: 1601, 1602, 1603, 1606, 1608, 1613, 1615, 1617, 1630.

[342] Vietor, Jeremias. *Centum Conciones in Apocalypsim* (Frankfurt). Tresley, p. 236.

1600

[343] Furno, Vitalis de. *In Apocalypsim* (Venice). Another edition (ed. Jean de la Haye): 1647.

[344] Neelssius, Nicolaus. *Commentaria . . . in Genesim . . . et Apocalypsim* (c. 1600). Tresley, p. 208.

[345] Ponce de Leon, Basilius Oesa. *In Apocalypsim Commentarii* (Salamanca). Tresley, p. 218.

[346] Terry, John. *Theological logic, or the Trial of Truth: Containing a Discovery of the chiefest points . . . of the Great Antichrist* (Oxford, 1600–25).

1601

[347] Eglinus Iconius, Raphael. *Epilysis Apocalypseos S. Joannis* (Zurich). Another edition: 1611.

1602

[348] Richter, Balthassar. *Buch der heimlichen offenbarung Ioannis* (Leipzig).

[349] Salmeron, Alfonso. *Commentarii in Evangelicum Historiam . . . & Apocalypsim*, 16 vols (Cologne, 1602–4). Another edition: 1612–14.

1603

[350] Abbot, Robert. *Antichristi Demonstratio*. Another edition: 1608.

[351] Dent, Arthur. *The Ruine of Rome; or an Exposition upon the Whole Reuelation*. Other editions: 1607, 1611, 1622, 1628, 1631, 1633, 1644, 1828, 1841.

[352] Downham, George. *A Treatise Concerning Antichrist*. Another edition: 1620 N. B. Chapter VII is translated and printed by Richard Baxter in *The Safe Religion* (1657).

[353] Ferdinandus de las Infantadas. *Tractatus in quo exponitur horum trium Prophetarum visio Ezelielis, Esaï & Joannis* (Cologne). Tresley, p. 175.

[354] Hunnius, Aegidius. *Thesaurus apostolicus complectens commentarios in omnes novi testamenti epistololas et Apocalypsin Iohannis* (Wittenberg, 1705). N. B. This commentary was written about 1603.

[355] Leoninus, Albertus. *Contemplatio exegetica in Apocalypsim* (Amsterdam). Another edition: 1608. Tresley, p. 200.

1604

[356] Abbott, George. *The Reasons . . . for Unholding Papistry Unmasked*.

[357] Alcasar, Ludovicus. *Vestigatio Arcani Sensus in Apocalypsim* (Antwerp). Other editions: 1614, 1618.
[358] Bonus, Thomas. *Commentarius in Apocalypsim* (c. 1604). Tresley, p. 157.
[359] Eedes, Richard. *Six learned and godly Sermons*.
[360] Malvenda, Thomas. *De Antichristo Libri Undecim* (Rome). Another edition: 1621.
[361] Pacard, George. *Description de l'Antechrist, et de son royaumes* (Noirt).
[362] Perkins, William. *Lectures upon the Three First Chapters of the Revelation*. Other editions: 1606, 1607. And included in *Works*: 1608–9, 1612–13, 1616–17, 1625–6, 1631, 1635. N. B. These lectures were first delivered in 1595.
[363] Toussain, Daniel. *Commentarii in Novum Testamentum* (Hanau). Tresley, p. 233.

1605

[364] Broughton, Hugh. *Certayne Questions . . . between Mr H. Broughton and Mr Henry Ainsworth* (Amsterdam).
[365] Capell, Jacques. *In Apocalypsim D. Johannis* (Sedan). Other editions: 1657, 1660, 1698.
[366] Gardiner, Samuel. *A Sermon upon the 20. of the Reuelation the 12. vers*.
[367] Symonds, William. *Pisagh Evangelica . . . a Briefe Ecclesiasticall Historie*. Another edition: 1606.

1606

[368] Holland, Henry. *The History of Adam or the foure-fold State of Man*.
[369] Pereyra, Benito. *Disputationes super libro Apocalypsis* (Lyon). Other editions: 1607, 1620.
[370] Anon. *Newes from Rome*, tr. W. W. Another edition: 1607 (this time under the title, *A Jewes Prophecy*).

1607

[371] Alabaster, William. *Apparatus in Revelationem Jesu Christi* (Antwerp).
[372] Cuffe, Henry. *The Differences of the Ages of Mans Life*. Other editions: 1633, 1640.
[373] Dekker, Thomas, *The Whore of Babylon*.
[374] Remundus, J. C. *L'Antichriste* (Paris).
[375] Thomson, George. *Quatre harmonies sur la revelation de S. Jean* (n. p.).

1608

[376] Agellius, Antonius. *In tria priora capita Apocalypseos* (c. 1608). Tresley, p. 124.
[377] Draxe, Thomas. *The Worldes Resurrection*.
[378] Pullenius, Peregrinus. *In Canticum Centicorum et in Apocalypsim* (c. 1608). Tresley, p. 221.
[379] Anon. *Der von Gott bestimpten Zahlen dess Antichrists 1260. endlicher Aussgang und Ende Apocal. 11. 12. 13.* (n. p.).

1609

[380] Brightman, Thomas. *Apocalypsis Apocalypseos* (Frankfurt). Other editions: 1611, 1612, 1615, 1616, 1618, 1641, 1644. English translation: *A Revelation of the Apocalyps* (1611).
[381] Broughton, Hugh. *A Most Humble Supplication to the King* (Amsterdam). Another edition: 1611.
[382] Clapham, Enoch. *A Chronological Discourse of the Church, Christ, Antichrist, Gog and Magog*.

[383] Taffin, Jean. *Calire Exposition de l'Apocalypse de St. Jean* (Flessing). Another edition: 1614.
[*384] Victorinus. *Commentarius in Apocalypsin*. Other editions: 1618, 1652, 1654, 1677, 1680.
[385] Anon. *Against Symbolizing with Antichrist* (n. p.).

1610

[386] Brightman, Thomas. *Antichristum Pontificiorum monstram fictitium esse* (Hamburg).
[387] Broughton, Hugh. *A Revelation of the Holy Apocalyps* (Amsterdam).
[388] Graser, Conrad. *Plaga regia; hoc est, commentarius in Apocalypsin* (Zurich). Another edition: 1614.
[389] Taberna, Batolomo. *Commentarius in Apocalypsim* (c. 1610). Tresley, p. 230.
[390] Varin de Perrières, Paul. *Le Sommaire des Secrets de l'Apocalypse suivant l'ordre des chapitres* (Paris). Tresley, p. 235. This is another attack on Napier.
[391] Vignier, Nicolas. *Théâtre de l'Antichrist* (Rochelle).

1611

[392] Eudaemon-Joannes, Andreas. *Castigatio in Apocalipsin Apocalipseos, Thomas Brightmanni Angli* (Cologne).
[393] Lessius. *De Antichristo* (Amsterdam).
[394] Michaelius, Nicolaus. *Commentarius in Apocalypsim* (Copenhagen). Another edition: 1627. Tresley, p. 206.
[395] Wirth, Georgius. *Discursus in Acta Apostolorum . . . & Apocalypsim* (Frankfurt). Tresley, p. 238.

1612

[396] Becanus, Martinus. *In Plagam Regim, seu Commentarius in Apocalypsim* (Mainz). Tresley, p. 151.
[397] Brochmond, Jesper Rasmussen. *Commentarius in Apocalypsim et in Ecclesiasten* (Franeker). Tresley, p. 158.
[398] Brondo, Antioco. *Commentarium . . . in Joannis . . . Apocalypsim* (Rome).
[399] Drusius, Joannes (Jan van den Driesche). *Adnotationum in totum Jesu Christi Testamentum* (Franeker).
[400] DuMoulin, Pierre. *De l'accomplissement des prophéties . . . de l'Apocalypse* (Rochelle). English translation: *The Accomplishment of the Prophecies*, tr. J. Heath (1613).
[401] Helwig, Andreas. *Antichristus Romanus, in Proprio Suo Nomine, Numerum Illum Apocalypticum (DCLXVI) continente Proditus* (Wittenberg).
[402] Josse, Charles. *La déroute de Babylon descrite . . . en l'Apocalypse* (Paris).
[403] Reuter, Adam. *Oratio demonstrons Papam esse Bestiam in Apocalyps. XVII. 8.*

1613

[404] Forbes, Patrick. *An Exquisite Commentarie upon the Revelation of Saint John*. Other editions: 1614, 1646.
[405] Lucius, Ludovicus. *Notae textualis et exegesis analytica in Apocalypsim* (Hanau).
[406] Piscator, Johannes (Johann Fischer). *Commentaria in Omnes Libros Novi Testamenti* (Herborn). Other editions: 1638, 1643–5.
[407] Price, Sampson. *Londons Warning by Laodicea's luke-warmnesse*.

[408] Williamson, Thomas. *The Sword of the Spirit to Smite in Pieces . . . the Pope.*

1614

[409] Alexander, William. *Doomes-day or the great day of the Lords Judgement* (Edinburgh).
[410] Fridericus, Daniel. *Expositio 12. priorum capitum Apocalypseos* (Wittenberg). Another edition: 1625. Tresley, p. 126.
[411] Maxwell, James. *Admirable and Notable Prophecies . . . Concerning the Church of Romes Defection, Tribulations and Reformation.* Another edition: 1615.
[412] Price, Sampson. *A Heavenly Proclamation to Fly Romish Babylon* (Oxford).
[413] Rainolds, John. *The Discovery of the Man of Sinne* (Oxford). Another edition: 1616.
[414] Raleigh, Sir Walter. *The History of the World.* Many subsequent editions.

1615

[415] Cooper, Thomas. *A Familiar Treatise, Laying Downe Cases of Conscience.*
[416] Cottière, Matthieu. *Apocalypseos, Domini Nostri Jesu Christ exposito* (Saumur). Another edition: 1625.
[417] Draxe, Thomas. *An Alarum to the Last Judgement.*
[418] Ferrier, Jeremy. *De l'Antichrist et de ses marques* (Paris).
[419] Grenfield, Nathaniel. *The Great Day, or, a Sermon, Setting Forth the Desperate Estate and Condition of the Wicked at the Day of Judgment.*

1616

[420] Benefield, Sebastian. *A Latin Sermon on Rev. V. 10* (n. p.).
[421] d'Aubigne, Agrippa. *Les Tragiques* (Paris). N. B. This piece was composed over the preceding forty years.
[422] James VI of Scotland and I of England. *A Paraphrase upon the Revelation of the Apostle S. John.* Another edition: 1619. N. B. The preface is by Isaiah Winton.
[423] Prideaux, John. *A Premonition to All Most Mighty Monarches.*
[424] Sengebaehar, Frideticus. *Tractatus circum cisus de septem spiritibus quorum mentio fit Apocalyp.* (Goslar). Tresley, p. 227.
[425] Sharpe, Lionel. *A Looking Glass for the Pope: Being the Image of Antichrist* (n. p.).
[426] Anon. *A Short Compend of the Growth of the Romaine Antichrist* (Edinburgh).

1617

[427] Belgicus. *De regno Christi* (Gouda).
[428] Bernard, Richard. *A Key of Knowledge for the Opening of the Secret Mysteries of St. Iohns Mysticall Revelation.* Another edition: 1640.
[*429] Nicolaus de Lyra. *In Apocalypsim* (Antwerp, 1617–34). Tresley, p. 210.
[430] Price, Sampson. *The Clearing of the Saints Sight* [Rev. 7.17].

1618

[431] Cramer, Daniel. *Apocalypsis oder Offenbarung S. Johannis* (Stettin).
[432] Ferey, Pierre. *L'aigle transcendant . . . sermons pour les advens sur le premier chapitre de l'Apocalypse* (Paris).
[433] Jungnitius, Christopherus. *Parallela sententiarum in Apocalypsim* (Frankfurt). Tresley, p. 197.
[434] Osiander, Andreas. *Biblia Sacra* (Frankfurt). Tresley, p. 213. N. B. This commentary was written about 1580.

[435] Pareus, David. *In divinam Apocalypsin* (Heidelberg). Other editions: 1622, 1642, 1644. English translation: *A Commentary upon the Divine Revelation of the Apostle and Evangelist John*, tr. Elias Arnold (1644). N. B. This commentary developed from lectures first presented in 1609.
[436] Selden, John. 'Of the Revelation' (c. 1618), in *Opera Omnia*, ed. David Wilkins, 3 vols. (1725), III, ii, 1401–4.
[437] Thompson, Thomas. *Anti-Christ arraigned*.

1619

[438] Cowper, William. *Pathmos: or, A Commentary on the Revelation of Saint Iohn*. Other editions: 1623, 1629, 1656, 1671.
[439] Gracian a Matre Dei, Hieronymus. *Liber in Apocalypsim* (c. 1619). Tresley, p. 180.
[440] Lautensack, Paul. *Offenbarung Jesu Christi* (Frankfurt).
[441] Mariana, Juan de. *Scolia in Vetus et Novum Testamentum* (Madrid). Other editions: 1620, 1624, 1745, 1905.
[442] Mason, Thomas. *A Revelation of the Revelation*.
[443] Montacutius, Jacobus. *Paraphrasis in Apocalypsin*.
[444] Paulutinas, Fabricius. *In actus et epistolas Pauli . . . et Apocalypsim commentarii* (Rome).
[445] Rhumel, Johann Conrad. *Apocalypsis Joannis Theologi poetica paraphrasis* (Nuremberg).
[446] Wilkinson, John. *An Exposition of the 13. Chapter of the Revelation* (Amsterdam).

1620

[447] Andreae, Johann Valentine. *Christianopolis* (1620), tr. and ed. Felix Emil Held. Ph. D. Thesis, Univ. of Illinois, 1914.
[448] Byfield, Nicholas. *The Marrow of the Oracles of God*.
[449] Cluverus, Johannes. *Primum diluculum apocalypticum; or the First Dawn of the Revelation of St. John* (Goslar). Another edition: 1647.
[450] Egard, Paul. *Explicatio viginti capitum Apocalypseos* (Luneburg).
[451] Felgenhauer, Paul. *Speculum temporis . . . der Offenbarung Johannis* (n. p.). Tresley, p. 173.
[*452] Gorranus, Nicolaus. *Commentarius in Apocalypsin* (Antwerp).
[453] Anon. *A prophecie of the Judgment Day*.

1621

[454] Alabaster, William. *Commentarius de Bestia Apocalyptica* (Delft).
[455] Bernard, Richard. *The Seven Golden Candlesticks*.
[456] Finch, Sir Henry. *The Worlds Great Restauration*. N. B. The preface is by William Gouge.
[*457] Huge de S. Caro. *In Apocalypsim*, in *Opera omnia* (n. p.). Another edition: 1703.
[458] Olearius, Johann. *Commentarius in Apocalypsim* (Goslar). Another edition: 1647. Tresley, p. 21.
[459] Piscator, Johannes (Johann Fischer). *In Apocalypsin Johannis Commentarius* (n. p.).
[460] Vecchiettus, Hieronymus. *De anno primitivo ab exordio mundi ad annum Juliarnum accommodate & de Sacrorum temporum ratione libri octo* (Augsburg). Tresley, p. 235.

1622

[461] Alsted, John. *Theologica Prophetica* (Hanover).

[462] Brandmueller, Jacob. *Analysis . . . libri Apocalypseos* (Basel).
[463] Cartwright, Thomas (?). *A Plaine Explanation of the Whole Revelation of Saint John.*
[464] Estius, Gulielmus. *Annotationes aureae in praecipua ac difficil ora Sacrae Scripturae loca* (Cologne).
[465] Olai, Nicolaus. *Analysis in Apocalypsim* (Stockholm). Tresley, p. 212. N. B. This commentary was written about 1599.
[466] Stephani, Willem. *Tuba belli sacri Apocalypseos beati Iohannis* (Campen). Another edition: 1623.
[467] Wilson, Thomas. *A Christian Dictionary . . . whereunto Is Annexed a Dictionary for the Revelation of St. John.*

1623

[468] Campanella, Tommaso. *De Antichristo* (c. 1623), ed. Romono Amerio (Rome, 1965).
[469] ——, *De Dictis Christi* (c. 1623), ed. Romano Amerio (Rome, 1969).
[470] Donne, John. 'Sermon . . . on Rev. 7.17' (c. 1623), in *The Sermons of John Donne*, ed. George R. Potter and Evelyn M. Simpson, 10 vols (Berkeley, 1962), V, 96–112.
[471] ——, 'Sermon . . . on Rev. 7.2, 3', *ibid.*, X, 41–64.
[472] Grossen, Isaac. *Antichristus Orientalis ex vaticiniis demonstratus* (Wittenberg).
[473] L., T. *An Exposition of the XI. XII. and XIII. Chapters of the Revelation*. Other editions: 1651, 1661.
[474] Rhonaeus, Erycius. *Idea reformondi Antichristi* (n. p.).

1624

[475] Abbott, George. *A Treatise of . . . the True Church.*
[476] Donne, John. 'Sermon . . . on Rev. 20.6', in *The Sermons of John Donne*, ed. George R. Potter and Evelyn M. Simpson, 10 vols. (Berkeley, 1953), VI, 62–80.
[477] ——, 'Sermon . . . on Rev. 7.9', *ibid.*, VI, 150–67.
[478] Gee, John. *Hold Fast, a Sermon* [on Rev. 3.11].
[479] Higgins, Theophilus. *Mystical Babylon; or, Papall Rome.*

1625

[480] Antoine de Saint-Michel. *Catechesis theologica in sanctam D. Joannis Apocalypsim* (Tournon).
[481] Beard, Thomas. *Antichrist the Pope of Rome.*
[482] Crugotius, Petrus. *Notae in Apocalypsin* (Frankfurt).
[483] Jansonius, Robertus Campensis (Agellius Vaesartus). *Brevis dissertatio de visionibus quae capitibus XIII et XVII Apocalypseos describuntur* (Clausenburg). Other editions: 1643, 1682.
[484] Mayer, John. *An Antidote against Popery.*
[485] Prideaux, John. *Orations . . . Apoc. 11: 3–5 . . . 13:8 . . . 20: 7–9* (Oxford). Another edition: 1672. Tresley, p. 219.
[486] S[andys], G[eorge] (?). *Sacrae heptades, or Seven Problems Concerning Antichrist* (Leiden).
[487] Sheldon, Richard. *A Sermon . . . Laying Open the Beast and His Masks.*
[488] Wolter, John. *Guldene arche, darinnen der wahre verstand der offenbarung Ioannis und in propheten Daniel* (Rostock). Another edition: 1629.
[489] Anon. *Prodromus Evangelij aeterni, seu Chilias sancta* (n. p.).

1626
[490] Prynne, William. *A Perpetuitie of a Regenerate Mans Estate.*

1627
[490] Alsted, John. *Diatribe de mille annis Apocalypticis* (Frankfurt). Other editions: 1630, 1643, 1647, 1675. English translation: *The Beloved City or; the Saints Reign on Earth a Thousand Yeares,* tr. William Burton (1643).

[492] Dieu, Ludovicus de. *Apocalypsis Sancti Johannis* (Leiden). Another edition: 1693.

[493] Donne, John. 'Sermon . . . on Rev. 4.8', in *The Sermons of John Donne,* ed. George R. Potter and Evelyn M. Simpson, 10 vols. (Berkeley, 1962), VIII, 37–60.

[494] Hakewill, George. *An Apologie or Declaration of the Power and Providence of God in the Government of the World* (Oxford). Other editions: 1630, 1635.

[495] Lapide, Cornelius à (Cornelius ven den Steen). *Commentaria in Apocalypsin* (Lyon). Other editions: 1631, 1717.

[496] Mayer, John. *Ecclesiastica Interpretatio: or the Expositions upon the Difficult and Doubtful Passages of the Seven Epistles Called Catholike, and the Revelation.* Another edition: 1631.

[497] Mede, Joseph. *Clavis Apocalyptica ex Innatis et Insitis Visionum Characteribus Eruta et Demonstrata* (Cambridge). Other editions: 1632, 1643, 1649, 1650, 1831, 1833. English translation: *The Key of the Revelation,* tr. Richard More (1643). N. B. The 1632 edition is an expanded version, with commentaries added; and the 1643 translation carries an introduction by Dr Twisse.

[498] Williams, Griffith. *On the Seven Golden Candlesticks* (n. p.).

1628
[499] Burton, Henry. *The Seven Vials. Or, a Briefe and Plaine Exposition upon the 15: and 16: Chapters of the Revelation.*

[500] Leighton, Alexander. *Speculum belli sacri; or the looking-glasse of the holy war* (Amsterdam).

[501] Smith, Henry. *One Great Asstae . . . four Sermons upon the 20th Chap. of Revelation.*

1629
[502] Adams, Thomas. 'Heaven-Gate: Or, the Passage to Paradise' [on Rev. 22.14], in *Workes . . . Being the Summe of His Sermons . . . and Other . . . Discourses,* pp. 651–60.

[503] ———, 'Presumption Running into Despair' [on Rev. 6.16], *ibid.,* pp. 751–60.

[504] ———, 'The Spiritual Navigator Bound for the Holy Land' [on Rev. 4.6], *ibid.,* pp. 392–413.

[505] Bazzius, Joan. *Comment. in Apocalypsin Joan* (Kalmar).

[506] Butterfield, Robert. *Maschil . . . For the Vindication of . . . H[enry] B[urton].*

[507] Cholmley, Hugh. *The State of the Now-Romane Church . . . by Way of Vindication . . . from the weake cavills of Henry Burton.*

[508] Deschaeus, Bartholomaeus. *Brevis Apocalypticae historiae collatio cum historia Ecclesiae* (Frankfurt). Tresley, p. 167.

[509] Laurentius, Jacobus. *Joann. Evang. & Apostoli Patmos; hoc est, Expositio septum epistolarum* (Amsterdam). Another edition: 1649.

[510] Tarnov, Paul. *In S. Johannis Evangelium Commentarius* (n. p.).

1631

[511] Beard, Thomas. *The Theatre of God's Judgements.*
[512] Borromeo, Federico. *Observationes in Apocalypsim, libri VII* (c. 1631). Tresley, p. 157.

1632

[513] Alcasar, Ludovicus. *In eas veteris testamenti partes, quas respicit apocalypsis, libri quinque* (Lyon). Tresley, p. 124.
[514] Prolaeus, Andreas. *Babylon. Das ist: Theologischer Schrifftmassiger Erklarung des sechsten General-Gesichtes der heiligen geheimen Offenbahrung S. Johannis 17. 18. 19. Capitels* (Leipzig).

1633

[515] Alabaster, William. *Ecce Sponsus venit . . . Tuba pulchritudinis.*
[516] Hall, Joseph. *A Plaine . . . Explication . . . of All the Hard Texts of Scripture*, 2 vols. N. B. See esp. II, 376–427.
[517] Lasena, Patrus. *Commentarius in Apocalypsim* (c. 1633). Tresley, p. 199.
[518] Taylor, Thomas. *Christs Victorie over the Dragon: or Satans Downfall*, ed. W. Jemmel. Another edition: 1653.
[519] Anon. *Explication de l'Apocalypse de Jesus Christ* (Leiden).
[520] Anon. τοῦ ἐν ἁγίοις καῖρος . . . ἑρμηνεία εἰς τὴν 'Αποκάλυψιν 'Ιωάννου (n.p.)

1634

[521] Fabricius, Georgius Andreas. *Catena Apostolica . . . Apocalypseos Johannis Analysis logico-topica* (Leipzig). Another edition: 1639. Tresley, p. 173.
[522] Pseudo-Nicolaus de Lyra. *In Prologum Gilberti in Apocalypsim* (Antwerp). Tresley, p. 210.
[523] Sheldon, Richard. *Man's Last End, The Glorious Vision and Fruition of God.*

1635

[524] Brightman, Thomas. *A Most Comfortable Exposition of Daniel* (Amsterdam).
[525] Crocius, Ludovicus. *Syntagma Theologiae* (n. p.).
[526] Ferrar, Nicholas. *Acta apostolorum elegantiss. monochromatis delineata.* Tresley, p. 142.
[527] Heironymus de Ghettis Oesa. *Super octo capita Apocalypseos* (c. 1635). Tresley, p. 188.
[528] Molinier, Etienne. *Les Douze Fondements de la Cité de Dieu* (Toulouse). Another edition: 1642.
[529] Pineton de Chambrun, Jacques. *Sermon sur deux versets du chapitre troisième de l'Apocalypse* (Orange).
[530] Rocha, Andreas. *Paraphrasis Apocalypsis S. Johannis* (Lumes).
[531] Sibelius, Caspar. *Apocalypseos Ioannis Evangelistae* (Amsterdam, 1635–6).
[532] Wither, George. *Ecchoes from the Sixth Trumpet.*

1636

[533] Amyrault, Moïse. *Sermon sur l'Apocalypse, II, 27* (Charenton).
[534] Burton, Henry. *A Divine Tragedie* (Amsterdam). Another edition: 1641.
[535] ———. *For God and the King* (Amsterdam).
[536] Prynne, William. *A looking-glasse for all lordly prelates.*

1637

[537] Trapp, John. *Gods Love-Tokens, and the Afflicted Mans Lessons.*
[538] Zapfius, Nicolaus. *Opusculum Theologicum* (Nuremberg). Tresley, p. 239.

1638

[539] Beard, Thomas. *The Beast Is Wounded* (Amsterdam, 1638?).
[540] Duerfeld, Jacob. *De duobus testibus veritatis, Apoc. 11: 11* (Rostock). Tresley, p. 170.
[541] Lilburne, John. *Come Out of Her My People* (Amsterdam).
[542] ——, *A Worke of the Beast* (Amsterdam).
[543] Ramsay, Andrew. *A Warning to Come out of Babylon* (Edinburgh).
[544] Anon. *A Briefe Relation* (Amsterdam).
[545] Anon. *A Guide unto Zion* (Amsterdam).
[546] Anon. *A licht for the Ignorant* (Amsterdam). Another edition: 1641.

1639

[547] Bordes, Jacques de. *Intelligence des révélations de sainct Jean* (Rouen).
[548] Lilburne, John. *To All the Brave Apprentises.* N. B. No copy survives.
[549] ——, *A Cry for Justice.* N. B. No copy survives.
[550] ——, *The Poore Mans Cry.* N. B. No copy survives.
[551] Micaelius, Nicolaus. *Gog et Magog, Abaddon et Apollyon* (Copenhagen). Tresley, p. 206.

1640

[552] Acetus de Portis. *Commentaria super Apocalypsim* (c. 1640). Tresley, p. 122.
[553] Alsted, John. *Trifolium propheticum . . . Prophetia Danielis & Apocalypseos explicata* (Herborn).
[554] Bayly, Richard. *The Shepheard's Starre: A Sermon.*
[555] Desmarets, Samuel. *Dissertatio de Antichristo* (Amsterdam).
[556] Grotius, Hugo. *Commentatio ad Loca Quaedam N. Testamenti Quae de Antichristo Agunt, aut Agere Putantur* (Amsterdam).
[557] Harford, Rapha. *Reverend Mr. Brightman His judgment on prophecies . . . collected out of his Exposition on the Revelation.* Other editions: 1642, 1643, 1644, 1650.

1641

[558] Archer, John. *The Personall Raign of Christ upon Earth.* Another edition: 1642, 1643, 1661.
[559] B., T. *News from Rome.*
[560] Bridge, William. *Babylon's Downfall.*
[561] Burroughs, Jeremiah. *A Glimpse of Sions Glory.* N. B. For this attribution, see Paul Christianson ([1354], pp. 251–2).
[562] ——, *Sions Joy.*
[563] Burton, Henry. *Englands Bondage and Hope of Deliverance.*
[564] ——, *The Sounding of the Two Last Trumpets . . . or, Meditations on Chapters IX–XI of the Revelation.*
[565] Byfield, Richard. *The Power of the Christ in God.*
[566] Chariciau, Nicolas. *La Jerusalem celeste* (Paris). Other editions: 1648, 1650.
[567] Coccejus, Johannis. *Brevis repetitio quorundam illustrium locorum veteris & Novi Testamenti, qui de Antichristo agunt* (Frankfurt).

[568] E., I. *The Land of Promise.*
[569] Ford, Thomas. *Reformation Sure and Steadfast.*
[570] Geree, John. *The Down-Fall of Anti-Christ: or, the Power of Preaching, to Pull Down Popery.*
[571] Holmes, Nathaniel. *The New World.*
[572] March, John de la. *A Complaint of the False Prophet's Mariners . . . Expounding Successive Turnes the Reuelation of St. J.*
[573] Mede, Joseph. *The Apostasy of the Latter Times.* Other editions: 1642, 1644, 1654, 1836, 1840, 1845, 1855.
[574] Montereul, Bernardin de. *Les Derniers combats d' l'Église, representez dans l'explication du liure de l'Apocalypse* (Paris).
[575] Overton, Richard. *Canterburys will.*
[576] ——, *Mercuries message.*
[577] ——, *Mercuries message defended.*
[578] ——, *Vox borealis.*
[579] P., R. *The Bishop's looking-glasse.*
[580] Prynne, William. *A New Discovery of the Prelates Tyranny.*
[581] Quintin, Michael. *A Brief Treatise Containing a Full Discovery . . . of Antichrist* (n. p.).
[582] Taylor, John. *The Hellish Parliament.*
[583] W., I. *A Discoverie of the Beasts* (Amsterdam).
[584] Wilkinson, Henry. *A Sermon against Lukewarmenesse in Religion.*
[585] Wilson, Thomas. *Davids zeal for Zion.*
[586] Anon. *The Bishops Manifest.*
[587] Anon. *Bloody News from Norwich.*
[588] Anon. *A Briefe Explanation of the XX. Chapter of the Revelation.*
[589] Anon. *Brightman's Predications and Prophecies.*
[590] Anon. *The Deliverance of the Whole House of Israel.*
[591] Anon. *Englands glory in her Royall King* (Amsterdam).
[592] Anon. *Napier's Narration: or, an Epitome of His Booke on the Revelation.* Another edition: 1642.
[593] Anon. *A Revelation of Mr. Brightmans Revelation.*
[594] Anon. *A Strange Prophecie against Bishops* (1641–2).
[595] Anon. *A True and Full Relation of the Horrible and Hellish Plot.*

1642

[596] Arrowsmith, John. *The Covenant-Avenging Sword Brandished.*
[597] Ashe, Simeon. *The Best Refuge for the Most Oppressed.*
[598] B., J. *The Last Will and Testament of Superstition.*
[599] Calamy, Edward. *Englands looking-glasse.*
[600] Caryl, Joseph. *The Workes of Epheus Explained.*
[601] Case, Thomas. *God Waiting to be Gracious Unto His People.*
[602] Cotton, John. *The Churches Resurrection, or the Opening of the Fift and Sixt Verses of the 20th Chap. of the Revelation.*
[603] ——, *The Powring Out of the Seven Vials: or an Exposition of the 16. Chapter of the Revelation.* Another edition: 1643, 1645.
[604] Corbet, Edward. *God's providence.*
[605] Diodati, John. *Pious Annotations upon the Holy Bible Expounding the Difficult Places.* Other editions: 1643, 1648, 1651, 1664.

[606] Duerfield, Jacob. *Disputatio theologica ... Apoc. 13: 18* (Rinteln). Tresley, p. 170.
[607] Duke, Francis. *The Fulnesse and Freenesse of Gods Grace.*
[608] E., E. *The Bishops downefalle or the prelats snare.*
[609] Fenwick, William. *Zions rights and Babels ruine.*
[610] Franklin, Thomas. *An Epistle Written from Lucifer.*
[611] Goodwin, Thomas. *Zerubbabels Encouragement to Finish the Temple.*
[612] Gouge, William. *The Saints Support.*
[613] Gross, Johann Georg. *Secreta Apocalypseos revelata* (Geneva). Another edition: 1663.
[614] Hodges, Thomas. *A Glimpse of Gods glory.*
[615] Hughes, Lewis. *Signes from Heaven.*
[616] Hunt, James. *Prophecy Concerning the Marriage of the Lamb, and Confounding the Whore of Babylon.*
[617] Laren, Daniel. *Notationes preoemiales in Apocalypsim* (Arnheim). Tresley, p. 199.
[618] Marshall, Stephen. *Reformation and Desolation.*
[619] Maton, Robert. *Israel's Redemption.* Another edition: 1646.
[620] Mocket, Thomas. *The Churches Troubles and Deliverance.*
[621] Overton, Richard. *New Lambeth fayre.*
[622] Potter, Francis. *An Interpretation of the Number 666.* Other editions: 1647, 1677, 1678, 1808. N. B. According to Joseph Mede, there may have been earlier editions, in 1626 and 1631, under the title *Bestia Apocalyptica.*
[623] Sedgwick, William. *Zions Deliverance and Her Friends Duty.*
[624] Spencer, John. *The Spiritual Warfare.*
[625] Tirinus, Jacobus. *Commentarius in S. Scripturam* (Antwerp). Other editions: 1668, 1688, 1723, 1738. Tresley, p. 232.
[626] Whittaker, Jeremiah. *Eirenopoios, Christ the Settlement of the Unsettled Times* (1642-3).
[627] Anon. *The Aphorismes of the Kingdome.*
[628] Anon. *The Camp of Christ, and the Camp of Antichrist* (n. p.).
[629] Anon. *The Discovery of the arch-whore.*
[630] Anon. *False Prophets Discovered.*
[631] Anon. *The Papists Petition in England.*
[632] Anon. *Six Strange Prophecies Predicting Wonderful Events.*
[633] Anon. *The Worlds Proceeding Woes and Succeeding Joyes.*

1643
[634] Artal, Johannes. *Commentarius in Apocalypsim* (c. 1643). Tresley, p. 148.
[635] B., T. *The Saints Inheritance after the Day of Judgement ... An Answer to ... The Personall Reigne of Christ upon Earth* (n. p.).
[636] Bailee, Robert. *Satan the Leader Is Chief.*
[637] Booker, John. *The Bloody Almanack.* Other editions: 1644, 1645, 1647, 1648, 1649, 1651, 1652, 1654.
[638] Bowles, Oliver. *Zeale for Gods House Quickened.*
[639] Burroughs, Jeremiah (?). *The Glorious Name of God.*
[640] Cheynell, Francis. *Sions memento, and Gods alarum.*
[641] Douglas, Lady Eleanor. *Apocalyps. chap. II. Its Accomplishment Shewed* (Oxford).
[642] ———, *Revelation's Interpretation.*
[643] Gerhard, Johann. *Adnotationes in Apocalypsin* (Geneva). Other editions: 1645, 1665.

[644] Greenhill, William. *The Axe at the Root.*
[645] Greislavius, Johannes. *Clavis Apocalypseos* (Leipzig).
[646] Hill, Thomas. *The Militant Church, Triumphant over the Dragon and His Angels.*
[647] Hunt, James. *A plaine and briefe Discovery of Those Two Beasts . . . Revelation 13.*
[648] Ley, John. *The Fury of Warre.*
[649] Marshall, Stephen. *The Song of Moses . . . and the Song of the Lamb.*
[650] Newcomen, Matthew. *Jerusalems Watch-men.*
[651] Wilkinson, Henry. *Babylons Ruine, Jerusalems Rising.*
[652] Wilson, Thomas. *Jerichoes down-fall.*
[653] Woodcock, Francis. *The Two Witnesses: Discovered in Several Sermons upon the Eleventh Chapter of the Revelation.*

1644

[654] Boden, Joseph. *An Alarme Beat up in Sion, to War against Babylon.*
[655] ——, *Sermon on Revelation.*
[656] Caryl, Joseph. *The Saints Thankfull Acclamation.*
[657] Case, Thomas. *Gods Rising, His Enemies Scattering.*
[658] Douglas, Lady Eleanor. *I Am the First and the Last.*
[659] Gower, Stanley. *Things Now-a-Doing.*
[660] Grotius, Hugo. *Annotationes in Novum Testamentum* (Amsterdam). Another edition: 1698.
[661] Hall, Henry. *Heaven Ravished.*
[662] Haye, John de la. *Commentarii litterales in Apocalypsin* (Paris). Another edition: 1647.
[663] Knox, John. *The Historie of the Reformation of the Church of Scotland.*
[664] Marshall, Stephen. *A Sacred Panegyrick.*
[665] Reyner, William. *Babylons Ruining-Earthquake.*
[666] Tesdale, Christopher. *Hierusalem: or a Vision of Peace.*
[667] Testard, Paul. *La Scene de l'Empire du monde et de l'Eglise de Christ . . . en l'esclareissement de l'Apocalypse de S. Jean* (Geneva). Tresley, p. 191.
[668] Woodcock, Francis. *Christs Warning-piece.*
[669] Anon. *A Brief Discovery of the Estate of the Church of Christ in the Apostles Times.*
[670] Anon. *Explanation . . . of the Mystical Number 666, applying it to the Pope of Rome* (Amsterdam).

1645

[671] Amyrault, Moïse. *Sermon sur ces mots de l'Apocalypse, I 4 et 5* (Saumur).
[672] Bailee, Robert. *A Dissuasive from the Errours of the Time.* N. B. See esp. chapt. IX.
[673] Burgess, Anthony. *Romes Cruelty and Apostacie.*
[674] Croy, Jean de. *Le dernier jugement, ou sermon la vision de . . . Apoc. XX* (Charenton).
[675] Denne, Henry. *Antichrist Unmasked.*
[676] ——, *The Man of Sin Discovered.*
[677] Hayne, Thomas. *Christs Kingdome on Earth.*
[678] L'Angle, Jean-Maximilien. *Sermon sur les paroles du second chapitre de l'Apocalypse* (Charenton).
[679] Lightfoot, John. *Discourse on Rev. XX. 1, 2.*
[680] Lilly, William. *A Collection of Ancient and Modern Prophecies.*
[681] Martinos, Didacus. *Commentarius in Apocalypsim* (c. 1645). Tresley, p. 203.

1646

[682] Cotignon, Pierre. *De l'estat de l'eglise en la loy de grace, comme elle nous est figurée en l'Apocalypse* (Troyes). Tresley, p. 165.
[683] Douglas, Lady Eleanor. *The Gatehouse Salutation . . . Revelat. cap. 4*.
[684] ——, *The Day of Judgements Modell*.
[685] ——, *Apocalyps. ch. 11* (1646?).
[686] Dury, John. *Israels Call to March out of Babylon unto Jerusalem*.
[687] Goodwin, Thomas. *The Great Interest of States and Kingdomes*.
[688] Maynard, John. *A Shadow of the Victory of Christ*.
[689] Pope, James. *The Unveiling of Antichrist*.
[690] Prynne, William. *Canterburies Doom*.
[691] White, John. *The Troubles of Jerusalems Restauration or the Churches Reformation*.
[692] Anon. *Commentarius in Apocalypsin* (Amsterdam).

1647

[693] Aresi, Paul of Milan. *Velitationes sex in Apocalypsin* (Milan, c. 1645).
[694] Carpenter, Richard. *Downfall of Antichrist*.
[695] Collier, Thomas. *The Glory of Christ and the Ruine of Antichrist Unvailed, as They Be Held Forth in the Revelation, by the Seales, Trumpets, and Vialls*. Another edition: 1651.
[696] Gravius, Gerhard. *Auslegung der Offenbarung Johannis* (Hamburg).
[697] Halsted, John. *Brightman Redivivus*.
[698] Hughes, George. *Vae-Euge-Tuba. Or, the Wo-Joy-Trumpet*.
[699] Mindgzies, Alexander. *The Downfall of Babylon, or the Ruin of Antichrist*.
[700] Rutherford, Samuel. *A Survey of the Spiritual Antichrist*.
[701] Salmon, Joseph. *Anti-Christ in Man*. Another edition: 1649.
[702] Saltmarsh, John. *Sparkles of Glory*.
[703] Strong, William. *A Way to the Highest Honor*.
[704] Trapp, John. *A Commentary or Exposition upon All the Epistles and the Revelation of John the Divine*. Another edition: 1656.
[705] Walther, Michael. *Prolegomena & Praecognita Apocalypticus* (Nuremberg).
[706] Winstanley, Gerrard. *The Breaking of the Day of God*.

1648

[707] Cary, Mary. *The Resurrection of the Witnesses*. Another edition: 1653.
[708] Erbery, William. *The Lord of Hosts*.
[709] Franciscus a Jesu Maria. *Commentarii literales & morales in Apocalypsin*, 2 vols (Lyon, 1648–55). Tresley, p. 175.
[710] Gott, Samuel. *Nova Solyma: The Ideal City; or Jerusalem Regained*. Another edition: 1649.
[711] Sterry, Peter. *The Clouds in which Christ Comes*.
[712] Winstanley, Gerrard. *The Saints Paradice*.
[713] Anon. *Light Shining in Buckinghamshire*.

1649

[714] Bacon, R. *The Labyrinth the Kingdom Is in*.
[715] Behmen, Jacob. *Mercurius Teutonicus; or a Christian Information Concerning the Last Times*.
[716] Blondel, David. *Des Sibylles celebrées* (Charenton).
[717] Coppin, Richard. *Antichrist in Man Opposeth Emmanuel or God in Us*.

[718] ——, *The Exaltation of All Things in Christ, and of Christ in All Things.*
[719] Douglas, Lady Eleanor. *The Everlasting Gospel.*
[720] Friedlieb, Phillip. *Theologica exegetica* (Stralsund). Tresley, p. 176.
[721] Held, Adolph. *Erklärung ubder die offenbarung Joannis und Ezechielis* (n. p.).
[722] Lilburne, John. *A Picture of the Councel of State.*
[723] Mercer, Richard. *Discourses of the Mysteries of the Last Times.*
[724] Salmon, Joseph. *A Rout, a Rout; or Some Rout of the Army's Quanters Besters.*
[725] Winstanley, Gerrard. *The New Law of Righteousnes Budding forth: A Glimpse of the new Heaven, and new Earth.*

1650

[726] Cominus, Scotus. *In Apocalypsim* (c. 1650). Tresley, p. 164.
[727] Foster, George. *The Sounding of the Last Trumpet.*
[728] ——, *The Pouring Forth of the Seventh and Last Viall upon All Flesh.*
[729] Grebnar, Paul. *A Brief Description of the Future History of Europe from Anno 1650 to An. 1710.*
[730] Hall, Joseph. *The Revelation Unrevealed.*
[731] Hammon, George. *Truth and Innocency and Zion's Redemption.*
[732] Hartlib, Samuel. *Apocalypsis Referata, or the Revelation of St. John Opened.* Another edition: 1653.
[733] Holland, Hezekiah. *An Exposition, or, a Short, but Full, Plaine, and Perfect Epitome of the Most Choice Commentaries upon the Revelation of Saint John.*
[734] Leigh, Edward. *Annotations upon all the New Testament Philological and Theological.*
[735] Lins, F. *Sharp, but Short, Noise of War: or the Ruin of Antichrist by the Sword.*
[736] Mede, Joseph. *Remaines on Some Passages in the Revelation.*
[737] Parker, Robert. *An Exposition of the Pouring out of the Fourth Vial.* Another edition: 1654. N. B. This work is, in part, an answer to Brightman.
[738] Pazzi, Antonius de. *Della divina providenza sopra le sette visioni dell' apocalisse* (c. 1650). Tresley, p. 128.
[739] Roxas, Alvares. *Commentarius in Apocalypsim* (c. 1650). Tresley, p. 224.
[740] Ussher, James. *Annales Veteris Testamenti . . . Novi Testamenti* (1650, 1654). Another edition: 1658.
[741] Winstanley, Gerrard. *Fire in the Bush . . . or The Great Battell.*

1651

[*742] Bruno of Segni. *Expositio in Apocalypsim,* in *Opera* (Venice).
[743] Cary, Mary, *The Little Horn's Doom and Downfal.*
[744] ——, *A New and More Exact Map, or Description of the New Jerusalem's Glory.*
[745] Hartlib, Samuel, et al. *The Revelation Reveled by Two Apocalyptical Treatises.* N. B. This volume includes a dedication by Hartlib, an epistle from John Drurie on Hartlib, and two commentaries: the first, *Clavis Apocalyptica,* is an adaptation of Mede; the second, *Apocalypsis Referata,* is a translation of Abraham von Frankenberg.
[746] Buttnerus, Johannes Paulus, *Paraphrasis expositiones Apocalypticae* (Geneva).
[747] Mauritius de Gregorio. *Anatomia totius Bibliae . . . & praecipuè Apocalypsis & de omnibus expositionibus suis* (c. 1651). Tresley, p. 204.
[748] Parker, Robert. *The Mystery of the Vialls Opened.*
[749] R., D. *The Morning Alarum,* tr. Nathaniel Johnson.
[750] Tillam, T. *The Two Witnesses.*
[751] Weldon, Robert. *Of Antichrist and the End of the World.*

[752] Anon. *Trias Mystica, in qua . . . speculum apocalypticum* (Amsterdam).

1652

[753] Danielis, Johannes Josephus. *Vrbs . . . Babylon apocalyptica mystica, Roma pro throno Antichrist ex Apoc. XVII. 5. 9. 18* (Wittenberg).

[754] Escobar et Mendoza, Antonius de. *Vetus et Novum Testamentum literalibus et moralibus*, 9 vols (Lyon). Tresley, p. 172.

[755] Houghton, Edward. *The Rise, Growth, and Fall of Antichrist.*

[756] Lowenius, Daniel. *Stricturae in Clavem Apocalypticam* (Cologne). Tresley, p. 200.

[757] Maton, Robert. *Christ's Personal Reign on Earth.* Another edition: 1665.

[758] Mede, Joseph. *Opuscula latina, ad rem apocalypticam spectontia* (Cambridge).

[759] Pinto, Ramírez Andrés. *Commentarius . . . in Apocalypsi* (Lyon). Tresley, p. 218.

[760] Reeve, Edmund. *The New Jerusalem: The Perfection of Beauty.*

[761] Tickell, J. *The Bottomless Pit Smoaking.*

[762] Venning, Ralph. *Mysteries and Revelations.*

1653

[763] Buttivant, Samuel. *A Brief Discovery of a Threefold Estate of Antichrist.*

[764] Durant, John. *The Salvation of the Saints by the Appearance of Christ.*

[765] Eston, John. *The Falling Stars.*

[766] Evehard, John. *Some Gospel Treasures Opened; in a Sermon on Rev. XI. 17*, ed. Rapha Harford. Another edition: 1657.

[767] Farnsworth, R. *Light Risen Out of Darkness.*

[768] Fox, George. *A Brief Discovery of a Threefold State of Antichrist.*

[769] Hall, E. *A Scriptural Discourse of the Apostasie and the Antichrist.*

[770] Hammond, Henry. *Paraphrases and Annotations upon All the Books of the New Testament.* Other editions: 1659, 1671, 1675, 1681, 1689, 1698.

[771] Holmes, Nathaniel. *The Resurrection Revealed: or, the Dawning of the Day-Star.* Another edition: 1661.

[772] Nayler, James. *The Power and Glory of the Lord Shining Out of the North.*

1654

[773] Coker, Matthew. *A Whip of Small Cords to Scourge Antichrist.*

[774] Duesbery, William. *A True Prophecy of the Mighty Day of the Lord.*

[775] Erbery, William. *An Olive Leaf; also the Reign of Christ.*

[776] Ferrarius, Gregorius. *Commentaria in sanctam Apocalypsin*, 3 vols. (Milan).

[777] Goodwin, Thomas. *A Sermon of the Fifth Monarchy.*

[778] Michel, James. *The Spouse Rejoicing over Antichrist.*

[779] More, J. *The Trumpet Sounded.*

[780] Nayler, James. *Discovery of the ———. The Great Earthquake, Rev. XVI. 18.*

[781] ———. *Man of Sin Acting in a Mystery of Inquisition.*

[782] ———. *The Old Serpent's Voice; or Antichrist Discovered* (n. p.).

[783] Robotham, John. *The Mystery of the Two Witnesses Unvailed.*

[784] Strong, William. *A Void from Heaven . . . Calling the People . . . from Mystical Babylon.*

[785] Tillinghast, John. *Knowledge of the Times, or, the Resolution of the Question, How Long It Shall Be unto the End of Wonders.*

[786] ———, *Generation-Work . . . the Second Part Being an Exposition of the Seven Vials, Rev. 16, and Other Apocalyptic Mysteries.* Another edition: 1655.

[787] Ursino, Johannes Henricus. *Die einleitung in die offenbarung Ioannis* (Frankfurt). Tresley, p. 234. N. B. This work is an attack on *Apocalypsis Referata*.

1655

[788] Cotton, John. *An Exposition upon the Thirteenth chapter of the Revelation*, ed. Thomas Allen. Another edition: 1656.
[789] Dorothée de Saint-René. *Commentaire theologique . . . sur les livres des Rogs et de l'Apocalypse* (Paris).
[790] Eustache, David. *Sermon sur Apocalypse XII. 13 et 14* (Orange).
[791] Farnsworth, R. *Antichrists Man of War*.
[792] Fox, George. *The Vial of the Wrath of God upon the Seat of the Man of Sin*.
[793] Guild, William. *Anti-Christ Pointed and Painted Out in His True Colours* (Aberdeen).
[794] Lightfoot, John. *The Harmony, Chronicle, and Order of the New Testament*.
[795] Miller, Joshua. *Antichrist in Man the Quakers Idol*.
[796] Nayler, James. *A Discovery of the Beast Got into the Seat of the False Prophet*.
[797] Nicolaus, Joannes. *Antichristus nova methodo, novis argumentis* (Amsterdam).
[798] Werensfelsius, Jacobus. *Homiliae in Apocalypsim* (c. 1655). Tresley, p. 237.

1656

[799] Crell, Johann. *Opera omnia exegetica* (Amsterdam). Tresley, p. 165.
[800] Duesbery, William. *Christ Exalted, and Alone Worthy to Open the Seals of the Book*.
[801] Guild, William. *The Sealed Book Opened*.
[802] Nayler, James. *Antichrist in Man, Christ's Enemy*.
[803] Raworth, Francis. *Work and Reward*.
[804] Reeve, John. *A Divine Looking-Glass*.
[805] Stephens, Nathaniel. *A Plaine and Easie Calculation of the Name, Mark and Number of the Name of the Beast*. Another edition: 1688.
[806] Venning, Ralph. *A Warning to Back-sliders; or, a Discovery for the Recovery of Fallen Ones*. Another edition: 1657.

1657

[807] Aspinwall, W. *A Brief Description of the Fifth Monarchy*.
[808] Baxter, Richard. *The Safe Religion*.
[809] Brensius, Daniel. *Tractatus de regno Ecclesiae glorioso . . .; addita sunt annotata in librum Apocalypseos S. Johannis* (Amsterdam).
[810] Canne, John. *The Time of the End*.
[811] Charpy, Nicolas. *De Sainte Croix ancienne nouveauté de l'écriture sainte, ou l'Eglise triomphante en terre* (Paris). Tresley, p. 162.
[812] Fromondous, Libertus (Libert Froidmont). *Commentarius in apocalipsin* (Louvain). Another edition: 1670.
[813] Gravius, Gerhard. *Au slegung der Offenbarung Johannis* (Hamburg).
[814] Haak, Theodore. *The Dutch Annotations upon the New Testament*.
[815] Wens, Johannes Baptista. *Commentarius in Apocalypsim* (c. 1657). Tresley, p. 237.

1658

[816] Amyraut, Balthazar Octavian. *Introduction a l'Exposition de l'Apocalypse* (The Hague).

[817] Bordes, Jacques de. *Elucidatio paraphrastica Apocalypsis beati Joannis*, 2 vols (Paris). Tresley, p. 157.
[818] Daillé, Jean. *Sermon . . . sur Apocalypse* (Charenton).
[819] Davies, John. *Apocalypsis; or the Revelation of Certain Notorious Advances of Heresies*.
[820] Desmarest, Jean. *Explicatio Apocalypseos Johannis* (Paris).
[821] Durham, James. *A Commentarie upon the Book of Revelation*, ed. John Carstairs. Other editions: 1660, 1680, 1739, 1764, 1788.
[822] Holzhauser, Batholomaeus. *Interpretatio in Apocalypsim* (c. 1658). Other editions: 1784, 1799, 1813, 1850. Tresley, p. 189.
[823] ———, *Compendium explanationis Apocalypseos* (c. 1658). Tresley, p. 189.
[824] ———, *In Apocalypsim* (c. 1658). Tresley, p. 189.
[825] More, Henry. *Paralipomena Prophetica*.
[826] Reeve, John. *Joyful News from Heaven*.
[827] Schmidt, Erasmus. *Notae et Animadversiones in Novum Testamentum*, 2 vols (Nuremberg). Tresley, pp. 226-27.

1659
[828] Bedell, William. *A Sermon on Rev. XVII. 4*.
[829] Bernard, Nicholas. *Certain Discourses, viz. of Babylon (Rev. 18.4) Being the Present See of Rome*.
[830] Bordes, Jacques de. *Explicatio omnium figurarum Apocalypse* (Paris).
[831] Fox, George. *The Great Mystery of the Great Whore Unfolded*.
[832] Hicks, William. Ἀποκάλυψις ἀποκαλύψεως. *The Revelation Revealed; Being a Practical Exposition on the Revelation of St. John* (Chs I–III). Other editions: 1661, 1662.
[833] Lee, Samuel. *De Exicido Antichristi*. Another edition: 1664.

1660
[834] Clarkson, L. *The Lost Sheep Found*.
[835] Grebnar, Ezekiel. *Visions and Prophecies Concerning Scotland, England, and Ireland*.
[836] More, Henry. *An Explanation of the Grand Mystery of Godliness*.
[837] Nelson, Abraham. *A Perfect Description of Antichrist and His False Prophet*.
[838] Price, John. *Commentarius in varios Novi Testamenti libros*. Tresley, p. 219.
[839] Schrylaeus, Antonius Maria. *Expositio in Apocalypsim* (c. 1660). Tresley, p. 227.
[840] Williams, Griffith. *The Great Antichrist Revealed*.

1661
[841] Hardy, Nathaniel. *The Hierarchy Exalted and Its Enemies Tumbled*.
[842] Nicolai, Philipp. *Viginti quinque conciones in capita quinque priora Apocalypseos*, in *Opera* (Hamburg). Tresley, p. 209.
[843] Anon. *An Essay to the Explaining of the Revelation*.
[844] Anon. *Key of Prophecy: . . . showing how the Little Horn of the Beast . . . Means the Parliaments of England which Killed the Two Witnesses and a Threefold King*.

1662
[845] Arcona, César d'. *L'interprétation des chapitres 4 et 5 de l'Apocalypse* (Bordeaux).
[846] Caryl, Joseph. *The White Robe; or, the Undefiled Christian Clothed in a White Garment*.

[847] E'Espagne. *Essay on the Wonders of God in the Harmony of the Times.*
[848] Drelincourt, Charles. *La ferveur d'esprit ou sermon sur l'Apocalypse* (Charenton).
[849] ——, *Le profit du châtiment, ou sermon sur l'Apocalypse* (Charenton).
[850] Kromayer, Hieronymus. *Commentarius in Apocalypsin* (Leipzig). Another edition: 1674.
[851] Muggleton, Lodowick. *A True Interpretation of the Eleventh Chapter of the Revelation of St. John.* Other editions: 1746, 1753, 1833.
[852] Spurstowe, William. *A Crown of Life, the Reward of Faithfulnesse.*
[853] Vane, Sir Henry. *The Face of the Times . . . from the Beginning of Genesis to the End of the Revelation.*

1663
[854] Bishop, George. *Two Treatises on the Judgement and the Man of Sin* (n. p.).
[855] Diest, Heinrich van. *Analysis Apocalypseos exegetica, ex commentario Davidis Parei cumprisis contexta* (Arnheim).
[856] Schilter, Johann. *Itemque de fatis ecclesiarvm s. Joanni revelatis dissertatio* (Geneva). Another edition: 1683.
[857] Sylveira, Joannes de. *Commentarius in Apocalypsim*, 2 vols. Another edition: 1700.

1664
[858] Brenius, Daniel. *Breves in Vetus & Novum Testamentum annotationes* (Amsterdam).
[859] Cirino, Andrea. *Commentarii in Apocalypsim* (c. 1664). Tresley, p. 163.
[860] Dannhauer, Johann Conrad. *Muhammedismus in Angelis Euphrataeis S. Johanni Apocal. IX, 13 ad 21* (Strassburg).
[861] Hamerstede, Johannes van. *Meretrix Babylonica et Sponsa Christi detectae* (Gorich).
[862] Mede, Joseph. *A Summary View of the Apocalyps*, in *Works*.
[863] More, Henry. *An Inquiry into the Mystery of Iniquity.*
[864] ——. *Synopsis Prophetica.*
[865] Petrie, Alexander. *Chiliasto mastix: or the Prophecies of the Old and New Testaments* (Rotterdam).
[866] Stigzelius, Laurentius Matthias. *Commentarius in Apocalypsim* (Uppsala, 1664–65). Tresley, p. 229.
[867] Anon. *Antichrist Unhooded.*

1665
[868] Arnaldus (?). *Remarques sur les erreurs d'un livre* [by Nicolas Charpy] (Paris).
[869] Beaumont, Joseph. *Some Observations upon the Apologie of Dr. Henry More for His Mystery of Godliness.*
[870] Bunyan, John. *The Holy City: or, the New Jerusalem.*
[871] ——. *Sermon on Rev. XXI. 10–XXII. 5* (n. p.).
[872] Coccejus, Johannis. *Cogitationes de Apocalypsin S. Johannis theologi* (Leiden).
[873] Muggleton, Lodowick. *A True Interpretation of All the Chief Texts, and Mysterious Sayings and Visions Opened, of the Whole of the Revelation of St. John.* Other editions: 1746, 1808.
[874] Seld, George. *Der bericht von der apocalypsi referata* (Danzig).
[875] Sherwin, William. $\Pi\rho o\delta\rho o\mu o\varsigma$, *the Forerunner of Christ's Peaceable Kingdom on Earth* (n. p.). Another edition: 1674.

[876] ——. Ειρηνικον, or a Peaceable Consideration of Christ's Peaceable Kingdom (n. p.). Another edition: 1676.

1666

[877] Cavendish, Margaret. *The Description of a New World, Called the Blazing World.*
[878] More, Henry. *Visionum apocalypticarum ratio synchronistica.*
[879] Lily, William. *Merlini Anglici Ephemeris or Astrological Judgments for the Year 1666.*

1667

[880] Episcopus, Simon. *Lectiones sacrae . . . in capita 2. & 3. Apocalypseos* (Amsterdam).
[881] Fox, George. *Something in Answer to Lodowick Muggletons Book.*
[882] Hutchinson, Samuel. *A Declaration of a Future Glorious Estate of a Church to be Here on Earth, at Christ's Personal Appearance for the Restitution of All Things.*
[883] Knollys, Hanserd. *Apocalyptical Mysteries, Touching the Two Witnesses, the Seven Vials, and the Two Kingdoms.*
[884] Pineton de Chambrun, Jacques. *La conversation et le renouvellement du monde en l'estat de la glorie, ou sermon sur ces paroles de l'Apocalypse* (Orange).
[885] Vincent, Thomas. *Christ's Certain and Sudden Appearance to Judgement.* Another edition: 1725.
[886] Williams, Griffith. *A Sermon on Rev. XXII. 12.*
[887] Anon. *Antichristi excidium.*
[888] Anon. *The Kingdom of Christ and Antichrist: A Sermon on Rev. XVI. 1* (n. p.).

1668

[889] Hoffmann, Matthias. *Chronotaxis Apocalyptica Visionibus Apocalypticis Certas Terporum Periodos Assignans* (Jena). Another edition: 1687.
[890] Meliton (?). *Sur l'Apocalypse* (Paris).
[891] More, Henry. *The Two Last Dialogues Treating of the Kingdom of God within Us and without Us.*
[892] Roth, Eberhard Rudolf. *Dissertatio historico-theologica . . . in Apocalypsi cap. II. 15* (Jena). Tresley, p. 224.

1669

[893] Bunyan, John. *Holy City or New Jerusalem.*
[894] More, Henry. *An Exposition of the Seven Epistles to the Seven Churches.*

1670

[895] DuBosc, Pierre. *Les censure et la condamnation des tièdes, en deux sermons sur les paroles . . . dans l'Apocalypse* (Charenton).
[896] ——. *Les estoiles du ciel de l'église, ou sermon sur ces paroles de S. Jean en l'Apocalypse* (Charenton).
[897] Harbie, Thomas. *What Is Truth? Or, the Patern in the Mount.* Other editions: 1670, 1671, 1673, 1674, 1678, 1679.
[898] Lucius, Johann Andreas. *Die Offenbahrung . . . Johannis* (Dresden).
[899] Newton, Sir Isaac. 'Fragments for a Treatise on Revelation' (c. 1670), in Frank E. Manuel, *The Religion of Isaac Newton* (Oxford, 1974).
[900] Ranew, Nathaniel. *Account Concerning the Saint's Glory after the Resurrection.*
[901] Schindler, Johann. *Sacra Vaticinia de Ecclesiae Christianae statu; oder, Kurtze*

delineatio des gantzen Buches der offenbahrung S. Johannis (Braunschweig).
[902] von Rosenroth, Christian Knorr (A. B. Peganius). *Eigentlich erklarung uber die gesichte der offenbarung Ioannis* (Amsterdam?). Another edition: 1674. English translation: *A Genuine Explication of the Visions of the Book of Revelation*, tr. Henry Oldenburg (1670).

1671

[903] Bachou, Jean. *Démonstration du divin théorème de la quadrature du cercle, du mouvement perpétuel et du rapport de ce théorème avec la vision d'Ézéchiel, l'Apocalypse de St. Jean* (Paris).
[904] Sherwin, William. *A Scheme of the Whole Book of the Revelation*.
[905] Vincent, Nathaniel. *A Covert from the Storm . . . Rev. 2.10*.

1672

[906] Chrytillus, Julius. *Commentarius in Apocalypsim*. Tresley, p. 163.
[907] Danvers, Henry. *Theopolis, or the City of God, New Jerusalem, in Opposition to the City of the Nations, Great Babylon*.
[908] Penn, William. *The New Witnesses Proved Old Hereticks*.
[909] Sherwin, William. *Tracts Concerning the Millennium*.

1673

[910] Gate, Theophilus. *Discourse Concerning Christ's Second Coming*.
[911] Hooke, William. *The Priviledge of the Saints on Earth Beyond Those in Heaven*.

1674

[912] Dury, Durce. *A New Explication of the Apocalypse* (Frankfurt).
[913] Molin, Peter. *Two Sermons on Rev. XVIII. 4, 5*.
[914] Sherwin, William. *On the Revelations and the Millennium* (1674–6).
[915] Wingendorpius, Hermannus. *Conjecturae in Apocalypsin* (Leyden).

1675

[916] Burroughs, Jeremiah. *Jerusalem's Glory Breaking Forth into the World*.
[917] Bussières, Jean de. *In Apocalypsin S. Joannis Apostoli* (Lyon).
[918] Franklin, Richard. *A Discourse on Antichrist, and the Apocalypse*.
[919] Grellot, Antonius. *Prodromus in D. Joannis Apocalypsin* (Leiden).
[920] Hacket, John. *A Century of Sermons* [on Rev. VI. 9, VI. 10]. N. B. See esp. pp. 992–1002, 1003–13.
[921] Hayter, Richard. *The Meaning of Revelation*. Another edition: 1676.
[922] Sherwin, William. *Chronbi Apokatastaseos Panton or The Times of Restitution of All Things*.
[923] ——, *The Scheme of the Gods Eternal Greate Designe*.

1676

[924] Kircher, Heinrich. *Prophetia apocalyptica S. Joannes apostoli accuratè, breviter, & clarè explanata* (Cologne).
[925] Mayer, Ulrich. *Oratio . . . Apoc. 12* (Leipzig).
[926] Poole, Matthew. *Synopsis Criticorum aliorumque Sacrae Scripturae Interpretum*. N. B. See vol. V, cols. 1659–2022.

[927] Sherwin, William. *The Saints First Revealed and Covenanted Mercies Shortly Approaching.*
[928] Smith, Thomas. *Septem Asiae ecclesiarum notitia.*
[929] Anon. *The Apocalyps Unveyl'd; or a Paraphrase on the Revelation . . . In Which the Synchronisms of . . . Mede Are Called into Question.*

1677

[930] Allen, William. *The Mystery of the Temple and the City.*
[931] Groenewegen, Henricus, *Sleuted der prophetien, ofte, Uitlegginge, van de openbaringe des Apostels Joannis,* 2 vols (n. p.).
[932] Marolles, Michel de. *Tradvction en vers de l'Apocalypse de saint Jean apostre* (Paris).
[933] Nicolai, Michael. *In Apocalypsim* (Copenhagen). Tresley, p. 209.
[934] Pictet, Benedict. *Dissertationes . . . Malach. 4.2 . . . Apoc. 2.17* (Leiden). Tresley, p. 218.
[935] Wirtz, Johannes. *Romae animale exemplum; oder Römisches contrafait apocalypdischen Figuren und Erklärungs-Gesprachen über dieselbigen fürgestelt* (n. p.). Tresley, p. 238. N. B. The commentary is an adaptation of Bullinger.

1678

[936] Brecklingius, Fridericus. *Compendium Apocalypseos referatae* (n. p.).
[937] Cock, William. *Revela[tio] revela[ta],* sive Apocalypsis Johannis theologi modo antehac incognito [*ex*]*plicata, vbi omnia eius operta sunt jam aperta* (Edinburgh).
[938] Lopez, Gregorio. *Vida, y escritos del venerable . . . Lopez* (Madrid).
[939] Phelpes, Charles. *A Commentary: or, an Exposition with Notes on the Five First Chapters of the Revelation of Jesus Christ.*
[940] Wilsius, Hermannus. *Diatribe de septem epistolarum Apocalypticarum sensu historico an prophetico* (Franeker, 1678). Another edition: 1692.

1679

[941] Knollys, Hanserd. *An Exposition of the Eleventh Chapter of the Revelation.*
[942] Kregel, John. *Vision and Prophecy.*
[943] ——. *Mystical Babylon Unvailed.*
[944] Ness, Christopher. *A Discovery of the Person and Period of Antichrist.*
[945] Nigrinus, Georgius. *Pugna ac victoria Michaëlis cum dracone, Apoc. 12.9* (Wittenberg). Tresley, p. 227.
[946] Anon. *Eigentliche Erklärung über die Offenbahrung S. Johannis* (n. p.).

1680

[947] Garret, Walter. *A Discourse Concerning Antichrist.*
[948] Hill, John. *The Grand Apostacy of the Church of Rome . . ., on Rev. XVIII. 4* (n. p.).
[949] More, Henry. *Apocalypsis apocalypseos; or, The Revelation of St. John the Divine unveiled.*
[950] Ramsey, William. *The Lord of Rome the Antichrist.*
[951] Anon. *The Full and Final Proof of the Plot from the Revelations.*

1681

[952] Durham, James. *The Blessednesse of the Death of These That Die in the Lord.*
[953] Hooke, William. *A Discourse Concerning the Witnesses.*
[954] Lead, Jane. *Revelation of Revelations.* Other editions: 1683, 1701.

[955] More, Henry. *A Plaine and Continued Exposition of the Several Prophecies.*
[956] Orme, William. *The Best Guide in the Worst Times.*

1682
[957] Balthazar, Augustinus. *Disputatio de prisca haeresi Nico laitum Apo. 2: 15* (Greifswald). Tresley, p. 150.
[958] Bunyan, John. *The Holy War.*
[959] Drelincourt, Laurent. *Les étoiles de l'Église . . . ou sermon sur l'Apocalypse* (Leiden).
[960] Keach, Benjamin. *Troposchemalogia: Tropes and Figures . . . in the Old and New Testaments.*
[961] Mulerius, Nicolaus. *Exegesis in posteriora capita Apocalypseos* (Hardewijk).
[962] Woodhead, Abraham. *The Apocalyps Paraphrased.*

1683
[963] Abbadie, Jacques. *Sermon sur ces paroles de l'Apocalypse* (Cologne).
[964] Clarke, Samuel. *The New Testament with Annotations.*
[965] Cradock, Samuel. *A Brief and Plain Exposition and Paraphrase of the Whole Book of the Revelation.* Another edition: 1696.
[966] Goodwin, Thomas. *An Exposition of Revelation*, in *Works*. Another edition: 1842. N. B. this commentary derives from lectures delivered in Holland in 1639.

1684
[967] Baxter, Richard. *A Paraphrase on the New Testament.*
[968] Beverley, Thomas. *A Scripture-Line of Time, Drawn in Brief from the Lapsed Creation to the Restitution of All Things* (n. p.). Another edition: 1692.
[969] Burnet, Thomas. *The Theory of the Earth*, 2 vols (1684–90).
[970] Funck, John. *Future State of the Church.*
[971] Herveus, Daniel. *Apocalypsis Joannis Apostoli explanatio historica* (Lyon).
[972] Mulerius, Nicolaus. *Vaticinia Pathmi elucidata; sive revelationum propheticarum divinae Apocalypseos Ioannis explicatio* (Hardewijk).
[973] Pasch, Johann. *De numero bestiae Apocalypseos* (Wittenberg).
[974] Sandhagen, Caspar Hermann. *Synoptica introductio in Historiam Jesu Christi & Apostolorum, ut & nexum Prophetiae Novi Testamenti juxta temporum seriem è . . . Apocalypsi considerandum* (Luneburg). Another edition: 1688. Tresley, p. 226.
[975] Anon. *An Answer to Several Remarks upon Dr Henry More.* Tresley, p. 128.

1685
[976] Possinus, Petrus. *Apocalypsis Enarratio* (Toulouse). Tresley, p. 218.
[977] Anon. *An Illustration of Those Two Abstruse Books in Holy Scripture . . . Framed Out of the Expositions of Dr Henry More.*
[978] Anon. *Paralipomena prophetica; Containing Several Supplements and Defences of Dr H. More; His Expositions of the Prophet Daniel and the Apocalypse.*
[979] Anon. *Some Cursory Reflections Impartially Made upon Mr R. Baxter His Way of Writing Notes on the Apocalypse.*

1686
[980] Jurieu, Pierre. *L'accomplissement des propheties, ou la Delivrance prochaine de l'Eglise* (Rotterdam). Tresley, p. 197. English translation: *The Accomplishment of the Scripture Prophecies* (1687). Another edition: 1793.

[981] Mather, Increase. *A Discourse about the Day of Judgment* (Boston).

1687

[982] Beverley, Thomas. *The Grand Apocalyptical Vision of the Witnesses Slain.*
[983] Heidegger, Johann Heinrich. *In Divi Johannis Theologi Apocalypseos prophetiam de Babylone magna diatribae* (Leiden).
[984] Jansen, Hendrik. *Erklaerung der Offenbarung Johannis* (Amsterdam).
[985] Philipot, Jacques. *Eclaircissements sur l'Apocalypse* (Amsterdam). English translation: *A New Systeme of the Apocalypse* (1688).

1688

[986] Amelotte, D. *Le Nouveau Testament traduit sur l'ancienne édition*, 2 vols (Paris). Tresley, pp. 126–7.
[987] Beverley, Thomas. *The Command of God to His People to Come out of Babylon, Revel. 18.4.*
[988] Wesel, Henric van. *Verklaarung over de openbarung Enkhuisen.*
[989] Anon. *A Modest Inquiry into the Meaning of the Revelations.*

1689

[990] Allen, William. *A Discourse of the Nature, Series, and Order of Occurrences, as They Are Prophetically Represented in the 11 Chap. of the Revelation.*
[991] Atwood, William. *Wonderful Predictions of Nostredamus, Grebnar, and David Pareus.*
[992] Basonage. *L'Apocalypse* (n. p.).
[993] Beverley, Thomas. *The Kingdom of Jesus Christ Entering Its Succession at 1697* (n. p.).
[994] ———. *The Late Revolution to Be Applied to the Spirit Now Moving in the Fulfilling of All Prophecy.*
[995] ———. *The Prophectical History of the Reformation; or the Reformation to Be Reform'd.*
[996] Bossuet, Jacques Benigne. *L'Apocalypse avec une explication* (Paris).
[997] Cressener, Drue. *Judgements of God on the Roman Catholic Church . . . in Explication of the Trumpets and Vials in the Apocalypse.*
[998] Epiphanius de Moirana. *Clavis Apocalypseos, futura reserans Prophetarum* (c. 1689). Tresley, p. 172.
[999] Keach, Benjamin. *Antichrist Stormed; or Mystery, Babylon, the Great Whore, and Great City, Proved to Be the Present Church of Rome.*
[1000] ———. *The Pattern of the Divine Temple.*
[1001] Knollys, Hanserd. *An Exposition of the Whole Book of the Revelation.*
[1002] Marck, John. *In Apocalypsin Johannis commentarius*, 2 vols (Amsterdam). Another edition: 1699.
[1003] Patticks, Dr. *A Hymn out of . . . Revelation* (n. p.).
[1004] Anon. *Rome's Downfal; Wherein Is Shewed That the Beginnings Thereof Call for Praise and Thanksgiving.*

1690

[1005] Aubert, Nöel. *La Véritable clef de l'Apocalypse* (Cologne).
[1006] Beverley, Thomas. *The Catechism of the Kingdom of Our Lord Jesus Christ in the Thousand Years.*

[1007] Bossuet, Jacques Benigne. *Reflections sur l'explication de l'Apocalypse de M. de Meaux* (Amsterdam).

[1008] Butler, John. *Bellua Marina; or an Historical Description of the Papal Empire, as Originally Copied out of the Prophecies.*

[1009] Cressener, Drue. *A Demonstration of the First Principles of the Protestant Applications of the Apocalypse.*

[1010] Garret, Walter. *An Essay upon the Fourth and Fifth Chapters of the Revelation.* Another edition: 1698.

[*1011] Johannes de Ruprescissa. *Visiones seu Revelations.* Tresley, p. 195.

[1012] Necseus, Stephanus Ungarus. *Analytica D. Johannis Apostoli Apocalypseos paraphrasis* (Franeker).

[1013] Thomas Garzia de Villanova Oesa. *Expositio in Apocalypsim* (Antwerp). Tresley, p. 231. This commentary was written sometime before 1555.

[1014] Anon. *Remarks on Dr H. More's Expositions of the Apocalypse and Daniel.*

1691

[1015] Beverley, Thomas. *An Appeal Most Humble, Yet Most Earnestly, by the Coming of Our Lord Jesus Christ, and Our Gathering Together unto Him.*

[1016] ———. *The Thousand Year Kingdom of Christ in Its Free Scripture State.*

[1017] ———. *The Universal Christian Doctrine of the Day of Judgment: Applied to the Doctrine of the Thousand Years Kingdom of Christ.*

[1018] Boyer, Pierre. *La condamnation de Babylon . . . sur l'Apocalypse* (The Hague).

[1019] Funck, Christian David. *Dissertatio de calculo albo Apoc. 2: 17* (Leipzig).

[1020] Kleschius, D. *Schema septem candelabrum* (n. p.).

[1021] Mulerius, Nicolaus. *Exercitationes in Apocalypsin* (Hardewijk).

[1022] Pfeifferus, Augustus. *Antichiliasmus* (Lubec).

1692

[1023] Beverley, Thomas. *A Sermon upon Revel. 11.11 & c.*

[1024] Chetardie, Joachim. *L'Apocalypse expliquée par l'histoire ecclesiastique* (Paris).

[1025] Dent, Edward. *Everlasting Blessedness.*

[1026] Lee, Samuel. *A Summons or Warning to the Great Day of Judgment* (Boston).

[1027] Peterson, John W. *A Scriptural Exposition and Demonstration of the Millennarian Reign* (Frankfurt).

1693

[1028] Beverley, Thomas. *A Fresh Memorial of the Kingdom of Christ.*

[1029] Helmont, Franciscus Mercurius vonn. *Quarstiones aliquot in apocalypsin* (Leiden). English translation: *Seder Olam: . . . To Which Is Now Annexed Some Explanatory Questions of the Book of the Revelations,* tr. J. Clark (1694).

[1030] Melchoir, Johannes. *Dialogi Apocalyptic & quaestiones miscellanae in Apocalypsin* (Herborn). Tresley, p. 205.

[1031] Petto, Samuel. *The Revelation Unvailed.*

[1032] Waple, Edward. *The Book of the Revelation Paraphrased; with Annotations on Each Chapter.* Other editions: 1694, 1715.

1694

[1033] Beverley, Thomas. *A Discourse on the Powers of the World to Come.*

[1034] ——. *The Great Chapter for the Interpretation of Prophecy* (n. p.).
[1035] Clieu, Jean-Baptiste. *Le système du nouvel univers de l'Apocalypse*, 8 vols (Paris, 1694–1701).
[1036] Eskuche, Johann. *Miscellanea sacra maximam partem prophetica* (Emden). Tresley, p. 172.

1695
[1037] Beckmann, Johann Christoph. *Dissertatio de Angelo Goale, seu vindice . . . Apocal. 19: 25* (Frankfurt). Tresley, p. 152.
[1038] Bernard, Jean. *Sermon sur le verset 5 du second chapitre de l'Apocalypse* (Amsterdam).
[1039] Bull, Digby. *A Letter of a Protestant Clergyman to the Reverend Clergy . . . Advertising Them . . . the Sacred Revelation of St. John.*
[1040] Gebhardi, Brandamus Heinrich. *Apocalypsis 20: 8–9* (Greifswald).
[1041] ——. *Epistola ad amicum de Resurrectione prima, Apoc. 5–6.*

1696
[1042] Brunsmand, Johan. *Phospherus Apocalypticus* (Copenhagen). Another edition: 1699.
[1043] Gebhardi, Brandamus Heinrich. *Isagoge ad apocalypsin divi Ioannis apostoli* (Greifswald). Another edition: 1697.
[1044] Koch, Christopher. *Regnum Chiliasticum funditus deletum* (Leipzig). English translation: *New Divine and Heavenly Revelation Respecting the Millennial Kingdom* (1697).
[1045] ——. *Chiliasta plagiarius* (n. p., 1696?).
[1046] Lomeier, Johannes. *Exercitationes tres de septem sigillis Apocalypticis* (Zuften). Tresley, p. 201.
[1047] Peterson, Johanna Eleonora von. *Anleitung zu gründlicher Verständniss der Heiligen offenbahrung Jesu Christi* (Frankfurt).
[1048] Whiston, William. *A New Theory of the Earth, from Its Original, to the Consummation of All Things.*
[1049] Anon. *Gus Gottes Wort genommene, und nach demselben eingerichtete Meinung, was wol in der Offenbahrung Johannis Cap. XIV, 8. und Cap. XVIII, 1. 2. 3.* (n. p.).

1697
[1050] Fecht, Johann. *De Apocalypseos Johannis auctoritate* (Rostock). Tresley, p. 193.
[1051] Schroeder, Gustav. *Quod apocalypsis ad Joannem* (Rostock).
[1052] Sewall, Samuel. *Phaenomena Quaedam Apocalyptica* (Boston).
[1053] Winckler, John. *A Thorough Investigation of the XXth Chapter of the Revelation* (n. p.).

1698
[1054] Addison, Lancelot. *An Account of the Millennium.*
[1055] Garret, Walter. *Decimum Caput Apocalypseos: sive Reformatio Anglicana.*
[1056] ——. *De vera ecclesia hodierna Spiritus . . .: sive quarti quintique Apocalypseos capitum interpretatio paraphrastica.*
Hanneman, John. *Comment. in cap. VIII. 5, Apocalypseos* (Frankfurt).
Heunisch, Johann Friedrich. *Clavis universalis Apocalypseos* (Frankfurt).

1699

[1057] Beverley, Thomas. *Reflections upon the Theory of the Earth.*
[1058] Garret, Walter. *A Persuasive to the Study of the Revelations.*
[1059] ——. *Paraphrase upon the First Chapter of the Revelation.*
[1060] Lead, Jane. *Signs of the Times.*
[1061] ——. *The Ascent to the Mount of Vision.*
[1062] Muggleton, Lodowick. *The Acts of the Witnesses of the Spirit.*
[1063] Stanhope, George. *The Happiness of Good Men After Death.*
[1064] Anon. *A Short Survey of the Kingdom of Christ Here on Earth.*
[1065] Anon. *The Mysteries of God Finished: or an Essay toward the Opening of the Mystery of the Mystical Numbers in the Scripture.*

3 1700 TO THE PRESENT

1700

[1066] Garret, Walter. *A New Method of Demonstrating that Rome Christianity is the Woman called Babylon, in the XVII. chap. Rev.*
[1067] Anon. *Eclectical chiliasm; or, a Discourse Concerning the State of Things from the Beginning of the Millennium to the End of the World.*

1701

[1068] Fleming, Robert. *Discourses on Several Subjects. The First Containing a New Account of the Rise and Fall of Papacy.*
[1069] Garret, Walter. *The Usefulness of the Study of Revelation.*
[1070] La Chětardi, Joachim Trotti de. *L'Apocalypse expliquée, par l'histoire ecclésiastique* (Paris).

1702

[1071] Freke, William. *The New Jerusalem . . . Rev. ch. 21, & 22.*
[1072] Garret, Walter. *Exposition of the VIth, VIIth, IXth and XIth Chapters of the Revelation* (1702–03).

1704

[1073] Worthington, John. 'Observations Concerning the *Millennium* and Other Passages in the *Apocalypse*', in *Miscellanies*.

1705

[1074] Vitringa, Campegius. Ἀνάκρισις *Apocalypseos Joannis Apostoli* (Frankfurt).

1706

[1075] Whiston, William. *An Essay on the Revelation of St. John, so far as Concerns the Past and Present Times* (Cambridge).

1707

[1076] Allix, Peter. *The Prophecies Which Mr Whiston Applies to the Times.*
[1077] Lacy, John. *Prophetical Warnings.*

1708

[1078] Cromarty, George MacKenzie. *Synopsis Apocalyptica* (Edinburgh).

1717
[1079] Whiston, William. *Astronomical Principles of Religion Natural and Revealed.*

1720
[1080] Daubuz, Charles. *A Perpetual Commentary on the Revelation of St. John.*
[1081] Rogers, John. *The Book of the Revelation of Jesus Christ* (Boston).

1723
[1082] Abbadie, Jacques. *Le Triomphe de la Providence et de la religion* (Amsterdam).
[1083] Edwards, Jonathan. *Notes on the Apocalypse,* in *The Works of Jonathan Edwards: Apocalyptic Writings,* ed. Stephen J. Stein (New Haven, 1977), pp. 97–305.

1730
[1084] Abauzit, Firmin. *A Discourse Historical and Critical on the Revelations Ascribed to John.*
[1085] Robertson, James. καινά και παλαία; *Things New and Old, or an Exposition of the Book of Revelation* (Edinburgh).

1733
[1086] Newton, Sir Isaac. *Observations upon the Prophecies of Daniel, and the Apocalypse of St. John.*

1735
[1087] Pyle, Thomas. *A Paraphrase with Notes on the Revelation of St. John.*

1737
[1088] Lowman, Moses. *A Paraphrase and Notes on the Revelation of St. John.*

1739
[1089] Anon. *A Defense of Natural and Revealed Religion: Being a Collection of the Sermons Preached at the Lecture funded by . . . Robert Boyle . . . (from the year 1691 to the year 1732),* 3 vols.

1741
[1090] Anon. *Apocalyptica cabbala: or a History of the Millennium.*

1747
[1091] Edwards, Jonathan. *An Humble Attempt,* in *The Works of Jonathan Edwards: Apocalyptic Writings,* ed. Stephen J. Stein (New Haven, 1977), pp. 309–436.

1749
[1092] Clayton, Robert. *A Dissertation on Prophecy, Wherein the Coherence and Connexion of the Prophecies in Both the Old and New Testaments Are Fully Considered.*

1755
[1093] Saint Clair, J. *Observations on Certain Passages in the Apocalypse . . . Containing . . . a Defence of Sir Isaac Newton's General Interpretation.*

1757

[1094] Bengel, Johann A. *Bengelius's Introduction to His Exposition of the Apocalypse*, tr. John Robertson. N. B. This commentary was first published in German in 1740.

1758

[1095] Swedenborg, Emanuel. *De equo albo de quo Apocalypsi, cap. XIX*.

[1096] ———. *De ultimo judicio, et de Babylonia destructa* (n. p.). N. B. This commentary was translated into English in 1788 and published under the title, *A Treatise Concerning the Last Judgement and the Destruction of Babylon*.

1759

[1097] Newton, Thomas. *Dissertations on the Prophecies, Which Have Remarkably Been Fulfill'd, and at This Time Are Fulfilling in the World*, 2nd ed, 3 vols. N. B. The dates for the first edition are 1754–8.

1763

[1098] Taylor, Lauchlan. *An Essay on the Revelation of the Apostle John*.

1766

[1099] Swedenborg, Emanuel. *Apocalypsis revelata in qua deteguntur arcana quae ibi praedicta sunt, et hactenus recondita latuerunt* (Amsterdam). N. B. This commentary was translated in 1791 by Nathaniel Tucker and published under the title, *The Apocalypse Revealed*.

1771

[1100] Walmesley, Charles. *The General History of the Church . . . Chiefly Deduced from the Apocalypse* (n. p.).

1772

[1101] Hurd, Richard. *An Introduction to the Study of the Prophecies*, Warburton Lecture.

1774

[1102] Langdon, Samuel. *A Rational Explication of St. John's Vision of the Two Beasts, in the XIIth Chapter of the Revelation* (Portsmouth).

1776

[1103] Gill, John. *An Exposition of the Revelation of S. John the Divine*.
[1104] Hallifax, Samuel. *Twelve Sermons on the Prophecies*, Warburton Lecture.
[1105] Pothier, Remi. *Ouvrage sur l'Apocalypse*, 2 vols (Cologne).

1778

[1106] Murray, James. *Lectures upon the Book of the Revelation*, 2 vols (Newcastle).

1779

[1107] Backmair, John. *The Revelation of St. John Historically Explained and Compiled* (n. p.).

1780

[1108] Bagot, Lewis. *Twelve Discourses on the Prophecies*, Warburton Lecture (Oxford).

[1109] Bray, Thomas Wells. *A Dissertation on the Sixth Vial* (Hartford).
[1110] Lavater, Johann Casper. *Jesus Messias . . . Nach der Offenbarung Johannes* (Zurich).

1781
[1111] Lawrie, John. *The Completion of Prophecy* (Edinburgh).

1785
[1112] Reader, Thomas. *Remarks on the Three First Chapters of the Revelation of St. John* (Taunton).
[1113] Swedenborg, Emanuel. *Apocalypsis explicata secundum sensum spiritualem*. N. B. This commentary was translated by William Hill in 1811 and published under the title, *The Apocalypse Explained*.
[1114] Vivian, Thomas. *The Book of the Revelation of Saint John the Divine Explained* (Plymouth).
[1115] Anon. *A Key to the Mystery of the Revelation*.

1786
[1116] Apthorp, East. *Discourses on Prophecy*, Warburton Lecture, 2 vols.

1787
[1117] Bowdler, Henrietta Maria. *Practical Observations on the Book of the Revelation*.
[1118] Moody, Robert. *Observations on Certain Prophecies in the Book of Daniel, and the Revelation of St. John*.
[1119] Wood, Hans. *The Revelation of St. John*.

1789
[1120] Cooke, William. *The Revelations Translated, and Explained throughout, with Keys*.
[1121] Purves, James. *Observations on the Visions of the Apostle John*, 2 vols (Edinburgh, 1789–93).

1790
[1122] Anon. *A Paraphrase, Notes, and Observations, upon the Revelation of St. John*.

1791
[1123] Eichorn, Johann Gottfried. *Commentarius in Apocalypsin Johannis* (Göttingen).
[1124] Langdon, Samuel. *Observations on the Revelation of Jesus Christ to St. John* (Worcester, Mass.).

1793
[1125] Anon. *Prophetic Conjectures on the French Revolution, and Other Recent and Shortly Expected Events*.

1794
[1126] Bicheno, James. *The Signs of the Times: or, the Overthrow of the Papal Tyranny in France*, 4th (much enlarged) edn.
[1127] Garnham, Robert Edward. *Outline of a Commentary on Revelations I. 1–14*.
[1128] Johnston, Bryce. *A Commentary on the Revelation of St. John*, 2 vols (Edinburgh).
[1129] Osgood, Samuel. *Remarks on the Book of Daniel and on the Revelations* (New York).

[1130] Priestley, Joseph. *Present State of Europe, Compared with Ancient Prophecies.*
[1131] Winchester, Elehanan. *The Three Woe Trumpets* (Boston).
[1132] Winthrop, James. *An Attempt to Translate the Prophetic Part of the Apocalypse of Saint John into Familiar Language* (Boston).
[1133] Anon. *Conjectures on the Prophecies of Daniel and the Apocalypse . . . as They Appear to respect Russia, Germany, England, France, & c.*

1795
[1134] Paine, Thomas. *The Age of Reason.*
[1135] Pirie, Alexander. *The French Revolution Exhibited, in the Light of the Sacred Oracles* (Perth).
[1136] Whitaker, Edward. *A General and Connected View of the Prophecies Relating to the Times of the Gentiles* (Egham).
[1137] Winthrop, James. *A Systematic Argument of Several Scriptural Prophecies Relating to Antichrist* (Boston).

1796
[1138] Gilbert, E. *Reflection sur L'Apocalypse* (Guernsey).
[1139] Levi, David. *Dissertations on the Prophecies*, 3 vols (1796–1800).
[1140] Winchester, Elhanan. *A Defence of Revelation, in Ten Letters to Thomas Paine.*
[1141] Anon. *Illustrations of Prophecy, Together with Extracts from Mede.*

1798
[1142] Amner, Richard. *Considerations . . . on the Prophecies of Daniel and St John.*
[1143] Baggs, John. *A Scriptural View of the Millennium.*
[1144] Rosell, Manuel. *Reglas y observaciones para entender las Santas Escrituras, especialimente el libro del Apocalipsis escrito par San Juan* (Madrid).
[1145] Wrangham, Francis. *Rome Is Fallen! A Sermon* (York).

1799
[1146] Curtius, Henricus. *Specimen hermeneutics-theologicum de apocalypsi* (n. p.).
[1147] Faber, George Stanley. *An Attempt to Explain Five of the Seven Vials.*
[1148] Osgood, David. *The Devil Let Loose* (Boston).
[1149] Snodgrass, John. *A Commentary, with Notes, on Part of the Book of the Revelation* (Paisley).

1800
[1150] Hurdis, James. *Twelve Dissertations on the Nature and Occasion of Psalm and Prophecy.*
[1151] Mitchell, John. *The First Part of a New Exposition of the Revelation*, 4 vols (1800–1).

1801
[1152] Bicheno, James. *The Destiny of the German Empire; or an Attempt to Ascertain the Apocalyptic Dragon.*

1802
[1153] Evanson, Edward. *Reflections upon the State of Religion in Christendom* (Exeter).
[1154] Galloway, Joseph. *Brief Commentaries upon Such Parts of the Revelation and Other*

[1197] Frere, James Hartley. *On the General Structure of the Apocalypse.*
[1198] Irving, Edward. *Babylon and Infidelity Foredoomed of God: A Discourse on the Prophecies of Daniel and the Apocalypse* (Glasgow).
[1199] Maitland, Samuel R. *An Inquiry into . . . Daniel and St. John.*

1827
[1200] Brown, John Aquila. *The Jew, the Master-Key of the Apocalypse.*
[1201] Croly, George. *The Apocalypse of St. John . . . the Revolution in France . . . the Final Triumph of Christianity.*
[1202] Drummond, Henry. *Dialogues on Prophecy*, 3 vols (1827–9).

1828
[1203] Cuninghame, William. *A Summary View of the Scriptural Argument for the Second and Glorious Advent of Messiah* (Glasgow).
[1204] Drummond, Henry. *A Defense of the Students of Prophecy.*
[1205] Faber, George Stanley. *The Sacred Calendar of Prophecy: or a Dissertation on the Prophecies.*
[1206] Tudor, John. 'On the Structure of the Apocalypse', in *Papers Read before the Society for the Investigation of Prophecy*, pp. 1–22.
[1207] Anon. *The Nature of the First Resurrection . . . with . . . Extracts from Mr. Mede.*

1829
[1208] Cuninghame, William. *A Critical Examination of Some of the Fundamental Principles of the Rev. George Stanley Faber's Sacred Calendar of Prophecy.*
[1209] Evill, Thomas. *The Apocalypse of St John.*
[1210] Leifchild, J. *A Help to the Private . . . Reading of the . . . Scriptures; . . . Including . . . an Analysis of Mr. Mede's Scheme of the Apocalypse.*
[1211] Anon. *The Apocalypse of Jesus Christ, Briefly, yet Minutely, Explained and Interpreted.*

1830
[1212] Drummond, Henry. 'Popular Introduction to the Study of Apocalypse', in *Christian Observer* (March, 1830), 129–42.
[1213] Jones, William. *Lectures on the Apocalypse.*
[1214] Todd, James H. *Discourses on the Prophecies Relating to Anti-christ* (Dublin).

1831
[1215] Cuninghame, William. *Strictures on Certain Leading Positions and Interpretations of the Rev. Edward Irving's Lectures on the Apocalypse* (Glasgow).
[1216] Frere, James Hartley. *Eight Letters on the Prophecies Relating to the Last Times.*
[1217] Irving, Edward. *Exposition of the Book of Revelation, in a Series of Lectures*, 4 vols.
[1218] Anon., *Investigator, or Quarterly Exposition on Prophecy* (1831–5).

1832
[1219] Bush, George. *A Treatise on the Millennium* (New York).

1833
[1220] Cooper, Robert Bronsby. *Commentary on the Revelation of St. John . . . by a*

Follower of the Learned Joseph Mede. N. B. This volume contains a translation of Mede's *Clavis Apocalyptica*.
[1221] Frere, James Hartley. *Three Lectures on the Prophecies*.
[1222] Robertson, David. *Discourses Shewing the Structure and Unity of the Apocalypse* (Glasgow).
[1223] Smith, Ethan. *Key to the Revelation* (New York).
[1224] Waugh, John S. *Dissertations on the Prophecies of Sacred Scripture* (Annan).

1834
[1225] Roe, Richard. *Analytical Arrangement of the Apocalypse* (Dublin).

1841
[1226] Bickersteth, Edward. *Practical Guide to the Prophecies* (Philadelphia).

1845
[1227] Faber, George Stanley. *Eight Dissertations . . . on Prophetical Passages*.
[1228] Stuart, Moses. *Commentary on the Apocalypse* (Andover).

1846
[1229] Frere, James Hartley. *The Harvest of the Earth Prior to the Vintage of Wrath*.
[1230] Anon. 'The Structure of the Apocalypse', in *Christian Observer* (February, 1846), 65–70.

1848
[1231] Frere, James Hartley. *The Great Continental Revolution Marking the Expiration of the Times of the Gentiles*.

1849
[1232] Cumming, John. *Apocalyptic Sketches; or Lectures on the Book of Revelation*.
[1233] Lee, S. *An Inquiry into the Nature, Progress, and End of Prophecy*. N. B. A note explains the volume is concerned with 'the principles of prophetic interpretation generally, and of those of Mr. Mede . . . in particular'.
[1234] Maitland, C. D. *The Apostles' School of Prophetic Interpretation*.
[1235] Wordsworth, Christopher. *The Apocalypse*.

1850
[1236] Hengstenberg, Ernst Wilhelm. *The Revelation of St. John*, tr. Patrick Fairbairn, 2 vols (Edinburgh, 1850–1).

1852
[1237] Elliott, Edward Bishop. *Horae Apocalypticae: or, a Commentary on the Apocalypse, Critical and Historical*, 5th ed, 4 vols. N. B. The first edition appeared in 1844.
[1238] Williams, Isaac. *The Apocalypse*.

1853
[1239] Maitland, Samuel R. *An Attempt to Elucidate the Prophecies Concerning Antichrist*.

1854
[1240] Baldwin, S. D. *Armageddon: or the Overthrow of Romanism and Monarchy; the*

Existence of the United States Foretold in the Bible, rev. ed. (Cincinnati and Nashville).
[1241] Graves, R. *An Analysis of the Revelations, Chiefly Founded on the Commentaries of J. Mede.*

1855
[1242] Cumming, John. *The End: or, the Proximate Signs of the Close of This Dispensation* (Boston).
[1243] Keith, Alexander. *The Harmony of Prophecy; or, Scriptural Illustrations of the Apocalypse* (New York).

1859
[1244] Faber, George Stanley. *Napolean III: Man of Prophecy* (New York).

1860
[1245] Hennell, Sara. *The Early Christian Anticipation of an Approaching End of the World, and Its Bearing upon the Character of Christianity as a Divine Revelation.*
[1246] Kelly, W. *The Revelation of St. John.*

1861
[1247] Call, W. M. W. 'The Apocalypse', in *Westminster Review* (October, 1861), 448–87.
[1248] Desprez, Philip S. *John, or the Apocalypse of the New Testament.*
[1249] Govert, Robert. *The Apocalypse Expounded by Scriptures*, 4 vols (1861–5).
[1250] Maurice, Frederick Denison. *Lectures on the Apocalypse* (Cambridge).

1863
[1251] Baxter, Michael P. *Louis Napolean, the Destined Monarch of This World*, 4th ed (Philadelphia).

1864
[1252] Davidson, Samuel. 'The Apocalypse of St. John', in *National Review* (April, 1864), 311–55.

1865
[1253] Fairbairn, Patrick. *Prophecy Viewed in Its Distinctive Nature, Its Special Function, and Proper Interpretation*, 2nd ed (Edinburgh). N. B. The first edition appeared in 1856.

1868
[1254] Grosart, Alexander B. *Key-bearer and the Opened Door* (Edinburgh).

1874
[1255] Lange, John Peter. *Revelation*, in *A Commentary on the Holy Scriptures*, X (New York).

1875
[1256] Bleek, Friedrich. *Lectures on the Apocalypse*, ed. L. T. Hossbach.

1877
[1257] Anon. *Apocalyptic Symbols and Figures Briefly Defined.*

188–
[1258] Baxter, Michael P. *Forty Coming Wonders . . . in Fulfillment of the Prophecies of Daniel and Revelation*, 5th edn.

1881
[1259] Seiss, Joseph Augustus. *The Apocalypse: A Series of Special Lectures*, 2 vols (Philadelphia).

1892
[1260] Shilling, G. J. *The Book of Revelation: Its Purpose and Structure* (New York).

1895
[1261] Milligan, William. *The Book of Revelation*, in *The Expositor's Bible* (New York).
[1262] Rossetti, Christiana G. *The Face of the Deep: A Devotional Commentary on the Apocalypse*.

1896
[1263] Bousset, Wilhelm. *Die Offenbarung Johannis* (Göttingen).

1900
[1264] Benson, Edward White. *The Apocalypse, an Introductory Study . . . Being a Presentment of the Structure of the Book* (London and New York).
[1265] Selwyn, Edward Carus. *The Christian Prophets and the Prophetic Apocalypse*.

1903
[1266] Palmer, Frederic. *The Drama of the Apocalypse* (New York).

1904
[1267] Ramsay, W. M. *The Letters to the Seven Churches . . . and Their Place in the Plan of the Apocalypse*.

1905
[1268] Hedges, Edwin Alvin. *The Epic of the Kingdom* (Cisco, Ill.).

1906
[1269] Swete, H. B. *Apocalypse of St. John*.

1912
[1270] Bird, Thomas Christopher. *Drama of the Apocalypse* (Boston).
[1271] Moulton, Richard G. *The Gospels, Epistles, and Revelation of St. John*.

1913
[1272] Charles, Robert Henry. *Studies in the Apocalypse* (Edinburgh).

1914
[1273] Boll, Franz. *Aus der Offenbarung Johannis* (Leipzig and Berlin).

1919
[1274] Case, Shirley Jackson. *The Revelation of John: A Historical Interpretation* (Chicago).

1920

[1275] Charles, Robert Henry. *Critical and Exegetical Commentary on the Revelation of St. John* (Edinburgh).

[1276] Levi, Eliphas. *The Mysteries of the Qabalah, or the Occult Argument of the Two Testaments, as Contained in the Prophecy of Ezekiel and the Apocalypse of St. John* (New York).

1921

[1277] Thomas, John. *Eureka: An Exposition of the Apocalypse*, 3 vols (Birmingham).

1922

[1278] Beckwith, I. *The Apocalypse of St. John* (New York).
[1279] Charles, Robert Henry. *Lectures on the Apocalypse.*
[1280] Welch, Adam Cleghorn. *Visions of the End: A Study in Daniel and Revelation.*

1931

[1281] Lawrence, D. H. *Apocalypse* (Florence).

1947

[1282] Claudel, Paul. *Introduction a l'Apocalypse* (Paris).

1949

[1283] Farrer, Austin. *A Rebirth of Images: The Making of St. John's Apocalypse* (Boston).

1951

[1284] Summers, Ray. *Worthy Is the Lamb: An Interpretation of Revelation* (Nashville).

1952

[1285] Claudel, Paul. *Interroge l'Apocalypse* (Paris).
[1286] Newbolt, M. R. *The Book of Unveiling: A Study of the Revelation.*

1957

[1287] Hoyt, Edyth Armstrong. *Studies in the Apocalypse of John of Patmos: A Non-Interpretative and Literary Approach*, 4th ed. (Columbus, Ohio). N. B. The first edition appeared in 1949.
[1288] Lilje, Hanns. *The Last Book of the Bible*, tr. Olive Wyan (Philadelphia).
[1289] Tenney, C. *Interpreting Revelation* (Grand Rapids, Mich.).

1958

[1290] Féret, H. M. *The Apocalypse of St. John*, tr. E. Corathiel (Paris).

1959

[1291] Torrance, Thomas F. *The Apocalypse Today.*

1961

[1292] Niles, D. T. *As Seeing the Invisible: A Study of the Book of Revelation* (New York).
[1293] Rist, Martin. *The Modern Reader's Guide to the Book of Revelation* (New York).

1964

[1294] Farrer, Austin. *The Revelation of St. John the Divine* (Oxford).

1965
[1295] Feuillet, André. *The Apocalypse*, tr. Thomas E. Crane (Staten Island, N.Y.).

1966
[1296] Caird, G. B. *The Revelation of St. John the Divine* (New York and Evanston).

1968
[1297] Bowman, John Wick. *The First Christian Drama* (Philadelphia).
[1298] Newman, Barclay M., Jr. *Rediscovering the Book of Revelation* (Valley Forge, Pa.).

1969
[1299] Morris, Leon. *Revelation: An Introduction and Commentary* (Leicester).

1971
[1300] Hobbs, Herschel H. *The Cosmic Drama* (Waco, Tex.).
[1301] Rousseau, François. *L'apocalypse et le milieu prophétique du Nouveau Testament: structoure et préhistoire du text* (Tournai).
[1302] Vanni, Ugo. *La struttura letteraria dell'Apocalisse* (Rome).

1974
[1303] Beasley-Murray, G. B. *The Book of Revelation*.
[1304] Constant, Alphonse Louis. *The Mysteries of the Qabalah*.
[1305] Prigent, Pierre. *Flash sur l'Apocalypse* (Neuchâtel).

1975
[1306] Ford, J. Massyngberde. *The Anchor Bible: Revelation* (Garden City, N. Y.).

1976
[1307] Strand, Kenneth Albert. *Interpreting the Book of Revelation: Hermeneutical Guidelines, with Brief Introduction to Literary Analysis* (Worthington, Ohio).

1977
[1308] Ellul, Jacques. *Apocalypse: The Book of Revelation*, tr. George W. Schreiner (New York).
[1309] Mounce, Robert H. *The Book of Revelation* (Grand Rapids, Mich.).
[1310] Rozanov, Vasily. *The Apocalypse of Our Time and Other Writings*, ed. Robert Payne (New York).

1978
[1311] Berrigan, Daniel. *Beside the Sea of Glass* (New York).

1979
[1312] Quispel, Gilles. *The Secret Book of Revelation* (New York).
[1313] Swete, John. *Revelation*.

II   ANCILLARY READING ON PROPHECY AND THE BOOK OF REVELATION

1   LITERATURE ON PROPHECY, ESPECIALLY WITH REFERENCE TO THE BOOK OF REVELATION

[1314] Ada, Michael. *Prophets of Rebellion: Millenarian Protestant Movements against the European Colonial Order* (Chapel Hill, 1979).

[1315] Alexander, Paul J. 'Medieval Apocalypses as Historical Sources', *American Historical Review*, 73 (1968), 1997–2018.

[1316] ——, 'The Medieval Legend of the Last Roman Emperor and Its Messianic Origin', *Journal of the Warburg and Courtauld Institutes*, 41 (1978), 1–15.

[1317] Anderson, Andrew R. *Alexander's Gate: Gog and Magog and the Enclosed Nations* (Cambridge, Mass., 1932).

[1318] Anon. *L'Apocalypse de Jean: Traditions exégétiques et iconographiques IIIe–XIIIe siècle* (Geneva, 1979).

[1319] Baille, John. *The Idea of Revelation in Recent Thought* (New York, 1956).

[1320] Baldwin, Edward Chauncey. *Types of Literature in the Old Testament* (New York, 1929).

[1321] Ball, Bryan W. *A Great Expectation: Eschatological Thought in English Protestantism to 1660* (Leiden, 1975).

[1321A] Barkun, Michael. *Disaster and the Millennium* (New Haven, 1974).

[1322] Bauckham, Richard. *Tudor Apocalypse: Sixteenth-Century Apocalypticism, Millennarianism and the English Reformation* (Appleford, Eng., 1978).

[1323] Bayly, Benjamin. *An Essay on Inspiration* (1708).

[1324] Becker, Carl. *The Heavenly City of the Eighteenth-Century Philosophers* (Ithaca, N. Y., 1932).

[1325] Bell, A. Robert. 'Muspilli: Apocalypse as Political Threat', *Studies in the Literary Imagination*, 8 (1975), 75–104.

[1326] Bellamy, H. S. *The Book of Revelation Is History* (1942).

[1327] Bernheim, Ernst. *Mittelalterliche Zeinanschauungen in ihrem Einfluss auf Politik und Geschichtsschreibung* (Tübingen, 1918).

[1328] Betz, H. D. 'On the Problem of Religio-Historical Understanding of Apocalypticism', *Journal for Theology and the Church*, 6 (1969), 134–56.

[1329] Bietenhard, Hans. 'The Millennial Hope in the Early Church', *Scottish Journal of Theology*, 6 (1953), 12–30.

[1330] Bloomfield, Morton W. 'Joachim of Flora: A Critical Survey of His Canon, Teachings, Sources, Biography, and Influence', *Traditio*, 13 (1957), 249–311.

[1331] ——, and Reeves, Marjorie. 'The Penetration of Joachimism in Northern Europe', *Speculum*, 19 (1954), 772–93.

[1332] Boettner, Louise. *The Millennium* (Philadelphia, 1958).

[1333] Boismard, M. E. 'L'Apocalypse ou "Les Apocalypses" de Saint Jean', *Revue Biblique*, 56 (1949), 507–41.

[1334] Bonner, Gerald. *Saint Bede in the Tradition of Western Apocalyptic Commentary* (Jarrow on Tyne, 1968).

[1335] Bousset, Wilhelm. *The Antichrist Legend: A Chapter in Christian and Jewish Folklore*, tr. A. H. Keane (1896).

[1336] Brady, David. 'The Number of the Beast in Seventeenth- and Eighteenth-Century England', *Evangelical Quarterly*, 45 (1973).

[1337] Brown, Louise. *The Political Activities of the Baptists and Fifth Monarchy Men in England during the Interregnum* (Washington, D. C., 1912).

[1338] Brueggemann, Walter. *The Prophetic Imagination* (Philadelphia, 1978).
[1339] Buber, Martin. 'Prophecy, Apocalyptic, and the Historical Hour', in *Pointing the Way* (1957), pp. 192-207.
[1340] ——. *The Prophetic Faith* (New York, 1949).
[1341] Bultmann, Rudolf. *History and Eschatology: The Presence of Eternity* (New York, 1962).
[1342] Burch, Vacher. *Anthropology and the Apocalypse* (1939).
[1343] Burkitt, Francis Crawford. *Jewish and Christian Apocalypses* (1914).
[1344] Burr, David. 'The Apocalyptic Element in Olivi's Critique of Aristotle', *Church History*, 40 (1971), 15-29.
[1345] Burrell, S. A. 'The Apocalyptic Vision of the Early Covenanters', *Scottish Historical Review*, 43 (1964), 1-24.
[1346] Burridge, Kenelm. *New Heaven, New Earth, A Study of Millenarian Activities* (Oxford and New York, 1969).
[1347] Cadman, Samuel Parkes. *The Prophets of Israel* (New York, 1933).
[1348] Capp, Bernard S. *Astrology and the Popular Press: English Almanacs 1500-1800* (Ithaca, N. Y., 1979).
[1349] ——. *The Fifth Monarchy Men: A Study in Seventeenth-Century English Millennarianism* (1972).
[1350] Carroll, Robert P. *When Prophecy Failed: Reactions and Responses to Failure in the Old Testament Prophetic Traditions* (1979).
[1351] Case, Shirley Jackson. *The Millennial Hope* (Chicago, 1918).
[1352] Chamberlain, Eric Russell. *Antichrist and the Millennium* (New York, 1975).
[1353] Charles, Robert Henry. *Eschatology: The Doctrine of a Future Life in Israel, Judaism and Christianity* (1899).
[1354] Christianson, Paul. *Reformers and Babylon: English Apocalyptic Visions from the Reformation to the Eve of the Civil War* (Toronto, 1977).
[1355] Clements, Ronald Ernest. *Prophecy and Tradition* (Oxford, 1975).
[1356] Clouse, Robert G. 'The Apocalyptic Interpretation of Thomas Brightman and Joseph Mede', *Journal of the Evangelical Society*, 11 (1968), 181-93.
[1357] ——. 'The Influence of John Harvey Alsted on English Millenarian Thought in the Seventeenth Century'. Ph. D. thesis, State Univ. of Iowa, 1963.
[1358] ——. 'Johann Heinrich Alsted and English Millennialism', *Harvard Theological Review*, 62 (1969), 189-207.
[1359] ——. 'John Napier and Apocalyptic Thought', *Sixteenth-Century Journal*, 5 (1974), 101-14.
[1360] Cohen, Alfred. 'Two Roads to the Puritan Millennium', *Church History*, 32 (1963), 322-38.
[1361] Cohn, Norman. *The Pursuit of the Millennium: Revolutionary Millenarians and the Mystical Anarchists of the Middle Ages*, rev. ed. (New York, 1970).
[1362] Cole, C. Robert, and Moody, Michael, eds. *The Dissenting Tradition* (Athens, Ohio, 1975).
[1363] Collins, Adela Yarbra. *The Combat Myth in the Book of Revelation* (Missoula, Mont., 1976).
[1364] ——. 'The Political Perspective of the Revelation of John', *Journal of Biblical Literature*, 96 (1977), 241-56.
[1365] Collins, John. 'Apocalyptic Eschatology as the Transcendence of Death,' *Catholic Biblical Quarterly*, 36 (1974), 21-43.
[1366] ——. *The Apocalyptic Vision of the Book of Daniel* (Missoula, Mont., 1977).

[1367] ——. 'Cosmos and Salvation: Jewish Wisdom and Apocalyptic in the Hellenistic Age', *History of Religion*, 17 (1977), 121–42.
[1368] ——. 'Pseudonymity, Historical Reviews and the Genre of the Apocalypse of John', *Catholic Biblical Quarterly*, 39 (1977), 329–43.
[1369] ——. *Semeia*, XIV (*Apocalypse: The Morphology of a Genre*) (1979).
[1370] ——. 'The Symbolism of Transcendence in Jewish Apocalyptic', *Biblical Research*, 19 (1974), 5–22.
[1371] Collinson, Patrick. *The Elizabethan Puritan Movement* (Berkeley, 1967).
[1372] Consult, John L. P. *The Millennial Kingdom of the Franciscans in the New World*, 2nd rev. ed (Berkeley, 1970).
[1373] Cooper, Brian G. 'The Apocalyptic Re-Discovery of Apocalyptic Ideas in the Seventeenth Century', *Baptist Quarterly*, N. S. 18–19 (1960–61), 351–62, 29–34.
[1374] Count, John M. *Myth and History in the Book of Revelation* (1979).
[1375] Cowherd, R. G. *The Politics of English Dissent, 1815–1848* (1959).
[1376] Crenshaw, James A. *Prophetic Conflict: Its Effect upon Israelite Religion* (New York, 1971).
[1377] Crone, Theodore M. *Early Christian Prophecy: A Study of Its Origin and Function* (Baltimore, 1973).
[1378] Daniel, E. Randolph. 'Apocalyptic Conversion: The Joachite Alternative to the Crusades', *Traditio*, 25 (1969), 127–54.
[1379] Daniélou, Jean. *The Theology of Jewish Christianity* (Chicago, 1964).
[1380] Davidson, James West. *The Logic of Millenial Thought: Eighteenth-Century New England* (New Haven, 1977).
[1381] Davies, J. C. *Utopia and the Ideal Society: A Study of English Utopia Writing 1516–1700* (Cambridge and New York, 1981).
[1382] DeJong, J. A. *'As the Waters Cover the Sea'*: *Millennial Expectations in the Rise of Anglo-American Missions* (Kampen, 1970).
[1383] DeVries, Simon John. *Prophet against Prophet* (Grand Rapids, Mich.).
[1384] Dillistone, Frederick William. *Drama of Salvation* (1967).
[1385] Dollinger, John J. I. von. *Prophecies and the Prophetic Spirit in the Christian Era*, ed. Alfred Plummer (1873).
[1386] Edersheim, Alfred. *Prophecy and History in Relation to the Messiah* (1885).
[1387] Eliott, Emory. *Power and the Pulpit in Puritan New England* (Princeton, 1975).
[1388] Ellis, Edward E. *Prophecy and Hermeneutic in Early Christianity: New Testament Essays* (Grand Rapids, Mich., 1978).
[1389] Fairfield, Leslie Parke. *John Bale, Mythmaker for the English Reformation* (Lafayette, Ind., 1976).
[1390] Fawcett, Arthur. *The Cambuslang Revival: The Scottish Evangelical Revival of the Eighteenth Century* (1971).
[1391] Faye, Eugène. *Les Apocalypses juives. Essai de critique littéraire et théologique* (Paris, 1895).
[1392] Fiorenza, Elizabeth Schüssler. 'Composition and Structure of the Book of the Revelation of John', *Catholic Biblical Quarterly*, 39 (1977), 345–50.
[1393] ——. *Invitation to the Book of Revelation* (Garden City, N. Y., 1981).
[1394] Firth, Katharine R. *The Apocalyptic Tradition in Reformation Britain 1530–1645* (New York, 1979).
[1395] Froom, LeRoy Edwin. *The Prophetic Faith of Our Fathers: The Historical Development of Prophetic Interpretation*, 4 vols (Washington, D. C., 1946–54).
[1396] Frost, Stanley B. *Old Testament Apocalyptic: Its Growth and Origins* (1952).

[1397] Funk, R. W., ed. *Journal for Theology and the Church: Apocalypticism* (1969).
[1398] Garrett, Clarke. *Respectable Folly: Millenarianism and the French Revolution in France and England* (Baltimore, 1975).
[1399] Gaussen, Louis. *Geneva and Rome: Rome Papal as Portrayed by Prophecy and History*, ed. E. Bickersteth (New York, 1844).
[1400] Giet, S. *L'Apocalypse et l'histoire* (Paris, 1957).
[1401] Gilsdorf, Joy B. *The Puritan Apocalypse: New England Eschatology in the Seventeenth Century.* Ph. D. thesis, Yale Univ., 1964.
[1402] Gruenwald, Ithamar. *Apocalyptic and Merkavah Mysticism* (Leiden and Cologne, 1980).
[1403] Guy, H. A. *New Testament Prophecy: Its Origin and Significance* (1947).
[1404] Haller, William. *Foxe's 'Book of Martyrs' and the Elect Nation* (1963).
[1405] ———. *The Rise of Puritanism, or, the Way to the New Jerusalem* (New York, 1938).
[1406] Hanning, Robert W. *The Vision of History in Early Britain* (New York, 1966).
[1407] Hanson, Paul D. *The Dawn of Apocalyptic* (Philadelphia, 1975).
[1408] Harbison, Craig. *The Last Judgment in Sixteenth-Century Northern Europe: A Study in the Election between Art and the Reformation* (New York, 1976).
[1409] Harrison, J. F. C. *The Second Coming: Popular Millenarianism 1780–1850* (New Brunswick, N. J., 1979).
[1410] Hartman, Lois. *Prophecy Interpreted* (Lund, 1966).
[1411] Harvey, John. *A Discoursive Probleme Concerning Prophesies* (1588).
[1412] Hatch, Nathan O. *The Sacred Cause of Liberty: Republican Thought and the Millennium in Revolutionary New England* (New Haven, 1977).
[1413] Headley, John. *Luther's View of Church History* (New Haven, 1963).
[1414] Heaton, E. W. *The Old Testament Prophets* (1977).
[1415] Hellholm, D., ed. *Apocalypticism in the Mediterranean World and Near East* (Uppsala, 1982).
[1416] Herner, C. J. 'A Study of the Letters to the Seven Churches of Asia with Special Reference to Their Local Background'. Ph. D. thesis, Manchester Univ., 1969.
[1417] Henn, Thomas Rice. *The Bible as Literature* (New York, 1970).
[1418] Herder, Johann Gottfried. *The Spirit of Hebrew Poetry*, tr. James Marsh, 2 vols (Burlington, 1833).
[1419] Heschel, Abraham J. *The Prophets* (New York, 1962).
[1420] Hickes, George. *The Spirit of Enthusiasm Exorcised* (1680; enlarged ed., 1709).
[1421] Hill, Christopher. *Antichrist in Seventeenth-Century England* (1971).
[1422] ———. *Intellectual Origins of the English Revolution* (Oxford, 1965).
[1423] ———. *Puritanism and Revolution* (1962).
[1424] ———. *The Religion of Gerrard Winstanley* (Oxford, 1978).
[1425] ———. *The World Turned Upside Down: Radical Ideas During the English Revolution* (New York, 1972).
[1426] Hill, D. 'Prophecy and Prophets in the Revelation of St. John', *New Testament Studies*, 18 (1972), 401–18.
[1427] Hobsbawn, Eric J. *Primitive Rebels: Studies in Archaic Forms of Social Movement in the Nineteenth and Twentieth Centuries* (Manchester, 1959).
[1428] Holtz, T. *Die Christologie der Apokalypse des Johannes* (Berlin, 1962).
[1429] Howard, Henry, Earl of Northampton. *A Defensative against the Poyson of Supposed Prophecies* (1583).
[1430] Hughes, Richard T. 'Henry Burton: A Study in Religion and Politics in Seventeenth-Century England'. Ph. D. thesis, Univ. of Iowa, 1972.

[1431] Hutchinson, Francis. *A Short View of the Pretended State of Prophecy* (1708).
[1432] Isani, Mukhtar Ali. 'The Growth of Sewall's *Phaenomena Quaedam Apocalyptica*', *Early American Literature*, 7 (1972), 64-75.
[1433] Jacob, J. R. 'Boyle's Circle in the Protectorate: Revelation, Politics, and the Millennium', *Journal of the History of Ideas*, 38 (1977), 31-40.
[1434] Jacob, Margaret C., and Lockwood, W. A. 'Political Millenarianism and Burnet's Sacred Theology', *Science Studies*, 2 (1972), 265-79.
[1435] James, Montague R. *The Apocalypse in Art* (1931).
[1436] Jarvis, Frank W. *Prophets, Poets, Priests, and Kings* (New York, 1974).
[1437] Jones, William. *A Course of Lectures on the Figurative Language of Holy Scriptures* (1786).
[1438] Juretic, George. 'Digger No Millenarian: The Revolutionizing of Gerrard Winstanley', *Journal of the History of Ideas*, 36 (1975), 263-80.
[1439] Kallas, James. *Revelation: God and Satan in the Apocalypse* (Minneapolis, 1973).
[1440] Kaminsky, H. *A History of the Hussite Revolution* (Berkeley, 1967).
[1441] Kamlah, Menachem Marc. 'Maimonides and Gersonides on Mosaic Prophecy', *Speculum*, 52 (1977), 62-79.
[1442] Kamlah, W. *Apokalypse u. Geschichstheologie* (Berlin, 1935).
[1443] Kingston, Richard. *Enthusiastick Imposters No Divinely Inspired Prophets* (1709).
[1444] Koch, Klaus. *The Growth of the Biblical Tradition: The Form-Critical Method*, tr. S. M. Cupitt (1969).
[1445] ——. *The Rediscovery of Apocalyptic*, tr. Margaret Kohl (Naperville, Ill., 1972).
[1446] Kurze, Dietrich. 'Prophecy and History', *Journal of the Warburg and Courtauld Institutes*, 21 (1958), 63-85.
[1447] Lacy, John. *The General Delusion of Christianity* (1713).
[1448] Lambert, E. *The Apocalypse of History: Problems of Providence and Human Destiny* (1948).
[1449] Lamont, William M. *Godly Rule: Politics and Religion 1603-1660* (1969).
[1450] ——. *Richard Baxter and the Millennarians* (1979).
[1451] Laneau, A. *L'Histoire du Salut chez les Pères de l'Eglise. La doctrine des âges du monde* (Paris, 1964).
[1452] Lanternari, Vittorio. *The Religions of the Oppressed*, tr. Lisa Sergi (New York, 1963).
[1453] Leff, Gordon. *Heresy in the Later Middle Ages* (Manchester, 1967).
[1454] Lerner, Robert E. 'Medieval Prophecy and Religious Dissent', *Past and Present*, 72 (1976), 3-24.
[1455] ——. 'The Refreshment of the Saints: The Time after Antichrist as a Station for Earthly Progress in Medieval Thought', *Traditio*, 23 (1976), 97-144.
[1456] Lindblom, Johannes. *Prophecy in Ancient Israel* (Philadelphia, 1976).
[1457] List, Günther. *Chiliastische Utopie und Radikale Reformation* (Munich, 1973).
[1458] Liu, Tai. *Discord in Zion: The Puritan Divines and the Puritan Revolution 1640-1660* (The Hague, 1973).
[1459] Löwith, Karl. *Meaning in History* (Chicago, 1949).
[1460] Lowth, Robert. *Lectures on the Sacred Poetry of the Hebrews*, tr. G. Gregory (Boston, 1815). N. B. The first English edition was published in 1787.
[1461] Maclear, James F. 'New England and the Fifth Monarchy', in *Puritan New England*, ed. Alden T. Vaughan and Francis J. Bremer (New York, 1977), pp. 69-91.
[1462] ——. 'The Republic and the Millennium', in *The Religion of the Republic*, ed. Elwyn A. Smith (Philadelphia, 1971).

[1463] Manuel, Frank. *The Prophets of Paris* (Cambridge, Mass., 1962).
[1464] ——. *The Religion of Isaac Newton* (Oxford, 1974).
[1465] ——. *Shapes of Philosophical History* (Stanford, Calif., 1965).
[1466] ——, and Manuel, Fritzie P. *Utopian Thought in the Western World* (Cambridge, Mass., 1979).
[1467] Matthews, Ronald. *English Messiahs* (1936).
[1468] McDonald, Duncan Black. *The Hebrew Literary Genius* (Princeton, 1933).
[1469] McDonald, H. D. *Ideas of Revelation: An Historical Study* (1959).
[1470] ——. *Theories of Revelation: An Historical Study* (1963).
[1471] McGinn, Bernard. 'Apocalypticism in the Middle Ages: An Historiographical Sketch', *Mediaevel Studies*, 37 (1975), 252–86.
[1472] ——. *Visions of the End: Apocalyptic Traditions in the Middle Ages* (New York, 1979).
[1473] McKeon, Michael. *Politics and Poetry in Restoration England: The Case of Dryden's 'Annus Mirabilis'* (1975).
[1474] Meer, Frederick van der. *Apocalypse: Visions from the Book of Revelation in Western Art* (1978).
[1475] Meinardus, O. F. A. *The Twenty-Four Elders of the Apocalypse in the Iconography of the Coptic Church* (Cairo, 1968–9).
[1476] Minear, Paul S. *Images of the Church in the New Testament* (1961).
[1477] ——. 'Ontology and Ecclesiology in the Apocalypse', *New Testament Studies*, 12 (1966), 89–105.
[1478] Moltmann, Jürgen. *The Theology of Hope* (New York, 1967).
[1479] Monloubou, L. *Apocalypses et théologie de l'espérance* (Paris, 1977).
[1480] Moorhead, James H. *American Apocalypse* (New Haven, 1978).
[1481] Morgan, Edmund Sears. *Visible Saints: The History of a Puritan Idea* (New York, 1963).
[1482] Morton, A. L. *The Matter of Britain: Essays in a Living Culture* (1966).
[1483] ——. *The World of Ranters: Religious Radicalism in the English Revolution* (1970).
[1484] Mowinckel, S. *Prophecy and Tradition* (Oslo, 1946).
[1485] Murray, Iain H. *The Puritan Hope: A Study in the Revival and Interpretation of Prophecy* (1971).
[1486] Mussies, G. *The Morphology of Koine Greek as Used in the Apocalypse of St. John* (Leiden, 1971).
[1487] Neuss, W. *Die Apokalypse des hl. Johannes in den Altspanischen und Altchristlichen Bibel-Illustrationen*, 2 vols (Münster, 1931).
[1488] Niebuhr, H. Richard. *The Meaning of Revelation* (New York, 1941).
[1489] Nuthall, Geoffrey F. *Visible Saints: The Congregational Way 1640–1660* (Oxford, 1957).
[1490] Olsen, V. Norskov. *John Foxe and the Elizabethan Church* (Berkeley, 1973).
[1491] Orlinsky, Henry M., et al. *Interpreting the Prophetic Tradition* (New York, 1969).
[1492] Oyer, John S. *Lutheran Reformers against Anabaptists* (The Hague, 1964).
[1493] Pannenberg, Wolfhart, et al. *Revelation as History* (1969).
[1494] Paton, Lucy Allen. *Les Prophecies de Merlin*, 2 vols (New York, 1926).
[1495] Peake, Arthur S. 'The Roots of Hebrew Prophecy and Jewish Apocalyptic', *Bulletin of the John Rylands Library*, 7 (1923), 233–55.
[1496] Pelikan, Jaroslav. *The Emergence of the Catholic Tradition, 100–600* (Chicago, 1971).
[1497] Perkins, William. 'The Art of Prophecying', in *The Works of . . . Mr W. Perkins*, 3

vols (Cambridge, 1608–9), II, 473–646.
[1498] Perrin, Norman. *The New Testament: An Introduction* (1974).
[1499] Phelan, John Leddy. *The Millennial Kingdom* (Berkeley, 1956).
[1500] Phillips, James Emerson. *Images of a Queen: Mary Stuart in Sixteenth-Century Literature* (Berkeley, 1964).
[1501] Plöger, Otto. *Theocracy and Eschatology*, tr. S. Rudman (Richmond, Va., 1968).
[1502] Pocock, J. G. A. *Politics, Language and Time* (New York, 1971).
[1503] Prigent, Pierre. *Apocalypse et liturgie* (Neuchâtel, 1964).
[1504] ——. *Apocalypse 12: Histoire de l'exégèse* (Tübingen, 1959).
[1505] ——. *The Message of the Prophets*, tr. D. M. G. Stalker (1968).
[1506] Rad, Gerhard von. *Old Testament Theology*, tr. D. M. G. Stalker (1965).
[1507] ——. *Wisdom in Israel*, tr. James A. Marton (1972).
[1508] Reeves, Marjorie. 'History and Prophecy in Medieval Thought', *Medievalia et Humanistica*, N. S. 5 (1974), 51–75.
[1509] ——. *The Influence of Prophecy in the Later Middle Ages: A Study in Joachimism* (Oxford, 1969).
[1510] ——. *Joachim of Fiore and the Prophetic Future* (1976).
[1511] ——. 'Some Popular Prophecies from the Fourteenth to the Seventeenth Centuries', *Studies in Church History*, 8 (1972), 107–34.
[1512] ——, and Hirsch-Reich, Beatrice. *The Figurae of Joachim* (Oxford, 1972).
[1513] ——. 'The Seven Seals in the Writings of Joachim of Fiore', *Recherches de théologie ancienne et médiévale*, 21 (1954), 211–47.
[1514] Reid, Mary Esson. *The Bible Read as Literature* (Cleveland, 1959).
[1515] Reines, Alvin J. *Maimonides and Abrabanel on Prophecy* (Cincinnati, 1970).
[1516] Rissi, Mathias. *Time and History: A Study of the Revelation*, tr. Gordon C. Winsor (Richmond, Va., 1966).
[1517] Robertson, Edward. 'The Role of the Early Hebrew Prophets', *Bulletin of the John Rylands Library*, 42 (1960), 412–31.
[1518] Robinson, H. Wheeler. *Inspiration and Revelation in the Old Testament* (Oxford, 1962).
[1519] Robinson, Theodore H. *Prophecy and the Prophets in Ancient Israel*, 2nd edn. (1960).
[1520] Rogers, Philip G. *The Fifth Monarchy Men* (New York, 1966).
[1521] ——. *The Sixth Trumpeter* (1963).
[1522] Rowley, H. H. *The Relevance of Apocalyptic: A Study of Jewish and Christian Apocalypses from Daniel to the Revelation*, rev. edn. (New York, 1963).
[1523] Russell, David Syme. *Apocalyptic, Ancient and Modern* (Philadelphia, 1978).
[1524] ——. *The Message and Method of Jewish Apocalyptic* (1964).
[1525] Sandeen, Ernest Robert. *The Roots of Fundamentalism: British and American Millenarianism 1800–1930* (Chicago, 1970).
[1526] Sands, P. C. *Literary Genius of the Old Testament* (Oxford, 1926).
[1527] ——. *Literary Genius of the New Testament* (Oxford, 1932).
[1528] Schall, J. V. 'Apocalypse as a Secular Enterprise', *Scottish Journal of Theology*, 29 (1976), 357–73.
[1529] Scholem, Gershom. *Sabbatai Zevi: The Mystical Messiah, 1626–1676*, tr. R. J. Zwi Werblowsky (Princeton, 1973).
[1530] Schmithals, Walter. *The Apocalyptic Movement: Introduction and Interpretation*, tr. John E. Steely (New York and Nashville, 1975).
[1531] Schnur, Harvey C. *Mystic Rebels* (New York, 1949).

[1532] Schwartz, Hillel. 'The End of the Beginning: Millenarian Studies 1969–1975', *Religious Studies Review*, 2 (1976), 1–15.
[1533] ——. *The French Prophets: The History of a Millenarian Group in Eighteenth-Century England* (Berkeley, 1980).
[1534] Scott, Nathan A., Jr. 'New Heav'ns, New Earth': The Landscape of Contemporary Apocalypse', *Journal of Religion*, 53 (1973), 1–35.
[1535] Seibt, F. *Utopica* (Cologne, 1972).
[1536] Shepherd, Massey Hamilton. *The Paschal Liturgy and the Apocalypse* (Richmond, Va., 1960).
[1537] Sherlock, Thomas. *The Use and Intent of Prophecy, in the Several Ages of the World* (1749). N. B. The first edition was published in 1725.
[1538] Smith, David E. 'Millenarian Scholarship in America', *American Quarterly*, 17 (1965), 535–49.
[1539] Smith, John. 'Of Prophecy', in *A Collection of Theological Tracts*, ed. Richard Watson, 6 vols (1785), IV, 297–362. N. B. The first appearance of this tract is 1631.
[1540] Solt, Leo F. *Saints in Arms: Puritanism and Democracy in Cromwell's Army* (Stanford, Ca., 1959).
[1541] Southern, R. W. 'Aspects of the European Tradition of Historical Writing', *Transactions of the Royal Historical Society*, 20–3 (1970–3), 173–96, 159–79, 159–80, 243–63. N. B. The essay is in four parts.
[1542] Stein, Stephen J. 'An Apocalyptic Rationale for the American Revolution', *Early American Literature*, 9 (1975), 211–25.
[1543] Stonehouse, N. B. *The Apocalypse in the Ancient Church* (Goes, 1929).
[1544] Strong, Roy C. 'The Popular Celebration of the Accession Day of Queen Elizabeth', *Journal of the Warburg and Cortauld Institute*, 21 (1953), 86–103.
[1545] ——. *Portraits of Queen Elizabeth I* (Oxford, 1967).
[1546] Talman, J. L. *Political Messianism: The Romantic Phase* (New York and Washington, D. C., 1960).
[1547] Talmon, Yonina. 'Pursuit of the Millennium: The Relation between Religious and Social Change', *Archives européanes de sociologie*, 3 (1962), 125–48.
[1548] ——. 'Millenarian Movements', *Archives européanes de sociologie*, 7 (1966), 159–200.
[1549] Taylor, Henry Osborn. *Prophets, Poets, and Philosophers of the Ancient World* (New York, 1915).
[1550] Taylor, Rupert. *The Political Prophecy in England* (New York, 1911).
[1551] Thomas, Keith V. *Religion and the Decline of Magic* (1971).
[1552] Thompson, Edward P. *The Making of the English Working Class* (1963).
[1553] Thrupp, Sylvia L., ed. *Millennial Dreams in Action: Studies in Revolutionary Religious Movements* (New York, 1962).
[1554] Tonkin, John. *The Church and the Secular Order in Reformation Thought* (1971).
[1555] Toon, Peter, ed. *Puritans, the Millennium, and the Future of Israel: Puritan Eschatology 1600–1660* (Cambridge, 1970).
[1556] Trevor-Roper, Hugh Redwald. *Religion, the Reformation and Social Change* (1967).
[1557] Tuveson, Ernest. *Millennium and Utopia: A Study in the Background of the Idea of Progress* (Berkeley, 1949).
[1558] ——. *Redeemer Nation: The Idea of American Millennial Role* (Chicago, 1968).
[1559] Vasiliev, A. A. 'Medieval Ideas of the End of the World: West–East', *Byzantion*, 16 (1942–3), 462–502.

[1560] Vawter, Bruce. 'Apocalyptic: Its Relation to Prophecy', *Catholic Biblical Quarterly*, 22 (1960), 33–46.
[1561] Verhelst, D. 'La préhistoire des conceptions d'Adson concertant l'Antichrist', *Recherches de Théologie ancienne et médiévale*, 39–40 (1973), 52–103.
[1562] Vos, L. A. *The Synoptic Traditions in the Apocalypse* (Kampen, 1965).
[1563] Waldegrave, Samuel. *New Testament Millenarianism* (1855).
[1564] Walzer, Michael. *The Revolution of the Saints: A Study in the Origins of Radical Politics* (1966).
[1565] Weber, Max. *The Sociology of Religion*, tr. Ephraim Fischoff (Boston, 1963).
[1566] Webster, Charles, ed. *The Intellectual Revolution of the Seventeenth Century* (1974).
[1567] Weinstein, Donald. *Savonarola and Florence: Prophecy and Patriotism in the Renaissance* (Princeton, 1970).
[1568] Werner, Martin. *The Formation of Christian Dogma* (Boston, 1965).
[1569] West, Delno C., ed. *Joachim of Fiore in Christian Thought: Essays on the Influence of the Calabrian Prophet*, 2 vols (New York, 1975).
[1570] Westermann, Claus. *Basic Forms of Prophetic Speech*, tr. Hugh Clayton White (Philadelphia, 1967).
[1571] White, B. R. *The English Separatist Tradition* (Oxford, 1971).
[1572] Widengren, G. *Literary and Psychological Aspects of the Hebrew Prophets* (Uppsala, 1948).
[1573] Wilder, Amos N. 'The Rhetoric of Ancient and Modern Apocalyptic', *Interpretation*, 25 (1971), 436–53.
[1574] ——. *Theopoetic: Theology and the Religious Imagination* (Philadelphia, 1976).
[1575] Williams, Ann, ed. *Prophecy and Millenarianism* (1980).
[1576] Williams, G. H. *The Radical Reformation* (1962).
[1577] Williamson, Arthur H. 'Antichrist's Career in Scotland: The Imagery of Evil and the Search for a Scottish Past'. Ph. D. thesis, Washington Univ., 1973.
[1578] ——. *Scottish National Consciousness in the Age of James VI: The Apocalypse, the Union and Shaping of Scotland's Public Culture* (Edinburgh, 1979).
[1579] Williamson, J. W. *The Myth of the Conqueror* (New York, 1978).
[1580] Wilson, Bryan R. *Magic and the Millennium* (1973).
[1581] Wilson, John F. 'Comment on "Two Roads to the Puritan Millennium"', *Church History*, 32 (1963), 339–43.
[1582] ——. *Pulpit in Parliament: Puritanism During the English Civil War, 1640–1643* (Princeton, 1969).
[1583] ——. 'Studies in Puritan Millenarianism under the Early Stuarts'. Ph. D. thesis, Union Theological Seminary, 1962.
[1584] Worsley, Peter. *The Trumpet Shall Sound* (1957).
[1585] Yates, Frances Amelia. *Astraea: The Imperial Theme in the Sixteenth Century* (1975).
[1586] ——. *The Rosicrucian Englightenment* (1972).

2 LITERATURE AS PROPHECY, ESPECIALLY LITERATURE AND THE BOOK OF REVELATION

[1587] Abrams, M. H. 'English Romanticism: The Spirit of the Age', in *Romanticism Reconsidered*, ed. Northrop Frye (New York, 1963), pp. 26–72.

[1588] ——. *Natural Supernaturalism: Tradition and Revolution in Romantic Literature* (New York, 1970).
[1589] Allen, Margaret J. 'The Harlot and the Mourning Bride', in *The Practical Vision*, ed. Jane Campbell and James Doyle (Waterloo, 1978), pp. 13–28.
[1590] Altizer, Thomas J. J. *The New Apocalypse: The Radical Christian Vision of William Blake* (East Lansing, Mich., 1967).
[1591] Argüelles, José A. *The Transformative Vision: Reflections on the Nature and History of Human Expression* (Berkeley, 1975).
[1592] Baroway, Isabel. 'Studies in the Bible as Poetry in the English Renaissance'. Ph. D. thesis, Johns Hopkins Univ., 1930.
[1593] Bayly, Anselm. *The Alliance of Musick, Poetry, and Oratory* (1789).
[1594] Bennett, Josephine Waters. *The Evolution of 'The Faerie Queene'* (Chicago, 1942). N. B. See esp. pp. 109-22.
[1595] Bercovitch, Sacvan. *The American Jeremiad* (Madison, 1979).
[1596] ——. 'Emerson the Prophet', in *Emerson: Prophecy, Metamorphosis, and Influence*, ed. David Levin (New York, 1975).
[1597] ——. *The Puritan Origins of the American Self* (New Haven, 1975).
[1598] ——, ed. *Typology and Early American Literature* (Amherst, 1977).
[1599] Berger, Harry J. 'Spenser's *Faerie Queene*, Book I: Prelude to Interpretation', *Southern Review* (Adelide), 2 (1966), 18–48.
[1600] Blackburn, William. 'Spenser's Merlin', *Renaissance and Reformation*, 4 (1980), 179–98.
[1601] Bloom, Harold. *Blake's Apocalypse: A Study in Poetic Argument* (Garden City, N. Y., 1963).
[1602] ——. 'Blake's *Jerusalem*: The Bard of Sensibility and the Form of Prophecy', *Eighteenth-Century Studies*, 4 (1970), 6–20.
[1603] ——. *Shelley's Mythmaking* (New Haven, 1959).
[1604] ——. *The Visionary Company: A Reading of English Romantic Poetry* (Garden City, N. Y., 1962).
[1605] Bloomfield, Morton. *'Piers Plowman' as a Fourteenth-Century Apocalypse* (New Brunswick, N. J., 1961).
[1606] Bowra, Maurice. *The Prophetic Element* (1959).
[1607] Buxton, Charles Roden. *Prophets of Heaven and Hell: Virgil, Dante, Milton and Goethe* (Cambridge, 1945).
[1608] Cambon, Glauco. *The Inclusive Flame: Studies in Modern American Poetry* (Bloomington, Ind., 1963).
[1609] Chadwick, Nora Kershaw. *Poetry and Prophecy* (Cambridge, 1942).
[1610] Chambers, Jane. 'Divine Justice, Mercy, and Love: The 'Mutabilitie' Subplot and Spenser's Apocalyptic Theme', *Essays in Literature*, 8 (1981), 3–10.
[1611] Clausen, Christopher. 'Poetry as Revelation: A Nineteenth-Century Mirage', *Georgia Review*, 23 (1979), 89–107.
[1612] Cook, A. S. 'Milton's View of the Apocalypse as a Tragedy', *Archiv*, 129 (1912), 74–80.
[1613] Corke, Helen. *Lawrence and Apocalypse* (1933).
[1614] Costa, Dennis. *Irenic Apocalypse: Some Uses of Apocalyptic in Dante, Petrarch and Rabelais* (Stanford, Ca., 1981).
[1615] Curran, Stuart, and Wittreich, Joseph, eds. *Blake's Sublime Allegory: Essays on 'The Four Zoas', 'Milton', and 'Jerusalem'* (Madison, 1973).
[1616] Cutts, John P. 'The Fool's Prophecy—Another Version', *English Language Notes*,

9 (1972), 262–65.

[1617] DeLuca, Vincent. 'The Style of Millennial Announcement in *Prometheus Unbound*', *Keats–Shelley Journal*, 28 (1979), 78–101.

[1618] Dobbins, Austin C. *Milton and the Book of Revelation: The Heavenly Cycle* (University, Ala., 1975).

[1619] Dorsten, J. A. van. *The Radical Arts* (1975).

[1620] Dudley, Guilford. *The Recovery of Christian Myth* (Philadelphia, 1967).

[1621] Emmerson, R. K. *Antichrist in the Middle Ages: A Study of Medieval Apocalypticism, Art and Literature* (Manchester, 1981).

[1622] Erdman, David V. *Blake, Prophet against Empire: A Poet's Interpretation of the History of His Own Times* (Princeton, 1954).

[1623] Evans, James G. 'The Apocalypse as Contrary Vision: Prolegomenon to an Analogical Reading of *The Four Zoas*', *Texas Studies in Language and Literature*, 14 (1972), 313–28.

[1624] Falls, Mother Mary Robert. 'Spenser's Legend of Redcrosse in Relation to the Elizabethan Religious Milieu'. Ph. D. thesis, Catholic Univ., 1951.

[1625] Farrer, Austin. *The Glass of Vision* (1948).

[1626] Fisch, Harold. *Jerusalem and Albion: The Hebraic Factor in Seventeenth-Century Literature* (1964).

[1627] Fisher, Peter. *The Valley of Vision: Blake as Prophet and Revolutionary*, ed. Northrop Frye (Toronto, 1961).

[1628] Fishman, Sylvia Barack. 'The Watered Garden and the Bride of God: Patterns of Biblical Imagery in Poems of Spenser, Milton, and Blake'. Ph. D. thesis, Washington Univ., 1980.

[1629] Fixler, Michael. 'Apocalypse' and 'Millennialism', in *A Milton Encyclopedia*, ed. William B. Hunter, Jr, *et al.* (Lewisburg, Pa., 1978–9), I, 57–60; V. 132–4.

[1630] ——. 'The Apocalypse within *Paradise Lost*', in *New Essays on 'Paradise Lost'*, ed. Thomas Kranidas (Berkeley, 1969).

[1631] ——. *Milton and the Kingdoms of God* (1964).

[1632] Fletcher, Angus. *The Prophetic Moment: An Essay on Spenser* (Chicago, 1971).

[1633] ——. *The Transcendental Masque: An Essay on Milton's 'Comus'* (Ithaca, N. Y., 1971).

[1634] Friedman, Lee M. '"The Jewes Prophecy" and Caleb Shilock', *More Books*, 22 (1947), 43–56.

[1635] Frontain, Raymond-Jean, ed. *Prophetic Voice and Vision in Western Literature* (Lewisburg, Pa., 1984).

[1636] Frye, Northrop. *Fearful Symmetry: A Study of William Blake* (Princeton, 1947).

[1637] ——. *The Great Code: The Bible and Literature* (New York, 1982).

[1638] Gette, L. W. 'Agrippa d' Aubigne: Prophetic and Apocalyptic in the Structure and Imagery of 'Les Tragiques'. Ph. D. thesis, Univ. of Wisconsin, 1975.

[1639] Gezari, Janet K. '*Romola* and the Myth of Apocalypse', in *George Eliot: Centenary Essays and an Unpublished Fragment*, ed. Anne Smith (Totowa, N. J., 1980), pp. 77–102.

[1640] Gilpin, W. Clark. *The Millenarian Piety of Roger Williams* (Chicago, 1979).

[1641] Globe, A. V. 'Apocalyptic Themes in the Sibylline Oracles, Langland, Spenser, and Marvell'. Ph. D. thesis, Univ. of Toronto, 1970.

[1642] Goen, C. C. 'Jonathan Edwards: A New Departure in Eschatology', *Church History*, 28 (1959), 25–40.

[1643] Gorfain, Phyllis. 'Contest, Riddle, and Prophecy: Reflexivity through Folklore in

King Lear', Southern Folklore Quarterly, 41 (1977), 239–54.
[1644] Grierson, Herbert J. C. *Milton and Wordsworth, Poets and Prophets: A Study of Their Reactions to Political Events* (1950).
[1645] Groff, Richard. *Thoreau and the Prophetic Tradition* (Los Angeles, 1961).
[1646] Hankins, John Erskine. *Source and Meaning in Spenser's Allegory: A Study of 'The Faerie Queene'* (Oxford, 1971). N. B. See esp. pp. 99–118.
[1647] Harper, George Mills. 'Apocalyptic Vision and Pastoral Dream in Blake's *Four Zoas', South Atlantic Quarterly,* 64 (1965), 110–24.
[1648] Harwood, A. C. *Shakespeare's Prophetic Mind* (Southampton, 1964).
[1648A] Hassett, Constance W. 'Browning's Caponsacchi: Convert and Apocalyptist', *Philological Quarterly,* 60 (1981), 487–500.
[1649] Hawkes, Terence. 'The Fool's "Prophecy" in "King Lear"', *Notes and Queries,* N. S. 7 (1960), 331–2.
[1650] Hayes, T. Wilson. *Winstanley the Digger: A Literary Analysis of Radical Ideas in the English Revolution* (Cambridge, Mass., 1979).
[1651] Helms, Randel. 'Ezekiel and Blake's *Jerusalem*', *Studies in Romanticism,* 13 (1974), 127–40.
[1652] Hill, Christopher. *Milton and the English Revolution* (New York, 1977).
[1653] ——. 'Marvell and Milton', in *Approaches to Andrew Marvell,* ed. C. A. Patrides (1979).
[1654] Hirst, Desiree. 'On the Aesthetics of Prophetic Art', *British Journal of Aesthetics,* 4 (1964), 248–52.
[1655] Hough, Graham. *The First Commentary on 'The Faerie Queene'* (Folcroft, Pa., 1964).
[1656] Hulst, Cornelia Steketee. *Homer and the Prophets* (Chicago, 1925).
[1657] Hunter, William B., Jr. 'The War in Heaven: The Exaltation of the Son', in *Bright Essence: Studies in Milton's Theology,* ed. Hunter *et al.* (Salt Lake City, 1971), pp. 115–30.
[1658] Jay, Elizabeth. *The Religion of the Heart, Anglican Evangelicalism and the Nineteenth-Century Novel* (Oxford, 1979).
[1659] Kaske, Carol V. 'Spenser's *Faerie Queene* and Exegetical Tradition: Nature, Law and Grace in the Episode of the Nymph's Well'. Ph. D. thesis, Johns Hopkins Univ., 1964.
[1660] Kelly, Robert A. 'The Failure of Prophecy in Melville', *Christianity and Literature,* 27 (1978), iii, 18–27.
[1661] Kermode, Frank. *The Sense of an Ending* (New York, 1967).
[1662] ——. *Shakespeare, Spenser, Donne: Renaissance Essays* (1971). N. B. See esp. pp. 12–59.
[1663] ——. 'Spenser and the Allegorists', *Proceedings of the British Academy,* 48 (1962), 261–79.
[1664] Kerrigan, William. *The Prophetic Milton* (Charlottesville, Va., 1974).
[1665] King, John N. *English Reformation Literature: The Tudor Origin of Poetical Tradition* (Princeton, 1982), esp. pp. 209–70.
[1666] ——. 'Robert Crowley's Editions of *Piers Plowman*: A Tudor Apocalypse', *Modern Philology,* 73 (1976), 342–52.
[1667] Klinck, Dennis. 'Calvinism and Jacobean Tragedy', *Genre,* 11 (1978), 333–58.
[1668] Korshin, Paul J. *Typologies in England 1650–1820* (Princeton, 1981).
[1669] Kragelund, Patrick. *Dream and Prediction in 'The Aeneid'* (Copenhagen, 1976).
[1670] Kramer, Aaron. *The Prophetic Tradition in American Poetry, 1835–1900*

(Rutherford, N. J., 1968).

[1671] Kranidas, Thomas. 'Milton's *Of Reformation*: The Politics of Vision', *English Literary History*, 49 (1982), 497–513.

[1672] Kremen, Kathryn R. *The Imagination of the Resurrection: The Poetic Continuity of a Religious Motif in Donne, Blake, and Yeats* (Lewisburg, Pa., 1972).

[1673] Lagorio, Valerie M. 'The Apocalyptic Mode in the Vulgate Cycle of Arthurian Romances', *Philological Quarterly*, 57 (1978), 1–22.

[1674] Lakshmi, Mani. *The Apocalyptic Vision in Nineteenth-Century Fiction: A Study of Cooper, Hawthorne, and Melville* (Washington, D. C., 1981).

[1675] Landow, George P. *Victorian Types, Victorian Shadows: Biblical Tradition in Victorian Literature, Art, and Thought* (Boston, 1980).

[1676] Lanoue, David G. "History as Apocalypse: The Prologue of Machaut's *Jugement dou roy de Navarre*," *Philological Quarterly*, 60 (1981), 1–12.

[1677] Lascelles, Mary. '*King Lear* and Doomsday', *Shakespeare Survey*, 26 (1973), 69–79.

[1678] LaValley, Robert J. *Carlyle and the Idea of the Modern: Studies in Carlyle's Prophetic Literature and Its Relation to Blake, Nietzsche, Marx, and Others* (New Haven, 1968).

[1679] Lewalski, Barbara K. '*Samson Agonistes* and the Tragedy of the Apocalypse', *PMLA*, 85 (1970), 1050–62.

[1680] Lewis, R. W. B. *Trials of the Word: Essays in American Literature and the Humanistic Tradition* (New Haven, 1965).

[1681] Lindsay, Jack. '*Antony and Cleopatra* and the Book of Revelation', *Review of English Studies*, 23 (1947), 66.

[1682] Lovelace, Richard F. *The American Pietism of Cotton Mather: Origins of American Evengelism* (Grand Rapids, Mich., 1979).

[1683] Lowance, Mason I., Jr. *The Language of Canaan: Metaphor and Symbol in New England* (Cambridge, Mass., 1980).

[1684] ——, and Walters, David, eds. 'Increase Mather's *New Jerusalem*: Millennialism in Late Seventeenth-Century New England', *Proceedings of the American Antiquary Society*, 87 (1977), 343–408.

[1685] Matar, N. I. 'Prophetic Traherne: A Thanksgiving and Prayer for the Nation', *Journal of English and Germanic Philology*, 81 (1982), 16–29.

[1686] Maurois, André. *Poets and Prophets*, tr. Hamish Miles (1936).

[1687] Mendl, Robert William. *Revelation in Shakespeare* (1964).

[1688] Montgomery, Marion. 'The Prophetic Poet and the Loss of the Middle Earth', *Georgia Review*, 23 (1979), 61–83.

[1689] Morris, Helen. 'Shakespeare and Dürer's Apocalypse', *Shakespeare Studies*, 4 (1968), 252–62.

[1690] Morson, Gary Saul. *The Boundaries of Genre: Dostoevsky's Diary of a Writer and the Traditions of Literary Utopia* (Austin, Tex., 1981).

[1691] Mueller, William Randolph. *The Prophetic Voice in Modern Fiction* (New York, 1959).

[1692] Murrin, Michael. *The Veil of Allegory: Some Notes Toward a Theory of Allegorical Rhetoric in the English Renaissance* (Chicago, 1969).

[1693] Nolan, Barbara. *The Gothic Visionary Perspective* (Princeton, 1977).

[1694] O'Connell, Michael. *Mirror and Veil: The Historical Dimension of Spenser's 'Faerie Queene'* (Chapel Hill, 1977).

[1695] O'Dyer, Patrick. 'The Poet Historical: A Study of Renaissance Methods and Uses of History'. Ph. D. thesis, Univ. of Tennessee, 1963.

[1696] Os, A. B. van. *Religious Visions: The Development of the Eschatological Elements in Medieval English Literature* (Amsterdam, 1932).
[1697] Pappas, John N. 'The Role of the Poet in Eighteenth-Century French Society', in *French Literature Series: Authors and Their Centuries*, ed. Phillip Grant (Columbia, S. C., 1974).
[1698] Patrides, C. A. *The Grand Design of God: The Literary Form of the Christian View of History* (Toronto, 1972).
[1699] ——. 'Till Time Stand Still: The Eschata of History', in *Milton and the Christian Tradition* (Oxford, 1966).
[1700] Paz, Octavio. *The Bow and the Lyre*, tr. Ruth L. C. Simms (New York, 1975).
[1701] Parker, Patricia A. *Inescapable Romance: Studies in the Poetics of a Mode* (Princeton, 1979).
[1702] Pearce, Roy Harvey. *The Continuity of American Poetry* (Princeton, 1961).
[1703] Pease, Donald. 'Blake, Crane, Whitman and Modernism: A Poetics of Pure Possibility', *PMLA*, 96 (1981), 64–85.
[1704] Pedworth, Ted-Larry, and Summers, Claude J. 'Herbert, Vaughan, and Public Concerns in Private Modes', *George Herbert Journal*, 3 (1979–80), 1–21.
[1705] Porter, David. *Emerson and Literary Change* (Cambridge, Mass., 1978).
[1706] Prendergast, John Brittain III. 'England as the City of God and the Third Troy in *The Faerie Queene*, I–III'. Ph. D. thesis, Univ. of Toronto, 1976.
[1707] Rasmussen, Carl J. 'Quietnesse of Minde': *A Theatre for Worldlings* as a Protestant Poetics', *Spenser Studies*, 1 (1980), 244–70.
[1708] Reeves, Marjorie. 'Dante and the Prophetic View of History', in *The World of Dante*, ed. C. Grayson (Oxford, 1980), pp. 44–60.
[1709] Regosin, Richard. 'D' Aubigne's *Les Tragiques*: A Protestant Apocalypse', *PMLA*, 81 (1966), 363–8.
[1710] ——. *The Poetry of Inspiration: A. d'Aubigne's 'Les Tragiques'* (Chapel Hill, 1970).
[1711] Revard, Stella. *The War in Heaven: 'Paradise Lost' and the Tradition of Satan's Rebellion* (Ithaca, N. Y., 1980).
[1712] Rivero, Albert J. 'Typology, History, and Blake's *Milton*', *Journal of English and Germanic Philology*, 81 (1982), 30–46.
[1713] Rogers, Arthur. *Prophecy and Poetry: Studies in Isaiah and Browning* (New York, 1909).
[1714] Rosenblatt, Jason P. 'Structural Unity and Temporal Concordance: The War in Heaven in *Paradise Lost*', *PMLA*, 87 (1972), 31–41.
[1715] Roston, Murray. *Prophet and Poet: The Bible and the Growth of Romanticism* (Evanston, Ill., 1965).
[1716] Rostvig, Maren-Sofie. 'Structure as Prophecy: The Influence of Biblical Exegesis upon the Theories of Literary Structure', in *Silent Poetry: Essays in Numerological Analysis*, ed., Alastair Fowler (New York, 1970), pp. 32–72.
[1717] Ryken, Leland. *The Apocalyptic Vision in 'Paradise Lost'* (Ithaca, N.Y., 1970).
[1718] Santi, Enrico Mario. *Pablo Neruda: The Poetics of Prophecy* (Ithaca, N.Y., 1982).
[1719] Schechter, Abraham. *'King Lear': Warning or Prophecy* (New York, 1956).
[1720] Schleiner, Louise. 'Emerson's Orphic and Messianic Bard', *ESQ: Journal of the American Renaissance*, 25 (1979), 191–202.
[1721] Schorer, Mark. *William Blake: The Politics of Vision* (New York, 1946).
[1722] Schultz, Howard. 'Christ and Antichrist in *Paradise Regained*', *PMLA*, 67 (1952), 790–808.

[1723] Schwartz, Susan Martha. 'The Prophecies of Merlin and Medieval Political Propaganda in England: From Geoffrey of Monmouth to Henry VII'. Ph. D. thesis, Harvard Univ. Press, 1975.

[1729] Scoufos, Alice-Lyle. 'The Mysteries in Milton's Masque', *Milton Studies*, 6 (1974), 113–42.

[1725] Seaton, Ethel. '*Antony and Cleopatra* and the Book of Revelation', *Review of English Studies*, 22 (1946), 219–24.

[1726] Sewall, Elizabeth. *The Orphic Voice* (New Haven, 1960).

[1727] Shaffer, E. S. '*Kubla Khan' and the Fall of Jerusalem: The Mythological School in Biblical Criticism and Secular Literature 1770–1900* (Cambridge, 1975).

[1728] Shaheen, Naseeb. *Biblical References in 'The Faerie Queene'* (Memphis, Tenn., 1976).

[1729] Sherill, Rowland A. *The Prophetic Melville: Experience, Transcendence, and Tragedy* (Athens, Ga., 1979).

[1730] Snare, Gerald. 'The Poetics of Vision: Patterns of Grace and Courtesy in *The Faerie Queene, VI*', in *Renaissance Papers 1974*, ed. Dennis G. Donovan and A. Leigh Deneef (Spain, 1975).

[17831] Spacks, Patricia Meyer. *The Poetry of Vision: Five Eighteenth-Century Poets* (Cambridge, Mass., 1967).

[1732] Spencer, Benjamin T. '*King Lear:* A Prophetic Tragedy', *College English*, 5 (1944), 302–8.

[1733] Stillman, Carol Ann. 'Spenser's Elect England: Political and Apocalyptic Dimensions of *The Faerie Queene*'. Ph. D. thesis, Univ. of Pennsylvania, 1979.

[1734] Stone, Walter B. 'Shakespeare and the Sad Augurs', *Journal of English and Germanic Philology*, 52 (1953), 457–79.

[1735] Stoneburner, Tony. 'Notes on Prophecy and Apocalypse in a Time of Anarchy and Revolution: A Trying Out', in *Literature in Revolution*, eds. George Abbott White and Charles Newman (New York, 1972), pp. 246–82.

[1736] Summers, Joseph H. 'Some Apocalyptic Strains in Marvell's Poetry', in *Tercentenary Essays in Honor of Andrew Marvell*, ed. Kenneth Friedenreich (Hamden, Conn., 1977), pp. 180–203.

[1737] Tannenbaum, Leslie. *Biblical Tradition in Blake's Early Prophecies: The Great Code of Art* (Princeton, 1981).

[1738] Tichi, Cecelia. *New World, New Earth: Environmental Reform in American Literature from the Puritans through Whitman* (New Haven, 1979).

[1739] Tresley, Richard M. 'Renaissance Commentaries on the Book of Revelation and Their Influence on Spenser's *Faerie Queene* and d'Aubigne's *Les Tragiques*'. Ph. D. thesis, Univ. of Chicago, 1980.

[1740] Tucker, E. F. J. 'Donne's Apocalyptic Style: A Contextual Analysis of *Devotions upon Emergent Occasions*', *Interpretations*, 12 (1980), 92–9.

[1741] Tuve, Rosemond. *Allegorical Imagery: Some Medieval Books and Their Posterity* (Princeton, 1966).

[1742] Vogler, Thomas. *Preludes to Vision: The Epic Venture in Blake, Wordsworth, Keats, and Hart Crane* (Berkeley, 1971).

[1743] Waddington, Raymond B. *The Mind's Empire: Myth and Form in George Chapman's Narrative Poems* (Baltimore, 1974).

[1744] Waggoner, Hyatt. *American Poets from the Puritans to the Present* (Princeton, 1968).

[1745] ——. *Emerson as Poet* (Princeton, 1974).

[1746] Watt, James Timothy. 'The Prophecy of the Hero's Children in English Renaissance Epic'. Ph. D. thesis, Univ. of North Carolina Press, 1977.
[1747] Weintrab, Wiktor. *Literature as Prophecy: Scholarship and Martinist Poetics in Mickiewicz's Parisian Lectures* ('–Gravenhage, 1959).
[1748] Williams, Kathleen. 'Vision and Rhetoric: The Poet's Voice in *The Faerie Queene*', *English Literary History*, 36 (1969), 131–44.
[1749] Wilner, Eleanor. *Gathering the Winds: Visionary Imagination and the Radical Transformation of Self and Society* (Baltimore, 1975).
[1750] Wittreich, Joseph. *Angel of Apocalypse: Blake's Idea of Milton* (Madison, 1975).
[1751] ———, ed. *Milton and the Line of Vision* (Madison, 1975).
[1752] ———. *Visionary Poetics: Milton's Tradition and His Legacy* (San Marino, Calif., 1979).
[1753] Woodman, Ross. *The Apocalyptic Vision in the Poetry of Shelley* (Toronto, 1964).
[1754] Yoder R. A. *Emerson and the Orphic Poet in America* (Berkeley, 1978).
[1755] Zaslove, Jerald. 'Fiction Extended: The Genre of Apocalypse and Dead Ends' *Genre*, 3 (1970), 17–39.
[1756] Ziff, Larzer. *The Career of John Cotton: Puritanism and the American Experience* (Princeton, 1962).
[1757] Zitner, Sheldon P. 'The Fool's Prophecy', *Shakespeare Quarterly*, 18 (1967), 76–80.

ADDENDA

[422A] Price, Sampson. *Ephesus Warning Before Her Woe* [Rev. 2.5].
[465A] Snodham, Thomas. *A Plaine Explanation of the Whole Revelation.*
[676A] Douglas, Lady Eleanor. *For Whitsontyde Last Feast.*
[744A] Douglas, Lady Eleanor. *Hells Destruction.*
[766A] Evans, Arise. *A Voice from Heaven to the Commonwealth of England.*
[996A] Claubergh, Andreas. *Die Thiere in und umb den stuhl Gottes . . . Apoc. IV. V. 6, 7.*
[1056A] Hanneman, John. *Comment. in cap. VIII. 5, Apocalypseos* (Frankfurt).
[1056B] Heunisch, Johann Friedrich. *Clavis universalis Apocalypseos* (Frankfurt).
[1202A] Croly, George. *The Englishmen's Polar Star* (East Moreland).
[1224A] Croly, George. *Divine Providence; or Three Cycles of Revelation.*
[1225A] Jones, Thomas. *The Interpreter: . . . Founded on . . . H. Gauntlett's Exposition of That Book.*
[1395A] Frost, Stanley Brice. 'Apocalyptic and History', in *The Bible in Modern Scholarship*, ed. J. Philip Hyatt (New York, 1965).
[1606A] Brooks-Davis, Douglas. *Spenser's 'Faerie Queene'* (Manchester, 1977).
[1628A] Fitch, Raymond E. The Poison Sky: Myth and Apocalypse in Ruskin (Athens, Ohio, 1982).
[1750A] Wittreich, Joseph. *'Image of that Horror'*: History, Prophecy, and Apocalypse in *'King Lear'* (San Marino, Calif., 1984).

Index nominum

Abbo of Fleury, 46, 67
Abbot, Archbishop George, 103
Abelard, Peter, 67
Abelove, Henry, 297
Abrams, M. H., 177, 201, 299
Achmetes ben Seirim, 145
Acton, Lord, 366
Adams, S. L., 119, 120, 121
Adams, Thomas, 213
Adas, Michael, 263
Addison, Joseph, 253
Adémar de Chabannes, 67
Adso, Abbot, 45, 46, 67
Agobard of Lyons, 43, 66
Albanese, Catherine L., 298
Alcazar, Ludovicus, 139, 146
Alexander the Great, 43, 52
Alexander, P. H., 37, 66, 67
Alford, Dean Henry, 320
Alley, Henry, 302
Alphandéry, P., 67, 144
Alsted, Joannes, 101, 110, 120, 134, 138, 145, 146, 226
Altmann, St, 46
Alvarus of Cordova, 44, 66
Ames, William, 107, 121, 268
Anderson, Andrew R., 66
Andreae, Johann Valentine, 201
Andrew of Caesarea, 138, 145
Andrewes, John, 235
Andrews, William D., 296
Angelo Clareno, 56
Anne, Queen of England, 280

Anselm of Havelberg, 48, 67, 68
Anselm, St, 47
Antiochus IV Epiphanes, 6, 8, 15, 20, 50, 212, 233
Antipas of Pergamum, 143
Appel, Helmut, 79, 90
Archer, John, 107, 110, 121, 122
Aristotle, 56
Arnold, Matthew, 312, 318, 321
Arnold of Villanova, 54
Athanasius, St, 354
Atzberger, Leonhard, 37
Auden, W. H., 324, 340
Augustine, St, 27, 28, 29, 31, 40-1, 44, 47, 49, 50, 66, 82, 90, 94, 151, 163, 329, 339, 349, 353-4
Augustus, Emperor, 127
Aulen, Gustaf, 90
Aylmer, John, 95, 96, 118, 119

Bacon, Sir Francis, 181, 217, 350, 366, 367
Bacon, Roger, 52, 68
Baethgen, F., 70
Baillie, Robert, 236
Bale, John, 93, 94, 95, 96, 118, 144, 145, 157-8, 160, 166, 173, 200, 232
Ball, Bryan W., 119
Banaster, Thomas, 113, 123
Banks, Theodore H., 234
Barbour, Hugh, 123
Barker, Arthur E., 236

Bar Kochba, 24
Barkun, Michael, 34
Barnes, Robert, 158, 160
Barnet, Sylvan, 203
Bartlett, David, 39
Bastwick, John, 105
Battenhouse, Roy W., 193, 203, 204, 205
Bauckham, Richard J., 37, 118, 119, 128, 143, 144, 145, 146, 172, 173, 185, 232
Bauer, W., 38
Bayly, Benjamin, 248
Beard, Thomas, 104, 121
Beaseley-Murray, G. R., 35
Beatus of Liebana, 44, 49, 66
Becker, Carl, 197, 205
Becket, St Thomas, 157
Becon, Thomas, 95, 96, 118, 199, 232
Bede, St, 66, 67, 129, 189
Belknap, Jeremy, 292, 298
Bellamy, Joseph, 286, 297
Bellarmine, St Robert Cardinal, 145
Benedict, St, 51
Benivieni, Girolamo, 63
Bentley, G. E., 202
Benzo of Alba, 47, 67
Bercovitch, Sacvan, 294, 295, 296, 298, 341
Berger, Klaus, 37, 39
Bernard, Richard, vii, 102, 106, 120, 121, 145, 228, 233, 237
Bernard of Clairvaux, St, 47, 51
Bernard the hermit, 45
Besborough, Lord, 165
Bettini, Luca, 63
Betz, H.-D., 14, 19, 33, 351
Bickersteth, Edward, 314, 319
Bickersteth, Edward Henry, 300, 319
Bietenhard, H., 38
Bignami-Odier, J., 70
Bihel, S., 69
Billingsley, Nicholas, 233
Blackwood, Adam, 162
Blake, William, 195, 299, 334, 346, 347, 355–6, 359, 360, 363, 364
Blatt, Thora B., 173
Bloch, Ernst, 327
Bloomfield, Morton W., 60, 71
Boas, F. S., 179
Boccaccio, Giovanni, 171, 174

Boehme, Jakob, 241, 245, 262
Boethius, 42
Boismard, M. E., 36
Bonaparte, Felicia, 317, 319
Bonaventure, St, 55, 70
Boniface III, Pope, 132, 144
Bornkamm, G., 36
Bornkamm, Heinrich, 233
Botticelli, Sandro, 63
Bousset, Wilhelm, 13, 20, 21, 35, 36, 43, 66, 90, 142, 144, 145
Boyle, Robert, 240
Bradshaw, John, 106, 113
Bradstreet, Anne, 267, 271–2, 293, 294
Bramante, Donato di Angelo, 233
Bransom, J. S. H., 201
Bray, Thomas, 289, 298
Bredero, A., 67
Breech, E., 33
Bremer, Francis J., 294
Breslow, M. A., 120, 121
Bridge, William, 109, 122
Brightman, Thomas, 93, 100–1, 102, 106, 108, 110, 117, 118, 120, 121, 134, 138, 145, 146, 149, 189, 204, 208, 231, 236, 269
Brocardo, Giacopo, 96, 119
Brooke, Robert Greville, Lord, 109, 111
Brothers, Richard, 244
Broughton, Hugh, 134, 149
Brown, Peter, 41, 66
Browne, Sir Thomas, 210, 222, 235
Buckingham, George Villiers, Duke of, 104, 105
Bugenhagen, Johann, 74, 88
Bulkeley, John, 263
Bullinger, Heinrich, 144, 190, 207, 233, 235, 237
Bultmann, Rudolf, 89
Bunyan, John, 214, 233, 244, 245, 255–6, 257, 354
Burdach, Konrad, 71
Burg, B. R., 293
Burges, Cornelius, 122
Burghley, see Cecil, Sir William
Burnet, Thomas, 243, 263
Burr, D., 56, 70
Burridge, Kenelm, 261
Burroughes, Jeremiah, 109, 111, 122
Burt, John, 287, 297

Index

Burton, Henry, 105, 107, 110, 121, 122, 235
Bushman, Richard, 296
Butler, Samuel, 250, 252, 257
Byles, Mather, 288, 297
Byron, Lord, 195, 367

Calamy, Edmund, 222
Call, W. M. W., 309–10, 311
Callistus III, Pope, 74
Calvin, Jean, 75–92, 148, 172, 175, 210, 212, 226, 232, 233, 235, 339
Campbell, Alexander, 341
Campbell, Joseph, 188
Campbell, Lily B., 201
Capp, Bernard, 142, 146, 236
Carlyle, Thomas, 198, 300, 301, 303, 310, 318, 333, 361, 362, 363, 364, 367
Cary, Henry, 123
Cary, Mary, 112, 122
Casaubon, Meric, 260
Cassiodorus, 42
Catherall, Samuel, 263
Caudwell, Christopher, 184
Cecil, Sir Robert, Earl of Salisbury, 101
Cecil, Sir William, Lord Burleigh, 165
Cecill, Thomas, 174
Celestine V, Pope, 57
Chadwick, Owen, 305, 320
Chambers, R. W., 201
Charlemagne, Emperor, 42, 46, 62, 63, 86
Charles, R. H., 15, 21, 32, 34
Charles I of England, 101, 103–14 *passim*, 116, 117, 127, 212, 251, 270, 353
Charles II of England, 117, 251, 253
Charles IV, Emperor, 59
Charles IV of Bohemia, 59
Charles V, Emperor, 64, 87
Charles VI of France, 59
Charles VIII of France, 62, 63
Charlton, Kenneth, 231
Charney, Maurice, 204
Chastel, André, 71
Chaucer, Geoffrey, 151
Cherry, Conrad, 296
Chew, Samuel C., 233
Cheynell, Francis, 111, 122
Christianson, Paul, 118–22 *passim*, 144,
146, 172, 203, 235
Cibber, Colley, 260
Cicero, 34
Clapham, Henoch, 232
Clement VII, Pope, 65
Clement of Alexandria, St, 38
Clouse, Robert G., 120, 236
Clovis of the Franks, 42
Cockayne, George, 113, 123
Coffman, Ralph J., 296
Cogswell, James, 287, 297
Cohn, Norman, 34, 118
Cola di Rienzo, 59
Coleridge, Samuel Taylor, 191, 242, 263, 350–1, 359, 360, 366, 368
Colet, John, 150, 151, 152, 172
Colie, Rosalie L., 174
Collado, Nicolaus, 145
Collier, Thomas, 113, 123
Collins, Adela Y., 16, 24, 36, 37, 143
Collins, Anthony, 249
Collins, John J., 6, 15, 17, 31, 32, 33, 34, 36, 143
Colman, Benjamin, 281
Columbus, Christopher, 65, 281, 357, 358
Comenius, Johannes Amos, 111
Commodian, 27, 29, 38, 39
Constantine the Great, Emperor, 42, 57, 61, 85, 95, 96, 128, 159
Cooper, William, 282
Coppe, Abiezer, 114, 123
Corbert, Richard, 104, 120
Cortes, Hernando, 64, 72
Cotton, John, of Boston, 110, 122, 269–70, 272
Cotton, John, of Hampshire, 103
Cotton, John, of Warblington, 120
Court, John M., 23, 36
Cranach, Lucas, the Elder, 83
Cranmer, Archbishop Thomas, 101, 158
Crawford, Michael J., 297
Crocker, Josiah, 284
Cromwell, Oliver, 104, 113–17, 123, 127, 212, 226, 250–1, 270
Cromwell, Thomas, 94, 95, 101, 157
Cross, F.M., 13, 16, 33, 34
Cumming, John, 308, 321
Cuninghame, William, 320
Cyprian, St, 31, 38

Cyrus the Great, 62

Dallison, A. R., 236
Danby, John, 194, 203
Danforth, Samuel, 273, 294
Daniel, Samuel, 181
Daniélou, Jean, 27, 38
Dante Alighieri, 59, 354
Darwin, Charles, 335, 337
Davenport, John, 268-9
Davidson, David, 311
Davidson, James W., 297, 298, 341
Davidson, Samuel, 320
Defoe, Daniel, 245, 262
Deios, Laurence, 97, 119
Dekker, Thomas, 181
Dell, William, 114, 123
Demaray, John G., 237
Denis, A. M., 37
Dent, Arthur, 98, 101, 119, 204, 207, 235
De Wette, W. M. L., 320
Dieu, Ludovicus de, 146
Diodati, Charles, 214
Diodati, Giovanni, 214, 215, 226, 233, 236, 237
Dixon, John, 165-6
Dobbins, Austin C., 234
Dodd, C. H., 35
Domitian, Emperor, 22, 143
Donckel, E., 70
Donne, John, 175, 176, 177, 189, 191, 199, 207, 209, 229, 233
Dowey, Edward A., Jr, 89
Dowland, John, 164
Downham, George, 102, 120, 232, 233
Draper, John W., 181, 201
Draxe, Thomas, 235
Dryden, John, 250, 251-3, 257, 260, 261
Dubois, Pierre, 58, 70
Dudley, Ambrose, 119
Dudley, Guilford, 206
Duensing, H., 37
Dunn, Richard S., 295
Durden, Ralph, 99
Dury, John, 111
Dwight, Timothy, 286, 290-1, 292, 297, 298
Dyke, Daniel, 233

Ebeling, Gerhard, 30, 39
Eck, Johann, 79, 89
Eddy, Mary Baker, 334-5
Edward VI of England, 94, 99, 106, 150, 158, 165, 172
Edwards, Jonathan, 282-3, 284, 285, 287, 290, 296, 297, 357, 366
Edwards, Thomas, 122
Eicksteth, Edward, 320
Ekkehard of Aura, 67
Elert, Werner, 80, 90
Eliot, George, 301-22
Eliot, John, of Roxbury, 271, 273, 294
Eliot, T. S., 215
Elizabeth I, 94-102 passim, 105, 106, 109, 149, 156-66 passim, 181
Elizabeth of Bohemia, 103, 104, 105-6
Elliott, E. F., 306, 307-8, 321
Elliott, Emory, 295
Ellul, Jacques, 198, 206
Elton, William, 178, 189, 202, 203, 205
Emmerson, Richard K., 35
Emser, Hieronymus, 79
Engels, Friedrich, 325 ff., 352
Erasmus, Desiderius, 149-53 passim, 154, 155, 168, 172, 175, 226, 233
Ermini, F., 68
Ernst, Josef, 35, 38
Erskine, John, 286, 297
Essex, Robert Devereux, Earl of, 99
Ethelbert of Kent, 42
Eulogius, St, 44
Eusebius of Caesarea, 27, 38, 41, 88, 257, 264
Evans, Mary Ann, see Eliot, George
Evelyn, John, 117
Ewald, H. G. A., 320

Faber, George Stanley, 320
Fallowes, Thomas, 261
Farrer, Austin, 177, 233, 234
Fatio de Duillier, Nicolas, 243
Fawcett, Arthur, 297
Featley, Daniel, 226, 236
Fichte, J. G., 346, 360, 361, 362
Ficino, Marsilio, 62, 63, 64
Field, John, 99
Finke, H., 69
Fiorenza, Elizabeth S., 36
Firth, Katharine R., 119, 120, 142,

144, 145, 146, 172, 173, 185, 201, 231, 235
Fisch, Harold, 237
Fitzmyer, Joseph, 34
Fixler, Michael, 145, 234, 235
Flaccianus, 60
Flacius Illyricus, Matthias, 88, 158
Focillon, H., 66, 67, 68
Folliet, G., 38
Fox, George, 116, 123
Foxcroft, Thomas, 280, 296
Foxe, John, 93, 94, 95, 96, 98, 118, 119, 120, 133, 138, 144, 146, 149, 151, 158–61, 165, 171–2, 175, 179, 194, 232
Francesco da Meleto, 63
Francis of Assisi, St, 54 ff., 74
Fraser, Russell, 205
Frederick Elector Palatine, 103, 104, 106
Frederick I (Barbarossa), Emperor, 47
Frederick II, Emperor, 53–4
Frend, W. H. C., 39
Frere, James H., 305, 320
Frey, David, L., 201
Freyham, R., 68
Froom, LeRoy E., 202
Frost, S. B., 13, 33
Frugoni, A., 70
Frye, Northrop, 193, 194
Fuchs, Ernst, 30, 39
Fulke, William, 119, 144
Funk, R. W., 18, 19, 35

Gager, John, 39
Galatinus, Petrus, 145
Galba, Emperor, 127
Galfridus Le Baker de Swynebroke, 60, 71
Gallagher, Edward J., 295
Gamaleon, 59
Gardiner, Samuel, 235
Gardiner, Stephen, 164
Garrett, Clarke, 365, 367
Gataker, Thomas, 112
Gaustad, Edwin S., 297
Gay, Peter, 296
Gebhart, E., 67
Gennadius of Marseilles, 28
Geoffrey of Monmouth, 193
Gerard of Borgo San Donnino, 54–5, 69

Gerberga, Queen, 45
Gerhard, Johann, 88
Gerhoh of Reichersberg, 47–8, 67
Gerrish, Brian A., 89
Gheerye, G. S., 341
Gifford, George, 98, 99, 119, 144, 183
Giles of Viterbo, 64, 72
Gilpin, W. Clark, 294
Gilpin, William 357
Glaber, Ralph, 46, 67
Godfrey of Viterbo, 47, 67
Goen, C. C., 297
Goldberg, S. L., 204
Goodman, Godfrey, 221
Goodwin, Thomas, 107, 114, 115, 121, 122, 123, 145, 146
Gottfried, Paul, 340
Gouge, William, 106, 121
Grant, R. M., 39
Graunt, John, of Bucklersbury, 122
Gregory of Tours, 42, 66
Gregory the Great, Pope, 42, 66
Gregory VII, Pope, 132, 136, 144
Gregory IX, Pope, 53
Grotius, Hugo, 133, 139, 144, 146
Gruenwald, Ithamar, 9, 13, 25, 31, 33, 37
Grundmann, Herbert, 70
Gui, B., 70
Guibert of Nogent, 46, 67
Guicciardini, Lodovico, 119
Gunkel, H., 13
Gustavus Adolphus of Sweden, 106, 128
Guthke, Karl S., 205
Guyse, John, 282

Hacket, William, 99
Hahn, T., 38
Haight, Gordon S., 321
Hall, Edmund, 117, 123
Hall, Joseph, 236
Haller, William, 95, 119, 121, 171
Hamilton, A. C., 172, 173
Hanford, James H., 235
Hankins, John E., 144, 173
Hanson, Paul D., 13, 31, 32, 33, 34
Harbert, William, 181
Harrison, John F. C., 319, 332, 366
Harrison, Major General Thomas, 114, 115, 198

Hartlib, Samuel, 111, 222
Hartman, Lars, 18–19, 21, 35
Harvey, Gabriel, 175
Harvey, Richard, 97
Harwood, A. C., 202
Hatch, Nathan O., 287, 341
Hausmann, Nikolaus, 89
Hayes, T. Wilson, 205
Haymo of Halberstadt, 42, 66, 67
Heaton, E. W., 179
Hegel, G. W. F., 324, 337, 346, 348, 358–67 *passim*
Heimert, Alan, 297, 298
Hellwis, Edward, 97, 98, 119
Henderson, J., 68
Heninger, S. K., 174
Hennell, Sara, 309, 316, 321
Henry, James I's heir apparent, 103, 105, 106
Henry II of England, 157
Henry IV, Emperor, 47
Henry VIII of England, 94, 95, 99, 105, 155, 157, 159
Henry of Harclay, 54
Henry of Langenstein (Hassia), 59, 71
Herbert, George, 175
Herbert, Thomas, 122
Herder, J. G. von, 360
Hesychius, 28
Heydon, Sir Christopher, 99
Hickes, George, 248
Hicks, William 208, 232
Higginson, John, 273, 294
Hildegard, St, 59
Hill, Christopher, 119–23 *passim*, 236, 260–1, 264
Hilliard, Nicholas, 164
Hinckmar of Rheims, 42
Hippolytus, St, 26, 29, 31
Hirsch-Reich, B., 68
Hitler, Adolf, 353
Hobson, Paul, 112
Hoekema, Anthony A., 264
Hoffmansthal, Hugo von, 347
Hölderlin, Friedrich, 358–65 *passim*
Holl, Karl, 80, 90
Holland, Hezekiah, 145, 237
Holloway, John, 203, 322, 368
Holmes, Nathaniel, 110, 122, 123
Honorius of Autun, 47, 67
Hooker, Thomas, 268, 272

Hopkins, Samuel, 286, 297
Horne, Thomas Hartwell, 304
Hough, Graham, 172
Howden, Roger, 68
Huillard-Bréholles, J., 69
Huit, Ephraim, 108, 121
Hull, John, 232
Hunt, William Holman, 300
Hunter, Robert, 194
Hunter, William B., 237
Huntley, Frank L., 233
Huss, John, 159, 162
Hutchinson, Francis, 248

Ignatius Loyola, St, 65
Innocent III, Pope, 46, 67
Irenaeus, St, 27, 31, 36, 38, 257, 264, 310
Isani, Mukhtar Ali, 295
Isidore of Seville, St, 42

Jack, Jane H., 203
Jackson, Martha, 305
Jacob, Margaret C., 123, 124, 262, 263
Jacobus de Paradiso, 59, 71
Jakoubek of Stříbro, 61
James, Montague R., 68
James I of England (VI of Scotland), 99, 102–4, 105, 106, 120, 173, 179–90 *passim*, 193, 194, 196, 207
James II of England, 117, 243
Jarrott, Catherine, 172, 173, 174
Jay, Elisabeth, 319
Jean de Meung, 69
Jedin, Hubert, 91, 92
Jerome, St, 28, 47, 66, 67
Jewel, John, 94, 95, 98, 118, 149, 163, 174
Joachim of Fiore, 49–51, 52 ff., 58 ff., 64–5, 70, 96, 102, 321, 349, 357
John of England, 157
John of Leyden, 351
John of Paris, 54, 69
John of Parma, 55, 69
Johnson, Edward, 270, 275, 294, 357, 366
Johnson, Samuel, 179
Jones, B. W., 35
Jones, Rufus M., 348
Joye, George, 119
Judson, Alexander C., 174

Julius Caesar, 43, 127
Jung, Carl, 188
Junius, Franciscus (François du Jon), 144, 237
Jurieu, Pierre, 245, 264
Justin Martyr, St, 27, 31

Kaminsky, H., 71
Kamlah, W., 67, 68
Kant, Immanuel, 360, 361, 363, 367
Käsemann, Ernst, 2, 18, 30
Kawerau, Georg, 83, 91
Keach, Benjamin, 244, 245
Keble, John, 300, 314, 315, 321
Kelly, Henry A., 201
Kermode, Frank, 173, 185, 196, 201, 204, 205, 365
Kernan, Alvin B., 202
Kildahl, John P., 264
Kingston, Richard, 248
Kittel, Gerhard, 90
Knibb, M. A., 32
Knight, G. Wilson, 193, 202, 203, 205
Knoepflmacher, U. C., 302, 319, 322
Koch, Klaus, 31, 65
Kohls, Ernst-W., 172, 173
Konrad, E., 67
Kott, Jan, 204
Kotting, B., 37
Kozintsev, Grigori, 188, 201, 204
Kümmel, W. G., 35, 36

Lacocque, Andre, 32, 34
Lactantius, 27, 29, 38, 39
Lacy, John, 246–9, 257, 258
Lamont, William M., 120, 121, 122, 123, 143, 144, 172
Langdon, Samuel, 288–9, 297, 298
Lanternari, Vittorio, 366
Lascelles, Mary, 203
Laski, J. H., 334, 341
Lathbury, John, 60
Latimer, Hugh, 94, 158
Laud, Archbishop William, 105–9 *passim*, 212, 267
Lawenus, Daniel, 146
Lawrence, D. H., 343, 365
Leach, Douglas E., 296
Lead, Jane, 244–5, 263
Lee, H., 69
Lefèvre d'Étaples, Jacques, 172

Leff, Gordon, 71
Lehmann, Paul, 91
Leicester, Robert Stanley, Earl of, 99, 165
Leigh, Edward, 237
Leighton, Alexander, 104–5, 107, 121
Lenin, V. I., 335
Lennard, Sampson, 103
Leo X, Pope, 64, 85
Leo the Wise, 57
Lerner, Robert E., 33, 67
Leslie, John, 162
Lessing, G. E., 360
Levin, David, 295
Lewalski, Barbara K., 234, 237, 294
Lewis, C. S., 233
Lewis, Maria, 305
Lilburne, John, 107, 121
Lilje, Hanns, 90
Lindsay, Jack, 204
Lisle, Francis, 123
Liu, Tai, 122, 123
Lockwood, W. A., 263
Lodge, Thomas, 233
Louis VII of France, 47
Louis XIV of France, 117, 245, 246
Louis the Pious, 43
Lovelace, Richard F., 295
Lowance, Mason I., Jr, 294, 296, 298
Löwith, Karl, 346, 365
Lucius, 96
Lukács, Gyorgy, 327
Luke, Sir Samuel, 122
Luneau, A., 41, 66
Luther, Martin, 65, 74–92, 138, 145, 148, 151, 158, 172, 175, 210, 226, 232, 233, 339

MacCaffrey, Isabel G., 172
McFarland, Thomas, 197, 204
McGinn, Bernard, 53, 69, 70, 194, 205, 311, 322
Mackay, Robert, 303, 321
McKeon, Michael, 123, 264
Maclear, James F., 120, 121, 122, 293, 294, 298
MacLure, Millar, 233
McNeill, John T., 90
Madsen, William G., 237
Mahomet (Mohammed), 44, 46, 132, 144

Mâle, Émile, 66
Malory, Thomas, 150, 151
Malvy, A., 91
Malynes, Gerard de, 174
Manselli, R., 68, 69
Manuel, Frank E., 123, 242, 263, 365
March, John de la, 122
Marlorat, Augustine, 119, 144, 226, 233, 236
Marlowe, Christopher, 236
Marshall, Stephen, 111, 122, 222
Marten, Anthony, 97, 118, 119, 121
Martin, John, 319
Marvell, Andrew, 175, 250–1, 257
Marx, Karl, 323–41, 352, 366
Mary Queen of England, 95, 158, 159, 165
Mary Queen of Scots, 162, 166, 173
Mason, Thomas, 235
Massa, E., 72
Mather, Cotton, 266, 268, 269, 271, 275, 276–9, 280, 281, 283, 286, 291, 292, 293–8 *passim*
Mather, Increase, 273–4, 293, 294, 295
Mather, Richard, 267
Mathesius, Johann, 74
Mathias of Janov, 61, 71
Maurice, F. D., 308–9, 320
Maxwell, James, 102, 120
Mayer, John, 204
Mayhew, Jonathan, 287, 297
Mede, Joseph, 101, 106, 108, 110, 111, 117–18, 121, 122, 124, 125–46, 149, 208, 227, 229, 232, 235, 237, 242, 266, 275, 281, 293, 308, 312, 321
Medwin, Thomas, 367
Meier, Karl, 313, 321
Meinhold, Peter, 89
Melanchthon, Philip, 75, 77, 78, 88
Mellen, John, 287, 297
Melville, Herman, 358, 366
Mendietta, Geronimo de, 64, 65, 72
Merchant, W. Moelwyn, 194
Methodius, St, 27
Middlekauff, Robert, 293
Migne, J. P., 66
Mildmay, Sir Walter, 119
Miller, Perry, 296
Milton, John, 74, 111, 122, 125, 134, 139, 142, 144, 145, 164, 175, 196, 200, 207–37, 253–5, 256, 257, 259, 300, 345, 347, 352, 353, 364, 368
Mohammed, *see* Mahomet
Moody, Samuel, 287
Moorehead, John, 284
Moorhead, James, 341
Morawski, K., 71
More, Henry, 125, 127–46 *passim*, 200, 208, 243, 260–1
More, Sir Thomas, 217
Morgan, Edmund S., 294
Morgan, Lewis, 338, 341
Mornay, Philippe de, 119, 120
Morris, Helen, 204
Mottu, H., 70
Mowinckel, Sigmund, 13
Mueller, Martin, 145
Muggleton, Lodowick, 248
Müller, H. P., 33
Munday, Anthony, 181
Müntzer, Thomas, 351
Murdock, Kenneth B., 296
Murray, Iain H., 297
Murrin, Michael, 234
Myers, Jacob M., 33

Napier, John, 100, 101, 103, 120, 182, 183, 184, 189, 200, 207, 208, 214, 226, 231, 235, 236, 237
Napoleon, Emperor, 336
Narne, William 233
Nayler, James, 123, 198, 248
Nepos of Arsinoe, 27, 38
Nero, Emperor, 28, 29, 36, 38, 42–3, 50–1, 43, 127
Nerval, Gérard de, 209
Nesi, Giovanni, 63
Newcomb, Thomas, 263
Newton, Sir Isaac, 117, 124, 200, 207, 242–3, 263, 335, 343
Newton, Thomas, 313, 321
Nicholas III, Pope, 57
Nicholas of Cusa, 60, 71
Nicholas of Dresden, 61
Nicholas of Lyra, 54, 138
Nickelsburg, G. W. E., 32
Nicolson, Marjorie H., 233, 235
Nietzsche, Friedrich, 196
Novalis, 360, 361, 363, 364, 367
Noyes, Nicholas, 273, 276, 294

Index

Nuttall, G. F., 121

Occam, William of, 30
Odalric, 46
Old, John, 118
Olivi, Petrus, 56–7, 70
Olsen, V. Norskov, 172, 173
Orgel, Stephen, 180
Origen, 25, 28, 81, 134, 151, 152
Ornstein, Robert, 201
Orosius, Paulus, 41
Osiander, Andreas, 119, 138, 145
Osorius, Jeronimo, 65
Owen, John, 113, 114, 123
Owen, Robert, 330–40 *passim*, 351

Pagitt, Ephraim, 122
Paine, Tom, 292
Palmer, Thomas, 122
Pannenberg, W., 18
Papias, 27
Pareus, David, 125–46, 215, 227–8, 232, 234, 237
Paris, Matthew, 52, 68
Parker, Patricia A., 172, 201
Parker, Robert, 122
Parker, Samuel, 260, 261
Parker, William R., 233
Pascal, Blaise, 207
Patai, Raphael, 341
Patrides, C. A., 201, 205, 264
Pelayo, Alvaro, 74, 88
Pelissier, L., 72
Pelster, F., 69
Pembroke, Philip Herbert, Earl of, 111
Pepys, Samuel, 232
Perkins, William, 236
Perrin, Norman, 18, 20, 32, 35
Phelan, John L., 72
Philip II of Spain, 163, 166
Phillips, James E., 173
Phillips, Samuel, 280, 296
Philpott, John, 94
Pico della Mirandola, Gianfrancesco, 63
Pico della Mirandola, Giovanni, 62–3, 65
Pipini, F., 70
Pius II, Pope, 74
Pius V, Pope, 166
Plato, 34, 40, 334
Pliny, 43

Pope, Alexander, 257, 259–60, 261
Portoghesi, Paolo, 234
Potter, Francis, 120, 232
Poulet, Georges, 233
Powel, Gabriel, 202
Powell, Vavasor, 116
Preusz, Hans, 90, 91
Priestley, Joseph, 342, 359, 365, 367
Primasius, 67
Prince, F. T., 236
Prince, Thomas, 279, 280, 282, 296
Prince, Thomas, Jr, 284
Proudhon, Pierre, 343–4, 365
Prynne, William, 105, 112, 122, 123
Purvey, John, 61
Pym, John 111

Quanbeck, Warren A., 232
Quispel, Gilles, 32
Quistorp, Heinrich, 232, 235

Rabil, Albert, Jr, 173
Rad, Gerhard von, 3, 13, 31, 33, 143, 144
Radzinowicz, Mary Ann, vii
Ralegh, Sir Walter, 133, 144, 145, 156, 212, 233
Rangheri, M., 67
Ratzinger, J., 69, 70
Rauh, H. D., 39
Ray, Mary A., 297
Reed, John, 334
Reeves, Marjorie, 118, 120, 226
Regiomontanus, Johannes, 97
Reimarus, Samuel, 2
Reu, Michael, 88
Revard, Stella, 237
Ribera, Francisco, 145, 146
Ribner, Irving, 202, 203
Rich, Sir Nathaniel, 108
Richard I of England, 49
Ridley, Nicholas, 95, 118, 158
Rietschel, Ernst, 90
Ritschl, Albrecht, 90
Robert of France, 46
Roberts, Michael, 121
Robinson, H. C., 346, 355, 365
Roche, Thomas R., Jr, 203
Roebuck, J. J., 331
Rogers, Thomas, 97
Roquetaillade, Jean de, 58–9

Rosenblatt, Jason P., 237
Rous, Francis, 235
Rousseau, Jean Jacques, 338
Rowley, H. H., 13, 31, 33
Rozanov, Vasily, 197
Rudwin, Maximilian, 233
Rupert of Deutz, 48, 68
Ruskin, John, 300, 301, 303, 318, 322
Russell, D. S., 13, 31, 33, 38

Saccio, Peter, 201
Sadoleto, Jacopo Cardinal, 80
Salimbene, 53, 54, 69
Salmon, Joseph, 113, 123
Sancroft, Archbishop William 113, 117
Sandeen, Ernest R., 263, 319, 340
Sanders, Nicholas, 162
Sandford, James, 96, 119
Sandys, Archbishop Edwin, 95, 96, 119
Sandys, George, 208
Savonarola, Girolamo, 62, 63, 303, 311 ff.
Saye and Sele, William Fiennes, Lord, 108
Schechter, Abraham, 202
Scheick, William J., 297
Schelling, Friedrich, 346, 348, 358–62 passim, 364, 367, 368
Schiller, J. C. F. von, 360, 362, 367
Schlegel, Friedrich, 326
Schlichtenberger, Eyriak, 202
Schloer, Friedrich, 121
Schmidt, R., 37
Schmithals, Walter, 6, 32, 33, 237
Scholem, Gershom S., 263
Schorer, Mark, 319
Schwartz, Barry, 263
Schwartz, Hillel, 246, 263
Schweitzer, Albert, 35
Scott, Thomas, 106, 121
Scoufos, Alice-Lyle, 235
Seaton, Ethel, 204
Sedgwick, William, 110, 122
Seferis, George, vii
Settle, Elkanah, 259
Sewall, Arthur, 203
Sewall, Joseph, 281, 282
Sewall, Samuel, 275–6, 277, 281, 295
Shakespeare, 175–206
Shaw, George Bernard, 35
Shawcross, John T., 237

Sheldon, Archbishop Gilbert, 242
Sheldon, Robert, 104, 121
Shelley, Mary, 367
Shelley, Percy Bysshe, 195, 253, 359, 360, 363, 365, 367
Sherwin, William, 244, 245
Sherwood, Samuel, 288, 298
Sibbes, Richard, 212
Sidney, Sir Philip, 181
Siegel, Paul, 186
Sigebert of Gemblours, 67
Silverstein, Theodore, 37
Simon Magus, 43, 51, 53
Simpson, John, 113, 123
Sims, James H., 234
Sitwell, Edith, 193, 201
Sleidanus, Johann Philippson, 158
Smalley, Beryl, 60, 71
Smith, Henry Nash, 366
Smith, John, the Cambridge Platonist, 235
Smith, Jonathan Z., 5, 14, 32, 34, 39
Smith, Joseph, 321
Smith, Marshall, 263
Smith, Samuel, 234
Snyder, Susan, 193, 205
Southcott, Joanna, 244, 304
Southern, R. W., 66, 203
Southey, Robert, 358, 359
Spalatin, Georg, 91
Spencer, Benjamin T., 202
Spencer, John, 252
Spenser, Edmund, 133, 148–74, 175, 176, 181, 194, 196, 199, 200, 212, 213, 354
Spinckes, Nathaniel, 247
Spoure, Edmund, 234
Stange, Carl, 89, 90
Stauffer, Donald A., 203
Stiles, Ezra, 289, 290, 298
Stillingfleet, Edward, 242
Stoddard, Solomon, 281, 282, 296
Stone, Michael E., 3, 6, 7, 15, 31, 32, 33, 34
Stone, Walter B., 119, 203
Stonehouse, N. B., 36, 38
Stoughton, John, 109
Strabo, 43
Street, Nicholas, 289, 298
Strich, Fritz, 368
Strong, Nathan, 292, 298

Strong, Roy, 163, 174
Stuart, Moses, 320
Suleiman the Magnificent, 212
Sulpicius Severus, 29
Sundén, K., 71
Suter, D., 32
Swan, John, 233
Swedenborg, Emanuel, 335
Swift, Jonathan, 248, 257–9, 260, 261
Swinburne, A. C., 175
Sylvester II, Pope, 160
Symonds, William, 183

Talfourd, Thomas Noon, 359–60, 367
Tappan, David, 290, 298
Tate, Nahum, 179
Tatian, 81
Taylor, Edward, 276
Taylor, Gary, 202
Taylor, Thomas, 237
Tcherikover, Avigdor, 34
Telesphorus of Cosenza, 59, 70
Tenison, Archbishop Thomas, 242
Tennyson, Alfred Lord, 300–1, 310, 326
Tennyson, G. E., 321
Tertullian, 27, 31
Thacher, Peter, 284
Theobald, Lewis, 259
Theodoric of the Goths, 42
Thomas of Celano, 68
Thomas of Pavia, 53, 69
Thomas of Wimbledon, 60
Tichi, Cecelia, 295
Tierney, Brian, 56
Tillinghast, John, 115, 123
Tillotson, Archbishop John, 117, 123, 242
Tillyard, E. M. W., 201
Tocco, F., 70
Tondelli, Leone, 68
Toon, Peter, 294
Torrance, David W., 75
Torrance, Thomas F., 75
Traheron, Bartholomew, 188
Trapp, Joseph, 263
Trevor-Roper, H. R., 121, 122
Tuttle, Jules H., 297
Tuveson, Ernest L., 195, 235, 298, 351, 366

Twisse, William, 108, 109, 121, 122, 232
Tyconius, 28, 29, 39, 131, 141
Tyndale, William, 144, 175, 208–9

Ubertino da Casale, 56, 69, 88
Udall, Nicholas, 95
Urban II, Pope, 46
Ussher, Archbishop James, 108, 145

Valla, Lorenzo, 85
Vanni, Ugo, 32
Vaughan, Dorothy M., 233
Venner, Thomas, 116, 248, 250
Verhelst, D., 66
Vespasian, Emperor, 127
Vicars, John, 102, 120
Victorinus of Pettau, 27, 28, 38, 138, 145
Vielhauer, P., 21, 36, 37
Villari, Pasquale, 313, 321
Vincent Ferrer, St, 74
Vincent of Beauvais, 51, 68
Virgil, 95, 251, 253, 257, 357, 365
Voegelin, Eric, 340
Voltaire, 292, 324
Volz, Hans, 88

Wadding, L., 68
Walpole, Michael, 232
Walther, C. F. W., 75, 88
Warwick, Robert Rich, Earl of, 99, 109, 111, 119
Washington, George, 289, 291
Watts, Isaac, 279, 282
Watts, Michael R., 263, 265
Webb, John, 282
Webster, Charles, 122
Weinel, Heinrich, 36
Weinstein, Donald, 62, 63, 71
Wesley, John, 241, 256
West, Samuel, 288, 298
Westfall, Richard S., 263
Whichcote, Benjamin, 218
Whiston, William, 240, 243–4, 249 263, 278
Whitefield, George, 283
Whiting, George W., 234
Whitman, Walt, 326
Wickham, Glynne, 202
Widengren, Geo, 13, 33

Wigglesworth, Michael, 272, 274-5, 294, 295
Wigglesworth, Samuel, 280, 296
Wikenhauser, A., 38
Wilcox, Thomas, 99
Wilkinson, Henry, 109, 111-12, 122
Willard, Samuel, 274, 295
Willet, Andrew, 209, 212
William III of England, 243
William of St Amour, 52, 55, 68
Williams, George H., 89
Williams, Granville, 173
Williams, Isaac, 320
Williams, John, 104
Williams, John, of Deerfield, 281-2, 296
Williams, Roger, 270-1
Williams, William, of Hatfield, 281
Williamson, Arthur H., 202
Williamson, J. W., 120
Willison, John, 286, 296
Wilson, John, of Boston, 268
Wilson, John F., 297
Wilson, Thomas, 237

Winstanley, Gerrard, 114, 123, 198, 354-5
Winthrop, John, 267, 270, 272, 293
Winton, Isaiah, 183
Wittreich, Joseph, 88, 142, 145, 234, 235, 321
Wood, Anthony a, 121
Woolrych, Austin, 123
Wordsworth, William, 299, 356-68 *passim*
Wotton, William, 264
Wycliffe, John, 60, 159, 162

Yates, Frances, 118, 119, 120, 164, 173, 174
Yeats, William Butler, 215
Young, Edward, 262, 263

Zeeden, Ernst W., 88
Zeno, Emperor, 42
Ziff, Larzer, 293
Zwingli, Huldreich, 175